Lorna L. Hecker, PhD
Joseph L. Wetchler, PhD
Editors

An Introduction to Marriage and Family Therapy

ONE WEEK LOAN

"**A**n *Introduction to Marriage and Family Therapy* raises the bar for books in this genre. This book easily takes the place of five or six other resources on my bookshelf. The chapter glossaries alone are worth the price of the book. If a better all-around text exists, I assure you, I haven't come across it."

Howard G. Rosenthal, EdD
Program Coordinator
and Professor of Human Services,
St. Louis Community College
at Florissant Valley; Author,
Encyclopedia of Counseling
and *The Human Services Dictionary*

"**L**orna Hecker and Joseph Wetchler have edited a dynamic book that brings together the expertise of the best thinkers in marriage and family therapy today. Each contributor writes a summary on his or her area of expertise. The editors bring these chapters together by introducing the reader to the primary concepts of family therapy in the first two chapters.

The authors write in a way that engages beginning therapists and provides helpful learning tools such as glossaries, summaries, bold terms in the text, and interesting case examples. I am confident that my students will find this book user-friendly and that we will use it as a required text in our master's-level marriage and family therapy program."

Jo Ellen Patterson, PhD
Professor,
Marriage and Family Therapy,
University of San Diego, CA

More pre-publication
REVIEWS, COMMENTARIES, EVALUATIONS . . .

"**W**hat an amazing collection of knowledge Lorna Hecker, Joe Wetchler, and their colleagues have managed to squeeze into *An Introduction to Marriage and Family Therapy*. This book does exactly what an introductory text should do—introduce students to the sometimes daunting landscape of marriage and family therapy (MFT) with clear, concise chapters that cover all the major issues. Set against the excellent introductory chapters on the history of our field and its theoretical foundations, the contributing authors examine the major models of MFT as well as special issues (domestic violence and legal issues, for instance) and allied fields such as sex therapy. This book will help introduce a new generation of students to the excitement and clinical promise of the field of marriage and family therapy."

Eric E. McCollum, PhD
Professor and Clinical Director,
Marriage and Family Therapy
Master's Program,
Virginia Tech, Falls Church

The Haworth Clinical Practice Press
An Imprint of The Haworth Press, Inc.
New York • London • Oxford

An Introduction to Marriage and Family Therapy

HAWORTH Marriage and the Family
Terry S. Trepper, PhD
Executive Editor

An Introduction to Marriage and Family Therapy

Lorna L. Hecker, PhD
Joseph L. Wetchler, PhD
Editors

The Haworth Clinical Practice Press
An Imprint of The Haworth Press, Inc.
New York • London • Oxford

Published by

The Haworth Clinical Practice Press, an imprint of The Haworth Press, Inc., 10 Alice Street, Binghamton, NY 13904-1580.

PUBLISHER'S NOTE
Identities and circumstances of individuals discussed in this book have been changed to protect confidentiality.

Cover design by Lora Wiggins.

Library of Congress Cataloging-in-Publication Data

An introduction to marriage and family therapy / Lorna Hecker, Joseph Wetchler, editors.
      p. cm.
   Includes bibliographical references and index.
   ISBN 0-7890-0276-0 (alk. paper)—ISBN 0-7890-0277-9 (alk. paper)
   1. Family psychotherapy. 2. Marital psychotherapy. I. Hecker, Lorna L. II. Wetchler, Joseph L.

RC488.5 .I5875 2003
616.89'156—dc21   2002027291

CONTENTS

PART II: SPECIAL ISSUES AND TOPICS IN MARRIAGE AND FAMILY THERAPY

ABOUT THE EDITORS

Lorna Hecker, PhD, is Professor in the Marriage and Family Therapy master's program and Director of the Marriage and Family Therapy Center at Purdue University Calumet in Hammond, Indiana. She is a contributing author and editor of *The Therapist's Notebook: Homework, Handouts, and Activities for Use in Psychotherapy Practice* (1998, Haworth), co-editor of *The Therapist's Notebook for Children and Adolescents: Homework, Handouts, and Activities for Use in Psychotherapy,* founding editor of the *Journal of Clinical Activities, Assignments, and Handouts in Psychotherapy Practice* (The Haworth Clinical Practice Press), and also founding editor of the Haworth Practical Practice in Mental Health: Guidebooks for Inpatient, Outpatient, and Independent Practice book program. A resident of Munster, Indiana, she maintains a private practice. Her interests include trauma recovery, ethics, and professional issues in family therapy, and gender and multicultural issues in family therapy.

Joseph L. Wetchler, PhD, is Professor of Marriage and Family Therapy, and Director of the Marriage and Family Therapy program at Purdue University Calumet. He is editor of the *Journal of Couple and Relationship Therapy* and serves on the editorial boards of the *American Journal of Family Therapy,* the *Journal of Family Psychotherapy,* the *Journal of Feminist Family Therapy,* and the *Journal of Clinical Activities, Assignments, and Handouts in Psychotherapy Practice* (The Haworth Clinical Practice Press). He is co-author (with Fred Piercy and Douglas Sprenkle) of the *Family Therapy Sourcebook, Second Edition.*

Dr. Wetchler received the Indiana Association for Marriage and Family Therapy Award for Outstanding Contribution to Research in Family Life in 1997 and is a clinical member and approved supervisor of the American Association for Marriage and Family Therapy. He maintains a family therapy practice and regularly consults to social service agencies and therapists in private practice.

Contributors

Jerome Adams, PhD, is Professor of Human Development and Family Studies at the University of Rhode Island. He has a specialized degree in child development and family studies from Purdue University and more than fifteen years of experience as a family therapist and clinical psychologist. His clinical skills include child and family assessment, diagnosis, and expertise in interviewing and intervening with families who have problematic children and who are at risk. His research interests include the evaluation of programs and interventions designed to assist children and families, and the impact of stress on family functioning. He has served as a principal investigator on a personnel preparation grant study for elderly families funded by the National Institute of Mental Health; he is an investigator on the effectiveness of interventions to reduce the stressful impact of stroke on family functioning. He has served as primary principal investigator on an evaluation project assessing the effectiveness of parenting programs provided statewide by the Rhode Island Parent Education Center. This four-year project is funded by the U.S. Department of Education. Dr. Adams is the faculty director of the University of Rhode Island's Family Resource Partnership, a consortium of faculty providing technical assistance, program evaluation, and training to regional agencies that provide services to children and families.

Joan D. Atwood, PhD, is Director of Graduate Programs in Marriage and Family Therapy at Hofstra University, Hempstead, New York. She is also Director of the Marriage and Family Clinic located in the Saltzman Community Center at Hofstra. She is a past president of the New York State Association for Marriage and Family Therapists and was awarded the Long Island Family Therapist of the Year award for outstanding contributions to the field. Dr. Atwood holds a bachelor's degree in psychology; master's degrees in psychology, sociology, and social work; and a doctorate in social psychology. She has published over 100 journal articles and six books in the field of marriage and family therapy. Her clinical work was with clinical psychologist John Neale and cognitive psychologist Marvin Goldfried (Department of Psychology, State University of New York [SUNY] Stony Brook); her academic work was with social psychologists John Gagnon and

Eugene Weinstein (Department of Psychology/Sociology, SUNY Stony Brook); family therapists Jay Haley (advanced workshops) and Salvador Minuchin (advanced clinical supervision program), and imago therapist Harville Hendrix (clinical training program). She also studied sex therapy with Richard Green (Department of Psychiatry, SUNY Stony Brook), William Masters and Virginia Johnson (advanced training workshops), and James Geer (Department of Psychology, SUNY Stony Brook). More recently, she has been influenced by Kenneth Gergen and Michael White. Her interests include theory and its application, the nature of therapeutic change, couple research, single-parent families, and identity transitions and adolescents.

Gary H. Bischof, PhD, LMFT, is Assistant Professor and Director of marriage and family therapy education in the Department of Counselor Education and Counseling Psychology at Western Michigan University in Kalamazoo, Michigan. He obtained a master's degree in marriage and family therapy (MFT) from Virginia Tech's Northern Virginia program, and a PhD in MFT from Purdue University. Gary is a clinical member and approved supervisor with the American Association for Marriage and Family Therapy (AAMFT). He has over ten years of clinical experience in a variety of private and public mental health and medical settings. He has been actively involved with the Collaborative Family Healthcare Coalition, a multidisciplinary group of professionals committed to family-oriented, collaborative approaches to health care. His research and professional interests include medical family therapy, couple therapy, preventive approaches, brief solution-oriented therapy, and families of adolescent sex offenders. He has published over a dozen articles in professional journals and five book chapters on these and other topics.

Richard J. Bischoff, PhD, is Associate Professor in the Department of Family and Consumer Sciences at the University of Nebraska—Lincoln. He is also a clinical faculty member and Director of the Marriage and Family Therapy Program at UNL. Dr. Bischoff received his doctoral degree from Purdue University (specializing in marriage and family therapy) in 1993, his master's degree from Auburn University (specializing in marriage and family therapy) in 1990, and his bachelor's degree from Weber State College (with a major in family relations) in 1988. In addition to his work at UNL, he was also on faculty at the University of San Diego (1993-1998) and with the Sharp HealthCare Family Practice Residency Program (1995-1998). His research interests have included professional development in therapists, frequent users of medical services, and collaborative health care. He currently maintains a private practice.

Shelly R. Boughner, PhD, NCC, LPC, is Associate Professor and Counseling Program Chair at the University of South Dakota. Dr. Boughner specializes in the areas of counselor supervision, couple and family counseling, and social constructionist approaches to counseling, supervision, and counselor education. Dr. Boughner is an active member of the South Dakota Counseling Association as well as regional and national professional organizations.

Norman Epstein, PhD, is Professor in the Department of Family Studies at the University of Maryland, College Park. He is a fellow of the American Psychological Association, a clinical member and approved supervisor of the American Association for Marriage and Family Therapy, a member of the American Board of Assessment Psychology, and a founding fellow of the Academy of Cognitive Therapy. His teachings and research focus on the development of assessment and treatment approaches for couple and family problems, family stress and coping, psychopathology in the family context, and cross-cultural studies of couple and family functioning. As a faculty member in the accredited Marital and Family Therapy Program at the University of Maryland, he teaches graduate courses in couple and family therapy, sexual issues, and research methods, as well as supervising students' clinical training in the outpatient Family Service Center within the Department of Family Studies. Among his publications are the books *Cognitive-Behavioral Marital Therapy* (with Donald Baucom), *Cognitive-Behavioral Therapy with Families* (edited with Stephen Schlesinger and Windy Dryden), and *Depression in the Family* (edited with Arthur Freeman and Karen Simon), plus numerous book chapters and journal articles. He is currently completing a new volume on couple therapy with Donald Baucom, expanding their cognitive-behavioral model, and is conducting research on family stress with colleagues at Shanghai Second Medical University. In addition to his teaching and research, he maintains a part-time private practice with individuals, couples, and families in Rockville, Maryland.

Shelley A. Haddock, PhD, is Assistant Professor in the Human Development and Family Studies Department at Colorado State University (CSU) and Director for the Center for Family and Couple Therapy. She is currently coprincipal investigator on a large, qualitative research study of dual-earner couples who successfully balance family and work, which is funded by the Alfred P. Sloan Foundation. Clinically, she practices from a feminist-informed model, utilizing the Mental Research Institute model (MRI), solution-focused, and narrative models of therapy. Her supervision is primarily feminist informed.

Karen B. Helmeke, PhD, LMFT, is Assistant Professor in the Family and Consumer Sciences Department and a part-time faculty member in the Department of Counselor Education and Counseling Psychology at Western Michigan University, and a marriage and family therapist in Kalamazoo, Michigan. She was formerly Assistant Professor and Director of the Marriage and Family Therapy Training Program at Christian Theological Seminary in Indianapolis, Indiana. Karen is a clinical member and approved supervisor with AAMFT. She received her MDiv degree from Princeton Theological Seminary and was an ordained Evangelical Lutheran Church of America (ELCA) minister before returning to graduate school to earn her PhD in MFT from Purdue University. Her research and professional interests, reflected in several publications in professional journals and book chapters, include couple therapy, spirituality, and training issues in MFT.

Kevin P. Lyness, PhD, is the newest member of the CSU MFT faculty and Assistant Professor in the Human Development and Family Studies Department. His PhD is in marriage and family therapy, and his bachelor's and master's degrees are in family studies. Dr. Lyness currently serves on the editorial boards of the *Journal of Couple and Relationship Therapy* and the *Journal of Feminist Family Therapy* and is book review editor for the *Journal of Couple and Relationship Therapy.* Clinically, he works from a contextual and solution-focused perspective, and his supervision is also contextual and solution focused. In addition, he has taught workshops on narrative therapy and brief therapy within managed care and community mental health settings. His research interests include studying both the process of marriage and family therapy, which examines what works and what does not, as well as the outcomes of marriage and family therapy. Additional areas of interest include substance abuse treatment and prevention, and problems of adolescence.

Grace Ann Mims, PhD, is Associate Professor at the University of South Dakota. Her PhD is in counselor education and supervision. Dr. Mims holds certification as a national certified counselor (NCC) and approved clinical supervisor (ACS). She also holds a South Dakota license as a professional counselor (LPC) and a marriage and family therapist (LMFT). Dr. Mims specializes in couple, family, and group counseling. She has published several articles and book chapters in these areas. Dr. Mims is currently involved in community research partnerships on violence prevention in South Dakota schools and diversity sensitivity training in the schools and community. Research in the area of counselor supervision is also an interest. Dr. Mims has held such leadership positions as President of the South Dakota Counseling Association (SDCA) and President of the South Dakota Mental Health Counselors Association (SDMHCA). She serves on the editorial board of the *Journal of Clinical Activities, Assignments & Handouts in Psychotherapy Practice.*

Thorana S. Nelson received her PhD in counselor education with an emphasis in marriage and family therapy from the University of Iowa. She taught in Purdue's accredited MFT doctoral program before going to Utah

State University to develop and lead their master's program. She and her husband live in the mountains of northern Utah with their two cats.

Anne Rambo, PhD, is Associate Professor at Nova Southeastern University where she teaches systemic family therapy. Her undergraduate degree is in child development, and her first job after college was as a preschool teacher in a Head Start program. There she became interested in working with families after noticing the profound effect a stressed or discouraged parent has on even a very young child. Dr. Rambo holds a master's degree in social work and interned at San Antonio Community Guidance Center (where multiple impact family therapy was still being practiced, under the direction of Al Serrano). She worked as a master's level family therapist for eight years in child guidance centers with high-risk children and their families, and on a research team seeking new treatments for psychotic adolescents. During this time, she received postgraduate supervision and training (over 200 hours) from the Galveston Family Institute (now the Houston Galveston Institute). Dr. Rambo earned her PhD in systemic family therapy just one week before her daughter was born, and a few months later she began teaching at Nova Southeastern University, where she has remained since. Dr. Rambo's research and writing now center on encouraging and affirming "different" children and those who care for them. Her most recent research project is ChildFit, a program designed to help parents find the right educational context for their special-needs children. She also works in the community to make changes in the educational system and has written the book *"I Know My Child Can Do Better": A Frustrated Parent's Guide to Educational Options* (2001), designed to encourage parents all over the country to become active advocates. Dr. Rambo also teaches and trains other therapists and is co-author of the book *Practicing Therapy: Exercises for Growing Therapists* (1994).

Karen H. Rosen, EdD, is Associate Professor in the Marriage and Family Therapy Program at Virginia Tech's Northern Virginia Campus. She is an AAMFT clinical member and approved supervisor and is also licensed as a marriage and family therapist in the Commonwealth of Virginia. Dr. Rosen trained with Haley and Madanes at the Family Therapy Institute in Rockville, Maryland, in 1985-1986. Her primary research interest is partner violence. She has published numerous articles in a variety of journals, including the *Journal of Marriage and the Family, Journal of Marital and Family Therapy, Journal of Social and Personal Relationships, Family Relations, American Journal of Family Therapy, Journal of Contemporary Families,* and the *Journal of Family Psychotherapy*. She has also published several book chapters and co-edited a book on domestic violence, *Violence Hits Home: Comprehensive Treatment Approaches to Domestic Violence,* with her colleague Sandra M. Stith.

Connie J. Salts, PhD, is Professor and Director in the Marriage and Family Therapy Program, the Department of Human Development and Family Studies, at Auburn University. She is a clinical member and approved supervisor of AAMFT and a licensed marriage and family therapist, approved supervisor, and supervisor of supervision in the state of Alabama.

Thomas A. Smith Jr., PhD, is Associate Professor in the Marriage and Family Therapy Program, the Department of Human Development and Family Studies, at Auburn University. He is a clinical member and approved supervisor of AAMFT and a licensed marriage and family therapist, approved supervisor, and supervisor of supervision in the state of Alabama.

Volker Thomas, PhD, is a native of Germany. He received a BS in national economics in 1972 from the University of Goettingen, Germany, an MSW in clinical social work in 1979 from the University in Kassel, Germany, and a PhD in family social science with a specialization in marriage and family therapy from the University of Minnesota. Dr. Thomas is a clinical member and approved supervisor of the American Association for Marriage and Family Therapy. He has been a commissioner of the Commission on Accreditation for Marriage and Family Therapy Education since 1999. Currently Dr. Thomas is Associate Professor and Director of the marriage and family therapy program in the Department of Child Development and Family Studies at Purdue University.

Lee Williams, PhD, is Associate Professor and Director of the Marriage and Family Therapy Program at the University of San Diego. His PhD and master's degree are in marriage and family therapy, and his bachelor's degree is in chemical engineering. Dr. Williams has conducted research in premarital counseling, family therapy supervision, and has most recently studied couples who belong to different denominations or churches. His clinical interests include premarital counseling, couple therapy, gender issues, and working with homeless individuals. Dr. Williams currently serves on the editorial boards of the *Journal of Couple and Relationship Therapy* and the *Journal of Clinical Activities, Assignments & Handouts in Psychotherapy Practice.*

Toni Schindler Zimmerman, PhD, is Associate Professor in the Human Development and Family Studies Department and Director of the Marriage and Family Therapy (MFT) Program at CSU. She is widely published in the areas of women's issues, gender equity, diversity, parenting, and work-family balance. She is currently coprincipal investigator on a large, qualitative research study of successful dual-earner couples, which is funded by the Alfred P. Sloan Foundation. She is editor of the *Journal of Feminist Family Therapy* and serves on the editorial boards of the *Journal of Marital and Family Therapy* and the *Journal of Couple and Relationship Therapy*. She is past chair and current member of the CSU Women's Studies and Programs Office and of the President's Commission for Gender Equity and Diversity. Clinically, she practices from a feminist-informed model, utilizing MRI, solution-focused, and narrative models of therapy. Her supervision is primarily feminist informed as well.

Programs in Marriage and Family Therapy

Auburn University's Master of Science Program in Marriage and Family Therapy (see Chapter 14) was first accredited in 1978. The two-year curriculum is designed to offer a theoretically integrated program with the overall goal of training professionally competent and ethical marriage and family therapists. A secondary goal of the program is to provide a foundation in marriage and family therapy for students who wish to pursue a doctoral degree. Auburn University is located in Auburn, Alabama. The MFT program is located in the Department of Human Development and Family Studies, within the College of Human Sciences. Information specific to the program may be obtained online at <www.humsci.auburn.edu/hdfs/mft.html>.

Colorado State University's Human Development and Family Studies' Marriage and Family Therapy Program (see Chapter 13) resides within the Department of Human Development and Family Studies in the College of Applied Human Sciences. The MFT program has been accredited by the Commission on Accreditation for Marriage and Family Therapy Education since 1990. This program has three primary components. First, students receive extensive course work in marriage and family therapy and developmental processes of individuals and families. Second, throughout the two-year program, students participate in a closely supervised clinical experience in the on-site clinic and off-site internships. The clinic is equipped with one-way mirrors and dual-screen video cameras, which serve to enhance students' training experience. Third, students complete a thesis based on original research. In addition to this research, many opportunities exist for students to participate in research activities in the clinic and with faculty members.

A major focus throughout all program activities is the infusion of meta-theories, including gender and culture, as described in Chapter 13. The program and departmental faculty have a sincere and sophisticated approach to fully infusing these topics in the various daily interactions of training. A key aspect of this approach resides in ensuring that the *process* of training is consistent with its *message* or *content*. Faculty members believe that the atmosphere is critical in allowing students to understand and embrace the material. In this way, the program and department take a holistic approach to infusing gender and culture—not just disseminating information, but providing students with opportunities to experience these principles in the everyday interactions of the program.

Hofstra University's Marriage and Family Therapy Training Program (see Chapter 12) was established in 1982 by Dr. Don David-Lusterman, then an adjunct professor of therapy. In 1983, Dr. Joan D. Atwood became the first full-time faculty member to coordinate the program, which at that time numbered three students. In 1983 and 1984, Dr. Atwood rewrote the master of arts degree, the certificate in family therapy, the advanced certificate in sex therapy, and introduced the professional diploma with the specialization in marriage and family therapy.

In 1990, the Marital and Family Therapy Clinic was opened in the Saltzman Community Services Center, with state-of-the-art equipment and settings, providing the MFT students clinic rooms with one-way mirrors and up-to-date video and audio equipment. The MFT Clinic serves as the clinical arm of the academic programs, enabling students to practice therapy in a supervised environment. Individual, couple, and family therapy as well as groups and workshops for the community are available at the MFT Clinic on a sliding-scale basis.

The philosophy and model of the MFT programs at Hofstra are balanced and integrated. Students are exposed to a wide range of theories in their first year, including structural, strategic, communication, object relations, solution focused, and social constructionist. This broad approach familiarizes students not only with the traditional models of family therapy but also exposes them to leading edge family therapy theory and practice, especially toward the end of their studies. This integration of theory and practice is further illustrated by the two-year internship that students begin after the first year of classes. Thus, students are provided with an intense training experience both academically and clinically. In total, the students experience 900 clinical supervision hours by the time they graduate.

Hofstra has seven graduate and advanced certificate programs in marriage and family therapy: (1) Master of arts in marriage and family therapy is a sixty-one-credit master's degree that provides the skills necessary to function as a marriage and family therapist. (2) Professional diploma in marriage and family therapy provides the student with a diploma beyond the master's level. (3) Professional diploma in sex therapy is a program in progress consisting of twenty-four credits, specifically designed for the practicing professional who wishes further specialization in sex therapy. (4) Advanced certificate in family therapy is available for those professionals who wish to add a family approach to their individual training background. (5) Advanced certificate in sex therapy is available for experienced practitioners already working in the field who wish to add sex therapy knowledge to their training. (6) Advanced certificate in divorce mediation is a nineteen-semester-hour certificate available to practicing professionals who wish to incorporate divorce mediation into their practice. (7) Advanced certificate in addiction studies offers a unique approach to the study of chemical dependence.

The marriage and family therapy courses are taught through seminars, clinical courses, and supervised internships. The curriculum is specifically designed to expose students to an increasingly more sophisticated theoretical base, beginning with traditional family therapy schools and culminating in constructivist/social constructionist approaches.

Nova Southeastern University (see Chapter 6) enrolled its first doctoral class in systemic family therapy in 1988, under the leadership of Brad Keeney. Although Keeney subsequently left to pursue his anthropological interests, several of the original faculty (Ron Chenail, Douglas Flemons, Anne Rambo, and Sharon Boesl) still teach in the program. Another original faculty member, Wendel Ray, is now Director of the Mental Research Institute (MRI). The department has grown to include a master's program in family therapy, started in 1991, which is now fully accredited by the Commission on Accreditation for Marriage and Family Therapy Education (COAMFTE). The doctoral program has candidacy status with COAMFTE.

From their inception, the family therapy programs at NSU have been centered around the collaborative language-based models of family therapy. The faculty's shared philosophical base creates a collaborative atmosphere, with faculty and students on a first-name basis, working together on projects of mutual interest. Supervision and training are a constant and interesting challenge for faculty. Similar to the Mental Research Institute and the Brief Therapy Center, the one-way mirror is used extensively in supervision. When such live supervision is not possible, and as an adjunct to this, Harlene Anderson of the Houston Galveston Institute developed what she calls the "as if" method of group supervision. A therapist gives his or her perspective of a clinical situation, and listeners (usually other supervisees) take turns voicing what they think may be the perspectives of each client involved in the situation—trying to speak "as if" they were that person. The therapist is then encouraged to reflect on the many different possible ways to see the situation. This is a model used in practicums as well, and it is the focus of one entire class in the program. Joe Wetchler developed solution-focused supervision, in which the supervisor comments upon and reinforces what the supervisee is doing right, rather than focusing on any errors. This focus on what is working is consistent with solution-focused therapy. Michael White developed a training exercise in which therapists take turns telling their supervision group the stories of how they decided to enter the therapy field, and of their professional careers to date. Listeners are encouraged to affirm each storyteller. This emphasis on personal narrative is consistent with the narrative model. Both of these supervision models are used by NSU faculty members as well.

In addition, some unique models of training and supervision have evolved at NSU. NSU family therapy faculty member Lee Shilts developed a model of client-informed supervision, in which the supervisor invites the client to take the lead in coaching the beginning therapist on what is useful to the client and what is not. NSU family therapy faculty members Pat Cole, Jim Hibel, and Anne Rambo have developed a model of consultative supervision that focuses on the personal narrative of the supervisee and encourages active reflection. Although working within the collaborative models does place additional constraints on supervisors, these constraints can lead to innovative approaches that combine fostering collaborative relationships with setting high standards.

NSU's department of family therapy was joined in 1993 by a department of conflict analysis and dispute resolution (DCAR), which applies the collaborative viewpoint to larger systems issues, including regional and national conflicts. This department administers such community-based programs as ChildFit and VOICES, an innovative domestic violence treatment program that combines therapy and mediation, as well as grants master's and doctoral degrees in the field of dispute resolution/violence prevention. DCAR has also sponsored relief efforts in Northern Ireland, Bosnia, and the Mideast. DCAR and family therapy together make up the Graduate School of Humanities and Social Sciences (SHSS). SHSS graduates are internationally recognized in their fields and have made significant contributions to research and clinical practice. For more information, visit their Web site, <http://www.nova.edu> (click on academic programs, and then on family therapy or dispute resolution). Their online newsletter, *Center Pointe,* contains interviews with graduates, information regarding recent faculty and graduate publications, and news of general interest. It may be accessed online at <http://www.nova.edu/ssss/center-pointe>.

Purdue University Calumet's Marriage and Family Therapy Program (see Chapters 1, 2, 3, and 15) is accredited by the Commission on Accreditation for Marriage and Family Therapy Education of the American Association for Marriage and Family Therapy. The program produces master's-level graduates who are trained in a variety of systemic orientations and are versed in the three-part model of theory, research, and practice. Students are prepared to work in a variety of clinical settings and/or to pursue doctoral training. Students spend a year doing clinical training in the campus Marriage and Family Therapy Center where various client problems are addressed, including couple or marital problems such as communication difficulties, infidelity, and domestic violence. A training subclinic on sexual disorders has also been established. In addition, family concerns, such as a child acting out, family communication problems, school-related problems, and drug use are also addressed. Individual issues presented, such as depression, loneliness, substance abuse, and gender or sexuality concerns, are all addressed utilizing a systemic perspective (understanding the problem in terms of the family or relational system in which it is embedded). Students then spend their second semester training at community agencies, which generally provide a diverse clientele. Numerous student theses have won research awards on both the university and state levels. Further, the majority of students present at a professional conference and/or publish in a professional journal by the time they graduate.

The program aims to develop scholar-clinicians who are excited about the possibility of making significant contributions to the field of marriage and family therapy. The marriage and family therapy program reflects a spirit of encouragement, cooperation, and collegiality. It is dedicated to nurturing the best in each student. This program seeks students that will become skilled clinicians interested in moving the profession forward through their clinical work, research, scholarly writing, and professional involvement. The Purdue MFT program supports the professionalization of students, as reflected in the large number of student-authored publications and student presentations at state and national conferences. The program admits an average of six students per year, which means that it has about thirty students enrolled at any given point in time. Students in the program have won many intramural, state, and national research awards, including a large number of prestigious AAMFT research awards. Graduates of the program may be found in colleges, universities, hospitals, community mental health centers, private practice, rehabilitation programs, and freestanding institutes involved in therapy training, clinical service, and research. Faculty members work well together and promote collegiality among themselves and their students. Each year, the program provides opportunities for students to have sustained contact with some of the best-known authorities in the field of family therapy. Also, teleconferencing is used to allow students to interact with well-known family therapists across the country. The program is part of the strong, nationally recognized Department of Child Development and Family Studies.

University of Maryland's Marriage and Family Therapy Program (see Chapter 8) was established in 1978 and initially accredited by COAMFTE in 1983. Its mission is to educate and train diverse, sensitive, competent, and ethical marital and family therapists who are able to apply the most current knowledge of the profession of marital and family therapy, and who will also make contributions to the profession. The master's degree MFT program consists of twenty required courses in family studies and marital and family therapy. These courses surpass the criteria of the standard curriculum required by COAMFTE and integrate course work in family, family therapy theory, and research with experience in supervised couple and family therapy practice. The Marriage and Family Therapy (MFT) Program and Family Service Center, its primary clinical training site, are housed within the Department of Family Studies on the University of Maryland College Park campus, in the greater Washington, DC, metropolitan area.

The Department of Family Studies emphasizes a systems or ecological approach to professional education by combining the concepts of a number of interrelated professional fields, including marital and family therapy, human services, program development and evaluation, policy analysis, and family sciences. The institution of the family is perceived as embedded in larger cultural, political, and economic contexts that influence the functioning and well-being of its members. The MFT curriculum includes courses on family theory; theories of family therapy; couple therapy; ethical, legal and professional issues; sexual issues in family therapy and service delivery; gender and ethnicity; research methods; statistics and clinical assessment; diagnosis; and treatment. Students also complete a minimum of 500 supervised direct client-contact hours, with a minimum of 100 hours of clinical supervision.

The MFT clinical faculty consists of four members, Dr. Ned Gaylin (professor and program director), Dr. Carol Werlinich (instructor and director of the Family Service Center), Dr. Norman Epstein (professor), and Dr. Leigh Leslie (associate professor). All are AAMFT-approved supervisors. All of the faculty members teach courses in the program, supervise students in the Family Service Center, conduct clinical research, and maintain private practices in couple and family therapy. During their clinical training, MFT students rotate through supervisors, each of whom represents at least one of the major paradigms in the practice of marital and family therapy (e.g., structural strategic, feminist, cognitive behavioral, person centered, experiential, and narrative). Supervision takes place in both individual and group formats. The faculty also consistently involves graduate students in research, focusing on topics such as couple and family therapy process and outcome, community violence, depression, anxiety, work/family issues, family stress and coping, domestic abuse, cross-cultural studies of marital and family functioning, and gender and ethnicity issues.

The Family Service Center (FSC) provides clinical and educational services to families from the metropolitan Washington, DC, area. Services include couple therapy, family therapy, and family education. In addition, the FSC provides continuing education programs for professionals. The FSC operates on a twelve-month-calendar-year basis and is a fully comprehensive facility with twelve interview rooms, a waiting room, and a playroom, in addition to a large office area and a separate locked room for the storage of client files. The clinical interview rooms are equipped with comfortable furniture, artwork, state-of-the-art videotaping equipment, one-way mirrors, intercoms, and a phone system for supervision. On the average, 350 families seek services at the FSC each year, and are seen on a sliding scale of fees basis. FSC clients represent a wide diversity in presenting problems, socioeconomic status, race, ethnicity, age, and religion. Clients are referred to the FSC from a variety of sources, including county and municipal social service agencies, schools, courts, mental health professionals, and current and former clients. MFT students typically spend fours semesters and a summer working as staff focusing on a special interest (e.g., working with elderly clients). The broad ethnic diversity of the metropolitan Washington, DC, area presents many excellent opportunities for clinical and research experience.

MFT students in this program represent diverse ethnic backgrounds, in terms of characteristics such as gender, age, race, religion, and ethnicity. Upon completion of the program, students typically find employment in therapeutic and other human service agencies, public policy settings, and educational settings. Others continue their education in doctoral programs, including the PhD program in the Department of Family Studies at the University of Maryland.

University of Nebraska–Lincoln's Marriage and Family Therapy Program (see Chapter 16) is nationally accredited by the Commission on Accreditation for Marriage and Family Therapy Education (COAMFTE). The MFT program is one of six options within the Department of Family and Consumer Sciences and the only specialization within this department. (other options include family science, child development, family economics and resource management, family and consumer science education, and employee assistance). Approximately six students are admitted into the MFT program each year to begin course work in the fall semester. Admitted students complete the program in approximately two years (including summers) and progress through course work as a cohort. During the program, students complete approximately fifty-six university credits and a research thesis. Students also complete a twelve-month continuous enrollment practicum and 500 hours of clinical contact, and receive at least 100 hours of supervision from AAMFT-approved supervisors. Students obtain this clinical experience through the program-operated, on-campus marriage and family therapy clinic and through placement at community-based facilities in Lincoln and Omaha.

The three clinical faculty members assigned to the program have designed curriculum and training experiences that address the realities of modern mental health practice. In addition to courses that emphasize theory development and clinical skill training, the curriculum also includes courses on psychopathology, collaborative health care, psychopharmacology, and group counseling. The program faculty members have an established relationship with the behavioral science faculty at the University of Nebraska Medical Center (UNMC), Department of Family Practice, and conduct joint training with this faculty. Each year, some MFT students obtain clinical experience by working at the family practice clinics associated with UNMC. Faculty members have also recently developed a postdegree training program with the faculty at UNMC in medical family therapy, for those interested in more specialized training.

University of Rhode Island (see Chapter 5) offers a two-year program leading to the master of science degree in human development and family studies with a specialization in marriage and family therapy. This program has been accredited by the Commission on Accreditation for Marriage and Family Therapy Education since 1985 and has graduated more than 120 students during its two-decade history. The URI program is proud of its 100 percent postgraduate employment rate. Graduates of the program are now employed in various parts of the country in mental health agencies, family services agencies, state departments, and corporate settings.

The marriage and family therapy program consists of (1) conceptual instruction in family systems, family development, research methods, and therapy; (2) supervised clinical experience with individuals, couples, and families having a wide range of problems; and (3) contextual learning in a professional setting that includes family therapy and family-based evaluation and preventative work. Students take between fifty-four and sixty credit hours exclusive of prerequisites. The number of graduate hours required depends on previous graduate course work in related fields, but usually averages about sixty hours. It takes a minimum of two years of full-time study to complete the program. Although licensure requirements vary somewhat from state to state, in general, graduates of this program are qualified to take the national licensing examination. In Rhode Island, one must have two years of postgraduate professional experience, 2,000 hours of clinical work, and 100 hours of clinical supervision to qualify for the licensing exam.

Students have the opportunity to participate in several funded research initiatives through URI's Family Resource Partnership <www.uri.edu/frp>. The mission of the partnership is to strengthen children, families, and communities by bringing research-based support to those organizations providing services to children, families, and communities.

The University of Rhode Island has about 10,600 undergraduate and 2,300 graduate students on the Kingston campus, and about 750 full-time and 100 part-time faculty. Because URI is a state university, the faculty is involved not only in teaching but in wide-ranging research and in reaching out with practical information to help the people of the state. Given the wide diversity of families in the United States, the program is particularly interested in attracting minority graduate students. See their Web site at <www.uri.edu/hss/mft> for more information.

University of San Diego's Marital and Family Therapy Program (see Chapter 11) is one of three master's programs in California fully accredited by the Commission on the Accreditation for Marriage and Family Therapy Education (COAMFTE). The program has been accredited since 1993. The program also meets the educational requirements necessary for therapists seeking licensure in California. Students in the program are exposed to a variety of family system theories, and are encouraged to integrate these theories in a manner that makes sense to each therapist. Although the primary emphasis is on family systems theories, students in the program are also taught to consider how biological, psychological, and spiritual factors, as well as larger social systems (e.g., gender socialization, culture, social class), can influence their work with clients. Students in their second year are placed in community agencies where they provide 500 hours of therapy. The community agencies provide students an opportunity to work with clients of diverse ethnic and racial backgrounds, and to develop experience working in a variety of areas (e.g., couple therapy, children and adolescents, chronically mentally ill, bereavement, child and adolescent inpatient). Students receive extensive supervision during their clinical work from both faculty and agency supervisors.

University of South Dakota's graduate counseling program (see Chapter 2) has three master's-level tracks—community agency, school counseling, and students affairs—and a doctoral program in counselor education and practice. The program has been fully accredited by the Council on the Accreditation of Counseling and Related Educational Programs (CACREP) since 1993. This is one of only thirty-five accredited doctoral programs in the country. The program also meets the educational requirements necessary for counselors seeking licensure and national certification as professional counselors. The program features a faculty committed to students' personal and professional development. The faculty members hold diverse theoretical orientations and bring a variety of professional experiences to their teaching and research. Program goals emphasize ethical and professional practice as well as counseling skills training with an extensive and diverse three-step clinical training component, including practicum and field-based experiences. A broad range of possibilities for specialization is available, such as couple, marriage, and family therapy; child and adolescent counseling; play therapy; group counseling; mental health and substance abuse counseling; and brief and narrative therapy. Diverse client experiences are provided through the on-site Individual and Family Counseling Center. Active membership in the local chapter of Chi Sigma Iota, the international counseling honorary, as well as other professional counseling organizations is encouraged and mentored.

Utah State University's Marriage and Family Therapy Program (see Chapter 9) is an accredited master's program in USU's Department of Family and Human Development. Located in the middle of the Bear River Range of the Rocky Mountains in beautiful Cache Valley, northern Utah, the program specializes in training excellent master's level clinicians. The faculty members provide a strong depth and breadth of education and training, focusing on helping students develop their own styles and models of therapy. Learn more about the program at their Web site: <http://www.usu.edu/fhd/index.html>.

Virginia Tech's Master's Program in Marriage and Family Therapy (see Chapter 4) is located on the Northern Virginia campus, which is ten miles from Washington, DC. It is accredited by the Commission on Accreditation for Marriage and Family Therapy Education of the American Association for Marriage and Family Therapy and currently has about thirty master's students enrolled from all over the country. This program is noted for its emphasis on both research and clinical practice, providing excellent supervision to students in an on-site clinic which serves a diverse community in Northern Virginia and the greater Washington, DC, metropolitan area. The program has agreements with several agencies in the area that also provide first-rate clinical training to students as well as potential job placements. Three program students have won AAMFT Student Research Awards, and one, the National Council on Family Relations (NCFR) Family Therapy Section Student Research Award. Faculty members not only are actively involved in research and in publishing their work, but they also truly enjoy working with students. Several ongoing projects are in progress at any given time to provide students with good experience and opportunities to earn money as graduate assistants and to work closely with faculty. Some well-known and experienced adjunct faculty include Drs. Eliana Gil, Linda Rogers, Mary Linda Sara, and Ronald Federici, offering students a chance to take courses in play therapy, sex therapy, psychopathology, and couple therapy from experts in their specialty areas. Perhaps one of the program's most significant strengths is its engendered sense of family. The program is relatively small, faculty and students support each other, and everyone stays closely connected through the newsletter, alumni conferences, and a mailing list, as well as annual picnics and holiday parties at the homes of faculty. For more information, see the program Web site: <http://www.nvgc.vt.edu/mft/aop-intro.html>.

The **Department of Counselor Education and Counseling Psychology** at **Western Michigan University** in Kalamazoo, Michigan, has a long history of training counselors and counseling psychologists for work in a variety of settings. The department has a strong reputation for its sensitivity to multicultural and diversity concerns. Students may obtain a master's degree from among a range of options, including community/agency counseling, with an emphasis in marriage and family therapy. Since fall 2002, the department has also offered a master's degree program specifically in MFT, with plans to seek accreditation through AAMFT. The department also offers two doctoral degrees, one in counseling psychology, accredited by the American Psychological Association (APA), and one in counseling, leadership, and student affairs, with three options, all CACREP accredited. Additional faculty specializing in MFT include Alan J. Hovestadt, EdD, and Karen R. Blaisure, PhD. You may visit the departmental Web site at: <www.wmich.edu/cecp/>.

Foreword

Family therapists agree that the family is a powerful source of support and change. Yet so many ways to help families are available that it is hard to know where to begin. New students of family therapy face myriad theories and interventions, and names to put with each. They need a kind, wise guide to walk them through the field and introduce them to the experts and their theories.

Master family therapy educators Lorna Hecker and Joseph Wetchler, and their associates, do just that. Their accessible introductory text is a gift to the field of family therapy. In it, they present the past and present of family therapy in a manner that informs and engages but does not overwhelm. Readers learn first about the history and major theories of family therapy, and then critical topics such as gender, culture, ethics, and research, and how family therapists address presenting problems such as alcohol abuse, family violence, and sexual dysfunction.

There is a stand-alone quality to each chapter. For example, if the reader wants to learn about cognitive-behavioral therapies, Epstein's chapter is a rather complete primer. At the same time, if readers spend an entire semester cuddling up to this book, they will gain a big-picture view of the field and the many ways family therapy is practiced. Some authors of introductory texts ramble, focus on one pet theory, put you to sleep, insult your intelligence, or use dense, jargon-filled insider language. In contrast, this book does exactly what an introductory text should do: it introduces the reader, step by step, theory by theory, topic by topic, to the expanding field of family therapy. The contributors describe how family therapists think and what they do to make a difference in people's lives. Nobody can ask more from an introductory text. Thank you, Lorna Hecker, Joseph Wetchler, and associates, for your wonderful gift to the field.

Fred Piercy, PhD
Professor of Family Therapy and Department Head
Department of Human Development
Virginia Polytechnic Institute and State University
Blacksburg, Virginia

Preface

Family therapy is an often-undernoticed branch of the mental health disciplines. Yet most behavior that follows us into adulthood developed within the context of our families of origin. Indeed, as you learn about family therapy, you will begin to understand how we re-create in our adult relationships the patterns that we learned in childhood. Family therapy departs radically from traditional mental health in that it looks to the family to understand mental health issues, rather than looking solely at an individual as the source of mental health problems. This was a dramatic shift from the more reductionistic thinking of the early to middle 1900s. Yet another shift occurred in the field in the 1980s when feminists led a revolt citing that family therapy had failed to address the larger social context in which families are embedded. They cited that the field had ignored the politics of gender, and that all people in a family system did not have equal power based on that larger social context. Soon after in this tumultuous period, multicultural family therapists also reminded us that ethnicity and race also play a factor in that context. In yet another revolution against the traditional psychodynamic therapy model on which psychology was founded, the inclusion of spirituality issues in family therapy has occurred. Advocates cite that the majority of families believe in God, and that the field had also ignored how this larger context influences and is influenced by families.

In this book, you will learn about the revolution against traditional mental health treatment led by those who embraced systems theory and applied it to families. In addition, in response to the advocates of looking at larger systemic issues, you will learn about the contexts in which families are embedded—including gender, culture, and spirituality. You will see departures from traditional psychology, but you will also see the integration of traditional psychology with family systems concepts, such as in Chapter 8, "Cognitive-Behavioral Therapies for Couples and Families". You may even learn about yourself and explore the context in which you grew up as you read through these chapters. This can be both an exhilarating and anxiety-provoking process at times, as we sometimes have to shift beliefs we hold near and dear to us in order to learn new ways of thinking. Last, you will see the results of one more rebellion within the field led by social construction-ist advocates. Chapter 6, "The Collaborative Language-Based Models of Family Therapy: When Less Is More," reflects yet another change in think-ing that has recently become popular in the field of marriage and family therapy. In what is termed *postmodern therapy* the belief is that reality is so-cially constructed, and that one person's view of a situation is as valid as the next person's. This view of therapy is collaborative and focuses on client language, and not necessarily on the family system.

The book is organized into two parts. Part I is a theoretical section, in which the history of family therapy (and the theories generated therein) is explored, and then systems theory is detailed for the reader as a base to most subsequent family therapy models discussed in Part I. Theories commonly used in family therapy are presented. Case examples are sprinkled through-out to bring the theories to life for the reader.

Next, specific treatment areas common to marriage and family therapists are discussed in Part II. This includes the ingredients to couple therapy, communication training, marital enrichment, and premarital counseling. Larger contextual issues are covered, such as gender, culture, and spiritual-ity. Also included in Part II are topics that a marital and family therapist will commonly find in practice, such as substance abuse, divorce, and family vi-olence. In addition, sexual dysfunctions are covered, and the reader is intro-duced to sex therapy treatment. The interface of ethics and the legal system in family therapy is often constant. These and other professional issues are covered in Chapter 15. One final question the reader should be able to an-swer after reading this book is "Does family therapy work?" Chapter 16 ad-dresses this issue eloquently.

How is this text different from others in the field of family therapy? Most textbooks are written by only one or two authors who detail the approaches to family therapy. In this book, we have invited experts from each important area of family therapy to contribute chapters in their area of expertise. Twenty professionals from across the United States have come together to present their knowledge in the treatment areas in which they have expertise. This brings to the reader a blend of approaches and styles that is often lack-ing in other texts.

The intent of this text is to introduce the reader to the rich history and practice of marriage and family therapy. You might imagine yourself in an airplane flying over the field of marriage and family therapy. In this text, you will get a good but slightly distant look at important areas of family therapy. However, in each area, to fully understand it, you would need to study each of them much more closely. This is best done in graduate training programs. For the undergraduate reader, a special section in Chapter 15 gives advice on applying to graduate school so that one might further study these dynamic ways of treating individuals, couples, and families. In addition, contributors provide information on themselves and the marriage and family therapy programs where they teach. We hope you will enjoy this opportunity to familiarize yourself with training opportunities in this important field.

Acknowledgments

It has been a long and laborious task to assemble our panel of experts and put together this textbook. We would like to first thank all of our contributors for the painstaking efforts they have put into each chapter. Their efforts and patience are appreciated to no end. We are excited that so many volunteered to share their expertise with you, the reader. Since both of us have previously done considerable editing, it was a joy to work with these authors who showed such expertise and professionalism in their writing. To them we owe immense gratitude.

In addition to our contributors, we would like to acknowledge those who helped us along in our project. Much of our load was helped by dedicated. graduate assistants, including Meghan Ryan, Theresa Petersen, Carley Flores, Gina Gutenkunst, Christina Dust, and Cézanne Haas. We would also like to thank the undergraduate students who gave us clarity in their feedback of a draft of the manuscript, which we forced upon them! Pat Geiger and Judy Bates have held a lantern of technical skills throughout the project that illuminated our way to completion. We also would like to thank imprint editor Terry Trepper for his encouragement and very occasional nagging on the way to our finish line. We would also like to thank our friends and family who helped us traverse the many developmental and situational crises encountered on the way to finishing this book.

I (LH) would like to thank my partner Jonathan Lee for both his twisted humor and moral support, and my children for making family life not just a concept in a book, but something real, rewarding, and a constant adventure in living. In addition, good friends Anna Bower and Kate Sori also deserve thanks. Thanks are extended to my co-editor for his patience and perseverance.

The editing of a book is often a labor of love. In other words, the labor of the task takes time away from the ones you love, and the labor of the task could not be completed without the support of the ones who love you. I (JW) want to thank my wife, Carole Schwartz, for being my best friend and teaching me to think about the future; my stepchildren, Ryan and Jessica Marie, for giving me energy and helping me to laugh at life's absurdities; my family of origin, Bernie, Jorie, Diane, and Sherry, for picking me up when I was down; and my daughter, Jessica Lily, for being the light of my life. In addition, I want to thank Terry Trepper for his wise words and unlimited patience. Finally, I want to thank and congratulate my co-editor for her courage in working with me.

PART I:
THEORIES IN MARRIAGE AND FAMILY THERAPY

Chapter 1

The History of Marriage and Family Therapy

Joseph L. Wetchler

The whole is greater than the sum of its parts.

Gregory Bateson

Welcome to *An Introduction to Marriage and Family Therapy*. This book serves as an introduction to and overview of the fastest-growing arm of the mental health field, marriage and family therapy. Perhaps this would be a good time to present a preliminary definition. **Marriage and family therapy** is a model of mental health treatment that takes a family perspective toward emotional problems and psychopathology. It places individual pathology in a relational context and views treatment as encompassing the environment in which it is maintained, namely, the family.

The marriage and family therapy movement was started by several charismatic mavericks who became disenchanted with the traditional individually oriented mental health models (Guerin, 1976; Kaslow, 1980). For many, the psychoanalytic approach that dominated the field did not fit the patients or the problems they treated. Marriage counselors and family therapists began experimenting with their new ideas in isolated pockets around the United States. In fact, with some notable exceptions in England, the marriage and family therapy movement was initially an American phenomenon.

Although you would think that these new approaches to treating emotional problems would be embraced by the mental health field, in fact the opposite occurred. Marriage and family therapists found themselves shunned by the mental health establishment. Much of what they did was shared privately with trusted colleagues and students. Kaslow (1980) reflects about the early family therapy movement:

> From 1950 to 1954 much work in family therapy took place underground. The ideas of the leaders were considered heresy and no plat-

form was readily available to them at major professional conferences. Their writings were not welcome in the standard journals. (p. 93)

If anything, this initial rejection by the mental health field probably helped to spark the revolutionary zeal of the original marriage and family therapists. John Elderkin Bell (1976), one of the founders of family therapy, beautifully summarizes his experience during this time:

> I began to be confronted by experienced psychotherapists and theoreticians who disapproved of my practice and were uncomfortable with my concepts. I learned that these critics were not to be won over easily by simple endorsements of working with the whole family, and usually answered their arguments by saying I would take their comments into account, as I did; but I also learned I could not fit older theories to my new experiences. I realized that, fundamentally, I had to find the rationale for family therapy from my own experiences, in private reflections on the actions of which I was a part. As a result, more and more I found myself avoiding the ideas and language of individual therapy and traditional group therapy. I found, also, the formulations and terms mastered for my university teaching on personality and abnormal psychology had little pertinence to my new activities. (p. 130)

As we begin the twenty-first century, marriage and family therapy has gained acceptance by the mental health establishment and the lay population in general. Family therapy is provided at most mental health centers and family service associations, and graduate degrees are available at numerous universities across the United States and around the world. Marriage and family therapy was influenced by four major movements: early social work, sex therapy, marriage counseling, and family therapy. The following pages summarize their impact on the field.

THE EARLY SOCIAL WORK MOVEMENT

Although marriage and family therapy is a relatively new idea, working with families is not. The early social workers first pioneered interventions with marriages and families (Broderick and Schrader, 1991). The field of **social work,** a branch of the mental health field that focuses on the impact of societal issues on human problems, grew out of the charity movements in Great Britain and the United States in the late nineteenth century (Nichols and Schwartz, 1998). The initial thrust of the movement was to minister to the needs of the underprivileged members of society. The first social caseworkers proposed that effective interventions must begin with the family. As early as 1890, Zilpha D. Smith wrote to the mental health establishment:

> Most of you deal with poor persons or defective individuals, removed from family relationships. We deal with the family as a whole, usually working to keep it together, but sometimes helping to break it up into units and to place them in your care. (p. 377)

Perhaps the greatest early champion of family intervention was Mary Richmond. In her influential book, *Social Diagnosis* (1917), she wrote about the importance of treating the family as a whole unit if one hoped to alleviate the problems of the poor. She believed that seeing the family at the beginning of treatment and specifically intervening in their process was the best way to achieve lasting results. She also foreshadowed the family therapy movement in her ability to see family systems as nested in larger societal systems (Nichols and Schwartz, 1998). This led to interventions in larger units, such as neighborhoods, and government policies to effect change for families. It also led to a greater appreciation for the role that culture plays in an individual family's life.

Unfortunately, although social workers were some of the most influential pioneers in family intervention, they returned to an individual focus when they joined forces with psychiatry in the 1920s (Broderick and Schrader, 1991). Although, with notable exceptions, they did not play a dominant role in the initial development of either marriage counseling or family therapy, they were influential members of both movements from the 1960s onward. Notable social workers who have made valuable contributions to marriage and family therapy include Virginia Satir, Peggy Papp, Lynn Hoffman, Steve de Shazer, Insoo Kim Berg, Michael White, Froma Walsh, Richard Stuart, Braulio Montalvo, Betty Carter, and Monica McGoldrick. Many of the contributions of these influential social workers will be discussed in later chapters.

THE SEXUAL REFORM MOVEMENT

Following World War I, several Europeans and Americans participated in a movement to establish human sexuality as a science and to provide sexual education to the general population (Broderick and Schrader, 1991). At the forefront of this movement were Havelock Ellis of Great Britain and Magnus Hirschfeld of Germany.

Havelock Ellis wrote widely on the area of human sexuality, including homosexuality, and provided counseling to people with sexual problems.

Many of his clients were women who may have been attracted to him as much for his good looks as for his sexual knowledge. Although his practice consisted primarily of listening and providing readings, he would sometimes initiate women into his own version of nondemand sexual pleasuring (Broderick and Schrader, 1991). He felt he could do this without being controversial as he was impotent for most of his adult life. It is interesting to note that he restricted his practice to individuals and did not see couples. Although his methods could be considered simplistic and ethically questionable, his pioneering efforts must be applauded. Further, he probably was quite helpful to several individuals in that, considering the times, a good proportion of the problems suffered by his clientele may have been related to a lack of education as much as anything else.

Magnus Hirschfeld founded the Institute of Sexual Science in Berlin in 1918 and, together with August Forel and Ellis, founded the World League for Sexual Reform. His institute was a Mecca for physicians the world over wishing to learn more about human sexuality. His definitive tome, *Geschlechtskunde* (Sex education) (1930) reported his findings based on 10,000 questionnaires completed by the men and women whom he consulted (Broderick and Schrader, 1991). He also founded the first German Marriage Consultation Bureau to provide counseling to German families and couples (Hirschfeld, 1940). Sadly, when Hitler came to power in Germany, he closed Hirschfeld's centers and turned them into institutions to evaluate couples for fitness to marry and reproduce.

Three American pioneers were instrumental in continuing the work of Ellis and Hirschfeld. Gynecologist Robert Dickinson was active as a scientist and counselor in the area of human sexuality. He systematically sketched the pelvic area of each of his patients, men as well, several of which he included in his landmark book, *Human Sex Anatomy* (1933). He also published his findings from thousands of interviews with his patients on their sex histories and current practices (Dickinson and Beam, 1931, 1934). Further, Robert Dickinson was one of the founders of the fledgling marriage counseling movement that started in the early 1930s.

When we think about the history of human sexuality in the United States, the first name that typically comes to mind is that of Alfred Kinsey, a professor at Indiana University. He and his colleagues published two of the most important and controversial books of their time. *Sexual Behavior in the Human Male* (Kinsey, Pomeroy, and Martin, 1948) and its companion *Sexual Behavior in the Human Female* (Kinsey et al., 1953) created a whirlwind of both praise and criticism for their frank presentations of the sexual practices of a wide range of Americans. Most surprising about Kinsey's work, perhaps, is that as most of his contemporaries were conducting their research in large metropolitan areas where they were surrounded by like-minded individuals, he conducted his studies in a small university town in the conservative Midwest. It must have been a lonely existence at times for this important pioneer.

The third member of the American sexual trilogy is the research team of William Masters and Virginia Johnson. Working out of Washington University Medical School in Saint Louis, Missouri, they conducted a vast body of scientific research in both the areas of sexual problems and treatment. Although written for professionals, their book *Human Sexual Response* (1966) was a popular success, selling over 300,000 copies (Broderick and Schrader, 1991). However, it was their second book, *Human Sexual Inadequacy* (1970), that promoted and popularized the field of sex therapy. Many couples today continue to receive treatment at their Saint Louis clinic.

MARRIAGE COUNSELING

Marriage counseling, a form of therapy in which a clinician sees both spouses together to resolve problems in their relationship, was virtually nonexistent within the mental health establishment during the early part of the twentieth century. A person complaining about marital problems would likely be seen in individual therapy by a psychiatrist, or psychologist, with his or her spouse being treated by another therapist if their problems were too difficult. Although this may seem a bit naive, we must remember that the psychoanalytic model was the dominant approach at the time. It was through individual long-term therapy that clients transferred their past issues onto their therapists and subsequently worked them through. Having one's spouse in the room was thought to hinder the development of transference onto the therapist and was not advised.

Early marriage counseling became the domain of a variety of professionals outside the mental health establishment. Couples with marital problems were more likely to meet with a member of the clergy, a physician, or an educator to get some semblance of help. Broderick and Schrader (1991) recall:

> Marriage and premarriage counseling was often the auxiliary activity of a college professor. It was equally likely to be the auxiliary occupation of a range of other professionals, including lawyers, social workers, and physicians. One group of physicians that played a particularly central role in the early shaping of the field of marriage counseling were members of the growing specialty of obstetrics and gynecology. (p. 9)

In 1930, the first two marriage counseling centers opened in the United States (Broderick and Schrader, 1991). Paul Popenoe, a biologist specializing in human heredity, founded the American Institute of Family Relations in Los Angeles, California. He claims to be the first to coin the term *marriage counseling,* which he translated from the German *Eheberatunsstellen,* the term used for marital consultation centers in Germany (Popenoe, 1975). That same year, physicians Abraham and Hannah Stone, finding themselves often providing marital counseling in their practice, officially opened their center in the New York Labor Temple. In 1932, they moved their operation to the Community Church of New York where they ran an ecumenical marriage center for many years (Broderick and Schrader, 1991).

A third center, The Marriage Council of Philadelphia, opened its doors under the directorship of Emily Mudd in 1932. This historic institution was the first to conduct a continuing program of research on the marital process (Broderick and Schrader, 1991). The Marriage Council of Philadelphia exists today as The Penn Council for Relationships. It continues to be a major force in the marriage and family therapy field, training thousands of clinicians and publishing numerous papers and books.

In 1938, husband and wife David and Vera Mace formed the first Marriage Guidance Council in London. Their idea was to use a few professionals to train and supervise several paraprofessionals who could provide counseling at a much-reduced cost to the numerous working-class families of England. By 1943 it had become the National Guidance Council of Great Britain and regularly provided counseling to couples throughout the British Commonwealth (Mace, 1945, 1948).

Although the 1930s brought about the development of several important marriage counseling centers, the field remained on shaky ground. If marriage counseling was to survive, it needed a professional association to develop guidelines for training clinicians and to conduct conferences that presented the latest findings. In 1942, Drs. Lester Dearborn, Robert Laidlaw, Ernest and Gladys Groves, Emily Mudd, Abraham Stone, Robert Dickenson, and Valerie Parker gathered together to organize what would become the American Association for Marriage Counseling (AAMC). The organization became a reality in 1945, with Ernest Groves elected the first president (Mudd and Fowler, 1976).

Unfortunately, although marriage counseling had a bright beginning, it was slow in developing as a profession. As late as 1960, the modal interview at the pioneering centers was still the one-on-one interview (Michaelson, 1963). Further, even up to the early 1970s the field still lacked a coherent body of scholarship (Gurman, 1973). Perhaps this is best explained by the fact that, as of 1965, only 25 percent of the members of the AAMC considered themselves to be primarily marriage counselors. For the rest, it still was an auxiliary activity (Alexander, 1968).

If the development of professional marriage counseling was somewhat sickly in the 1960s, its cure came in the form of the family therapy movement (Broderick and Schrader, 1991). The fields were a natural marriage as both took a relational approach to problem resolution. Family therapists' belief that individual pathology was best treated by working with the family was a perfect match to the marriage counselors' dictum to work with couples. In 1970, the AAMC changed its name to the American Association of Marriage and Family Counselors, and subsequently to the American Association for Marriage and Family Therapy (AAMFT) in 1979, to reflect this expanded perspective.

THE FAMILY THERAPY MOVEMENT

Perhaps the greatest push within the field of marriage and family therapy came from the family therapy movement (Broderick and Schrader, 1991; Guerin, 1976; Kaslow, 1980; Nichols and Schwartz, 1998). The early family therapists were researchers and clinicians working with intractable problems such as schizophrenia and delinquency. Traditional individual models such as psychoanalysis, play therapy, and client-centered approaches were either not helpful for or applicable to these problems. The mental health field was restless and looking for new ways to treat these problems.

It is not surprising that family therapy had a stronger impact than marriage counseling. Historically, the mental health profession was built on treating pathological disorders. Even today, training in psychopathology and knowledge of the *Diagnostic and Statistical Manual of Mental Disorders* (DSM) is considered a crucial part of a clinical education. Often in marital problems there is no **identified patient,** or individual family member identified as having a specific problem; instead, there is a marital problem between two basically healthy people. It has always been viewed within the mental health establishment, whether correctly or incorrectly, that it is more important to treat diagnosable problems than relational issues that cause extreme pain. This is further supported by the number of insurance policies that do not reimburse marital therapy, but will provide payment if one of the spouses suffers from depression due to marital problems.

The family therapy movement started with a focus on the family as causing the patient's problem and eventually moved to a view of the patient's problem as part of a relational process among the members (Gale and Long, 1996; Guerin, 1976). This development made it a perfect fit with marriage counseling as both place a strong emphasis on treating relational processes.

Further, treating certain family problems involves working with the parents' marriage, and some children's problems have been found to diminish without treatment when the parents receive marital counseling (e.g., Bowen, 1978; Haley, 1987; Kramer, 1980).

Who actually founded family therapy is open to debate; however, the distinction can probably be shared by four individuals: Nathan Ackerman, Murray Bowen, John Elderkin Bell, and Don Jackson (Nichols and Schwartz, 1998). Several other pioneers also played significant roles in the development of this movement. Gregory Bateson, Theodore Lidz, Ivan Boszormenyi-Nagy, Jay Haley, Salvador Minuchin, Virginia Satir, Carl Whitaker, and Lyman Wynne provided important contributions to this growing field. Further, more recent names such as Betty Carter, Steve de Shazer, Monica McGoldrick, Peggy Papp, Mara Selvini Palazzoli, and Michael White have taken the field in directions that the original founding parents may never have imagined.

John Bell

John Elderkin Bell, a psychologist at Clark University in Worchester, Massachusetts, began seeing families in 1951. Although he may be considered the first family therapist (Broderick and Schrader, 1991; Nichols and Schwartz, 1998), he did not publish his ideas for several years and did not develop a clinical center or train well-known students. As a result, many of his ideas remained on the periphery of the field.

His most noteworthy contribution was a book, *Family Group Therapy* (1961), in which he described an approach to families based on the ideas of **group therapy,** a form of treatment in which individuals discuss their problems in a group setting, allowing them to receive support and feedback from other group members. Rather than thinking about a family as an **interactional system,** or a single unit in which all members interact as parts of a larger whole, he treated each family member as he would an individual group member. He would prod silent members to speak up and encourage more dominant members to speak less often. Some of his ideas led to the early belief that family therapy was similar to group therapy, but many issues distinguish the two.

First of all, group therapy brings several individuals together to form a temporary support group in which individuals work through their problems. Their relationship is temporary and often terminates when an individual leaves the group or the group disbands. On the other hand, family therapy operates on the assumption that the family in treatment has both a past and a future, as well as the current relationship. Issues from the past as well as future concerns of the family are often tied up in present issues. Although group therapy often encourages an open expression of feelings and ideas, it may not be advisable for complete disclosure in family therapy. In a group of strangers with no connection other than the group, open discussion of feelings and issues is done in the presence of a therapist who can handle and redirect the emotional fallout.

In family therapy, certain disclosures can have serious consequences for the emotional well-being and history of a family. For example, it would be very unwise for a therapist to encourage overwhelmed parents to admit to their young children that they wish they had never had them. Discussing this issue would be appropriate with the children out of the room, but sharing this information openly would certainly cause unnecessary pain for both the children and parents and could cause future relational problems regarding family trust. Group therapy issues are dealt with in the presence of a therapist and the individuals then go to their respective homes, but family members must spend the time between sessions dealing with one another and acknowledging what was shared without a therapist to referee their conflicts (Nichols and Schwartz, 1998).

A second difference relates to how a therapist approaches a group versus a family. In group therapy, the therapist brings together a group of strangers to develop a support network. Their initial relationship is to the therapist and then expands to the group. Other group members do not have as big a stake in an individual's problems and are willing to help the therapist in getting members to talk about their problems. In family therapy, the therapist is confronted with an organized system in which the members have a history of assuming specific roles and following a certain culture. Rather than getting support from other family members to help a member disclose an issue, the therapist may find that all members collude to keep the issue a secret. Further, how therapists talk to one family member may affect the success they have in developing relationships with the rest of the family. For example, Carl Whitaker (1976) believes it is important for family therapists to quickly develop a playful relationship with small children. It reassures the rest of the family members that the therapist is safe when they can see him or her being playful with their most vulnerable members. However, if the child does not respond to the therapist, it is best to quickly move on to a different family member to avoid their growing feeling of concern.

Nathan Ackerman

Nathan Ackerman was a dynamic individual who did much to introduce family therapy to the mental health profession. Originally trained as a child psychiatrist, he developed a method of family therapy that reflected his original psychoanalytic orientation. Ackerman believed that although a family may appear united, its members are often split into competing factions and coalitions—similar to how Freud saw the human psyche caught in a battle among the components of id, ego, and superego.

In 1937, Ackerman became chief psychiatrist of the Child Guidance Clinic at the Menninger Clinic in Topeka, Kansas. He initially followed the traditional child guidance model in which a psychiatrist saw the child in therapy while a social worker consulted with the mother. He began to question this approach and in the 1940s experimented with having the same therapist treat both. It was also during this time that he became concerned with the legitimacy of the individual approach to mental illness and started to view it as a family phenomenon. In 1950 he wrote "Family Diagnosis: An Approach to the Preschool Child" (Ackerman and Sobel, 1950), which some consider to be the article that started the family therapy movement (Kaslow, 1980).

Ackerman was a daring and innovative clinician. He was an "agent provocateur" (Nichols and Schwartz, 1998) who promoted the open and honest expression of feelings and the confrontation of issues within the family. He was known for his ability to use wit and personal charisma to enable families to develop new ways of relating; this was more closely related to modern family therapy approaches of changing family interaction than to the psychoanalytic and group format that dominated the early approaches. His style later evolved more fully through the work of his student Salvador Minuchin, whose **structural family therapy** approach attempted to alter the organization of a family to enable them to solve their problems.

During the later part of the 1950s, Ackerman held many positions within this growing field. In 1955, he organized and chaired the first session on family diagnosis at the American Orthopsychiatric Association. Two years later, he opened the Family Mental Health Clinic at Jewish Family Services in New York City and joined the faculty at Columbia University. In 1958, he published *The Psychodynamics of Family Life,* which was the first book on the diagnosis and treatment of family relationships (Broderick and Schrader, 1991). In 1960, he founded the Family Institute, which was renamed the Ackerman Institute following his death in 1971. This institute continues to serve as a prominent center for training family therapists and promoting clinical innovation within the field. In 1960, he founded the first journal in the field, *Family Process,* with Don Jackson of Palo Alto. His legacy lives on: *Family Process* continues to be the most influential and unifying journal in the field.

Palo Alto: Gregory Bateson, Don Jackson, Jay Haley, Virginia Satir, and the Mental Research Institute

During the 1950s, Palo Alto, California, became a foundational hotbed for the family therapy movement. Two important projects—a study on schizophrenia under the directorship of Gregory Bateson, and the Mental Research Institute headed by Don Jackson—dovetailed together to have an impact that still affects the field today. It is difficult to document in a coherent manner all of the important people who emerged through these projects, especially since many of them went on to influence the field differently than their original work while in Palo Alto would have suggested. Still, besides Bateson and Jackson, this is where family therapy innovators such as Richard Fisch, Jay Haley, Virginia Satir, Carlos Sluzki, Paul Watzlawick, and John Weakland got their start.

Gregory Bateson

Family therapy owes a major debt to Gregory Bateson, yet he was not a family therapist and was opposed to therapeutic interventions of any kind. Bateson was an anthropologist with an interest in applying ideas from the emerging field of cybernetics to communication patterns in living organisms. **Cybernetics** is the science of communication and control in humans and machines. It looks at how humans and machines maintain stability through feedback. A good example is how a thermostat maintains the temperature in a room. As the temperature rises, the thermostat receives this information and turns on the air-conditioning. When the temperature drops to the desired setting, the thermostat receives this information and shuts off the air-conditioning. This idea was used to explain how a family member's symptoms would get worse to cool off an escalating family crisis and subside when the crisis settled down. For example, an adolescent might begin stealing to deflect attention from his or her parents' marital problems, and stop when their marriage was doing better.

In 1952, Bateson was funded by a Rockefeller Foundation grant to study paradoxes in communication (Gale and Long, 1996). **Paradoxes** are statements that tend to disqualify themselves. For example, a wife ordering her husband to be more spontaneous disqualifies her demands, because the husband cannot behave spontaneously if he follows his wife's orders. The very root of spontaneity is to be free to act as one pleases.

Bateson invited two former students, John Weakland, an anthropologist and former chemical engineer, and Jay Haley, a communications major, to join him in this study. Their project was housed at the Menlo Park Veterans

Affairs Hospital in California and it was here that they developed an interest in the communication patterns of schizophrenics (Weakland, Watzlawick, and Riskin, 1995). Their initial concern was with the origin of schizophrenia. Because they were unable to get accurate descriptions of the history of their schizophrenic patients or their families, they decided to study their communication patterns by interviewing them and taping their sessions (Weakland, Watzlawick, and Riskin, 1995). This led to their desire to provide treatment and to their receiving a subsequent grant from the National Institute of Mental Health to study the effects of family therapy on schizophrenics and their families.

During this period, Bateson invited Don Jackson, a psychiatrist at the VA hospital, to serve as a consultant to their project. He later became a core member and jointly authored a paper, "Toward a Theory of Schizophrenia" (Bateson et al., 1956), which revolutionized the thinking about severe psychopathology. The paper posited that schizophrenic behavior is caused by paradoxical, or double-bind, family communication patterns in which verbal messages are often contradicted at the nonverbal level. For example, the team observed a situation in which a schizophrenic patient on the ward attempted to hug his mother when she visited him. Seeing her cross her arms and back away, he withdrew his gesture. The mother then admonished her son about how he *should* show more affection when she came to visit, which led to his having a psychotic episode after she left. The team believed that the only way a person continuously exposed to paradoxical messages could behave was through schizophrenic expression (Bateson et al., 1956). Although this paper garnered much discussion, it was primarily theoretical in nature. In fact, the team began to interview families with a schizophrenic member only around the time of the paper's publication. Haley candidly reflects (in Simon, 1992):

> When Bateson came up with the double-bind hypothesis, he had never seen a family. He developed it in 1954, and we didn't see a family until about 1956 or 1957. We wrote the double-bind paper in June 1956; it was published in September 1956—the fastest journal publication ever done, I think. (p. 5)

Although a theoretical paper of this type would not be published today without some form of clinical support, it is noteworthy how it influenced schizophrenia research, and therapy practices in general, for the next several decades.

Unfortunately, although the mental health establishment was uplifted by these ideas, the same may not be said for the families of schizophrenics.

Nichols and Schwartz (1998) provide a dissenting opinion on the double-bind theory:

> This 1956 double-bind paper proved to be one of the most influential and controversial in the history of family therapy. The discovery that schizophrenic symptoms made sense in the context of some families may have been a scientific advance, but it had moral and political overtones. Not only did these investigators see themselves as avenging knights bent on rescuing "identified patients" by slaying family dragons, they were also crusaders in a holy war against the psychiatric establishment. Outnumbered and surrounded by hostile critics, the champions of family therapy challenged the orthodox assumption that schizophrenia was a biological disease. Psychological healers everywhere cheered. Unfortunately they were wrong.
>
> The observation that schizophrenic behavior seems to fit in some families doesn't mean that families *cause* schizophrenia. In logic, this kind of inference is called "Jumping to Conclusions." Sadly, . . . families of schizophrenic members suffered for years under the assumption that they were to blame for the tragedy of their children's psychoses. (pp. 29, 30; italics in original)

Gregory Bateson's subsequent books, *Steps to an Ecology of Mind* (1972) and *Mind and Nature* (1979), continue to have a major impact on family therapy theory and practice today. However, true to his training as an anthropologist, he remained skeptical about therapeutic intervention. He often observed how anthropologists and missionaries accidentally destroyed the cultures they attempted to study, or help, by teaching them the cultural practices of their home countries. Although these new gifts were often valued by the host culture, they often did not fit with traditional practices and ended up destroying their society (A good example is the introduction of alcoholic beverages to Native Americans.). Bateson's greatest fear was that therapists would intervene too much with families and destroy their inherent strengths while attempting to resolve their problems. These concerns eventually led him away from family therapy to study animal behavior. Bateson died in 1980 at age seventy-six.

Don Jackson

Don Jackson was a brilliant psychiatrist and charismatic personality who amazed his colleagues with his clinical insights. He was a major influence on many of the key family therapy figures of the time. While working at the VA hospital in Menlo Park, he served as a consultant to the Bateson project, and subsequently became a core member. Prior to coming to the VA hospital he spent the preceding three years as a psychiatric resident at Chestnut Lodge under the supervision of Harry Stack Sullivan, who taught him about the interactional nature of psychosis (Guerin, 1976).

While working with Bateson on the communications project, Jackson founded the independent Mental Research Institute (MRI) in 1959 where he was joined by Virgina Satir (Broderick and Schrader, 1991). Although Bateson was more interested in research, the MRI was more focused on family therapy. The MRI has served as one of the most influential centers for family therapy in the entire world. It was here that the strategic school of family therapy was founded (see Chapter 4), and to date, the MRI has produced over fifty completed research projects, more than forty books, and over 400 other publications (Weakland, Watzlawick, and Riskin, 1995). That same year, Jackson published the paper "Family Interaction, Family Homeostasis, and Some Implications for Conjoint Family Therapy" (Jackson, 1959), in which he argued that seeing families together was more effective than conducting therapy with individual members alone.

In 1960, Jackson joined with Nathan Ackerman to form a journal, *Family Process,* and appointed Jay Haley the first editor. The first issue of *Family Process* was published in 1962 and continues today to set the standard for the rest of the field.

Don Jackson was an amazing diagnostician. Paul Watzlawick (in Weakland, Watzlawick, and Riskin, 1995) recalls that the researchers at the MRI

met with Don for many, many weeks for several hours per week, and we played him blind segments of structured interviews—that is, the couple's response to "How, out of the millions of people in the world, did you two get together?" We had 60 such examples which ranged from two to five minutes approximately. Don did not know the people. He had never seen them; we did not give him any information, not even the ages. Don would come up with the most incredibly concrete interchanges, of which, of course, he only had the verbal and paralinguistic parts; he did not see the facial expression and the body language or anything. He just listened to the tape. He would then say something as concrete as, "All right, if they have a son, he is probably delinquent. If they have a girl, she probably has some psychosomatic problem." He was right every bloody time. And we would say, "For God's sake, Don, how do you do it? What made you say this?" He would say, as if it was the most obvious thing in the world, "Well, because of the way they laugh here." We still did not know what was the thing that made him say it, but he was always right. I remember one funny incident in particular. We tried to get a control group of so-called normals, and we rounded up three normal couples. I remember one was a father and a mother, whose marriage seemed to be very much all right after something like 17 years. They had a 15-year-old daughter and she was doing well at school and there were no problems. So they qualified for our idea of normal. We played this particular part of "how did you meet" for Don, and for the first time Don said, "I don't know; to me they sound normal." (pp. 13-14)

In 1962, at the close of the Bateson project, Jay Haley and John Weakland joined Jackson at the MRI. In 1967, with Paul Watzlawick and Janet Beavin, he published *Pragmatics of Human Communication* (Watzlawick, Beavin, and Jackson, 1967), which was the first book-length treatise on the interactional theories of the MRI. Don Jackson's premature death in 1968 deprived the field of a major leader and innovator; however, his name will continue to live on through the ongoing accomplishments of the MRI.

Jay Haley

Jay Haley remains one of family therapy's most controversial and most influential leaders (Simon, 1992). With a master's degree in communications, he began as an outsider to the mental health establishment. Perhaps it was this outsider perspective that enabled him to so easily challenge the traditional psychoanalytic approach of the time and to focus on patterns of family interaction. In fact, none of the original members of the Bateson team held a degree in the mental health field (both Bateson and Weakland were anthropologists).

Although clearly identified as one of the original founders of the strategic school of family therapy, Haley served equally important roles as both a promoter and synthesizer of the ideas in family therapy and a critic of the mental health establishment (Simon, 1992). While a member of the Bateson project, Haley traveled to Phoenix, Arizona, to observe the work of Milton Erickson, a noted psychiatrist and hypnotherapist. Erickson practiced a brief form of hypnotherapy; patients from across the country then would work with him for a few weeks and return home with their problems resolved. It was through these observations that Haley and the other members of the MRI were able to develop **strategic family therapy,** a brief approach that focuses on observing and altering the interactional sequences in which a problem is embedded. Further, this association led to Haley becoming the chief chronicler of Erickson's work (e.g., Haley, 1973, 1985a,b,c).

During his tenure as the first editor of *Family Process,* Haley traveled around the country observing others' work and encouraging them to submit

articles to the new journal. During this period, he observed five family therapists conducting therapy and discussed with them how they conceptualized
cases and why they intervened in the ways they did. These interviews, along
with verbatim transcripts of their sessions were published in book form as
Techniques of Family Therapy (Haley and Hoffman, 1967). This book was
the first to clearly show readers how family therapy was practiced. However, it was *Strategies of Psychotherapy* (Haley, 1963) in which Haley de-
clared all-out war on the traditional mental health establishment by refuting
such ideas as patient-therapist transference and therapist nondirectiveness.
He presented a therapy based on interaction, relational power, and therapist
directiveness. Haley continues to create controversy among students and
mental health practitioners with his direct and provocative writing style.

In 1967, Haley left the MRI to join Salvador Minuchin at the Philadelphia Child Guidance Clinic where he helped develop structural family therapy (see Chapter 3), a form of therapy in which the therapist uses an organizational approach to treat families. He then moved on to found the Family
Therapy Institute of Washington, DC, which he directs with his ex-spouse
Cloe Madanes. Jay Haley continues to be a leader in the strategic school of
family therapy.

Virginia Satir

While Virginia Satir was one of the original members of the MRI, her relationship to Strategic Family Therapy is tangential at best. She began seeing families in the early 1950s as a social worker in Chicago; however, it
was through reading Bateson et al.'s (1956) "Toward a Theory of Schizophrenia" that she developed a systems perspective (Satir, Stachowiak, and
Taschman, 1977). This made her a natural to join Jackson in Palo Alto,
which was becoming a hotbed for the emerging field. During the mid-1960s
she left the MRI to become involved with the human potential movement at
the Esalan Institute in Big Sur, California, where she became associated
with **experiential family therapy,** a school of family therapy that is more
focused on human emotions and growth than interactional sequences. Similar to Haley, Satir was a major force in popularizing this new movement;
however, she recruited followers through her warmth and charisma in contrast to Haley's criticism and controversial stances. Broderick and Schrader
(1991) recall:

> Probably more than any other early founder, she was responsible for
> popularizing the movement. She had a flair for clear, nontechnical ex-
> position and charismatic presentation that led her to address tens of

thousands in person, hundreds of thousands through her books, and millions through the media. (p. 29)

Murray Bowen

Murray Bowen was a child psychiatrist who specialized in treating psychotic children. After World War II, Bowen served on the staff of the Menninger Clinic in Topeka, Kansas, which at the time was a bastion of the psychoanalytic movement. He was initially influenced by the writings of Freida Fromm-Reichman on the role of the schizophrenogenic mother in child psychosis. Fromm-Reichman postulated that these mothers were needy, insecure women who smothered and overprotected their children to the point at which they had a schizophrenic break, an idea no longer believed to be credible. In 1951, Bowen began hospitalizing schizophrenic children and their mothers at the Menninger Clinic in the hope of observing and eventually treating this phenomenon. It was during this period that he began to question the psychoanalytic notion of schizophrenia as existing in the "head" of the patient, and began to assess the interactional dynamics of the mother/child relationship. His new ideas about schizophrenia as an interactional disorder rather than an intrapsychic one drew the wrath of many of his colleagues at Menninger's and eventually led to his departure (Wylie, 1992).

In 1954, he moved to Washington, DC, to join the staff of the National Institute of Mental Health (NIMH). This was a creative wellspring for bright young mental health mavericks who were interested in studying emotional phenomena that ran counter to traditional mental health ideas. During this period, Bowen questioned the interactional pattern that maintained schizophrenia belonged solely to the mother/child dyad and began to examine the role of fathers in this relationship. He and his research team were able to hospitalize four families and study several others in the community. They found these families engaged in a pattern in which the mother and child were unusually close and the father was distant; however, in times of stress, the alliance would shift to the father and child, with the mother on the outs. This finding led Bowen to study how these behavioral sequences were transmitted through the generations in families, which he called the **multigenerational transmission process**.

Bowen's desire was to develop a natural systems model of human behavior—a model that showed how all living systems behave according to innately programmed patterns. As the years passed, he turned more toward the field of biology and the natural sciences than to the traditional psychological models that pervaded the mental health literature (Bowen, 1978).

In 1958, Bowen left the NIMH to go to the Georgetown University School of Medicine where he set up his family therapy training program. In 1967, he experimented with his ideas for altering entrenched multigenerational family patterns with his own **family of origin,** the family in which he grew up (Anonymous, 1972). This was an important undertaking for Bowen, as he found this experience so profound that he mandated all of his family therapy trainees have a similar experience with their own families. In fact, having family therapy students understand their own families of origin continues to be a hallmark of training in **Bowen systems therapy,** the family therapy approach named after Murray Bowen that views problems as maintained through multigenerational patterns.

Throughout his career, Bowen showed a greater interest in theory than in therapy. He felt that too great of an emphasis on therapeutic technique led many therapists to replicate problem-maintaining patterns with their treatment families because they did not understand the theoretical underpinnings of their problems (Bowen, 1978). This focus on theory made Bowen somewhat unique within the family therapy field and also kept him somewhat separated and misunderstood (Wylie, 1992). Many of Bowen's key ideas are presented in his book, *Family Therapy in Clinical Practice* (Bowen, 1978), which is a collection of important articles written and presentations made throughout his career. His legacy has continued beyond his death in 1990, through the ongoing work of the faculty at the Georgetown Family Therapy Center.

Theodore Lidz

Theodore Lidz was a psychoanalytically oriented researcher interested in the role of families in schizophrenia. At Johns Hopkins University, he discovered that schizophrenic individuals came from homes with numerous family and marital problems (Lidz and Lidz, 1949). This certainly was a significant finding for its day, and opened the door for other family models of severe mental illness. After entering Yale University in 1951, he began to study hospitalized schizophrenics and their families more closely. Similar to Bowen, he questioned the role of the schizophrenogenic mother, and emphasized the role of fathers in the process of mental illness (Lidz, Perker, and Cornelison, 1956).

Lidz also hypothesized that the parents' marital relationship was as important in the development of a schizophrenic child as either of the parents' individual characteristics (Lidz et al., 1957). Two dominant marital patterns he observed were **marital schism,** in which the husband and wife fail to accommodate each other, and constantly attack each other and compete for their children's affection, and **marital skew,** in which one spouse is dominant and the other is submissive and dependent. Although these patterns were associated with schizophrenia in children, it must be noted that they also exist in families with no child pathology. Many couples who struggle with problems that are similar in structure to marital schism and marital skew will come to marital therapy but report no problems with their children.

Lyman Wynne

Of all the founders of the field, perhaps none was so fully trained to become a family therapist and researcher as Lyman Wynne (Broderick and Schrader, 1991). Having earned both a medical degree in psychiatry and a PhD in social relations from Harvard University, he was easily able to move beyond the individual perspectives on mental health to a more contextual approach. In 1952, he joined the staff at the National Institute of Mental Health (NIMH) and began to see the families of schizophrenic patients as part of the standard course of treatment.

Wynne believed that certain interpersonal characteristics pertained to schizophrenic families. Specifically, he noticed that some exhibited **pseudomutuality,** the loss of personal identity to maintain a false sense of family togetherness. For example, family members would sacrifice important personal needs to maintain the façade of family harmony. For the schizophrenic, this meant giving up a hold on reality to preserve peace in the family. He also noticed a different pattern in which some families expressed **pseudohostility,** or the expression of false anger to mask family members' needs for intimacy or deeper issues of conflict and alienation. In other words, they would have false fights to cover up more important areas of family conflict. He also noticed that schizophrenic families acted as if they were surrounded by a **rubber fence;** they remained impervious to interventions from outside agents. Typical therapist comments bounced off them as if they were surrounded by rubber (Gale and Long, 1996; Wynne, 1961; Wynne et al., 1958).

In 1954, Murray Bowen joined Wynne at the NIMH. Although they worked in separate sections, they were colleagues with a mutual fascination in the role of family phenomena in mental illness. During the 1956 and 1957 meetings of the American Psychiatric Association, Wynne and Bowen met with Don Jackson, Theodore Lidz, and Nathan Ackerman, which began a series of interchanges among these prominent pioneers. In 1971, Wynne moved to the University of Rochester Medical School where he still conducts research on schizophrenic families.

Carl Whitaker

Of all of the charismatic mavericks who founded the family therapy field, Carl Whitaker is considered the most irreverent and colorful (Gale and Long, 1996; Nichols and Schwartz, 1998). He used an innovative approach to families that forced them to use their dormant creative powers to resolve their problems. Whitaker viewed therapy as a countercultural process in which clients and therapists need to be free to regress and explore themselves apart from societal constraints (Whitaker and Ryan, 1988).

Perhaps Whitaker's belief that therapy promotes personal growth at the expense of societal expectations stemmed from his own tendency to buck the system. He initially began his medical career in obstetrics and gynecology; however, he left it for the world of psychiatry due to his growing concerns with the emotional lives of his patients. During World War II, he worked as a staff psychiatrist in the hospital at the Oak Ridge Plutonium Facility in Tennessee. This was a top-secret base; at the time no one knew that the purpose of the facility was to create plutonium for nuclear bombs. It was here that Whitaker joined forces with John Warkentin, another innovative therapist and free spirit, and began experimenting with two therapists interviewing a patient, seeing patients' relatives in sessions, and developing a creative approach to therapy. The flavor of Whitaker's work is best expressed by recounting a story in which a schizophrenic patient once threatened to kill him with a knife. The patient threatened Whitaker: "You will never know when it will happen; you could be walking down the street, sleeping, going to the bathroom, and suddenly there I'll be!" Whitaker sincerely responded to the patient: "I want to thank you for giving me something else to think about at the urinal rather than worrying if I will get my shoes wet." It was this no-holds-barred, irreverent attitude to therapy that characterized Whitaker's work throughout his life.

Although Whitaker could be both creative and daring with his patients, he was not free from his own medicine. He once asked Warkentin to consult with another patient who had threatened to kill him. Whitaker recalls that, "[Warkentin] took one look at the patient and said, 'You know, I don't blame you. There have been times when I wanted to kill Carl myself.' Then he walked out!" (Whitaker and Ryan, 1988, p. 18).

Following the war, Whitaker became chair of the psychiatry department at Emory University in Atlanta, Georgia. He brought Warkentin with him and hired a new colleague, Thomas Malone. It was here that Whitaker and

Malone wrote *The Roots of Psychotherapy* (1953), which documented their new approach to the treatment of mental illness. This was a very provocative book for its time. The mental health establishment was aghast at their break from traditional psychiatric practice and not so subtly suggested that the team members receive therapy themselves. It was here that they experimented with seeing families of schizophrenics due to their disenchantment with the individual approach to treatment.

Some credit Whitaker for calling the first meeting of family therapy (Broderick and Schrader, 1991). At Emory, his staff would have a semi-annual conference in which they would observe one another working with families of schizophrenics and share their observations. In 1955, Whitaker invited Don Jackson and Gregory Bateson, to participate with them. Whitaker recalls with typical aplomb that, "[Jackson] was a 'brain' who sparked a lot of new thinking and [Bateson] was an elder statesman anthropologist—a sage who smelled of people (Whitaker and Ryan, 1988)." During this meeting, the group came to a clear definition of schizophrenia as a family phenomenon.

In 1965, Whitaker left Atlanta to join the Department of Psychiatry at the University of Wisconsin. It was here that he solidified his thinking about families and family therapy and named his approach **symbolic-experiential family therapy** (Whitaker and Keith, 1981) to represent the experiential form of encounter between therapist and client that operates at the symbolic level. In other words, the therapist interacts with the family at a metaphorical level to bypass their resistance. As Whitaker's ideas were more creative than practical, he was not initially as well known as the other early pioneers; however, he was always respected by the leaders in the field. It was in his later years that Whitaker became a sage to the rest of the family therapy community and a constant fixture at conferences and workshops. His daring, creativity, and respect for the inherent strength in humans served as a model for other family therapists. His death in 1995 left a hole in the field that may never be filled.

Philadelphia: Ivan Boszormenyi-Nagy, James Framo, Ross Speck, Carolyn Attneave, and the Eastern Pennsylvania Psychiatric Institute

Across the country from Palo Alto, California, another important family therapy think tank was developing in Philadelphia. Although perhaps not as well known as the Mental Research Institute, the family therapists and researchers who worked at the Eastern Pennsylvania Psychiatric Institute (EPPI) have provided substantial contributions to the family therapy field.

Ivan Boszormenyi-Nagy

Similar to many of the early family therapists, Ivan Boszormenyi-Nagy was a psychoanalytically trained psychiatrist with an interest in schizophrenia. He founded the family therapy department at the EPPI to study the relationship between family process and psychosis. This became a major East Coast training institute which spawned numerous leaders in the field. Boszormenyi-Nagy co-edited with James Framo *Intensive Family Therapy: Theoretical and Practical Aspects* (1965), which was one of the first books in the field. More important, he wrote one of the first books on **transgenerational family therapy,** a school of therapy which believes that problems are maintained by patterns spanning several generations in families, *Invisible Loyalties: Reciprocity in Intergenerational Family Therapy* (Boszormenyi-Nagy and Spark, 1973). Boszormenyi-Nagy moved to Hahneman University in 1980 when the EPPI was closed by the state of Pennsylvania. He continues today to refine his model of **contextual family therapy,** which focuses on the role of ethics in family relationships (Boszormenyi-Nagy and Krasner, 1986).

James Framo

James Framo was one of the few psychologists to gain a prominent role in the early days of family therapy. He initially gained national recognition at EPPI and then moved on to Temple University. During this period, he began asking adult patients to bring their entire family of origin, no matter how far away, for intensive weekend marathon sessions to work on transgenerational issues (Framo, 1981). He has since moved to United States International University in San Diego, California, where he remains one of the most important voices in the transgenerational family therapy movement.

Ross Speck and Carolyn Attneave

If James Framo expanded the scope of family therapy by conducting sessions with the families of origin of his adult patients, Ross Speck and Carolyn Attneave obliterated the notion of individual and family therapy by having patients include their entire social support system (family, relatives, friends, and sometimes co-workers) in a bold venture known as **network therapy** (Speck and Attneave, 1973). In this approach the therapist used group process to stimulate the network to come up with innovative ideas to solve the problem and support the identified patient and family.

Network therapy did not have a large impact on the field and remains a historical footnote. However, it is noteworthy because it was one of the first family therapy models to look at the impact of larger systems on the family and ties directly to the social work perspective on the importance of community organization. It is also noteworthy because this model had an impact on the work of Murray Bowen (Guerin, 1976) and can be seen in his emphasis on the function of interlocking triangles between family of origin and society.

Salvador Minuchin

While Salvador Minuchin was not one of the founders of family therapy, he remains one of the most influential of the pioneers (Wetchler, 1988). In fact, it is almost impossible to conceptualize the field of family therapy without Minuchin's contributions. Minuchin was a child-oriented psychiatrist who came to the United States as an immigrant from Argentina. He initially worked under the tutelage of Nathan Ackerman who taught him the rudiments of family therapy.

During the early 1960s, Minuchin worked with inner-city delinquent youths at the Wiltwyck School in New York. Here he faced the challenge of working with minority families who were not interested in insight and were more concerned with the real-world problems of keeping their children away from crime. He noticed that these families tended to be under-organized, with no one in charge. This posed a major problem for Minuchin as traditional therapies did not seem appropriate for these families. Minuchin recalls (in Simon, 1992):

> Like everyone else back then, I was thrashing around trying to find something that worked, since everything I had been trained to do—child psychiatry, play therapy, psychoanalysis—had shown itself to be ridiculously ineffective with the tough inner-city kids we were seeing. (p. 76)

As necessity is often the mother of invention, Minuchin developed a therapy that focused more on action than insight and was geared to help these families place the parents in a leadership position with their children. The results of this project lead to the publication of the book *Families of the Slums* (Minuchin et al., 1967). This book is especially noteworthy, in that it is one of the first family therapy texts to examine issues of culture and race in therapy.

In 1965, Minuchin took over the directorship of the Philadelphia Child Guidance Clinic. There, joined by Braulio Montalvo, a colleague at the

Wiltwyck School, and Jay Haley, from the Mental Research Institute in Palo Alto, they further refined Minuchin's earlier ideas and developed structural family therapy, a form of treatment that applies organizational principles to family interaction. The goal of structural family therapy is to reorganize a family's structure so that parents can become effective leaders and resolve their children's problems. The ideas of structural family therapy were first presented in Minuchin's groundbreaking book *Families and Family Therapy* (1974), which continues to be the most popular family therapy text in the world (Nichols and Schwartz, 1998).

Among the programs Minuchin started was the Institute for Family Counseling. This groundbreaking experiment involved training minority members from the community to work as paraprofessional family therapists with other minority families. Minuchin hoped that minority clients would be more open to the therapy process with therapists of similar background than they had been to the predominantly white professionals they had seen in the past. To accomplish a project of this nature meant that Minuchin and colleagues had to present the ideas of structural family therapy in a straightforward manner without professional jargon. Their training manual was later published by Jay Haley as the influential book *Problem-Solving Therapy* (1987).

To gain legitimacy for this project among the professional community, Minuchin and colleagues also provided intensive supervision for these paraprofessionals. They developed a new form of training called **live supervision,** in which a supervisor behind a one-way mirror observed the trainee conduct therapy and suggested interventions while the session was in progress. This form of training has been synonymous with family therapy supervision ever since.

In 1981 Minuchin founded Family Studies Inc. in New York City, where he continued to train family therapists and became involved in the foster care system. In 1996, he retired and moved to Boston with his wife Pat.

The Milan Group: Mara Selvini Palazzoli, Luigi Boscolo, Gianfranco Cecchin, and Giuliana Prata

During the 1960s and early 1970s, family therapy was primarily an American phenomenon. This changed dramatically when a team of Italian family therapists burst upon the scene in the mid-1970s. The Milan Group, composed of psychiatrists Mara Selvini Palazzoli, Luigi Boscolo, Gianfranco Cecchin, and Giuliana Prata, initially borrowed their ideas from American family therapists, but later became some of the foremost teachers to the family therapy community throughout the world.

Mara Selvini Palazzoli was an internist who became interested in the phenomenon of anorexia nervosa following World War II (Simon, 1992). She switched her specialty to psychiatry, as this disorder had all of the physicians in Italy stumped. Selvini Palazzoli was sure that this was not a physical malady but an emotional disorder. The problem was how to treat it. Over time, she became one of the most prominent psychoanalysts in all of Italy; however, her frustration with the traditional psychoanalytic approach led her to the United States in 1967 to learn about family therapy.

Upon returning to Italy, she formed a team of psychiatrists to experiment with family therapy in the treatment of anorexia and schizophrenia. The group split in 1971, with Selvini Palazzoli, Boscolo, Cecchin, and Prata remaining. Their initial attempts at family therapy derived from a psychoanalytic perspective, but they now drew their inspiration from the Palo Alto group, the text *Pragmatics of Human Communication* (Watzlawick et al., 1967), and the writings of Gregory Bateson.

The group was interested not only in the interactional patterns in families but also in the interaction that existed between therapist and family. Their concern with therapists being co-opted by family patterns led to their development of a team approach to treatment with two therapists interviewing the family in the room and two therapists observing behind a one-way mirror. The team would then meet without the family during the middle of the session to discuss the first part of the therapy and devise an intervention for the second half.

As word of the Milan Group's ideas and clinical prowess spread, they were invited to present their work at an invitation-only conference at the Ackerman Institute in New York. The conference attendees were a veritable who's who of family therapy innovators. Needless to say, the somewhat skeptical audience was impressed with the Milan Group's team approach, their use of paradoxical intervention, and their flair for the dramatic. Family therapist Peggy Papp recalls (in Simon, 1992):

> They turned everything into a theatrical presentation. With all their detailed questioning, they managed to take the hidden subjective life of the family and turn it into a heightened performance. Eventually each family's situation would take on the dimensions of a great opera. (p. 143)

Their "hit" presentation was followed by the eagerly awaited text *Paradox and Counterparadox* (Selvini Palazzoli et al., 1978) which focused on the use of paradox in the treatment of severe psychosis and the use of their team format. Although this book was read worldwide, much of their theoretical impact came from an article they wrote in 1979 just before they disbanded their team, "Hypothesizing—Circularity—Neutrality: Three Guidelines for the Conductor of the Session" (Selvini Palazzoli et al., 1980). It was this article in which they moved away from paradoxical interventions and began to focus on the interactional process between family and therapist. They posited that the therapist was not an objective observer of a family's interactions, but that all hypotheses were due to the interaction between therapist and family. In other words, a feedback loop existed between the therapist's questions, the family's answers, and the subsequent questions the therapist would ask. Hypotheses were not grounded in fact, but on how useful they were for the therapist and family (Selvini Palazzoli et al., 1980). At this time, their approach became known as **Milan systemic family therapy** because of its focus on the interactional nature of the therapist-client relationship.

After the split, Boscolo and Cecchin held to the tenets originally presented in "Hypothesizing—Circularity—Neutrality" and focused on teaching their approach. They now refer to themselves as the Milan Associates to differentiate themselves from the original group and Selvini Palazzoli's new work. Selvini Palazzoli and Prata began to research a new method for treating psychotic processes in families. They referred to their approach as the **invariant prescription,** as they asked the parents in every family they treated to develop a secret alliance, separate from the other members, to break up the interactional patterns that existed in their families (Selvini Palazzoli et al., 1989). Selvini Palazzoli broke with Prata in 1982 and continues to work on the invariant prescription with a new team.

Feminist Family Therapy

By the late 1970s, it was evident that many of family therapy's basic assumptions were at odds with the ideas in the feminist movement. Rachel Hare-Mustin's provocative article "A Feminist Approach to Family Therapy" (1978) challenged many of the family therapy ideas as being at odds with women's issues. For example, viewing behavior as interactional can obscure the fact that women are typically the recipients of beatings in spouse abuse, and that historically women have had less power to determine societal policy, and subsequently their own fates, than men.

The Women's Project, comprised of Betty Carter, Peggy Papp, Olga Silverstein, and Marianne Walters, formed to study the issues of gender in families and family therapy. This team was especially remarkable in that it brought together members with orientations in strategic, Milan systemic, structural, and transgenerational family therapies. Their landmark book, *The Invisible Web: Gender Patterns in Family Relationships* (Walters et al.,

1988), presented new ways of viewing families and conducting family therapy. Another important individual was Deborah Luepnitz, whose book *The Family Interpreted: Feminist Theory in Clinical Practice* (1988) showed how several of the leading family theories promoted traditional male and female stereotypes. These and other feminist theoreticians altered the way family therapy was conceptualized, which led to numerous revisions of the original theories.

Social Constructionist Family Therapy: Michael White and Steve de Shazer

The late 1980s through the 1990s marked a radical shift for family therapy. Following on the heels of the Milan Group's ideas that hypotheses arise through interaction between the family and therapist, some clinicians began to question whether any therapist could objectively diagnose a family and intervene in its process separate from the therapist's values and worldview. **Social constructionist family therapists** believe that therapists have no better ideas about how to solve problems than their treatment families. They believe that reality is not an objective phenomenon, but is subject to the interpretations of various groups. This means that all ideas about how a family should look, or how it should solve its problems, are subjective. Therefore, social constructionist family therapists do not tell families how to change, but rather help them find their own solutions (Wetchler, 1996). As these ideas have gained prominence only in the last few years, their historical significance for the field of family therapy is yet to be determined. Nevertheless, they had a major impact during the 1990s. Two notable leaders in the social constructionist movement are Michael White and Steve de Shazer.

Michael White

Michael White is an Australian family therapist who has critiqued the role of diagnosis in limiting more positive views of families and individuals (White, 1995; White and Epston, 1990). Diagnoses tend to focus on problems and not on how families can resolve their problems. In fact, focusing on problems keeps people from identifying potential strengths that enable them to solve their problems.

With his colleague David Epston, he has developed **narrative therapy,** which helps clients challenge their views of themselves as having a problem and helps them develop alternative stories about themselves based on their strengths. These strengths then enable them to solve their problems. Narrative therapists avoid diagnosis as this hinders them and their families from identifying previously unperceived strengths.

Steve de Shazer

Steve de Shazer directs the Brief Family Therapy Center in Milwaukee, Wisconsin. Along with his wife, Insoo Kim Berg, he has developed **solution-focused therapy,** which de-emphasizes problems and focuses on the role of solutions in treatment (de Shazer, 1985, 1988). Similar to the work of the Mental Research Institute, de Shazer's ideas initially stemmed from the teachings of hypnotherapist Milton Erickson. In fact, de Shazer's ideas were originally considered to be a form of strategic therapy. However, he does not look at interactional sequences that maintain a problem. Instead, he works with families to identify exceptions to the problem and have them utilize these exceptions in solving their problem. Because his approach focuses on solutions rather than problems, it tends to take fewer sessions than traditional therapies.

SUMMARY

The field of marriage and family therapy has its roots in four sources: early social work, the sexual reform movement, marriage counseling, and family therapy. Although early social work and the sexual reform movement served as influences, it was the push within marriage counseling and family therapy that organized the field. Perhaps the greatest impetus for growth came with family research on schizophrenia in the 1950s.

Much of the growth in the field has been due to charismatic leaders who rebelled against the typical mental health establishment. Early marriage counselors, such as Paul Popenoe and Abraham and Hannah Stone, and early family therapists, such as John Elderkin Bell, Nathan Ackerman, Don Jackson, and Murray Bowen, fought numerous battles to have their ideas accepted. Even in recent years the field has maintained its revolutionary zeal. Modern contributors such as feminist family therapists and social constructionists continue to challenge how we view and treat families.

SUGGESTED READINGS

Broderick, C. B. and Schrader, S. S. (1991). The history of professional marriage and family therapy. In A. S. Gurman and D. P. Kniskern (Eds.), *Handbook of family therapy* (Volume 11) (pp. 3-40). New York: Brunner/Mazel.

Gale, J. E. and Long, J. K. (1996). Theoretical foundations of family therapy. In F. P. Piercy, D. H. Sprenkle, and J. L. Wetchler (Eds.), *Family therapy sourcebook* (Second edition) (pp. 1-24). New York: Guilford.

Guerin, P. J. (1976). Family therapy: The first twenty-five years. In P. J. Guerin (Ed.), *Family therapy: Theory and practice* (pp. 2-22). New York: Gardner.

Kaslow, F. W. (1980). History of family therapy in the United States: A kaleidoscopic overview. *Marriage and Family Review, 3,* 77-111.

Nichols, M. P. and Schwartz, R. C. (1998). *Family therapy: Concepts and methods.* Boston: Allyn and Bacon.

GLOSSARY

Bowen systems therapy: A form of transgenerational family therapy, founded by Murray Bowen, that views patterned behavior as being innate in all of nature.

contextual family therapy: A form of transgenerational family therapy, founded by Ivan Boszormenyi-Nagy, that focuses on the role of ethics in family relationships.

cybernetics: The science of communication and control in humans and machines.

experiential family therapy: A school of family therapy that focuses on human emotions and growth rather than interactional sequences.

family of origin: The family in which an individual is raised.

group therapy: A form of treatment in which individuals discuss their problems in a group setting, allowing them to receive support and feedback from the group members.

identified patient: An individual family member identified as having a specific problem and who, in fact, is representative of a larger family problem.

interactional system: A single unit in which all members interact as parts of a larger whole.

invariant prescription: A technique in which a marital couple is instructed to form a secret alliance separate from the other family members to break up the interactional patterns that exist in their family.

live supervision: A form of training in which a supervisor behind a one-way mirror observes the trainee conduct therapy and suggests interventions while the session is in progress.

marital schism: A dysfunctional marital pattern in which the husband and wife fail to accommodate to each other, constantly attack each other, and compete for their children's affection.

marital skew: A dysfunctional marital pattern in which one spouse is always dominant and the other is submissive and dependent.

marriage counseling: A form of therapy in which a clinician sees both spouses together to resolve problems in their relationship.

marriage and family therapy: A model of mental health treatment that takes a family perspective toward emotional problems and psychopathology.

Milan systemic family therapy: A form of therapy, founded by Mara Selvini Palazzoli, Luigi Boscolo, Gianfranco Cecchin, and Guiliana Prata, that focuses on both the interactional nature of the family and the therapist-client relationship.

multigenerational transmission process: A process by which behavioral sequences are transmitted through several generations within a family.

narrative therapy: A form of social constructionist family therapy, founded by Michael White, that helps clients challenge their views of themselves as having a problem and helps them develop alternative stories about themselves based on their strengths. These strengths then enable them to solve their problems.

network therapy: A type of therapy that uses group process to stimulate the family's network of friends, relatives, and social services to come up with innovative ideas to solve the problem and support the identified patient.

paradoxes: Statements that tend to disqualify themselves. For example, a wife ordering her husband to be more spontaneous disqualifies her demands, because the husband cannot behave spontaneously if he follows his wife's orders.

pseudohostility: The expression of false anger to mask family members' needs for intimacy or for help with deeper issues of conflict and alienation.

pseudomutuality: The loss of personal identity in the attempt to maintain a false sense of family togetherness.

rubber fence: Schizophrenic families acted as if they were surrounded by a rubber fence, in that they remained impervious to interventions from outside agents. Typical therapist comments bounced off them as if they were surrounded by rubber.

social constructionist family therapists: This school of family therapy believes there is no objective reality, and that it is subject to the interpretations of various groups. This means that all ideas about how a family should look, or how it should solve its problems, are subjective. Therefore, social constructionist family therapists do not tell families how to change, but rather help them find their own solutions.

social work: A branch of the mental health field that focuses on the impact of societal issues on human problems.

solution-focused therapy: A form of social constructionist family therapy, founded by Steve de Shazer, that helps clients solve their problems by identifying naturally occurring solutions within their lives and helping them to utilize them.

strategic family therapy: A brief approach, founded by the members of the Mental Research Institute, that focuses on observing and altering the interactional sequences in which a problem is embedded.

structural family therapy: An approach, founded by Salvador Minuchin, that alters the organization of a family to enable them to solve their problems.

symbolic-experiential family therapy: A specific form of experiential family therapy, founded by Carl Whitaker, in which the therapist attempts to have an experiential form of encounter with the client operating at the symbolic level. This is done to bypass typical patient resistance.

transgenerational family therapy: A school of therapy which believes that problems are maintained by patterns that span several generations in families.

REFERENCES

Ackerman, N. (1958). *The psychodynamics of family life.* New York: Basic Books.

Ackerman, N. W. and Sobel, R. (1950). Family diagnosis: An approach to the preschool child. *American Journal of Orthopsychiatry, 20*(4), 744-753.

Alexander, F. (1968). An empirical study on the differential influence of self-concept on the professional behavior of marriage counselors. Unpublished doctoral dissertation, University of Southern California.

Anonymous (1972). Toward the differentiation of a self in one's own family. In J. Framo (Ed.), *Family interaction* (pp. 175-200). New York: Springer.

Bateson, G. (1972). *Steps to an ecology of mind: A revolutionary approach to man's understanding of himself.* New York: Ballantine Books.

Bateson, G. (1979). *Mind and nature: A necessary unity.* Toronto, New York, London: Bantam Books.

Bateson, G., Jackson, D. D., Haley, J., and Weakland, J. H. (1956). Toward a theory of schizophrenia. *Behavioral Science,* 251-264.

Bell, J. E. (1961). *Family group therapy. Public Health Monograph, 64,* Washington, DC: U.S. Government Printing Office.

Bell, J. E. (1976). A theoretical framework for family group therapy. In P. J. Guerin Jr. (Ed.), *Family therapy: Theory and practice* (pp. 129-143). New York: Gardner Press.

Boszormenyi-Nagy, I. and Framo, J. L. (Eds.) (1965). *Intensive family therapy: Theoretical and practical aspects.* New York: Hoeber Medical Division, Harper and Row.

Boszormenyi-Nagy, I. and Krasner, B. R. (1986). *Between give and take: A clinical guide to contextual therapy.* Bristol, PA: Brunner/Mazel.

Boszormenyi-Nagy, I. and Spark, G. (1973). *Invisible loyalties: Reciprocity in intergenerational family therapy.* New York: Harper and Row.

Bowen, M. (1978). *Family therapy in clinical practice.* New York: Jason Aronson.

Broderick, C. B. and Schrader, S. S. (1991). The history of professional marriage and family therapy. In A. S. Gurman and D. P. Kniskern (Eds.), *Handbook of family therapy* (Volume 2) (pp. 3-37). New York: Brunner/Mazel.

de Shazer, S. (1985). *Keys to solutions in brief therapy.* New York: W. W. Norton and Company.

de Shazer, S. (1988). *Clues: Investigation solutions in brief therapy.* New York: W. W. Norton and Company.

Dickinson, R. L. (1933). *Human sex anatomy* (Revised edition). Baltimore: Williams and Wilkins.

Dickinson, R. L. and Beam, L. (1931). *A thousand marriages.* Baltimore: Williams and Wilkins.

Dickinson, R. L. and Beam, L. (1934). *The single woman.* Baltimore: Williams and Wilkins.

Framo, J. L. (1981). The integration of marital therapy with sessions with family of origin. In A. S. Gurman and D. P. Kniskern (Eds.), *Handbook of family therapy* (pp. 133-158). New York: Brunner/Mazel.

Gale, J. E. and Long, J. K. (1996). Theoretical foundations of family therapy. In F. P. Piercy, D. H. Sprenkle, and J. L. Wetchler, *Family therapy sourcebook* (Second edition) (pp. 1-24). New York: The Guilford Press.

Guerin, P. J. Jr. (1976). Family therapy: The first twenty-five years. In P. J. Guerin Jr. (Ed.), *Family therapy: Theory and practice* (pp. 2-22). New York: Gardner Press.

Gurman, A. S. (1973). Marital therapy: Emerging trends in research and practice. *Family Process, 12,* 45-54.

Haley, J. (1963). *Strategies of psychotherapy.* New York: Grune and Stratton.

Haley, J. (1973). *Uncommon therapy.* New York: W. W. Norton and Company.

Haley, J. (1985a). *Conversations with Milton Erickson, M.D.* Volume 1: *Changing individuals.* New York: W. W. Norton and Company.

Haley, J. (1985b). *Conversations with Milton Erickson, M.D.* Volume 2: *Changing couples.* New York: W. W. Norton and Company.

Haley, J. (1985c). *Conversations with Milton Erickson, M.D.* Volume 3: *Changing children and families.* New York: W. W. Norton and Company.

Haley, J. (1987). *Problem-solving therapy* (Second edition). San Francisco: Jossey-Bass.

Haley, J. and Hoffman, L. (1967). *Techniques of family therapy.* New York: Basic Books.

Hare-Mustin, R. T. (1978). A feminist approach to family therapy. *Family Process, 17,* 181-194.

Hare-Mustin, R. (1987). The problem of gender in family therapy theory. *Family Process, 26,* 15-27.

Hirschfeld, M. (1930). *Geschlechtskunde* (Sex education) (5 volumes). Stuttgart: J. Puttman Verlag.

Hirschfeld, M. (1940). *Sexual pathology: A study of derangements of the sexual instinct* (J. Gibbs, Trans.). New York: Emerson Books. (Original work published 1932.)

Jackson, D. D. (1959). Family interaction, family homeostasis, and some implications for conjoint family therapy. In J. Masserman (Ed.), *Individual and family dynamics* (pp. 122-141). New York: Grune and Stratton.

Kaslow, F. W. (1980). History of family therapy in the United States: A kaleidoscopic overview. *Marriage and Family Review, 3* (1/2), 77-111.

Kinsey, A. C., Pomeroy, W. B., and Martin, C. E. (1948). *Sexual behavior in the human male.* Philadelphia: W. B. Saunders.

Kinsey, A. C., Pomeroy, W. B., Martin, C. E., and Gebhard, P. (1953). *Sexual behavior in the human female.* Philadelphia: W. B. Saunders.

Kramer, C. H. (1980). *Becoming a family therapist: Developing an integrated approach to working with families.* New York: Human Sciences Press.

Lidz, R. W. and Lidz, T. (1949). The family environment of schizophrenic patients. *American Journal of Psychiatry, 106,* 332-345.

Lidz, T., Cornelison, A. R., Fleck, S., and Terry, D. (1957). The intrafamilial environment of the schizophrenic patients II. Marital schism and marital skew. *American Journal of Psychiatry, 113,* 241-248.

Lidz, T., Perker, B., and Cornelison, A. (1956). The rule of the father in the family environment of the schizophrenic patient. *American Journal of Psychiatry, 113,* 126-132.

Luepnitz, D. A. (1988). *The family interpreted: Feminist theory in clinical practice.* New York: Basic Books.

Mace, D. R. (1945). Marriage guidance in England. *Marriage and Family Living, 7,* 1-2, 5.

Mace, D. R. (1948). *Marriage counseling.* London: Churchill.

Masters, W. H. and Johnson, V. E. (1966). *Human sexual response.* Boston: Little, Brown.

Masters, W. H. and Johnson, V. E. (1970). *Human sexual inadequacy.* Boston: Little, Brown.

Michaelson, R. (1963). An analysis of the changing focus of marriage counseling. Unpublished doctoral dissertation, University of Southern California.

Minuchin, S. (1974). *Families and family therapy*. Cambridge, MA: Harvard University Press.

Minuchin, S., Montalvo, B., Guerney, B., Rosman, B. L., and Schumer, F. (1967). *Families of the slums*. New York: Basic Books.

Mudd, E. H. and Fowler, C. R. (1976). The AAMC and AAMFC: Nearly forty years of form and function. In B. N. Ard Jr. (Ed.), *Handbook of marriage counseling* (Second edition). Palo Alto, CA: Science and Behavior Books.

Nichols, M. P. and Schwartz, R. C. (1998). *Family therapy: Concepts and methods* (Fourth edition). Needham Heights, MA: Allyn and Bacon.

Popenoe, P. (1975). Foreword. In American Institute of Family Relations (Ed.), *Techniques of marriage and family counseling* (Volume IV). Los Angeles: American Institute of Family Relations.

Richmond, M. E. (1917). *Social diagnosis*. New York: Russell Sage.

Satir, V., Stachowiak, J., and Taschman, H. (1977). *Helping families to change*. New York: Jason Aronson.

Selvini Palazzoli, M., Boscolo, L., Cecchin, G., and Prata, G. (1978). *Paradox and counterparadox*. New York: Jason Aronson.

Selvini Palazzoli, M., Boscolo, L., Cecchin, G., and Prata, G. (1980). Hypothesizing—circularity—neutrality: Three guidelines for the conductor of the session. *Family Process, 19*(1), 3-12.

Selvini Palazzoli, M., Cirillo, S., Selvini, M., and Sorrentino, A. M. (1989). *Family games: General models of psychotic processes in the family*. New York: W. W. Norton and Company.

Simon, R. (1992). *One on one: Conversations with the shapes of family therapy*. New York: The Guilford Press.

Smith, Z. D. (1890). *Proceedings of the National Conference in Charities and Corrections, 1890,* 377.

Speck, R. and Attneave, C. (1973). *Family networks: Retribalization and healing*. New York: Pantheon.

Walters, M., Carter, B., Papp, P., and Silverstein, O. (1988). *The invisible web: Gender patterns in family relationships*. New York: The Guilford Press.

Watzlawick, P., Beavin, J. H., and Jackson, D. D. (1967). *Pragmatics of human communication*. New York: W. W. Norton and Company.

Weakland, J. H., Watzlawick, P., and Riskin, J. (1995). MRI—A little background music. In J. H. Weakland and W. A. Ray (Eds.), *Propagations: Thirty years of influence from the Mental Research Institute* (pp. 1-15). Binghamton, NY: The Haworth Press.

Wetchler, J. L. (1988). Primary and secondary influential theories of family therapy supervisors: A research note. *Family Therapy, 15*(1), 69-74.

Wetchler, J. L. (1996). Social constructionist family therapies. In F. P. Piercy, D. H. Sprenkle, and J. L. Wetchler (Eds.), *Family therapy sourcebook* (Second edition) (pp. 129-152). New York: The Guilford Press.

Whitaker, C. A. (1976). The hindrance of theory in clinical work. In P. J. Guerin Jr. (Ed.), *Family therapy: Theory and practice* (pp. 154-164). New York: Gardner Press.

Whitaker, C. A. and Keith, D. V. (1981). Symbolic-experiential family therapy. In A. S. Gurman and D. P. Kniskern (Eds.), *Handbook of family therapy* (pp. 187-225). New York: Brunner/Mazel.

Whitaker, C. A. and Malone, T. P. (1953). *The roots of psychotherapy.* New York: Blakiston.

Whitaker, C. A. and Ryan, M. O. (Eds.). (1988). *Midnight musings of a family therapist.* New York: W. W. Norton and Company.

White, M. (1995). *Re-authoring lives: Interviews and essays.* Adelaide, South Australia: Dulwich Centre Publications.

White, M. and Epston, D. (1990). *Narrative means to therapeutic ends.* New York: W. W. Norton and Company.

Wylie, M. S. (1992). Family therapy's neglected prophet: A profile of Murray Bowen. In R. Simon, C. Barrilleaux, M. S. Wylie, and L. M. Markowitz (Eds.), *The evolving therapist: Ten years of the family therapy networker* (pp. 24-38). New York: The Guilford Press.

Wynne, L. (1961). The study of intrafamilial alignments and splits in exploratory family therapy. In N. W. Ackerman, F. L. Beatman, and S. N. Sherman (Eds.), *Exploring the base for family therapy* (p. 95). New York: Family Service Association of America.

Wynne, L., Ryckoff, I., Day, J., and Hirsch, S. (1958). Pseudo mutuality in the family relations of schizophrenics. *Psychiatry, 21,* 205-220.

Chapter 2

General Systems Theory, Cybernetics, and Family Therapy

Lorna L. Hecker
Grace Ann Mims
Shelly R. Boughner

"But I don't want to go among mad people," Alice remarked.
"Oh, you can't help that," said the Cat: "we're all mad here. I'm mad.
  You're mad."
"How do you know I'm mad?" said Alice.
"You must be," said the Cat, "or you wouldn't have come here."
Alice didn't think that proved it at all; however, she went on. "And
  how do you know that you're mad?"
"To begin with," said the Cat, "a dog's not mad. You grant that?"
"I suppose so," said Alice.
"Well, then," the Cat went on, "you see, a dog growls when it's angry,
  and wags its tail when it's pleased. Now I growl when I'm pleased,
  and wag my tail when I'm angry. Therefore I'm mad."

Lewis Carroll
Alice's Adventures in Wonderland

Family systems theory allows family therapists to examine the context in which individuals live. It is this context that shapes meaning in the lives of individuals, couples, and families. Individual psychology has traditionally focused on the mind as the source of mental illness, and family therapy focuses on the family system as the source of problematic behaviors. As Alice quickly found in encountering the Cheshire Cat and others in Wonderland, mental illness is defined by the context by which one is surrounded.

39

In this chapter you will learn about general systems theory and cybernetic theory and the application of these theories to families. Following is a look at how these two theories came to be.

REDUCTIONISM VERSUS HOLISM

As early as the 1920s and into the 1940s scientists from many disciplines began to question the usefulness of **reductionism** in science. Reductionism is a theory or procedure that reduces complex data to simple terms. Reductionism is a powerful tool for understanding reality by breaking complex identities down into constituent parts, allowing scientists significant insight into how things work. Reductionism asks us to think about things mechanistically, or as a machine. A machine is built up from distinct parts and can be reduced to those parts without losing its machinelike character. This idea is called *Cartesian reductionism.* The success of reductionism in science cannot be ignored. Most of modern science and technology is the result of it.

However, this notion of everything being reduced to machinelike qualities does not generally apply to complex (real) systems. One cannot reduce complex systems; it only reduces them to simple mechanisms. The human brain similarly displays unique properties that are unrecognizable in a reductionistic study of neurons and transmitters. In some sense, then, the whole is more than the sum of its parts. The same is true in understanding human beings and mental illness. Gregory Bateson (1972) pointed out that to understand a mentally ill person, one should look at the web of family communications with which that person lives.

In order to understand families, we cannot reduce them to their distinct parts. That is, we cannot study families by looking at individual members. In order to understand families, we must study the family members in relationship to one another. It is this relationship between family members that makes each family unique. When studying families, it was found that using a reductionist approach was not helpful, and that a more holistic approach better captured the complexity of families.

Although many people advanced our thinking toward a more holistic approach in mental health, three historic figures in particular were perhaps most influential in paving the way for our modern notions of family therapy. The first of these was Ludwig von Bertalanffy (1968), a biologist who developed **general systems theory** (GST). General systems theory focuses on the relationship and interaction between the objects in a system. GST provided a model for understanding living systems that was focused on how apparently unrelated events or phenomena could be seen as interrelated parts or components of a larger whole or system. The second important scientist, Norbert Wiener (1954), advanced cybernetic theory. **Cybernetics** is a term derived from the Greek word *kubernetes*, which means "steering" or "governing." Cybernetics was used to describe Wiener's theory of communication and control. According to this theory, humans (as well as machines) attempt to control entropy (disorganization) in systems through feedback that influences future performance. Cybernetic theory considers the organization of systems and the mechanisms that regulate the system's functioning. Third, the most influential thinker in the field of family therapy, Gregory Bateson (1972), an anthropologist, was the person most responsible for applying both general systems theory and cybernetic theory to families.

The integration of general systems theory and cybernetics theory as applied to families shall be referred to in this chapter as systems theory. Learning about systems theory not only means studying new terms and concepts but involves a **paradigm shift** (Kuhn, 1962), which is a shift in thinking similar to the change in thinking that occurred when Galileo proposed that the earth revolved around the sun—challenging the commonly held belief of the time that the earth was the center of the universe. A **paradigm** is a model or conceptual scheme through which people make sense of such things as "reality" or "the world." Each paradigm provides a particular way of viewing and understanding its subject, along with corresponding methods for gaining this understanding. When family therapy originated, it provided an entirely new approach to viewing and understanding people, which contrasted greatly with individually oriented paradigms. Systems theory is a scientific paradigm applied to both biological and social systems. In this chapter systems theory is applied to families.

The basic **tenets** of systems theory include the following (adapted from Minuchin, 1985):

1. Any system is an organized whole; objects within the system are necessarily interdependent.
2. The whole is greater than the sum of its parts.
3. Systems are composed of subsystems.
4. Patterns in a system are circular rather than linear.
5. Complex systems are composed of subsystems.
6. Systems have homeostatic mechanisms that maintain stability of their patterns.
7. Evolution and change are inherent in open systems.

ANY SYSTEM IS AN ORGANIZED WHOLE; ELEMENTS WITHIN THE SYSTEM ARE NECESSARILY INTERDEPENDENT

What Is a System?

A **system** is a set of elements standing in interaction. Each element in the system is affected by whatever happens to any other element. Systems are composed of three elements: objects, attributes, and relationship among the objects within an environment (Littlejohn, 1978, p. 31). Within a family, the "objects" are the family members. Attributes may include goals, energy, attitudes, ethnicity, and other characteristics of the family. The "relationship among objects" is how family members communicate with one another. The environment includes the surroundings that are simultaneously shaped by the family, and shaping the family. For example, the community in which a family resides, or the social class to which a family belongs, would provide the family with particular opportunities or limitations, and would also reflect the family's participation as members of the community or social class. The success of the family depends on the existence and connection with other family members. Family therapists are most concerned with looking at the relationship between the "parts" or family members (see Figure 2.1). Interaction (communication) among the parts reflects the dynamic nature of families. The study of the family must begin with the relationships, and interactions among family members.

What Is a Family System?

A **family system** includes family members, the unique attributes of the family members, and the relationships between family members. This small group of closely interrelated and interdependent individuals is organized into a unit with specific purposes, functions, or goals. Our society has historically defined family in a fairly restricted fashion. We may think of the typical American family consisting of a mother, a father, and their children. Although this **nuclear family** form is prevalent in our depictions of families in movies or on television programs, and although it is still the dominant form, it is not the only form that family therapists will encounter by any means. Fortunately, systems theory comprises all sorts of relationships among people, their attributes, and their environments. Thus for the purposes of thinking about families from a systemic perspective, families are defined by the people in them. One person's definition of a family may not look like a family to another. Perhaps you come from a traditional nuclear

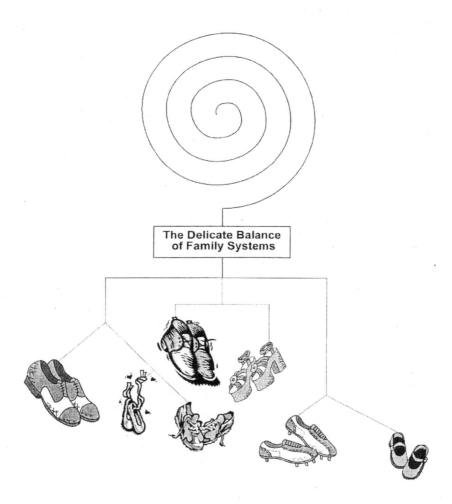

FIGURE 2.1. Understanding Interdependence. Virginia Satir encouraged people to think of families as interdependent systems and imagine them as hanging mobiles. Perhaps you had a mobile as a child that had airplanes or shapes or planets on it. Instead of objects, visualize each person hanging from the mobile. Now imagine that the wind blows a bit. Interdependence is illustrated each time one person on the mobile moves. When one person on the mobile is impacted by the wind, it impacts all the others in the mobile, and they in turn also move. The mobile is more than each hanging object; it is also the delicate balance of each part with the others. When one visualizes a mobile, one can understand the systems concept that a change in one part of the system affects all parts of the system.

family. Or you may come from a stepfamily, foster family, single-parent family, cohabiting family, a three-generation family, a grandfamily, or you may come from a family in which one or more of your parents is gay. Couples without children are also families. Family systems theory encompasses all types of families and examines the relationships among the members. Family systems also include **extended families,** or relatives of those making up the primary nuclear family. We all grow up in some type of a family system. The family you grew up in is referred to as your **family of origin.** Some people who do not have family-of-origin support or extended families may make up their own family configurations based on friendships; this is termed a **family of choice.**

The Impact of Suprasystems

Larger systems also impact the family system. Unfortunately, family therapy often ignored the impact of the larger system on the family until recent years. Larger systems, or **suprasystems,** impacting families include cultural, political, and economic contexts, environment (social and physical), and any other contextual systems that impact the daily workings of the family, school, ethnicity, religion, culture community, and so on (see Figure 2.2).

For example, some find it difficult to understand why women in abusive relationships do not leave their spouses. Yet if the impact of the larger systems on a woman in an abusive relationship are taken into account, we may find that culture dictates that she stay—her ethnicity and/or religious background may place pressure on her to remain in the marriage. In addition, because of political and economic constraints, women in our society generally have fewer economic opportunities than men. Perhaps this woman has few ways in which she can support herself and her family without the income of her abusive partner. Many larger systemic factors may be influencing this woman to stay in an abusive situation. An abused male partner may face their own unique suprasystem factors, such as societal shaming for allowing a woman to beat him; thus he also develops a cloak of secrecy and reasons to tolerate his abusive situation.

Context Alters Meaning

Those who practice family systems theory examine the context of individuals and their families in order to fully understand a problem. Context alters meaning. A reductionistic paradigm would cause one to assume the problem exists alone; a holistic family systems paradigm explores the con-

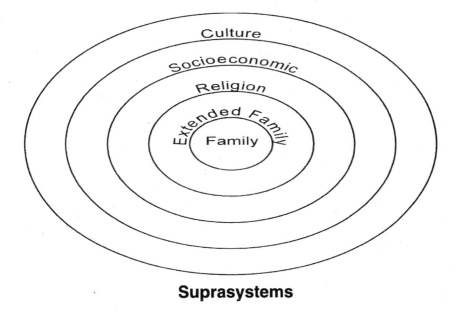

Suprasystems

FIGURE 2.2. Larger Systems Impact the Family

text of the problem within family and social relationships. Because the parts of a system are interdependent for survival, family therapists look at this context and examine the relationships of those in the family system.

For example, if a man came to therapy who complained of obsessive behaviors, it might seem very strange that he inspects the light switches, electrical sockets, and fire alarms several times daily. You learn he is driving his wife to the point of desperation because of his incessant checking behaviors and his inability to keep a job due to his compulsivity. In addition, he continually wakes their children in the night just to be sure they are breathing. This client, if seen individually, might be diagnosed with obsessive-compulsive disorder. Yet when we learn that his first wife and children died in a house fire, we may reconsider his behaviors in light of this new information. His behaviors may make further sense when examining his present relationship. We learn his wife occasionally has had too much too drink, and has fallen asleep smoking; on one occasion, they had to throw a smoldering couch cushion out of their home. She, in response to his hypervigilant behaviors, tries to "loosen up" with alcohol. All of the behaviors we see as problematic make sense in the context of the relationship system.

Interdependence

Systems (or subsystems) are interdependent and do not exist in isolation. Interdependence may be thought of as every part of the system having an effect on every other part of the system. Change in one part of the system will result in change in another part of the system. Capuzzi and Gross (1999) describe the interrelatedness of systems using the metaphor of the ripple effect seen when a rock is thrown into a pond. At first, the ripple will be very small, but eventually it spreads throughout the entire pond. For example, if a teenage girl becomes pregnant, the event will probably impact the teenager's life, the life of her baby, her parents, perhaps her grandparents who may be involved in helping to care for the new baby while the teenager attends school, possibly the social welfare system may become involved if the family needs assistance, the father of the baby, the father's family, and so on. There is a ripple effect from this event. Because family systems therapists believe in interdependence, they believe that change in one family member necessitates change in other members.

THE WHOLE IS GREATER THAN THE SUM OF ITS PARTS

A concept related to interdependence within systems theory is that the whole is greater than the sum of its parts. One could study hydrogen and oxygen in isolation from each other forever, yet never discover water. Hydrogen and oxygen must interact before water can be achieved (Bellinger, 2000). In a human example, although a team may have very good baseball players, they may not be a winning team unless they have just the right mix of players. The combined skills and the ability of the team to work together shows synergy, or what is often referred to as nonsummativity. **Nonsummativity** is the assertion that a system is its own entity which is greater than the mere sum of its parts; this is often explained by using the math equation, $1 + 1 = 3$. If a system has two people, then it has three parts. One part consists of each person in the system and one part consists of the interaction between the two people in the system. Within families, although several individuals make up a family, the family system takes on a life of its own when the familiy gets together. Each family has its own "personality." The sum, the relationships among members, is greater than the simple contribution of individual family members.

PATTERNS IN A SYSTEM ARE CIRCULAR
RATHER THAN LINEAR

Feedback

Feedback in a family system is the process by which the input of each family member leads to a more complex, systems-oriented output. In order to understand the family, the output is not individually determined, but the whole becomes more than the sum of its parts. With systems feedback, we assume that the malfunction of any one person is not caused by an intrapsychic breakdown, but by failure of the system itself to function properly. Typically, one person is labeled by the system as the problem. Family therapists call this person the **identified patient,** or IP. Family therapists see this person as the symptom bearer for dysfunction in the family system.

Feedback loops are the cycles by which individuals influence one another's actions. The impact that a behavior has on the system and the response of the system to that behavior is viewed in terms of positive and negative feedback. "Positive" and "negative" are not value judgments about the behavior but rather indicate whether a change has occurred in the system. A positive feedback loop reinforces itself. If a change has occurred and has been accepted by the system, a positive feedback loop has occurred. The status quo was not maintained, so the process is referred to as positive feedback. Negative feedback, on the other hand, can lead to nearly stable behavior with gentle fluctuations, similar to a thermostat that maintains a certain room temperature. If a couple gets into a fight, but both go to different parts of the house to cool off so they avoid saying hurtful things to each other, negative feedback has occurred. The couple became aware that the "temperature" was getting higher in the relationship than was comfortable, so they took action to correct the situation to maintain a comfortable stance with each other. Evaluating the usefulness of positive or negative feedback loops must be done contextually. Both processes may refer to something that is either helpful or not helpful to the family.

The whole system will behave differently with positive or negative feedback. Negative feedback controls positive feedback. Negative feedback helps the system maintain itself over the course of time. However, if negative feedback stops all change, it can also cause the system to crash. Although a system needs stability, it must also be able to accept change and to adapt.

Negative Feedback Example

Maria and Julio, a couple, present for couple therapy. The couple complains of low sexual desire. The therapist learns that whenever Julio begins to exhibit sexual interest in Maria, which he expresses by asking her if she wants to "get it on" or "do the horizontal mambo," Maria becomes anxious. When Maria becomes anxious she tends to do things that turn Julio off, such as talk incessantly, bite her nails, and smoke more. The level of sexual desire remains low. In this example the output (sexual interest) of one object of the system, Julio, becomes the input of the other object, Maria. Maria's output (doing unattractive things) becomes Julio's input (Maria's unattractive behaviors decreases Julio's sexual desire). The result is that no change occurs. The more sexual interest Julio displays, the more anxious Maria becomes, and thus the more she engages in behaviors that turn Julio off. No matter how sexually turned on Julio becomes, the result is always the same: low sexual interest on the part of both spouses. This is an example of negative feedback—the input led to output that leads to input that maintains the status quo.

Positive Feedback Example

Dwayne is jealous and suspicious of his wife LaShonda. When LaShonda has a business lunch with a male colleague, Dwayne becomes suspicious and distrustful of LaShonda. Dwayne's jealousy makes LaShonda defensive and antagonistic, and causes her to try to conceal innocent things from Dwayne to avoid arousing his jealousy. In turn, LaShonda's defensiveness and concealment fuel Dwayne's jealousy. The more jealous Dwayne becomes, the more defensive and surreptitious LaShonda becomes. Thus, Dwayne becomes more and more jealous. Here Dwayne's output, jealousy, becomes input for LaShonda: she responds with defensiveness. LaShonda's output (defensiveness) becomes input for Dwayne, who responds with increased jealousy. The result is that an original small jealousy is magnified and becomes raging jealousy.

Distinguishing Positive and Negative Feedback

Whenever Ben begins to become angry, it makes his partner Norman becomes more detached. The angrier Ben becomes, the more detached Norman acts. If Norman's detachment has the result of cooling Ben down, we would have an example of negative feedback: As Ben becomes angry, Norman backs off and this decreases Ben's anger, and soon neither party is angry (the feedback system eliminates the anger). If, on the other hand, Norman's detachment just makes Ben angrier, we have an example of positive feedback: the angrier Ben becomes, the more detached Norman becomes, and Norman's increasing detachment and coolness fuels Ben's anger, so that Ben's anger continues to escalate (the feedback system magnifies the anger).

Stability/Adaptability

Change is something that families must embrace as well as avoid. It is a difficult balancing act. In order to avoid disintegration and chaos, a system must balance stability with adaptability. A system's ability to remain stable in the context of change and to change in the context of stability is central to its survival. A system has two mechanisms that operate simultaneously to achieve this balance. **Morphostasis** is a system's tendency toward stability or a steady state. The system must engage in regulation and control as well as manage its position in the supra-system. Such regulation and control contribute to order and to a state of dynamic **equilibrium** for the system. At the same time, the system has a mechanism that allows for growth, creativity, innovation, and change called **morphogenesis.** A balance between these two mechanisms is necessary for a well-functioning system. Becvar and Becvar (1996) describe this balance as two sides of the same coin. Keeney (1983, p. 70) illustrates the interrelatedness of morphostasis and morphogenesis with his statement "change cannot be found without a roof of stability over its head. Similarly, stability will always be rooted to underlying processes of change" (as quoted in Becvar and Becvar, 1996).

Linear versus Circular Causality

As in the previously noted negative and positive feedback examples, input in a family system leads to output that is fed back into the system, thus becoming input to the family's or couple's next output. This circular process is important in understanding family systems. In family systems thinking, a circular process is involved in the feedback model of causality. Viewing reality from this circular model of causality means that events are multicausal and reciprocal. Reciprocal causality is very different from how our society typically understands events. Most of us are trained to think in terms of **linear causality,** or *A causes B* (see Figure 2.3). The reader can make the paradigm shift from linear to circular thinking by thinking about two or more people rather than one. Whenever we describe a person we are also describing one part of an interaction. For example, if someone describes the father in a particular family as "controlling," we can't stop with that "one-way" (i.e., linear) description of the interaction. Systems thinkers also want to understand what father is reacting to—perhaps a teenage son whose behavior the father believes is "careless." Now we can broaden our descriptions to include a "two-way" interaction. When the son behaves carelessly, the father becomes controlling; the more controlling the father becomes, the more careless the son becomes. Understanding the reciprocal component of any interaction is central to circular, systemic thinking. This is often more formally referred to as **reciprocal causality** (see Figure 2.3). A's behavior is the logical outcome of B's behavior and B's behavior is the logical outcome of A's behavior. In this case, the son's carelessness is the outcome of the father's overcontrolling behaviors, and the overcontrolling behaviors are a

Linear Causality   **Reciprocal Causality**

FIGURE 2.3. Linear versus Reciprocal Causality

function of the son's carelessness. Both influence and are influenced by each other simultaneously.

Consider reciprocal causality in terms of a coin (see Figure 2.4). Father's "controlling" behavior is related to son's "careless" behavior in that both behaviors can be described as different approaches to risk taking (the coin). One side of the coin represents minimum risk taking while the other side of the coin represents maximum risk taking. One way reciprocal causality concepts are utilized in family therapy practice is through **positive connotation** (see Box 2.1 for further explanation of positive connotation).

Family therapists understand relationships from a circular causality perspective. If a woman comes to therapy complaining about that her husband just watches television and does little with the children, linear causality would cause us to think that her husband's behavior is causing her unhappiness. But with circular causality, we look further and examine the relation-

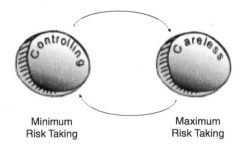

Minimum   Maximum
Risk Taking   Risk Taking

FIGURE 2.4. Reciprocal Causality. This figures represents two sides of the same coin. The father takes minimum risks; the son takes maximum risks. The more careless the son becomes, the more controlling the father becomes in his efforts to protect his son. The more controlling the father becomes, the more the son rebels by taking more risks. The more the son rebels, the more the father controls the son, and so on, causing a vicious cycle. This mutual influence is called reciprocal causality.

**BOX 2.1. Putting Theory into Practice:
The Art of Positive Connotation**

One final helpful tip for understanding systems theory is to utilize the art of positive connotation. As in the case presented involving a father and son, if we want to influence the interaction between father and son we will need to alter the connotation of each of their behaviors so they can think differently about their interactions. For example, if we continue to call the father "controlling" and the son "careless" then we are discounting the positive intentions each one has toward the other. As an alternative perspective we might say that the father is frightened about his son's safety and would be devastated and unable to forgive himself if anything were to happen to his son. The son now can view his father as deeply concerned for him, which allows the son to respond to his father differently than when he believed his father was trying to control him. In this situation, the therapist can remind the father that he had to take risks in order to attain the success he has in life. Likewise, his son is taking risks. If the therapist reframes the son's "carelessness" as an attempt to learn how to take risks, the father may see him as capable and behaving in a way that ultimately could lead to the teen's success in his adult life. The therapist could then encourage the father to teach the son methods of risk taking that are likely to have good results. Once the positive intention is uncovered, the son now views his father as deeply concerned for him rather than intending to control him, and the father views his son as trying to succeed and make him proud rather than being careless.

Positive connotation is central to the work of family therapy as we seek to understand a system and how each part affects and is affected by every other part. The use of positive connotation helps us to have empathy for a family rather than blaming or criticizing particular family members or the entire family. Systems theory views a problem as an indication that something is not working effectively within the family structure or process. A structural symptom points to problems in the systems hierarchy, boundaries, subsystems, rules, etc. A process symptom points to problems in the family interaction, such as emotional reactivity and ineffective communication. The goal is to understand the context within which a problem fits, examine the patterns maintaining that problem, and then change the context.

ship pattern. We might find that when the husband has become more involved in chores and interaction with his wife, she criticizes his performance. Therefore, he withdraws in response to this criticism. The more he withdraws, the more lonely and unsatisfied the wife feels, and the more she complains. The more she complains, the more he withdraws into the solace of television programs, and so the reciprocal process continues.

COMPLEX SYSTEMS ARE COMPOSED OF SUBSYSTEMS

Within a family system are also smaller, self-contained, but interrelated systems called **subsystems.** For example, parents in a family constitute a **parental subsystem** that has its own set of rules, boundaries, and goals. The same parents may also be married and form yet another subsystem known as a **spousal subsystem.** Brothers and sisters, stepbrothers and stepsisters, half brothers and half sisters all are different formations of the **sibling subsystem.** The concept of **hierarchy** (as you shall see in the structural family therapy chapter) refers to the fact that any complex system is also a subsystem of a higher-order system. For example, the local school district, religious community, medical community, and business community are subsystems of the larger community for each town or city in the United States. Just as cities have within themselves subsystems, so do families.

One other subsystem is the **personal subsystem** and its components. Each person has biological, cognitive, emotional, and behavioral components that constitute the individual (Kantor and Lehr, 1976) and impact the other subsystems and systems, and conversely these systems impact the individual's personal subsystem.

SYSTEMS HAVE HOMEOSTATIC MECHANISMS
THAT MAINTAIN STABILITY OF THEIR PATTERNS

Family Patterns

All systems exhibit patterns that are recursive in nature. Patterns are habitual, redundant ways of behaving and communicating in relationships. Systems are made up of interactional patterns that tend to repeat themselves. All systems want to maintain equilibrium or a steady state. As a result, these patterns lead to predictability that an interaction will end the same regardless of the way it began, regardless of the topic or content (i.e., input) of the interaction. For example, most teens could predict how their parents would react to them staying out all night without calling home. These teens understand how their family system would show a pattern they are likely to be able to predict. Another salient example is when a family member or partner just has to give you a "look" and it seems to start an argument. The "look" itself is a predictor of an upcoming interactional pattern reflecting circular causality. All systems have patterns of interaction that can become predictable over time. **Homeostasis** in a family is the desire to maintain stability or the status quo. Humans tend to like predictability; this predictability lends itself to homeostasis.

Rules and Roles

Family rules and roles help maintain stability. **Family rules** are understandings or agreements in families that organize the family members' interactions. Rules may be overt or covert. Examples of such **overt rules** include "In our family we go to church every Sunday" or "Those who do not do their chores do not get their allowance." **Covert rules** are those that are implied but not overtly stated, such as "Never challenge your mother," or "Don't have sex until you are married."

Family **roles** are individually prescribed patterns of behavior reinforced by the expectations and norms of the family. These roles may be defined by gender, or by talents, or abilities, and so on. A father's role may be to stay up late with sick children because he can manage on less sleep than his wife. Roles can be about tangible tasks, or they can be more about ascribed traits such as the role of the "black sheep," the "clown," "the achiever," and so on.

Boundaries

Boundaries are the defining parameters of both individuals and systems. A system boundary may be thought of as the point at which data flow (e.g., output) from one system into another (e.g., input). In family systems theory, boundaries determine who is in and who is out of the system. Boundaries may separate subsystems, generations, or the identity of families.

The degree to which data are free to flow from one system to another is known as the **permeability** of the boundary. A permeable boundary allows data to flow freely, resulting in an open system. An impermeable boundary is one that strictly controls (or even refuses) the acceptance or dispensing of data, resulting in a closed system.

In family systems it is sometimes difficult to distinguish between subsystems, which may point to a lack of boundaries or **diffuse boundaries.** For example, it is not uncommon to see a child as part of a parental subsystem. A child may have been "parentified" because he or she is the oldest and is expected to take care of younger siblings with little consideration for his or her needs by the parents. Or perhaps one parent is not functioning in the parental role, as may be the case if one parent is struggling with a substance abuse problem. In such a case, a child may try to fill the role and become part of the parental subsystem. In other instances, **rigid boundaries** exist and family members are so separate that it is difficult to tell that members are part of the same family. For example, there may be little communication between parents and children as depicted in the saying, "Children are to be seen and not heard!" See Figure 2.5 for a continuum that demonstrates the range of family boundary variations.

EVOLUTION AND CHANGE ARE INHERENT IN OPEN SYSTEMS

Systems can be closed or open. **Closed systems** have no interchange with their environments. For example, machines are closed systems. They do not exchange energy with the environment. Consider a windup alarm clock. The system of this alarm clock is closed. The alarm clock does not exchange energy with its environment. Without the help of a human hand to wind it, it will stop running. **Open systems** exchange matter, energy, or information with their environments. Most biological and social systems are open systems. Plants are an example of open systems. The environment provides the plant with moisture and food, and the plant provides the environment with oxygen. Each influences the other.

Family systems are open systems. "An open system is a set of objects with attributes that interrelate in an environment. The system possesses qualities of wholeness, interdependence, hierarchy, self-regulation, environmental interchange, equilibrium, adaptability, and equifinality" (Littlejohn, 1983, p. 32). Families have constant interchange with their environment. Values encouraged at school, work, or religious institutions influence values at home and vice versa. For example, a child may come home from school one day making fun of a schoolmate for being different. The parents may discuss tolerance and compassion for those who are different with the child, who in turn goes back to school and shares these ideas with other children,

Boundaries

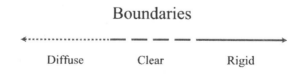

Diffuse   Clear   Rigid

FIGURE 2.5. The Range of Possible Boundaries Within a Family

who then filter this information to their families. Families influence their environments and at the same time the environments influence families. **Adaptability** is the ability of a family to change patterns in response to changing conditions, such as developmental or situational crises or occurrences. For example, a family that makes curfew later for a teenager who has been responsible but desires to stay out a little later is showing adaptability to the child's changing developmental needs. Families must change and restructure themselves in order to survive and thrive. **Equifinality** is the ability of a family to achieve similar goals, but in different ways. For example, not all parents parent alike. Yet families with different parenting styles may have children who behave in an acceptable manner. This illustrates the ability of family systems to achieve the same goals, but from various different routes. The opposite of equifinality is **equipotentiality**. Equipotentiality occurs when the same cause can produce different results. Both equfinality and equipotentiality refer back to the notion that there are no single causes or effects in systems theory.

Sometimes families minimize interchange with their environment, especially if that environment is seen to threaten the integrity of the system. For example, the Amish have strong boundaries between the outside world and their world in order to preserve cultural and religious ideals. On the negative side of a closed system, some families may wish to protect a secret, such as physical or sexual abuse, and thus avoid the outside world so that no one will know what is occurring in the family (see Figure 2.6).

A system at either extreme of openness/closedness is in maximum disorder and disintegration, referred to as **entropy.** A system must find a balance of permeable boundaries so that it can be open to receive the information it requires to survive and close out information that threatens the system's integrity. Such a balance is called **negentropy;** it indicates a system at maximum order. Typically, family therapists encounter families in a state of entropy, and it is their job to help restore negentropy to the family system.

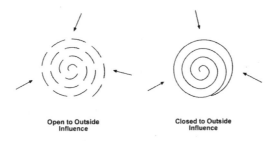

Open to Outside
Influence

Closed to Outside
Influence

FIGURE 2.6. Open and Closed Family Systems

Information Exchange

Open systems exchange information with their environment. Families exchange information through behavior and communication. All behavior is communication, and it is impossible to not communicate (Watzlawick, Beavin, and Jackson, 1967). Even as you are sitting reading this book right now, you are communicating to those around you—perhaps you are showing that you are studying (by your silent reading), that you are bored (by yawning), or that you are interested (by the look on your face as you read). Communication serves as input and output in the system.

There are two types of communication: digital and analogic. **Digital communication** is the verbal mode of communication, the spoken word or content of the communication. **Analogic communication** is the combination of nonverbal communication mode (e.g., voice tone, voice inflection, gestures, facial expression, and body posture) and the context of the message. It is the analogic communication or process of communication that is of most interest to family therapists because this communication tells us about interpersonal relationships.

In family therapy, the therapist is typically focused much more on the analogic communication in the family therapy session. He or she is looking at the **process** of communication and deciphering it in terms of what it means regarding the relationship of the family members to each other. The **content** of what is said is much less important than how it is said.

For example, consider that the digital communication (content) is the same in the following messages, but the analogic communication is different in all three examples:

- If someone says, "Hey, we should get together some time," in a cheery tone with a friendly smile, you would probably consider that an invitation to do something fun with this person.
- If someone says, "Hey, we should get together sometime," with little passion or interest in his or her voice while looking away, you might think he or she is being polite but is uninterested in truly getting together.
- Yet again, "Hey, we should get together sometime" might hold a very different message if the context is that you are walking up a prison aisle and the person sending the message is an inmate.

If the process and content of the message are not *congruent,* a **double message** can occur. If someone says, "You really look nice today," but rolls his or her eyes sarcastically while saying it, you are receiving a double message. Communication is key to any form of psychotherapy.

Family therapists look to communication to regulate the family system. Although content is important for the family therapist to consider, he or she will be continually monitoring the communication process of the family, since this is where input and output in the system occur.

FROM SYSTEMS THEORY TO FAMILY THERAPY THEORIES

Systems theory is the foundation for understanding the majority of family therapy theories presented in the remainder of this book. This theory is provided as the starting point for you to begin an important paradigm shift from linear to circular thinking, so that when you conceptualize a family you will focus on interrelatedness of family members and their interactions rather than the individual family members. In addition, systems theory helps us to understand the tremendous balancing act families must perform to achieve being close and yet separate, stable yet adaptable, open yet closed, and the same yet different—all at the same time. Finally, systems theory orients us to discover the context of any family problem or symptom to give it meaning and understand its function for the entire system.

Each model of family therapy presented in this book represents an emphasis on a different part of systems theory, with the exception of the social constructionist theories presented in Chapter 6, and to an lesser extent, the cognitive-behavioral theories discussed in Chapter 8. For example, structural family therapy attends to the family structure by looking at its rules, boundaries, and hierarchies. Strategic family therapy attends to interactional patterns and positive feedback mechanisms. Because each theory has a different emphasis on a specific part of a family's process or structure, unique interventions from each theory are designed to impact various aspects of the family system. Some models of family therapy emphasize the importance of having all family members in the room; others believe that there is a ripple effect with the system, so having all family members in therapy together is unimportant. The latter believe that changing one or more family members will create change in the entire system. One may think of this emphasis on various family therapy theories or models from the systemic viewpoint of equifinality. One can have similar outcomes from different origins—family change can occur through many different types of family therapy.

Whatever the theoretical model of treatment chosen, family therapy typically has the following hallmarks:

- No family member is singled out as the patient or "sick one."
- Family therapists usually see families conjointly rather than individually.
- Diagnosis and goals are based on the family, not on individuals.

This chapter has introduced you to family systems theory, which was derived both from general system theory and cybernetic theory. Systems theory was derived from a revolt against the reductionist thinking that permeated science fifty-plus years ago. It provided science with a more holistic way to look at complex phenomena. Gregory Bateson, basing his work on the ideas of Norbert Wiener (1954) and Ludwig von Bertalanffy (1968), did much to bring these theories to the forefront of families, and was a pioneer in beginning to understand mental illness in the context of the family system.

GLOSSARY

adaptability: The ability of a family to change patterns concurrent with the changing conditions.

analogic communication: Communication not with words, but of nonverbal, paraverbal, and contextual aspects of interaction. Analogic communication has connotative meanings. In family therapy it is the process of communication.

boundaries: Abstract or physical dividers between or among systems and subsystems. Boundaries define who is in and who is out of a system.

closed system: A system that has no interchange with its environment.

content: Verbal or written words in communication; what is said. *See* DIGITAL COMMUNICATION.

covert rules: Rules that are implied but not overtly stated.

cybernetics: Science of communication, control, and feedback; the study of the self-regulating properties of systems.

diffuse boundaries: Boundaries that are overly permeable. This causes distance to decrease in families and boundaries to become blurred.

digital communication: Verbal mode of communication, with denotative meaning. Digital communication takes place via words said verbally or in written language.

double message: When the process and content aspects of a message are not congruent.

entropy: A system's tendency to move toward disorganization.

equifinality: The principle that similar outcomes may result from different origins. In family systems theory this refers to the ability of a family or families to achieve similar goals in different ways.

equilibrium: Balance in a system that keeps it stable.

equipotentiality: The same process can produce different results.

extended family: Relatives of those making up the primary nuclear family.

family of choice: Individuals outside of one's biological family that one also chooses to consider family.

family of origin: The family one grew up in.

family rules: Understandings or agreements in families that organize the family members' interactions.

family system: Includes family members, the unique attributes of the family members, and the relationships among the family members.

feedback: Any reciprocal flow of influence.

feedback loop: A circular causal process in which a system's output is returned to its input.

general systems theory: Theory that defines relationship of objects or individuals within biological, economic, or physical systems.

hierarchy: Having an organization of a higher-order system.

homeostasis: When a system maintains stability or the status quo. In family systems this typically occurs through families developing recurring interactional patterns to maintain stability and balance.

identified patient: The symptom bearer for dysfunction in the family.

linear causality: The idea that one event is the cause and another is the effect.

morphogenesis: Tendency of a system to evolve and to change its structure; constructive, system-enhancing behaviors.

morphostasis: The tendency of a system to retain its organization or to maintain the status quo.

negentropy: Emergence of organizational patterns.

nonsummativity: The assertion that a system is a separate entity greater than the sum of its parts. A synergistic effect that occurs in systems.

nuclear family: A family consisting of a father, a mother, and child (or children) triad.

open system: A system that exchanges matter, energy, or information with its environment.

overt rules: Rules that are stated.

paradigm: A model or conceptual scheme through which people make sense of their reality or world.

paradigm shift: A shift in thinking when one conceptual worldview is replaced by another.

parental subsystem: The parents of a family make up the smaller, self-contained, but interrelated systems of a family.

permeability: Degree to which data are free to flow from one system to another through boundaries.

personal subsystem: Systems are composed of individuals. Each person has a system that includes his or her biological, cognitive, emotive, and behavioral components, making that individual a subsystem of the larger system. The individual impacts the family system, and the family system impacts the individual, including his or her biology, cognitions, behaviors, and emotions.

positive connotation: Occurs when a therapist relabels a behavior positively so that the family can see the symptom in a new light.

process: How one communicates and the context in which one communicates. Process gives one information on how to interpret content. *See* ANALOGIC COMMUNICATION.

reciprocal causality: Refers to a nonlinear, circular sequence of events whereby one event modifies another event, which in turn modifies another event, which eventually modifies the original event.

reductionism: A theory or procedure that reduces complex data to simple terms.

rigid boundaries: Boundaries that are nonpermeable whereby communication across subsytems becomes difficult.

roles: Individually prescribed patterns of behavior reinforced by the expectations and norms of the family.

sibling subsystem: A family subsystem made up by the siblings of the family.

spousal subsystem: A family subsystem made up of the two spouses.

subsystems: Within a family the smaller, self-contained, but interrelated systems.

suprasystems: The larger systems that surround the family.

system: An entity that maintains its existence through the mutual interaction of its parts.

tenets: Principle beliefs or doctrine.

REFERENCES

Bateson, G. (1972). *Steps to an ecology of the mind.* New York: Ballantine.

Becvar, D. S. and Becvar, R. J. (1996). *Family therapy: A systemic integration* (Third edition). Boston, MA: Allyn and Bacon.

Bellinger, G. (2000). *Systems: Understanding the way.* Retrieved on November 23, 2001, online <http://www.outsights.com/systems/systems/systems.htm>.

Capuzzi, D. and Gross, D. R. (1999*). Counseling and psychotherapy: Theories and interventions* (Second edition). Upper Saddle River, NJ: Merrill.

Kantor, D. and Lehr, W. (1976). *Inside the family.* San Francisco: Jossey-Bass.

Keeney, B. P. (1983). *Aesthetics of Change.* New York: The Guilford Press.

Kuhn, T. S. (1962). *The structure of scientific revolutions.* Chicago, IL: University of Chicago Press.

Littlejohn, S. W. (1978). *Theories of human communication.* Columbus, OH: Charles Merrill.

Littlejohn, S. W. (1983). *Theories of human communication* (Second edition). Belmont, CA: Wadsworth Publishing Company.

Minuchin, P. (1985). Families and individual development: Provocations in the field of family therapy. *Child Development, 36,* 289-302.

von Bertalanffy, L. (1968). *General systems theory: Foundations, development, applications.* New York: George Braziller.

Watzlawick, P., Beavin, J. H., and Jackson, D. D. (1967*). Pragmatics of human communication.* New York: W. W. Norton and Company.

Wiener, N. (1954). *The human use of human beings: Cybernetics and society.* New York: Avon.

Chapter 3

Structural Family Therapy

Joseph L. Wetchler

> Minuchin: What is the problem? . . . So who wants to start?
> Mr. Smith: I think it's my problem. I'm the one that has the problem . . .
> Minuchin: Don't be so sure. Never be so sure.
>
> Salvador Minuchin
> *Families and Family Therapy*

During the late 1960s an Argentine-born psychiatrist named Salvador Minuchin challenged patients, family members, and mental health professionals to view emotional problems from a family perspective rather than an individual one. His clinical flair and personal charm enabled him to seduce families to change in an often startling and provocative fashion. However, although his methods were certainly dramatic, they were based on solid theoretical tenets.

Structural family therapy views families and emotional distress from an organizational perspective. Individual problems are maintained not through personal pathology but rather through flaws in a family's organizational design. Structural family therapists do not attempt to resolve an individual's problems as much as they work to alter the family's organizational structure. Family members are then able to relate to one another in new ways that enable them to solve their problems themselves (Minuchin, 1974; Minuchin and Fishman, 1981).

MAJOR FIGURES IN STRUCTURAL FAMILY THERAPY

In the early 1960s, Salvador Minuchin joined the staff of the Wyltwick School, in upstate New York, to work with juvenile delinquents. It was here that he discovered the limits of a traditional psychotherapy background. Basically, insight-oriented, individual approaches did not work with a non-motivated teenage population. Physically active boys who are cut off from their feelings are highly resistant to the quiet reflection required for individ-ual therapy. Further, talking about feelings and problems often seemed fu-tile when parents were concerned with stopping their child's violent behav-ior. With colleagues Braulio Montalvo and Bernice Rosman, he developed an action-oriented approach that utilized a family perspective to treatment (Minuchin et al., 1967).

Based on his success at the Wyltwick School, Minuchin moved on to be-come the director of the Philadelphia Child Guidance Clinic. From its hum-ble beginnings as an inner-city child guidance center, under Minuchin the Philadelphia Child Guidance Clinic grew to become one of the foremost centers for family therapy training in the 1970s and early 1980s (Nichols and Schwartz, 1998). With Braulio Montalvo and Bernice Rosman from the Wyltwick School, Minuchin joined forces with Jay Haley, Harry Aponte, Charles Fishman, Jorge Colapinto, Cloe Madanes, and Marianne Walters to develop and refine structural family therapy.

In 1976, Minuchin resigned as director of the Philadelphia Child Guid-ance Clinic, but remained as director of training until 1981. From there he moved to New York City to start his own small center, Family Studies Inc., with colleagues George Simon and Wai-Yung Lee. Following his retirement in 1996, the center in New York City was renamed the Minuchin Center for the Family in his honor. Minuchin now lives in Boston, where he consults with the Massachusetts Department of Health on home-based therapy pro-grams and continues his writing (Nichols and Schwartz, 1998).

Although the first pioneers at the Philadelphia Child Guidance Clinic have since moved on, several members of the original team and its students continue to make notable contributions to the structural family therapy liter-ature. Braulio Montalvo, Jorge Colapinto, and Harry Aponte are considered elder statesmen within the family therapy community, and second-generation structural family therapists Charles Fishman and George Simon have con-tinued to develop the theory (e.g., Fishman, 1993; Simon, 1995). Jay Haley and Cloe Madanes have developed their own school of strategic family ther-apy (see Chapter 4) and Marianne Walters has become a major figure in the feminist family therapy movement (see Chapter 13).

THEORETICAL CONCEPTS
OF STRUCTURAL FAMILY THERAPY

Family Structure

Similar to other schools of family therapy, structural family therapy fo-cuses on the role of context in maintaining and solving individual problems.

It is unique in its focus on family organization and the active role assigned to the therapist as an agent of change (Colapinto, 1991). In fact, it is from this view of the family as an organizational entity that the theory derived the name structural family therapy. Minuchin and Fishman (1981) state:

> The family is a natural group which over time has evolved patterns of interacting. These patterns make up the family structure, which governs the functioning of family members, delineating their range of behavior and facilitating their interaction. (p. 11)

Structural family therapists believe that problems are maintained, not caused, by a dysfunctional family organization. Therefore, they are less concerned with the root cause of the problem than they are with how the family is structured in its attempts to solve the problem. Rather than focusing on the history of the problem, structural family therapists are interested in present-centered issues such as who is in charge in the family, who are the allies in a family and who is on the outs, how much personal space exists for people to assume responsibility for their actions, who has power over whom, and how much flexibility exists for family members to change roles in new and different situations.

Structural family therapists view families similarly to how an organizational consultant looks at a corporation. Every family has an unspoken structural flowchart that shows who is in charge and what are the responsibilities of each member. Various family structures dictate the patterns in which families communicate (Aponte and VanDeusen, 1981). The manner in which a family is organized affects who takes the leadership role in specific situations and who talks to whom about certain subjects. For example, in many families the parents are in charge of setting limits on their young children's behavior; they discuss and set the rules and values for raising their children. However, although these children are excluded from disciplinary discussions, they may be included in family decisions about where they will go on family outings.

When a family comes to therapy, a structural family therapist assesses how the family organizes itself regarding solving the problem. Does an effective leadership pattern exist in dealing with this problem? Do people talk directly to one another about the problem, or are others inappropriately involved as mediators? Are problems maintained because certain family members are in secret alliance against other family members? Are some people unable to solve their own problems because other family members intrude on the resolution process? Is the family flexible enough to change their organization to solve the problem, or do they attempt to resolve it with an outmoded structure? The answers to these types of questions about a family's organization enable structural family therapists to develop treatment plans and interventions to meet a family's specific needs.

All families have a variety of structures to handle different situations (Minuchin, 1974). For example, although the mother and father might handle the majority of housework in a family, some of the older children might have to assume more of this responsibility if one of the parents becomes laid up with a serious illness. As the parent recovers, he or she can return to the previous position of authority, or perhaps the family might renegotiate their roles around who handles which responsibilities at home. Similarly, it is also important for various subgroups to handle different tasks. One parent and child might be the best subgroup to work on problems with math homework, and the two brothers who share a room might be the best subgroup to decide on what posters they hang on their walls (of course, parental supervision might be necessary depending on the type of posters they choose, or whether their deliberations result in a physical altercation).

Family Competency

At the heart of structural family therapy is a fundamental belief in the basic competency of families (Simon, 1995). Problems do not exist because of a core dysfunction in the family, but rather because the family is unable to access a workable structure to solve the problem. As Minuchin states (in Minuchin and Nichols, 1993):

> When families come to me for help, I assume they have problems not because there is something inherently wrong with them but because they've gotten stuck—stuck with a structure whose time has passed, and stuck with a story that doesn't work. (p. 43)

All families have the potential to solve their problems. In fact, the ability to access appropriate structures already exists in their repertoire. It is the therapist's task to convince families to risk searching for alternatives they already possess (Simon, 1995).

Boundaries and Subsystems

In keeping with its organizational approach, structural family therapy breaks families down into various **subsystems,** or groupings of family members concerning specific tasks. For example, husbands and wives form the spouse subsystem which provides mutual support, sex, and companionship, and they also serve as the parental subsystem in making executive decisions about child rearing, discipline, and nurturance. Children, on the other hand, form the sibling subsystem in which they learn about mutual cooperation, peer problem solving, and how to support one another (Colapinto, 1991). Other subsystems can serve a temporary function, as when a father and daughter work on a school project together or a mother coaches her son's Little League team.

Individuals are both a subsystem by themselves and are members of numerous other subsystems. In fact, all subsystems belong to even larger subsystems. For example, the family is a subsystem of the extended family and the community in which it lives. The term **holon** refers to a subsystem that is both a system in its own right and a subsystem of a larger system. "Every holon—the individual, the nuclear family, the extended family, and the community—is both a whole and a part, not more one than the other, not one rejecting or conflicting with the other" (Minuchin and Fishman, 1981, p. 13). Structural family therapists would say that an individual's identity is formed by being a member of numerous subsystems. Within such various roles as spouse, parent, employee, lover, and child to one's own parent, we develop different aspects of personality and develop a sense of self.

Boundaries are the rules that govern who is included and excluded from a specific subsystem. It is as if these rules form an invisible fence around each group and define its membership. However, these subsystems do not exist in isolation but, following the idea of holons, are in constant interaction with other subsystems within a family. **Clear boundaries,** those that successfully enclose a subsystem yet enable communication with other subsystems, are important for optimum family functioning (see Figure 3.1). "They must be defined well enough to allow subsystem members to carry out their functions without undue interference, but they must allow contact between the members of the subsystem and others" (Minuchin, 1974, p. 54). The composition of a subsystem is not as important as the clarity of a subsystem's boundaries. Therefore, optimum functioning in one family might include two parents working together to run the family, while the **executive subsystem,** the subsystem that takes the leadership role, in another family might be composed of a mother and grandmother, and a third family might have a **parental child,** an older child with occasional family leadership tasks, to take charge of the younger children while the parents are at work. Because this is an organizational model, the emphasis is on the successful functioning of a family as opposed to how a family should look.

In fact, the clarity of a family's boundaries is an extremely useful parameter for assessing family functioning. Some families have highly **enmeshed boundaries** in which there is little autonomy between individuals and other subsystems (see Figure 3.1). It is as if there is no internal support structure

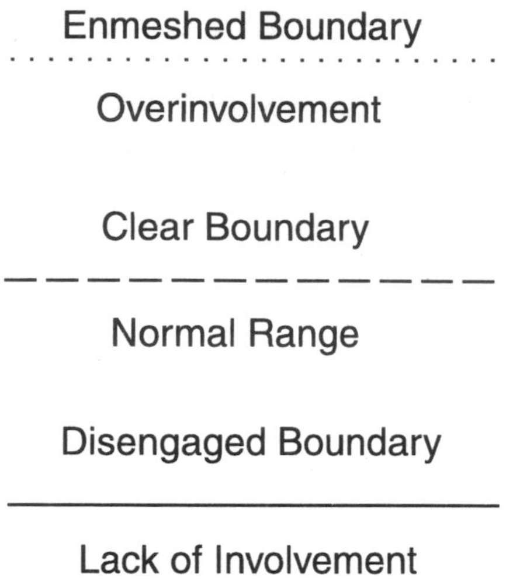

Enmeshed Boundary

. . . .

Overinvolvement

Clear Boundary

— — — — — — — — — — — —

Normal Range

Disengaged Boundary

Lack of Involvement

FIGURE 3.1. Boundaries

for the family. It is impossible to develop effective subsystem productivity as everyone keeps intruding in everyone else's business. Children's issues become confused with marital issues, and no one has a sense of self because it is impossible to tell where one person ends and another begins. Minuchin and Fishman (1981) present a brief example of a dysfunctionally enmeshed system:

> The therapist presses a diabetic girl's wrist. "Do you feel this?" he asks the parents.
> "Yes, I do," the father says, indicating his own wrist. "Here. It feels like pins and needles."
> "I have very poor circulation today," the mother says, apologizing for not sharing the experience. (p. 142)

How could a father actually believe that he feels a therapist squeezing his daughter's wrist and a mother believe she should feel it? Enmeshment at this level is extremely rare. Yet this situation happened in a family in which a diabetic child had to be hospitalized numerous times for diabetic acidosis even though the child received regular doses of insulin. This type of enmeshment is not typical of families with diabetic children, but it was found in several of the families Minuchin, Rosman, and Baker (1978) treated for **psychosomatic diabetes,** cases of diabetes that consistently have to be hospitalized even though the child is on insulin. Although the diabetes is physiological in nature, the flare-ups are thought to be due to psychological or family issues.

Of course, enmeshed boundaries can also be appropriate in certain situations. Parent-infant relationships must be enmeshed as babies have no way of fending for themselves and are dependent on their parents' abilities to understand their needs based on the tiniest shift in expression. Further, parents must be thoroughly intrusive in all aspects of their baby's life until their child begins to function autonomously. Until that time, however, they must feed, clothe, bathe, diaper, and nurture their young one. At the opposite end of the spectrum are **disengaged boundaries,** which successfully enclose a subsystem but are impermeable to outside information (see Figure 3.1). Families with disengaged boundaries are often closed off from the rest of their community. They do not discuss their problems with others and do not voluntarily partake of outside services such as counselors or family-life educators. Again, a disengaged family structure can often be quite helpful. Many families believe that parents should promote autonomy in their teenage children. For example, many parents give their teenagers chores to do on their own and let them make their own decisions on how to spend their allowance. An extremely disengaged family, on the other hand, might have absolutely no idea where their teenagers go when they leave home, who their friends are, or how they are doing in school.

Many families show a mixture of boundaries within their organization. Minuchin, Rosman, and Baker (1978) found that several of the families with an anorexic child that they treated had highly enmeshed internal boundaries and overly disengaged external boundaries. Although it was virtually impossible to distinguish the child's issues from the parents', these families were particularly immune from the outside interventions of professionals. Trepper and Barrett (1989) report a similar phenomenon in incest families in which no sexual boundary exists between the perpetrator and the child; however, these families are so secretive that often no one reports the abuse until several years have passed.

Structural family therapists are also aware that it is useful for families to use multiple types of boundaries at different times. Further, it is also desirable for boundaries to change according to different situations. For example, when a mother and father make love, it is desirable for them to be enmeshed so they can freely engage in the give and take of sex. The mutual touching, caressing, and kissing require an extreme level of closeness to be mutually satisfying. It is also desirable that they have a disengaged boundary between themselves and their children by not allowing them in the room while they make love or by waiting until their children are asleep. However, in a healthy family, these rules should change to allow the children to enter their parents' room in case of an emergency, such as an injury to one of the children. It should be noted that a child accidentally intruding on their parents' lovemaking, while embarrassing, is not problematic if dealt with effectively; however, a boundary problem may exist if it continues without resolution.

Hierarchy

Hierarchy refers to a boundary that distinguishes the leadership subsystem from the rest of the family. Structural family therapists believe that an individual, or a group of family members, must assume the leadership role for a family to successfully resolve a given task. Those members within the leadership hierarchy have more power in the decision-making process than the rest of the family. For example, parents typically have a greater role in determining their young children's bedtimes than do the children themselves. Although young children may have input in some situations, such as asking for later bedtimes to watch special television programs, it is still up to the parents to make the final decision. The term **parent-child hierarchy** refers to the specific boundary that demarcates the parents' responsibility in child-rearing issues. Figure 3.2 shows an example of a parent-child hierarchy with a clear boundary.

As families use different structures to meet the demands of different situations, they must also have different hierarchical arrangements. Typically, the person who is responsible for a specific task assumes the leadership function for that task. The father might be at the top of the hierarchy for cooking meals if he is in charge of preparing supper, and the mother would assume the leadership function for mowing the lawn if she is in charge of yard care. Children also can assume leadership roles. For example, an older son might take care of the younger children while a single mother is out, but relinquishes his role when she returns. Figure 3.3 shows various hierarchical arrangements that could exist in families.

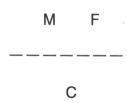

FIGURE 3.2. Parent-Child Hierarchy with a Clear Boundary

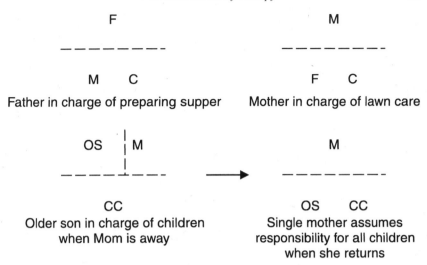

FIGURE 3.3. Typical Hierarchical Arrangements in Families

No hierarchical arrangement is written in stone. In fact, families must often rearrange their structure to meet the demands of specific crises. When the mother is away at work, a grandmother might care for the father and the children while he recovers from a heart attack. Children might receive increased responsibilities for chores and meal preparations following the divorce of their parents. When a family fails to appropriately change the leadership hierarchy in times of crisis, severe problems can arise. A family that is lost in the woods would be best advised to let their Eagle Scout son be in charge of getting them to safety instead of relying on parents, the usual leaders, who have minimal outdoors skills. Then, when they return to civilization, the parents can again assume responsibility for the family.

Problems arise when families fail to adopt a functional leadership subsystem. For example, a parent-child hierarchy may be so enmeshed that the parents are unable to apply appropriate punishment when their children misbehave. The parents are so concerned about losing their children as friends that they are afraid to set appropriate limits. In other families, this boundary might be so disengaged that, although effective rules exist, the parents are unable to respond to their children's personal concerns. A crisis can develop because the parents are unaware that their child has a problem. This sometimes happens when parents do not monitor their child's school performance until they discover that he or she has to repeat a grade. In this case, the family must open the lines of communication between the parents and child. Perhaps the parents might create a study time at home, have the child show them his or her work, do homework with the child, or have the school send progress notes to keep them aware of the child's in-class behavior and performance.

Alliances, Coalitions, and Triangles

Families have many tasks that are more easily accomplished when several members participate. For example, a mother and her daughters raking the leaves and a father and his sons washing the dishes often make the chores go faster. An **alliance** exists when two or more family members join together to handle a specific problem. Family alliances are typically known to most members and are generally viewed positively. For example, everyone in the family usually knows if two brothers like to go fishing together or that Mom and Dad work together on paying the bills.

Alliances often shift as family members deal with various tasks. They can exist across family hierarchies and are not limited by a particular subsystem. In fact, a new subsystem exists each time a new alliance is formed. Mom and Dad may be the most effective team to work on parenting issues; however, Dad and the two daughters, who share a mutual interest in rare stamps, might be better suited for having a joint hobby of stamp collecting. Expecting Mom to join in simply because she and Dad are part of the "parenting" alliance would probably diminish the joy for everyone involved. Then again, Mom and Dad would probably most enjoy a night out together without the children, and the kids would feel stifled if their parents regularly intruded on their play time.

Coalitions exist when two or more family members join forces against one or more family members. This usually happens when two family members have a disagreement and a third member joins forces with the perceived weaker member to balance the score (Aponte and VanDeusen, 1981). Besides being adversarial, coalitions tend to be secretive in nature. In fact, coalitions are most likely to exist when family members are unable to openly discuss a particular problem. The more overt a coalition is, the easier it is to resolve. For example, families can easily recognize and handle situations in which the big sister punches the middle son for breaking the youngest son's toy. It is clear to everyone that the big sister is defending her youngest brother. It is an entirely different matter when one of the children consistently breaks one of Dad's possessions every time Dad wins an argument with Mom. Dad may not even be aware that his son has aligned with Mom against him. This is especially problematic if Mom and Dad do not discuss the problems in their relationship that led to the child becoming Mom's champion.

Triangles are a specific type of coalition in which two family members join forces against a third member. Although triangles within a subsystem can be relatively benign and are often easily handled, they can be especially problematic when they exist across generations. A **cross-generational coalition** is a specific type of triangle in which two family members from different generations ally against a third member. The two most common types are when a parent and child join forces against the other parent or when an in-law and spouse ally against the other spouse. Of course it is not uncommon for a child and grandparent to form a coalition against a parent. Cross-generational coalitions typically exist when a power imbalance exists between two family members that cannot be mediated by discussion. The weaker member typically joins forces with a family member of a different generation to balance the power discrepancy. Problems between an in-law and a spouse usually exist for two reasons. In the first instance, one spouse complains to his or her parent about his or her spouse's behavior. The parent then retaliates by openly criticizing that spouse. Rather than the husband and wife resolving their problem, a third person serves as the focus of attack. This pattern, although highly uncomfortable for the members of the triangle, is not as uncomfortable as the two spouses dealing with the core issues in their relationship. Unfortunately, although this type of interaction balances the power in the family, it does not resolve the core problem. In fact, once started, cross-generational coalitions often maintain the problem. The only way for a problem such as this to be resolved is for the two spouses to openly and mutually discuss the problems in their relationship.

The second type of cross-generational coalition exists when a child is involved as the third party in a parental dispute. Typically, one parent allies with the child against the other parent; however, another pattern involves both parents attempting to involve the child in a coalition against the other. This second pattern can be highly stressful for the child because to ally with one parent automatically earns the disfavor of the other parent. The child must constantly walk a fine line between the needs of both parents (Minuchin, 1974).

A third type of cross-generational triangle is called **detouring,** in which the two parents shift their focus to one child every time a problem arises between them. This action happens so fast that the parents may not be overtly aware of a relationship problem between them, and simply assume they have a problem child. Minuchin, Rosman, and Baker (1978) explicitly revealed this pattern in a landmark study of psychosomatic diabetics, or diabetic children who had to be consistently rehospitalized for diabetic acidosis despite being on insulin. Hospitalization is usually an unlikely occurrence once treatment has begun, yet these children constantly returned with no organic reason for their crisis.

In this study, the parents and child all had intravenous blood sampling units attached to their arms from which blood samples were unobtrusively taken at specific intervals and which were later evaluated for the concentration of free fatty acids (FFA) in the bloodstream. Although certain amounts of FFA are normal, the buildup of FFA is a precursor to ketoacidosis in diabetics. FFA levels are also known to rise when an individual is under stress.

The researchers conducted a three-part experiment. During the first stage, a researcher elicited and maintained an argument by the parents while the child watched from behind a one-way mirror. In the second phase, the child was brought into the room to help the parents resolve the problem. In the third phase, the discussion ended and the family met with a researcher who debriefed them and made sure the experiment had no undesirable effects.

The psychosomatic diabetic families showed the most striking physiological examples of detouring compared to normal diabetic families and physiologically and emotionally normal families. During the parent argument phase, both the parents and child showed highly elevated FFA levels. When the child entered the room, the parents' levels dropped markedly as they focused on the child, yet the child's levels continued to rise. Afterward, the parents' FFA levels continued to drop while the child's were still on the rise.

In contrast, in the normal diabetic family the parents showed a small rise in FFA during the parent argument phase while the child showed none at all. The child's FFA rose slightly when he or she entered the room while the parents returned to normal. Afterward, both the parents' and child's FFA levels were maintained at the normal level. The reason for the lack of change in FFA levels in the normal diabetic families is that disagreement was not a major form of stress for these families. For the psychosomatic families, however, parental disagreement was very stressful and was detoured onto the diabetic child, who carried the brunt of the family anxiety (Minuchin, Rosman, and Baker, 1978).

NORMAL FAMILY DEVELOPMENT

Minuchin (1974) claims that no single family structure is indicative of health; however, the best sign of functionality is a family's ability to change structures to meet the new demands of various life cycle stages or family crises. Problems are an inherent part of life and often require organizational shifts for families to resolve them (Nichols and Schwartz, 1998). This is certainly true for life cycle development. Specific structures are idiosyncratic to individual families, yet some general assumptions can be made.

The primary task of a newly married couple is to develop both external and internal boundaries that define them as a spousal system. Through continuous negotiations, they develop a set of rules that distinguishes them from their families of origin. Initially, each will attempt to shape the couple according to the rules they learned in their families of origin. This includes what they eat, when they eat, what they do for fun, when they make love, how many children they have or whether they have children, whether they go to church, and many more decisions both large and small. Through discussion, they develop the rules and procedures that define them as a couple. Some will be similar to their families of origin and some will be unique to them. It is the ability to successfully negotiate these rules that creates a boundary that separates them from their families of origin. Although healthy couples should always maintain the option of returning to their families of origin for advice and help, they must now depend primarily on each other for decision making and problem solving.

Internally, the new couple must also learn to accommodate to each other and to develop internal boundaries. As they develop their rules, each must learn to compromise and recognize when his or her partner has a better idea. Further, they must also negotiate rules that enable each to maintain a unique personhood. Although the couple may choose activities such as going to church and the movies as joint activities, the wife can continue to go to the gym and the husband continue to fish as things they do for personal recreation. Couples are constantly renegotiating their internal boundaries as they change jobs, get promotions, develop new interests, and meet new friends.

The birth of children leads to the development of a parent-child hierarchy, a parental subsystem, and a sibling subsystem. The parents need to open the boundary of their couple system to include their newborn children. Failure to accommodate to their children's needs could lead to serious developmental problems for their offspring. Further, the parents need to work jointly in formulating decisions that affect their children without triangulating them into their problems.

The type of boundary that exists within a parent-child hierarchy changes as children mature. For example, an infant requires a well-defined hierarchy with an enmeshed boundary. Young children are totally dependent on their parents' decisions regarding their well-being. Further, parents need to be highly in tune to the most subtle clues as young children lack sufficient verbal communication to express their needs. On the other hand, the hierarchy between parents and normal adolescents becomes more egalitarian and less enmeshed as teenagers show increased ability to make appropriate decisions and become more personally responsible.

It is important that clinicians not mistake growing pains for pathology (Minuchin, 1974; Nichols and Schwartz, 1998). A heightened degree of stress and anxiety accompanies all life cycle transitions. The important issue is whether a family can modify its existing structure to meet the developmental changes. Nichols and Schwartz (1998) remind us, "Although no clear dividing line exists between normal and abnormal families, we can say that normal families modify their structure to accommodate to changed circumstances; pathological families increase the rigidity of structures that are no longer functional" (p. 249).

PATHOLOGY AND BEHAVIOR DISORDERS

If structural family therapy defines normality as a family's ability to change its structure to solve a specific problem, then at the most basic level pathology exists when a family is unable to alter its structure to handle an existing crisis. No family structure is a panacea for all situations. Inherent strengths and weaknesses are part of every structure. Although a disengaged boundary is highly appropriate for family members to work on personal pursuits, it is not appropriate when they need to communicate about a specific problem. Likewise, although having every member of the family involved in decision making can ensure a certain degree of unity for certain situations, such as going on a family outing, it can be cumbersome and even dangerous when an emergency arises. Then, having a subsystem choose the path of action may be the most expedient route.

Not only must families possess the ability to change their structure, but they must also have the wisdom to recognize when they should stay the same (Colapinto, 1991). A stable structure is often the best solution for many problems. For example, in many cases of childhood rebellion, the best strategy is for the parents to continue to take charge and punish the misbehavior. Although a child might be angry during the entire time he or she is grounded, this does not mean that the parents should not hold firm. In fact, altering their structure and giving in to the child may give the message that no offense was committed or that the child can get his or her way by simply having a tantrum.

Most important, structural family therapists do not see a one-to-one relationship between specific structures and individual symptoms (Aponte and VanDeusen, 1981). For example, cross-generational coalitions have been implicated in both anorexia nervosa (Minuchin, Rosman, and Baker, 1978) and adult male substance abuse (Stanton, Todd, and Associates, 1982). It is not viewed as abnormal when a girl starts to diet because she is concerned about her looks or when a person experiments with drugs. These situations happen all the time in families. From a structural perspective, many families find ways to handle these situations before they become problems. Anorexic and substance abusing families, however, could not find alternative structures to nip these problems in the bud. Specifically, the families could not create an appropriate parent-child hierarchy in which both parents worked together to deal with their child.

In essence, structural family therapy provides a highly optimistic view of families. Individual symptoms do not exist due to dysfunctional or punitive families, but rather happen due to an inability to access a workable structure. More important, it means that even long-standing problems can be solved if the family can find a workable organization. This does not mean that family members are not capable of doing terrible things to one another, or that they are absolved of taking responsibility for their actions. For example, Trepper and Barrett (1989) believe that it is a crucial part of treatment for fathers who sexually abuse their children to take responsibility and apologize for their actions as an initial part of treatment; however, long-term change is maintained only if these families are able to develop an appropriate boundary between the parent and child generations. Further, much structural renegotiation needs to happen within the spousal subsystem, especially in terms of opening up boundaries around communication and problem solving.

Alignments and coalitions are a normal part of family life. The father and daughter might conspire to throw a surprise party for the mother, or the younger brother and sister might occasionally ally together against the older brother who always watches the same television shows. The important point is that alliances and coalitions can shift to different members when appropriate (Aponte and VanDeusen, 1981). Although father and son might be the best twosome for discussing football, Dad and Mom would still be the most appropriate alliance to handle parenting issues.

Alliances and coalitions become problematic when they remain inappropriately stable across time. Let us return, for example, to the father and son who enjoy discussing football. Perhaps a wider view of the family reveals a power imbalance between the mother and father in which their inability to communicate leads to the mother typically making the family decisions. The father, being lower in the marital hierarchy, begins to rely on his son more for emotional support than as someone to discuss football. The father-son alliance now has the makings of a cross-generational coalition, especially if the son begins to challenge the mother on behalf of his father. Another variation of this problem is when the parents become ineffective disciplinarians because they cannot agree on how to deal with the son. Every time the mother wants to punish the boy for his mistakes, the father takes the son's side. Problems such as these can be dealt with by forming a more solid

parent-child hierarchy and having the parents become more open and egalitarian in their relationship. Another option is to create an alliance between
the mother and son that enables them to develop a positive relationship. One
single alternative structure is never perfect for solving all problems. Many
options are available. The important issue for implementing an alternative
structure is its fit with a specific family.

GOALS OF STRUCTURAL FAMILY THERAPY

Structural family therapists believe that problems are maintained by dysfunctional family structures. Therefore, the primary goal is to help the family develop a new structure. Problem resolution is a by-product of change, as
new, more appropriate structures lead to effective problem solving (Aponte
and VanDeusen, 1981).

Families with problems are not viewed as inherently flawed but rather as
suffering from an inability to switch to a more functional family structure.
One of the core assumptions of structural family therapy is that all families
possess the ability to change (Simon, 1995). Therefore, it is the therapist's
responsibility to help them find a more appropriate structure. At that point,
the family will begin generating potential solutions.

Structural family therapy is a process-oriented model. The therapist focuses more on altering the family's transactions and leaves the outcome to
the family. This is based on a belief that no therapist has the ability to know
what is the most effective solution for a family, but rather changes the process by which problems are solved. In fact, focusing on the content of a family discussion more than likely will hinder the change process. This is because a therapist who becomes bogged down deciding who is right and who
is wrong in a family negotiation has probably been triangled into a family
role usually reserved for another family member. It is hard to maintain clinical objectivity when a therapist takes sides on an issue (Minuchin and
Fishman, 1981). Further, it is difficult to both focus on content and the process involved in changing a family's structure.

Family assessment typically involves asking questions about how a family attempts to resolve its problems and observing the family members in action. From that information, the therapist then generates a **family map** in
which he or she diagrams the family's current dysfunctional structure. From
there, the therapist can develop a more suitable alternative structure. For example, Wetchler (1992) describes a family in which a boy consistently
missed school due to a psychosomatic stomach ailment with no physiological cause. The boy lived with his mother, but his stepmother made most of
the decisions concerning his health and school attendance. The family's

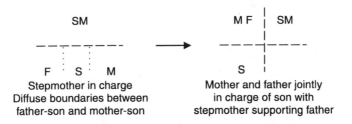

FIGURE 3.4. Change from Nonfunctional to Functional Hierarchy in Family of Boy with Stomach Pain

structure had the stepmother at the top providing most of the leadership for the boy, and the next level had the boy in between his two divorced parents who ineffectively argued about how to best take care of him. Most of the communication between the biological parents was carried out by the boy as the two did not speak to each other (see Figure 3.4). The goal of this therapy was to create an appropriate parent-child hierarchy with the two biological parents deciding how to handle their son's stomach problems and lack of school attendance with the stepmother off to the side as a support to the father. Having the parents negotiate a set of rules and consequences while the son stayed out of their discussions took several sessions. The parents initial responses were to triangle the son, or the stepmother, into their discussions when they began to disagree with each other. The results of the intervention were that the parents agreed to have the son live with the father and stepmother and that he was not to miss school unless he had a fever. The parents had to punish the boy for not attending, but he eventually went back to school and had perfect attendance.

STRUCTURAL FAMILY THERAPY TECHNIQUES

Structural family therapy techniques tend to be action focused rather than insight oriented (Minuchin and Fishman, 1981). This is consistent with its original development as a model for treating poverty-level delinquent families. Many of these children had no interest in discussing their problems and the families did not have the luxury of long-term discussions about possible origins for their problems. They needed to take action quickly. When parents are confronted by a son threatening them with a knife, they need to know how to safely get their son to give them the knife. Discussions about insight are better left for more calm and reflective times.

Joining

Families are often anxious when they begin therapy. They wonder if their therapist will understand them or blame them for their problems. They worry about how much to reveal about themselves and if they can trust their therapist with this information. They ask themselves questions such as, "Will my therapist like me?" or "What are we going to talk about?" or "Will my therapist think I am crazy?" and "Can therapy really help us?" All of these concerns are valid, and all must be addressed before a therapist can help a family change.

Joining is the process in which therapists let their client families know that they understand them and are working to help them (Minuchin and Fishman, 1981). A primary rule of structural family therapy is that therapists should first join with their families and then attempt to restructure them (Minuchin, 1974). No therapeutic plan, no matter how brilliant, will ever be effective if a family does not trust its therapist.

Joining includes such behaviors as making a family feel comfortable, listening to the concerns of all members, understanding each member's opinions and feelings, and treating everyone with respect. It goes beyond the bounds of simple courtesy to also include the understanding of a family's rules and unique structure. For example, therapists would not undermine a parent's credibility in front of a child and would treat important family members with extra respect.

Further, it is helpful for therapists to support a family's unique cultural values without creating stereotypical expectations of their behaviors. Normal families can engage in a wide array of religious, educational, sexual, marital, and behavioral practices. In some cases, a family's uniqueness may enable its members to solve certain problems that others will struggle with. It is problematic for therapists to assume that all African Americans have the same parent-child relationships or that all Catholics have the same religious beliefs. In fact, stereotyping families often leads to their feeling misunderstood and wanting to withdraw from therapy.

Accommodation

Accommodation is the manner in which a therapist adapts his or her behavior to fit a specific family. It is important for therapists to comprehend the importance of family uniqueness as well as respond in ways that show this understanding. This means that therapists must adjust their language, body posture, and pace to be consistent with a given family's mode of operating. For example, a boisterous family in which everyone interrupts one another would probably drown out a quiet therapist. That therapist would probably have to speak louder and block interruptions to be heard. On the other hand, behaving in a loud and directive manner might seem overbearing to a soft-spoken and thoughtful family. This is one way in which therapists might accommodate to different families. Of course, all therapist accommodations must stay within the style and culture of that given therapist. For example, it would be rude and disrespectful for a white therapist to talk "jive" to an African-American family; however, it would make sense to talk a bit faster if that family seemed put off by the therapist's "slow" pace.

Accommodation also means knowing when to challenge a given family and when to hold back. For example, one therapist found that one of her families failed to do a homework assignment every time she encouraged them. However, they always rose to the challenge when she questioned whether a given assignment was a bit beyond their abilities. Would this type of challenge work for every family? Definitely not! Structural family therapists must learn from each family how to get the best results (Minuchin and Nichols, 1993).

Finally, accommodation even pertains to the words a therapist uses to explain a concept to a family. For example, for parents who feel that saying "no" to a child means they don't love that child, a therapist might have to talk about giving their child "a different type of love" when encouraging them to punish inappropriate behaviors. On the other hand, Minuchin, Rosman, and Baker (1978) once had to describe a girl's refusal to eat as disrespect, rather than anorexia, to encourage her parents to enforce rules regarding her eating habits. The important thing to remember is that every family is different. What works for one family may be totally inappropriate for another. It is through joining and accommodation that clinicians learn to tailor therapy to meet an individual family's needs.

Structural Diagnosis

Structural diagnosis is the process by which a therapist identifies the dysfunctional family structure that maintains an individual's symptoms. It is within the assessment process that structural family therapists expand the idea of individual pathology to a focus on family transactions. Families are typically unable to describe their problematic structures. Therefore, therapists have to discover them through the course of several initial sessions. It is through interacting with families, asking questions, and making observations that therapists come to understand a family's structural makeup. As Minuchin (1974) states:

> Family structure is not an entity immediately available to the observer. The therapist's data and his diagnoses are achieved experientially in the process of joining the family. He hears what the family members tell him about the way that they experience reality. But he also observes the way that family members relate to him and to each other. The therapist analyzes the transactional field in which he and the family are meeting, in order to make a structural diagnosis. (p. 89)

It is usually helpful for therapists to ask questions—such as who is close to whom, how do the mother and father differ in terms of parenting styles, and who has the greatest say in making decisions—to get an initial sense of a family's structure. However, the way family members describe their behavior and how they act can be two different things. It is often helpful for therapists to observe family interactions. For example, if a problem child repeatedly sits next to one parent, while the other parent sits across the room, the therapist might infer that a coalition exists. Or if every time the parents discuss a disagreement, they either change the subject to the identified patient or the problem child distracts them through becoming disruptive, the therapist might assume that a detouring maneuver is taking place. Both verbal and observational cues are important in understanding a family structure.

A good structural diagnosis not only should contain the dysfunctional pattern but should also have a hypothesized alternative structure to resolve the problem. For example, if a therapist believes that a teenage boy's drug use is maintained by a cross-generational coalition with his mother against his father, then an alternative structure might propose shoring up the parental subsystem and creating a parent-child hierarchy. As an alternative, a therapist might propose developing an alliance between the father and son by having them engage in more activities together, such as washing the car, playing catch, or doing homework together.

No structural diagnosis is written in stone. In fact, further sessions may reveal that a different structure is, in fact, the dysfunctional one. A clue that one's diagnosis is faulty is when a proposed alternative structure fails to resolve the problem. In these cases, the therapist needs to make a new structural diagnosis and begin again the process of creating an alternative structure.

Restructuring

Structural family therapy is a process-oriented rather than content-oriented treatment approach. **Restructuring** refers to helping the family find a more appropriate structure for solving its problems. While the family's goal might be to get its child to stop stealing, the structural family therapist helps family members reorganize their transactional patterns so they can success-fully solve the problem themselves.

Although families are capable of developing numerous types of struc-tures, they limit themselves to those that feel most comfortable or are most useful. Some families begin repeating these structures even though they no longer work. It is not that the family is not trying to solve the problem; it is more that they are attempting to solve the problem in the "same old way." In many cases they might be using superhuman effort. The problem is they need a different structure to be successful. As Minuchin states (1974): "Families with chronic dysfunctional patterns can be helped only by chang-ing those patterns. The pain can be reduced only when the family's func-tioning improves" (p. 139).

Although joining and accommodation help the family feel understood and cared for by the therapist, they are not enough to bring about change. Restructuring requires that a therapist be active and directive. Old patterns die hard. Therefore, clinicians must be willing to take charge of the therapy to ensure that families change their structures. Remember, it is not that fami-lies do not want to change, it is that they are trapped in a structure that does not allow them to solve their particular problem. Even in therapy, they will initially try to maintain their old ways of doing things. It is the therapist's job to challenge the old structure in a way that the family has to try a differ-ent way of interacting (Colapinto, 1991). It is here that the relationship be-tween joining and restructuring is most obvious. It is scary to try out new structures, and no family will follow a leader if they do not feel safe with him or her. It is through joining that a therapist and family form a safe, emo-tional bond that enables them to face the challenge of restructuring rela-tional patterns.

Enactment

Enactment involves having family members engage in their problematic behaviors in the therapy room. Dating back to his early work with families of inner-city delinquents, Minuchin (Minuchin et al., 1967) believed that many people provide inaccurate accounts of their behavior. Their ability to retell an event is often blinded by their own perceptions. Further, different individuals would have different accounts of the events, which often led to heated arguments over who is right or wrong. To bypass this, Minuchin had family members enact their behaviors as a way of showing the therapist what happens at home. For example, a structural therapist might ask family members to talk among themselves about how to solve the problem of their son's truancy. This allows the therapist to observe the problematic structure as it actually unfolds. Minuchin and Fishman (1981) state:

> When the therapist asks the family questions, the family members can control what they are presenting. In selecting what material to communicate, they frequently try hard to put their best foot forward, as it were. But when the therapist gets the family members to interact with each other, transacting some of the problems that they consider dysfunctional and negotiating disagreements, as in trying to establish control over a disobedient child, he unleashes sequences beyond the family's control. The accustomed rules take over, and transactional components manifest themselves with an intensity similar to that manifested in these transactions outside of the therapy session. (pp. 78-79)

Although enactment provides a wonderful means of developing a structural diagnosis, it also can be used to restructure a family's behavior. As therapists observe a dysfunctional transaction, they can then invite other members to participate or block certain members from dominating the discussion. For example, Minuchin might disrupt an ongoing triangle involving the parents and a delinquent son by having the parents talk together about how to effectively discipline him, while the therapist blocks his interruptions.

Structural therapists also use enactments to support and encourage individual family members to express their views. For example, Minuchin and Fishman (1981) describe a situation in which they used enactment to help a mother form an effective parent-child hierarchy with her daughter. As the daughter began misbehaving in the session, the therapist asked the mother to control the girl's behavior. When the mother's initial tries proved fruitless, the therapist moved his seat next to the mother's and pushed her to continue confronting her daughter until she behaved appropriately. The therapist then complimented the mother on her ability to effectively discipline her daughter as a means of reinforcing her behavior.

Certainly having a person take a strong stand with his or her family members can be risky and anxiety producing. Students are cautioned that interventions such as this are not done in isolation. The therapist and mother must have already had a trusting relationship or the therapist could never have pushed her to discipline her child. Further, the therapist had to have faith in the mother's inherent ability to be successful. Finally, the therapist would have to be willing to continue this intervention, no matter how long it took for the mother to be successful. Ending this intervention with the mother failing to control her child could have deeply affected her confidence in ever being able to manage her daughter, and it could have led the daughter to conclude that her mother was an ineffective parent. No intervention is as easy as it looks. It takes a well-trained therapist, such as Minuchin, to successfully intervene in people's lives.

Boundary Marking

Boundary marking is a technique for creating new subsystems within a family. Therapists might want to create a boundary by having the parents work together without their children's interruptions, or open a disengaged boundary by helping a distant father become involved with his children. It is through boundary marking that therapists create new structures which enable families to solve problems.

Boundaries can be established through various means. For example, a therapist might disrupt a cross-generational coalition by having the over-involved father and distant mother negotiate rules for parenting their child. The therapist would then block the child's attempts to interrupt the parents' conversation and refocus the parents when they try to involve the child. An even simpler intervention would be to ask the child to leave the room while the therapist and parents discuss how to discipline the child. The walls of the office would then serve as a boundary between parents and child. The therapist could then meet with the child alone to discuss various concerns with the new rules the parents were implementing.

Even assigning different tasks to different subsystems can be an effective way to mark a boundary. For example, Wetchler (1990) created a parent-child boundary in a single-parent family in which the teenage son refused to leave his room by assigning the son the task of finding a job and giving the mother the job of monitoring his behavior. Her job was to make sure that he searched for a job and to enforce rules regarding how many applications he must complete in a day. The enmeshed boundary between mother and son was altered so that the son worked alone on his task of finding a job. He practiced interviewing skills, found job openings on his own, collected applications, and applied for jobs. His mother monitored his progress by having him show her a specific number of completed job applications each week and setting up a series of rewards and punishments, depending on whether he successfully met his quota.

Therapists can also manipulate the space in the treatment room to establish boundaries (Minuchin and Fishman, 1981). To help a disengaged father become closer to his son, the therapist might ask him to sit next to the boy while they plan a father-son outing. Further, the therapist might ask the mother to observe their conversation from the opposite end of the room as an additional means of marking the boundary surrounding father and son.

Unbalancing

Unbalancing is a technique in which a therapist temporarily sides with a specific individual, or family subsystem, to induce change. Sometimes a family's structure is so rigid that the members are unable to change either through discussions or new actions on their part. No matter what they do, they go back to behaving in the same way. In these situations, a structural family therapist might use his or her influence to support a specific member to behave differently for a long enough time so a new structure can be generated (Minuchin and Fishman, 1981). For example, unbalancing could be used in a marital case in which the couple is unable to successfully renegotiate their relationship because one spouse holds an inordinate amount of power over the other. Whether this is due to family-of-origin issues, gender stereotyping, or an imbalance of income that the spouses generate for the family, it seems that the more powerful spouse dominates the discussion while the less powerful spouse always gives in. In this situation, the therapist might support the less powerful spouse to continue to demand his or her needs in spite of the cues from the more powerful spouse to stop talking. For example, the therapist might sit next to the less powerful spouse during the negotiations, or he or she might keep encouraging the less powerful spouse to continue talking. At the most extreme, the therapist might actually confront the more powerful spouse about the need to listen to his or her mate.

Unbalancing techniques could be used in a child case when the therapist supports the parents to take charge of their child. The therapist might meet with the parents alone to help them develop a plan, or he or she could sit with them when they confront their child. Even simple statements such as "Because you are the parents, I will support your rules" can have a powerful impact on a stuck family structure.

Needless to say, an unbalancing technique could never work without the therapist being strongly joined with all members of the family (Minuchin, 1974). It is only through the development of a good relationship that a family member could tolerate the therapist temporarily taking sides against him or her. All family members need to feel safe in knowing that although their therapist may temporarily stand against them, he or she will eventually return to support them. In fact, whenever a therapist sides with one family member against another, he or she must always return to side with the opposed member so that person will feel supported. Failure to follow through with this important component could lead to either that member or the entire family dropping out of treatment. Needless to say, unbalancing is a highly sophisticated technique that should be done only by an advanced clinician or by a beginner under the supervision of a senior family therapist.

Enhancing Family Strengths

Underlying structural family therapy is a core belief in the inherent strength of families (Simon, 1995). If therapists approach families as if they are basically dysfunctional, they will only find problems and fail to see potential resources within the family that can solve their problem. Structural family therapists **enhance family strengths** when they help the family identify these hidden resources and promote their use in resolving the problem (Minuchin and Fishman, 1981). Through altering a family's structure, they usually are able to solve their own problems.

When therapists encourage a couple to discuss solutions to their marital problems, or push a parent to discipline a child, there is an inherent message that these individuals are *capable of being effective.* This is a very powerful message. Often families in crisis are able to identify only their faults. Opening their cognitive boundary to view themselves as competent people can create a world of new solutions. For example, in the case of the teenage son who never left his room, Wetchler (1990) strengthened the emerging boundary between parent and child by having the boy develop numerous ways to solve his problem as his mother observed. At the end of the session, both the mother and son agreed that he had the potential to get out of his room and on with his life. In fact, the son was later able to use these ideas to obtain a job and to eventually earn a promotion.

EVALUATING STRUCTURAL FAMILY THERAPY

Beginning with his early days at the Wyltwick School, Minuchin showed a commitment to testing his theories through research. His studies on psychosomatic children and delinquents, and Stanton, Todd, and Associates' (1982) work with drug addicts, are excellent examples of the effectiveness of structural family therapy (Nichols and Schwartz, 1998).

Structural family therapy appears to be a promising, if not effective, means of treating several childhood and adolescent problems. Further, it shows great potential in treating young adult drug addicts who remain in close physical contact with their families of origin. In his book *Families of the Slums,* Minuchin and colleagues (1967) found that structural family therapy was effective in seven of the eleven cases they treated at the Wyltwick School. Although they did not use a control group in their study, they found their results compared favorably to the 50 percent success rate that existed at Wyltwick during that time. Although readers are cautioned that the small number of cases actually treated at Wyltwick limits interpretations of overall effectiveness, the results provide a good start for further analysis and help to support the results found in more comprehensive studies.

In a most impressive study of structural family therapy, Minuchin, Rosman, and Baker (1978) summarized the results of treating fifty-three cases of **anorexia nervosa,** a disorder primarily found among young women in which they starve themselves to dangerous levels under the mistaken idea that they are overweight. They found that forty-three anorexic children "recovered," two were "improved," three showed "no change," two "relapsed after showing initial improvement," and three "dropped out of the study." Even though the researchers did not use a control group, due to ethical considerations, the 90 percent improvement rate for children who remained in the study (forty-three "recovered" and two "improved") is extremely compelling when compared to the typical 30 percent mortality rate for this disorder (Nichols and Schwartz, 1998).

Finally, Stanton, Todd, and Associates (1982) showed structural family therapy to be a highly effective treatment for drug addicts. They compared structural family therapy to a family placebo treatment and individual therapy, and found that the level of positive change in the structural family therapy group was twice as effective as the other two treatments, and that these changes persisted up to one year after therapy. Most important, even though the addicts ranged in age from nineteen to thirty, similar to the delinquent families at Wyltwick and the anorexic families, a primary intervention of the study was to place the parents in charge of controlling the addicts' behaviors.

A Case Example: Structural Family Therapy with a Teenage Drug Abuser

This section describes how a structural family therapist treated a case with a teenage drug abuser. As described in the research section, structural family therapy appears to be an ideal treatment for adolescent problems. The emphasis on boundaries and parental hierarchy are important when a child presents with school, behavioral, and drug-use problems.

All members of the family were present at the first session at the therapist's request. It is common for structural family therapists to request the entire family to attend the first session so they can assess family alliances and coalitions. The family consisted of a father, an electrician, the mother, a secretary, a teenage daughter, and a teenage son who was caught several times stealing money from his parents to purchase drugs.

The family members arranged themselves with the son seated between his parents and his sister seated across the room. Because structural family therapists rely heavily on spatial configurations to make their assessments, the therapist initially hypothesized that the son, Andy, was caught in a cross-generational coalition between his parents.

To further assess whether a cross-generational coalition actually existed, the therapist asked each parent separately how he or she dealt with the son when he stole money or used drugs. The mother reported that she attempted to ground the boy when he stole money from them; the father said the mother's method was too harsh and that he attempted to have discussions with Andy regarding his feelings about drugs and his self-esteem. Although a difference in parental opinion about how to discipline a child is further confirmation of a possible parent-child coalition, the final confirmation came during a spontaneous family enactment later in the session.

During the later part of the session, the son announced that he was tired of hearing his family complain about him and that he was leaving therapy. His mother immediately began to threaten him with grounding if he left, while his father said they could watch a football game on TV together if he stayed. This led to the parents arguing about the best way to deal with their son. The father argued that the mother was too harsh with him, and the mother accused the father of not supporting her. This type of enactment helped the therapist to further refine the hypothesis that the father and son were in a cross-generational coalition against the mother. The father's defense of the son against the mother's punishments and the mother's complaints that the father did not support her showed a structure in which the father and son are aligned against the mother.

From this structural diagnosis, the therapist decided to disrupt the cross-generational coalition by having the parents work together to parent the boy. Further, by having them work together, they would be forming a stronger parent-child hierarchy than currently existed. When two parents chronically fight over how to parent a child, especially when that child continues to misbehave, it can be assumed that the parents are not sufficiently in charge of that child to be effective as parents. By having the parents work together to parent their child, this disrupts the stability of the cross-generational coalition as well as shores up the parents and renews their authority with their child. Since the daughter was not involved in the parent-son triangle, and was doing well in school and drug free, she was excused from further therapy sessions unless she, the family, or the therapist felt her presence was needed.

The next session, the therapist began to intervene with the family. First, she asked to meet with the parents alone and then the son alone. This served to create a temporary boundary around the parental subsystem and the son subsystem. It gave a message to all family members that certain conversations are appropriate for parents only, and that certain issues would be talked about with the son only. During the parents' time, the therapist convinced them to work together in dealing with their son's drug use and theft. They agreed that they had fought each other too long and that they needed to work together for the sake of their son. During the son's session, the therapist and son talked about school, drugs, and the son's friends. The son told the therapist that he enjoyed drugs and had no desire to stop using them. This let the therapist know that, since the son had no desire to stop using drugs, most of the therapy work would be done with the parents; however, it would be important to continue to see the son to keep a therapeutic alliance with him. If the son thought the therapist was in a coalition with his parents against him, he would accelerate his problematic behaviors. If he felt the therapist also was aligned with him, he would be more likely to listen to his parents as they took control, knowing that this was being done in his best interest.

At the end of the session, the therapist met with the parents and son together and had the parents tell their son that they would start working together to get him off drugs. Consistent with his statement to the therapist, the son stated that he liked drugs, and there was nothing the parents could do to stop him. The therapist and family agreed to meet in one week to help the parents work together to deal with their son and to check up to see how the boy was doing.

The therapist met with the parents and son at the start of the next session, but quickly separated them to form a boundary around the parent subsystem and son subsystem. The therapist first met with the son to discuss how things were going at home and to support him regarding how hard it is to be in trouble with your parents.

In the parents' session, the therapist had them negotiate how they would handle the son's stealing money to use for drugs (the problem that brought them into therapy in the first place). Similar to their earlier roles, they tended to argue over how to punish the son. The father preferred lighter punishments and the mother preferred harsher punishments. As they continued to talk to each other and hear each other out, their positions softened and they began to compromise. They decided that the son would be grounded for a month, and that any future acts of stealing or drug use would be handled the same way. The therapist then brought the family together and had the parents jointly explain the son's punishment to him. By having the parents present this together, the son was able to see that the parents were working together and in a more authoritative relation to him.

Sessions continued in this manner with individual support to the son and meetings with the parents to discuss further joint parenting strategies. The parents also negotiated plans to help the son improve his school performance and to show more respect to the parents. As the parents became more united, the son stopped using drugs and his grades improved. He began talking about personal issues during his therapy sessions, especially his concerns about a girl he liked at school.

Near the end of therapy (a total of twelve sessions) the son announced he was now dating the girl he admired and they were going steady. As the cross-generational coalition that existed in the family was disrupted and the parents were able to join together to form a successful parent-child hierarchy, the son stopped using drugs, improved his grades, and developed an age-appropriate dating relationship.

SUMMARY

Structural family therapy takes an organizational approach to families. It focuses on altering dysfunctional hierarchies, boundaries, coalitions, and triangles. Its most important tenet is that a specific family structure can be called dysfunctional only if it keeps a family from solving a particular problem. As a result, it takes a present-centered and problem-focused stance to treatment. Structural family therapy appears to be most effective with childhood and adolescent problems, especially substance abuse, delinquency, and psychosomatic problems such as anorexia nervosa. Less information is available on its use with couple and marital problems.

SELECTED READINGS

Fishman, H.C. (1988). *Treating troubled adolescents: A family therapy approach.* New York: Basic Books.

Fishman, H.C. (1993). *Intensive structural therapy: Treating families in their social context.* New York: Basic Books.

Minuchin, S. (1974). *Families and family therapy.* Cambridge, MA: Harvard.

Minuchin, S. and Fishman, H.C. (1981). *Family therapy techniques.* Cambridge, MA: Harvard.

Minuchin, S., Lee, W., and Simon, G. (1996). *Mastering family therapy: Journeys of growth and transformation.* New York: Wiley.

Minuchin, S., Rosman, B., and Baker, L. (1978). *Psychosomatic families: Anorexia nervosa in context.* Cambridge, MA: Harvard.

GLOSSARY

accommodation: The manner in which a therapist adapts his or her behavior to fit a specific family. For example, a therapist might talk more quickly with a fast-talking family and more slowly with a slow-talking family to fit their individual styles.

alliance: When two or more family members join together to handle a specific problem.

anorexia nervosa: A disorder, primarily found among young women, in which they starve themselves to dangerous levels under the mistaken idea that they are overweight.

boundaries: The rules that govern who is included and excluded from a specific subsystem.

boundary marking: A technique for creating new subsystems within a family.

clear boundaries: Boundaries that successfully enclose a subsystem yet enable communication with other subsystems. Clear boundaries are often important for optimum family functioning.

coalitions: When two or more family members join forces against one or more family members.

cross-generational coalition: A specific type of triangle in which two family members from different generations ally against a third member.

detouring: A defensive pattern in which the two parents shift their focus to one child every time a problem arises between them that they are unable to handle.

disengaged boundaries: Boundaries that successfully enclose a subsystem but are impermeable to outside information.

enactment: A technique in which a therapist has family members engage in their problematic behaviors in the therapy room to assess their family structure.

enhance family strengths: A technique in which a therapist helps a family identify hidden resources and promotes their use in resolving the problem.

enmeshed boundaries: Boundaries in which there is little autonomy between individuals and other subsystems.

executive subsystem: The subsystem within a family that takes the leadership role. In most cases, this is typically the parents.

family map: A diagram of a family's current dysfunctional structure.

hierarchy: A boundary that distinguishes the leadership subsystem from the rest of the family.

holon: A subsystem that is both a system in its own right and a subsystem of a larger system. For example, a marriage is both a system in its own right and a subsystem of the entire family.

joining: The process in which therapists let their client families know that they understand them and are working to help them.

parental child: An older child with occasional family leadership tasks.

parent-child hierarchy: The specific boundary that demarcates the parents' responsibility in child-rearing issues.

psychosomatic diabetes: Cases of diabetes that consistently have to be hospitalized even though the child is on insulin.

restructuring: A therapeutic technique to help the family find a more appropriate structure for solving their problems.

structural diagnosis: The process by which a therapist identifies the dysfunctional family structure that maintains an individual's symptoms.

Structural family therapy: A family therapy theory that views emotional distress from an organizational perspective. Individual problems are maintained not through personal pathology, but rather through flaws in a family's organizational design.

subsystems: Grouping of family members to accomplish specific tasks.

triangles: A specific type of coalition in which two family members join forces against a third member.

unbalancing: A technique in which a therapist temporarily sides with a specific individual, or family subsystem, to induce change.

REFERENCES

Aponte, H.J. and VanDeusen, J.M. (1981). Structural family therapy. In A.S. Gurman and D.P. Kniskern (Eds.), *Handbook of family therapy* (Volume I) (pp. 310-360). New York: Brunner/Mazel.

Colapinto, J. (1991). Structural family therapy. In A.S. Gurman and D.P. Kniskern (Eds.), *Handbook of family therapy* (Volume II) (pp. 417-443). New York: Brunner/Mazel.

Fishman, H.C. (1993). *Intensive structural therapy*. New York: Basic Books.

Minuchin, S. (1974). *Families and family therapy*. Cambridge, MA: Harvard.

Minuchin, S. and Fishman, H.C. (1981). *Family therapy techniques*. Cambridge, MA: Harvard.

Minuchin, S., Montalvo, B., Guerney, B.G., Rosman, B.L., and Schumer, F. (1967). *Families of the slums*. New York: Basic Books.

Minuchin, S. and Nichols, M.P. (1993). *Family healing: Tales of hope and renewal from family therapy*. New York: Free Press.

Minuchin, S., Rosman, B.L., and Baker, L. (1978). *Psychosomatic families: Anorexia nervosa in context*. Cambridge, MA: Harvard.

Nichols, M.P. and Schwartz, R. (1998). *Family therapy: Concepts and methods*. Boston: Allyn and Bacon.

Simon, G.M. (1995). A revisionist rendering of structural family therapy. *Journal of Marital and Family Therapy, 21*, 17-26.

Stanton, M.D., Todd, T.C., and Associates (1982). *The family therapy of drug abuse and addiction*. New York: Guilford.

Trepper, T.S. and Barrett, M.J. (1989). *Systemic treatment of incest: A therapeutic handbook*. New York: Brunner/Mazel.

Wetchler, J.L. (1990). Family treatment of a fifteen-year-old social isolate. *Journal of family psychotherapy, 1*(2), 29-38.

Wetchler, J.L. (1992). Family treatment of a thirteen-year-old with chronic stomach pain. *Journal of Family Psychotherapy, 3*(4), 1-14.

Chapter 4

Strategic Family Therapy

Karen H. Rosen

A strategic therapist must have a strategy. The issue is choosing the strategy that is best suited to each different kind of problem. . . . What makes a therapist choose a particular strategy is how he conceptualizes a problem brought to therapy as well as the specific characteristics of the problem itself or of the people who present it.

Cloe Madanes
Behind the One-Way Mirror

The purpose of this chapter is to acquaint readers with strategic family therapy—strategic in the sense that the therapist designs specific strategies to create change. Strategic family therapy is an approach that is associated with more than one individual or group. Although these schools of strategic therapy have many similarities, they also have a number of differences. This chapter focuses on two of these schools: the Mental Research Institute (MRI) approach, which was founded on the West Coast by Fisch, Weakland, and Watzlawick in the 1960s, and the Washington School, which was founded by Jay Haley and Cloe Madanes at the Family Therapy Institute on the East Coast in the 1970s.

This chapter will introduce readers to the major leaders of the strategic therapy approach and the basic theoretical concepts, views of pathology, and techniques. Case examples are used to illustrate how therapists might actually apply strategic therapy principles in working with clients. Relevant research will also be cited to familiarize readers with the effectiveness of this approach.

MAJOR FIGURES IN STRATEGIC THERAPY

The two primary schools of strategic therapy have common roots. They are an outgrowth of a research project headed by Gregory Bateson in Palo Alto, California, in the 1950s and 1960s. Bateson, who is sometimes considered to be the grandfather of family systems theory, conducted a research project that applied ideas from **cybernetics** and **systems theory** to the study of communication. The project evolved into a study of communication patterns common to schizophrenics and their families and produced the seminal concept of the **double bind** theory of **paradoxical communication,** which was highly controversial. Haley and Weakland were among the researchers working on this project along with Don Jackson. Some of the thinking that emerged from this research project was subsequently applied to treating clients when the Mental Research Institute was founded by Jackson, who was joined by Fisch, Weakland, Watzlawick, and Haley, among others.

Strategic therapy was also largely influenced by the unique therapeutic approach of Milton Erickson who is considered by some the father of strategic therapy. Haley and Weakland visited Erickson many times over a period of seventeen years to record his thoughts and study his work (Haley, 1985). At that point in time, Erickson was considered a maverick in the field of psychiatry because he tended to use **hypnosis** and **paradoxical interventions.** He was also considered unconventional because he viewed symptoms as resulting from clients' failure to take action or from their taking the wrong action when confronted with difficulty. He used many different techniques to help people resolve their problems and believed that action often preceded understanding, rather than the other way around.

Although work at the Brief Therapy Center at the MRI continued and the therapy approach conceived there continued to evolve, Haley left the MRI to work with Salvador Minuchin and Braulio Montalvo at the Philadelphia Child Guidance Clinic where **structural family therapy** was developed (see Chapter 3). There he met Cloe Madanes, a clinician from Argentina, and after working and learning with the leaders of the Philadelphia Child Guidance Clinic for several years, Haley and Madanes started the Family Therapy Institute in the Washington, DC, area. There they developed and refined their own approach to strategic therapy, which has commonality with both the MRI model and structural family therapy. The Haley-Madanes approach to therapy is sometimes referred to as the Washington School of strategic therapy.

THEORETICAL CONCEPTS

Only by understanding the general conceptions of problems and treatment—in short, the theory—to which specific practices are related can one go beyond such blind response, either to judiciously reject or judiciously accept and apply such an approach to therapy. (Fisch, Weakland, Segal, 1982, p. 5)

Theory is a provisional **conceptual map** that helps therapists understand and treat problems. It is a tool that allows therapists to integrate observation and action in a consistent way. At the same time, theory is an "acknowledged oversimplification" (Keim, 1999) of complex processes, which is in part what makes it useful in working with families. What therapists believe about the nature of problems and how people change strongly influences the kind of information they pay attention to, who is seen in treatment, and what interventions they use. It helps them to make these decisions in a consistent, timely way in the face of myriad information that clients often provide.

Focus on Interactions

Similar to other schools of family therapy, strategic therapy subscribes to the **interactive view of problems,** which explains behavior in terms of what happens between people rather than within them (Haley, 1976; Fisch, Weakland, and Segal, 1982). When strategic therapy was initially developed it was considered revolutionary because traditional **psychoanalysis** was the mainstream approach to treating mental disorders at the time. From the interactive perspective, problems and their treatment are viewed in terms of what happens between the identified client and his or her primary social context—the family. A focus on communication and interaction within the family leads to an emphasis on what is happening in the present rather than what happened in the past. Therapists attempt to obtain a step-by-step account of what happens between people regarding the presenting problem and to help clients move from unsatisfactory sequences of interaction to satisfactory ones.

In addition to placing emphasis on the interactions between the **identified patients** and their social systems, MRI strategic therapists also tend to pay close attention to what is being said and done to try to resolve the problem (Weakland and Fisch, 1992). According to this approach, problems are a result of attempts to change a real or imagined difficulty. Attempted solutions sometimes become the problem; families get stuck in **vicious cycles** involving some inappropriate behavior and well-intentioned efforts to get rid of it. In other words, MRI strategic therapists tend to view problems as resulting from applying a solution that does not work and continuing to do more of the same despite undesirable results. Therefore, interventions tend to interrupt the continuation of the misguided solution behavior: "Since one cannot just cease any given behavior, such interventions often involve the prescription of some new alternative behavior, but the crucial element remains stopping the performance of the attempted solution" (Weakland and Fisch, 1992, p. 309).

The Washington School's Map

The Washington School is noted for describing problems in terms of what is called the **PUSH system**—protection, unit, sequences of interaction, and hierarchy (Keim, 1999). PUSH is a helpful way for therapists to describe presenting problems because it emphasizes solutions rather than causes.

Protection

With the exception of abuse, Washington School therapists often view symptoms as being motivated at some level by a desire to help a loved one. In other words, symptoms serve a protective function either to stabilize the family or to help another family member who is experiencing difficulty (Madanes, 1984). For example, a child's symptom may be viewed as providing an opportunity for parents to behave competently in their parental role as an alternative to focusing on a failure in another area of life. When it is suspected that a child's symptom serves a protective function, the therapist may substitute a sequence of interaction for the family that serves the same purpose without necessitating the symptom.

Viewing problems as being unsuccessful attempts to help is useful for therapists for two major reasons. First, a therapist who believes that problem behavior is positively motivated tends to view the client in a positive light and to intervene in a much more empathic manner than a therapist who believes that a client is negatively motivated. Second, a therapist who views problematic efforts as protection is open to investigating issues and relationships that may otherwise be overlooked.

Unit

When viewing problems interactionally rather than intrapsychically, the preferred unit of focus is the **triangle** (see Chapter 9). In other words, when working with a problem that seems to be between two people, from this perspective a therapist would be curious about the possible involvement of a third person, such as an in-law or a child. The therapist would also consider the role that a third person may play in the solution to the problem and the impact of change on this third person. In either case, therapists from the Washington School also tend to view themselves as a new point in a triangle and to consider their effect on a two-person relationship (Haley, 1976).

Sequence of Interaction

As already discussed, for Washington School therapists, the sequence of interaction is crucial to conceptualizing the presenting problem. The sequence of interaction not only describes the problem but points the way to a solution as well. In general, negative escalating sequences of interaction are replaced with soothing ones; thus, a preferred sequence replaces a destructive one. Further, within the interactional frame of reference, solving one problem sequence may result in a change in other sequences as well. For example, a husband and wife who learn to be more effective parents may also learn to deal more effectively with their differences regarding financial issues.

Hierarchy

From the Washington School perspective, people who have a history and future together follow organized ways of behaving with one another. When people are organized together, they form a status, or **power ladder,** where each has a place with someone above and someone below. In the marital hierarchy, for example, there is a balance of influence between spouses with each spouse contributing equivalently, and each spouse open to the influence of the other. In the parental hierarchy parents are in charge of children. Strategic therapists pay attention to the degree to which the people involved in the problem interact in age- and role-appropriate ways (Haley, 1976).

Dysfunction is viewed as a manifestation of an **incongruent hierarchy.** In other words, people are not behaving in age- or role-appropriate ways toward one another. For example, although by their position parents may be leaders of the family, children through their repetitive misbehavior may, in effect, be in charge of the parents. Further, the helplessness of a drug-addicted husband may be both a source of power in relation to his wife and, at the same time, a source of weakness. When the couple's marital life is organized around his addiction, he is powerful; to the extent that he is incapable of fulfilling his adult role in the family, he is weak relative to his wife

(Madanes, 1984). Washington School strategic therapists assess the family's hierarchical arrangement by carefully observing the family's interactions. Who speaks first? Who interrupts whom? Who tells whom what to do? Around whom does the family seem to be organized? Whose opinion is discounted? When the hierarchy is incongruent, a strategic therapist tries to correct this hierarchy and reorganize the family so family members interact in ways that are appropriate to their relationship. For example, therapists arrange to help parents take charge of children and to help symptomatic spouses become powerful in appropriate ways.

Client Position

A key concept from the MRI perspective is **client position,** a term that refers to strongly held beliefs, values, and priorities that determine how clients behave. These are values that the client is committed to and have likely been made public, similar to a politician's platform (Segal, 1991). For example, parents' position about why their children misbehave usually determines their response. A father who expresses concern that his son is having difficulty adjusting to a new school may take the position that his son misbehaves because he is sad, and therefore the father tends to be overly gentle rather than enforce consequences. A father who describes his son as lazy probably takes the position that his son misbehaves because he is bad, and therefore he might tend to be overly punishing.

Why is it important to understand the client's position with regard to the problem, therapy, or the therapist? Much of the success of strategic therapy depends on the therapist's ability to persuade the client to do something differently. If therapists want to successfully influence clients, they must understand their clients' positions. Knowing their clients' positions allows therapists to frame their suggestions in ways that clients are most likely to accept or respond to. For example, clients who view themselves as caregiving will be more motivated to undertake tasks that are framed as self-sacrificing and constructive than tasks framed as self-care (Fisch, Weakland, and Segal, 1982). Therapists pay attention to clients' specific wording, tone, and emphasis when they talk about problems, themselves, or therapy in general in order to assess their clients' positions.

Symptoms As Metaphors

A therapist can focus on concrete facts, observations, and information, or he can be interested in covert, implied, or indirect references. (Madanes, 1984, p. 145)

Strategic therapists from the Washington School may sometimes view presenting problems as **metaphors** for the actual problem (Haley, 1976; Madanes, 1981). For example, the marital problem presented by a couple may be both the focus of fighting and a way of avoiding conflict in another area. A child's refusal to go to school may be viewed as a metaphor for the mother's difficulty finding a job. The strategy developed to solve the family's problem is based on the therapist's thinking about what sequence of interaction might be able to replace another sequence of interaction. The therapist may think in terms of the symptom as metaphor yet choose to take a direct approach to therapy and focus on the symptom that is presented, or the therapist may choose to respond to the metaphor.

PROBLEM DEVELOPMENT, PATHOLOGY, AND NORMALCY

Both schools of strategic family therapy view deviant behavior in an individual as a social phenomenon reflecting a dysfunction in the system. Problems arise primarily as an outcome of everyday life, usually involving an adaptation to a **family life cycle transition** that requires a major shift in personal relationships (Haley, 1973; Weakland et al., 1983). Symptomatic behavior is not viewed as pathological but rather as unfortunate behavior that makes sense given the social context in which the client is a part. For example, the symptom of depression is viewed as logical in a dysfunctional context. Strategic therapists avoid labeling their clients' behavioral disorders. Labeling clients' thoughts, feelings, or actions (diagnosing) is viewed as an obstacle to resolving their problems because it tends to give clients the sense that their problems are deep-rooted and fixed, rather than fluid and contextual.

From the view of the Washington School, symptoms are described as communicative acts that have a function within the family system. In essence, they are "a style of behavior adaptive to the ongoing behavior of other people in the system" (Haley, 1976, p. 98). The communication of the identified patient is functional within the system. In order for the identified patient's communication to change, the situation or family system must change.

Further, when an individual has a symptom, it may be an indication that the family has a confused hierarchical arrangement. Every family organizes itself in a hierarchical fashion in which the rules are worked out about who is primary in status and power and who is secondary. When a hierarchy becomes confused, it may be because no one knows exactly who is in charge. It may also be confused because a person at one level of the hierarchy consistently joins with a member at another level against a peer, thus forming a dysfunctional coalition. For example, one parent may consistently take the side of a child against the other parent. When the hierarchy is confused, repetitive dysfunctional sequences of interaction develop that stabilize the system. Pathology is defined as rigid, repetitive sequence of a narrow range of interaction. Pathological behavior develops when the repetitive sequence of interaction confirms two opposite hierarchies at the same time or when the hierarchical arrangement fluctuates from one time to another. Therapeutic change introduces greater diversity into the system.

In addition, from the Washington School perspective, symptoms are viewed as being inevitable based on the way the family develops over time (Haley, 1973). Therapists must be sensitive to family life cycle stages (e.g., young adult, marriage, having children, etc.) and the tasks common to different ages and stages. Clients may have difficulty as they try to adjust to the changes required when moving from one life cycle stage to another. Thus, therapists help clients move from one stage of life to another. It is helpful for therapists and clients alike to know that problems are normal challenges faced by people going through similar life cycle stages rather than indicators of pathology (Keim, 1999).

The MRI approach does not try to impose any standards on clients (Heath and Ayers, 1991). Nor is there an ideal standard of family structure or communication. From the MRI perspective, dysfunction is not viewed as an aspect of the system's organization that requires fundamental changes. Instead it is believed that fairly minor changes in behavior are often enough to initiate progressive developments in a positive direction. As in the Washington School, the MRI approach is also nonpathological in that clients are viewed as caught in unhelpful (for the clients) interactional patterns.

Further, problems are likely to develop when ordinary difficulties are either overemphasized or underemphasized. Over- or underemphasis of life's difficulties may depend on general cultural attitudes as much as on personal or family characteristics. For example, normal adolescent limit testing may become a problem when incidents are blown out of proportion by parents and teenagers are inappropriately punished or lectured.

In addition, inappropriate handling of life's difficulties is often multiplied by the interactions between various family members. Once the difficulty is seen as a problem, behaviors that are designed to resolve the problem inadvertently serve to intensify the difficulty. Thus, the cure becomes worse than the disease. Although potentially disturbing and painful, symptomatic behavior can have its advantages or payoff. For example, symptoms can provide leverage in controlling relationships (e.g., they may organize the family). However, this potential function of the symptom is not considered a major factor in the change process by the MRI school of strategic therapy. Resolution of problems primarily requires a substitution of behavior patterns that disrupt the vicious cycle which has developed around the initial life difficulty.

GOALS OF THERAPY

What the therapist wants is a clear focus on a problem so that family relationships can be changed by using that problem as the lever. (Haley, 1976, p. 27)

Another revolutionary perspective adopted by the leaders of strategic therapy is that therapeutic interventions focus on resolving those problems which are most stressful for clients. Although considered mainstream thinking today, this approach went counter to the mainstream thinking of the time, which was dominated by psychoanalysts who focused on uncovering the **subconscious roots of problems.** The goal of the initial therapeutic interview from a strategic therapy perspective is to negotiate a presenting problem that can be defined in clear, solvable behavioral terms. The therapist negotiates a detailed behavioral statement of the problem and goals for therapy in order to check outcome and determine whether therapy has been successful.

In focusing on the presenting problem, strategic therapists tend to emphasize the importance of behavioral change rather than change in feelings or insight and, as a result, **brief therapy** tends to occur. In fact, the belief is that change can happen without understanding and that self-understanding does not necessarily produce change. Thus, the primary goal of therapy is to solve the presenting problem by getting clients to do something different rather than getting clients to express their feelings or to understand their problem better. In addition to changing behavior, strategic therapists may also try to get clients to look at their problems differently. This may entail **redefining the problem** so that it is viewed as simply one of life's many difficulties (Weakland and Fisch, 1992).

STRATEGIC THERAPY TECHNIQUES

The strategic therapist first joins (see Chapter 3) with the family and collects information about the presenting problem, the goals for change, and interactions that maintain the symptomatic behavior. With this information, the therapist then develops a plan (strategy) for solving the presenting problem. The **strategy for change** may include giving the family (or individual) one or more directives or tasks with the intent of changing the problematic interactional sequence. Informing the choice of directive from the Washington School point of view might be the sense of hierarchy and triangles involved in the problematic interactional sequence. What informs the choice of directive from the MRI point of view might be the ineffective solutions that the family has tried or the clients' position.

After the therapist gives a directive designed to shift interactions, he or she assesses the family's response to the directive and plans a new depending on that response. If the directive does not produce the intended result, the therapist may need to change the strategy or to develop a different tactic to implement the strategy. This process continues until the presenting problem is solved.

Who to Invite to the Session

Strategic therapists practicing from the Washington School perspective prefer to work with all the individuals involved in the problem (Haley, 1976). For example, when the identified client is an adolescent, the whole family would be engaged in treatment from the beginning. When marital problems are the focus, both the husband and wife would be asked to attend the first session of therapy. Seeing everyone involved in the problem helps the therapist understand the problem and the social situation that maintains it. It is believed that clients are incapable of accurately reporting their own social system. In contrast, MRI strategic therapists tend to direct their therapeutic efforts toward whomever is most motivated to see change happen instead of routinely seeing all members of a family (Weakland and Fisch, 1992).

Role of the Therapist

Strategic therapists actively take charge of what happens in the sessions. The therapist decides how therapy should be conducted including who to invite to the sessions, who will be asked to speak about the problem first, and what interventions to apply (Haley, 1976). In both the MRI and the Washington School approaches, therapists tend to remain **outside the family system** and avoid directly challenging the family's defenses. Thus interventions are viewed as the therapist taking action on behalf of the family. Further, they do not stress using or eliciting the expression of the client's or the therapist's feelings.

Strategic therapists observe the family's interactions and mood and, rather than commenting on what is occurring in the session, develop **hypotheses** about what maintains the problem based on the information collected. Therapists direct the session based on hypotheses developed as well as their own thinking about what brings about change. For example, a therapist may purposely speak to the leader of the family first to show differential respect to the member who has the most power to bring the family back to therapy. In taking leadership of the therapeutic process, the strategic therapist also take full responsibility for solving the presenting problem (Haley, 1976; Weakland and Fisch, 1992).

Strategic therapists create the change necessary to solve the presenting problem by giving directives. Giving directives may involve telling people what to do directly or implicitly—by vocal intonation, body movement, well-timed silence, or commenting on something a client has said or done (Haley, 1976).

Therapist-Client Relationship

While the therapist is in charge of the session, the relationship between therapist and client is hierarchically balanced because the client has hired the therapist and is therefore the boss, yet the therapist has special training and is in the position of expert (Keim, 1999). Essentially, the **therapist-client clinical contract** forms the basis of the relationship.

Another aspect of the therapist-client relationship is the **therapeutic alliance.** Although developing a positive therapeutic alliance for its own sake is not a goal of strategic therapy, a strong therapeutic alliance is an important aspect of creating a cooperative atmosphere, one in which the client and therapist work together to solve the presenting problem. The therapist must establish a trusting relationship with the client in which the therapist is viewed as being helpful and on the side of the client (Haley, 1976).

Toward this end, a strategic therapist is concerned with understanding the client's beliefs, values, priorities, and feelings, and conveying understanding and empathy, which is critical to developing a strong therapeutic alliance. To accomplish this, therapists must be able to communicate to clients that they have been heard, understood, and respected (Fisch, Weakland, and Segal, 1982). Therefore, the **joining** process would probably look much the same for a strategic therapist as for other schools of family therapy (e.g., structural) in which the therapist uses empathic communication to build rapport with the client. Accepting clients where they are and proclaiming their thoughts, feelings, and behaviors normal given the situation facilitates clients' abilities to move to a more productive stage. Along the same vein, strategic therapists tend to highlight clients' strengths rather than their liabilities, which empowers the clients to make change quickly rather than to feel overwhelmed by pathology.

Empirical research supports the notion that strategic therapists place importance on a positive therapist-client relationship. Lucy Mabrey (cited in Keim, 1999) conducted **qualitative interviews** with clients who were treated by Washington School therapists to find out how connected they felt to their therapists. All clients interviewed, which included adults, adolescents, and children, reported that they felt accepted and affirmed by their therapists. Therapists were given credit for the trust that developed, and clients tended to feel empowered and hopeful. The MRI school stresses the importance of the therapist maintaining **therapeutic maneuverability.** In other words, therapists try to maintain their ability to determine whom to see in therapy, what questions to ask, and the timing and pacing of treatment. For example, when a client will not include his or her spouse in treatment or discuss certain topics that he or she would rather keep secret, the therapist's maneuverability is reduced (Segal, 1991). Treatment success depends on clients providing concrete information and therapists getting clients to carry out suggestions or tasks. To be successful, therapists need to be in charge of the therapeutic process.

In addition, strategic therapists tend to discourage clients' dependence on the therapist and instead to stress the clients' strengths and abilities to take charge of their problem. An assumption is that clients come to therapy feeling discouraged and incompetent after trying unsuccessfully to solve their problems. By highlighting clients' strengths, their sense of competence is reinforced, and they become empowered to try something new or to resurrect healthy behavior that had been attempted in the past but perhaps forgotten.

First Session

Although perhaps not a technique per se, much is written about the first session in strategic therapy literature since it is a critical first step in establishing a working client-therapist relationship and in collecting vital information needed for developing a strategy. In other words, the first session sets the stage for treatment. Therapy that begins well will more likely end well (Haley, 1976). Haley recommends beginning therapy by inviting the entire family to the initial interview and following a highly structured approach that has four stages: a social stage, a problem stage, an interaction stage, and a goal-setting stage. The goal of the **social stage** is to help everyone relax. The therapist greets everyone and tries to make each feel comfortable and welcome as he or she observes how the family interacts. During the **problem stage,** the therapist tells the family what is already known, explains why the entire family was invited to the session (to get everyone's perspective about the problem), and asks each person to give his or her perspective about the problem. Strategic maneuvering begins with the decision about which person to turn to first at this point. The therapist considers such factors as who has the most power to bring the family back to more therapy sessions, who is most concerned about the problem, and who is least involved. During this phase the therapist is observing the family's interactions with the intent of assessing interaction sequences and family structure (triangles and hierarchy). After each person has a chance to express his or her point of view, the therapist invites them to talk among themselves about how they view the problem **(interaction stage),** which provides the opportunity to observe their interactions regarding the problem. After the family has had a chance to interact with one another, the therapist negotiates a reasonable, clear statement of the changes the family wants to make **(goal-setting stage).** The therapist may end the first session by giving a directive that can be done as **homework** to be completed before the next session. This may be a simple task that keeps the family involved with the therapist until the next session.

From the MRI perspective, the main aim of the initial interview is to gather information about the problem, how the problem is being managed, the clients' goals, and the clients' positions and language (Fisch, Weakland, and Segal, 1982). When the problem is stated in vague terms, such as, "Mom is depressed," the therapist helps the clients to define a concrete, behavioral goal by perhaps asking, "What will be a sign that things are getting better?" When the problem and goals are defined clearly, the therapist asks what the clients have done so far to try to solve the problem. The therapist wants to have an understanding of what people say and do to solve the problem and who is involved. In this way, the therapist can get an understanding of the attempted solutions that may be maintaining the problem. Getting the clients' cooperation in letting go of their solution may be a challenge.

As has already been discussed, understanding the clients' position is critical to gaining their cooperation. The therapist notices the clients' wording and tone in relation to the presenting problem, treatment, and the therapist. For example, do clients view themselves and their situation as unique or commonplace? Do they view the identified patient as mad, sad, or bad? Do they view themselves as angry, frustrated, or hurt? Making an accurate assessment of the clients' positions on these and other matters related to the presenting problem will help the therapist decide what is the best approach to take with the clients in terms of strategies to use and ways to deliver them.

Reframe

A basic tool of both schools of strategic family therapy is **reframing** problematic behavior in order to solve the presenting problem. Getting the clients to let go of their own solution to the problem and to try a new approach that may seem uncomfortable at best, or bizarre at worst, is an important step to solving the presenting problem (Fisch, Weakland, and Segal, 1982). Changing the meaning or reframing the situation is often an important first step, because sometimes the way a problem is viewed helps to keep the client stuck. The therapist must listen carefully to the words a client uses to describe a problem to understand the client's view of it. For example, does a wife talk about her husband who does not have a job as if he were depressed and therefore deserving pity, or lazy and therefore deserving disrespect and criticism? Reframing involves altering the client's experience of a situation that fits the facts of the situation, but it changes the meaning in a way that invites change (Watzlawick, Weakland, and Fisch, 1974). In essence, the therapist uses language to give new meaning to a situation. When new meaning is given to a situation, this new meaning can sometimes lead to the development of new action.

The change in meaning may be directed toward a behavioral sequence of interactions, the client's perception of what is causing the problem or who is responsible, the client's perception of the seriousness of the problem, and/or the client's perception of the solution to a problem. Sometimes the weak are relabeled as powerful and the powerful as weak (Madanes, 1984). In the case of parents who are convinced that their child is not going to school because he or she is depressed and therefore too sad to be forced to behave appropriately, it may help the parents to take action if the child's behavior is reframed as laziness or rebelliousness rather than depression.

Case Study 1: A Case of Mismatched Confrontational Styles (Part I)

Mr. and Mrs. Jones, parents of Beth, age fourteen, were referred to family therapy by Beth's school counselor because she had been disrespectful to teachers and cutting class. Beth was also confrontational at home and seemed to enjoy having head-to-head arguments with her parents.

The whole family (parents, Beth, and two younger children) was invited to the first session in order to hear everyone's description of the problem and to see the family in action. The therapist listened carefully to all family members and made them feel comfortable, heard, and supported. When the therapist met with the parents alone, they confessed that they were afraid Beth was turning into an evil person and that her teacher had called her a "bad seed." They felt guilty, frustrated, and powerless to change Beth's behavior.

Based on the family's description of events, the therapist hypothesized that the family had a confused hierarchy in which Beth acted as though she had authority over the adults, and the adults behaved as if they were arguing with a peer. A vicious cycle was repeated several times each week with increasing intensity. When one of the parents asked Beth to do something, she would talk back. When the parent tried to explain or insist, Beth would become even more belligerent, leading to a screaming match or slammed doors.

First, it was necessary to shift the parents' position that Beth was a "bad seed" and that they were at fault. The strategy chosen to accomplish this task was a reframe. The parents were told that this kind of problem often occurs when parents and children have different confrontational styles. The parents were told that most parents are outcome oriented in their confrontational style, as they are, and children are sometimes process oriented. That is, for children who are process oriented, winning an argument means controlling the process and keeping the argument going if they so choose, while parents are interested in the outcome— getting the child to behave appropriately. The therapist told the parents that although they were doing what normally works with children, parents with a child who has this kind of confrontational style need to do something different.

Once the parents accepted this reframe they were able to relax and to consider changing the way they responded to Beth. The focus shifted from "who is at fault" to "what can we do about it?" The parents were given the homework assignment to observe the degree to which Beth was invested in determining the process of their arguments by controlling the timing, the content, or the mood of their confrontations. This homework assignment began to shift the hierarchy by putting the parents in charge because they became observers of their child's be-. havior and knew something that Beth did not know.

Directives

Directives are techniques the therapist uses to help the family change. A hallmark of strategic therapy is that each therapy is individually created depending on the presenting problem and how the family views it. Unique directives are developed to help clients solve the presenting problem. In addition to bringing about change, a directive may also serve the purpose of providing more information to the therapist. When the therapist tells the family what to do, whether or how family members respond gives the therapist information about how the family interacts and/or how family members respond to the changes sought. In a sense, everything a therapist does can be considered a directive (Haley, 1976). For example, when a mother is explaining in session how she talks to her daughter about the problem and the therapist nods, smiles, or says "tell me more," the therapist is encouraging certain behavior. If a client says or does something that the therapist does not think is helpful, she or he may tell the client to stop or simply turn away from the client and change the subject. Telling the client to stop is an **explicit directive;** turning away and changing the subject is an example of an **implicit directive.**

When giving an explicit directive, the first step is to motivate the family to follow it (Madanes, 1981). The way therapists motivate their clients depends on the therapist-client relationship, the nature of the task, and family dynamics. Haley (1976) suggests that therapists give directives that go directly to the goal. If such a direct approach does not work, therapists can use another approach to motivate the family toward the goal. Developing a clear problem and goal for therapy makes it easier to design directives. There are two basic types of explicit directives: (1) **straightforward directives**— those the therapist hopes the client will do, and (2) **indirect directives**— directives the therapist hopes the client will rebel against and not do.

Often strategic therapists give directives that are to be carried out at home between sessions. This approach helps to keep the family engaged with the therapist over the course of the week (Haley, 1976). Family members end up thinking about the therapy and whether they will do the task prescribed or whether they will not, and if not how the therapist will respond if the task is not done. When therapists assign homework, they should be precise and include all the members of the family if possible. The assignment may be rehearsed in the session prior to their leaving. The therapist should ask for a report about the task during the next session.

Straightforward Directives

Therapists give a straightforward directive to help clients change interactional sequences and/or hierarchical structure (Haley, 1976). They give these kinds of directives when they think that they have enough power to get clients to do what they want them to do. These **compliance-based directives** may be in the form of advice giving, explanations, providing information that the family lacks, or suggestions that promote open communication. They may also take the form of coaching parents on how to control children, establish family rules and consequences, and redistribute jobs and privileges among family members. Therapists may simply ask clients to stop doing something they are doing that is unproductive or to begin to do something they are not doing. For example, a therapist may ask parents to follow through with consequences or to stop reminding their teenage son to do his homework. With minor problems or situations, helping clients change may be fairly easy. However, with more serious or with chronic problems this may be difficult—such as asking an alcoholic to stop drinking. A straightforward directive often needs to accompany other messages or other actions in order to obtain the clients cooperation. For example, therapists may need to raise clients' anxiety about the problem to motivate them to cooperate, or the therapist may need to enlist the help of other family members. The therapist may describe the task as small or as a major thing, depending on the situation. In general, directives should be clearly stated rather than suggested. If possible, a directive should involve all family members participating in therapy to put emphasis on the family unit as a whole. As discussed, the

MRI school recommends taking into account the clients' position when giving a directive.

Typically, strategic therapists will help family members **negotiate and contract** with one another to reach agreements (Madanes, 1990). The therapist helps family members express their preferences and compromise with one another about money, rules, relatives, leisure time, and sex. They may develop a contract that formalizes agreements and encourages family members to respect the terms agreed upon.

Case Study 1: A Case of Mismatched Confrontational Styles (Part II)

The therapist began to help Beth's parents change their behavior in response to Beth. Their task was to prevent Beth from controlling the timing, content, or mood of their confrontations and conversations. The parents were asked to describe a typical argument and to think of process-sensitive strategies that would allow them to control the conversation. The goal of this straightforward directive was to strengthen the appropriate hierarchical arrangement in which parents are in charge of children and competent enough to think of their own solutions.

The next series of steps focused on helping the parents change their interactions with Beth. After each session, the parents left with a homework assignment to try a strategy they had developed to take charge of the conversation (straightforward directive). They were also asked to record the results of their efforts so that adjustments could be made during the next session. For example, the mother and father were asked what kind of mood they wanted to have during confrontations with Beth. They said that they would like to stay calm and caring, yet firm. With coaching from the therapist, the parents decided that they would help each other remain calm when talking to Beth by holding hands when the intensity began to rise. The therapist congratulated the parents on every small success, and the parents became more confident in their ability to control the mood of their conversations with Beth. Once the parents began to do this consistently, the focus shifted to developing a process-sensitive system of rules and consequences. The parents were directed to develop a basic list of rules and consequences and ways to time their delivery in the most effective manner. Beth slowly became more amenable to their efforts to discipline her, and became a competent student as well (case study adapted from Keim, 1998).

Indirect Directives

Strategic therapists give indirect directives when they think they might not have the power to gain the cooperation of family members to follow a straightforward directive or when the family is resistant to changing despite asking for help with a problem (Haley, 1976). These directives are sometimes called **paradoxical directives.** Both Washington School and MRI strategic therapists use therapeutic paradoxes when appropriate. Therapeutic paradoxes are seemingly illogical interventions that appear contradictory to the goals of therapy, yet are designed to achieve the goals of therapy. When the client proves the therapist wrong and makes changes, the therapist might be surprised, confused, or suggest that the change is probably temporary. It is important that these directives are given in a thoughtful, respectful manner, and in a way that makes sense in the therapeutic context.

Prescribing the symptom is one type of therapeutic paradox that has several variations. Basically, the family is told to continue having the problem behavior, sometimes in such a way that it exposes family interactional sequences that maintain the problem (Haley, 1976). The therapist may also prescribe where, when, and how the symptom will happen. For example, the therapist may encourage a couple that regularly fights in unproductive ways to practice fighting at a certain time every evening, in a specified manner, and in a particular room in the house. Perhaps a depressed man may be encouraged to continue to be depressed because his wife needs someone to care for.

Madanes (1984) developed several variations to prescribing the symptom, many of which are done in a playful way and may be practiced in the session and then given as homework. In one variation, the therapist prescribes the symptom in such a way that it shifts the hierarchical arrangement of family members. For example, a parent might be asked to encourage the child to purposely have the presenting problem instead of trying to prevent it, and by so doing when the child has the symptom, he or she becomes compliant and the parent is in charge. Therefore, in addition to shifting interactions between parent and child regarding the symptom, the incongruent hierarchy between parent and child is also realigned. In another variation, family members are directed to behave in ways that represent what the therapist thinks is the function of the symptom.

Restraining change or asking the clients to go slowly is a paradoxical intervention frequently used by MRI strategic therapists (Fisch, Weakland, and Segal, 1982). This intervention might be used when clients are anxious and impatient about solving the presenting problem and apt to rush assignments, or when clients see improvement as having negative as well as positive consequences. It might also be used when the therapist suspects that a client might be thrown by a slip that occurs after change begins (Segal, 1991). The client may be encouraged not to change or to change slowly because change might have negative effects for someone in the family. A critical determiner of the success of this intervention is the therapist's skill in offering a believable rationale for suggesting that the client go slowly. This directive will most often be given early in the treatment, perhaps in the first session, particularly with clients who are trying too hard to solve the problem. Another appropriate time to use this intervention is when a client comes to a session feeling elated after experiencing definite, welcome improvement. In this event, a therapist may want to avoid indicating overt optimism and instead caution the client to go slowly, perhaps because changing too fast might be dangerous or scary. In fact, the therapist might even encourage the client to have a relapse (prescribing the symptom). This tactic is useful because if the therapist is relatively uncommitted to changing the client quickly, it takes away the sense of urgency to solve the problem quickly and puts implicit pressure on the client to cooperate with any suggestion the therapist may give.

Prescribing a symbolic act is an intervention that might be used when clients are involved in compulsive self-destructive behaviors that are seemingly out of their control (Madanes, 1990). Because self-destructive behaviors are often performed in an attempt to punish someone else who does not provide enough love and attention, asking clients to perform a repetitive action that is symbolic of the self-destructive act may symbolically punish that person without the client actually being self-destructive. For example, a bulimic client may be encouraged to mash up all her favorite foods with her hands and, in the presence of the family, flush it down the toilet.

The **pretending technique** is a therapeutic intervention that originated from the Washington School of strategic therapy (Madanes, 1981). When prescribing the symptom is ethically inappropriate or impractical, the therapist may direct the client to pretend to have the symptom. For example, a child may be asked to pretend to have the symptom each evening and the parents may then be asked to criticize the child's performance, make sure the pretending is accurate, and then behave the way they usually do when the child has the symptom. This strategy might be used when the therapist hypothesizes that the symptom has a function in the family and that pretending to have the symptom can fulfill that function without having to actually have the symptom. Asking a symptomatic client to pretend to have the symptom also makes a seemingly involuntary behavior become voluntary. In addition, pretending to have the symptom provides the opportunity for the family to respond differently to the symptom, thus interrupting patterns of interaction that have developed concerning the symptom. For example, the therapist may arrange for a child who has stomachaches (in order to get love and attention from a parent) to pretend to have a stomachache and for the parents to comfort her.

Case Study 2: The Anxious Violinist

A young adult male music teacher came to therapy because he had trouble performing on the violin during concerts due to nervousness. The therapist's first task was to clearly understand the problem and what the young man was doing to deal with it. To accomplish this task, the therapist asked specific questions about the problem, attempted solutions, and who was involved in the problem and its solution. The therapist discovered that nervousness was primarily experienced as sweating and shaky hands, and it sometimes had a serious detrimental effect on the young man's performance. The therapist asked what eased the nervousness and what made it worse.

The therapist learned that the client was beginning a new career as a concert violinist after spending several years pursuing an architect career. The young man had ended his music career several years earlier after a poor performance due to nerves during his second year at a conservatory. He had wanted to be a violinist despite the fact that his father thought that a music career was frivolous. The young man thought he had the support of his mother no matter what career he chose, as long as he was successful.

After much discussion, the therapist had some guesses about the young man's position in terms of his problem. He admitted that he tended to be skeptical and pessimistic about most things. Although he was following the advice of his music teacher, who told him that he would improve if he performed more often, he doubted that he was improving despite the fact that some of his friends told him that they saw improvement. Therefore, from his perspective, his efforts to try harder to play better were as yet unsuccessful.

Other positions held by the young man were that it was wrong for him to be nervous and he was skeptical about the possibility of improvement. To cast doubt on this position, the therapist reframed his skepticism as healthy skepticism. The therapist cautioned him to be careful not to put too much stock in what others say in terms of noticing improvement because of the risk of over-reaching himself, which could result in a bad setback. In effect, the therapist was issuing a paradoxical directive to the young man by suggesting that he go slow, which was counter to his efforts to correct the problem by trying harder, according to the advice of others.

The therapist also suggested that improvement may have mixed blessings. The young man was encouraged to be more thoughtful about pursuing his goal of being a concert violinist because success could have some disadvantages that may not have occurred to him yet. The young man was asked to think about what the disadvantages might be. After some discussion, the therapist then offered another possible problem: he suggested that a certain amount of anxiety goes along with performing even if the person is talented enough to be a professional performer. Thus, the therapist reframed the problem as normal and again confirmed the necessity to go slowly because pursuing this kind of career could have some disadvantages.

The therapist also suggested that it might be difficult to distinguish between the kind of anxiety that is natural and useful to good performance and the kind of anxiety that is not. To help the young man further part with his attempted solution, the therapist made an implicit suggestion to deliberately try to play badly. He suggested that he might learn something by trying to play badly. However, the dilemma was posed that trying to play badly might actually lead to the beginning of improvement, which could have a snowball effect—leading to even more improvement, possibly putting him on a road that he does not really want to be on. The client was then given the homework task of thinking about the dangers of change. When, during the next session, the client reported that he experienced some improvement in his playing when playing for himself, the therapist resisted the urge to be optimistic and instead said that he shouldn't attach too much meaning to that improvement. After a few sessions the client terminated, and in a follow-up interview several years later, reported that he had become a success- ful businessman and enjoyed playing the violin as a hobby (adapted from a case presented by Fisch, Weakland, and Segal, 1982).

Ordeal

An **ordeal** is an intervention that directs clients to do something that is mildly disagreeable yet also good for them in response to engaging in symp- tomatic behavior (Haley, 1984). These interventions are based on the prem- ise that if it is more difficult for a person to have a symptom than to give it up, the person will likely give up the symptom. There are two types of or- deals: straightforward and paradoxical. When the therapist prescribes a **straightforward ordeal,** he or she requires that each time the symptom occurs the client must go through a specific ordeal. For example, when a symptom occurs during the day, a client may be directed to get up in the middle of the night to do something distasteful but healthy (e.g., write or ex- ercise). In a **paradoxical ordeal,** the therapist directs the client to have the symptom at a time when he or she might rather be doing something else. For example, a client who is troubled by ruminations during work hours may be directed to get up an hour early each morning to ruminate for a specific amount of time. An ordeal may also involve more than one person. For ex- ample, a couple that is having problems getting past an extramarital affair may be directed to conduct a ritualized ordeal together that is designed to make the offender suffer appropriately.

When ordeals are used skillfully, they can have positive effects on prob- lem resolution. The problem must be clearly defined, the client must be very motivated to get over the problem, an appropriate ordeal must be selected, and a rationale that makes sense must be given to the client. Generally, the therapist directs the client to continue the ordeal until the problem is solved.

RELEVANT RESEARCH

It is safe to say that the development and dissemination of family therapy approaches has outstripped the collection of research evidence to support the usefulness of these approaches. Strategic therapy is no exception. For the most part, information about the success of strategic therapy is limited to anecdotal evidence provided in case studies.

However, there have been a few instances in which strategic therapy out- come has been tracked more systematically. For example, in one study follow- up, telephone interviews were conducted three to six months after treatment ended with ninety-seven clients treated from the MRI perspective for an average of seven sessions. These clients sought therapy for a wide range of problems. Interviewers found that 40 percent of these clients said they experienced complete symptom relief; 33 percent said they had considerable but not complete relief; and 27 percent said there was no change in their symptoms, which represents a 73 percent success rate (Watzlawick, Weakland, and Fisch, 1974).

Haley (1980) reported on the outcome of his model with schizophrenic young adults who had issues about leaving their families of origin. He and his colleagues treated schizophrenic young adults who had been hospitalized for the first time. He used rehospitalization as a measure of whether therapy helped the clients. In two to four years after the completing therapy, three of the fourteen clients tracked had been rehospitalized, and one had committed suicide, which represents a 71 percent success rate. Madanes (1995) reported on the outcome of her work with a large sample of male adolescent sex offenders. She and her colleagues obtained two-year follow-up information for seventy-two of the seventy-five adolescents treated. Of these individuals, four had reoffended, which represents a 96 percent success rate.

Several researcher-clinicians have reported on therapy outcomes achieved with family therapy models that integrate strategic therapy and other approaches. For example, Stanton, Todd, and associates (1982) treated drug addicts with a family therapy approach that combined structural and strategic techniques. In comparing their approach with individual therapy and a family-based placebo, these researcher-clinicians found that their approach was nearly twice as effective as the other two approaches. Another team of researchers (Szapocznik et al., 1986) found that Hispanic drug abusing adolescents and their families improved their individual and family functioning after being treated with a brief structural-strategic family therapy approach.

GLOSSARY

brief therapy: Approaches to therapy that maintain a focus on the present rather than the past and on solving the presenting problem as quickly as possible.

client position: Beliefs, values, and priorities that clients hold which are related to the presenting problem.

compliance-based directive: Directives that therapists expect clients will follow.

conceptual map: A mental model that represents how an individual perceives reality and by which an individual is guided.

cybernetics: A scientific discipline interested in the interrelationship between stability and change.

directives: An encouragement by the therapist to the client to think or act in a certain way.

double bind: A communication in which an individual is given two mutually exclusive messages by another person in which any response will inevitably result in a failure to please.

explicit directive: The therapist asks the client to do something that he or she thinks will lead to change.

family life cycle transition: Phases in the family developmental evolution that mark periods of change primarily when a member enters or exits the family.

goal-setting stage: The final stage of the initial session when strategic therapists help family members set goals for therapy.

homework: Activities or tasks relating to the presenting problem that the therapist asks the client to do between sessions.

hypnosis: A technique in which a person is put into a trance or dreamlike state.

hypotheses: The ideas and/or guesses that a therapist makes regarding what maintains the presenting problem.

identified patient: The person who is viewed by the family as the focus of therapy; the person who has a problem or is a problem for the family.

implicit directive: The therapist indirectly influences the client's behavior, e.g., changing the subject when the topic seems counterproductive to the goals of therapy.

incongruent hierarchy: A term used to describe families in which family members do not behave in age- or role-appropriate ways in relation to one another.

indirect directive: A task that implicitly influences the client's positive change.

interaction stage: The third stage of the initial session in which strategic therapists ask family members to discuss their various points of view about the problem so that they can observe how the family interacts regarding the problem.

interactive view of problems: The belief that problems are maintained by the repetitive negative interchanges of family members.

joining: A therapeutic skill of establishing rapport with clients in which therapists develop a personal relationship with families thus becoming accepted, trusted helpers.

metaphor: Symbolic language or behavior that links two events, ideas, characteristics, or their meaning.

negotiate and contract: Therapist helps clients to reach a satisfactory agreement regarding specific goals or changes in behavior.

ordeal: A therapeutic technique in which the therapist asks the client to do a set of tasks that is appropriate for the problem but causes distress that is equal to or greater than the problem.

outside the family system: The therapist maintains distance from the family.

paradoxical communication: A set of contradictory messages.

paradoxical directives: Therapeutic tasks that seem contradictory to the goals of therapy whereby family members change by either accepting or rejecting the therapist's suggestion.

paradoxical interventions: Therapists direct clients to continue their symptomatic behavior.

paradoxical ordeal: The client is instructed to go through the experience of having the symptom at a time or place that is different than when he or she might ordinarily have the symptom.

power ladder: Relative influence each family member has in relation to other family members.

prescribing a symbolic act: A type of directive in which the therapist asks a family member to do something that represents the symptom.

prescribing the symptom: A strategy in which the therapist asks the client to have the symptom, which forces the client to rebel against the prescription or to obey, thus putting the client more in control of the symptom.

pretending technique: The therapist directs a client to pretend to have a symptom thereby making the symptom more under the client's control.

problem stage: The second stage of the initial session in which strategic therapists ask each family member to share ideas about the problem and his or her involvement in it.

psychoanalysis: A form of therapy usually accredited to Sigmund Freud in which the patient's past and unconscious inner life is the focus of treatment.

PUSH system: A way of viewing a family system used by some strategic therapists who think about how a symptom might be protective (P) of someone in the family, who is involved in maintaining the problem (U), what behavior patterns are involved in maintaining the problem (S), and what is the power structure of the family (H).

qualitative interview: A conversation for the purpose of collecting information from a person about a topic that will subsequently be analyzed.

redefining the problem: Changing the client's belief about the problem.

reframing: Using language to give new meaning to a situation and thereby helping clients see their situation in a new way, which may entail developing a more positive interpretation of the problem.

restraining change: A type of paradoxical directive in which the therapist discourages change, often citing the drawbacks of improving.

social stage: The first stage of the initial session in which strategic therapists greet family members and try to make them feel comfortable.

straightforward directive: A task given to a client that the therapist hopes he or she will do because it encourages the client to correct the presenting problem.

straightforward ordeal: The client is instructed to go through a specific ordeal (something he or she should do more of anyway) each time the symptom occurs.

strategy for change: A plan or approach for solving the presenting problem.

structural family therapy: The family therapy approach, developed by Salvador Minuchin and his colleagues, that focuses on how families operate (structure and communication patterns).

subconscious roots of problems: Problems that stem from feelings or motivations that are outside a person's awareness and therefore based in the subconscious.

systems theory: A theoretical framework that suggests individuals in a system affect and are affected by one another and cannot be understood without understanding the interrelationships.

therapeutic alliance: The therapist and client develop a collaborative working relationship.

therapeutic maneuverability: A technique in which therapists maintain their ability to take action.

therapist-client clinical contract: The therapist and client together negotiates an agreement related to the presenting problem and goals for change.

triangle: A three-person system that develops when stress between two people becomes so great that a third person is drawn in to decrease the tension, thus creating a triangle.

vicious cycles: Destructive, repetitive patterns of interaction.

REFERENCES

Fisch, R., Weakland, J. H., and Segal, L. (1982). *The tactics of change: Doing therapy briefly.* San Francisco, CA: Jossey-Bass.

Haley, J. (1973). *Uncommon therapy.* New York: W. W. Norton.

Haley, J. (1976). *Problem-solving therapy.* San Francisco, CA: Jossey-Bass.

Haley, J. (1980). *Leaving home: The therapy of disturbed young people.* New York: McGraw-Hill.

Haley, J. (1984). *Ordeal therapy: Unusual ways to change behavior.* San Francisco, CA: Jossey-Bass.

Haley, J. (Ed.) (1985). *Conversations with Milton. H. Erickson. M. D.* (Volumes I, II, and III). New York: Triangle Press.

Heath, A. W. and Ayers, T. C. (1991). MRI brief therapy with adolescent substance abusers. In T. Todd and M. Selekman (Eds.), *Family therapy approaches with adolescent substance abusers* (pp. 49-69). Boston: Allyn and Bacon.

Keim, J. (1998). Strategic family therapy. In F. M. Dattilio (Ed.), *Case studies in couple and family therapy* (pp. 132-157). New York: Guilford Press.

Keim, J. (1999). *Brief strategic marital therapy.* In J. M. Donovan (Ed.), *Short-term couple therapy* (pp. 265-290). New York: Guilford Press.

Madanes, C. (1981). *Strategic family therapy.* San Francisco: Jossey Bass.

Madanes, C. (1984). *Behind the one-way mirror: Advances in the practice of strategic therapy.* San Francisco: Jossey Bass.

Madanes, C. (1990). Strategies and metaphors of brief therapy. In J. K. Zeig and S. G. Gilligan (Eds.), *Brief therapy: Myths, methods, and metaphors* (pp. 18-35). New York: Brunner/Mazel.

Madanes, C. (1995). *The violence of men: New techniques for working with abusive families: A therapy of social action.* San Francisco: Jossey Bass.

Segal, L. (1991). Brief therapy: The MRI approach. In A. Gurman and D. Kniskern (Eds.), *Handbook of family therapy* (pp. 171-199). New York: Brunner/Mazel.

Stanton, M. D., Todd, T. C., and Associates (1982). *The family therapy of drug abuse and addiction.* New York: The Guilford Press.

Szapocznik, J. Kurtines, W. M., Foote, F., Perez-Vidal, A., and Hervis, O. (1986). Conjoint versus one-person family therapy: Further evidence for the effectiveness of conducting family therapy through one person with drug-abusing adolescents. *Journal of Consulting and Clinical Psychology, 54* (3), 395-397.

Watzlawick, P., Weakland, J. H., and Fisch, R. (1974). *Change: Principles of problem formation and problem resolution.* New York: W. W. Norton.

Weakland, J. H. and Fisch, R. (1992). Brief therapy—MRI style. In S. Budman, M. Hoyt, and S. Friedman (Eds.), *The first session in brief therapy* (pp. 306-323). New York: Guilford Press.

Weakland, J. H., Fisch, R., Watzlawick, P., and Bodin, A. M. (1983). Brief therapy: Focused problem resolution. In R. J. Green and J. L. Framo (Eds.), *Family therapy: Major contributions* (Second edition) (pp. 493-525). New York: International Universities Press, Inc.

Chapter 5

Milan Systemic Therapy

Jerome Adams

Milan therapy brings the future—or rather, many possible futures—
into the present, and allows clients to choose the ones they prefer. The
possibility of a future not determined by necessity, but open to sometimes unpredictable choices, gives clients hope; it helps them . . . em-
bark on a new journey.

Luigi Boscolo
The Times of Time

Theories are, by definition, works in progress. Nowhere is the evolving
nature of therapy models more apparent than in the Milan approach. Indeed,
its numerous revisions over time represent perhaps its most obvious characteristic. Based initially on the ideas of the early Palo Alto Mental Research
Institute group, with its emphasis on family rules and homeostasis-seeking
interactive patterns, the Milan approach has itself undergone continuous
change in its thirty-year history (Goldenberg and Goldenberg, 2000; Campbell, Draper, and Crutchley, 1991).

After a decade of work together, the four original Milan team members
separated into two autonomous groups (Selvini Palazzoli and Prata; Boscolo
and Cecchin) in 1979, each pair pursuing differing emphases in their systemic thinking and practices. Selvini Palazzoli and Prata (separately since
1982) have engaged in family systems research, particularly directed at developing techniques for interrupting the destructive games they believe psychotic individuals and their families play. Selvini Palazzoli's work at this
stage, carried out in collaboration with a group of colleagues, is called *Family Games* (Selvini Palazzoli et al., 1989); in it she proposes a **universal
strategic intervention** designed to break up repetitively resistant patterns
in families with severely disturbed members. In the early 1990s Selvini
Palazzoli abandoned this strategic approach and returned to long-term insight-oriented individual therapy until her death in 1999.

On the other hand, Boscolo and Cecchin began training family therapists worldwide and have continued to elaborate their own systemic ideas. Departing from strategic techniques, they have developed a more collaborative therapeutic intervention style based on the interviewing process itself, particularly the use of circular questioning. Consistent with those views, their most recent efforts have been directed at fine-tuning such questioning techniques. In seeking to advance a new **systemic epistemology,** Boscolo and Cecchin have become central players in advancing the approaches of **constructivism** that are now so popular in the family therapy field. In the United States, they have found a particularly receptive audience among some members of the Ackerman Institute for Family Therapy in New York, particularly Peggy Papp (1983), Peggy Penn (1982), and Joel Bergman (1985). Lynn Hoffman, formerly at Ackerman, has since relocated to Amherst, Massachusetts, and now ascribes to a social construction viewpoint (Hoffman, 1985). Elsa Jones (1993), as well as David Campbell and Rosalind Draper (1985) in England, are enthusiastic supporters of the Milan viewpoint. In Canada, Karl Tomm of the University of Calgary is a leading interpreter of the Milan (and post-Milan) systemic approach. A description of the work of Boscolo and Cecchin can be found in *Milan Systemic Family Therapy* (Boscolo et al., 1987).

MAIN PROPONENTS AND THEORETICAL CONCEPTS

As are many well-known therapists in the family therapy field, Mara Selvini Palazzoli was initially trained as a psychoanalyst. In 1967 she became the leader of a group of eight fellow psychiatrists—including Luigi Boscolo, Gianfranco Cecchin, and Guiliana Prata—to treat families of severely disturbed children, many of whom were suffering from **anorexia nervosa.** However, their initial efforts to apply psychoanalytic concepts to the family proved to be very time consuming and produced limited results (Selvini Palazzoli, 1974). Turning to the published accounts of the works of the Palo Alto group, particularly the book *Pragmatics of Human Communication* (Watzlawick, Beavin, and Jackson, 1967), the four formed a study group to better understand strategic theories and techniques in the hope that such an outlook would lead to better interventions in families with entrenched interactive patterns.

In 1971, the group split from their analytic colleagues. They established the Milan Center for the Study of the Family in order to work more exclusively with family systems. Although Watzlawick was their major consultant in these early years and visited them periodically in Italy, the group gradually developed its own theory and set of strategic intervention techniques over the next decade (Boscolo et al., 1987). They published their first article in English in 1974 (Selvini Palazzoli et al., 1974), introducing a team approach along with a set of powerful and innovative intervention techniques, such as positive connotation and therapeutic rituals (both described in detail later in this chapter), designed to overcome the paradoxical interactive sequences that deadlocked families and resulted in therapeutic impasses. What is now referred to as the "classic" Milan approach quickly captured the imagination of family therapists around the world. Working with families with a wide range of the most severe emotional problems, they reported particular success in treating anorexic children as well as schizophrenics with their team approach.

By 1980, the four were beginning to de-emphasize the use of therapeutic paradoxes, and in a landmark paper "Hypothesizing—Circularity—Neutrality: Three Guidelines for the Conductor of the Session" (Selvini Palazzoli et al., 1980) revealed their thinking to be moving in a systemic direction and away from strategic techniques. They contended that **hypothesizing,** a continual interactive process of speculating and making assumptions about the family situation, provides a guide for conducting a systemic interview. They stressed that this guide to the family system is not true or false, but rather is useful as a starting point and open to revision or abandonment by the family as well as the therapist as new data accumulate. The technique allows the therapist to search for new information, identify the connecting patterns that sustain family behavior, and speculate on how each participant in the family contributes to systemic functioning. Beginning with the family's first telephone contact and continuing throughout the therapeutic process, hypothesizing represents therapeutic formulations regarding family functioning and is carefully constructed to elicit a picture of how the family is organized around the symptom or presenting problem. When asked for a description of the problem at the start of the first interview, the family might point to the symptom bearer as the one with the problem. The Milan therapist will ask, "Who noticed the problem first?" This redefines the problem as relational— it does not exist without a "noticer," and thus it does not belong to one person alone. Moreover, the problem is depicted as an event between two or more family members, thus involving the wider family system (Boscolo et al., 1987). Thus, hypothesizing permits the therapist to present a view of the family's behavior that is different from their own established self-picture. The therapist is offering a conceptualization—of the family's communication patterns, the meaning of a member's symptoms, the way in which the family organizes itself to deal with problems, and the family game. In doing so, the therapist identifies himself or herself as an active participant, someone who does not necessarily have all the answers but, with his or her unique view of the family's reality, intended to open the family up to considering a new perspective on their lives.

As Burbatti and Formenti (1988) contend, *the goal of therapeutic hypotheses is change, not truth.* In the Batesonian tradition, hypothesizing offers information, allowing the family members to choose or reject the therapeutic message from an active therapeutic partner. If, instead, the therapist were simply a passive observer, the Milan group believes the family would impose its own punctuations and resume its own games; little if any new information would be forthcoming to initiate change, and the system would tend toward entropy. Hypothesizing, on the other hand, offers a structured viewpoint, organizing data provided by the family and encouraging the family to rethink their lives and together begin to form new hypotheses (for example, regarding previously denied coalitions) about themselves and their interactions.

Neutrality is different from noninvolvement; it means the therapist is interested in, and accepts without challenge, each member's unique perception of the problem (if not necessarily accepting the problem itself). No one family member's view is seen as more correct than any other view. Thus, each family member may repeatedly experience the therapist being allied with one or another member as that person's views are elicited, but never allied solely with any one participant. Cecchin (1987) characterized the notion of neutrality as **curiosity,** as a result of widespread misunderstanding that neutrality demonstrated coldness or aloofness. As currently used, the curious therapist is open to numerous hypotheses about the system and invites the family to explore those which increase the number of options or possibilities for the changes they seek.

When Milan therapists speak of **circularity** they are referring both to interactional sequences within the family and, because the therapist is part of the system, to the therapist's interactional relationship with the family. The therapist's hypotheses lead to questions, and the family's responses lead to refined hypotheses and new questions, all leading to changes in the family's belief system. As Selvini Palazzoli et al. (1980) define it in their paper,

> By circularity, we mean the capacity of the therapist to conduct his investigation on the basis of feedback from the family in response to the information he solicits about relationships and, therefore, about differences and change. (p. 3)

Circular questioning, destined to be a significant influence on future therapists, has become the cornerstone of Boscolo and Cecchin's later modifications of the original systemic outlook. Circular questioning involves asking each family member questions that help address a difference or define a relationship between two other members of the family. These differences are intended to expose recursive family patterns. These interviewing techniques will be defined and illustrated later, but for now it will suffice to state that the therapist is trying to construct a map of the interconnections among family members, and is assuming that asking questions about differences in viewpoints is the most effective way of creating such a map (Campbell, Draper, and Crutchley, 1991). One major gain is that each family member is continually exposed to the ideas and opinions of the others throughout the therapy.

After the four separated, Selvini Palazzoli and a new set of associates (Selvini Palazzoli et al., 1989) began to elaborate on the concept of **family games,** the destructive, collusive parent-child patterns they believe psychotic individuals and their families play. She and her colleagues suggested the controversial proposal that therapists offer a solitary prescription or task to the parents. Selvini Palazzoli proposed that this universal or invariant prescription be applied to all families with schizophrenic or anorexic children. Their intervention techniques at this stage represent a return to some of the Milan group's earlier strategic and structural ways of working (Simon, 1987).

In the early 1990s, Selvini Palazzoli reinvented her therapy once more, this time abandoning any form of short-term strategic therapy (invariant prescription included) for long-term therapy with patients and their families. Thus she has come full circle, beginning with psychodynamic roots, then abandoning any concerns with the individual to focus on family patterns, and now returning to long-term therapy that emphasizes insight and focuses again on the individual. This new therapy revolves around the denial of family secrets and suffering over generations. In this way it is linked conceptually to her former models (Nichols and Schwartz, 2001).

Following the group split in 1979, Boscolo and Cecchin continued to elaborate their own systemic ideas, and have developed a more **collaborative** therapeutic intervention style based on the interviewing process itself, particularly the use of circular questioning. Unlike Selvini Palazzoli's direct, take-charge therapeutic style, offering parents prescriptions, their efforts emphasize neutrality as a more effective device for quietly challenging an entire family to reexamine its epistemology. In effect, they temporarily join the family, becoming part of a whole system from which they can begin to offer information and perspectives on reality. In essence, the therapists and family members influence each other, producing the opportunity for change as a by-product.

Boscolo and Cecchin now argue that perhaps it is better to do away with the concept of family systems entirely, and think of the treatment unit as a meaning system in which the therapist is as active a contributor as anyone else. Any intervention, then, should not be directed at a particular outcome but rather should be seen as perturbing the system, which will then react in terms of its own structure. Consistent with postmodern ideas, therapists do not have the answers but, together with the family, can coconstruct or co-evolve new ways of looking at the family system, creating the possibility of new narratives or versions of reality that are less saturated with past problems or past failed solutions. For example, Cecchin (Cecchin, Lane, and Ray, 1993) has suggested that in addition to remaining curious, the therapist should maintain an attitude of **irreverence.** By this he means not becoming too attached to any model or belief and helping families become more irreverent toward the beliefs that constrain them (Nichols and Schwartz, 2001).

Karl Tomm, in a series of papers (1987a,b, 1988), has elaborated on these ideas, arguing that the therapist should carry out continuous **interventive interviewing.** More than simply seeking workable interventions, Tomm (1987a) urges therapists to attend closely to the interviewing process, especially their own intentionality, adopting an orientation in which everything an interviewer does and says—and does not do and say—is thought of as an intervention that could be therapeutic, nontherapeutic, or countertherapeutic.

Tomm adds **strategizing** to the original set of Milan techniques of hypothesizing, circularity, and neutrality. His circular questions are carefully constructed—not simply for information-gathering purposes but also as a change-inducing technique (Slovik and Griffith, 1992). Strategizing refers to a therapist's ongoing cognitive activity—evaluating the effects of past therapeutic actions, developing new plans of action, anticipating the consequence of possible interventions, and deciding, moment to moment, how to achieve maximum therapeutic influence most effectively. More specifically, Tomm is interested in the kinds of questions a therapist asks to help families exact new levels of meaning from their behavior in the service of enabling them to generate new ways of thinking and behaving on their own.

Of greatest relevance are what Tomm (1987b) refers to as **reflexive questions.** Intended to be facilitative, they are designed to move families to reflect on the meaning they extract from their current perceptions and actions and stimulate them to consider alternative options. For example, the therapist may suggest a useful course of action by asking, "What would happen if you told her when you were hurt or angry instead of withdrawing?" The client is given the idea and invited to speculate on the implications of acting on it. These questions are described in more detail later.

NORMAL FAMILY DEVELOPMENT

Because the Milan team was closely associated with the MRI group in its early stages, they share a **nonnormative stance** toward family development. By nonnormative, MRI therapists mean that "we use no criteria to judge the health or normality of an individual or family. As therapists we do not regard any particular way of functioning, relating, or living as a problem if the client is not expressing discontent with it" (Fisch, 1978, p. 109). This relativism has deep roots (Nichols and Schwartz, 2001). As early as 1967 Don Jackson wrote an essay called the "Myth of Normality," cautioning against taking any position regarding how families should behave.

The Milan associates strive to maintain a nonnormative posture through their attitude of neutrality or curiosity (Cecchin, 1987) regarding families. They aspire to no preconceived goals or normative models for their client families. Instead, by raising questions that help a family examine itself and its belief system, they trust that the family will reorganize on its own in a better way, even if that does not conform to some normative map (Nichols and Schwartz, 2001). However, despite their rejection of normative goals, Boscolo and Cecchin imply that healthy families are resourceful enough to modify beliefs and attitudes that do not work, and that this flexibility is needed not only with everyday difficulties but also to navigate transitional points in the family's development.

Selvini Palazzoli and her colleagues came closer to a normative blueprint of family functioning, although this is not explicitly stated. Their hypotheses about family games involve any number of covert, **cross-generational alliances,** so one could infer that they believe families should have clear generational **boundaries.** Nichols and Schwartz (2001) caution against making this inference, however, since normality is not always the converse of abnormality.

PATHOLOGY AND BEHAVIOR DISORDERS

The Milan team's explanation of problematic behavior parallels the group's evolution. The team's first book, *Paradox and Counterparadox: A New Model in the Therapy of the Family in Schizophrenic Transaction* (Selvini Palazzoli et al., 1978), reveals the strong influence of **cybernetics** on their thinking. Dysfunctional families exhibited paradoxical behavior—the moves each member of the system made seemed to keep change from occurring. As Tomm (1984a) observed, it was as though the family were asking the therapist to change its symptomatic member at the same time that it was insisting the rest of the family was fine and had no intention of changing.

For example, in this early work, the Milan group focused on the rules of the game in psychotic families—tactics by which family members struggle against one another as, together, they act to perpetuate unacknowledged family games in order to control one another's behaviors. That is, they conceptualized the family as "a self-regulating system which controls itself according to the rules formed over a period of time through a process of trial and error" (Selvini Palazzoli et al., 1978, p. 3). The symptoms in a family member, then, were not accidental, but were "skillfully fabricated to achieve particular systemic purposes" (Seltzer, 1986). A schizophrenic individual, trapped by these family rules, is powerless to effect change. That is, the rules of the family's game, rather than any individual input, define and sustain their family position and pathology.

Recognizing from a systems perspective that it is impossible for a part to change without a complementary change in the whole, the group began to design interventions in the form of **counterparadoxes** directed at breaking up such contradictory patterns, thus freeing up the family to change. Palazzoli, in her work *Family Games* (Selvini Palazzoli et al., 1989), describes her experiments with interventions such as the invariant prescription designed to disrupt these pathological family games. Most recently Selvini Palazzoli focused her research on intergenerational secrets as the source of symptomatic behavior in families.

Boscolo and Cecchin's thinking moved away from the MRI version of families as self-correcting systems governed through rules, and began to regard systems as evolving and unfolding rather than seeking a return to previous **homeostasis**. Extrapolating from Bateson's (1972) work, they theorized that dysfunctional families are making an "epistemological error"—they are following an outdated or erroneous set of beliefs or maps of their reality, which is why they appear to be stuck or in homeostatic balance. Put another way, the family was having problems because it had adopted a set of beliefs that did not fit the reality in which it was living. In effect, they were being guided by an out-of-date map when the signs and streets had changed since the map's publication.

According to this new perspective, the family's beliefs about itself were not the same as the actual behavior patterns of its members, so that they only gave the impression of being stuck; in reality their behavior was changing continuously. Boscolo and Cecchin decided they needed to help families differentiate between these two levels—meaning and action. Therapeutically, they began to introduce new information, new distinctions in thought and action, carefully introducing differences into the family's belief system.

Relying on circular questioning to present differences for the family to consider, the team attempted to activate a process in which the family creates new belief patterns and new patterns of behavior consistent with those beliefs.

TECHNIQUES

Long Brief Therapy

Two distinguishing characteristics of classic Milan systemic family therapy have been its **spacing of therapeutic sessions** and its use of a **team** of therapists who work together with a family. The original Milan team method has been described as "long brief therapy" (Tomm, 1984a), since relatively few sessions (generally about ten) were held approximately once a month and thus treatment might extend up to a year or so. Initially, this unusual spacing of sessions was instituted because so many of the families seen at the Milan Center had to travel hundreds of miles by train for treatment. Later, the therapy team realized that their interventions—often in the form of paradoxical prescriptions aimed at changing the way an entire family system functioned—took time to incubate and finally take effect. Once the frequency was determined, the therapists did not grant an extra session or move up a session to shorten the agreed-upon interval. Such requests by families were seen as efforts to disqualify or undo the effects of a previous intervention (Selvini Palazzoli, 1980). The early Milan group was adamant in its determination that the therapist not submit to the family's "game" or become subjugated to its rules for maintaining sameness and controlling the therapeutic relationship. Even under pressure from the family, these therapists would remain unavailable in the belief that a request for an exceptional meeting actually meant the family was experiencing rapid change and needed the time to integrate any subsequent changes in family rules.

During most of the 1970s, the Milan group worked in an unconventional but consistent way developed from their strategic-based research. The entire family was seen together by one or sometimes two therapists (typically a man and a woman), while the remainder of the team watched from behind a one-way mirror to gain a different perspective. From time to time during the session, the observers would summon one of the therapists out of the room to change therapeutic direction; while conferring with the therapist, they would make suggestions, share opinions, provide their own observations, and often issue directives that the returning therapist could then share with the family.

Following this strategy conference, the therapist rejoined the family group, discussed what had transpired with the other team members, and assigned the family members a task, usually a paradoxical prescription. Sometimes such an intervention took the form of a paradoxical letter, a copy of which was given to every family member. In the event that a key member missed a session, a copy of the letter would be sent by mail, frequently with comments (again, often paradoxically stated) regarding his or her absence. Prescriptions took the form of opinions ("We believe Father and Mother, by working hard to be good parents, are nevertheless . . .") or requests that certain behavioral changes be attempted by means of rituals carried out between sessions ("The immediate family, without any other relatives or outsiders, should meet weekly for one hour, with each person allowed fifteen minutes to . . ."). By addressing the behavior of all the members, the therapists underscored the connections in the family patterns. Prescriptions usually were stated in such a way that the family was directed not to change for the time being. Thus, the therapist might say, "I think the family should continue to support Selma's behavior for the present" (Selvini Palazzoli et al., 1978).

Structured Family Sessions

The classic Milan therapeutic interview format was divided into five segments: the presession, the session, the intersession, the intervention, and the postsession discussion. Family therapy would begin with the initial telephone call from the family. The team member who took the call would talk to the caller at length, recording the information on a fact sheet. Who called? Who referred the family? What is the problem? How disturbed is the caller's communication? What tone of voice is used? What is the caller's attitude regarding the forthcoming treatment? What special conditions, if any, does the caller attempt to impose? These intake issues are then discussed with the entire team in the presession, prior to the first interview, in a lengthy and detailed way, and tentative hypotheses regarding the family's presenting problem were proposed by the various team members. Particularly noteworthy is the fact that the referring person or agency was kept involved throughout treatment, a recognition of his or her part in the **larger system.**

In a similar fashion, such team conferences occurred before each session, as the group met to review the previous session and together planned strategies for the upcoming one. All of these tactics affirmed the Milan therapists' belief that the family and therapist(s) are part of one system. During the session itself, a major break in the family interview (the intersession) would occur so that the observer team could have an active discussion with the therapist outside of the hearing of the family, during which hypotheses would be validated or modified. The therapist would then return to offer the team's intervention (usually a prescription or ritual) to the family. The team postsession discussion would focus on an analysis of the family's reaction to the intervention as well as providing a chance to plan for the following session (Boscolo et al., 1987).

This early version of the Milan model was more concerned with family processes than with family structure. Members of dysfunctional families were seen as engaging in self-perpetuating games in which members tried to control one another's behaviors. The identified problem was seen as serving the system in the best way possible at the moment. Since the family members, through their communication patterns, maintained the system's rules and thus perpetuated the transactions in which the symptomatic behavior was embedded, the therapist tried to change the rules in order to change that behavior (Selvini Palazzoli et al., 1978).

As the Milan therapeutic procedures changed over time, the classic method—male and female cotherapists, two team members behind the one-way mirror—was amended so that a single therapist was likely to work with the family while the rest of the team (often students learning the technique) observed. The observers were free to call the therapist out of the room to share ideas and offer hypotheses. The **five-part session** division (presession, session, intersession, intervention, and postsession discussion) has been maintained by and large, although the fixed month-long interval between sessions has become more flexible, depending upon feedback from the family and consultants. Generally speaking, a ten-session limit extended over an indeterminate period of time still qualifies the approach as long brief therapy (Jones, 1993).

Interviewing Techniques

Two early Milan therapeutic interventions included the use of positive connotation and ritualized prescriptions.

Positive connotation is a form of reframing the family's problem-maintaining behavior in which symptoms are seen as positive or good because they help maintain the system's balance and thus facilitate family cohesion and well-being. By suggesting a good reason for behavior previously viewed as negatively motivated ("Your child refuses to go to school because he wants to provide companionship for his lonely mother"), the systemic therapist is indicating to the family that the unwanted symptomatic behavior may actually be desirable. Instead of being considered "bad" or "sick" or "out of control," the symptomatic child is considered to be "well intentioned" and behaving volitionally. Note that it is not the symptomatic behavior (school refusal) that is connoted to be positive but rather the intent behind that behavior (family cohesion or harmony).

All members are considered to be motivated by the same positive desire for family cohesion, and thus all are linked participants in the family system. Because the positive connotation is presented by the therapist as an approval rather than a reproach, the family does not resist such explicit confirmation and accepts the statement. As a result of **reframing,** the symptomatic behavior is now viewed by the family as voluntary, greatly enhancing the possibilities for change. However, the positive connotation has implicitly put the family in a **paradox:** Why must such a good thing as family cohesion require the presence of symptomatic behavior in a member?

One other important function of positive connotation deserves mention: it prepares the family for forthcoming paradoxical prescriptions. That is, when each member's behavior is connoted as positive, all view one another as cooperative and thus are more willing to join in complying with any tasks they may be assigned by the therapist, reducing family resistance to future change. If the therapist adds a **no-change prescription** ("And because you have decided to help the family in this way, we think that you should continue in this work for the time being") (Tomm, 1984b, p. 266), an additional paradox of "no change in the context of change" further increases the impact of the intervention. The seemingly innocuous phase "for the time being" implies that the current family pattern need not always occur in the current manner, leaving open the possibility of future spontaneous change. The family is left to resolve the paradoxical absurdities on its own.

Family rituals, such as weddings, birthday parties, baptisms, bar and bat mitzvahs, graduations, and funerals, often play a central role in a family's life. Such transitions are designed to mark and facilitate family developmental transitions and changes. Therapeutically, rituals may be designed to intervene in established family patterns, promoting new ways of doing things, which in turn may alter thoughts, beliefs, and relationship options (Imber-Black, 1988). Rather than offer a direct prescription, which the family may fear or resist or otherwise oppose, ritualizing the prescribed behavior offers a new context and is thus more likely to be carried out by the family. Rituals usually are assigned in paradoxical prescriptions describing in detail what act is to be done, by whom, when, and in what sequence. Typically, carrying out the ritual calls for the performance of a task that challenges some rigid, covert family rule (see Box 5.1).

Therapeutic rituals address aspects of family relationships that the therapist or team hypothesizes to be significant for family functioning, based on how the team views the family's current difficulty. Generally, they are cere-

---

BOX 5.1. Family Ritual Example

Family rituals have many uses. One example is using family rituals for a case in which parents are inconsistent or competitive with each other in an attempt to maintain behavioral control of a disruptive child. The therapist may suggest an alternating day ritual wherein the mother takes full charge of discipline on odd days (with father observing and taking exact notes on the ensuing mother-child interaction), and the father takes charge on even days (with mother playing the opposite role). Each is directed to carry out the assigned roles for a certain number of days and to behave "spontaneously" for the remaining days of the week. Carrying out the ritual clarifies differences in approach for the parents and provides greater awareness of how their differences can cause confusion in their child. It thus highlights the importance of two-parent consistency as a goal if the child is to achieve the comfort level necessary to abandon the disruptive behavior.

---

monial acts proposed by the therapist in a tentative way as suggestions or family experiments, and are not expected to become a permanent part of family life. The therapist does not insist the ritual be carried out but only indicates that he or she believes the gesture may be useful.

Generally speaking, the purpose of a ritual is to provide clarity where there might be confusion in family relationships; clarity is gained by the family's enactment of the directive (Tomm, 1984b).

In a ten-year evolution of their own therapeutic approach, Selvini Palazzoli and Prata (Prata, 1990; Selvini Palazzoli et al., 1989) sought to avoid end-of-session rituals tailored for each new family by specifically searching for a universal or invariant prescription that would fit all families. The **invariant prescription** is a ritualized sequence of directives families must follow if the therapist is to help them interrupt their dysfunctional interactions.

This ritualized prescription is based on their six-stage model of psychotic family games. Selvini Palazzoli contends that a single process takes place in all schizophrenic and anorexic families, beginning with a stalemated marriage (stage one) in which a child attempts to take sides (stage two). Eventually drawn into the family game, the child erroneously considers the actively provoking parent to be the winner over the passive parent, and sides with the perceived "loser." The subsequent development of disturbed behavior of symptomatology in the child (stage three), requiring parental attention, presents a demonstration to the passive parent of how to defeat the "winner." Instead of joining the child, however, the passive parent or "loser" sides with the "winner" parent (stage four) in disapproving of the child's behavior. The child, in this scenario, feels betrayed and abandoned and responds by escalating the disturbed behavior, determined to bring down the "winning" parent and show the "loser" what can be done (stage five). Ultimately, the family system stabilizes around the symptomatic behavior (stage six), all participants resorting to "psychotic family games" as each family member tries to turn the situation to his or her advantage (Selvini Palazzoli, 1986).

To break up the game, it is suggested that therapists offer a solitary prescription or task by which the parents mysteriously disappear for a time-limited period. Selvini Palazzoli proposed that the invariant prescription be applied to all families with schizophrenic or anorexic children. A case example illustrating the invariant prescription is described later in this chapter. As indicated earlier, Selvini Palazzoli later abandoned this idea.

Boscolo and Cecchin, on the other hand, focused on developing the three landmark intervention strategies—hypothesizing, circularity, and neutrality—developed near the end of the original Milan group's collaboration. Circular questioning in particular has become the cornerstone of Boscolo and Cecchin's later modifications of the original systemic outlook. Further refinements have been offered by Penn (1982, 1985) and Tomm (1987a,b).

Underscoring the notion of feedback loops, circular questions enable the therapist to construct a map of the interconnections among family members. More specifically, rather than rely on a free-form set of therapeutic questions based loosely on previously formulated hypotheses, Boscolo and Cecchin refined questions that (1) probed differences in perceptions about relationships ("Who is closer to Father, your daughter or your son?"); (2) investigated degrees of difference ("On a scale of one to ten, how bad do you think the fighting is this week?"); (3) studied now-and-then differences ("Did she start losing weight before or after her sister went off to college?"); and (4) sought views of family members on hypothetical or future differences ("If she had not been born, how would your marriage be different today?") (Boscolo et al., 1987, p. 11). The idea was to search for mutually causal feedback chains underlying family interactive patterns and to incorporate these findings into systemic hypotheses, which in turn would form the basis for asking further circular questions, leading to further refined hypotheses, and so forth. Particularly ingenious about this technique is that it allows very little room for a refusal to answer, because questions are given in multiple-choice format.

The technique focuses attention on family connections rather than individual symptomatology by framing every question so that it addresses differences in perception by different family members about events or relationships. Asking a child to compare his mother's and father's reactions to his sister's refusal to eat, or to rate each one's anger on a ten-point scale, or to hypothesize what would happen if they divorced—these are all subtle and relatively benign ways to compel people to focus on differences. By asking several people the same question about their attitude toward the same relationship, the therapist is able to probe more and more deeply without being directly confrontational or interrogating the participants in the relationship (Selvini Palazzoli et al., 1980).

Family members reveal their connections through the communication of information, expressed in verbal and nonverbal fashion. Information about the family lies in the different meanings each participant gives an event. Such differences in turn reflect differing views of family relationships. Circular questioning aims at eliciting and clarifying confused ideas about family relationships and introducing information about such differences back to the family in the form of new questions.

Such **triadic questioning** (addressing a person about the relationship between two other people) often produces change in the family in and of itself, as well as provides information to the therapist. Families learn in the process to think in circular rather than linear terms, and to become closer observers of family processes. Another member's perspective may prove enlightening when compared with one's own view of an event or relationship. Circular questioning always addresses significant family issues and not trivial or irrelevant differences. Such questions need to be guided by hypotheses, because hypotheses give order and coherence to the therapist's pattern of circular questioning (Tomm, 1984b) (see Box 5.2).

Neutrality refers to the therapist's efforts to remain allied with all family members, avoiding getting caught up in family coalitions or alliances. Such a position, typically low key and nonreactive, gives the therapist maximum leverage in achieving change by not being drawn into family games or appearing to side with one family member against another. More concerned with curiosity about how the family system works than with attempting to change it, the neutral therapist assumes that the system the family has constructed makes sense; the family could not be any other way than it is at the moment. By not offering suggestions as to how the family should be, the therapist activates the family's capacity to generate its own solutions (Boscolo et al., 1987).

Being neutral does not imply being inactive or indifferent. Actually, the therapist might display neutrality by listening without prejudice to what is being said, but at the same time asking thought-provoking, relationship-focused, circular questions. A report that the family argues a lot might be accepted by the neutral therapist as interesting information. Without joining the family in assuming arguing is bad, the therapist might inquire, "Who enjoys fighting the most?" or "What would be missing if all the arguing suddenly stopped?" (Tomm, 1984b). (Note that a hypothesis that the family is getting something out of the fighting is subtly being explored.) Nor should

---

BOX 5.2. Reflexive (Change-Inducing) Circular Questions

Reflexive (change-inducing) circular questions are intended to be facilitative to the therapeutic process. These questions are designed to move families to reflect on the meaning they extract from their current perceptions and actions, stimulating them to consider alternative options. Tomm (1987b) differentiates eight groups of reflexive questions:

1. *Future-oriented questions* are designed to open up consideration of alternative behavior in the future. For example, "If the two of you got along better in the future, what would happen that is not happening now?"
2. *Observer-perspective questions* are intended to help people become self-observers. For example, "How do you feel when your wife and teenage son get into a quarrel?"
3. *Unexpected counterchange questions* are questions that open up possibilities of choices not previously considered by altering the context in which the behavior is viewed. For example, "What does it feel like when the two of you are not fighting?"
4. *Embedded suggestion questions* allow the therapist to point clients in a useful direction. For example, "What would happen if you told her when you felt hurt or angry instead of withdrawing?"
5. *Normative-comparison questions* are questions that suggest the problem is not abnormal. For example, "Have any of your friends recently dealt with their last child leaving home, so that they would understand what you are going through now?"
6. *Distinction-clarifying questions* separate the components of a behavior pattern. For example, "Which would be more important to you— showing up your boss's ignorance or helping him so that the project can be successfully completed?"
7. *Questions introducing hypotheses* are those which use tentative therapeutic hypotheses to generalize outside behavior with others. For example, "You know how you become silent when you think your husband is angry with you? What would happen if next time you told him how you felt?"
8. *Process-interrupting questions* create a sudden shift in the therapeutic session. For example, "You just seemed to get quiet and upset, and I wonder if you thought I was siding with your partner?"

---

the therapist become too committed to the family's changing. As Selvini Palazzoli has observed, "If you wish to be a good therapist it is dangerous to have too much of a desire to help other people" (quoted in Simon, 1987, p. 28). Rather, the therapist's goal should be to *help the family achieve change in its ability to change.* They also have the right not to change. Neutrality precludes taking a position for or against any specific behavioral goals from therapy or that the therapist must somehow be the one to effect change.

An important aspect in the evolution of the Milan model is the attention given to the dimension of **time.** Although not directly identified, the Milan team always pays special attention to the dimension of time as a core component of the therapeutic interview. In *Paradox and Counterparadox* (Selvini Palazzoli et al., 1978) the Milan team describes the accidental way they discovered that giving families a longer time between sessions lessened resistance and provided for increased effective change. There was also a formal pause built in to the five-part session itself to give both families and therapist time to reflect. They also ritualized time in prescriptions, such as the **odd/even days prescription,** assigned to interrupt current family interactions. Milan therapy now prefers an orientation toward the future, in the sense that futures are constructed in the "here and now" of the sessions themselves. By means of future hypothetical questions, the therapist brings the future—or rather, many possible futures—into the present and allows clients to choose the ones they prefer (Boscolo and Bertrando, 1993).

RELEVANT RESEARCH

The Milan model has unique characteristics that set it apart from other approaches. Friedlander, Wildman, and Heatherington (1991) compared transcripts of structural and Milan approaches to confirm that their major proponents conduct therapy in ways that are consistent with their theory. Structural approaches rely on more direct comments from the therapist; they "mix it up" with families. The Milan therapist conveys his or her expertise through the use of questions to elicit comments from family members.

Whether the Milan model has any demonstrable superiority over other forms of family therapy remains an unanswered question. There are few comparative family therapy studies. The evidence to date suggests that, similar to the comparative studies of individual therapy, no one approach is better than the others (Shadish et al., 1995), particularly if only well-designed investigations are considered (Pinsof, Wynne, and Hambright, 1996). However, because of methodological limitations, it is unwise to assume that different family therapy approaches do not have different success rates. Different approaches may work for different reasons, with different families, and for different family problems (Pinsof, Wynne, and Hambright, 1996).

Marshal, Feldman, and Sigal (1989) conducted a two-year follow-up of fourteen families and five couples to determine the efficacy and degree of satisfaction with Milan therapy. Family outcome was found to be improved in 56 percent of parents and 89 percent of identified child patients at follow-up. The rates reported by the parents are marginally lower than the usual improvement rates of two-thirds (65 to 73 percent) reported for family systems therapy. One of the most interesting aspects of this study was the assessment of therapy delivery issues as well as outcomes. The researchers found (1) if parents reported liking the group behind the one-way mirror they also reported liking the therapy; (2) fathers who liked the time interval between sessions and were satisfied with the length of treatment tended to like the therapy; (3) mothers who reported liking the treatment also reported positive outcomes; (4) there was a greater likelihood of a family member seeking other treatment if mothers did not report enjoying therapy.

Most systemic treatment approaches focus on finding techniques to change families. Moreover, these interventions are tailored to the unique characteristics of each family. This may account for why so little research has been done evaluating the components of the Milan model. Although Selvini Palazzoli (1986) claimed a high success rate for the invariant prescription intervention technique, the therapeutic power of a single prescription for all disturbed families still remains to be established, as does its potential applicability to troubled families with less serious dysfunction (Nichols and Schwartz, 2001). This description of the psychotic process occurring in certain families is intriguing, and the use of this dramatic intervention procedure aimed at strengthening parental alliances and dislodging family coalitions is an admirable effort to break up a rigid, destructive family game and force family members to invent more flexible ways of living together. However, Selvini Palazzoli's move away from the use of the intervention may have reflected her own assessment of its results.

CASE EXAMPLES

Milan systemic therapy tries to discover, interrupt, and thus change the rules of the game before the behavior of the players (the symptomatic member as well as other family members) could change. For example, the therapist working with a family with an anorexic daughter must break the code inherent in a family game as each parent both insists upon and denies family leadership (Selvini Palazzoli, 1978):

> MOTHER: I don't let her wear miniskirts because I know her father doesn't like them.
> FATHER: I have always backed my wife up. I feel it would be wrong to contradict her. (p. 208)

Note the trap the therapist is drawn into if he or she tries to change such confusing and disqualifying statements. Direct interventions are likely to bring forth countermoves, as the family members fight off any challenge to their rules. Following Bateson's earlier work, Selvini Palazzoli and her colleagues in their early formulations contended that a family double-bind message, a paradox, can be undone only by a therapeutic double bind, which they call a counterparadox.

Consider another hypothesis about how the symptom of anorexia might provide a clue about the family game:

> A 13-year-old girl whose mother has recently returned to work goes on a diet to lose her "baby fat" and continues food refusal to the point of developing symptoms of anorexia. These symptoms and the resulting danger to the girl's health require that her mother leave her newly acquired job and become active in monitoring her daughter's eating habits. The father, who is 9 years older than the mother, encourages his wife in this diligent detective-like behavior. When viewed within the context of this family's relationship pattern the child's self-destructive behavior can be seen as an ingenious attempt, covertly supported by the father, to keep her mother dependent and tied into the role of wife and mother. Alternately it can be seen as supporting the mother's ambivalence regarding obtaining employment, and her need to pull the father closer to home with worries. Finally, as Selvini Palazzoli (1986) recently argued, the child's behavior may represent the culmination of concerted efforts among all family members to prove that competition leads nowhere. (Gelcer, McCabe, and Smith-Resnick, 1990, pp. 52-53)

A provocative therapeutic strategy in such a situation is to offer the parents an invariant prescription—a fixed sequence of directives they must follow if the therapist is to help them interrupt the family game. After an initial family interview, the therapist sees the parents separately from the child and gives them the following prescription intended to introduce a clear and stable boundary between generations (Selvini Palazzoli, 1986):

> Keep everything about this session absolutely secret at home. Every now and then, start going out in the evenings before dinner. Nobody must be forewarned. Just leave a written note saying, "We'll not be home tonight." If, when you come back, one of your (daughters) inquires where you have been, just answer calmly, "These things concern only the two of us." Moreover, each of you will keep a notebook, carefully hidden and out of the children's reach. In these notebooks

each of you separately, will register the date and describe the verbal and nonverbal behavior of each child, or other family member, which seemed to be connected with the prescription you have followed. We recommend diligence in keeping these records because it's extremely important that nothing be forgotten or omitted. Next time you will again come alone, with your notebooks, and read aloud what has happened in the meantime. (pp. 341-342)

The parental alliance, reinforced by joint action and by secretiveness, is strengthened by the prescription (Selvini Palazzoli et al., 1989; Prata, 1990), and previously existing alliances and family coalitions are broken. Parental disappearance exposes and blocks family games, over which none of the players had complete control but which nevertheless perpetuated psychotic behavior. The overall therapeutic thrust, then, is to separate the parents from the rest of the family, alter previous family interactive patterns, and then reunite the family in a more stable alliance at the conclusion of the treatment.

GLOSSARY

anorexia nervosa: Self-starvation leading to a loss of 25 percent or more of body weight, hyperactivity, hypothermia, and amenorrhea (found largely in females).

boundaries: A concept used in structural family therapy to describe emotional and information barriers that protect and enhance the integrity of individuals, subsystems, and families.

circular questioning: The technique of asking questions that focus on family connections. These questions highlight differences in perception about events and relationships among family members.

circularity: The idea that actions are part of a causal chain, each one influencing and being influenced by others.

collaborative: A therapeutic attitude that minimizes therapist expertise. In collaborative interviews the therapist's knowledge, experience, and values are viewed as no truer than the client's.

constructivism: A relativistic point of view that emphasizes the subjective construction of reality. Implies that what we see in families may be based as much on our preconceptions as on what is actually going on.

counterparadox: Placing the family in a therapeutic double bind in order to counter the members' paradoxical interactions.

cross-generational alliance (coalition): An inappropriate alliance between a parent and child who side together against a third family member.

curiosity: A term introduced by Cecchin to replace the idea of therapist "neutrality," which he believed had been misunderstood as aloofness and detachment.

cybernetics: The study of control processes in systems, especially the analysis of feedback of information in closed systems. The term was introduced as a concept to family therapy by Gregory Bateson.

family games: The concept that children and parents stabilize around disturbed behaviors in an attempt to benefit from them.

family rituals: Family ceremonies and traditions such as weddings and birthdays that symbolize important emotional events and transitions.

five-part session: The classic Milan therapeutic interview format, it was divided into five segments: the presession, the session, the intersession, the intervention, and the postsession discussion. The format has remained but more emphasis is now placed on interview questions rather than the team opinion at the end of the interview.

homeostasis: A dynamic state of balance or equilibrium within a system. In families, it is the tendency to remain in the same pattern of functioning and to resist change unless challenged or forced to do otherwise.

hypothesizing: The process by which a team of therapists forms suppositions, open to revision, regarding how and why a family's problems have developed and persisted.

interventive interviewing: An orientation in which everything a therapist says and does is viewed as a potential therapeutic intervention depending on its impact on the family.

invariant prescription: A therapeutic ritual designed by Selvini Palazzoli in which parents of anorexic or psychotic children are directed to mysteriously disappear. The goal is to disrupt the dysfunctional games or family interactions that sustain symptomatic behavior.

irreverence: An attitude in which ideas and beliefs are continually challenged.

larger system: The institutions and professional helpers with whom the family interacts.

neutrality: A balanced acceptance of all family members.

no-change prescription: A technique used in strategic therapy whereby a therapist recommends that problematic behavior should remain unchanged because it is helpful to the family. If they rebel, they give up their symptoms.

nonnormative stance: The therapist makes no assertions regarding ideal family health or functioning.

odd/even days prescription: A ritualized task in which a family is asked to alternate ideas or behaviors. For example, a father would manage a child on the even days of the week, the mother on the odd days. They would then note the differences and compare the merits of each approach.

paradox: A message that contradicts itself on a metalevel (higher level). A statement or proposition that seems contradictory. For example, "I always lie" is a paradoxical statement.

positive connotation: The technique of ascribing positive motives to family behavior in order to avoid resistance to therapy. *See* NO-CHANGE PRESCRIPTION.

reflexive questions: Questions designed by the therapist to induce change.

reframing: Relabeling a family's description of its behavior to make it more amenable to therapeutic change; for example, describing a parent as "intensely caring" rather than "overinvolved."

spacing of therapeutic sessions: The technique of spacing sessions over one-month intervals. This is explained to the clients as the amount of time needed for change to unfold.

strategizing: The posture of the therapist when actively attempting to induce a change.

systemic epistemology: A concept that stresses the interconnectedness of family members as well as the importance of organizational change in families.

team: Therapists observing an interview behind a one-way mirror who share their observations about the family.

therapeutic ritual: Technique used by Selvini Palazzoli that prescribes a specific act for family members to perform, designed to change the family system's rules. *See* ODD/EVEN DAYS PRESCRIPTION.

time: Used therapeutically both between and within sessions. For example, the Milan team would revise the past and create the future in the "here and now" by using circular questions and the temporal aspects of therapeutic rituals.

triadic questioning: Asking one family member how two other family members relate.

universal strategic intervention: *See* INVARIANT PRESCRIPTION.

REFERENCES

Bateson, G. (1972). *Steps to an ecology of mind.* New York: Dutton.

Bergman, J. (1985). *Fishing for barracuda: Pragmatics of brief therapy.* New York: W.W. Norton.

Boscolo, L. and Bertrando, P. (1993). *The times of time: A new perspective in systemic therapy and consultation.* New York: W.W. Norton

Boscolo, L., Cecchin, G., Hoffman, L., and Penn, P. (1987). *Milan systemic family therapy: Conversations in theory and practice.* New York: Basic Books.

Burbatti, G. L. and Formenti, L. (1988). *The Milan approach to family therapy.* Northvale, NJ: Aronson.

Campbell, D. and Draper, R. (Eds.) (1985). *Applications of systemic family therapy: The Milan approach.* London: Grune and Stratton.

Campbell, D., Draper, R., and Crutchley, E. (1991). The Milan systemic approach to family therapy. In A. S. Gurman and D. P. Kniskern (Eds.), *Handbook of family therapy* (Volume II) (pp. 325-362). New York: Brunner/Mazel.

Cecchin, G. (1987). Hypothesizing, circularity, and neutrality revisited: An invitation to curiosity. *Family Process, 26,* 405-413.

Cecchin, G., Lane, G., and Ray, W. (1993). From strategizing to nonintervention: Toward irreverence in systemic practice. *Journal of Marital and Family Therapy, 19,* 125-136.

Fisch, R. (1978). Review of problem solving therapy by Jay Haley. *Family Process, 17,* 107-110.

Friedlander, M. L., Wildman, J., and Heatherington, L. (1991). Interpersonal control in structural and Milan systemic family therapy. *Journal of Marital and Family Therapy, 17,* 395-408.

Gelcer, E., McCabe, A. E., and Smith-Resnick, C. (1990). *Milan family therapy: Variant and invariant methods.* Northvale, NJ: Aronson.

Goldenberg, I. and Goldenberg, H. (2000). *Family therapy* (Fifth edition). Belmont, CA: Wadsworth.

Hoffman, L. (1985). Beyond power and control: Toward a second-order family systems therapy. *Family Systems Medicine, 3,* 381-396.

Imber-Black, E. (1988). *Families and larger systems: A family therapist's guide through the labyrinth.* New York: Guilford Press.

Jackson, D. (1967). The myth of normality. *Medical Opinion and Review, 3*(11), 110-114.

Jones, E. (1993). *Family systems therapy: Developments in the Milan-Systemic therapies.* New York: Wiley.

Marshal, M., Feldman, R. B., and Sigal, J. J. (1989). The unraveling of a treatment paradigm. A follow-up study of the Milan approach to family therapy. *Family Process, 28,* 457-470.

Nichols, M. P. and Schwartz, R. C. (2001). *Family therapy* (Fifth edition). Boston: Allyn and Bacon.

Papp, P. (1983). *The process of change.* New York: Guilford Press.

Penn, P. (1982). Circular questioning. *Family Process, 21,* 267-280.

Penn, P. (1985). Feed-forward: Future questions, future maps. *Family Process, 24,* 299-310.

Pinsof, W. M., Wynne, L. C., and Hambright, A. B. (1996). The outcomes of couple and family therapy: Findings, conclusions, and recommendations. *Psychotherapy, 33,* 321-331.

Prata, G. (1990). *A systemic harpoon into family games: Preventive interventions in therapy.* New York: Bruner/Mazel.

Seltzer, L. F. (1986). *Paradoxical strategies in psychotherapy: A comprehensive overview and guidebook.* New York: Wiley.

Selvini Palazzoli, M. (1974). *Self-starvation.* London: Human Context Books.

Selvini Palazzoli, M. (1978). *Self-starvation.* New York: Aronson.

Selvini Palazzoli, M. (1980). Why a long interval between sessions? The therapeutic control of the family-therapist suprasystem. In M. Andolfi and I. Zwerling (Eds.), *Dimensions of family therapy.* New York: Guilford Press.

Selvini Palazzoli, M. (1986). Towards a general model of psychotic family games. *Journal of Marital and Family Therapy, 12,* 339-349.

Selvini Palazzoli, M., Boscolo, L., Cecchin, G., and Prata, G. (1974). The treatment of children through brief therapy of their parents. *Family Process, 13,* 429-442.

Selvini Palazzoli, M., Boscolo, L., Cecchin, G. F., and Prata, G. (1978). *Paradox and counterparadox: A new model in the therapy of the family in schizophrenic transaction.* New York: Aronson.

Selvini Palazzoli, M., Boscolo, L., Cecchin, G. F., and Prata, G. (1980). Hypothesizing—circularity—neutrality: Three guidelines for the conductor of the session. *Family Process, 19,* 3-12.

Selvini Palazzoli, M., Cirillo, S., Selvini, M., and Sorrentino, A. M. (1989). *Family games: General models of psychotic processes in the family.* New York: W.W. Norton.

Shadish, W. R., Ragsdale, K., Glaser, R. R., and Montgomery, L. M. (1995). The efficacy and effectiveness of marital and family therapy. A perspective from meta-analysis. *Journal of Marital and Family Therapy, 21,* 345-360.

Simon, R. (1987). Goodbye paradox, hello invariant prescription: An interview with Mara Selvini-Palazzoli. *Family Therapy Networker, 11*(5), 16-33.

Slovik, L. S. and Griffith, J. L. (1992). The current face of family therapy. In J. S. Rutan (Ed.), *Psychotherapy for the 1990s.* New York: Guilford Press.

Tomm, K. M. (1984a). One perspective on the Milan approach: Part I. Overview of development, theory, and practice. *Journal of Marital and Family Therapy, 10,* 113-125.

Tomm, K. M. (1984b). One perspective on the Milan approach: Part II. Description of session format, interviewing style, and interventions. *Journal of Marital and Family Therapy, 10,* 253-271.

Tomm, K. M. (1987a). Interventive interviewing: Part I. Strategizing as a fourth guideline for the therapist. *Family Process, 26,* 3-13.

Tomm, K. (1987b). Interventive interviewing: Part II. Reflexive questioning as a means to enable self-healing. *Family Process, 26,* 167-183.

Tomm, K. (1988). Interventive interviewing: Part III. Intending to ask lineal, circular, strategic, or reflexive questions? *Family Process, 27,* 1-15.

Watzlawick, P., Beavin, J. H., and Jackson, D. D. (1967). *Pragmatics of human communication.* New York: W.W. Norton.

Chapter 6

The Collaborative Language-Based Models of Family Therapy: When Less Is More

Anne Rambo

All versions are neither right nor wrong. Our task is as much as possible to engage in a dialogue in order to understand how the various persons came to create their descriptions and their explanations. Thereafter, we invite them to a dialogue to discuss whether there might be other not yet seen descriptions, and maybe even other explanations not yet thought of. . . . The appropriate unusual questions are our best contributions. (Andersen, 1990, p. 52)

INTRODUCTION

In this chapter, reflexive family therapy (both languaging and reflecting models), solution-oriented family therapy, and narrative family therapy will be discussed. Together, these models of family therapy are the collaborative language-based models of family therapy. They are also sometimes called **postmodern** (Anderson, 1997) or **social constructionist** models (Hoyt, 1994), because they posit that agreed-upon cultural realities develop through conversation, and that different individuals and cultural groups may perceive reality very differently. Therapists working in these models consider all possible points of view and do not assume there is one "correct" reality.

The collaborative language-based models of family therapy are above all collaborative and conversational. They affect not just how family therapists work with clients, but how they work with colleagues and within the larger mental health system as well. These models have in common a philosophical stance that values respect for multiple realities, and focuses on **client-directed outcomes**. This gentle, collaborative approach will tend to affect how therapists converse with colleagues as well as how they converse with therapy clients.

149

HISTORY AND BASIC ASSUMPTIONS

The Galveston Connection

It will be apparent that the collaborative language-based models of family therapy are indebted to the earlier school of MRI therapy, with its focus on **nonpathologizing** and **multiple realities** (as discussed in Chapter 4). In addition, these models share a common connection to the Galveston Family Institute, now restructured slightly and known as the Houston Galveston Institute.

The **Galveston Family Institute** was founded by Harry Goolishian and his associates (Anderson, 1997; Sherman, 1992). Goolishian was present for the very beginnings of family therapy. He became interested in family therapy during the 1950s, as a young psychology student completing his internship at the University of Texas at Galveston Medical School clinic (Harry Goolishian, personal communication, September 15,1989). One of his therapy clients was a man who was seeking treatment because of what he described as his nagging, domineering wife. Goolishian saw this man individually for some time and felt very sympathetic toward him, suffering as the client did with such a difficult family life. One of Goolishian's friends and fellow interns was seeing the client's wife, also in individual therapy. In those days, it would have been seen as a breach of confidentiality to see the husband and wife together, or even for the two therapists to compare notes. But when his friend went on vacation, and his friend's client called in a crisis, Goolishian could not resist satisfying his curiosity by meeting with his friend's client—his client's wife—just to see what she was like in person. He was very surprised to find that he liked her just as much as he liked his own client, and that she had other ways of describing their marital problems that made just as much sense. Goolishian began to meet with both husband and wife. He had to do this secretly, because if his supervisor had known he was doing this he would have been fired from his internship. Many of the founding family therapists took risks such as this; it can be difficult to realize today, when it is so accepted, how controversial family therapy was in the beginning. At first, Goolishian wanted to find out which person was "right," the husband or the wife; he still thought there would be one correct way of understanding what was going on between them. However, after a while, he formulated the idea of multiple realities.

Goolishian participated in a research project called the **Multiple Impact Therapy Project** in 1954, also at the University of Texas Medical Branch at Galveston (UTMB at Galveston) (Anderson, 1997). This project was directed by Albert Serrano, MD, and experimented with assigning each member of a troubled family his or her own therapist for an intensive individual session. Over a period of days, each therapist met with the other therapists, and finally all the therapists and all the family members met together. This project also came to emphasize multiple realities.

Although he continued working at UTMB at Galveston with the research project after his graduation, eventually Goolishian wanted to explore family therapy in a less constraining environment. In 1977, together with Harlene Anderson, Paul Dell, and George Pulliam, he founded the Galveston Family Institute. Dell eventually left the institute, but Pulliam and Anderson remain. After Goolishian's death in 1991, Anderson became director. It was renamed the **Houston Galveston Institute** in the late 1980s because by that time most of its office locations were in Houston rather than Galveston, and because the term *family* misled people who did not understand that the institute also consulted with individuals, couples, and even organizations (personal communication, Harlene Anderson, September 19, 1989).

The Galveston Family Institute (GFI) was in an interesting position throughout the 1970s and 1980s, as one of the few training centers for family therapy located between the two coasts. GFI trained many people and became a stopping-off place for family therapists who were touring the United States and wanting to experience the heartland as well as the East or West Coast (Sherman, 1992). Goolishian and his colleagues were particularly influenced by, and an influence on, Bradford Keeney (who shared his ideas about the importance of nonpathologizing while in Texas teaching at Texas Tech University), Luigi Boscolo and Gianfranco Cecchin (two of the founding members of the Milan team, who were frequent visitors to GFI during the 1980s), and Tom Andersen (a Norwegian family therapist whose work remains very closely tied with the work of the Houston Galveston Institute and will be discussed in this chapter). In addition, Goolishian corresponded with John Weakland of the Mental Research Institute. Being close to a large university as they were, the GFI staff were also influenced by developments in other fields, such as the physicist Ilya Prigogine and his groundbreaking work while at the University of Texas on the **dissipative nature of structures** (Anderson, 1997).

Out of all these influences, the GFI group evolved its own unique model of family therapy, which they call **collaborative language systems** or sometimes just **languaging.** They see the central change process in psychotherapy as a dialogical one, believing that problems naturally **dissipate through conversation** or in responsive dialogue. The task of the therapist, then, becomes to

- maintain a **not-knowing stance** (do not be the "expert" on the client's problem; let the client tell you what it is really like);
- embrace the **client's reality** (believe and trust in what the client says, even when it does not initially seem to make sense);
- ask **conversational** questions (keep the dialogue going); and
- listen responsively (provide plenty of affirmation and encouragement so that the client feels heard and understood. GFI therapists also talk about this as honoring the **client's story**).

Closely related to the GFI model of family therapy (which is also, as you can see, applicable to individuals and couples) is the work of Tom Andersen in Norway (1990, 1999), and Lynn Hoffman (1993) in Amherst, Massachusetts. Andersen adds a formal **reflecting team** to his work with families. The reflecting team format involves having a team of therapists observing behind a one-way mirror while a therapist works with a family in the therapy room. Such teams were a feature of the Milan school of family therapy, with whom Andersen trained (notice the link with Boscolo and Cecchin, and so with GFI) and are also common in family therapy training and research facilities. Andersen's innovation was to share the team discussions with the family. In a classic, Andersen-derived reflecting team format, a therapist converses with a family in the therapy room, while a team of other therapists observes silently behind a one-way mirror. The therapist confines himself or herself primarily to conversational questions and lets the family talk, while the observing therapists hold their comments until they can be shared with the family. At a specified time, usually midway through the session, the team behind the mirror changes places with the therapist and family. Then the therapist and family watch the team that has been observing as they comment freely on what they have noticed, careful only to keep their comments affirming and nonpathologizing. The family and therapist then trade again to their original positions, and the therapist invites the family to comment on what was useful to them about the discussion and what ideas they might like to pursue. This format is seen as less invasive and therefore more consistent with the not-knowing stance, while still allowing the therapeutic team to introduce some new ideas to the family. In this way, those ideas do not come directly from the therapist, and the family is free to pick and choose the ideas that appeal to them.

Hoffman has adapted this format for use in a less formal way, at times turning to a cotherapist to reflect in the presence of the family during the middle of the session. Hoffman has also emphasized a broader use of self-disclosure than has been normative in family therapy, calling for increased openness on the part of the therapist. It is Hoffman who coined the term **re-**

flexive therapy to describe her work, the work of her colleague William Lax in Brattleboro, Andersen's reflecting team work, and the work of the GFI—Anderson and Goolishian in particular (Hoffman, 1993). Reflexive here means the use of the formal reflecting team, but also includes informal **in-session reflections** among therapists and between therapist and client, the use of **self-disclosure,** and the commitment to affirming, accepting, nonpathologizing dialogue.

Review and Summary

Drawing and expanding on the MRI tradition, the Galveston Family Institute developed a model of family therapy that emphasizes dissipating problems through **dialogue.** Influenced by the work of the Galveston Family Institute, Tom Andersen in Norway and Lynn Hoffman in Massachusetts have added additional **reflecting** components to their practices. The work of the Galveston Family Institute—especially the work done by its two directors Harry Goolishian and Harlene Anderson—along with Andersen's work and Hoffman's work is collectively known as the reflexive model of family therapy.

Related Models: Solution-Focused and Narrative Therapies

Two other models of family therapy also emphasize collaboration and nonpathologizing. These are the solution-focused and narrative models of family therapy.

Solution-Focused Therapy

Solution-focused therapy is quite similar to MRI therapy (see Chapter 4) but with additional influence from Milton Erickson. Hypnotherapist Erickson was a major influence on the early communication research of the Palo Alto Project and later on the development of MRI. In the early 1980s, two young therapists began corresponding about integrating still more of Erickson's work into their practice (visit <www.possibilitycenter.com> and <http://www.brief-therapy.org>). They were Steve de Shazer, who had been trained by John Weakland at MRI, and Bill O'Hanlon, who had studied directly with Milton Erickson. Together with his wife Insoo Kim Berg at the **Brief Family Therapy Center** in Milwaukee, Wisconsin, de Shazer came up with the term *solution-focused therapy.* In this model of therapy, the therapist begins by embracing the client's reality about the problem, but then starts to shift that reality to its hidden opposite, the absence of the problem.

In other words, if a client comes in complaining that he and his wife frequently quarrel, the solution-focused therapist will draw the client's attention to the times the two do *not* quarrel and what is different about those times. (Certain specific techniques for doing this will be discussed.) In hypnotherapy, the client's attention is shifted to where the hypnotherapist wants it to go. This is why the solution-focused model borrows more from hypnotherapy than from the original MRI model. Other important solution-focused therapists are Yvonne Dolan (1994) and Eve Lipchik (1993), who expanded the model to the difficult areas of recovery from traumatic abuse and domestic violence (respectively), and Scott Miller (1994), who with Insoo Kim Berg expanded the model to the area of alcohol abuse and now concentrates on therapy outcome research in this area (Hubble, Duncan, and Miller, 1999).

O'Hanlon originally called his similar model **solution-oriented therapy** but now, to avoid confusion, calls it **possibility therapy.** He also shifts the client's attention away from the problem to the absence of the problem, but in addition he widens the conversation to include social, political, and cultural forces. (**Narrative therapy** also does this, as will be discussed.) For example, if a client came in complaining about his quarrels with his wife, O'Hanlon would shift the conversation to the times the husband and wife do *not* quarrel, but would also possibly raise the issue of what in the client's cultural background led him to think that quarreling was always negative or was not supposed to happen in marriage. Michele Weiner-Davis is a well-known solution-oriented therapist who has worked with both de Shazer and O'Hanlon, and whose work goes a step further in actively encouraging the client to **focus on the positives** about his or her marriage, even when the client does not want to talk about those positive at first. (Her agenda is clear in the title of her best selling 1992 book *Divorce Busting.*) Ben Furman and Tapani Ahola (1994), in contrast, take a less directive but still solution-oriented approach, blending solution talk and elements of reflexive family therapy in their native Finland.

Review and summary. Solution-focused and solution-oriented or possibility therapy redirect the client's attention away from the presenting problem toward the absence of that problem. They do this through techniques that borrow from hypnotherapy. They share with the MRI and the reflexive models an emphasis on **collaboration,** nonpathologizing, and change through dialogue, but they are more directive in their solution focus.

Case Examples. Working from published case studies, we can see the similarities and differences between the models in practice. For example, when a mother sought treatment from Ben Furman and Tapani Ahola, mentioning that she did not always feel competent to set limits with her four-year-old, they asked her to visualize the times when she did feel competent and give that experience a name (Furman and Ahola, 1994). In contrast, when Harlene Anderson (1997) consulted with a client who was also feeling guilty about being a bad mother, she would have found this approach too directive. She instead commiserated with the client and mused aloud about the difficulty of figuring children out. However, she limited herself to this kind of **curious stance** and reflection, and avoided giving the client any direct suggestions. She expected that the problem would eventually dissipate through dialogue.

Narrative Therapy

In the late 1980s, therapists Michael White and David Epston were trying to adapt the family therapy theory they had learned from MRI and the Milan team to their practices in Australia (White and Epston, 1989). The politics of therapy in Australia and New Zealand are particularly compelling, as the oppression of the native Australian Aborigine and New Zealand Maori peoples by the European settlers of Australia and New Zealand is in the quite recent past, and too present in memory to allow for therapists, especially those of European descent, to embrace their client's reality without discussing these larger political issues, especially when the client is of Aborigine or Maori descent. It may be that we are naive in the United States to think that European-American therapists can work with Native American or African-American clients without discussing issues of historical oppression, and this has been suggested (Hardy and Laszloffy, 1995); be that as it may, it was the Australian and New Zealand schools of family therapy which first made such discussions a cornerstone of their therapy. White and Epston argued that in order to truly embrace the client's reality, the family therapist must bring into the conversation larger issues of **historical oppression,** including issues of language, culture, historical persecution, and gender and economic inequities (White and Epston, 1989; White, 1991). They reiterated the emphasis of the early MRI on nonpathologizing, adding an additional technique, **externalizing,** to help meet this goal. They moved away from giving directives, preferring to concentrate on hearing the client's story. White and Epston with their model of narrative therapy established the **Dulwich Centre** in Australia and have been influential in the United States as well. Jeffrey Zimmerman and Victoria Dickerson (1994) saw the possibilities in this approach for more fully embracing the client's reality, and have explored narrative therapy while on the teaching faculty of MRI. Also in California, at Berkeley, Jennifer Freeman and Dean Lobovits combine narrative therapy with expressive play therapy, and David Epston is visiting faculty when not in Australia (Freeman, Epston, and Lobovits, 1997).

Stephen Madigan and Heather Elliott, both graduates of the Nova Southeastern University family therapy program, formed the influential **Yaletown Family Therapy Centre** in Canada after their graduation. Narrative therapy spoke strongly to Madigan in part because of his father's background as a labor union organizer (personal communication, Stephen Madigan, March 15, 1999). Madigan has been active in the Canada branch of the **Anti-Anorexia League,** an informal union of young women diagnosed with anorexia that allows them to offer one another support and comfort against what is seen as a politically oppressive cultural focus on weight and appearance (Madigan, 1994). Similar leagues operate in New Zealand and Finland. Elliott draws on her interest in feminism to encourage clients to explore less oppressive gender-related life stories for themselves (Elliott, 1998).

Narrative therapists use **deconstructing questions** and **unique outcomes** to broaden the **conversation** into social, political, and cultural areas. They also use externalizing to further guard against pathologizing. These specific narrative techniques will be discussed further in the Techniques section.

Review and summary. Similar to reflexive therapy and solution-focused/possibility therapy, the narrative therapy model emphasizes nonpathologizing, embracing the client's reality, and change through conversation. Narrative therapists' emphasis on the importance of the **client's voice,** however, leads them to avoid explicit directives. They may shift the conversation to the absence of the problem, as do solution-focused therapists, but they do so in a particular way (through unique outcomes, which differ slightly from the solution-focused therapist's exceptions). They differ from reflexive therapists in that they will introduce into the conversation issues of gender, politics, and culture, even if the client does not bring up these issues or seem to want to pursue them.

Case examples. Earlier, case examples featuring Anderson (1997) and Furman and Ahola (1994) were discussed. Both cases involved clients who were concerned that they might not be competent mothers. You may wonder why it seems that many clients are mothers who feel guilty; narrative therapists would explicitly address that commonality. When Zimmerman and Dickerson (1994) saw such a client, they explicitly commented on how often mothers get blamed for their children's behavior in Western culture, and cautioned the client: "A lot of parents get sucked into the notion that they're to blame for this. I don't know if you've tortured yourself with this. I hope not. I run into that a lot" (p. 310), thus broadening the conversation to consider maternal guilt as a cultural theme.

Joseph Eron and Thomas Lund (1996) integrate elements of traditional MRI work with narrative therapy. Gene Combs and Jill Freedman (1994) integrate some solution-focused aspects into their narrative approach. Jennifer Freeman (Freeman, Epston, and Lobovits, 1997) has developed a narrative play therapy approach. Thus the narrative innovation has inspired considerable creativity. To fall under the narrative umbrella, an approach needs to remain embracing of the client's reality and fundamentally nonpathologizing, while incorporating an attentiveness to the sociocultural context.

CONSTRAINTS AND LIMITATIONS

Because there is no one correct reality, none of these models can be considered the one correct model of therapy. By and large, therapists working within the collaborative language-based models are consistent with their philosophy in that they will freely admit that their particular model can be imperfect, limited, and applicable only when it fits the client. Beginning therapists trying one or more of these models of therapy tend to experience difficulties in the following areas in particular.

Social Control Issues

Although the client's reality is paramount in these models, the client's reality may be at variance with what is culturally and legally permissible. At times, therapists become agents of **social control.** For example, a parent convinced of the need to discipline his or her child by beating the child with a belt poses a difficulty for the collaborative language-based therapist. This difficulty is typically raised in one or more of three ways. First, an outside agency may be invoked. For example, if child welfare authorities are involved, the client may be reminded that such discipline techniques are not legal and invited to consider alternatives, with the goal of ending child welfare's involvement in the client's life. (This is usually very much a goal of the client.) Second, particularly if no outside agency is presently involved, the therapist may need to make what Lynn Hoffman (1993) calls a **citizen's protest.** In other words, the client may be told that although the therapist understands how this behavior makes sense to the client, as a person and a citizen the therapist cannot approve of this behavior and must indeed report it if legally mandated to do so. Third, particularly after the issue of outside social control is settled, or if the behavior is objectionable but not immediately dangerous or illegal, the therapist may use deconstructing and **curious**

questions to lead the client to question the behavior on his or her own. For example, Harry Goolishian used to defuse potentially explosive child welfare referred situations by simply asking the client, "Leaving aside for the moment whether or not it was legal, was the method of discipline you were using [before the child welfare involvement] working? Did you feel that your child was really listening to you?" Typically, physically abusive parents are also frustrated parents. In Goolishian's experience, this question was always answered with a resounding "*No,* it wasn't. My child doesn't listen," which then opened up other avenues of conversation (personal communication, Harry Goolishian, September 15, 1989).

Strongly Held Therapist Values and Beliefs

It can be difficult to listen openly to clients whose worldview differs dramatically from your own. Therapists working in these collaborative language-based models certainly have their own cherished beliefs and convictions. It is neither necessary nor desirable to abandon these beliefs. It is necessary, however, to hold as an equally cherished conviction the idea that listening nonjudgmentally can be a healing experience for therapist and client alike. When faced with a client whose particular ideas are abhorrent, a beginning therapist should try to understand: how does it happen that this worldview makes sense to the client? Where would the client have gotten such ideas? Are there times the client thinks in other ways? This curiosity is both a fundamental value and a key technique for these models of therapy. It is also worth noting that at times the therapist may need to make a citizen's protest to ease his or her own discomfort in the room. As Tom Andersen notes, the therapist should not be the dominant voice in the room, but neither should the therapist feel silenced as a person, any more than the client should (Andersen, 1990). All voices should be valued in the therapy room. Beginning therapists, however, are usually wise to err on the side of listening, as it is easy for the therapist's voice to be overvalued and to unwittingly silence the client.

NORMAL FAMILY DEVELOPMENT

The question of normative individual and family development is an interesting one for the collaborative language-based models. It should be clear by now that a rigid set of "correct" life stages, predetermined by the therapist, would be not in keeping with the nonpathologizing stance of these models and with the focus on multiple realities. Some reflexive family therapists go so far as to discount the entire notion of development: Hoffman

(1993) states that to posit a predetermined developmental path within any human group or for any human individual dangerously downplays both individuality and the role of chaos (random chance). However, more recently narrative family therapists have offered rite-of-passage suggestions for life passages common within a particular culture, embracing the client's perceived transitions. Freeman, Epston, and Lobovits (1997) envision coming-of-age and graduation ceremonies created by the extended family and **published** with the therapist's help. However, any concept of "norms" and "stages" for the collaborative language-based therapist must be tempered with a respect for the client's perceptions and for the possibility of multiple interpretations.

PATHOLOGY AND BEHAVIOR DISORDERS

Diagnosis that describes the client in a way with which the client has not agreed is anathema to collaborative language-based therapists. It is on this topic that they write most passionately, and are most willing to separate from their fellow family therapists. A few examples will suffice to establish the deep distrust with which diagnosis is regarded. (The first comment points out the strongest underlying bond between MRI and collaborative language-based therapies, their mutual dislike of the expert "diagnostic" role.)

- John Weakland (Weakland, de Shazer, and Hoyt, 1994): "It's [MRI therapy] a helluva lot more respectful than knowing better than the client what ails them, which I think is the most basic comparison. And that's what the whole damn other psychiatric and psychotherapeutic scheme is based on." (p. 24)
- Harlene Anderson (1997): "To my way of thinking, a problem does not have a cause that needs to be discovered; it does not need to be diagnosed, labeled, fixed, resolved, or solved . . . the traditional diagnostic processes and categories are of little use." (p. 76)
- Ben Furman and Tapani Ahola (1994): "The term *depression* can be used to refer to the condition known in psychiatry as *major depression,* but there are many alternatives, such as *down in the dumps* or *feeling blue.* It is possible to develop even more inventive names, such as *doing one's life inventory, hatching,* or *latent joy* . . . perhaps we should start by giving this problem a nice optimistic name." (pp. 42-43)
- Jeffrey Zimmerman and Victoria Dickerson (1994): "[Therapists and clients] have been subjected to normalizing judgments, and evaluated

as objects . . . furthermore, anorexia (and other psychiatric diagnoses) seems to reflect many of the techniques of power that are in evidence when one group dominates another: techniques of isolation, evaluation (through surveillance and comparison), and promotion of a lack of entitlement to one's own experience." (p. 295)

A dislike and distrust of conventional psychiatric diagnosis is found across the collaborative language-based models. Yet given their emphasis on collaboration, these therapists are often also not comfortable giving up the possibility of collaborating with physicians and other mental health professionals who do use diagnosis (Anderson, 1997). Also, as Lynn Hoffman sagely points out, even reflexive family therapists need to get paid (Gergen, Hoffman, and Anderson, 1996) and diagnosis is a requirement of insurance companies. The resulting uneasy accommodations are a frequent topic of discussion among collaborative language-based family therapists.

TECHNIQUES

The following techniques are common to all the collaborative language-based models.

1. *Maintaining a curious stance:* It may seem strange to think of curiosity as a technique, but the ability to keep an open mind and convey genuine interest in what the client has to say is central to keeping a collaborative conversation going. A good therapist working in this model, when confronted with a comment or a behavior he or she does not understand, will continue asking questions until understanding is achieved. This is sometimes referred to as the not-knowing position, meaning that the therapist does not act as if he or she knows more than the client, but as if what the client has to say is truly fascinating and the therapist's best source of information. This is consistent with a nonpathologizing approach, which downplays diagnosis and therapist evaluations of the client.

2. *Conveying respect for the **client's own resources:*** Equally central to these models is the ability to convey that the therapist and client are a team, working together to meet the client's goals. Even in the more directive models, the client should experience therapy as a partnership, not as receiving instruction from an authority figure. The therapist conveys respect for the client's goals, and for the client's ability to solve problems, and uses the client's language whenever possible.

3. *Asking engaging questions:* To keep the collaborative conversation going, the therapist must ask interesting questions that "invite a client into a

shared inquiry" (Anderson, 1997, p. 145). These questions should come from a genuinely curious, not-knowing perspective. These questions should also utilize the client's language.

4. *Affirming and conveying hope:* A long string of questions with no comments can begin to seem like an interrogation, not at all what the collaborative therapist wants to convey. To guard against this, to build hope for change, and to create a healing therapeutic space for conversation, the collaborative therapist is generous with what Lynn Hoffman (1993) calls the "three A's": affirmation, affiliation, and appreciation. The therapist avoids blame and negativity, and frequently points out examples of the client's progress, hard work, and/or courage in struggling with life difficulties. When it is possible to interpret a client's action in several different ways, the collaborative therapist will choose to interpret the action in the most positive way. For example, Furman and Ahola (1994), consulting with a teenage boy whose parents disapprove of his friends, suggest that the boy is trying to help his more delinquent buddies, rather than that he is descending to their level.

In addition to these basic skills common to all the collaborative models, some techniques are specific to each of the models discussed in this chapter.

1. *Reflexive therapists reflect.* That is, they constantly wonder about their own thinking, as well as the client's, and they share their thoughts and reactions with the client on an ongoing basis (being careful to stay consistent with an affirming context).

2. *Solution-focused therapists look for* **exceptions.** That is, they direct their own attention and the client's attention to the times when the client is *not* experiencing the problem. Their way of being affirming includes conveying great optimism about these exceptions. To this end, *solution-focused therapists typically ask the* **miracle question**—"What if you woke up one morning and the problem was gone?"—to get the focus on the positive as quickly as possible. They may also use **scaling questions,** asking the client to rate the intensity of the problem from one to ten, in order to track even small progress from session to session, and so expand upon it.

4. *Narrative therapists ask deconstructing questions.* That is, they ask questions (and make comments) designed to draw the client's attention to larger social and cultural issues. In addition, *narrative therapists externalize,* meaning that they are careful to talk about the problem as a thing apart from the person of the client. For example, a client diagnosed with anorexia would be asked how the anorexia was terrorizing him or her (Zimmerman and Dickerson, 1994) to underline the point that the diagnosis is *not* the client, but rather an annoying (or terrorizing) outsider. *Narrative therapists also look for exceptions, which they call unique outcomes.* The difference is

that the narrative therapist prefers unique outcomes that are exceptions to larger social and cultural patterns also, while the solution-focused therapist is content with any identified exception (Elliott, 1998). For example, a wife may notice that she and her husband fight less about housework when she calmly but firmly asserts her belief that housework should be shared, but that they also fight less when she gives up and hires outside cleaning help. Either exception will work for the solution-focused therapist, but the narrative therapist would typically prefer the first of these two exceptions (and would label it a unique outcome).

In summary, it is worth stressing that all of these auxiliary techniques rely on the central techniques of *respect for the client's own resources, affirming,* and *conveying hope,* as well as the conversational skills of *maintaining curiosity* and *asking engaging questions.* Research suggests that these central techniques, "low tech" as they may seem, are actually the most effective interventions of all (Hubble, Duncan, and Miller, 1999).

RELEVANT RESEARCH

Research on these collaborative models falls into four general areas:

1. *Case studies,* in which each individual case is viewed as its own research project and compared only with itself. Not surprisingly, this is the preferred research methodology of both reflexive and narrative family therapists, as it allows them to avoid a focus on any specific outcome than the moment-to-moment one the client desires, to focus on the client's individual story, and to avoid putting clients into categories. This approach has led to a rich library of case histories and videotapes (Anderson, 1997). However, generalizations are next to impossible, and ultimate interpretation depends on the viewer—as Combs and Freedman (1994) comment, "Our colleagues, guided by different metaphors, did not see or hear [our] tape as we did" (p. 68).

2. *Ongoing outcome surveys,* in which the clients of a particular center are periodically surveyed to determine their satisfaction with services. Clients are generally asked if their problem has gone away or lessened, and if they were pleased with the services received. Following in the footsteps of the original MRI Brief Therapy Project, the Brief Family Therapy Center in Milwaukee, the originating point of solution-focused therapy, has kept such records, and now reports an average of around 80 percent of clients with problems resolved satisfactorily after six months.

3. *Controlled outcome studies:* Considered the most valuable evidence for efficacy by most funding sources, these have been in short supply for the collaborative language-based models and are somewhat at variance with the

premises of the models. However, the outcome focus of solution-focused therapy makes it the most likely candidate for study using this method, and the recent intense interest in solution-focused therapy has indeed resulted in a small but significant number of traditional double-blind experimental research studies in which solution-focused approaches were compared with a control group or with another form of treatment, and the outcome was evaluated not by the client but by the researcher, using preestablished criteria. Fifteen of these studies were reviewed by Gingerich and Eisengart (2000). Of the fifteen research studies, one did not clearly report posttreatment results for either group; thirteen reported positive outcomes for the group receiving solution-focused therapy; and only one did not report positive results. The study without positive outcomes used high school guidance counselors given only very minimal training in solution-focused therapy who may thus have been less than clear on the techniques to be used. Of the thirteen studies that did report positive outcomes, eleven permitted a comparison between solution-focused and other models of family therapy. In seven of these eleven studies, solution-focused therapy resulted in either more positive results or equally positive results in less time than the comparison method. Thus, solution-focused therapy has received recent empirical support.

4. *Research across all models,* which at present provides indirect support for collaborative language-based models. The trio of Scott Miller, Barry Duncan, and Mark Hubble have taken a leading role in the family therapy field in systematically investigating factors in successful therapy outcome (Duncan, Hubble, and Miller, 1997; Hubble, Duncan, and Miller, 1999). The three factors they (and other outcome researchers such as Lambert and Bergin [1994]) identify as most significant are

- *extratherapeutic factors*—the client's own resources;
- *relationship with the therapist*—the client feels validated and affirmed in the therapy context; and
- *expectancy*—the degree of hope generated by the therapy process.
- *The technique of the therapist* is also a factor, but a far less significant one. This finding fits nicely with the beliefs of collaborative therapists, who have long stressed respect for the client's own resources, affirmation, and conveying hope.

5. *Client-directed outcome research:* Most recently, Barry Duncan and colleagues have begun a large-scale outcome research project, utilizing both quantitative and qualitative measures, which uses clients as coinvestigators, thus combining all four of the previously noted research areas (Duncan

et al., 2000). Early results have been promising, as clients are able to identify salient factors in their own progress and fold this back into their therapy.

CASE EXAMPLE

I saw Linda through our university-run ChildFit program, a program specifically for parents who are having difficulty relating to their child's schoolteachers and administrators, and/or to their child about school. Broward County, the county in which Nova Southeastern University is located, is the fifth-largest school district in the nation, and a most complex one. Reaching out to parents with school-age children as a group is a community-based intervention, influenced by faculty interest in narrative therapy and its social/cultural concerns. Linda was a beleaguered single mother who would not have come for the "luxury" of family therapy, had the ChildFit program not offered a chance for specific help in negotiating with her child's school. She was very distressed about her son's chronic truancy and, consistent with Florida law, had herself been threatened with jail time if she could not make him attend middle school on a more consistent basis.

She stated her problem succinctly. "I *have* to get my son in school," she explained. "He is fifteen, and the school district is saying I will be liable if I allow him to be truant. I agree; he ought to be in school. I don't much like the school we're zoned for, but I can't afford a private school. So he just has to go to this school! I've told him over and over. I've tried everything to make him—but he won't stay in school. I have to make him, but I can't."

The first intervention I made with Linda was simply to believe her. I did not assume she was at fault for her son disliking school, and I affirmed her hard work raising him as well as she had. I commiserated with her on the close to impossible bind she was in with the school system. This seems minor as I write it, yet it was what Linda most appreciated about therapy. For clients in general, and clients in distress in particular, the intense relief of being believed and affirmed is difficult to overestimate. The collaborative, reflexive training I received as a beginning therapist at what was then the Galveston Family Institute reminds me in every clinical situation to begin by affirming the client's reality.

With some ChildFit clients, that intervention alone would be enough. In Linda's case, in view of her crisis situation with respect to her son's truancy, I also broadened the conversation to include the larger social and cultural system. I invited her to consider how parents can be held responsible yet have little real authority. We discussed the growing home schooling movement, in which she was interested, and the changes in Florida law which now permit parents to take back control over their children's education. In nudging the conversation onto this path, I was following her interests yet also being influenced by the narrative therapy perspective.

Linda and I also identified what had worked for her in the past with her son. She preferred offering him alternatives, with each alternative carrying a clear, logical consequence. This parenting approach had worked for her up until this year, when faced with her son's skipping school. Under pressure from school authorities, she had resorted to techniques such as physically forcing him into her car, pouring water over his head to wake him up in the mornings, and other strategies that left them both upset and angry. These attempts had not worked and had left her feeling that her generally positive relationship with her son had been weakened. In asking questions about what had worked for her, I was using solution-focused therapy techniques. I also hoped to reawaken her memories of happier parenting days.

After our second session, Linda went home and outlined a clear choice for Charlie. First, she dramatically conceded, "Charlie, you are too big and I cannot force you to go to school." This opening remark compelled the boy's attention in a new and different way. Then she explained that if he wanted to be treated as an adult, that option was open to him. Under Florida law, once she notified the school board of her intention to home school Charlie, he would no longer be legally truant. As she pointed out, however, that would put the responsibility on her to guide and supervise Charlie's education and locate resources for him on the Internet. In return, she suggested, Charlie could begin to earn his own keep, helping her out more with household chores, and working in her home-based business. There would be, of course, the other alternative, she mentioned casually, that it would still be possible for Charlie to attend his local public school regularly. However, Charlie would need to attend daily or she would be forced to conclude that home schooling was the better option for him. Although I helped her consider alternatives, and encouraged her new ideas, this plan was entirely Linda's own. She let me know that she would call me if she needed more help, but that she felt comfortable with her plan. That was three months ago.

In a follow-up phone call recently, Linda told me that Charlie has not missed a day of school since, nor has he been late to school in the past three months. In fact, she now goes out to her health club in the early morning, knowing she can count on Charlie to get himself up to catch the school bus. The days of her frantic involvement with his morning schedule are over. As she commented, "The important thing is just to know that, as a parent, you do have choices. The parent is the one with the big picture, the one who knows the child best. You helped me realize I really did know what I was doing after all."

In helping Linda feel newly empowered and respected, I drew on the training I received from the Galveston Family Institute, which continues to enrich my work with its emphasis on affirming clients. I enjoyed my work with Linda and feel privileged to have been a part of her experience for a while. This sense of productive partnership is perhaps the most rewarding aspect of practicing within the collaborative language-based family therapy models.

GLOSSARY

Anti-Anorexia League: A group of clients organized by narrative therapists to support one another as they recover from eating disorders. The clients are viewed as supporting one another against a "sick" culture with unrealistic and undesirable ideals of femininity.

Brief Family Therapy Center: The clinic founded by Steve de Shazer and Insoo Kim Berg, considered a headquarters of solution-focused therapy in the United States. Its Web site is <www.brief-therapy.org>.

citizen's protest: Lynn Hoffman's idea about how to resolve social control issues in therapy.

client-directed outcomes: Treatment outcomes that fit with the client's goals, rather than being set by the therapist alone.

client's own resources: What collaborative language-based therapists like to focus on—the strengths and capabilities of the client, rather than any pathology or present difficulty.

client's reality: How the client understands the situation.

client's story: What the client wants the therapist to hear about the situation and about the client's life to date.

client's voice: The client's own unique perspective, which the client may be able to share only if assured the therapist will be supportive.

collaboration: Working together with one or more other people in such a way that everyone's ideas are valued and everyone puts forth the same or a similar amount of effort.

collaborative language systems: Those models of family therapy that focus on conversation and collaboration between therapist and client.

conversation: A verbal exchange in which at least two people share ideas and feelings in a mutually supportive atmosphere

conversational: One is conversational when one encourages a verbal exchange with another.

curious questions: Genuine, open requests for new information, not accusations or statements disguised as questions. (Example: "What did you do today?" may be a genuinely curious question; "Why didn't you mow the lawn as you promised?" is probably an accusation in disguise.)

curious stance: A collaborative therapist takes a curious stance; he or she genuinely want to find out the client's reality

deconstructing questions: These take apart assumptions in order to understand them better. When you ask yourself why you do something the way that you have always done it, you may for the first time realize you have choices and could do it differently.

dialogue: Genuine back-and-forth conversation between two or more people. A dialogical question encourages this.

dissipate through conversation: Reflexive therapists believe that talking about problems in a supportive atmosphere helps people to deconstruct those problems. The problems then dissolve, or dissipate, upon being examined, and the person realizes he or she has more options than was previously thought.

dissipative nature of structures: Structures in the natural world that tend to dissolve and reform over time, such as sand dunes on beaches.

Dulwich Centre: The clinic started by Michael White and David Epston, considered the headquarters of narrative family therapy in Australia. Its Web site is <www.dulwichcentre.com.au>.

exceptions: Times when the problem is not a problem. Identifying these times is a goal of solution-focused therapists.

externalizing: Talking about a problem in such a way that it is clear the problem is outside the person, not a part of the person. For example, if we externalize, we say that anger sometimes makes problems for Johnny, not that Johnny is an angry boy.

focus on the positives: Focus on what is working, rather than on what is not working; on the absence of the problem, not on the problem. This is a central tenet of solution-focused therapy.

Galveston Family Institute (GFI): The clinic started by Harry Goolishian, Harlene Anderson, Paul Dell, and George Pulliam, which has been a central influence on collaborative language systems models of family therapy. Its Web site is <www.neosoft.com/~hgi>.

historical oppression: Throughout the world, throughout time, certain groups of people have had unfair advantages compared to other groups. Women, people of color, the poor, members of minority religious groups, the disabled, and those who are seen as too different in any way, among others, have been disadvantaged, and narrative family therapists remind us to be sensitive to the resulting pain when we work with families.

Houston Galveston Institute: The present name of the Galveston Family Institute. Its Web site is <www/neosoft.com/~hgi>.

in-session reflections: When the therapist muses or wonders aloud, sharing his or her thoughts with the clients openly.

languaging: The name of the model of family therapy most associated with the Galveston Family Institute.

miracle question: "What would happen if a miracle occurred and the problem disappeared?" Asking this question is a favorite technique of solution-focused therapists, to shift the client's focus away from the problem.

Multiple Impact Therapy Project (1954): An early research project investigating the multiple realities within families. This project influenced the collaborative language-based models.

multiple realities: The philosophical idea that everyone sees the world a little differently and that everyone's point of view has validity.

narrative therapy: The name of the school of therapy most associated with the work of the Dulwich Centre and the Yaletown Family Therapy Center.

nonpathologizing: Avoiding labeling, demeaning, or patronizing your client, and focusing on the client's strengths instead.

not-knowing stance: Staying curious and not thinking you know all the answers.

possibility therapy: Bill O'Hanlon's variation on solution-focused therapy. Visit <www.possibilitycenter.com>.

postmodern: After the modern age; no longer thinking that science and technology have all the answers or that there will ever be definitive answers to life's mysteries. This is a philosophical term often used by academics.

published (-ing): When used by narrative therapists, this means publicizing and celebrating a client's triumphs, for example, mailing out a newsletter to everyone in the extended family announcing a child's improved grades.

reflecting: Wondering, thinking aloud, pondering in a curious way.

reflecting team: A technique of reflecting family therapists in which those who have been observing a therapy session from behind a one-way mirror come into the therapy room and share their thoughts in a nonjudgmental way.

reflexive therapy: The school of family therapy incorporating both languaging and reflecting family therapists.

scaling question(s): A technique of solution-focused family therapists. Clients are asked how bad the problem is, on a scale of one to ten (or how much improvement there has been), and then these numbers are compared later in therapy to help the client notice improvement. For example, the therapist might say, "Well, the school problem was an eight when you first came in, but this week you say it's down to a four. That's great progress!"

self-disclosure: In an appropriate way, the therapist reveals something about himself or herself to the client, perhaps that the therapist has struggled with similar problems.

social constructionist: The idea that one's view of the world is largely formed by one's context. As you grow, develop, and explore the world, the reality you experience is shaped through your conversations with those around you. Similar to the term *postmodern,* the term *social constructionist* is often used by family therapists as a reminder that there is more than one way to look at the world. However, while *postmodern* is primarily a term used by academics in the liberal arts, *social constructionist* is a term psychologists and sociologists are more likely to use.

social control: The duty of the therapist to act, even against the client's wishes, if such action is judged necessary to prevent suicide, homicide, child abuse, elder abuse, or other potentially dangerous behavior.

solution-focused therapy: The name of the model of family therapy most associated with the Brief Family Therapy Center.

solution-oriented therapy: Bill O'Hanlon's variation on solution-focused therapy. *See also* POSSIBILITY THERAPY.

unique outcomes: Times when the problem is not a problem, and the client is not being disadvantaged by historical oppression. Identifying these times is a key technique of narrative family therapists.

Yaletown Family Therapy Centre: An important narrative family therapy center in Canada. Its Web site is <www.yaletownfamilytherapy.com>.

BIBLIOGRAPHY

Andersen, T. (1990). *The reflecting team: Dialogues about the dialogues.* Broadstairs, Kent, United Kingdom: Borgmann Publishing.

Andersen, T. (1999). *The reflection of light and sound: Gecko #2.* Adelaide, Australia: Dulwich Centre Publications.

Anderson, H. (1997). *Conversation, language, and possibilities.* New York: Basic Books.

Combs, G. and Freedman, J. (1994). Narrative intentions. In Hoyt, M. (Ed.), *Constructive therapies* (pp. 67-91). New York: Guilford Press.

Dolan, Y. (1994). Solution focused therapy with a case of severe abuse. In Hoyt, M. (Ed.), *Constructive therapies* (pp. 276-294). New York: Guilford Press.

Duncan, B., Hubble, M., and Miller, S. (1997). *Psychotherapy with "impossible" cases: The efficient treatment of therapy veterans.* New York: W.W. Norton.

Duncan, B., Miller, S., Shilts, L., Sparks, J., Sara, C., Bishop, P., Coleman, S., Reynolds, L., Nedlin, M., Singer, M., and Krepps, J. (2000). The client as researcher and supervisor. In Duncan, B. and Miller, S. *The heroic client* (pp.175-191). San Francisco: Jossey-Bass.

Elliott, H. (1998). Ex-gendering distinctions: Postmodernism, feminism, and family therapy. In Madigan, S. and Law, I. (Eds.), *Praxis: Situating discourse, feminism, and politics in narrative therapies* (pp. 35-64). Vancouver: Yaletown Family Therapy Publications.

Eron, J. and Lund, T. (1996). *Narrative solutions in brief therapy*. New York: Guilford Press.

Freeman, J., Epston, D., and Lobovits, D. (1997). *Playful approaches to serious problems: Narrative therapy with children and their families*. New York: W.W. Norton.

Furman, B. and Ahola, T. (1994). Solution talk: The solution oriented way of talking about problems. In Hoyt, M. (Ed.), *Constructive therapies* (pp. 41-66). New York: Guilford Press.

Gergen, K., Hoffman, L., and Anderson, H. (1996). Is diagnosis a disaster? A constructionist trialogue. In Kaslow, F. (Ed.), *Handbook of relational diagnosis and dysfunctional family patterns.* Retrieved in original draft form (before editorial revisions, direct from authors) February 1, 2000, online <http://www. california.com/~rathbone/pmth.htm>.

Gingerich, W. and Eisengart, S. (2000). Solution focused brief therapy: A review of the outcome research. *Family Process, 39,* 477-498.

Hardy, K. and Laszloffy, T. (1995). The cultural genogram: A key to training culturally competent family therapists. *Journal of Marital and Family Therapy, 21,* 227-237.

Hoffman, L. (1993). *Exchanging voices: A collaborative approach to family therapy.* London: Karnac Books.

Hoyt, M. (1994). *Constructive therapies.* New York: Guilford Press.

Hubble, M., Duncan, B., and Miller, S. (1999). *The heart and soul of change: What works in therapy.* Washington, DC: APA Press.

Lambert, M. and Bergin, A. (1994). The effectiveness of psychotherapy. In Bergin, A. and Garfield, S. (Eds.), *Handbook of psychotherapy and behavior change* (Fourth edition) (pp. 143-189). New York: John Wiley.

Lipchik, E. (1993). "Both/and" solutions. In Friedman, S. (Ed.), *The new language of change: Constructive collaboration in psychotherapy* (pp. 25-49). New York: Guilford Press.

Madigan, S. (1994). Body politics. *Family therapy networker, 18* (6), 18-29.

Miller, S. (1994). Some questions (not answers) for the brief treatment of people with drug and alcohol problems. In Hoyt, M. (Ed.), *Constructive therapies* (pp. 92-110). New York: Guilford Press.

Sherman, E. (1992). *Playing with language: A historical and clinical study of a languaging model of family therapy.* Unpublished dissertation, Nova Southeastern University.

Weakland, J., de Shazer, S., and Hoyt, M. (1994). An interview with John Weakland and Steve de Shazer. In Hoyt, M. (Ed.), *Constructive therapies* (pp. 11-40). New York: Guilford Press.

Weiner-Davis, M. (1992). *Divorce busting: Revolutionary and rapid program for staying together.* New York: Summit Books.

White, M. (1991). Deconstruction and theory. *Dulwich Centre Newsletter, 3,* 21-40.

White, M. and Epston, D. (1989). *Literary ends to therapeutic means.* Adelaide, Australia: Dulwich Centre Publications.

Zimmerman, J. and Dickerson, V. (1994). Tales of the body thief: Externalizing and deconstructing eating problems. In Hoyt, M. (Ed.), *Constructive therapies* (pp. 295-318). New York: Guilford Press.

Chapter 7

Experiential Approaches to Family Therapy

Volker Thomas

When I first begin to work with someone, I am not interested in changing them. I am interested in finding their rhythms, being able to join
with them, and helping them go inside to those scary places.

Virginia Satir
In "Reaching Out to Life"

It is experience, not education that changes families.

Keith and Whitaker
In *Family Counseling and Therapy*

Imagine family therapists such as Virginia Satir and Carl Whitaker walking into your classroom and telling you that education, knowledge, cognitive skills, etc., do not change families, but that it is *experience.* What does
this mean? Whose and what experience is Whitaker talking about? Is Virginia Satir really not interested in changing client families? Change is what
family therapy is all about, right? What does Satir mean by "finding their
rhythms" and going "inside to those scary places"? What scary places does
she have in mind?

Experiential approaches to family therapy originated in the humanistic
movement of the 1960s and combined this with the unique personalities of
several mavericks of the early family therapy movement. Oriented on the
tenets of systemic thinking and individually and group-based approaches
such as gestalt therapy, psychodrama, Rogerian client-centered therapy, and
encounter groups, the experiential approaches to family therapy almost reflect the rebellious nature of some of their proponents (as some of you may
have guessed reading the quotes that begin this chapter). Thomas (1992)

suggests that the experiential approaches to family therapy are character-ized by

- a philosophy of growth;
- an emphasis on expression of feeling and meaning;
- the therapist sharing personal feelings and thoughts in the therapy ses-sion;
- action-oriented techniques within the therapy session;
- improvement of basic communication skills;
- an orientation toward increased physical and emotional health, lead-ing to wholeness and balance; and
- each person taking responsibility for self. (pp. 202-229)

This chapter presents three orientations of the experiential approach to marriage and family therapy, Virginia Satir's humanistic/experiential and Carl Whitaker's symbolic/experiential approaches to family therapy, and Leslie Greenberg and Susan Johnson's emotion-focused approach to couple therapy.

PROPONENTS OF THE MODEL

When I participated in my first family therapy conference in the 1980s I had a powerful and career-changing experience. I went to a plenary session in which Virginia Satir was going to present her work to a larger group of professionals. Usually, speakers at these large sessions give rather boring speeches in which they present the tenets of the approaches more or less by reading from prepared notes. Satir proceeded differently. With her warm and genuine charisma, she had 400 to 500 family therapists stand up, hold hands, and feel their inner love for one another. Sounds phony, right? It was not phony with Virginia Satir (if I tried this, it probably would seem phony). She had the ability to connect with people and to help them connect with one another in ways that felt sincere and genuine. She not only talked about how her humanistic-experiential approach to family therapy worked, she lived it and made her audience experience it—and what an experience that was.

Many consider Virginia Satir to be the mother of family therapy in the United States. She was the only woman among the mainly white, male psy-chiatrists of the founding generation of family therapists in the 1950s, and 1960s. Having worked as a clinical social worker with families in the early 1950s, Satir joined Gregory Bateson and his group at the Mental Research Institute (MRI) in Palo Alto, California. Under the influence of the MRI,

Satir focused in her early work on improving the communication patterns among family members. More interested in training than in research, Satir left the MRI and published the groundbreaking first description of her work in *Conjoint Family Therapy* (1964). Until her death in 1988, Satir continued to emphasize the importance of clear communication. She included issues of spiritual growth and world peace in her approach (Brothers, 1991; Satir, 1988), which she identified as the human validation process model (Satir, 1986; Satir and Bitter, 1991).

During my training as a marriage and family therapist, I had group supervision with Carl Whitaker once a month. I was in graduate school at the time at the University of Minnesota. Every first Friday afternoon Whitaker would make the five-hour car trip from Madison, Wisconsin, to Minneapolis, Minnesota, and meet with twelve family therapists for three hours. At times, we all were tired after a long week of engaging in therapy and graduate school. One day, when the energy in the group was extremely low with long periods of silence, I noticed Carl drifting off in a nap, his head tilted to the side. When he woke up after a few minutes, I thought he would be embarrassed and apologize for his inappropriate behavior. Instead, he got up, stretched his arms a couple of times, and proceeded to walk to the door. On his way out, he said calmly, "When you guys decide that you have something meaningful to discuss during supervision, send one of you out to get me. You put me right to sleep with your boredom. Until then I'll have better things to do." We were shocked, oscillating between disgust and embarrassment. We quickly noticed the increased energy in the room. Carl's falling asleep and his leaving the room confronted us with our low level of energy and our unconscious desire to sit back and relax rather than work. When Carl came back, he thanked us for the nap, talking about his "craziness" when he gets tired. In a very different way, this was a similarly powerful experience as the one with Virginia Satir described previously. By being himself (or allowing himself to be rude and to fall asleep on us), Whitaker confronted us with our own tiredness and ambiguity about the supervision session. This was a first-hand experience (I could feel my low energy level at the beginning of the session and the rising energy after Carl left the room) of our process in the here and now. It was not something taught through insight.

Learning through experience, giving meaning to experiences through emotional and affective involvement in the relational process between therapist and family member, is at the core of Whitaker's approach to family therapy. As did Virginia Satir, Carl Whitaker had the rare ability to find and foster **connections** between and among people. With his genuine openness he got away with his sometimes outrageous violations of the social etiquette regarding how therapists were expected to behave. Whitaker was not only a maverick of family therapy, he was a maverick of life. Some of his contemporaries thought he acted highly unprofessionally, even unethically, but many appreciated his charismatic, often paradoxical ways of saying what everybody in the room thought but did not dare tell.

Based on his early work with traumatized soldiers during World War II, Whitaker developed a symbolic/experiential approach to psychotherapy in the 1950s that also expressed his frustration with the limitations of classical psychoanalysis. With a group of colleagues, Whitaker (Whitaker and Malone, 1953) developed an approach that focused on the *experiential processes* within both client and therapist as well as between the two. After his move to the University of Wisconsin Medical School in 1965, Whitaker expanded his approach to working with whole families, frequently including multiple generations, until his death in 1995 (Roberto, 1991; Whitaker and Keith, 1981).

In the late 1990s, I invited Susan Johnson to present a workshop at a regional conference on the approach she had developed with Leslie Greenberg— emotionally focused couple therapy (EFCT) (Greenberg and Johnson, 1988; Johnson and Greenberg, 1995; Johnson, 1998). I had read her work, but had never met her. From my encounters with Virginia Satir and Carl Whitaker I knew that their approaches were closely connected to their personalities and their individual idiosyncrasies. Many have tried to copy their approaches; nobody has even come close to their abilities to work with couples and families. However, Susan Johnson is different. She is an energetic academician and researcher who is not only concerned about advocating a particular approach but also providing empirical data that prove the efficacy and effectiveness of the approach. During her workshop, Johnson presented the major tenets of her approach and reported on research findings which showed evidence that the approach actually works with couples.

THEORETICAL ASSUMPTIONS AND CONCEPTS

Satir's Humanistic-Experiential Approach

According to Satir and Bitter (1991), the **humanistic-experiential** approach bases its concepts on several underlying assumptions:

- Dysfunctional behavior is the result of a deficit in *growth.*
- *Growth* is a natural process occurring in all human beings.
- Human beings have within them all the resources they need to grow.
- *Subjective perceptions* rather than external/objective facts constitute a family's reality.

- Individual symptoms are viewed as the "price" paid to keep the family balanced and is usually associated with *low self-esteem* on part of the symptom bearer.
- Because relationships are highly communicational, a person's self-esteem manifests itself in *poor communication*. Low self-esteem leads to dysfunctional communication patterns.

Satir and Baldwin (1983) summarize these assumptions with a wonderful image. People are similar to *blossoms in the spring*. They are part of fully developed plants that have made it through the hard times of winter. They have slowly grown as the spring sun increases its intensity. All they need in order to open up and show their colorful beauty and reveal their attractive smell is a little nurturance from Mother Nature, the warm beams of the sun, a soft spring breeze, and a gentle soaking rain. Then the blossoms can unfold their beauty and transform into wonderful spring flowers.

The humanistic-experiential approach includes the following concepts:

- *Individual growth and development.* All humans strive for growth and development and have the resources within themselves to grow. Three factors influence human development:
  1. the genetic makeup;
  2. things learned during the growth process; and
  3. the constant mind-body interaction.
- *Self-esteem and self-worth.* Satir (1986) believed that the core of every person or the self consists of eight different aspects that all have to be attended to and nourished in order for the human potential (i.e., flower) to unfold to its fullest (i.e., bloom). Thus, Satir worked on the following levels:
  1. physical (the body);
  2. intellectual (thoughts, cognitions);
  3. emotional (feelings, intuition);
  4. sensual (sound, sight, touch, taste, smell);
  5. interactional (I-thou, communication between oneself and others);
  6. contextual (colors, sound, light, temperature, space, time);
  7. nutritional; and
  8. spiritual (relationship to life's meaning).

Satir (1972) believed that self-esteem is one of the most fundamental concepts of the human condition that is learned in the family from verbal and nonverbal messages. Self-worth is comprised of the *feel-*

ings (**self-esteem**) and the *ideas* (**self-concept**) people hold about
themselves (Satir, 1988).

- *Communication.* The way people in families communicate reflects the
  way they feel about themselves. Family members with high self-esteem communicate in direct, open, clear, genuine, and authentic ways.
  People who feel bad about themselves (i.e., low self-esteem and self-
  worth) tend to use dysfunctional ways of communication (e.g., indirect, covert, unclear, distorted, inappropriate). Satir (1972) developed
  a classification of communications styles:

Communication Style		Role Taken Under Stress
placater	→	service
blamer	→	power
super reasonable	→	intellect
irrelevant	→	spontaneity

A congruent communicator uses all four styles in accordance with
specific relationship requirements. under stress most people tend toward one style that they distort and apply predominantly. for example, a **placater** tries to please at all costs, acts weak, always agrees,
and apologizes for everything. the **blamer** blames others for his/her
own mistakes, dominates, and is self-righteous. the **super reasonable**
remains emotionally detached and controlled, rigid in his/her thinking.
finally, the **irrelevant** becomes a distracter, totally non-committal to
the process.

Watching Virginia Satir do therapy was a treat. Her warm and engaging
style, her big and open heart going out to families, found pathways to
their hearts in pain and in joy. Once I saw her holding hands with a couple that were afraid of their deadly rage that had separated them. In another session she demonstrated how to connect and communicate with
a three-year-old girl who had been diagnosed as autistic.

Whitaker's Symbolic-Experiential Approach

Underlying Whitaker's **symbolic-experiential** approach to family therapy are several assumptions (Keith and Whitaker, 1982):

- *Reciprocity of therapist and family:* The therapist has to grow and get in touch with her or his issues to help the family work on its problems.
- *Distrust of cognitive insight;* active use of physical contact.
- Affective energy of *unconsciousness* is used as fertile ground of growth.
- *Flexibility of roles* in family is central notion (kids may be parents temporarily and vice versa; parents/kids may be therapists temporarily and vice versa).
- *Cotherapy* is crucial for two reasons: (1) to protect therapists from getting "hooked"; and (2) to learn by doing.
- *Goal of therapy is to trigger anxiety* in family which they can use as energy to change; the therapist has to separate his or her own anxiety from the family's; the therapist cannot make the family change; change must come out of the family's own desperation and motivation.

These assumptions translate into several key concepts that are crucial if therapy is to be successful:

- *Battle for structure.* Assuming that the family seeks therapy because it is out of control, Whitaker assumes control over the structure of therapy (Whitaker and Keith, 1981). He is very firm that he decides who attends the first session and when it is held. This provides a framework for the family to regain structure within its family life.
- *Battle for initiative.* Once Whitaker has defined the structure of therapy, he allows the family to take the initiative for the course of therapy (Whitaker and Keith, 1981). He believes the family's creative forces will unfold when he provides the space.
- *Nontheory.* Whitaker believes that theory hinders therapist and client creativity.
- *Emotional experience.* Instead, he encourages families and therapists to affectively engage with one another.
- *Depathologizing of human experience.* Whitaker views families as stuck in patterns of interaction they are unable to change. Experiencing this "stuckness" is the first step to changing the pattern.
- *No preplanned techniques.* Therapist spontaneity that develops from the spontaneous connection with clients helps families change; preplanned techniques are not necessary for this process. They may even hinder the change process.

- *Use of self by therapist.* Whitaker encourages therapists to draw from their own life experiences and the affective reaction during the session when working with families.
- *Use of cotherapy.* Whitaker promoted cotherapy for two reasons: (1) therapists get so deeply involved with clients in the therapy process that a cotherapist may keep some distance to observe the process and step in when necessary to support the other therapist; (2) since no theory or techniques are used to prepare for doing therapy, cotherapy is the main teaching tool of Whitaker's approach ("learning by doing").

Observing Carl Whitaker in a therapy session frequently appeared bizarre. For example, interviewing a multigenerational family, he would sit on the floor while talking to the grandmother who had great wisdom about what was going on in the family. When asked why he sat on the floor in front of the grandmother's chair, Whitaker replied that he was so at awe with her wisdom that he felt like a little boy who would sit in front of her, looking up to her. In another session, he would give a long monologue about his own "craziness" to a family who wanted to know from him whether their sixteen-year-old son was mentally ill. Whitaker would do outrageous things other therapists would never do, but he did them in engaging and genuine ways that made the families feel supported and understood.

Johnson's Emotionally Focused Couple Therapy

Emotionally Focused Couple Therapy (EFCT) is a newer model of experiential therapy that Greenberg and Johnson (1985, 1986, 1988) developed in the 1980s and primarily applied to their work with couples. It draws from Rogers' (1951) client-centered and Perls' (1961) gestalt therapy, integrates some of Satir's (1972) ideas, and adds aspects of family systems theory (Fisch, Weakland, and Segal, 1983). EFCT is brief and empirically validated through many research projects (Johnson, 1998). It helps couples change dysfunctional interactional patterns (e.g., attacking-withdrawing, pursuing-distancing) by modifying the inner experience of both partners. EFCT builds on **attachment** theory (Bowlby, 1969), which proposes that people need accessibility and responsiveness of attachment figures in order to achieve a sense of personal security, which many dysfunctional couples do not possess.

EFCT offers two central concepts:

- **Primary emotions.** These emotions express our *core feelings.* They are authentic and genuine. Once therapists have helped couples to bond and alter their dysfunctional interactional pattern, partners have access to their primary emotions and can relate in open and genuine ways.

- **Secondary reactive emotions.** These emotions act as defenses of the more vulnerable primary emotions. When there is a lack of attachment bonds in the relationship, partners rely on secondary reactive emotions because they do not feel safe to express their primary emotions. For example, a husband may get very angry with his wife to mask his fear and hurt that she came home two hours late from work without telling him in advance.

NORMAL FAMILY DEVELOPMENT

All three approaches to experiential couple and family therapy discussed in this chapter have something in common: they focus on growth and human **development** rather than dysfunction and pathology. They look at the world from a positive perspective, viewing the glass of human life as half full rather than half empty. Virginia Satir's aforementioned metaphor of the flower blossom that needs some nurturing to bloom summarizes how experiential therapists view family development. We all are a family of flowers ready to bloom when sufficiently nurtured.

Satir's Humanistic-Experiential Approach

In Satir's human validation process model (1986), she uses the analogy of the wheel to delineate human development. The hub of the wheel represents the potential health of a person's self. Attached to the hub are the spokes as components that foster personal growth. These components include physical, intellectual, emotional, sensual, interactional, nutritional, contextual, and spiritual aspects. Families who attend to all components have the greatest chance to secure healthy development for all members over time. Using a mathematical metaphor Satir (1986) proposed a formula for healthy development:

A (body) + B (brain) + C (emotions) + D (senses) + E (interactions) + F (nutrition) + G (context) + H (soul) = S (self) (p. 287)

Whitaker's Symbolic-Experiential Approach

For Whitaker, health is a continuous process of becoming that is never finished (Whitaker and Bumberry, 1988). Healthy families always change and have the ability to adapt their rules and roles accordingly. Parents flexibly deal with their children as they grow older, and the children gain the necessary independence without losing their parents as dependable and reliable guides. During the course of healthy development all family members maintain a balance between connectedness and autonomy, between community and individuality. Flexibility serves as the regulating mechanism in this process. Families develop rituals to move through the different phases of their life cycles. For example, birthday celebrations put one family member in the center of everyone's attention to mark the developmental transition from one year to the next. "Today is my birthday, so I am the leader," my youngest son used to say when he was four or five years old. The birthday ritual gave him the opportunity to temporarily assume the rule of the "family leader" usually reserved for the parents.

Johnson's Emotionally Focused Couple Therapy

Securely attached partners characterize healthy development in this approach. When both partners in the couple relationship get their primary emotional needs met, they naturally progress through the life cycle. Both are able to identify their primary emotions and accept each other's needs. The couple engages in a close relationship that includes intimacy and connectedness as well as separateness and autonomy. Both feel secure and respond to each other with caring love.

PATHOLOGY AND BEHAVIOR DISORDERS

Although all three experiential approaches focus mainly on growth and development, they do have some notion of pathology and associated behavior disorders.

Satir's Humanistic-Experiential Approach

From Satir's point of view, **pathology** is the absence of growth. When a family system is out of balance, some family members may pay the price of behavioral symptoms to rebalance the system. Thus, Satir sees the symptom in a family member as signaling a **blockage of growth.** The symptoms may take on one of the four communication styles mentioned previously (e.g., placater, blamer, super reasonable, irrelevant). The lack of growth and development of symptoms are associated with low self-esteem in family members. For example, the pregnant stepmother of three- and four-year-old boys is afraid for her unborn baby's life because the boys have been caught severely beating a dog. She requests that her husband give up custody of the boys and transfer them to their mother, who has been known to abuse the boys. The stepmother is so insecure about herself and the future of her baby that she blames the boys for their behavior. The more she worries, the more the boys act out; the more the boys act out, the more the stepmother worries. They all pay the price of unhappiness to keep the family together when the father tries to negotiate with his wife regarding how to control the boys.

Whitaker's Symbolic-Experiential Approach

Whitaker assumes that symptoms develop when dysfunctional family structures persist over a period of time and interfere with the family's ability to carry out its life tasks (Roberto, 1991). Thus, psychopathology arises from the same mechanisms that produce normal behavior. For example, many years ago, a young family came into my office consisting of two parents in their early thirties and their nine-year-old daughter whom they could not control. When they entered my office, the girl sat down on a comfortable recliner while the parents chose hard and uncomfortable chairs. The girl misbehaved throughout the session by interrupting and correcting the parents frequently, leaving the room whenever she pleased, and refusing to answer my questions. I understood the girl's behavior as an expression of her discomfort with having too much power (symbolized by sitting on the recliner) and running the parents' lives rather than being a normal nine-year-old girl with limits.

Johnson's Emotionally Focused Couple Therapy

Pathology arises when couples are *insecurely attached* (Bowlby, 1969). Then they hide their primary emotions and instead engage in secondary reactive emotions, which are defensive or aggressive in character. Thus, **negative interactions create negative cycles.** These cycles develop (e.g., pursue-distance, blame-withdraw) because both partners do not trust in the emotional availability of the other and try to protect themselves from revealing their fears and other vulnerable feelings. The continuation of these negative interactions increases the fear that the partner is not worthy of trust and that primary emotions have to be hidden (Greenberg and Johnson, 1986, 1988). For example, consider this couple in their midtwenties: she loves to get together with her girlfriends; after awhile, he becomes obsessed with the idea that she is cheating on him instead of seeing her girlfriends. He accuses her of lying and her girlfriends of covering up her lies. She feels treated unjustly and begins to dislike him. The more she withdraws because she is afraid of him hurting her, the more he controls and threatens her. He does not share his fear of abandonment with her, and she withholds her feelings of fear and intimidation.

TECHNIQUES

Satir's Humanistic-Experiential Approach

Satir used the following techniques (Satir and Baldwin, 1983):

- *Family sculpturing:* Family members demonstrate closeness and distance as well as communication patterns by moving people into specific bodily positions. These positions represent the relationships within the family.
- *Metaphor:* The therapist and/or client suggests an idea that represents an interactional pattern. For example, parental nurturance is symbolized by the metaphor of the sun warming a budding tree in the spring.
- *Reframing:* Using a positive label for a behavior or feeling that was negatively framed. For example, I reframed the nine-year-old girl taking a seat in the recliner while the parents sat on hard chairs as the girl's attempt to tell the parents that she had too much power in the family from which she wanted to be released.
- *Humor:* The use of humor often makes therapist's comments more easily acceptable. For example, I told the nine-year-old girl how awkward she looked in the "huge chair" while Mom and Dad "squeezed their big bodies" on the little hard chairs. The family members looked at one another and began to laugh.
- *Touch:* Touch is a central technique in Satir's approach. Because many people feel personal boundaries are violated by touch, the therapist has to use it carefully. Asking clients for permission allows them to check their boundaries. Applied respectfully, touch is a wonderful way to connect with clients, to validate their experience, to reinforce a therapeutic intervention, and to foster the therapeutic relationship. Gentle touch (e.g., putting a hand on a client's shoulder, holding a client's hand, a brief patting on the back) nonverbally supports the client and increases his or her self-esteem.
- *Communication stances:* Satir invited families to sculpt the four communication styles of placater, blamer, super reasonable, and irrelevant. Then she would work with the family to change these stances

into that of a congruent person and have family members sculpt this stance.

- *"I" statements:* Satir encouraged families to own their feelings and communicate them clearly. Instead of using indirect language, clients learned to begin sentences with "I" and make eye contact with the other person for congruent communication.
- ***Family reconstruction:*** One family member becomes the "star" that engages in the reconstruction of his or her family. During the reconstruction at least three scenes are role-played: (1) the family history of each of the star's parents, (2) the story of the relationship of the star's parents from their meeting to the present, and (3) the birth of the children to the star's parents, especially the star's birth.

Whitaker's Symbolic-Experiential Approach

Contrary to Satir, Whitaker did not address symptoms directly. He believed that doing so might increase the family's distress (Whitaker and Keith, 1981). Instead, a symbolic-experiential therapist uses techniques which address the family's emotional states that underlie the symptoms. Whitaker viewed the following seven techniques as important vehicles that facilitate the therapeutic process (Whitaker and Keith, 1981):

- ***Redefining*** *symptoms as an effort for growth:* This technique is similar to Satir's reframing. In general terms, Whitaker considered symptoms as family members' attempts to get unstuck and grow. For example, Whitaker might have told the nine-year-old girl in the recliner that she wants to be a big person and sit in a big chair because she has all the adult responsibilities in the family.
- ***Modeling*** *fantasy alternatives to real-life stress:* The therapist relies on creative ideas to model alternative behaviors to the ones the family members exhibit. In the case of the nine-year-old girl, I got up from my chair, picked up my toy box, placed it in front of the recliner, and began to play with toys on the floor while talking to the parents. The girl watched me for a few minutes then got up and joined me on the floor. Then I invited the parents to also join us, which they hesitantly did. Eventually, we all played with the toys on the floor, which decreased the tension among the family members considerably.
- *Separating* ***interpersonal*** *stress and* ***intrapersonal*** *stress:* Whitaker believes that many people act out the stress they internally feel in their relationships with family members. However, because they are unaware of the internal stressors, they blindly project them onto others,

which increases the interpersonal stress among family members. Using humor and exaggeration are ways to uncover these unconscious processes. For example, when I told the nine-year-old girl that she wanted to sit in the recliner because she felt the pressure to be a grown-up (intrapersonal stress), it reframed the parents' complaints that they could not control the girl's behavior (interpersonal stress).

- *Adding practical bits of* **intervention:** At times it is very important to suggest very practical behavioral changes to client families. One of those practical bits was my invitation to the parents of the nine-year-old girl to come down and play with us on the floor.
- *Augmenting the despair of a family member:* Whitaker loved to increase family members' anxiety and add to their despair with the goal that it would trigger the desired change process. For example, in one of the classic books on symbolic-experiential family therapy (Napier and Whitaker, 1978), Whitaker engages in a wrestling match with a young defiant boy, which makes the parents feel so bad that they finally take charge of their son's behavior and set clearer limits to what he may or may not do.
- **Affective confrontation:** This intervention is similar to the previous one. Confronting denied or invalidated affect in a paradoxically supportive environment was one of Whitaker's favorite interventions. For example, he would call a father who would not stand up to his adolescent son's provocations a "lame duck who would be too scared to show his son how a man acts."
- *Treating children as children and not as peers:* Whitaker considered it extremely important to keep the boundaries between the generations clear. He believed that children needed the parents' protection and permission to be children and should not be treated as equals, because that would put too much responsibility on them. For example, the fact that the nine-year-old girl sat in the recliner and the parents on the hard chairs symbolized that the parents did not treat the girl as a child but wanted to avoid a confrontation with her in front of the therapist. Thus, the goal of therapy was to relieve the girl of her burden of being a peer to her parents and to allow her to be and act like a nine-year-old girl.

These techniques were emphasized differently in the four stages of therapy Whitaker described (Whitaker, 1977):

- *Pretreatment or engagement phase:* During this phase, symbolic-experiential therapists mainly rely on redefining the symptom and modeling fantasy alternatives. The therapists establish that they have control over the sessions but that the family makes its own life decisions.

- *Middle phase:* During this phase, family members get increasingly involved in the therapeutic process. The therapists put more emphasis on the other techniques discussed. They especially try to increase the family members' anxiety and augment their despair. They aim at affective confrontation and help family members separate interpersonal and intrapersonal stress.

- *Late phase:* During this phase, the family needs less guidance and confrontation from the therapists. Members have learned to implement their progress during the sessions and outside of the office visits. Flexibility on part of the therapists fosters the family's growth process.

- *Separation phase:* During this final phase, therapists and family members work through the pending loss of the termination of therapy. The family uses mostly its own resources and lets go of the therapists. The famly members work through their own sense of loss and grief.

As unstructured as Whitaker's therapy appears in his original writings, he put a great deal of thought and systematic reflection in the therapeutic process. When asked how he came up with some of his outrageous yet extraordinarily creative interventions, Whitaker replied, in essence, "I have no idea what I am doing when I am doing it. A good therapist does not need to know ahead of time what he is going to do. But he must be able to provide a sound rationale for what he did afterward."

Johnson's Emotionally Focused Couple Therapy

Instead of specific interventions or techniques, EFCT offers a step-by-step treatment manual that suggests a prototype for the therapy process that different therapists and couples can replicate:

- *Delineating conflict issues in the core struggle:* Once the secondary emotions have been identified, the therapist focuses in on the core struggle and delineates the pertinent conflict issues in detail. For example, during the first session with the midtwenties couple mentioned previously, the therapist identifies the wife's fear of violence and the husband's anger and obsession that his wife is cheating on him.

- *Identifying the negative interaction cycle:* The delineation of the core struggle leads to the identification of the couple's negative interaction cycle, such as pursue-distance or blame-withdraw. The couple learns how the husband pursues and intimidates his wife, and she tries to distance herself out of fear of being hurt. The couples also identifies the reciprocity of this negative cycle—that is, the more the husband pursues, the more the wife distances; and the more the wife distances, the more the husband pursues.

- *Accessing the unacknowledged feelings underlying interactional positions:* During this step the therapist helps the couple to access the primary feelings that they try to protect when they pursue, blame, distance, or withdraw. Once the couple has gained some understanding of the negative cycle feeding their secondary emotions, the therapist works with each partner on getting in touch with the primary emotions. In our case example, the husband experiences his fear of abandonment when he gets angry and controlling, as the wife gets in touch with the loneliness she feels when her husband does not want to talk and cuddle up with her.

- *Reframing the problem in term of underlying feelings, attachment needs, and negative cycles:* The therapist reframes the fear of abandonment that expresses attachment needs and often leads to blaming or withdrawing as an attempt to protect oneself from another loss and emotional betrayal. This helps the couple to identify the negative cycles in terms of their attachment needs. The therapist reframes the wife's fear of her husband as her strong need to feel emotionally connected with him. The husband's anger is relabeled as his need to be close to his wife, a feeling that she longs for but also fears.

- *Promoting identification with disowned needs and aspects of self, and integrating these into relationship interactions:* Once the couple has identified the disowned attachment needs, the therapist works with the couple to express the needs to each other and so bring them directly into the relationship. During this stage, the therapist coaches the husband to share his fears and concerns when his wife wants to go out with her girlfriends. The wife learns to acknowledge her husband's fear and validate it rather than get defensive and push it aside. Conversely, the wife is encouraged to express her need to have relaxed conversations with her husband (which she instead seeks with her girlfriends) and to feel close to him. The therapist coaches the husband to accept his wife's expressed needs, even if it is difficult for him to meet the need.

- *Promoting acceptance of partner's experiences and new interaction patterns:* When one partner has the courage to bring the needs and fear into the relationship, the therapist encourages the other partner to accept him or her, which leads to new patterns of interaction in the couple's relationship. Once the two learned to accept each other's experience, the husband became less anxious and angry and let go of his unfounded fear of infidelity. The wife felt more secure and safe with her husband and stopped distancing herself.

- *Facilitating the expression of needs and wants, and creating emotional engagement:* Once both partners have made the first step to express their primary emotions, they need coaching to emotionally connect by continuing to express their needs and wants to their partner and by being open to respond to the partner's needs and wants. Now the example couple was ready to have more closeness—having dinner together, going for walks. They even talked about having a baby for the first time in their marriage. In role-plays, the therapist practiced with the couple to stay engaged in conversation, even when they felt anxious and uncomfortable.
- *Establishing the emergence of new solutions:* At this point most couples are ready to find new solutions to the daily problems they face without falling back into the negative cycles that brought them to therapy. The safer the example couple felt and the more they engaged with each other, the less the wife wanted to go out with her girlfriends, and the less the husband felt threatened when his wife did go out.
- *Consolidating new positions:* During this final phase of therapy the couple can stay emotionally connected even when dealing with stress, and can openly express their needs and meet each other's needs. Eventually, the example couple learned to have fun with each other and eventually had a baby.

RELEVANT RESEARCH

Little empirical research has been conducted to validate the efficacy and effectiveness of Satir's humanistic-experiential and Whitaker's symbolic-experiential approaches. The only **experiential** approach that has yielded relevant outcome research is Johnson's emotionally focused couple therapy. For example, Greenberg and Johnson (1988) found that helping an angry and attacking (secondary emotions) partner reveal his or her softer feelings (primary emotions) was associated with positive therapy outcome. In another study, Greenberg et al. (1993) concluded that when couples expressed primary emotions in therapy they have more productive sessions and feel more intimate with each other. In a comparison of several empirically based treatment approaches derived from several methodological rigorous research studies, Alexander, Holtzworth-Munroe, and Jameson (1994) reported that EFCT was one of the effective approaches for treating distressed couples. In a meta-analysis that included many outcome studies within and across different treatment approaches, Dunn and Schwebel (1995) also confirmed the efficacy and effectiveness of EFCT.

CASE EXAMPLES

At the conclusion of this chapter we revisit three previously discussed case examples in more detail by applying them to the three approaches. Imagine you are Virginia Satir, Carl Whitaker, and Susan Johnson for a few minutes as you read the following case examples.

Satir's Humanistic-Experiential Approach

Remember the family with the two little boys whose stepmother was pregnant and feared that they would hurt the baby? Following is the Smith family's story from the perspective of Virginia Satir.

Jim is in his midthirties and has two boys, four-year-old Bob and three-year-old Cody. Jim divorced two years ago after his mentally ill ex-wife had severely abused the boys while they were staying with her. Since the incident, Jim has had sole custody of Bob and Cody. Jim is remarried to Sue, who is twenty-seven years old and pregnant with their first child. When Sue heard from the boys' baby-sitter that they had attempted to choke a baby also in the baby-sitter's care, she became afraid for her own unborn child and requested that Jim remove the boys from their home. Jim felt torn between taking care of his two sons and protecting his new wife and unborn child. Attempts to more effectively manage Bob and Cody had failed because most of the parenting was left up to Sue, who was afraid of and angry with the boys at the same time. Jim and Sue were quite desperate, fearing that they were not able to create a safe environment for their new family. Satir saw the whole family that was currently living together—Jim, Sue, Bob, and Cody—and made sure to connect with all four family members. When talking with one of the boys, Satir would move her chair in front of him and establish eye contact by gently holding his chin to lift his head so that he would look at her while they were talking. This gesture was particularly important, because the parents complained that the boys do not listen. By making sure that each boy made eye contact and by gently touching them, Satir modeled effective communication with the boys for the parents.

When it became clear that the boys were threatening the safety of the family, Satir reframed their violent behavior as attempts to reach out and ask the parents to stop the violence they had suffered at their biological mother's house. Then Satir asked Jim to face each of the boys, hold their hands, establish eye contact, and tell each of them that he loved them, that he wanted them to be part of the family, and that he wanted them to mind and behave better. While Jim talked to his sons, Satir would sit next to him, put her hand on his shoulder, and help him to effectively communicate with his sons. While talking to his sons Jim began to cry softly and Cody gave his dad a kiss to comfort him. Satir calmly praised both father and son for their emotional connection and encouraged them to continue on this route. Sue watched the exchange with great interest and tears in her eyes. During this process, Satir made sure that the parents used "I" statements when they talked to the boys and that they did not blame the boys' biological mother for abusing them.

Then Satir turned to Jim and Sue and suggested to them to find a way out of the dilemma by either having the baby and staying together as a new family (thus removing Bob and Cody from the home) or for Sue to leave once she had the baby. Again, Satir modeled clear communication when she asked Jim and Sue to move their chairs so that they could squarely face each other. During the ensuing emotional conversation, Satir introduced the metaphor of the "bottom line," representing the safe ground needed for this family. Sue's bottom line was that the boys' violent behavior had to stop. Jim defined his bottom line as having one family in which he could raise his three children with Sue. Satir acknowledged how far apart the two bottom lines were and asked Jim and Sue to sculpt the families they envisioned once the boys' behavior had change in the desired direction. To the parents' surprise, their ideal families looked almost identical. Then Satir asked the couple to sit down again and face each other. Sue and Jim held hands and Jim told Sue that he would do the best he could to "make the boys mind" (those were his words) and protect the baby. Sue openly stated her doubts whether this would ever happen and repeated her fear for the baby's safety. After a few minutes, the couple felt stuck again and turned to Satir. She put her hands on their hands that were still connected and repeated their bottom lines. Then she asked both whether they would be willing to consider the possibility of putting their doubts aside for a moment and looking into each other's eyes. They agreed and began to cry. In their pain, they began to emotionally connect in a way they had not connected before. They hugged and were silent for some time. Satir placed one of her hands on each of their shoulders. The boys observed the process quietly and with great interest. After the parents had collected themselves, the boys calmly went over to them and the whole family engaged in a big family hug with Satir.

During the ensuing conversation, Sue expressed her relief to see the boys so passionate and calm, stating, "Sometimes they seem like untamable monsters, now I see them as sweet little boys who need as many hugs as I do and their daddy does." This is a wonderful summary of the change Sue experienced. Unfortunately, therapy is not quite as easy as this case might indicate. It took many sessions for Jim and Sue to permanently overcome their doubts and fears and to be firm and supportive parents in light of the additional stress of having a baby. Yes, they stayed together and worked through their fears with the coaching and support of Satir (or another similar therapist). The more secure and confident the parents felt about their parenting, the safer the boys felt, even in the presence of this new little rival for attention—their sister Melanie, who was born after the ninth session. Actually, Bob became quite affectionate and protective of his little sister when Cody wanted to play rough with her. In his four-year-old voice he would say, "When Daddy is at work and Mommy is in the other room, then I watch Melanie." Although the boys' behavior remained difficult to manage for the parents at times, they never hurt their little sister, as Sue had feared. This increased her self-esteem and self-confidence considerably, which made her a more effective stepmother. Jim dealt successfully with his guilt about the boys' abuse, which had previously kept him from setting firm limits with them. This increased his self-esteem and self-confidence, which made him a more effective father. Sue and

Jim's increased self-esteem also helped them as a couple to communicate more effectively and to avoid getting stuck in irreversible positions.

Whitaker's Symbolic-Experiential Approach

Now let's find out how a therapist such as Carl Whitaker (and his cotherapist) would work with the nine-year-old girl who came into my office and sat down in the comfortable recliner while her parents took the hard chairs. Following is a little more information about the Brown family and their treatment.

Jack and Jill are both in their early thirties. They married right after college graduation, after Jill had gotten pregnant with Anna during her senior year. Jill stayed home after college and Jack went on to graduate school for his MBA. Jill grew up as the middle child of five children. Both of her parents were professionals working full time when Jill was born. She was partly raised by her two older sisters and was used to having people around at home. Jack, on the other hand, was the only child of older parents who had struggled with infertility until they finally conceived. When Jack's mom got pregnant with him, she quit her job and put all her energy into what became her most precious accomplishment in life. Jack consequently grew up well nurtured and protected. Coming from very different family backgrounds, the Browns had little time to adjust to each other and to learn about those differences. They had a rather casual courtship and had starting living together only a few months before Jill's pregnancy occurred. In addition, Jack's parents were especially upset that he "had to" get married and had implied to Jack that they were concerned that Jill had "tricked" him into the marriage by getting pregnant. After Anna's birth, Jill wanted to pursue a graduate career, but Jack opposed this, wanting her to stay home as his mom had done. Jill resented Jack's lack of support and felt isolated and lonely with a small child at home. During Anna's early childhood Jill would accept odd jobs, against Jack's wishes, to get out of the house and have adult contact. The tension between the two grew. Jack accused Jill of being a "neglectful" mother and withdrew into his studies and his job more and more. Jill resented Jack's withdrawal, accusing him of not doing his share around the house and with Anna. Both Jack and Jill were very achievement oriented and rather competitive. Both felt shorted when it came to their marriage. Both considered getting a divorce several times. However, Jack did not want to give his parents the satisfaction of being correct that the marriage would not work out, as they had predicted and Jill's value system did not include divorce as a viable option.

Thus, Anna grew up amid this tension about parental roles and accomplishments. She became quite achievement oriented herself. She picked up on her parents' strong wills and their tendency to engage in open arguments. Over the years, she learned to take advantage of her parents' stuckness by playing them against each other. For example, she would complain to Dad that Mom would leave her alone too much, which would make him angry at Jill, and he would spoil Anna with the intent to make up for Jill's neglect. When Mom found out about Dad taking Anna places behind her back, she would get angry with Jack. Or Anna would complain to Mom that Dad had yelled at her unjustly. Jill would get angry at

Jack and withdraw into her bedroom with Anna to read to her for hours, both giving Jack the "silent treatment." In turn, Jack would get angry and withdraw even more into his job and graduate school.

Over the years, this cycle became so powerful that eventually Anna ran the family by manipulating her parents as she pleased. Although she was very unhappy that her parents would get angry so frequently and be unhappy as well, she thought that was how life was supposed to be and did not know what else to do. When Jill finally was so desperate that she threatened to divorce Jack despite her values, Jack agreed to seek family therapy.

This background helps us understand how the family ended up in my office. Before they came we went through a battle for control. Jill, who had made the initial phone call and scheduled the appointment, called back the next day reporting that Jack was so busy with school and work he could not make the appointment. According to Jill, Jack had suggested that Jill and Anna go ahead with the session, because it would be more important to them anyway. I insisted that I would see them only if all three would come in at the time of the scheduled appointment and suggested that Jill talk it over with Jack and call me back. The following day, Jack called and tried to make his case with me personally. I stayed firm and insisted on seeing all three of them because I considered Jack a crucial part of the family. Finally Jack gave in and the family showed up at the scheduled time.

As mentioned, Jack and Jill entered my office in a depressed and discouraged mood and sat down helplessly on the hard chairs, while Anna placed herself in the recliner. This picture in my office reflected the way they had seen their family world. I engaged Anna in playing with toys on the floor (something the parents had rarely done), which Anna greatly enjoyed. When I finally succeeded in getting the parents off the chairs and they awkwardly kneeled down next to Anna on the floor, I had found a way to join with them. At the end of the first session, I gave them homework: play with Anna once a day for fifteen minutes until our next session.

When the family came back the following week, I could feel the increased tension in my office. They reported that the daily playtime had been a disaster. Anna argued with the parents about what to play, dictated and controlled their actions, and threw tantrums when they did not do what she had demanded. After two attempts, the parents discontinued playtime, which also led Anna to throw tantrums. Apparently, the negative cycle had escalated and the family felt more desperate than before. I decided to listen to the family members and let them take the initiative at the beginning of the second session (battle for initiative). The longer we sat there with the family not knowing what to do, the more the intensity in room increased. Finally, Jill suggested trying the playtime again, hoping that I would help to facilitate the process and keep Anna from "running the show." Jill got down on the floor and asked Jack and Anna to join her, which Jack did after a few moments. However, Anna refused to get up from the recliner, accusing her parents of being bad playmates. In response, the parents accused each other of being insensitive to Anna's needs. Imagine this grotesque picture: two adults on the floor with toys arguing about their child, while she sits in the recliner cussing at her parents.

At this point I was so disgusted with them that I rose from my chair and announced that I would leave the room until they were ready to do therapy. I told them that I understood how they were acting at home and that they did not have to waste their time and money to do the same in my office. I would take a book and read in the waiting room. When they were ready to do therapy, one of them could come and get me. As all three family members sat in quiet shock, their mouths and eyes wide open, I left my office. After five minutes, Anna came out and politely asked me to come back. She promised that they would not fight any longer and wanted to try to be a happy family. When I entered my office I saw Jill in tears and Jack looking furious. They were sitting on the hard chairs, full of emotions they did not know how to handle. Anna went quietly to the floor and began to play with the dollhouse.

I ignored the parents and asked Anna what she wanted to show me. She took a male doll and put it in a big box on the attic. Then she placed a female doll in a bed in the basement. Another female child-size doll started preparing meal in the kitchen. "This is my family after a big fight," Anna exclaimed. I shared with Anna how impressed I was that she kept taking care of the family even after a fight and asked what would happen next. She cooked for awhile, then brought a plate with food to the basement and quietly handed it to Mom (the female doll). She repeated the same with another plate and brought it to the attic and placed it quietly on top of the closed box in which Dad (the male doll) had been placed. "How nice of you to bring Mom and Dad something to eat when they are sad," I commented and added, "What a responsibility for a nine-year-old girl—to take care of her Mom and Dad!" Anna looked at me, surprised, and teared up. She turned and looked at her mom who was still quietly crying. Their eyes met in sadness. Mom got up and went to her daughter, who was now sobbing. While Mom was holding Anna on the floor, I went over to Jack, sat down next to him, and put my arm around his shoulder. He fought his tears as hard as he could, but they were too insistent to be held back. "You may join them if you like. There is room for everybody in this family, even in pain and sadness." Relieved by my permission, Jack got up and joined Jill and Anna in their embrace. Without any reluctance, they welcomed him. When they got up from the floor, something astonishing happened. Anna asked to sit on her dad's lap. After some awkward tiptoeing around each other, Dad ended up in the recliner with Anna on his lap, and Mom moved one of the hard chairs next to the recliner and sat there.

When I asked what had happened, Anna responded first. "I want to be a little girl and not have so much responsibility. It's much more fun sitting on Dad's lap than bringing him food he does not eat anyway." Jack and Jill looked at each other and confirmed that they both had forgotten that Anna was just nine years old, and that they wanted to learn to be better parents and to be better husband and wife.

As with the Satir family, it took several months of weekly and later bi-weekly sessions for Jack and Jill to accomplish their goals and for Anna to fully accept being a nine-year-old girl rather than a parentified child that runs the house. She had to learn to let go of the power that came along with the parentification and to accept the limits her parents set. Jack and Jill had to learn to work through their family-of-origin issues that had led them into their negative cycles. That freed up energy so that Jack and Jill could attend to each other's needs, and most of all, to recognize and meet Anna's needs according to her developmental stage. I learned how to deal with the intensity of three people who had greatly unmet needs and to appreciate the power of emotional connections that arise out of fear and pain.

Johnson's Emotionally Focused Couple Therapy

Finally, Joe and Cindy are the couple in their midtwenties who lived together bound by Joe's fear of Cindy's perceived infidelity and by Cindy's fear of possible violence perpetrated by Joe.

Joe grew up as the youngest of seven children. His father was an alcoholic who died of liver problems when Joe was ten years old. His mom, although severely depressed at times, raised the children by herself and never remarried. When Joe was fourteen years old he went to live with his mother's sister's family until he graduated from high school and went away to college. Since he moved in with his aunt, Joe has always worked and also supported himself through college. He quit college after his junior year and worked for a landscaping company because he loved to be outdoors.

Cindy grew up as the eldest sister with two brothers in a lower-middle-class home. Both of her parents worked to make ends meet, which left Cindy with the responsibility to take care of the house and her younger brothers until her mom returned home from work. Cindy's parents instilled a very strong sense for education in their children so that they would have a better life than their parents had as high school graduates. Cindy was a good student and also succeeded in college despite having to work her way through.

Cindy and Joe met in a class at the beginning of their junior year. Since Joe was struggling with school at that time, Cindy would help him with assignments and study with him. They dated for about six months and then moved in together because Joe thought they could save some money. Cindy felt that Joe was clingy and controlling from the first day they lived together. He always wanted to know where she was and did not show any interest in spending time with other people. Cindy hoped that Joe would change once they had lived together for awhile. When Cindy realized that Joe would not change, she began to resent him and accused him of holding her hostage in her own house. At the same time, she felt guilty for wanting to be away from him because she genuinely loved Joe. Because she needed somebody to talk about her dilemma, she increasingly went out with her girlfriends in the hope of figuring out how to make things better with Joe. However, the more she went out, the more difficult Joe became, until he finally accused her of having an affair and of trying to get rid of him.

At the beginning of their relationship Joe was so in love with Cindy that he wanted to spend as much time with her as possible. He was convinced that he had finally found a person who would unconditionally be there for him for the rest of his life. He pushed Cindy to move in with him so that they could be together all the time. He quit college so that he could make more money and become a "good man" who could provide well for Cindy. That was something his father had never managed to do because most of the money he earned went toward alcohol. From the beginning, he sensed Cindy's discomfort at staying home every night. He tried to tolerate her need to go out and see her girlfriends. One day, he found a pack of condoms in her car, which convinced him that Cindy had an affair. Her explanation—that one of her girlfriends had left the pack in her car—only increased Joe's resentment toward Cindy when she wanted to go out with them. He began to check up on Cindy and would get very angry when she would come home later than they had agreed upon. The resentment and tension between Joe and Cindy increased until one day he hit her when she stayed out late and Joe could not find her at the place where she was supposed to be. Cindy threatened to leave him if he did not agree to engage in couple therapy.

Joe was so afraid of losing Cindy that he called an EFCT therapist (such as Susan Johnson), to set up the first appointment. He felt comfortable that the therapist was a woman, hoping that she would convince Cindy to be more open and honest and to quit the affair he was still convinced she was having. Cindy also wanted to have a female therapist, hoping that she would receive support in dealing with this clinging, insecure man. Using the step-by-step treatment manual as discussed, the therapist met with Cindy and Joe for twelve sessions over a three-month period.

During the first session, the therapist identified Cindy's fear of violence and Joe's anger and obsession that Cindy was cheating on him. Then the couple learned how Joe pursues and intimidates Cindy, while she tries to distance herself out of fear of getting hurt. The couple also identified the reciprocity of this negative cycle—that is, the more Joe pursues, the more Cindy distances; and the more she distances, the more he pursues. Once the couple gained some understanding of the negative cycle feeding their secondary emotions, the therapist worked with each partner on getting in touch with their primary emotions. Joe experienced his fear of abandonment when he got angry and controlling, while the Cindy got in touch with the loneliness she felt when Joe did not want to talk and cuddle with her. Then the therapist reframed the fear of abandonment, which expressed attachment needs and often led to blaming or withdrawing, as an attempt to protect oneself from another loss and emotional betrayal. This helped the couple to identify the negative cycles in terms of their attachment needs. The therapist reframed Cindy's fear of Joe as her strong need to feel emotionally connected with him. Joe's anger was relabeled as his need to be close to his wife, a feeling that she longed for but also feared.

Once the couple had identified their disowned attachment needs, the therapist worked with them on expressing these needs to each other and to bring them directly into the relationship. During this stage, the therapist coached Joe to share his fears and concerns when Cindy wanted to go out with her girlfriends. Cindy learned to acknowledge Joe's fear and validate it rather than get defensive and push it aside. Conversely, the therapist encouraged Cindy to express her need to have relaxed conversations with Joe (which she instead seeks with her girlfriends) and to feel close to him. The therapist coached Joe to accept Cindy's expressed needs, even if it is difficult for him to meet the need. Once the couple learned to accept each other's experience, Joe became less anxious and angry, and let go of his fear that Cindy was being unfaithful. Cindy felt more secure and safe with Joe and did not distance herself as much as before.

Now the couple was ready to have more closeness, having dinner together, going for walks. They even talked for the first time in their marriage about having a baby. The therapist practiced helping the couple to stay engaged in conversation, even when they felt anxious and uncomfortable. After a few more sessions Cindy and Joe were ready to find new solutions to the daily problems they faced without falling back into the negative cycles that brought them to therapy. The safer the couple felt and the more they engaged with each other, the less Cindy wanted to go out with her girlfriends and the less Joe felt threatened when she did go out. During this final phase of therapy, Cindy and Joe were able to stay emotionally connected even when dealing with stress, openly expressed their own needs, and met each other's needs. Eventually, the couple learned to have fun with each other and eventually had a baby.

CONCLUSION

This chapter gave you an impression of what experiential couple and family therapy is about and how three schools of thought conceptualize and apply experiential therapy. As in other schools, the experiential approaches depend very much on the personality of their proponents. The human growth experience was so important to Virginia Satir and she felt so comfortable being with clients on so many levels that her humanistic-experiential approach to therapy replicated her approach to life. Similarly, Carl Whitaker was so strongly convinced that therapists should emotionally engage with family members and he felt so comfortable doing so that he shaped a unique approach that fit his personality. Finally, Susan Johnson, influenced by the push for empirical validation of our approaches to therapy, developed a step-by-step procedure that has been successfully tested as having sufficient efficacy and effectiveness and at the same time fits her personality strengths of getting clients involved emotionally and working with these emotions.

GLOSSARY

affective confrontation: One of Whitaker's techniques to challenge denied or invalidated emotions.

attachment: The most basic need for emotional and physical connection.

battle for initiative: Allowing the family members the freedom and giving them the responsibility to determine the course of therapy (used by Whitaker after the battle for structure is won).

battle for structure: Therapist taking control of the structure of therapy in order to establish an effective working relationship with the family.

blamer: One of Satir's communication types that describes a person who holds others responsible for his or her own mistakes by being dominating and self-righteous.

blockage of growth: Internal and external forces that keep people from growing emotionally.

connections: A form of relating between people that has emotional, cognitive, and sensual aspects.

cotherapy: Two therapists working at the same time with an individual, couple, or family for training purposes.

depathologizing of human experience: To put human behavior and feelings in a context that is not related to problems or disease.

development: The movement from one stage to the next over time.

Emotionally Focused Couple Therapy (EFCT): An experiential approach, based on humanistic, systemic, and attachment foundations, that helps couples to change negative interactional cycles and to express their primary emotions.

experiential: The therapeutic approach in which therapists reveal their real person and use the self to change the family (proponents include Susan Johnson, Virginia Satir, and Carl Whitaker).

family reconstruction: Families reenact key family situations in order to gain new insights into their family and their own lives.

family sculpturing: Physical arrangement of family members in space as determined by one family member who is called "director"; the sculpted constellation represents the relationships among family members.

flexibility of roles: A person may temporarily take on the role of another person.

humanistic-experiential: Virginia Satir's approach to family therapy that has a life-affirming view and emphasizes each person's uniqueness and worth, the potential for positive human interaction, and personal growth.

interpersonal: Between or among persons.

intervention: A therapist's statement or question that has the goal to change a client's behavior and/or affective state.

intrapersonal: Within a person.

irrelevant: One of Satir's communication types that describes a person who is a distracter and remains noncommittal toward interaction processes.

metaphor: A figure of speech in which a term is transferred from the object it ordinarily designates to an object it may designate only by implicit comparison or analogy.

modeling: Exhibiting behavior and affect a therapist would like the client to adopt.

negative interactions create negative cycles: When partners distrust each other and try to protect themselves, they engage in negative behaviors that elicit negative responses.

pathology: Behavior and affect that is associated with problems and disease.

placater: One of Satir's communication types that describes a person who tries to please at all costs, always agrees, and apologizes for everything.

primary emotions: Expressing one's core emotions that are related to the true genuine self.

reciprocity: A mutual condition or relationship.

redefining: Putting the meaning of a term into a different context in which its meaning changes.

reframing: Relabeling behavior by putting it into a new and positive context with the goal of eliciting a different behavior.

secondary reactive emotions: Emotions that serve as defenses to protect the vulnerable primary emotions. Couples rely on secondary emotions when they have insecure attachments to each other and do not trust their partners.

self-concept: Thoughts and ideas people hold about themselves.

self-esteem: Feelings and emotions people hold about themselves.

super reasonable: One of Satir's communication types that describes a person who remains emotionally detached, controlled, and rigid in his or her thinking.

symbolic-experiential: Carl Whitaker's approach to family therapy that focuses on the symbolic meanings of relationships.

REFERENCES

Alexander, J.F., Holtzworth-Munroe, A., and Jameson, P. (1994). The process and outcome of marital and family therapy: Research review and evaluation. In A. Bergin and S. Garfield (Eds.), *Handbook of psychotherapy and behavior change* (Fourth edition) (pp. 366-392). New York: Wiley.

Bowlby, J. (1969). *Attachment and loss.* Volume 1: *Attachment.* New York: Basic Books.

Brothers, B.J. (1991). Introduction. In B.J. Brothers (Ed.), *Virginia Satir: Foundational ideas* (pp. 1-15). Binghamton, NY: The Haworth Press.

Dunn, R.L. and Schwebel, A.I. (1995). Meta-analysis of marital therapy outcome research. *Journal of Family Psychology, 9,* 58-68.

Fisch, R., Weakland, J.H., and Segal, L. (1983). *Tactics of change.* New York: Norton.

Greenberg, L.S., Ford, C.L., Alden, L., and Johnson, S.M. (1993). In-session change in emotionally focused therapy. *Journal of Consulting and Clinical Psychology, 61,* 78-84.

Greenberg, L.S. and Johnson, S.M. (1985). Emotionally focused couples therapy. In N.S. Jacobson and A.S. Gurman (Eds.), *Clinical handbook of marital therapy* (pp. 313-317). New York: Guilford Press.

Greenberg, L.S. and Johnson, S.M. (1986). Affect in marital therapy. *Journal of Marital and Family Therapy, 12,* 1-10.

Greenberg, L.S. and Johnson, S.M. (1988). *Emotionally focused therapy for couples.* New York: Guilford Press.

Johnson, S.M. (1998). Emotionally focused couples therapy. In F.M. Dattilio (Ed.), *Case studies in couple and family therapy* (pp. 115-148). New York: Guilford Press.

Johnson, S.M. and Greenberg, L.S. (1995). The emotionally focused approach to problems in adult attachment. In N.S. Jacobson and A.S. Gurman (Eds.), *Clinical handbook of couple therapy* (pp. 121-141). New York: Guilford Press.

Keith, D.V. and Whitaker, C.A. (1982). Experiential/symbolic family therapy. In A.M. Horne and M.M. Ohlsen (Eds.), *Family counseling and therapy* (pp. 43-74). Itasca, IL: F. E. Peacock.

Napier, A.Y. and Whitaker, C.A. (1978). *The family crucible.* New York: Harper and Row.

Perls, F.S. (1961). *Gestalt therapy verbatim.* Lafayette, CA: Real People Press.

Roberto, L.G. (1991). Symbolic-experiential family therapy. In A.S. Gurman and D.P. Kniskern (Eds.), *Handbook of family therapy* (Volume 2) (pp. 444-476). New York: Brunner/Mazel.

Rogers, C.R. (1951). *Client-centered therapy.* Boston: Houghton Mifflin.

Satir, V.M. (1964). *Conjoint family therapy.* Palo Alto, CA: Science and Behavior Books.

Satir, V.M. (1972). *People making.* Palo Alto, CA: Science and Behavior Books.

Satir, V.M. (1986). A partial portrait of a family therapist in process. In H.C. Fishman and B.L. Rosman (Eds.), *Evolving models of family change: A volume in honor of Salvador Minuchin* (pp. 138-155). New York: Guilford Press.

Satir, V.M. (1988). *The new people making.* Palo Alto, CA: Science and Behavior Books.

Satir, V.M. and Baldwin, M. (1983). *Satir step-by-step.* Palo Alto, CA: Science and Behavior Books.

Satir, V.M. and Bitter, J.R. (1991). The therapist and family therapy: Satir's human validation model. In A.M. Horne and J.L. Passmore (Eds.), *Family counseling and therapy* (Second edition) (pp. 189-202). Itasca, IL: F. E. Peacock.

Thomas, M.B. (1992). *An introduction to marital and family therapy: Counseling toward healthier family systems across the lifespan.* New York: McMillan.

Whitaker, C.A. (1977). Process techniques of family therapy. *Interaction, 1,* 4-19.

Whitaker, C.A. and Bumberry, W.M. (1988). *Dancing with the family: A symbolic-experiential approach.* New York: Brunner/Mazel.

Whitaker, C.A. and Keith, D.V. (1981). Symbolic-experiential family therapy. In A.S. Gurman and D.P. Kniskern (Eds.), *Handbook of family therapy* (pp. 187-225). New York: Brunner/Mazel.

Whitaker, C.A. and Malone, T.P. (1953). *The roots of psychotherapy.* New York: Blakiston.

Chapter 8

Cognitive-Behavioral Therapies for Couples and Families

Norman Epstein

Couples are often adept at dealing with people outside the relationship, but few people enter an intimate relationship with the basic understandings—or the technical skills—that make a relationship blossom. They frequently lack the know-how to make joint decisions, to decipher their partners' communications. . . . Because of the strength of the feelings and expectations, the deep dependency, and the crucial, often arbitrary, symbolic meanings that they attach to each other's actions, partners are prone to misinterpret each other's actions. When conflicts occur, often as a result of miscommunication, partners are likely to blame each other rather than to think of the conflict as a *problem* that can be solved.

Aaron T. Beck, MD
Love Is Never Enough

Behavioral treatments for couple and family problems are based on the assumption that dysfunctional behaviors are learned and can be reduced or replaced with more constructive behaviors through new learning processes. Behavioral approaches for a wide range of human problems had their roots in laboratory research on learning processes in animals and humans. Ivan Pavlov (1932) demonstrated how emotional and behavioral responses could be conditioned so that they would be elicited by a **neutral stimulus,** by pairing the neutral stimulus with an existing **reflexive response.** For example, a dog could be conditioned to salivate at the sound of a bell if the bell was rung a number of times as the dog was salivating to the smell and taste of food. John Watson's publicized case of "Little Albert," in which a phobia was established in a child through such **classical conditioning** (Watson and Raynor, 1920), increased interest in applying learning principles to understand a variety of human clinical disorders. However, it was not until Joseph Wolpe (1958) developed **systematic desensitization** as a treatment for phobias that therapeutic interventions based on learning principles gained significant credibility as effective treatments. Based on the concept that a phobia is a classically conditioned response to a stimulus that is not dangerous, systematic desensitization involves pairing the anxiety-producing stimulus (e.g., a mouse) with relaxation, assertiveness, or some other response that is incompatible with anxiety. The exposure of the individual to the anxiety-provoking stimulus is done in steps, or a hierarchy, beginning with a mildly distressing aspect of the feared stimulus, such as looking at a caged mouse from across a room, and eventually progressing to holding a mouse. At each step, the individual practices the relaxation or other response that counteracts the anxiety response, and moves to the next higher step in the hierarchy only when he or she has **deconditioned** the anxiety at the current step. Wolpe's work advanced the field of behavior therapy and has contributed to the development of effective treatments for a variety of clinical problems, such as anxiety disorders and sexual dysfunctions. Nevertheless, the focus of the behavioral assessment and interventions tended to be on the individual, and potential application to interpersonal problems was unclear.

B. F. Skinner's (1953) work on **operant conditioning** had a more extensive impact on the development of behavioral approaches to couple and family problems. Skinner demonstrated that one could increase or decrease an animal's specific action by controlling the consequences of the action. Thus, a rat could be taught to press down a bar in a box if pressing the bar dispensed a food pellet (i.e., positive reinforcement was provided). In contrast, a behavioral response could be decreased by following it with conditions that are assumed to be aversive (punishment), or by discontinuing the reinforcement. Skinner (1953, 1971) argued that all human behavior could be explained in terms of such learning processes, and concepts about internal processes such as feelings, beliefs, etc., as causes of behavior are superfluous. Skinner considered all responses, including overt behaviors and internal responses such as emotions and thoughts, as acts that are controlled by consequences in the individual's environment, so treatment of problematic responses should involve changing the environmental conditions. Similar to Wolpe's work, Skinner's theoretical model was in opposition to the psychodynamic models (e.g., psychoanalytic theory) that dominated the field of psychology in the first half of the twentieth century with their focus on intra-psychic causes of behavior. Unlike psychodynamic propositions that an individual's current problems were caused by residual issues from childhood and other earlier life experiences, learning theories such as Skinner's emphasized present conditions that affect the occurrence of particular positive and negative behaviors. Equally important for clinical intervention was the idea that learned responses could be modified or eliminated through learning procedures. Skinner's ideas about the impact of one's environment (the specific consequences received for one's responses) had a major influence on the development of behavioral therapies, including early versions of behavioral couple and family therapy.

Even though operant conditioning principles were helpful in understanding how animals and people learn a variety of responses, it became clear that they had some limitations in accounting for the rapid and varied learning that takes place in humans during childhood and beyond. Clearly, humans learn complex responses without having to wait for reinforcement of the small acts that constitute them. Social learning theorists such as Rotter (1954) and Bandura (1977; Bandura and Walters, 1963) described observational learning processes in which an individual can imitate a complex behavior demonstrated by another person, particularly if the observer sees that the model has high status or receives reinforcement for the behavior. For example, Bandura and Walters's (1963) research showed that a child who observed an adult hitting a large toy clown was likely to imitate the behavior. Beginning early in life, a child learns many complex skills, such as speaking a language, playing sports, etc., by observing and imitating others who are modeling the skills. Social learning theorists began to focus on the interpersonal context in which behaviors are adopted and maintained, and the relevance of such learning processes for **mutual influences** between members of an intimate relationship began to be noted.

As described in more detail later, the earliest behavioral conceptualizations of couple and family relationships focused on ways in which two members of a relationship **shape** each other's behavior by providing consequences for particular responses. Thus, as two people interact, they reinforce each other for certain responses and either ignore or provide punishment for others. Over time, each person will increase the frequencies of responses that were reinforced and decrease frequencies of those that were ignored or punished. Goldstein (1971) and Stuart (1969) developed somewhat different treatments for marital distress, based on this concept of mutual influence. Goldstein worked with women whose husbands refused to take part in marital therapy, and instructed the wives in reinforcing their spouses for desired changes in specific behaviors without informing the husbands about this procedure. Stuart intervened jointly with both members of a couple, guiding them in devising behavioral "contracts" in which each person agreed to perform particular behaviors desired by the other person in return for receiving reinforcements from the partner. Such procedures were also based on social exchange theory developed by social psychologists

(Thibaut and Kelley, 1959) in which an individual's satisfaction with a relationship is a function of the ratio of benefits to costs that he or she experiences in the relationship.

Behavioral marital therapists such as Liberman (1970), Weiss, Hops, and Patterson (1973), O'Leary and Turkewitz (1978), Jacobson and Margolin (1979), and Stuart (1980) further developed techniques for increasing couples' mutual exchanges of positive behavior using social learning principles to teach communication skills and set up behavioral contracts between partners. Similarly, Patterson (1971) developed behavioral interventions for families with children who exhibited aggressive and other problematic behavior, based on social learning principles such as operant conditioning. Behavioral family therapists commonly have focused on developing parents' skills for decreasing their children's problematic behaviors and increasing their desirable behaviors (Barkley and Benton, 1998; Blechman, 1985; Graziano, 1971; Patterson and Forgatch, 1987; Webster-Stratton and Herbert, 1994). By the end of the 1970s, behavioral approaches to couple and family therapy had become established treatment modalities with growing evidence of their efficacy.

Even though behaviorists focused on changing family members' overt acts in order to establish more satisfying relationships, they increasingly acknowledged that there is **subjectivity** in individuals' experiences of what behaviors by other family members are pleasing or displeasing. For example, marital treatments by Margolin and Weiss (1978) and Jacobson and Margolin (1979) took into account partners' attributions for each other's behavior. Thus, if an individual intends to behave positively toward a partner, but the partner makes an inference (attribution) that the individual had negative motives for the behavior, the partner will be upset by the actions, whether or not the attribution is accurate. Nevertheless, publications on behavioral marital and family therapy did not provide much information on how clinicians could assess and modify family members' negative cognitions that were contributing to relationship conflict and distress.

Beginning in the 1980s, behaviorally oriented couple and family therapists began to integrate into their behavioral model of relationships some concepts and methods from the rapidly developing **cognitive therapies** of Ellis (1962), Beck (1976), and Meichenbaum (1977). Whereas behaviorists had largely focused on family members' overt actions, cognitive therapists emphasized how internal thought processes that are subject to distortion influence individuals' emotional and behavioral responses. Consideration of these subjective internal experiences posed a challenge for behaviorists who often had rejected intrapsychic explanations of behavior offered by psychodynamic theorists. However, findings from basic research on human cognition, research on the effectiveness of cognitive therapy for individual problems such as depression, and evidence that strictly behavioral interventions for couples' relationship problems produced had limited effectiveness all contributed to a growing acceptance of cognitive interventions among behaviorists (Baucom and Lester, 1986; Epstein and Williams, 1981; O'Leary and Turkewitz, 1978).

In turn, the tradition in cognitive therapies has been to focus on assessing and modifying individuals' cognitive distortions and other **inappropriate thought processes.** Thus, if an individual is unhappy in his or her marriage, a cognitive therapist would be most likely to help the person distinguish between views of the relationship that are distorted versus those that are accurate. Cognitive restructuring procedures could be used to change the distorted cognitions, but if the individual's views of the relationship were accurate, the implications for treatment were less clear. A cognitive therapist could help the individual devise alternative solutions to the problem of living in a distressing relationship, such as requesting change from the partner or perhaps ending the relationship. However, attempting to improve the relationship by working only with one member presented significant limitations. Consequently, as cognitive therapists have increasingly considered how individuals' interactions with significant others affect their well-being, they have integrated behavioral interventions for those relationships into their treatments (Beck, 1988; Epstein, 1982).

Thus, two converging trends have led to increasing integration of behavioral and cognitive theories and clinical techniques in the field of couple and family therapy. On one hand, behaviorally oriented therapists have adopted concepts and methods from cognitive therapies as a means for taking into account family members' subjective responses to one another's actions. On the other hand, cognitive therapists have adopted the behaviorists' focus on interaction processes among family members, which influences each person's subjective thoughts and emotions. Resulting **cognitive-behavioral approaches** to couple and family treatment attend to both the overt interactions among family members and the internal experiences of each member.

Both behavioral and cognitive models of couple and family therapy have been challenged by some adherents of systems theory as being limited to linear rather than **circular concepts of causality** in family relationships. They have argued that behaviorists' learning concepts, such as operant conditioning, involve **linear causal thinking,** in that reinforcement of a person's action causes an increase in that action. Similarly, systems-oriented theorists have argued that cognitive therapists see a linear causal relationship between a person's cognitions and his or her emotional and behavioral reactions (for example, a parent views a child as intentionally disobeying him or her, and this inference leads to anger toward the child and a spanking). Although these critiques have been accurate to some degree, they have overlooked aspects of cognitive-behavioral theory and practice that take into account mutual, circular influences involving members of a couple or family, which will be described in this chapter. For example, Bandura's (1977) social learning model takes into account how individuals who are interacting with one another mutually influence the probabilities that the other person will respond in particular ways.

During the 1970s, James Alexander and his colleagues (e.g., Barton and Alexander, 1981) developed **functional family therapy** as an integration of systems and behavioral approaches, based on the recognition that both models focus on interaction patterns among family members. Similar to other behavioral approaches, functional family therapy identifies specific sequences of behavior among family members and is intended to modify problematic patterns. Consistent with systems theory, it is based on a premise that understanding an individual's behavior requires identifying its interpersonal context—how the person influences and is influenced by other family members. Functional family therapists tend to differ from other behaviorists by assuming that a person's behavior is intentionally designed to produce particular consequences, even if the person is not fully aware of that intent. Thus, Barton and Alexander (1981) argue that if an individual's aversive behavior creates distance from other family members, the individual continues to behave in that manner because he or she desires that outcome, even if the person says otherwise. This premise has been debated, but it has challenged behaviorists to identify why members of families continue to engage in negative behaviors that seem to be at odds with their positive goals for their relationships. Functional family therapists do not view the function of an interpersonal behavior (creating distance or closeness) as inherently good or bad, but instead they focus on how particular behaviors that people use to achieve their goals create problems. For example, a couple that generally has difficulty achieving intimacy may feel close only when they make up with each other after verbally abusive arguments. A function of the arguments is to produce some intimate feelings, but the abusive arguments themselves also involve significant costs to the individuals and couple. Consequently, a functional family therapist will not try to change the function of the problematic behavior, but will use behavioral interventions to help the couple develop more constructive ways of achieving the end goal. Functional family therapy has contributed to the development of cognitive-behavioral approaches that take into account interpersonal processes and circular causality in family relationships.

This chapter describes the current state of cognitive-behavioral therapy with couples and families. Following a summary of the model's major theoretical concepts and identification of major proponents of the approach, both normal and dysfunctional family processes are described. Typical ways of assessing and treating couple and family problems from a cognitive-behavioral perspective are described, with illustrative case examples, and the current status of research on the efficacy of these methods is summarized.

THEORETICAL CONCEPTS

As described in the introduction, cognitive-behavioral approaches to couple and family therapy focus on the behavioral interactions and family members' subjective thoughts that contribute to relationship problems. The following sections describe the major behavioral and cognitive aspects of family interactions that are relevant in a cognitive-behavioral approach to understanding and treating relationship problems. In addition, the role of emotions in couple and family relationships is described, in relation to behavioral and cognitive factors.

Behavioral Factors in Couple and Family Relationships

Based on social learning principles (Bandura, 1977), it is assumed that when two adults form a couple relationship they each bring a personal learning history that affects how they relate to each other. In past relationships, especially in the family of origin, each person learned particular styles of communicating and relating to significant others, by observing parents, siblings, etc., and through being reinforced for certain actions and punished for others. In addition, the family of origin is a primary setting in which the child learns a variety of interpersonal skills, such as those for expressing thoughts and emotions clearly and constructively, and for listening effectively to others' expressions. In addition, parents implicitly model and explicitly teach their children skills for solving both small and large life problems. Some parents model effective problem-solving skills, whereas others model ineffective and even destructive approaches. For example, a child may observe a parent responding to conflict with extended family members and friends by behaving aggressively, or by cutting off contact with the other people. This **observational learning** may result in the child lacking constructive skills for dealing with conflictual relationships in his or her own life.

Problematic Couple and Parent-Child Interaction Patterns

Given the behavioral tendencies and skills that they bring to their relationship, the members of a couple develop patterns for interacting with each other. These patterns can vary considerably in their effectiveness in meeting the needs of the couple and of each partner. Cognitive-behavioral couple therapists (e.g., Baucom and Epstein, 1990; Jacobson and Christensen, 1996) have noted that at least some conflict is inevitable in intimate relationships, due to differences in the two partners' needs, personalities, temperaments, etc. One of the risk factors for marital distress is poor skills for identifying and implementing effective solutions to such relationship problems (Gottman, 1994; Weiss and Heyman, 1990). Gottman's research has indicated that distressed couples tend to respond to conflicts with negative behaviors such as criticism, defensiveness, contempt, and stonewalling (withdrawal).

Couples who engage in high rates of negative behavior toward each other tend to lack adequate skills for communicating their needs and for solving relationship problems in a cooperative way. In one common pattern, the partners develop an almost "automatic" response pattern in which a perceived negative behavior by one person results in **negative reciprocity** from the other person. In negative reciprocity, a person who receives a negative from his or her partner reciprocates with a negative act toward the partner. Sometimes the reciprocation is immediate, as an argument between partners escalates with mutual insults and threats, but at other times an individual waits until a later time to "get even." Distressed couples are more likely than satisfied ones to engage in negative reciprocity (Baucom and Epstein, 1990; Weiss and Heyman, 1990). A second common problematic couple interaction pattern involves one person pursuing the other, while the other person is withdrawing (Christensen, 1988). This **demand/withdraw** pattern typically becomes a repetitive cycle. Although family therapists are able to see the circular causal process in mutual attack and demand/withdraw patterns, the members of such couples typically perceive linear causality in their interactions, with the other person being at fault. For example, the individual who keeps pursuing a partner says, "I pursue only because my partner withdraws," but the other person's view is "I withdraw only because my partner keeps pursuing me." The cognitive-behavioral therapist's job is to help the couple understand the circular nature of their interaction problem, and to motivate each person to modify his or her contribution to it.

Parents' marital conflict and distress have been found to be associated with a variety of child problems, including **conduct disorders** and **depression** (e.g., Hetherington, Bridges, and Insabella, 1998; Jenkins and Smith,

1991). The research suggests that a major way in which a couple's conflict influences their children is through its effect on parenting behavior. Thus, a parent who is upset and distracted by couple relationship problems is less likely to guide and discipline a child in a patient, consistent, and constructive manner. Furthermore, a couple may express conflict in the area of parenting by openly counteracting each other's attempts to discipline a child and by trying to form an alliance with the child against the other parent. Consequently, when presented with a family with child emotional and behavioral problems, a cognitive-behavioral therapist may intervene with parental conflict to the extent that the couple is open to doing so, but his or her primary interventions are likely to focus on the ways that the two parents interact with the child.

Research also indicates problem-solving skills deficits and negative interaction patterns in distressed parent-adolescent relationships (Robin and Foster, 1989). Patterson (1982) has described how aggressive children commonly grow up in **coercive family systems,** in which their parents use criticism, threats, and various forms of punishment to try to control the children's behavior, and in turn the children use aversive behavior to influence the parents. Thus, the parents and children engage in a pattern of negative reciprocity, in which they exchange negative acts in a retaliatory manner.

If a child receives little attention or other reinforcement for his or her positive behavior, but receives considerable attention from parents (even if it is criticism, etc.) for negative actions, such as verbal and physical aggression, it is likely that the attention will reinforce and thus strengthen the negative behavior. Based on operant conditioning principles, the reinforcement of negative behavior is likely to produce a stronger effect if the parents provide it to the child inconsistently. Research by learning theorists such as B. F. Skinner indicated that an individual who receives **intermittent reinforcement**—in which the reinforcement occurs occasionally or unpredictably rather than every time—will keep behaving in the way that has produced the reinforcement even when there is no reinforcement for a long time. In essence, the individual has learned that sooner or later some reinforcement is likely to occur, so he or she should keep trying to elicit it. Those who doubt the power of intermittent reinforcement need only observe the persistence of individuals who use slot machines and other forms of gambling.

Furthermore, parents can unwittingly teach a child to use verbal and physical aggression through modeling, if they use those types of behavior in their discipline of the child. Although a parent may feel tempted to vent his or her frustration toward a child by using aversive words and actions, particularly if the parent lacks more effective parenting skills, that approach tends to backfire, in that it contributes to more coercive exchanges between the child and parents. As will be described, one of the tasks facing a cognitive-behavioral family therapist is changing some parents' beliefs about the usefulness of verbal and physical aggression in developing more positive behavior in their children.

An alternative form of punishment that is commonly advocated by cognitive-behavioral family therapists, at least for younger children, is the use of **time-out** procedures. Time out involves removing the child physically from all available sources of reinforcement, such as having him or her sit in a chair in a corner, away from TV, games, siblings, and even the attention of parents. The power of the technique is based on the child's tendency to seek reinforcement, and the unpleasant experience of being deprived of it. Sometimes parents report to a family therapist that they are familiar with and use time-out procedures (which are described in detail later) to punish a child for negative behavior, but the therapist discovers that they use the procedure inconsistently. On one hand, some parents send the child to a location in which there is still plenty of enjoyable activity to be found, such as the child's room. On the other hand, other parents may effectively cut off the child temporarily from reinforcement occasionally, but fail to do so consistently (perhaps yelling at the child instead). The principle of intermittent reinforcement helps explain why inconsistent use of time outs is ineffective.

Effective parenting also includes reinforcement of positive behavior. Often a parent is so focused on a child's negative behavior that he or she either fails to notice the instances in which the child behaves well or fails to provide reinforcement, such as praise, for those acts. Unfortunately, the systematic ignoring of positive behavior follows the operant learning principle of **extinction,** in which an act that has no positive consequences will decrease. Thus, if parents want children to behave less negatively, they need to use a combination of techniques to decrease negative acts and techniques to increase positive acts.

As previously noted, providing reinforcement for a child's positive behavior necessitates that the parent notice those actions. Jacobson and Margolin (1979) have labeled an individual's tendency to notice another's negative behavior and overlook positive behaviors as **negative tracking.** This biased perception is one of the forms of cognition described in the next section. Once a parent does notice a child's positive behavior, the parent faces a decision about how he or she should respond. Parents who believe that children should behave well "just because it is the right thing to do" and view reinforcement of positive behavior as "bribes" are unlikely to use praise and other rewards. These beliefs constitute assumptions and standards, two other forms of cognition that influence family relationships and are described in the next section. A third factor in parents' failure to provide reinforcement for their children's positive acts is **deficits in communication skills.** Some parents are unfamiliar with ways to phrase positive feedback messages to their children effectively. Rather than giving a vague, general message such as "You had a better day yesterday," the parent may need to learn how to give the child specific behavioral feedback, such as "I was very happy to see you putting your dirty clothes in the hamper, cleaning up the dinner table, and not hitting your sister when she interrupted your game."

Inconsistency in parenting behavior may be due to various factors. Although some factors involve deficits in the parents' behavioral skills, others involve the ways that they think about their parenting roles. Some parents feel ambivalent about setting firm limits on their children's behavior, because they equate strictness with harshness. In some cases, a parent has bought into a child's complaint that the parent is being unloving or unfair by setting limits on what is acceptable child behavior. Other parents, such as those who have experienced separation or divorce, or who work long hours and have limited time to spend with their children, may feel guilty that their children have experienced aspects of these family situations. Still others feel overwhelmed by various stresses in their lives, such as trying to balance their work and family, and do not believe that they can tolerate the effort involved in consistent parenting behavior. These factors involve the **cognitions** that the parents have about parenting, and in cognitive-behavioral family therapy the clinician helps each parent identify and modify such thought patterns that interfere with constructive interactions with their children. A more detailed description of cognitive factors in family interaction follows.

Cognitive Factors in Couple and Family Relationships

As described, cognitive therapies are based on the premise that a person's emotional and behavioral responses to life events depend on the particular thoughts the person has about those events. Virtually the same event might happen to two people, but the two individuals might react differently because they interpret the event differently.

Bonnie and Fred were eating breakfast together and talking about ideas for a family summer vacation when their sixteen-year-old son Mike walked into the kitchen. When Bonnie told Mike that they were thinking about all of them—including Mike and his younger brother Rick—spending ten days at a beach resort, Mike simply responded, "I don't want to go to any resort. I just want to stay home and spend time with my friends." Bonnie's immediate reaction was a strong feeling of sadness, and she sat quietly, but Fred became quite angry and yelled at Mike, telling him he was "ungrateful for the nice things we try to do for you." When Bonnie and Fred discussed the incident later, Bonnie described how Mike's comment made her feel sad because it made her think that their days as a whole family were ending, as their son was moving toward independence. In contrast, Fred noted that his anger had been associated with thoughts that Mike should be grateful that his parents were willing to spend a lot of money to take him to a special place, and that Mike's comment was disrespectful. Thus, each parent interpreted Mike's behavior somewhat differently, and their subjective interpretations led to different emotions and behaviors.

Aaron Beck's cognitive therapy (Beck, 1976; Beck et al., 1979; Beck, 1995; Leahy, 1996) focuses on helping individuals learn to identify aspects of their thinking that are contributing to negative emotions and behavior, to test the validity of their thoughts, and to replace distorted cognitions with more realistic ones. In Beck's model, two major types of cognitions influence individuals' responses to events in their lives: automatic thoughts and schemas.

Automatic Thoughts

Automatic thoughts are the stream-of-consciousness thoughts that spontaneously run through one's mind and seem plausible at the time, even if they are distorted. People typically do not stop to question their automatic thoughts, so the thoughts can control their moods and behavior. Beck (1976) originally developed cognitive therapy based on his observation that depressed individuals had frequent overly negative thoughts about themselves, the world, and their futures. These negative thoughts are shaped by particular **cognitive distortions,** or errors in processing information. For example, **overgeneralization** is a cognitive distortion in which the individual observes one instance of an event and views it as representing a general characteristic. For example, when five-year old Amanda disobeyed Tim's instruction to put her toys away, he thought, "She *never* listens to what I tell her to do," and this thought made him angry. Later, he was able to take a broader perspective on the event and acknowledged that sometimes Amanda is obedient, and sometimes not. Some other types of cognitive distortions identified by cognitive therapists (e.g., Beck et al., 1979) include **personalization** (assuming that events involve you when in fact they do not), **mindreading** (making unwarranted inferences about others' thoughts and emotions), **dichotomous thinking** (placing experiences into distinct, opposite categories, such as "good child" versus "bad child"), **selective abstraction** (biased perceptions such as negative tracking, described earlier), **magnification** (viewing something as more important than it is, such as seeing a relatively minor mistake as a catastrophe), and **minimization** (viewing something as less important than it is, such as seeing one's own or another's improved behavior as "no big deal"). Cognitive therapists help their clients become aware of upsetting distortions in their thinking and teach them ways to challenge their negative automatic thoughts.

Theorists and researchers who have studied forms of cognition affecting couple and family relationships (see reviews by Baucom and Epstein, 1990; Baucom et al., 1989; Epstein and Baucom, 1993; Fincham, Bradbury, and Scott, 1990) have identified three types of cognition that can involve the information-processing errors involved in cognitive distortions. **Selective perception** is equivalent to the distortion of selective abstraction, in which an individual notices only some aspects of his or her interactions with a family member. Thus, Tim's selective perception of his daughter Amanda's disobedience contributed to his anger. Research on couples has indicated that partners, especially those in distressed relationships, commonly disagree on what events have occurred in their interactions within a twenty-four-hour period (Christensen, Sullaway, and King, 1983; Jacobson and Moore, 1981).

Attributions are inferences that individuals make about causes of events that they observe, and these inferences may be accurate or distorted. Some attributions concern the characteristics of a cause, i.e., whether it is global versus specific, stable versus unstable, and internal to a person or relationship versus external.

When Denise told Sam that she had lost her job, he said little to her. Her attribution that his lack of support for her was due to "his self-centered personality" was global, stable, and internal to Sam. It was global because she viewed his lack of support as due to a broad personality characteristic that is likely to influence many areas of Sam's functioning (i.e., if he is self-centered, it is likely to affect other ways in which he relates to Denise and others). It was stable because it involves a personality characteristic that is likely to be present over a long period of time. Finally, as part of Sam's personality it was an internal characteristic rather than an outside cause. In contrast, Denise might have attributed Sam's behavior to his being distracted by a stressful project at his job. Such a cause is more external to Sam, it is unstable to the extent to which work stresses at his job tend to be temporary, and it is specific to the extent that it adversely affects his ability to listen to Denise when the topic of conversation is their jobs.

Research on couples' attributions has generally found that members of distressed couples are more likely than satisfied couples to attribute their partners' negative behaviors to global, stable characteristics of the partner (Bradbury and Fincham, 1990; Baucom and Epstein, 1990). These attributions concerning negative traits in the partner are associated with individuals' future levels of distress and negative communication with their partners (Bradbury and Fincham, 1992; Fincham and Bradbury, 1987; Fincham, Harold, and Gano-Phillips, 2000). Barton and Alexander (1981) note that when family members attribute relationship problems to negative traits of other members, it reduces the chance that they will work toward changing the ways they interact with one another. Blaming problems on another person typically leads to waiting for the other person to change and failing to recognize ways in which one can contribute to change oneself. In addition, viewing problems as being caused by global, stable traits is likely to result in the individual feeling hopeless about change.

Other attributions affect relationships because of their particular content. For example, Pretzer, Epstein, and Fleming (1991) found that individuals who attributed their couple relationship problems to a lack of love or malicious intent by their partners were more dissatisfied in their relationships. Similarly, Morton, Twentyman, and Azar's (1988) clinical observations of child-abusing parents indicated that these parents commonly believe that their children's misbehavior is caused by intentional efforts to be annoying and spiteful.

Expectancies are the third type of cognition that potentially involves the distorted processing of information. An expectancy is a prediction that an individual makes about the probability that particular events will occur in the near or distant future.

Dave may tell his son Robby that he cannot play outside before dinner, because he has an expectancy that Robby will run off with his friends. As with other types of inferences, expectancies can vary in their accuracy, and to some degree a person's expectancies about family members are shaped by past experiences with those individuals. Thus, Dave's expectancy may be due to several past episodes of Robby disappearing with friends at mealtimes. However, perhaps Robby has never run off in that way, and Dave's expectancy is based on his general belief that "young boys are impulsive and mostly pay attention to having fun with their friends."

Research studies have indicated that couples' negative expectancies about their abilities to solve relationship problems are associated with higher levels of relationship distress (Pretzer, Epstein, and Fleming, 1991; Vanzetti, Notarius, and NeeSmith, 1992). Cognitive-behavioral therapists help family members identify their expectancies and test their validity.

Schemas

Whereas cognitive distortions shape the *form* of a person's thoughts, cognitive-behavioral therapists examine how the *content* of the thoughts is based on **schemas,** long-standing beliefs or "knowledge structures" that the individual has about characteristics of people, objects, relationships, etc. In contrast to selective perceptions, attributions, and expectancies, which tend to focus on events occurring at a particular moment or in a particular situation, schemas are relatively stable ways in which a person understands his or her world. They include basic beliefs about how human beings function and how they relate to one another. It is thought that many of these schemas begin to develop during an individual's childhood, based on experiences that he or she has with other people and other aspects of the world. Later life experiences can alter an existing schema, but research indicates that strongly established beliefs can be highly resistant to change (Fiske and Taylor, 1991). Examples of schemas relevant to couple and family relationships are beliefs about **gender roles** and characteristics of females and males, beliefs about how love "feels," beliefs about appropriate behavior of individuals in particular family roles such as "child," and beliefs about the characteristics of a "good marriage." Two major categories of schemas that affect couple and family relationships are assumptions and standards (Baucom and Epstein, 1990; Baucom et al., 1989; Epstein and Baucom, 1993).

Assumptions are beliefs that an individual has about typical characteristics of people and objects, as well as the relationships among them. In essence, assumptions are concepts about how particular aspects of the world are and how they work. For example, as a child observes people over a period of time, he or she develops a set of concepts about human thoughts, emotions, and behavior. Those concepts vary from one person to another, depending on the particular people the individual observed and the idiosyncratic inferences that he or she made about what was observed. A child who is raised in a home in which parents and older siblings frequently vent anger through sudden verbal and physical outbursts may develop a basic assumption that the expression of strong emotions is automatic and uncontrollable. Such an assumption may affect the way the child deals with his or her own emotions in relationships with others, during childhood and adulthood. Eidelson and Epstein identified some assumptions that tend to be associated with marital distress, including the beliefs that (1) disagreement between partners is destructive to their relationship, (2) problems in male-female relationships are due to innate differences between the sexes, and (3) once patterns have developed in a relationship, the partners cannot change them (Eidelson and Epstein, 1982; Epstein and Eidelson, 1981).

Standards are beliefs about ways that people, relationships, and events "should" be. Similar to assumptions, it is likely that individuals develop personal standards for themselves and their relationships on the basis of life experiences. Those experiences can involve family-of-origin relationships, observation of other people's characteristics and relationships, mass media (e.g., television, movies, books, magazines, popular songs), peer relationships, teachers, clergy, etc. Holding standards is not inherently problematic, in fact, people typically have some basic standards that make up their personal moral codes (e.g., "Parents should nurture their children and avoid abusing them"). However, standards can vary in how realistically they represent the possibilities of real life, and unrealistic beliefs may lead to frustration, disappointment, and other negative experiences. For example, Eidelson and Epstein (1982) found that the more individuals adhered to standards that (1) partners should be able to mind-read each other's thoughts and emotions, and (2) partners' sexual relationship should be perfect (always trouble free and highly satisfying), the more they were unhappy in their relationships. The concept of extreme or **unrealistic beliefs** is similar to the **irrational beliefs** that are a focus of **rational-emotive therapy** (Ellis, 1962; Ellis et al., 1989), which has more recently been renamed rational-emotive behavior therapy due to its increased focus on clients' behaviors. Ellis and his colleagues have emphasized that when an individual holds unrealistic beliefs about the ways that people and life experiences should be, he or she is likely to be upset and to behave negatively when the realities of daily life fall short of those desires.

Two other ways in which standards might be problematic are when (1) two partners' standards are in conflict, and when (2) a person's standards are potentially realistic but are not being met to his or her satisfaction in the couple's relationship. Baucom et al. (1996) developed a questionnaire to assess individuals' standards for their couple relationships, focusing on standards about **boundaries** (how much autonomy versus togetherness partners should have), the degree of **investment** of time and energy that partners should make for their relationship, and how **power/control** should be distributed and used in the couple's relationship. Their Inventory of Specific Relationship Standards (ISRS) assesses these three types of standards that each member of a couple has concerning twelve different areas of their relationship, such as affection, sex, household tasks, finances, and the expression of positive and negative feelings. Baucom and colleagues found a modest relationship between lack of consensus between partners' standards and the individuals' levels of relationship distress. The strongest predictor of distress was the degree to which the individual reported that he or she was not satisfied with the ways in which personal standards were being met in the relationship.

Thus, a cognitive-behavioral model of couple and family functioning takes into account a number of types of cognitions that individuals have about themselves and their close relationships. To a significant degree, the types of behavior patterns described in the previous section are influenced by the ways that family members interpret one another's actions. For example, in negative reciprocity, two family members are more likely to reciprocate each other's negative acts if they selectively notice the negatives and overlook the positives, or if they attribute the negative behavior to causes such as the other person having malicious intent. Similarly, an individual may withdraw from another family member if he or she has an expectancy that any attempt to communicate with the other person will be ineffective. Concerning personal standards, a parent may fail to use positive reinforcement for a child's good behavior if the parent believes that children should naturally behave well because "they know it's the right thing to do," and that rewarding children "only spoils them." The parent's standard results in dissatisfaction with the child's behavior, and it influences how the parent chooses to respond to the child's failure to live up to what the parent expects. Consequently, understanding and treating problems in couple and family relationships necessitates paying attention to both the ways that family members interact and the members' cognitions which influence those interactions.

These emphases on behavior and cognition in the literature on cognitive-behavioral therapies sometimes creates an impression that emotions of family members are neglected in these approaches. In fact, family members' emotional responses are central aspects of their satisfaction or distress in their relationships and are of major concern to cognitive-behavioral therapists. The next section describes important emotional factors in couple and family relationships.

Emotional Factors in Couple and Family Relationships

Much of the literature on cognitive therapy has focused on thought processes as causes for depression, anxiety, anger, and other emotions (e.g., Beck, 1988; Beck et al., 1979; Beck and Emery, 1985; Dattilio and Padesky, 1990; Deffenbacher, 1996; Ellis et al., 1989), whether the individual is responding to family relationships or other life events. Similarly, behavioral couple and family therapists commonly have emphasized how exchanges of positive and negative behavior between members of a relationship affect the individuals' satisfaction with the relationship. Thus, it is easy to get the impression that cognitive-behavioral models take a linear causal view, in which emotions are results, but not causes, of family members' cognitions and behaviors. However, considerable clinical and research evidence suggests that individuals' emotions about their relationships influence their thoughts and behavior as well. Weiss (1980) described a process of **sentiment override,** in which a person's preexisting overall feelings about a spouse determines the person's cognitions and behavior toward the spouse more than the spouse's current behavior does.

Ken had built up a high level of resentment toward Sarah based on a number of incidents over the past two years in which she had made personal choices that seemed selfish to him. Sarah was aware of Ken's being upset about those past events, and she was committed to improving their relationship. Consequently, she had begun to make special efforts to ask Ken about his preferences about decisions she was considering. However, each time Sarah asked to talk to Ken about such a decision, even when she began the discussion by emphasizing that she wanted to consider his input, Ken quickly reacted with anger and criticized her for being selfish. His strong emotion interfered with his ability to listen to her and led to his negative behavior toward her.

Similarly, Nikki had become depressed about her relationship with James, because their work shifts and child-rearing activities left them very little time as a couple. Unfortunately, whenever they did have an opportunity to do something together, her depressed mood made it difficult for her to enjoy herself. James would notice her lack of enthusiasm and comment on it. Nikki would react defensively, and they would have an argument.

Cognitive therapists also have noted how an individual's emotional states can influence his or her perception and behavior. They have described how an individual may engage in **emotional reasoning,** wherein he or she relies on cues of his or her emotions as signs of some "truth." For example, depressed individuals commonly experience symptoms of low energy, inertia, and low motivation to engage in even basic daily activities such as getting out of bed and getting dressed. If the person concludes, "I don't feel that I can do anything," it is likely that he or she will become inactive, which tends to worsen the depression. Cognitive therapists help the individual understand that it is important not to trust the physical and emotional cues that he or she is experiencing, and that it is possible to engage in activities even when one feels that way. Similarly, people who experience panic attacks often interpret the symptoms (e.g., rapid heart rate, sweating, shortness of breath) as signs of a serious physical problem such as a heart attack, or a sign of "going crazy." Cognitive-behavioral treatment of panic disorders includes teaching the individual that those symptoms may be uncomfortable but are not dangerous.

Thus, emotion has a crucial role in cognitive-behavioral approaches to couple and family relationships, and therapists typically gather a lot of information about the emotions that each family member experiences during their interactions. It is important to differentiate various types of emotions, rather than asking family members how happy versus unhappy, or satisfied versus dissatisfied, they are. Individuals' negative emotions regarding their relationships can include anger, sadness, depression, anxiety, etc., or a combination of emotions, and each type of emotion may require a different form of intervention. For example, an individual's anxiety may be associated with negative expectancies that communicating directly with his or her partner will lead to criticism by the partner and emotional tension between the two people. The individual may find anxiety symptoms so unpleasant that he or she generally avoids expressing important thoughts and emotions to the partner. Intervention is likely to include exploration of how valid the negative expectancies are. To the extent that communicating with the partner appears to be tension provoking but otherwise safe, and that direct communication would be advantageous for meeting the person's needs in the relationship, therapy may focus on reducing the person's avoidant behavior and increasing open communication.

In contrast, another individual may primarily experience anger, associated with sentiment override from past unpleasant experiences with the partner. Rather than avoiding the partner, this person quickly becomes upset whenever the partner discusses their relationship, and the anger leads him or her to attack the partner verbally. In this case, the therapy is like to focus on moderating the individual's strong, global anger response and helping him or her practice listening to the partner. The past events that have contributed to the person's pervasive anger also would be explored, with a goal of seeing whether conditions in the couple's relationship that led to the anger have changed or could be changed.

PROPONENTS OF THE MODEL

As described previously, current forms of cognitive-behavioral therapy for couples and families represent an integration of behavior therapy and cognitive therapy traditions, along with systems theory concepts. Behavioral marital and family therapists (in alphabetical order) such as James Alexander, Ileana Arias, Donald Baucom, Steven Beach, Gary Birchler, Andrew Christensen, Norman Epstein, Ian Falloon, Frank Floyd, Sharon Foster, Kurt Hahlweg, W. Kim Halford, Richard Heyman, Amy Holtzworth-Munroe, Neil Jacobson, Gayla Margolin, Howard Markman, Clifford Notarius, K. Daniel O'Leary, Jill Rathus, Arthur Robin, William Sanderson, Stephen Schlesinger, Scott Stanley, Richard Stuart, Dina Vivian, and Robert L. Weiss have integrated assessment and modification of cognitions in their treatments. Sometimes these authors' publications describe cognitive interventions as **adjunctive interventions** to their primary focus on behavioral interactions. For example, if the members of a couple are resistant to practicing constructive communication skills because they attribute each other's past negative communication to a lack of caring about their relationship, the therapist might shift from the behavioral intervention to challenging the negative attributions. At other times, therapists whose background was primarily behavioral have shifted toward giving cognition relatively equal weight as behavior in their approaches.

On the other hand, therapists whose background focused on cognitive processes within individuals (in alphabetical order) such as Aaron T. Beck, Frank Dattilio, Windy Dryden, Albert Ellis, Arthur Freeman, and Christine Padesky have embraced concepts and clinical methods involving behavioral interactions and systems theory. Sometimes they use behavioral interventions primarily as means for producing cognitive changes, such as when training in constructive communication is used to modify partners' hopelessness that their relationship can improve, or to increase their ability to give each other feedback that can challenge other negative cognitions about each other.

Thus, the proponents of cognitive-behavioral couple and family therapy represent a mix of individuals whose original primary theoretical orientation tended to be either behavioral or cognitive. However, as behavior and cognition have been integrated in cognitive-behavioral clinical training programs, more therapists are entering their clinical careers with a view that treatment of relationship problems necessarily involves attention to complex relations between behavior and cognition, as well as family members' emotional responses. Publications by Baucom and Epstein (1990); Dattilio (1998a,b); Epstein, Schlesinger, and Dryden (1988); Morris, Alexander, and Waldron (1988); Rathus and Sanderson (1999); Robin and Foster (1989); and Schwebel and Fine (1994) reflect the trend toward integrative cognitive-behavioral approaches to couple and family therapy.

NORMAL FAMILY DEVELOPMENT

Within a cognitive-behavioral model, normal couple and family development depends on the fulfillment of each member's personal needs, as well as some core functions of the relationship. Among the major needs of individual members are those involving connection with significant others (e.g., intimacy, nurturance, altruism) and those involving individual functioning (e.g., autonomy, achievement, power) (see Prager, 1995, for an excellent discussion of these **communal needs** and **agentic or individually oriented needs,** respectively). Major relationship functions include those that provide for the physical and economic security of the couple or family, as well as those that allow the family to interact successfully with aspects of the outside world, such as schools. Needs and relationship functions are likely to be fulfilled to the extent to which the members of a couple or family (1) are aware of those needs and what types of actions are involved in meeting them, (2) communicate in clear, constructive ways that facilitate those actions, (3) can engage in effective problem solving when their current interactions are inadequate for meeting their needs, and (4) have cognitions that facilitate all of these processes. In normal family development, the members are relatively free of distortions in their appraisals of the events that occur in their relationship, have realistic standards for the ways in which they interact, approach each other in the spirit of collaboration and mutual support (rather than as adversaries), and have good skills for communicating and working together to resolve conflicts and problems.

Communal and individually oriented needs sometimes conflict with each other, either within an individual or between family members (Baucom and Epstein, 1999; Epstein and Baucom, 1999). For example, Janice was strongly motivated to have close relationships with her husband and children, but she also was highly motivated to achieve in her career. Although these two needs were in no way incompatible in principle, Janice sometimes found herself feeling stressed when the time demands of family and career pulled her in different directions, so she experienced internal conflict. In addition, her husband Paul had more traditional views of gender roles than Janice did, and he periodically pressed her to decrease her work hours, which led to some conflict between the spouses. Similarly, it is common for adolescents to move toward greater autonomy from their parents, which often creates some parent conflict as the parents may be unprepared for the change in the relationship. Such intrapersonal and interpersonal conflicts over normal human needs commonly pose challenges for couples and families.

In normal family development, the individuals have a realistic understanding of their owns needs and those of the other family members, and have flexible ways of thinking about and relating to one another in order to solve problems that arise. Their cognitive flexibility and relative rationality allow them to engage in creative problem solving. Thus, the parents of an adolescent who has become argumentative and less interested in family activities may be able to interpret (i.e., make attributions about) the child's behavior in nonthreatening ways and experiment with new ways of letting him or her balance some autonomy and family connectedness. Consistent with **social exchange theory** (Thibaut and Kelley, 1959), if a relationship begins to become less satisfying over time because the ratio of positives to negatives exchanged has decreased, normal family development involves the members' identifying the shift and interpreting it in a relatively benign way rather than as a sign that the relationship is no longer viable. Their ability to communicate clearly and collaborate in problem solving allows them to increase the positive behaviors and decrease the negative behaviors, thus restoring a more satisfying balance.

PATHOLOGY AND BEHAVIOR DISORDERS

In contrast to normal couple and family development, dysfunction develops in close relationships when the behaviors that meet the members' needs and fulfill the relationship's basic functions decrease, become less effective, or are outweighed by behaviors that interfere with fulfillment of needs. In a cognitive-behavioral model, these changes may be influenced by the family members' cognitions as well as the specific behaviors that occur. For example, a husband may exhibit fewer affectionate and caring actions toward his wife because he has become busier and distracted by his job, or he may be behaving about the same as in the past, but his wife finds his "predictable" behaviors less meaningful than she did years ago.

Consistent with family systems concepts, dysfunction occurs when the patterns in a relationship fail to help the members adapt to changing life circumstances (Carter and McGoldrick, 1999). Thus, if parents have relatively rigid standards about how an adolescent should relate to the family, attribute the adolescent's autonomous behavior as disrespectful to them, and tend to respond in a coercive, authoritarian manner to the adolescent's violations of their rules, parent-adolescent conflict is likely to escalate. As described, research on distressed couples and families has indicated high levels of both unrealistic assumptions and standards, negative attributions regarding one another's motives, and **aversive control** strategies such as threats, punishment, and other negative behavior. Unfortunately, as members of a relationship rely on aversive control in order to try to change one another's behavior (and often one another's "bad attitude"), that approach typically backfires, contributing to negative reciprocity of escalating negative behavior exchanges, or a demand/withdraw pattern. Gottman's (1994, 1999) research has identified behavioral sequences or **cascades,** in which attacking, defensive, and withdrawing behaviors increase distress among members of a relationship, and increase the probability that the partners will end the relationship.

A combination of negative cognitions, emotions, and behaviors among members of the relationship results in either a relatively chronic level of dissatisfaction or a deterioration over time. Even when an individual attempts to behave positively toward other family members, the others are unlikely to notice or appreciate it, due to their overall negative sentiment toward the person. Thus, each individual's negative behavior tends to be reinforced in the family interactional system, and his or her positive behaviors are ignored or even punished. In the absence of good expressive and listening communication skills, as well as problem-solving skills, the family is unable to disengage itself from these destructive patterns.

When an individual family member is experiencing personal difficulties such as psychopathology symptoms, those symptoms can place stress on family relationships and, in return, family stress and conflict can exacerbate an individual's personal adjustment problems (Halford and Bouma, 1997; Miklowitz, 1995). This bidirectional causality necessitates that couple and family therapists assess the degree to which an individual's development of psychological and behavioral disorders affects the development of relationship problems, and vice versa. A cognitive-behavioral model focuses on both processes, and decisions about combinations of individual therapy and couple or family therapy depend on the evidence concerning the causal processes in a particular family.

TECHNIQUES

Cognitive-behavioral techniques for couple and family therapy tend to emphasize **cognitive restructuring** and changes in the members' behavior. Cognitive restructuring techniques are designed to help family members increase their awareness of their cognitions that are contributing to distress and conflict, and to test their validity or appropriateness (Baucom and Epstein, 1990; Epstein, Schlesinger, and Dryden, 1988). Behavior change techniques focus on increasing family members' positive actions toward one another, decreasing negative actions, and developing their skills for effective communication and problem solving. Although they have received less attention in cognitive-behavioral therapy publications, treatment includes techniques for improving the family members' awareness of their emotions, their skills for expressing their emotions in clear and constructive ways, and their ability to regulate their emotional responses. **Emotional regulation** involves an individual's ability to control the strength of his or her emotions, for example, using **relaxation techniques** so that one feels moderate anger rather than rage. In clinical practice, interventions for cognitions, behaviors, and emotions commonly are combined during treatment sessions, as well as for homework assignments between sessions, but for clarity here they are described separately in the following sections.

It is important to note that cognitive-behavioral therapists are not restricted to any particular interventions and can use any approach that is designed to modify problematic family interactions, is objectively measurable, and is subjected to empirical evaluation of its effectiveness (Wetchler and Piercy, 1996). As noted by Wetchler and Piercy, the role of the therapist in this model is one of teacher/consultant, in which he or she provides didactic information, instructions, modeling of constructive responses, and coaching as family members try new skills and responses with one another. Treatment is designed to teach families skills that they can continue to use long after therapy has ended.

Cognitive Assessment and Interventions

Effective cognitive restructuring begins with systematic assessment of family members' selective perceptions, attributions, expectancies, assumptions, and standards concerning their relationships. The major approaches to the assessment are (1) detailed interviews with the family, (2) observation of the thoughts that they spontaneously express as they speak to one another, (3) probing for cognitions associated with particular emotional and behavioral responses of family members during sessions, and (4) use of questionnaires.

Interviews Concerning Cognitions

A therapist can assess an individual's selective perceptions of other family members' behavior by asking questions about what specific acts he or she observes, when they occur, in what circumstances, and how often. Sometimes it becomes clear that the individual is leaving out important information because he or she has failed to notice it. For example, a parent may initially report that a child "fails to obey directions." When asked for examples, the parent describes instances in which the child was told to "clean his room" and in which he was instructed to "stop interrupting adults when they are talking to each other." When the therapist asked the parent to describe any instances in which the child did obey a directive, the parent replied, "I can't think of any. He's a very willful child." However, the therapist then asked, "When you send him in to clean his room, are there any things he does to clean up?" The parent hesitated and then replied, "He puts some toys away in his closet but he leaves dirty clothes on his bed and books on the floor instead of where they belong in the bookshelf." The therapist began to understand that the parent selectively fails to notice, or discounts, instances in which the child exhibited some obedient behaviors that could be praised in order to encourage the child.

In this example, the therapist also noticed that the parent used the **negative trait label** "willful child," and asked questions to determine the degree to which the parent assumed that "willfulness" was a broad characteristic affecting many areas of the child's life. Often parents in distressed families attribute their children's negative behavior to such traits rather than to **situational conditions.** For example, given the widespread publicity concerning **attention deficit hyperactivity disorder (ADHD),** many parents automatically attribute their children's distracted, active, or disobedient behavior to that disorder and fail to consider ways in which the child's environment may be eliciting and reinforcing the undesirable behavior. Differentiating between ADHD and a behavior problem that developed primarily through learning experiences requires careful observation of a child's behavior in a variety of situations. In general, a therapist can interview each family member about attributions for others' behavior by asking questions such as "When you see her behaving like that, what do you think causes that behavior? Why do you think that happens?"

Similarly, individuals' expectancies about events in their relationships can be tapped by asking questions such as, "When you think about [behaving in a particular way], how do you think [particular family members] will react?" It is important to identify how the person anticipates that others will respond in the short term *and* in the long term, because the expectancies may be different. For example, when Susan was asked how she believed her partner Michele would react if Susan said she wanted to discuss possible changes in their responsibilities for household tasks, she replied, "She would listen quietly, and would agree to do some chores more often." However, when asked what Michele might do later, Susan said, "She'd probably make me pay for it later by turning me down when I suggest going out to do something I really enjoy."

Assessing family members' assumptions about each other and their relationships involves asking questions about the characteristics that they believe certain types of people have, and about how they believe relationships function. For example, some parents assume that young children are incapable of depression, anxiety, and other strong emotions that adults feel, so they do not consider that their children's behavior problems or academic difficulties may be influenced by such emotional responses to life events. A therapist can interview a parent about his or her assumptions by using questions such as "Your family recently moved here and left relatives, friends, etc. behind. You mentioned that your son's school problems started soon after you moved. How do you think he has coped with the big changes in his life?" Perhaps the parent would reply, "He complained about moving, but within a couple days he was playing outside with the boy next door. Kids make new friends really easily, and they just move on with their lives." The therapist might continue the inquiry into the parent's assumption about the son's emotional life by saying, "You described how you have felt sad about leaving your friends. How do you think your son's experience of leaving his friends might compare with yours?"

An individual's relationship standards can be assessed with questions in the form of "How do you believe [some aspect of oneself, the partner, or the relationship] should be? If things could be just the way you want them to be, what would it be like?" Alternatively, when an individual describes a characteristic of the self, partner, or relationship, the therapist can ask, "How does that compare with the way you want it to be? In what ways is it similar, and in what ways different?"

Observation of Spontaneously Expressed Cognitions

As described, family members often spontaneoulsy express some of their cognitions as they speak to the therapist and one another. For example, clues to selective perception include language such as, "You *always* . . ." and "You *never* . . ." Attributions are commonly expressed with trait labels such as, "You're so *selfish!*" and descriptions of others' motives, such as, "You want to control my life." Concerning expectancies, an individual might spontaneously voice a prediction such as, "If I count on you to pick up after yourself, in a few days I won't be able to see the floor of your bedroom." Assumptions tend to be expressed in terms of statements about the ways that things *are* (e.g., "Men are . . ." or "Women are . . ."), whereas standards tend to be expressed as conditions that *should* exist (e.g., "You should want to do your fair share of the chores"). However, a therapist must be cautious and not assume that he or she knows exactly what cognitions an individual's comments reflect, and needs to ask questions to pin down the specific meaning.

Probing for Cognitions Associated with Emotional and Behavioral Responses

During a couple or family therapy session, the therapist often will notice cues that an individual is reacting to something that another person has said or done. Sometimes there are verbal or nonverbal signs of an emotional response (e.g., a pained facial expression), and sometimes the individual's actions (e.g., turning away) suggest that he or she is interpreting the other's behavior in a negative way. At such times, a therapist can gently interrupt the interaction, point out the person's response, and ask what the person was just thinking. This kind of "here and now" probing for cognitions is valuable, in that it gives the therapist opportunities to identify specific types of thoughts that occur as family members interact. Catching the cognitions as they are occurring often is preferable to asking family members to try to recall how they were thinking during past upsetting experiences.

Meichenbaum's (1977) work with **self-statements** (similar to automatic thoughts) that influence individuals' abilities to cope with stressful situations is relevant for the assessment and treatment of spontaneously occurring cognitions in family interaction. Meichenbaum notes that the content of some cognitions interferes with the person's coping ability by fueling negative emotion and eliciting problematic behavior. For example, when Barbara told Luke that she wanted to discuss a problem in their relationship, Luke replied that he was too busy and began to walk out of the room. As Barbara thought to herself, "He can't get away with ignoring me. He's not getting out of here!" she felt her anger rising and moved quickly to block Luke's path to the door. It is important to help family members identify their **internal dialogue,** to see how it contributes to negative responses and to practice more constructive self-statements.

Questionnaires

A number of self-report questionnaires have been developed to assess particular types of relationship cognitions, for example, Eidelson and Epstein's (1982) Relationship Belief Inventory that assesses assumptions and standards; Roehling and Robin's (1986) Family Beliefs Inventory that assesses parents' and adolescents' unrealistic beliefs about their relationships; Pretzer et al.'s (1991) Marital Attitude Survey that assesses attributions and expectancies; Fincham and Bradbury's (1992) Relationship Attribution Measure; and Baucom et al.'s (1996) Inventory of Specific Relationship Standards. These scales have been used primarily in research, but therapists can administer them to family members as a way of surveying particular types of cognitions, which can be explored further during interviews.

Cognitive Restructuring Techniques

The overall goal of cognitive restructuring is to broaden each person's ways of thinking about his or her close relationships. Particular interventions tend to be most useful for intervening with each type of cognition described previously.

Reducing selective perception. When the assessment indicates that an individual is selectively attending to particular aspects of family interaction and overlooking others, the therapist can ask the person, as a homework assignment, to keep a daily written log of specific acts. This makes the person pay closer attention to other family members' behavior.

Brenda claimed that Carl rarely participated in child care activities such as dressing, feeding, and reading to their two young children. When she was asked to monitor his specific child care behavior each day for the next week, she returned with a log that indicated some days with few such behaviors but other days in which Carl had engaged in a several of them. Of course, because Carl was aware that Brenda was keeping track of his behavior, he may have increased his involvement (and Brenda did tell the therapist that she attributed his child care activity to "being on the spot" and wanting to impress the therapist). Nevertheless, the therapist can emphasize that Carl, in fact, did engage in child care activities, he apparently chose to do so, and that it will be helpful if Brenda can let him know that she appreciated it (rather than criticizing him about his motives). Similarly, the therapist can ask family members to monitor one another's behaviors during therapy sessions in order to counteract selective perception.

Modifying biased attributions. When it appears that an individual is making a biased attribution about the cause of another's responses, the therapist can ask him or her to think of other possible explanations.

When Brenda attributed Carl's child care behavior to his wanting to impress the therapist, the therapist said that she might be correct, but that it was important not to jump to conclusions and to consider other possible causes for his behavior. The therapist coached Brenda as she listed a few other explanations, including the idea that the therapy had opened Carl's eyes to how overburdened she felt, and that he was trying to improve their parenting relationship. Direct feedback from the other family member also can help challenge an individual's negative attribution. Thus, Carl told Brenda that he indeed increased his child care behavior, but it was primarily because their discussions during therapy sessions made him think how he was missing out on time with their children, who would be growing up quickly.

Modifying inaccurate expectancies. An individual who is making a negative prediction about one or more other family members can be asked to think back systematically to similar past situations and whether those events unfolded as he or she now expects. A second technique is to ask the person to keep a log of events during the next week, and to focus on the degree to which his or her predictions come true. Finally, the therapist can coach the person in setting up a "behavioral experiment" in which he or she intentionally tests the negative expectancy.

During a session with two parents, Ted predicted that their adolescent daughter would talk excessively on the phone with her friends if he and Lois stopped reminding her to keep her calls brief and gave her the responsibility for monitoring her phone use. When the couple agreed to experiment with this arrangement for a week, they returned and reported that their Karen had surprised them by talking only a little more than they would have preferred.

Challenging unrealistic or extreme assumptions and standards. Because these types of beliefs tend to be long-standing aspects of a person's worldview, it will likely take time and persistence to modify them. For example, an individual may hold a standard that in an intimate couple relationship the partners should spend virtually all of their free time together, and should share all of their thoughts and emotions with each other. This person may have become involved with a partner who initially seemed to value together-ness just as much (in the early stage of their relationship they were insepara-ble), but in fact the partner holds a standard that members of a couple should have opportunities to develop autonomous interests and activities. When the partner's desire for some autonomy eventually became clear, the individ-ual's responses were great disappointment, anger, and attempts to coerce the partner to spend more time together. A therapist might ask each member of this couple to describe his or her standard about togetherness versus auton-omy, how well the standard was being met in their relationship, and what specific behavior changes would be needed to meet the standard adequately. As described earlier, differences in two partners' standards for their rela-tionship are not necessarily problematic as long as both people believe that their standards are being met satisfactorily (Baucom et al., 1996).

The potential for meeting each person's standards depends on whether the standard is realistic and flexible, or extreme and inflexible. Thus, if the individual who wants a very high level of togetherness and open communi-cation is unwilling to accept that the partner wants some degree of auton-omy, the couple will likely have great difficulty finding a mutually accept-able solution. As Jacobson and Christensen (1996) have noted, resolving conflicts in one's relationship depends in part on each person's **acceptance** of differences between the two people's needs, personalities, etc. Cognitive-behavioral therapists explore with each person the advantages and dis-advantages of clinging firmly to a standard, versus trying to live by a "soft-ened" version of the standard. Thus, the individual who virtually demanded togetherness from his or her partner could be coached in considering a stan-dard such as "I value and greatly enjoy togetherness and open communica-tion with my partner, and I realize that I can have a close relationship with my partner even when he or she wants to have some independent activities and thoughts. The key is that we are still the most important people in each other's lives."

As with other types of cognitions, it often requires direct experience with living according to a revised standard before the person begins to deem it ac-ceptable. In the previous case, when the couple's therapist coached the indi-vidual in trying intentional planning of independent as well as shared activi-ties, the individual's partner was relieved by the reduced pressure and was in a better mood whenever the couple spent time together. The pleasant times together felt more intimate to the person with the strong togetherness stan-dard, which made the revised standard easier to accept.

These have been examples of cognitive interventions, but no set group of techniques is routinely used. The cognitive-behavioral therapist can be cre-ative in helping members of families consider the validity and appropriateness of their cognitions. The next section describes major behavioral interventions.

Behavioral Techniques

Based on social learning and social exchange theoretical principles, as well as research findings described earlier, the major types of behavioral interventions focus on (1) increasing exchanges of positive behavior and decreasing exchanges of negative behavior among family members, (2) training in communication skills, and (3) training in problem-solving skills. Each of these major types of intervention is summarized in this section. Therapists assess the particular behaviors that are in need of modification in each family by observing the family members interacting during sessions, as well as by asking the members to describe specific examples of their interactions that they find distressing. A **functional analysis** involves observing sequences of behaviors in family interaction and identifying what behaviors of other family members precede (tend to elicit) another's problematic behavior, and what behaviors of the other family members follow it (tend to reinforce or punish it).

Melody and Doug and their five-year-old son Kyle were referred to a family therapist because the parents were embarrassed, frustrated, and angry about Kyle's increasing tantrums, which were occurring more often in public places such as stores. The family therapist interviewed the parents in detail about the events that occur just before Kyle begins a tantrum and after he starts one. The parents described how typically a tantrum begins after they tell Kyle to stop doing something that he is enjoying (including taking packages of candy from store shelves). They also noted that they usually try to explain to Kyle why they want him to stop what he is doing, and that sometimes they give in (e.g., buy him the candy) in order to end his embarrassing public display. To observe the family interaction directly, the therapist asked the parents to instruct Kyle to stop playing with a toy in the therapy room and to sit in a chair. Not surprisingly, Kyle resisted Melody and Doug's instructions and began tantrum behavior. The parents tried talking to him more and then stared at the therapist in a helpless way. This assessment gave the therapist crucial information about the behavioral patterns that needed to be changed to improve the family's problem.

Changing frequencies of positive and negative behavior. The most widely used technique for increasing positive exchanges and decreasing negative ones involves setting up **behavioral contracts** among family members. Typically a behavioral contract is a formal agreement, commonly written, that each person will enact particular behaviors that another family member desires. Some contracts involve **quid pro quo agreements,** in which a person commits to behaving in particular ways that another person requests, with the understanding that in exchange, the other person will behave in ways that the first person requests. A potential limitation of this approach is that one person's failure to carry out his or her side of the contract will lead the other person to void the agreement. Couples can be coached in forming more informal **good faith agreements** in which each person agrees to work toward changing particular behaviors, whether or not the other person reciprocates (Baucom and Epstein, 1990; Jacobson and Margolin, 1979).

In **parenting training** (e.g., Gordon and Davidson, 1981; Patterson and Forgatch, 1987; Webster-Stratton and Herbert, 1994) parents are coached in setting up contracts with their children, in which the child is expected to behave in particular ways the parents desire, and avoid behaving in particular negative ways, in return for some specified types of reinforcement. This type of contract differs from a quid pro quo arrangement between two adults who have equal power in their relationship, in that in this case the parents have the authority to decide on the types of behavior to be changed, as well as the types of reinforcement to be earned. Therapists generally encourage parents to use reinforcements such as praise, time playing with the child, and other rewards that do not involve spending money, although reinforcements involving small expenses (e.g., renting a movie the child wants to see) can be effective. A contract can be formalized by creating a **behavior chart,** listing the specific behaviors to be monitored by the parents and creating spaces for each day of the week in which the parents indicate the frequency with which each behavior was exhibited. Parents can use a system in which occurrences of positive behaviors and days without particular negative behaviors earn points toward a larger reward. Punishments for negative behavior can include temporary removal of particular privileges, and use of time outs for younger children.

Communication skill training. Couples and families are coached in clear, constructive communication, involving both **expressive skills** and **listening skills,** based on an assumption that good communication requires effective sending as well as receiving of messages. Guerney's (1977) guidelines and procedures are among the most widely used for communication training. In Guerney's approach, two individuals practice taking turns as the person expressing his or her thoughts and emotions and the person listening empathically in order to understand each other's experience. The person in each role is coached in following particular guidelines for good communication. For example, the expresser is supposed to describe his or her thoughts briefly and using specific descriptive language. The expresser is to describe his or her thoughts and emotions as subjective rather than as "the truth," communicating that the listener has the right to have other views. When describing dissatisfaction with the listener's behavior, the expresser should convey empathy for the other's personal experiences. In turn, the listener's primary job is to try to understand the thoughts and emotions of the expresser (imagine how it feels to be in his or her position). The listener is to avoid interrupting the expresser, criticizing him or her, offering advice, etc. After the expresser has ended a brief description of personal experience, the listener's task is to "reflect" back what he or she has heard. The expresser gives the listener feedback about the accuracy of the reflecting, and they repeat the process until the communication has been effective.

In addition to these expressive and listening skills, cognitive-behavioral therapists observe each family and identify other specific verbal and nonverbal behaviors to target for change. For example, if members of a family make little eye contact with one another as they talk, the therapist will coach them in increasing it. Therapists teach families all of these communication skills by describing them briefly, demonstrating the skills, and then coaching the family members as they practice them during therapy sessions. Family members continue to practice the skills as homework between sessions. Communication skills training is widely used in cognitive-behavioral couple and family therapy (Baucom and Epstein, 1990; Epstein, Schlesinger, and Dryden, 1988; Falloon, 1991; Markman, Stanley, and Blumberg, 1994; Robin and Foster, 1989).

Problem-solving training. Whereas communication training focuses on messages about each family member's subjective thoughts and emotions, problem-solving training deals with specific steps that family members need to take in order to find mutually acceptable solutions to problems they face together. Some problems involve people and circumstances outside the family (e.g., a member lost a job), whereas others involve issues within the family (e.g., how to allot time with a couple's two extended families during holidays). Cognitive-behavioral therapists (e.g., Baucom and Epstein, 1990; Falloon, Boyd, and McGill, 1984; Jacobson and Christensen, 1996; Robin and Foster, 1989) teach couples and families to engage in a series of steps, including (1) defining the nature of the problem clearly and specifically, in behavioral terms (the "who, what, when, and where"), (2) brainstorming a variety of possible solutions to the problem (without evaluating them at this point), (3) discussing the advantages and disadvantages of each potential solution, in terms of costs and benefits to all of the involved parties, (4) choosing a solution (or combination of two or more solutions) acceptable to all, based on the cost-benefit analysis, (5) implementing the solution between sessions, and (6) evaluating its effectiveness. Solutions that turn out to be inadequate are reconsidered and revised as needed.

Techniques Focused on Emotions

When a therapist determines that an individual is failing to monitor his or her emotional states, and thus cannot communicate about them to other family members, the therapist coaches the person in paying attention to cues that he or she is having emotional experiences. For example, the therapist noticed that Alan sometimes showed nonverbal signs of sadness when his teenage children criticized his life philosophy and personal habits. When the therapist asked him how he was feeling, Alan replied that he was disappointed in them but did not feel any emotions about it. The therapist gave him feedback about his facial expressions and his slumped posture at such times, and asked him to pay attention to how his body felt. Alan began to notice a "heavy feeling" in his body and a tightness in his throat. The therapist continued to coach him in noticing his bodily cues and thinking about the thoughts and emotions associated with them.

Some other family members have difficulty with emotional regulation, or the ability to keep emotional arousal from reaching so high a level that it interferes with constructive thinking and behavior. In some individuals, deficits in emotional regulation constitute a lifelong personality characteristic that probably calls for individual therapy, whereas in others it may result from faulty learning of skills that can be practiced in family therapy. For example, some couples who engage in anger outbursts characterized by verbal abuse but who pose no danger of physical violence may be treated jointly with interventions focused on anger management (e.g., relaxation training, anger control self-statements, use of "time outs" in which partners temporarily go to separate locations and "cool off," and communication training). Meichenbaum (1977) and Deffenbacher (1996) use a **stress inoculation** approach to having individuals rehearse self-statements that calm them (e.g., "Stay calm. You don't have to react to his provocative behavior") and that direct their behavior (e.g., "Speak slowly and don't raise your voice").

RESEARCH ON COGNITIVE-BEHAVIORAL COUPLE AND FAMILY THERAPY

Because behavioral therapies had their roots in laboratory research on animal and human learning, with a focus on objectively measurable changes in specific behaviors, behaviorists have a tradition of emphasizing that therapy procedures should be based on sound evidence showing they are effective. A similar strong record of research on the role of cognition in individual and relationship problems has strengthened the foundations of cognitive therapies. Consequently, there has been much more empirical research on the effectiveness of behavioral and cognitive-behavioral couple and family treatments than on any other approach (Baucom et al., 1998; Dunn and Schwebel, 1995). In addition to studies of treatments clearly labeled as "behavioral" or "cognitive-behavioral," Alexander and his colleagues have conducted research on their "functional family therapy," which in practice is primarily a cognitive-behavioral approach involving communication training and behavioral contracting (Barton and Alexander, 1981).

Studies of behavioral marital therapy have consistently shown it to be more effective in improving self-reported marital satisfaction than a no-treatment "waiting list" control condition and placebo or "nonspecific" treatments (e.g., having couples discuss their issues without intervening actively). When studies have compared the effectiveness of the major components of behavioral marital therapy (communication training, problem-solving training, behavioral contracts), they have been found to be equally effective, although small samples in the studies may have limited their ability to detect treatment differences (Baucom et al., 1998; Hahlweg and Markman, 1988; Shadish et al., 1993). The positive effects tend to last through one-year follow-up assessments, but approximately one-third of the improved couples relapse over the next few years. When researchers have assessed not only statistically significant change but also how many treated individuals score in the nondistressed range on marital adjustment questionnaires, studies have shown that between approximately one-third and one-half met the latter criterion. It is important to note that the studies involved an average of eleven therapy sessions (based on research design considerations), which may not be adequate treatment for many distressed couples.

Behavioral marital therapy also has been evaluated as a sole treatment or a treatment component for a number of clinical disorders. For example, studies by Beach and O'Leary (1992) and Jacobson et al. (1993) indicated that behavioral marital therapy significantly improved both depression and marital distress among women who presented with both problems, and whose relationship problems appeared to contribute to their depression. Behavioral couples group therapy as a component of a treatment for male alcoholics and their partners has been evaluated by O'Farrell and his colleagues. Although the clients in the couple therapy condition did not improve significantly more than the treatment-as-usual clients on all outcome measures, overall the couple treatment demonstrated advantages, such as the percentage of days abstinent from drinking and decreased risk of domestic violence (O'Farrell et al., 1993; O'Farrell and Murphy, 1995).

Baucom and his colleagues conducted studies comparing behavioral marital therapy (including only behavioral interventions) with a treatment consisting of behavioral intervention sessions and cognitive restructuring sessions (Baucom and Lester, 1986; Baucom, Sayers, and Sher, 1990). Because the effects of the treatments were comparable, it has been concluded that cognitive restructuring does not enhance behavioral therapy. However, in order to keep the total number of treatment sessions equal in the conditions, adding cognitive restructuring meant decreasing the number of behavioral intervention sessions. Thus, cognitive restructuring appears to have been equally effective as behavioral intervention, but it is unclear whether couples that received the combined treatment got enough of either type of intervention. Clearly, more extensive research is needed to test whether a truly integrated cognitive-behavioral therapy is advantageous for treating distressed couples.

Reviews of behavioral parent-training interventions (e.g., Gordon and Davidson, 1981) have focused on three types of outcome measures: parents' subjective reports of improvements in their children's problematic behavior, parents' records of the frequencies of specific child behaviors, and records of children's specific behaviors by outside observers. Overall, although parental data do not reliably agree with outsiders' ratings, and parental measures show more improvement than outsiders' ratings, all three types of measures have indicated positive effects of behavioral parent-training programs. A review by Forehand and Atkeson (1977) pointed out that the improvements shown in particular behaviors that were treated with parent training did not consistently generalize to other problematic child behaviors that had not been addressed by the therapy. Such findings suggest that the conditions affecting each type of problematic behavior need to be assessed and treated.

Studies have been conducted on behavioral family therapy for families with a schizophrenic member, with the treatment emphasizing education for all family members on causes and treatments for the disorder, communication skill training, and problem-solving training. Overall, the studies have demonstrated its efficacy in reducing the patients' relapse rates or length of time hospitalized during follow-up periods (Baucom et al., 1998). Other support for the effectiveness of behavioral family therapy comes from evaluations of functional family therapy programs that primarily included communication training and behavioral contracting for families with delinquent children (Barton and Alexander, 1981). Compared to individual treatment or no treatment, the family treatment produced positive change in family communication and lower recidivism of delinquent behavior.

Thus, the research on cognitive-behavioral couple and family therapy is encouraging; yet a number of important questions remain. For example, none of the outcome studies matched the types of cognitive and behavioral interventions each couple or family received to the clients' particular needs and problematic patterns. Studies that provide the same treatment for all clients constitute good controlled research, but they probably do not meet every couple's or family's personal needs equally well. There is a need for research that tailors treatment to what is known about each family. In the meantime, couple and family therapists can have confidence that knowledge of cognitive-behavioral approaches to assessment and intervention can be very useful in their work.

CASE EXAMPLE

Earlier, Melody and Doug and their five-year-old son Kyle were described briefly as an example of how a therapist uses a functional analysis to identify how a family member's problematic behaviors may be influenced by the behaviors of other family members that typically precede and those that are **consequences** of it.

Kyle's tantrums in public places tended to occur after the parents instructed him to stop doing something that he was enjoying, such as handling packages of candy or pulling toys from store shelves. When the therapist asked Melody and Doug how they typically responded to Kyle's initial refusal to follow their directions, they reported that they try to explain to him why they want him to stop his behavior (for example, "Kyle, put the candy back. We already have a lot of candy at home, so you don't need anymore"). In addition, when Kyle continues his misbehavior in public Melody and Doug are embarrassed and cannot think of anything more effective to stop him, so they somtimes buy him what he wants, such as the toy or candy. The therapist took note of the associations between the parents' responses and the child's negative behavior and formed a hypothesis that two of the factors operating in this family's problem were that the parents (1) had no effective means of punishing Kyle for tantrum behavior and (2) were unwittingly reinforcing his tantrums by giving him things that he wants whenever he behaves aversively. In fact, it appeared that the parents were providing intermittent reinforcement for Kyle's whining and tantrum behavior by trying to ignore it for a while and then providing the rewards on some occasions.

As noted earlier, the therapist also conducted the functional analysis by observing the family interaction while Melody and Doug tried to get Kyle to stop playing with a toy in the therapy room and sit still. Consistent with the parents' reports of what occurs at home and in public, Melody began by saying, "Kyle, please put the truck down and come sit in this chair next to me. It's very important for us to all talk together about the problems we've been having." When Kyle ignored her, Melody repeated herself twice, each time with a little more forcefulness in her voice. "Kyle, listen to me now! Will you please put the truck down and come over here?" As Kyle continued to ignore Melody, Doug tried to back her up by standing up and firmly saying, "Kyle, if you don't listen to your mom I'm taking the truck away from you and you'll never be able to play with toys here again." Kyle began to whine loudly and darted away from his father. In a frustrated tone, Doug said, "Kyle, get over here!" At this point, both parents looked embarrassed as they sheepishly glanced in the therapist's direction.

Thus, in this **behavioral assessment,** the therapist gathered detailed information about the sequence of behavior involved with Kyle's problematic behavior, using both self-reports from the parents and direct observation of the parent-child interactions. The data suggested that there was a pattern of negative reciprocity in which the parents and child exchanged negative behaviors (e.g., the parents' threats, the child's whining and tantrum behavior) as means of aversive control of one another's behavior. In other words, there was a circular causal pattern in which the parents and child were influencing each other's negative behavior. Melody and Doug might benefit from some parenting training in the use of time outs and other forms of nonaggressive **punishment** for Kyle's negative behavior, and in the use of **positive reinforcement** whenever he behaved in desirable ways.

The therapist also assessed the parents' cognitions regarding their child, such as their assumptions and standards concerning appropriate parental and child behavior, as well as their attributions about possible causes of his behavior. For example, both parents held an unrealistic assumption that children of Kyle's age are able to understand and appreciate logical explanations for behavioral rules; thus they repeatedly but ineffectively tried to reason with him about proper behavior. They also held a standard that "loving parents try to protect their children from experiencing frustration and emotional distress," so they easily felt guilty about disciplining Kyle if it appeared that it made him very upset. Furthermore, Melody and Doug had read magazine articles about attention deficit hyperactivity disorder (ADHD) and believed that Kyle might have that disorder; consequently, they often made attributions that his disobedient behavior and tantrums were caused by ADHD and were beyond his control. In fact, they had consulted Kyle's pediatrician, who was unsure of the appropriate diagnosis and suggested that the couple take him to a behavioral specialist before the option of medication such as Ritalin was used. It was the pediatrician who had referred the family to the family therapist. Because the parents tended to attribute Kyle's behavior problems to ADHD, they believed that they could not have much impact on them and thought that medication was needed.

The therapist conducted a systematic behavioral assessment of Kyle's symptoms, including information from the parents, a phone consultation with Kyle's kindergarten teacher, and observation of Kyle during sessions. Based on standard diagnostic criteria from the *Diagnostic and Statistical Manual of Mental Disorders* published by the American Psychiatric Association (1994), the therapist determined that Kyle had some ADHD symptoms, but the pattern was inconsistent and he was too young for a reliable diagnosis to be made.

The therapist also noticed that Melody and Doug had difficulty working as a team in handling Kyle's behavior. They were both busy with their jobs and household chores, in addition to raising Kyle. Consequently, they rarely took time to have uninterrupted talks about their difficulties with Kyle and possible solutions to the problem. Each of them tended to try whatever occurred to him or her at the moment, and they often criticized each other's approach. Although there were no clear signs of general conflict and distress in Melody and Doug's marriage, the therapist did get the impression that there was some conflict and ineffective coordination of their efforts in their parenting roles.

The therapist discussed these findings and hypotheses from the assessment with Melody and Doug. When the therapist pointed out the pattern in which Kyle continued his negative behavior until his parents gave in, Melody and Doug readily agreed that it occurred frequently, and they could see how they were reinforcing the behavior that they wanted to decrease. Although they agreed with the therapist that decreasing such reinforcement would be a good goal, they voiced concerns that setting firmer limits with Kyle would make him so distressed that it might harm him psychologically. The therapist spent time challenging the parents' assumptions by discussing processes of normal child development, including the idea that a child needs to develop the ability to tolerate frustrations in life, and that parents can help a child develop that ability by setting limits on the child's behavior.

The therapist also discussed the parents' attributions that Kyle's behavior was caused by ADHD and was unlikely to respond to behavioral interventions. The therapist proposed that, based on the behavioral assessment, it was premature to conclude that Kyle had ADHD, and that even if he did there was substantial research evidence that children with attention and hyperactivity problems benefit from parents' use of behavioral approaches based on **learning principles**. Melody and Doug agreed to a trial period of working with the therapist on behavioral interventions with Kyle. First, they devised a simple behavior chart with a list of two types of behavior that they wanted Kyle to *increase* (make eye contact with parents when they address him, obey requests such as "put the toy back on the shelf" and "come to the table for dinner"), and three types of behavior that they wanted him to *decrease* (whining, stomping his feet, and screaming). With coaching from the therapist, the couple drew the chart on a sheet of paper, explained it to Kyle, and took it home to be posted on their refrigerator.

The therapist also guided Melody and Doug in thinking of specific consequences, involving punishment for instances of negative behavior and reinforcement of positive behavior, that they would use to implement the behavior chart program at home. The therapist described the use of time-out procedures, and the parents also agreed to try taking away some of Kyle's privileges for instances of negative behavior. At this point, the therapist coached the couple in a problem-solving discussion to identify types of privileges that they both felt comfortable withdrawing temporarily. Similarly, the therapist guided the couple in thinking of small but meaningful rewards that they could give Kyle when he exhibited desired behavior. For example, the couple agreed to use praise and hugs as *immediate* positive consequences. They also set up a system in which the parents would draw a star on his behavior chart each time he exhibited a particular type of desired behavior. He would earn special rewards (e.g., renting a movie, playing a game with a parent) for reaching particular point totals.

The therapist stressed the importance of gradually shaping Kyle's positive behaviors rather than expecting him to suddenly make major changes. Melody and Doug agreed that initially they would immediately praise Kyle if he complied at least partly with a request (e.g., putting *some* of his toys away). In contrast, the therapist emphasized the importance of being very consistent in providing negative consequences for *any* instances of noncompliance and tantrum behavior. The therapist frequently commented on the importance of the couple supporting each other in these efforts and consistently using the same approaches with Kyle. Although in some families there is sufficient conflict between parents that they require some separate couple sessions to resolve their issues before they are able to collaborate well as a parenting team, that was not the case with Melody and Doug. The therapist encouraged them to communicate more at home, using expressive and listening skills, and they decided to schedule at least a fifteen-minute "check in" with each other each evening after Kyle was asleep, during which they could review their parenting strategies and discuss successes and difficulties as needed.

GLOSSARY

acceptance: An individual's attitude that another family member's personal characteristic or behavior falls within the range of his or her personal standards of how the other person should be; in contrast to an attitude that the other person should change.

adjunctive intervention: A type of therapeutic technique that is added in order to enhance an existing treatment by addressing an aspect of clients' needs that are not adequately addressed by the primary treatment.

agentic or individually oriented needs: A person's basic needs that involve functioning and growth as an individual; for example, a need for autonomy.

assumption: A basic belief or schema that an individual holds about typical characteristics of people and objects, as well as about relationships among them; for example, an assumption that men are generally unaware of their feelings. Assumptions can vary in validity.

attention deficit hyperactivity disorder (ADHD): A disorder involving difficulty sustaining attention to tasks and other people, excessive motor activity and talking, and impulsive behavior. ADHD typically is first diagnosed during a child's elementary school years and may continue through adolescence and adulthood, although for the majority of individuals the symptoms decrease during adolescence. Subtypes involve primarily attention problems, primarily hyperactivity/impulsivity problems, and a combination of the two.

attribution: An inference, which can vary in validity, that an individual makes about an unobserved cause of an observed event, such as the cause of a spouse's or child's sarcastic remark.

automatic thoughts: Stream-of-consciousness thoughts that run through a person's mind and seem plausible to the person, whether or not they are accurate or valid.

aversive control: An individual's use of threats, criticism, and punishment to control other family members' behavior.

behavior chart: A chart that is constructed for the purpose of logging instances of specific behavior enacted by a family member each day; most often used to log a child's behaviors that parents want to increase and those that they want to decrease.

behavioral assessment: Monitoring the frequencies of family members' specific acts and the circumstances that precede and follow those acts, through family members' observations and logging of their interactions at home, or through therapist observation of family interactions during sessions.

behavioral contract: A formal or informal, written or oral agreement among members of a family for each person to enact particular behaviors that are desired by the others.

boundary: A degree of psychological or physical separation between people in a relationship, such as the degree to which two members of a family share or withhold personal thoughts and feelings from each other.

cascade: A sequence in which one type of behavior by a member of a couple or family leads to another type of behavior by another member, and over time there is a positive or negative trend to the pattern; for example, when criticism by one person leads to defensiveness by the recipient, which produces more criticism, more defensiveness, and so on.

circular concepts of causality: The idea that two people in a relationship have mutual effects on each other, in a circular manner; for example, person A withdraws because person B nags, and person B nags because person A withdraws.

classical conditioning: A learning process in which a stimulus that has been relatively neutral for an individual (e.g., the sound of squealing car tires) elicits an automatic reflexive response (e.g., anxiety symptoms) after the neutral stimulus has been associated with another stimulus that produces the reflexive response (e.g., a severe car accident).

coercive family system: A pattern of family interaction in which parents and children each use aversive behavior such as yelling and threats in attempts to control each other's actions.

cognitions: Forms and processes of thinking, such as attributions, expectancies, assumptions, standards, and selective perception, with which individuals process information about themselves and the world.

cognitive distortions: Automatic, involuntary thoughts that involve the distorted processing of information; for example, dichotomous thinking, emotional reasoning, maximization, minimization, mind-reading, overgeneralization, and personalization.

cognitive restructuring: Therapeutic interventions that have the goal of modifying an individual's distorted or inappropriate thoughts, by challenging their logic, presenting information concerning their validity, or examining their impact on the individual's personal life and close relationships.

cognitive therapies: Forms of psychotherapy focusing on identifying an individual's distorted, invalid, or inappropriate forms of thinking that are contributing to his or her psychological and/or interpersonal problems.

cognitive-behavioral approaches: Concepts and methods for understanding and treating individual and relationship problems in terms of behavioral patterns, individuals' cognitions about themselves and other people, and emotional responses associated with those behaviors and cognitions.

communal needs: A person's basic human needs that involve connections with other people; for example, a need for intimacy or deep sharing of personal experiences with another person.

conduct disorder: A pattern of problematic behavior in a child or adolescent that includes threats or actual harm to people or animals, damage to property, deceitfulness, theft, or serious violations of rules set by parents, schools, etc.

consequences: The results that occur following an individual's particular action, either consistently or intermittently, and which serve as reinforcement or punishment for the person's action.

deconditioned: A previously classically or operantly conditioned response is weakened or eliminated by reversing the conditions that initially established it; for example, using extinction procedures to reduce a child's tantrum behavior by eliminating a parent's attention that reinforced it.

deficits in communication skills: An individual's lack of abilities to express himself or herself verbally and nonverbally in a clear, direct, but nonaggressive manner, or a lack of abilities to pay close attention to another person's expression of thoughts and emotions, to understand the other person's perspective, and to reflect back that understanding to the expresser.

demand/withdraw: An interaction pattern between two people in which one person tends to approach the other and press for attention and communication, while the other person tends to withdraw, and each person's type of behavior elicits more of the other person's type of response.

depression: A clinical disorder that may be chronic or occur in episodes or discrete periods of time, and that typically includes a variety of emotional symptoms (e.g., low mood), cognitive symptoms (e.g., hopelessness, self-criticism), physiological symptoms (e.g., fatigue, poor appetite), and behavioral symptoms (e.g., withdrawal from other people).

dichotomous thinking: A type of cognitive distortion in which an individual categorizes people and events in all-or-nothing terms rather than considering gradations of characteristics along continua; for example, a parent who dichotomizes a child's school grades as "Either A or failure."

emotional reasoning: A cognitive distortion in which an individual interprets cues of his or her subjective emotions as objective facts; for example, when members of a couple who have had little available time together notice a lack of intimate feelings and conclude that they no longer love each other.

emotional regulation: An individual's ability to control the strength of the emotions that he or she experiences and expresses.

expectancy: An individual's inference involving a prediction about the probability that an event will occur in the future under particular circumstances.

expressive skills: The abilities to be aware of one's thoughts and feelings and to express them to another person clearly, succinctly, and in a nonjudgmental way that encourages the listener to consider them without becoming defensive.

extinction: An individual's behavioral response that previously was increased or maintained by reinforcing consequences now is decreased and possibly eliminated by the removal of the reinforcement.

functional analysis: Identification of the antecedent situational conditions that tend to elicit an individual's behavioral, cognitive, or emotional response, as well as the consequences that follow the response and serve to reinforce, punish, or extinguish it.

functional family therapy: A behaviorally oriented form of therapy that focuses on ways in which family members' responses toward each other exist due to the functions that the responses serve in producing outcomes consciously or unconsciously desired by the individuals.

gender roles: Behavioral, cognitive, and emotional responses that are commonly accepted in society as appropriate and desirable for a male or for a female, and those responses that are considered inappropriate for each sex.

good faith agreement: A behavioral contract in which each party agrees to enact at least some of the desired behaviors specified by the other party without an explicit agreement about which behaviors he or she will choose. The individual's compliance with the other person's requests is not contingent on whether the other person reciprocates behaviors that the individual desires. Each person provides his or her own reinforcement for such compliance rather than receiving reinforcement from the other person.

inappropriate thought processes: Cognitions that are irrelevant or extreme such that they do not realistically fit particular circumstances in an individual's personal life or relationships; for example, holding a standard that one's spouse or children should always share one's personal values and preferences.

intermittent reinforcement: An individual receives reinforcing consequences for his or her specific action occasionally or unpredictably rather than after every instance of that action.

internal dialogue: Conscious thoughts that an individual has concerning a current experience; for example, an internal debate about the pros and cons of behaving toward other family members in a particular way.

investment: The degree to which an individual puts time and energy into maintaining or enhancing a relationship.

irrational belief: An individual's unrealistic belief about characteristics that an individual or relationship should or must have, which leads the person to respond with emotional upset and negative behavior when actual events fail to meet the standard.

learning principles: Concepts concerning the processes by which individuals acquire new knowledge and behavioral and emotional responses, as well as concerning processes by which responses are weakened.

linear causal thinking: An individual's concept that the causal relationship between two people's responses exists in only one direction (i.e., person A's behavior produces person B's behavior); in contrast to circular causal thinking that focuses on mutual influences.

listening skills: Communication skills for the accurate receipt of information from another person who is expressing his or her thoughts and emotions; for example, the abilities to take another's perspective, to avoid thinking about one's own thoughts and feelings instead of focusing on those expressed by the other person, and to reflect back to the expresser what the listener has heard.

magnification: A cognitive distortion in which an individual exaggerates the qualities or effects of a person or event, beyond what evidence suggests is accurate; for example, catastrophic thinking such as, "My daughter was disciplined at school for talking in class. Her reputation is ruined and her grades will suffer."

mind-reading: A cognitive distortion in which an individual observes an aspect of another person's behavior and makes an arbitrary inference or attribution that he or she knows the other's unstated thoughts and emotions; for example, "She stayed at work later than she told me she would, so she obviously decided the work was more important than spending time with me."

minimization: A cognitive distortion in which an individual underestimates the qualities or effects of a person or event, beyond what evidence suggests is accurate; for example, an individual whose spouse turned down a job opportunity so the couple would not have to face moving might conclude, "It was no big sacrifice for her."

mutual influences: A process in couple or family interactions in which each person's behavior simultaneously affects and is effected by others' behavior; as when a child's tantrums elicit stress, frustration, and harsh punishment from parents, and in turn the parents' yelling and harsh punishment elicit frustration, anger, and tantrum behavior from the child.

negative reciprocity: The tendency for members of a relationship, especially a distressed one, to reciprocate negative actions toward each other, either immediately or at a later time.

negative tracking: A form of selective perception, particularly common in distressed couples and families, in which an individual notices a family member's negative behavior but overlooks the person's neutral or positive acts.

negative trait label: Using a concept of a broad, stable personal characteristic or trait to describe and explain an individual's reactions to life events; for example describing one's child as being a "selfish" *person* rather than exhibiting particular selfish *acts*.

neutral stimulus: A condition or event that has no natural, automatic impact on increasing or decreasing an individual's behavioral, cognitive, or emotional responses. Exposure to the neutral stimulus does not affect the individual's responses.

observational learning: A process through which an individual can learn how to perform particular responses merely by observing another person performing them; as when a child imitates a parent's ways of speaking and responding to frustrating events.

operant conditioning: A process through which an individual learns to enact particular behaviors more or less frequently, based on the reinforcing or punishing consequences that occur when he or she exhibits those behaviors.

overgeneralization: A cognitive distortion in which an individual generalizes that a behavior that actually occurs occasionally either *never* or *always* occurs; for example, a man whose wife periodically complains about his failing to clean up after himself may overgeneralize, "You always criticize me."

parenting training: Developing parents' knowledge of normal child development and teaching parents more effective, nonaggressive methods for increasing their children's positive behavior and decreasing the children's negative behavior.

personalization: A cognitive distortion of information processing in which an individual automatically interprets an event as related to his or her own actions or characteristics when in fact the event may have been caused by other factors.

positive reinforcement: Consequences provided for an individual's behavior that result in the person exhibiting that behavior more in the future, presumably because the individual experiences the consequences as pleasant.

power/control: The degree to which a member of a family has input and impact on decisions that the family makes about its priorities and activities.

punishment: Consequences provided for an individual's behavior that result in the person exhibiting that behavior less in the future, presumably because the individual experiences the consequences as aversive.

quid pro quo agreement: A behavioral contract in which one individual agrees to enact particular behaviors desired by another individual, in return for the latter party enacting particular behaviors that the former party desires. Each person's adherence to the agreement is contingent on the other's adherence to it.

rational-emotive therapy: A psychotherapy approach developed by psychologist Albert Ellis focusing on modifying irrational beliefs that elicit an individual's dysfunctional emotional and behavioral reactions to events in his or her life.

reflexive response: An individual's behavioral or emotional response that occurs naturally and automatically, such as fear that a person instantaneously feels at the moment when a truck is about to hit his or her car.

relaxation techniques: Procedures, such as tensing and relaxing muscles in each part of one's body, or practicing slow deep breathing, that an individual can use to increase overall physical relaxation and reduce tension.

schema: An individual's generally long-standing basic concept or belief about the characteristics of people, a particular object, a type of interpersonal relationship, or a type of event.

selective abstraction: A cognitive distortion, or biased information processing, in which an individual notices only certain aspects of the information available in a situation and overlooks other information.

selective perception: *See* SELECTIVE ABSTRACTION.

self-statement: A form of cognition in which an individual purposely gives himself or herself an instruction to guide thoughts (e.g., "Listen to my parents' instructions"), behavior (e.g., "Tell her how I am feeling, but don't blame her"), or emotions (e.g., "Stay cool, just relax").

sentiment override: An individual's emotional and behavioral responses to another family member are determined more by the individual's preexisting feelings toward the person than by the person's present behavior.

shape: Gradually develop an individual's new response by rewarding him or her for small approximations of the end goal; for example, reinforcing a child for success in cleaning part of his or her room.

situational conditions: The characteristics of the physical or interpersonal setting in which a behavioral, cognitive, or emotional response occurs; for example, the amount of structure in home and classroom settings associated with a child's controlled versus hyperactive behavior.

social exchange theory: A theory positing that members of any interpersonal relationship exchange actions that each person experiences as costs and benefits, and that each individual feels satisfied in the relationship to the extent to which he or she perceives the self receiving a favorable ratio of benefits to costs.

standard: A belief or schema that an individual holds concerning the characteristics that individuals and relationships "should" have. Standards can vary in their flexibility or extremeness, and the degree to which they are realistic.

stress inoculation: Methods used to prepare an individual to cope effectively with stressful situations; for example, training the individual to use self-statements focused on remaining relaxed and speaking calmly to upset family members.

subjectivity: The degree to which a person's experiences of life events involve idiosyncratic personal interpretations and beliefs rather than external reality that could be measured in an objective manner.

systematic desensitization: Gradually decreasing an individual's negative, cognitive, emotional, and behavioral responses to a stimulus situation that the person finds stressful, by means of exposing him or her to increasingly stressful aspects of the situation while having the person practice relaxation techniques during the exposure.

time out: A discipline technique that removes a child from sources of reinforcement by placing him or her in a place of isolation (e.g., a chair in a corner, with no access to entertainment or attention from others) for a fixed amount of time; commonly, one minute for each year of the child's age.

unrealistic beliefs: *See* IRRATIONAL BELIEFS.

REFERENCES

American Psychiatric Association (1994). *Diagnostic and statistical manual of mental disorders* (DSM-IV) (Fourth edition). Washington, DC: American Psychiatric Association.

Bandura, A. (1977). *Social learning theory*. Englewood Cliffs, NJ: Prentice-Hall.

Bandura, A. and Walters, R.H. (1963). *Social learning and personality development*. New York: Holt, Rinehart and Winston.

Barkley, R.A. and Benton, C.M. (1998). *Your defiant child: 8 steps to better behavior*. New York: Guilford Press.

Barton, C. and Alexander, J.F. (1981). Functional family therapy. In A.S. Gurman and D.P. Kniskern (Eds.), *Handbook of family therapy* (Volume I) (pp. 403-443). New York: Brunner/Mazel.

Baucom, D.H. and Epstein, N. (1990). *Cognitive-behavioral marital therapy*. New York: Brunner/Mazel.

Baucom, D.H. and Epstein, N. (1999). It takes two to tango: There are some individuals in there interacting with each other. Paper presented at the annual meeting of the Association for Advancement of Behavior Therapy, Toronto, November 13, 1999.

Baucom, D.H., Epstein, N., Rankin, L.A., and Burnett, C.K. (1996). Assessing relationship standards: The inventory of specific relationship standards. *Journal of Family Psychology, 10,* 72-88.

Baucom, D.H., Epstein, N., Sayers, S., and Sher, T.G. (1989). The role of cognitions in marital relationships: Definitional, methodological, and conceptual issues. *Journal of Consulting and Clinical Psychology, 57,* 31-38.

Baucom, D.H. and Lester, G.W. (1986). The usefulness of cognitive restructuring as an adjunct to behavioral marital therapy. *Behavior Therapy, 17,* 385-403.

Baucom, D.H., Sayers, S.L., and Sher, T.G. (1990). Supplementing behavioral marital therapy with cognitive restructuring and emotional expressiveness training: An outcome investigation. *Journal of Consulting and Clinical Psychology, 58,* 636-645.

Baucom, D.H., Shoham, V., Mueser, K.T., Daiuto, A.D., and Stickle, T.R. (1998). Empirically supported couple and family interventions for marital distress and adult mental health problems. *Journal of Consulting and Clinical Psychology, 66,* 53-88.

Beach, S.R.H. and O'Leary, K.D. (1992). Treating depression in the context of marital discord: Outcome and predictors of response for marital therapy vs. cognitive therapy. *Behavior Therapy, 23,* 507-528.

Beck, A.T. (1976). *Cognitive therapy and the emotional disorders.* New York: International Universities Press.

Beck, A.T. (1988). *Love is never enough.* New York: Harper and Row.

Beck, A.T. and Emery, G. (1985). *Anxiety disorders and phobias: A cognitive perspective.* New York: Basic Books.

Beck, A.T., Rush, A.J., Shaw, B.F., and Emery, G. (1979). *Cognitive therapy of depression.* New York: Guilford Press.

Beck, J.S. (1995). *Cognitive therapy: Basics and beyond.* New York: Guilford Press.

Blechman, E.A. (1985). *Solving child behavior problems at home and at school.* Champaign, IL: Research Press.

Bradbury, T.N. and Fincham, F.D. (1990). Attributions in marriage: Review and critique. *Psychological Bulletin, 107,* 3-33.

Bradbury, T.N. and Fincham, F.D. (1992). Attributions and behavior in marital interaction. *Journal of Personality and Social Psychology, 63,* 613-628.

Carter, B. and McGoldrick, M. (Eds.) (1999). *The expanded family life cycle: Individual, family, and social perspectives.* Boston: Allyn and Bacon.

Christensen, A. (1988). Dysfunctional interaction patterns in couples. In P. Noller and M.A. Fitzpatrick (Eds.), *Perspectives on marital interaction* (pp. 31-52). Philadelphia: Multilingual Matters, Ltd.

Christensen, A., Sullaway, M., and King, C. (1983). Systemic error in behavioral reports of dyadic interaction: Egocentric bias and content effects. *Behavioral Assessment, 5,* 131-142.

Dattilio, F.M. (Ed.) (1998a). *Case studies in couple and family therapy: Systemic and cognitive perspectives.* New York: Guilford Press.

Dattilio, F.M. (1998b). Cognitive-behavioral family therapy. In F.M. Dattilio (Ed.), *Case studies in couple and family therapy: Systemic and cognitive perspectives* (pp. 62-84). New York: Guilford Press.

Dattilio, F.M. and Padesky, C.A. (1990). *Cognitive therapy with couples.* Sarasota, FL: Professional Resource Exchange.

Deffenbacher, J.L. (1996). Cognitive-behavioral approaches to anger reduction. In K.S. Dobson and K.D. Craig (Eds.), *Advances in cognitive-behavioral therapy* (pp. 31-62). Thousand Oaks, CA: Sage.

Dunn, R.L. and Schwebel, A.I. (1995). Meta-analytic review of marital therapy outcome research. *Journal of Family Psychology, 9,* 58-68.

Eidelson, R.J. and Epstein, N. (1982). Cognition and relationship maladjustment: Development of a measure of dysfunctional relationship beliefs. *Journal of Consulting and Clinical Psychology, 50,* 715-720.

Ellis, A. (1962). *Reason and emotion in psychotherapy.* New York: Lyle Stuart.

Ellis, A., Sichel, J.L., Yeager, R.J., DiMattia, D.J., and DiGiuseppe, R. (1989). *Rational-emotive couples therapy.* New York: Pergamon.

Epstein, N. (1982). Cognitive therapy with couples. *American Journal of Family Therapy, 10* (1), 5-16.

Epstein, N. and Baucom, D.H. (1993). Cognitive factors in marital disturbance. In K.S. Dobson and P.C. Kendall (Eds.), *Psychopathology and cognition* (pp. 351-385). San Diego, CA: Academic Press.

Epstein, N. and Baucom, D.H. (1999). Advances in cognitive-behavioral couple therapy: Assessment and intervention with behavioral patterns and cognitive themes. Workshop presented at the annual meeting of the Association for Advancement of Behavior Therapy, Toronto, November 12, 1999.

Epstein, N. and Eidelson, R.J. (1981). Unrealistic beliefs of clinical couples: Their relationship to expectations, goals and satisfaction. *American Journal of Family Therapy, 9* (4), 13-22.

Epstein, N., Schlesinger, S.E., and Dryden, W. (Eds.) (1988). *Cognitive-behavioral therapy with families.* New York: Brunner/Mazel.

Epstein, N. and Williams, A.M. (1981). Behavioral approaches to the treatment of marital discord. In G.P. Sholevar (Ed.), *The handbook of marriage and marital therapy* (pp. 219-286). New York: Spectrum.

Falloon, I.R.H. (1991). Behavioral family therapy. In A.S. Gurman and D.P. Kniskern (Eds.), *Handbook of family therapy* (Volume II) (pp. 65-95). New York: Brunner/Mazel.

Falloon, I.R.H., Boyd, J.L., and McGill, C.W. (1984). *Family care of schizophrenia.* New York: Guilford Press.

Fincham, F.D. and Bradbury, T.N. (1987). The impact of attributions in marriage: A longitudinal analysis. *Journal of Personality and Social Psychology, 53,* 510-517.

Fincham, F.D. and Bradbury, T.N. (1992). Assessing attributions in marriage: The relationship attribution measure. *Journal of Personality and Social Psychology, 62,* 457-468.

Fincham, F.D., Bradbury, T.N., and Scott, C.K. (1990). Cognition in marriage. In F.D. Fincham and T.N. Bradbury (Eds.), *The psychology of marriage: Basic issues and applications* (pp. 118-149). New York: Guilford Press.

Fincham, F.D., Harold, G.T., and Gano-Phillips, S. (2000). The longitudinal association between attributions and marital satisfaction: Direction of effects and role of efficacy expectations. *Journal of Family Psychology, 14,* 267-285.

Fiske, S.T. and Taylor, S.E. (1991). *Social cognition* (Second edition). New York: McGraw-Hill.

Forehand, R. and Atkeson, B.M. (1977). Generality of treatment effects with parents as therapists: A review of assessment and implementation procedures. *Behavior Therapy, 8,* 575-593.

Goldstein, M.K. (1971). Behavior rate change in marriages: Training wives to modify husbands' behavior. *Dissertation Abstracts International, 32* (18), 559.

Gordon, S.B. and Davidson, N. (1981). Behavioral parent training. In A.S. Gurman and D.P. Kniskern (Eds.), *Handbook of family therapy* (Volume I) (pp. 517-555). New York: Brunner/Mazel.

Gottman, J.M. (1994). *What predicts divorce? The relationship between marital processes and marital outcomes.* Hillsdale, NJ: Lawrence Erlbaum.

Gottman, J.M. (1999). *The marriage clinic: A scientifically based marital therapy.* New York: W. W. Norton.

Graziano, A.M. (1971). *Behavior therapy with children.* Chicago: Aldine.

Guerney, B.G. Jr. (1977). *Relationship enhancement.* San Francisco: Jossey-Bass.

Hahlweg, K. and Markman, H.J. (1988). Effectiveness of behavioral marital therapy: Empirical status of behavioral techniques in preventing and alleviating marital distress. *Journal of Consulting and Clinical Psychology, 56,* 440-447.

Halford, W.K. and Bouma, R. (1997). Individual psychopathology and marital distress. In W.K. Halford and H.J. Markman (Eds.), *Clinical handbook of marriage and couples interventions* (pp. 291-321). Chichester, UK: Wiley.

Hetherington, E.M., Bridges, M., and Insabella, G.M. (1998). What matters? What does not? Five perspectives on the association between marital transitions and children's adjustment. *American Psychologist, 53,* 167-184.

Jacobson, N.S. and Christensen, A. (1996). *Integrative couple therapy: Promoting acceptance and change.* New York: W. W. Norton.

Jacobson, N.S., Fruzzetti, A.E., Dobson, K., Whisman, M., and Hops, H. (1993). Couple therapy as a treatment for depression. II: The effects of relationship quality and therapy on depressive relapse. *Journal of Consulting and Clinical Psychology, 61,* 516-519.

Jacobson, N.S. and Margolin, G. (1979). *Marital therapy: Strategies based on social learning and behavior exchange principles.* New York: Brunner/Mazel.

Jacobson, N.S. and Moore, D. (1981). Spouses as observers of the events in their relationship. *Journal of Consulting and Clinical Psychology, 49,* 269-277.

Jenkins, J.M. and Smith, M.A. (1991). Marital disharmony and children's behavior problems: Aspects of a poor marriage that affect children adversely. *Journal of Child Psychology, Psychiatry, and Allied Disciplines, 32,* 793-810.

Leahy, R.L. (1996). *Cognitive therapy: Basic principles and applications.* Northvale, NJ: Jason Aronson.

Liberman, R.P. (1970). Behavioral approaches to family and couple therapy. *American Journal of Orthopsychiatry, 40,* 106-118.

Margolin, G. and Weiss, R.L. (1978). Comparative evaluation of therapeutic components associated with behavioral marital treatments. *Journal of Consulting and Clinical Psychology, 46,* 1476-1486.

Markman, H., Stanley, S., and Blumberg, S. (1994). *Fighting for your marriage: Positive steps for preventing divorce and preserving a lasting love.* San Francisco, CA: Jossey-Bass.

Meichenbaum, D. (1977). *Cognitive-behavior modification.* New York: Plenum Press.

Miklowitz, D.J. (1995). The evolution of family-based psychopathology. In R.H. Mikesell, D.D. Lusterman, and S.H. McDaniel (Eds.), *Integrating family therapy: Handbook of family psychology and systems theory* (pp. 183-197). Washington, DC: American Psychological Association.

Morris, S.B., Alexander, J.F., and Waldron, H. (1988). Functional family therapy. In I.R.H. Falloon (Ed.), *Handbook of behavioral family therapy* (pp. 107-127). New York: Guilford Press.

Morton T.L., Twentyman, C.T., and Azar, S.T. (1988). Cognitive-behavioral assessment and treatment of child abuse. In N. Epstein, S.E. Schlesinger, and W. Dryden (Eds.), *Cognitive-behavioral therapy with families* (pp. 87-117). New York: Brunner/Mazel.

O'Farrell, T.J., Choquette, K.A., Cutter, H.S.G., Brown, E.D., and McCourt, W.F. (1993). Behavioral marital therapy with and without additional couples relapse prevention sessions for alcoholics and their wives. *Journal of Studies on Alcohol, 54,* 652-666.

O'Farrell, T.J. and Murphy, C.M. (1995). Marital violence before and after alcoholism treatment. *Journal of Consulting and Clinical Psychology, 63,* 256-262.

O'Leary, K.D. and Turkewitz, H. (1978). Marital therapy from a behavioral perspective. In T.J. Paolino and B.S. McCrady (Eds.), *Marriage and marital therapy: Psychoanalytic, behavioral and systems theory perspectives* (pp. 240-297). New York: Brunner/Mazel.

Patterson, G.R. (1971). *Families*. Champaign, IL: Research Press.

Patterson, G.R. (1982). *Coercive family process*. Eugene, OR: Castalia.

Patterson, G.R. and Forgatch, M.S. (1987). *Parents and adolescents living together: Part 1: The basics*. Eugene, OR: Castalia.

Pavlov, I.P. (1932). Neuroses in man and animals. *Journal of the American Medical Association, 99,* 1012-1013.

Prager, K.J. (1995). *The psychology of intimacy*. New York: Guilford Press.

Pretzer, J., Epstein, N., and Fleming, B. (1991). The Marital Attitude Survey: A measure of dysfunctional attributions and expectancies. *The Journal of Cognitive Psychotherapy: An International Quarterly, 5,* 131-148.

Rathus, J.H. and Sanderson, W.C. (1999). *Marital distress: Cognitive behavioral interventions for couples*. Northvale, NJ: Jason Aronson.

Robin, A.L. and Foster, S.L. (1989). *Negotiating parent-adolescent conflict: A behavioral-family systems approach*. New York: Guilford Press.

Roehling, P.V. and Robin, A.L. (1986). Development and validation of the Family Beliefs Inventory: A measure of unrealistic beliefs among parents and adolescents. *Journal of Consulting and Clinical Psychology, 54,* 693-697.

Rotter, J.B. (1954). *Social learning and clinical psychology*. Englewood Cliffs, NJ: Prentice-Hall.

Schwebel, A.I. and Fine, M.A. (1994). *Understanding and helping families: A cognitive-behavioral approach*. Hillsdale, NJ: Lawrence Erlbaum.

Shadish, W.R., Montgomery, L.M., Wilson, P., Wilson, M.R., Bright, I., and Okwumabua, T. (1993). Effects of family and marital psychotherapies: A meta-analysis. *Journal of Consulting and Clinical Psychology, 61,* 992-1002.

Skinner, B.F. (1953). *Science and human behavior*. New York: Macmillan.

Skinner, B.F. (1971). *Beyond freedom and dignity*. New York: Knopf.

Stuart, R.B. (1969). An operant-interpersonal treatment for marital discord. *Journal of Consulting and Clinical Psychology, 33,* 675-682.

Stuart, R.B. (1980). *Helping couples change: A social learning approach to marital therapy.* New York: Guilford Press.

Thibaut, J.W. and Kelley, H.H. (1959). *The social psychology of groups.* New York: Wiley.

Vanzetti, N.A., Notarius, C.I., and NeeSmith, D. (1992). Specific and generalized expectancies in marital interaction. *Journal of Family Psychology, 6,* 171-183.

Watson, J.B. and Raynor, R. (1920). Conditioned emotional reactions. *Journal of Experimental Psychology, 3,* 1-14.

Webster-Stratton, C. and Herbert, M. (1994). *Troubled families—Problem children: Working with parents: A collaborative process.* Chichester, UK: Wiley.

Weiss, R.L. (1980). Strategic behavioral marital therapy: Toward a model for assessment and intervention. Volume 1. In J.P. Vincent (Ed.), *Advances in family intervention, assessment, and theory* (pp. 229-271). Greenwich, CT: JAI Press.

Weiss, R.L. and Heyman, R.E. (1990). Observation of marital interaction. In F.D. Fincham and T.N. Bradbury (Eds.), *The psychology of marriage: Basic issues and applications* (pp. 87-117). New York: Guilford Press.

Weiss, R.L., Hops, H., and Patterson, G.R. (1973). A framework for conceptualizing marital conflict, a technology for altering it, some data for evaluating it. In L.A. Hamerlynck, L.C. Handy, and E.J. Mash (Eds.), *Behavior change: Methodology, concepts and practice* (pp. 309-342). Champaign, IL: Research Press.

Wetchler, J.L. and Piercy, F.P. (1996). Behavioral family therapies. In F.P. Piercy, D.H. Sprenkle, and J.L. Wetchler, *Family therapy sourcebook* (Second edition) (pp. 106-128). New York: Guilford Press.

Wolpe, J. (1958). *Psychotherapy by reciprocal inhibition.* Stanford, CA: Stanford University Press.

Chapter 9

Transgenerational Family Therapies

Thorana S. Nelson

Transgenerational or **intergenerational** family therapies typically are those that attend to dynamics across more than two generations. Although other family therapies, such as structural or strategic, may attend to dynamics across two generations (e.g., parent-child) in the present, the transgenerational therapies are more interested in how the past affects the present. These therapies are not interested in learning about individual pathology. Rather, they are interested in how families, across generations, develop patterns of behaving and responding to stress in ways that prevent healthy development in their members and lead to predictable problems. By understanding how certain patterns develop and changing the way they resolve past issues and interact in their families, troubled individuals and families can develop new ways of interacting that do not include symptoms.

Several key figures are identified with transgenerational family therapies. Murray Bowen (Bowen family systems theory) and Ivan Boszormenyi-Nagy (contextual family therapy), or Nagy (pronounced "najh"), as he is often referred to, are probably the most noted theoretical writers. James Framo also is included in this category and will be discussed briefly. Depending upon how transgenerational is defined, Carl Whitaker is sometimes considered a transgenerational therapist because of his insistence on focusing on multiple generations. He is included in Chapter 7 on experiential therapy in this book because of his focus on the ways people interact based on symbolic experiences and psychodynamic motives.

BOWEN FAMILY SYSTEMS THERAPY

Murray Bowen became interested in psychiatry as a physician in World War II. After the war, he trained and worked at the famous Menninger Clinic in Topeka, Kansas. The Menninger Clinic was founded by two brothers who used classic **psychoanalytic techniques** in psychiatry. Bowen discovered that he often felt confused and trapped in the dynamics at the Menninger, and was particularly distressed at the way the brothers and staff involved patients and other staff in "crazy-making" interactions. Bowen also discovered that he could think more clearly about what was going on at the clinic when he was traveling, but was quickly pulled back into the dysfunctional processes as soon as he returned to work.

Bowen also noticed that he could think more clearly about his own family-of-origin dynamics when he was not with his family of origin. He noticed that family members often complained to him about another family member without talking directly to that person about the problem. Again, he noticed that he could think clearly about what was happening when no one was communicating with him, but had more difficulty when he was interacting with them.

Based on these observations, Bowen set about to deliberately change his own ways of interacting in his family. He gave a speech at a professional meeting; however, instead of giving his intended speech, Bowen told the audience about these deliberate actions he had made in his family and their consequences. At that time (1967), therapists *never* disclosed personal family information. Thus, Bowen broke tradition and published his now-famous paper on his family of origin anonymously (Framo, 1972).

As a theorist, Bowen hypothesized that mentally ill individuals were caught up in patterns of family fusion or **undifferentiated ego mass** such that they were symptom bearers for the family rather than characterologically flawed or ill. He therefore hospitalized whole families in order to treat the emotional system rather than the individual.

Key Concepts

Differentiation of Self

The hallmark concept of Bowen theory, **differentiation of self,** refers to an individual's ability to maintain a strong sense of self while, at the same time, maintaining a connection with a strong emotional system. By being able to distinguish what one thinks and feels as separate from the system dynamics, an individual is able to have his or her own opinion and act on personal judgment without the undue influence of family members. A person with a differentiated self is able to use the opinions and advice of others, but makes independent decisions. Differentiation of self is a process and a part of family dynamics rather than a personality characteristic. This process can be observed in many kinds of systems including family, friendships, and work.

Closely tied to differentiation of self from the family is the concept of **differentiation of thinking from emotion.** Bowen believed that this is a biological and physiological as well as mental process. To the degree that a person is able to distinguish emotions from thinking, one is able to make decisions about behavior rather than reacting to the intensity of the emotional system.

The opposite of differentiation is **fusion.** Bowen believed that all of us are constantly balancing needs for intimacy and autonomy. Without autonomy, we are fused with others and unable to think for ourselves. We are easily swayed by other peoples' opinions and wishes. There is a natural tendency to want intimacy with others, to feel connected, understood, and important. At the same time, there is a natural aversion to too much fusion such that we get anxious when we begin to lose autonomy. This **fusion anxiety** is a motivator to separate and try to develop a separate self, to differentiate. Bowen believed that most behavior in relational systems reflects an attempt to balance the natural togetherness and separateness forces that we all have regarding fusion anxiety. Fusion anxiety leads to reactivity or emotionality under stress.

Bowen believed that anyone, even the most differentiated person, can become symptomatic under sufficient stress. More differentiated persons are less likely to develop severe symptoms from stress and are able to recover more quickly when they do develop symptoms. The ability to be **responsive** rather than **reactive** allows a person to more easily make thoughtful decisions about what to do. It's not that emotions are not present but that they are less likely to paralyze or inhibit thinking, which can lead to knee-jerk behaviors. For example, a differentiated person will still become angry under certain circumstances, but is more likely to decide after thinking about it whether to walk away, say something calmly, yell, or even act out physically.

Bowen talked about differentiation of self as a continuum and even wrote about a scale that went from 0 (no differentiation) to 100 (total differentiation). He later regretted this because it led people to attempt to quantify the concept in individuals. Bowen was more interested in the qualities that distinguished more and less differentiated persons and systems. In addition, he wrote about the scale as though the low end of the scale was characterized by a lack of **autonomy.** Although this is a reasonable understanding of what he wrote, Bowen's idea was much more complex. He believed that most of life's difficulties arise because we are ruled by emotion and depend on others' goodwill. Over time, we become more autonomous and **interdependent** rather than **dependent.** Therefore, we are more likely to be able to act on our own. However, we are always more or less susceptible to the opinions of others, which affects our ability to think clearly. To the extent that we have unresolved differentiation issues, we are ruled in reactive ways by our emotions and by what we believe others want us to do. We need to exercise our ability to think while under emotional strain, not focus on our feelings.

However, Bowen also believed that it is necessary for people to be in well-established intimate relationships, able to draw upon these relationships under stress, and able to appreciate and enjoy them as part of basic human needs and interactions. Bowen came under attack by feminists and others as overvaluing masculine traits of autonomy and undervaluing feminine traits. It is clear from his writings, however, that he believed **intimacy** is an important part of differentiation, and that differentiation and autonomy are not the same thing. We are so used to leading with our emotions that to focus more on our thinking takes direct effort.

Bowen also talked about **basic self** and **pseudoself.** The basic self is stable and is less likely to be affected by day-to-day situations. The basic self is established through the **nuclear family projection process** and does not change much after childhood. The pseudoself, on the other hand, is one's ability to distinguish a sense of self depending upon particular situations. We have all had the experience of feeling more in control of our emotions in some social situations, such as at work, than in highly intimate or stressful situations, such as in a family conflict or when hurt or ill. The concept of the pseudoself accounts for apparent changes in maturity or personality. We can be overconfident in some situations without being considered an arrogant person. We can act silly with our children or certain friends without being considered a childish person.

Finally, Bowen also believed that people tend to marry others with similar levels of differentiation of self. A newly engaged couple is at its most undifferentiated, or fused. That is, newly engaged people are immensely affected by their oneness and by each other's wishes and desires, and are quite vulnerable to each other's systemic needs. One may *appear* more differentiated than the other, perhaps by acting more emotionally stable, but this is due to the effects of pseudo rather than basic differentiation.

To summarize, differentiation of self is the hinge pin of Bowen's theory. The concept describes both the psychological ability to distinguish thinking from feeling and the relational ability to distinguish a self from others. It also describes the ability to maintain a sense of autonomy and intimacy at the same time. This ability is dependent upon three things: level of basic self, amount of stress and **anxiety,** and the emotional nature of the situation.

Triangles

Bowen was very systemic in his thinking although he had not attended much to the writings of other systems thinkers of his day. He very much believed that in nature, all things are affected by other things, including human relationships over multiple generations, and that this is a holistic or systemic rather than linear process. Using an analogy from physics, he described two-person systems as unstable depending upon the amount of stress and conflict in the system. His emphasis was on the system as a whole, not the individuals in the system. He believed that any system, given enough stress and anxiety, will attempt to stabilize by forming triangles. These **triangles,** the smallest stable unit of a system, may be formed by one or both of the persons' drawing a third person into the relationship. The third part of the triangle also can be work, a hobby, or an issue. All systems form triangles and this is sometimes good. For example, an arguing couple may become temporarily distracted by an interesting story that one of their children tells them and become very involved in talking about the story rather than their disagreement. It may even appear that they are *using* the story to avoid their disagreement. However, after a time, when they are both more calm and able to think clearly, they may be able to resolve their difference quite easily.

The third person in a triangle is favored and may enjoy special privileges or position when stress is high. When stress lessens, this person is the "odd one out" and may triangle another person to reduce his or her anxiety. In this way, systems are made up of multiple interlocking triangles with stress, anxiety, and tension dynamically moving around the system. The problem comes when there is a **rigid triangle,** always using the same person, issue, or problem, or when it is severe and prevents the system from dealing with the difference directly. For example, triangles may be as mild as the one described in the previous paragraph, or as destructive as an affair or drug or alcohol abuse, or involving a child or other person to such an extent that he or she becomes symptomatic.

Nuclear family emotional process. Individuals and families develop typical patterns of dealing with stress in order to reduce anxiety. Each of these patterns can be useful, if it is moderate and flexible. Each can be harmful if used severely or exclusively. In mild form, each allows emotions to cool down so that thinking processes are more available. When people are emotionally heated, it is difficult to think of alternatives and easy to be reactive. "I just couldn't think clearly" is an example of this. When people are able to think clearly, they can more easily control their emotions (not ignore or bury them) and choose actions that are likely to lead to desirable outcomes rather than more trouble. Reactivity is seldom if ever helpful.

The first pattern to reduce anxiety that Bowen described is **conflict.** When there is a difference of opinion, people can talk about it reasonably, heatedly, or, in its extreme, violently. A couple may disagree about where to eat out for dinner. They can decide to go with one person's choice because the other got to choose last time, a process that leads to resolution and is healthy. Another way they can handle conflicts is to let the discussion deteriorate with name-calling and hurt feelings. In this case, one person may give in to avoid further conflict at the expense of his or her own autonomy. The conflict may lead to a heated argument that includes past hurts and issues and further deteriorate into mental, emotional, or physical violence. It is often puzzling to hear about the seemingly irrational "causes" of violent arguments.

The second pattern is the appearance of a **symptom** in one person. Symptoms can be physical, emotional or mental, or social. For example, one person could develop a headache or become depressed. Another person could become anxious or turn to alcohol. In extreme cases of chronic unresolved anxiety, one person could develop "stress headaches," chronic back pain, or even a serious or fatal condition such as heart disease or cancer. According to Bowen, rigid family patterns over the generations can make an individual susceptible both physiologically and emotionally to some kinds of symptoms. That is how we may see patterns of illness in families: heart problems, "nervous" conditions such as depression, or alcoholism and drug abuse. Social symptoms include such events as alcohol or drug abuse and related activities, problems with the law, or poor school or work performance. We are not used to thinking of physical, mental, or social problems in this way. However, nearly all of us can think of an example or two that may fit this pattern—a not-so-obvious way of reducing anxiety between two people.

The third pattern described by Bowen is **distancing.** In its mildest and most helpful form, distancing may mean something as simple as a time out agreed upon by the people involved. It can be a way of reducing anxiety temporarily to prevent escalation of conflict that is not helpful. In moderate forms, distancing not only keeps people from becoming more anxious, it also keeps them from developing more intimate relationships that otherwise would lead to increased differentiation and intimacy as well as autonomy. In its most extreme form, distancing can mean divorce or cutting off from important others.

The fourth pattern in of the nuclear family emotional process is **triangling,** which happens when tensions or anxiety rise in a two-person system or dyad. One or both persons attempts to reduce his or her anxiety by involving a third party to which the anxiety can be spread. Bowen originally limited this idea to the involvement of a child; however, therapists have come to recognize that this process can involve other people, activities, and issues. In its mildest form, triangling may serve as a temporary distraction from the anxiety-producing stress. In more moderate forms, it can actually increase anxiety because issues do not get resolved or because the relationship with the triangled person becomes problematic itself. For example, a woman may complain to her mother about her husband. The mother, in turn, tries to give helpful advice and feels closer to her daughter. After the woman and her husband calm down and resolve their difference, the mother is no longer in such a favored position. She may complain to another daughter that the woman does not listen to her advice, thereby creating another triangle. Triangling can involve more than one party or person when the first attempt is not successful or is inadequate for reducing anxiety. Similarly, triangled persons may, in turn, triangle others to reduce *their* anxiety. In these ways, anxiety spreads throughout a system and appears "contagious."

In its most extreme form, triangles include such problems as affairs, preoccupation with work, or zealousness about some topic or issue—a "cause." Notice that these things are a way of reducing anxiety in the original dyad but also may spiral back into the dyad in the form of more stress and anxiety. When the same child is always used in the triangle, that child may become symptomatic in a physical, emotional, or social manner. In therapy, it is not uncommon to see parents arguing heatedly over differences while their child waits for their support and appropriate discipline. The child's behavior may serve to distract the parents from their marital issues, but it is at the expense of the child's growth, development, and personal differentiation.

All four of the mechanisms that are used by people to reduce anxiety are available to everyone. However, families sometimes "choose" one pattern or another as the family's "way," or they may elect certain individuals to carry certain patterns. These patterns may then become described as fixed characteristics of a person's personality. Each of us has a "typical" way of dealing with problems in general or with certain kinds of problems or relationships. I may tend to engage in conflict with my children but distance from my spouse. You may become depressed whenever your mother and you disagree. Difficulties arise when individuals or families use the same mechanism over and over or in extreme forms. Less differentiated people and systems are more likely to develop rigid or extreme patterns and to use them more often.

Family projection process. The family projection process helps explain how it is that children from the same family can be so different. Parents tend to project their unresolved differentiation issues onto one or more of their children. The children who are "elected" for this honor tend to be special to one or both parents for various reasons. The child may remind a parent of an important family member. The child may have been born at an important time in the family—when a grandparent died, for example, or after a period of infertility. The child may share a birth order position with the parent or other family member or have a physical vulnerability. These children then tend to be the recipients of parents' attention—negative or overtly positive—which may compromise their ability to develop and differentiate. Children in the family who are not treated in such a way may suffer from lack of attention, compromising their differentiation process, or they may be freed from negative attention in a way that allows them to mature beyond their parents and siblings.

Sibling birth order. Using the ideas of German psychologist Walter Toman (1961), Bowen hypothesized that a person's sex and birth order in the family affected the attention they received and their roles in the family. This often led to certain and particular characteristics and vulnerability to triangling by parents. For example, oldest children often tend to follow the family rules, to be more responsible, and to develop leadership skills. Conversely, younger siblings tend to be more carefree and irresponsible, and to march to their own drummers.

Multigenerational transmission process. Over several generations, different branches of family trees exhibit more and less differentiation. The cousins on one branch seem to do very well—graduate school, high-powered professions, philanthropists, and generous helpers. Cousins on another branch, however, have problems with drugs, the law, and the in-laws. To the extent that one or more children are the recipients of the parents' negative attention or triangling, these children are stunted in their own differentiation processes and develop with similar or less differentiation than their parents. They then tend to marry others with similar levels of differentiation and *their* triangled children develop with even lower levels of differentiation. Over many generations, according to Bowen, this process leads to individuals who are so unable to think for themselves that they develop symptoms of schizophrenia, a thought disorder.

Conversely, children who are spared the negative attention or triangling by their parents may develop higher levels of differentiation, marry, and produce some children who are even more differentiated. This branch of the family tree, over time, may produce a Ghandi or an Einstein.

Emotional cutoff. After developing his ideas about the concepts just described, Bowen developed two others. The first is called emotional cutoff and describes the process by which some people attempt to distance themselves in their families so much that they believe that their families have no influence on them. Cutoff people are not able to access the intimacy and other benefits of their families and believe that they are mature, autonomous, and unaffected by their family influences. These people may move to another part of the country or world or they may live across the street from their family members. They pretend, however, that they have no emotional involvement with their families. These people may take the opposite view on an issue, but they do not realize that this position is dictated by what the other person thinks, not their own independent perspective.

Societal emotional process. The last of Bowen's concepts was never fully developed. Bowen believed that the same processes that occur in all family systems and that lead to more and less differentiation in family branches, also occur in other societal systems. His idea, however, seemed very fatalistic in that he described the transmission of differentiation in only a negative direction. Over time, society is doomed to less and less differentiation and more and more conflict, according to Bowen.

Normal Family Development

Bowen believed that the same processes are found in all families. Differences in quantity rather than quality of the dynamic determine how well a family manages stress without symptoms. That is, *all* families use processes of triangling and conflict. All families struggle with unresolved issues and. problems that are exacerbated by poor differentiation. Typical families, in Bowen's view, are more or less functional, not "healthy" or "unhealthy." That said, for purposes of this chapter, we will examine **typical** (and relatively healthy) **family development.**

Healthier families are those that can balance the needs for autonomy and intimacy for each individual over time and across situations. Some stressful situations require that families give up "self" for a time—during grieving, for example. Healthier families are those that can pull together, assisting one another in the emotional morass of crisis, and then gradually redifferentiate, sometimes resulting in higher levels of differentiation for their members.

Fusion, or what Minuchin (1974) calls **enmeshment,** is normal in two situations: when a couple is first engaged to be married (or first make a commitment to each other—Bowen did not discuss possibilities of nonmarried commitment); and when children are first born. It is normal for newly committed persons and new parents to be totally consumed by the other and quite susceptible to the emotional flooding that naturally occurs. In healthier families, this state of fusion develops into a process of differentiation. The differentiation process is not a steady upward line. Rather, it is more like the waves of an incoming tide: some forward movement, some backward movement, but overall, forward.

Healthier families can move through the typical stages of the individual and family life cycles without undo difficulty. People are able to be flexible in their ability to tolerate conflict and difference and are able to adjust to the comings and goings of family members through birth, leaving home, marriage or commitment, death, and divorce. Children are involved in parental triangles, but not excessively and they are able to get on with their own lives when released or when they free themselves. Parents do not inappropriately involve children in their marital life nor do they overfocus on their children or each other, unduly giving up self for the sake of the other. There is a good balance of family, couple, and individual time. People are relatively symptom free and, when symptoms of system stress are evident, they are easily overcome and the family moves on in its evolution. Members of the extended families are neither overfocused upon nor cutoff.

Dysfunctional Family Development

The corollary of functional family processes is dysfunctional processes. This is where Bowen's view—that dysfunction is a matter of quantity rather than quality—differs so significantly from other theories' views. For example, Bowen believed that the processes that are evident in individuals diagnosed with schizophrenia or other problems are operating in all of us. We *all* "hear voices"; it's just that some of us hear them to a greater degree and with greater discomfort (or greater discomfort to others).

Whether a particular behavior is problematic is decided more by the individuals or situation than by some gold standard of health. For example, whether someone is given treatment for schizophrenia may depend on how well the symptom is succeeding at reducing anxiety in the triadic system in which it is embedded. If no one in the system is troubled and the system is otherwise stable, it may be that no treatment is necessary. However, if someone is troubled by the difficulty or if it does not decrease anxiety (indeed, it may *increase* anxiety), someone may decide that professional treatment is needed. It is at this point, when someone labels something as problematic that it *becomes* problematic. A behavior in and of itself would not be considered problematic, in Bowen's view. To say otherwise may say as much or more about the person doing the diagnosing or labeling and their position in some triangle.

Any of the four anxiety-reducing mechanisms described (conflict, distancing, triangling, and symptoms) can be problematic. This is more likely to happen when a family is caught in a generations-old pattern that uses one or two of the mechanisms excessively. We must remember also that any system, even the healthiest, may appear or become dysfunctional given enough stress. The key factor, in Bowen's view, would be how differentiated the individuals are and therefore how able they are to rebound from the stress with fewer, less severe, and shorter-lived symptoms.

There is another situation in which symptoms may appear. This situation involves a parental dyad that is so unstable and fraught with stress that the anxiety spills over onto more than one child. In these situations, each child develops his or her own way of absorbing or managing the anxiety. One may develop physical symptoms, another school problems. One may become anti-social and another may work so hard to be "good" and overfunction that she or he slips into depression or another emotional illness. Rarely, such a child may be able to detriangle and redirect the anxiety back onto the parents.

In couples that do not triangle their children, one partner may act as an "overfunctioner." Such a position requires a complementary "underfunctioner" in order to exist. That is, there can be no overfunctioner if no one is in need of such care. The overfunctioner often appears more healthy and is sometimes held up as a martyr. Examples include long-suffering husbands of depressed women and long-suffering wives of alcoholics.

However, recall that Bowen believed that people married others with similar levels of differentiation. One partner simply *appears* healthier. The overfunctioner is just that: *over* functioning. To be functional, a person is neither over- nor underfunctioning. This does not mean that people do not take care of each other. The process described refers to a habitual pattern in which one person must play his or her role to the exclusion of other roles and at the expense of self-differentiation. The difference between health and not-health in such situations is evident when the caretaker becomes overburdened and either obtains help from outside (healthier) or becomes dysfunctional (less healthy) himself or herself. In therapy, it is often helpful to remind women, who are usually socialized to be overfunctioners, that it does no one any good if they become ill themselves.

Goals of Bowen Systems Theory

The chief goal of Bowen family therapy is differentiation of self. Bowen believed that problematic behaviors ought not to be the focus of therapy except as they point toward habitual and unhelpful family processes or issues. Simply talking about problems will not make them go away because the underlying difficulty is the system's inability to handle stress without symptoms. Increasing differentiation helps people increase their ability to think rather than act and therefore to choose responses rather than using habitual, knee-jerk behaviors and to handle stress without overusing any of the four mechanisms.

A corollary goal of therapy is detriangling from a complex of relationships, particularly in the family of origin. Difficulties with partners and children often are directly tied to messy triangles in extended families. Pragmatically, it often is easier to calm emotions first in the family of origin and to pull oneself out of dysfunctional triangles. This often calms the nuclear family anxiety sufficiently so that the triangles there become less rigid and harmful. Bowen observed that his trainees' marriages often improved as their family-of-origin relationships improved.

Mere symptom removal is not a goal of Bowen family therapy. Symptoms can be removed, but without changes in triangles or differentiation of self, symptoms of one sort will be replaced by symptoms of another sort. Triangles in one situation may abate, but the need to reduce anxiety will not, and other triangles will appear. Some of these triangles may be less unfortunate than others. For example, a couple may stop triangling a child into their relationship and may use a therapist for a time to reduce their anxiety. If the therapist can maintain his or her own self and not become anxious, can remain a calm third and temporary point in the triangle, the system may become stable enough to allow the couple to resolve their difficulties directly and increase their differentiation. This allows healthier functioning in terms of separating emotion from thinking, self from other, and self from family of origin.

Bowen Family Therapy Techniques

The chief technique of Bowen therapy is the therapist herself or himself. People come to therapy because their usual ways of managing stress and anxiety are not working and usually involve high emotionality. From this perspective, therapy becomes the third point in a triangle, one way to reduce anxiety and stabilize the system. To the extent that a triangled person can remain calm and not get pulled into the anxiety of the dyadic system, the dyadic system can resolve its difficulty, which may increase differentiation for both persons. However, in most intense emotional systems such as families, it is very difficult for the third person to remain calm. Our tendency is to want to help people when they are upset. However, in our families, our ways of helping are often programmed and reactive, pulling us deeper into the emotional morass of the system and sometimes making things worse. In therapy, the differentiated therapist has the opportunity to help clients by remaining calm, not becoming activated by the clients' stress and anxiety, not getting caught up in the family's issues, and helping the clients think about what is going on. Therefore, the chief technique is the calm presence of a differentiated therapist.

Recall that Bowen believed that very few people, including therapists, are very well differentiated. Our tendency is to become reactive and search for answers, give advice, and *do* something. This is not helpful if it does not help the client increase his or her ability to think under stress. Therefore, therapists must increase their own differentiation of self through Bowen therapy. By learning about their own "toxic" issues and detriangling in their own families of origin, therapists are able to increase their ability to think and remain calm when they are invited to take on others' anxiety.

Genograms

Beyond the presence of a calm therapist as technique, a few practices are hallmarks of Bowen therapy. The first step is helping the clients understand the family system in which they are embedded. This is very much a "give away" type of therapy. Rather than protecting hypotheses and insights, the therapist explains the principles of the model to the clients so that they have a clearer picture of what is happening and a map to use for guidance. This map is sometimes called a **genogram** or **family map** (see Figure 9.1). It is like a family tree, but includes information about the emotional dynamics of the family as well as dates of birth and death.

The genogram gives a quick picture of what the family looks like: men and women, marriages and divorces, children, dates, and significant events. The genogram may also contain information about emotional functioning including overinvolved relationships, cutoffs, distance, and conflict. By drawing these relationships on the genogram, clients and therapists are able to see triangles and patterns of reacting to stress. This information may give clues to how and where clients can detriangle and change their own functioning in the family. According to systems thinking and Bowen theory, when a person changes his or her own position in the family, others *must* change in order to adapt to the first person's changes. The genogram also holds clues to probable reactions. The more rigid the family pattern, the more likely it is that family members will react to change with messages that suggest the client should "change back" to predictable ways. Knowing the typical family patterns and helping clients choose wisely in their strategies can reduce the likelihood of discouraging results.

The therapist also helps the client identify particularly loaded or toxic family issues. These issues are the ones that tend to get people stuck, and they are often less likely to be able to think independently about them. Some of these issues may include money, childbearing or child rearing, religion, alcohol, or affairs.

Detriangling

The therapist helps clients detriangle in sticky emotional systems by having them think about their positions in these systems when they are less

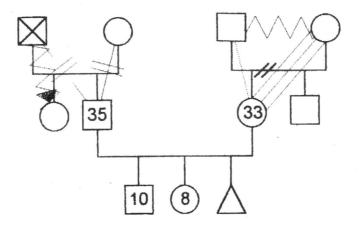

□ = male; ○ = female; X = death; △ = child in utero; // = cutoff; ∧∧∧ = conflicted relationship

FIGURE 9.1. Basic Genogram Showing Parents with Two Children and a Pregnancy. (Father is cut off from his mother and his father, who is dead. The mother has a fused relationship with her mother and a distant relationship with her father. Her parents are divorced and their relationship is conflictual.)

emotional and therefore more able to think clearly about them. This increases intellectual functioning but not at the expense of intimacy. By planning detriangling moves and anticipating family countermoves, the client is able to prepare for new family interactions, ones in which she or he is an actor and responder rather than reactor.

Therapeutic Mode

Bowen preferred to work with couples. He believed that child difficulties were symptomatic of the way the parents involved the child in their marriage. By replacing the child in the triangle, Bowen was able to free the child so that he or she could continue his or her normal development and, at the same time, assist the couple by being a calm rather than reactive part of the triangle. According to these ideas, the child's symptoms would disappear because the child was detriangled and because the parents would become more able to care for the child appropriately—better than any therapist could.

During the couple sessions, the therapist helps the clients maintain their self-positions with two important techniques. First, the clients are seldom instructed to talk with each other unless the therapist is sure that they can do so without being reactive to each other. Rather, the clients are instructed to talk to and through the therapist. One partner is able to listen less reactively to the other than when the partners are talking directly to each other, which tends to activate more emotions than rational thinking.

Second, the therapist asks each partner what he or she thinks about what is being discussed. By encouraging thinking and talking in the form of **"I" statements,** the therapist helps the clients differentiate their emotional and thinking systems, bringing thinking more into the forefront. Emotions are important, but because of our tendency to get caught up in them and to not think clearly, therapists encourage clients to talk about them rather than re-experience them. Experience alone, without thoughtful examination, does not help people change their lives, according to Bowen.

As couples become more able to talk calmly without resorting to their usual patterns of reacting, the therapist steps back and intervenes only when the system needs calming again. As the two increase their differentiation from each other (which is accompanied by both increased autonomy *and* increased intimacy), they are more able to help each other in differentiating in their families of origin. The genogram has helped them understand how they came to be the way they are and to plan new ways of interacting with each other. The genogram then becomes a tool for planning changes in the families of origin. At this point, therapy often becomes less frequent. It takes time for changes in families of origin to be accomplished. Also, at this time, many couples discontinue therapy. Their anxiety has been reduced and they sometimes do not see the need or the value of continuing. Sometimes, the idea of making changes in the family of origin produces enough anxiety to make therapy seem unnecessary, unduly difficult, and even dangerous for the individuals.

Bowen therapists also work with individuals, but in very systemic ways. Examining the genogram over multiple generations helps people understand past patterns and plan changes so that rigid patterns are not carried forth into future generations.

Research

Very little research has been done using Bowen theory. Bowen often stated that if people tried to research his theory, they did not understand it. However, several attempts have been made to develop differentiation scales. The most used is the Family of Origin Scale (Hovestadt et al., 1985). This scale purports to measure the balance of intimacy and autonomy as a measure of family health. The scale has been used to show differences in family health in a number of clinical and nonclincal samples.

Bray, Williamson, and Malone (1984) developed a scale to measure the extent of personal authority in an individual. Williamson (1981) hypothesized a life cycle stage called "personal authority," typically found during a person's midthirties. This life cycle stage is marked by the ability of an adult to see her or his parents as real and distinct people similar to other people. Personal authority allows people to have adult rather than parent-child relationships with their parents. The Family of Origin Scale measures a family's health in the past and the Personal Authority in the Family System measures current relationships. Nelson (1989) attempted to investigate Bowen's notions that (1) people tend to marry others with similar levels of differentiation and (2) the partner who exhibits symptoms is not necessarily less differentiated than the more functioning partner. She found that married people in her sample were similar in terms of personal authority and that people in therapy were more similar to their partners than to subjects in a nonclinical sample.

CONTEXTUAL FAMILY THERAPY

Contextual family therapy was developed by Ivan Boszormenyi-Nagy, a psychiatrist who was a contemporary of Murray Bowen, Carl Whitaker, Lyman Wynne, and other psychiatrists who also were developing ideas regarding the multigenerational nature of relationships and, particularly, problems. Nagy believed that individuals and families are governed not only by patterns of behavior that are developed over multiple generations but also by principles of relational fairness. The core concept of contextual therapy relates to the **trustworthiness of relationships** in terms of an oscillating balance of credits and debits, of give and take. A context of **fairness, mutuality,** and trustworthiness leads to individuation, **balanced relationships,** and personal fulfillment. This theory takes into consideration **ethical dimensions** of relationships and the way loyalties, legacies, entitlements, and obligations are balanced over time and over multiple generations.

Dimensions of Relational Reality

According to Nagy's ideas, there are four dimensions to an understanding of relationships and the parts played by the individuals in them. The first of these dimensions is **facts,** the undisputed things that have happened or that exist. These include birth, death, physical differences, marriages, divorces, and natural and human-made events such as hurricanes and war.

Different from other models of family therapy, **individual psychology** is an important dimension in contextual theory. Contextual therapy considers the dynamics of individuals' inner lives including thoughts, dreams and aspirations, intellectual ability, and emotions. Elements of individuals' psyches interact with others' in ways that encourage patterns in relationships, both good and bad, helpful and harmful. This is especially important when dynamics from one person's family are similar to a partner's and evoke certain expectations, emotions, and reactions.

Transactional patterns are the ways that people interact with one another. These processes are both simple and complicated, involving just two people and involving many people over multiple generations, even those that do not know each other. Interactional patterns are not used as a primary target in therapy as in other family therapy models. Rather, they give clues as to the legacies, entitlements, and **indebtedness** that constitute fair and just relatedness over time.

The final dimension that Nagy discussed is the ethics of due consideration, or **relational ethics.** This concept does not refer to ethics or morality as they typically are understood. Rather, it refers to what Nagy believed was the natural and fundamental basis for interactions: a balance of ethical consideration for others' interests as well as one's own. According to this idea, people both deserve and owe fairness in their relationships, sort of tit for tat. This dynamic is called trustworthiness and is considered over time and across generations. Something may not seem fair in the present interaction, and therefore must be and can be balanced at a later time. Failure to consider others' interests can lead to symptomatic behavior and relational problems. This concept does not refer simply to a *felt* sense of injustice, unfairness, or entitlement. Rather, it is in the **existential,** natural order of humanity that people are treated fairly and that they treat others fairly in relationships. Therefore, people who have not been treated fairly cannot simply "get over it," but must, in some way, be involved in **exoneration** through exonerating and/or being exonerated. This occurs in therapy in two ways: (1) the ability of the therapist to demonstrate consideration of all people and relationships that are involved, including past and future generations, and (2) the ability of the clients to understand the need for consideration on all parts and make efforts to balance the ledgers in the family.

To the extent that relationships are trustworthy, the individuals within them are involved in a dynamic of balanced give and take. Each person deserves and receives consideration of their interests by others. People are neither exploited nor scapegoated. No one must balance a ledger with negative behavior; relationships should serve as resources of trust for the people involved in them so that they can navigate other relationships without undue strain.

An important concept of contextual therapy is **loyalty.** Loyalty is not simply blind faithfulness, commitment, and dedication to another person. Rather, loyalty is what is owed to parents by virtue of what they have given their children through birth and care. Loyalty is fundamental and factual in parent-child relationships. Parents maintain a balance of fairness with their children, which reinforces the loyalty commitment of the children.

Overt or healthy loyalty is demonstrated when people are able to keep the lines open with their parents, even when the parents are difficult or require great amounts of care. Covert or **invisible loyalty** is destructive in that people are not consciously aware of the dynamic, but are nonetheless driven by it. Because they are not aware of the nature of the loyalty, they are unable to make choices about repayment. Repayment and demonstration of invisible loyalty is made through automatic, driven, and often destructive action. An invisible loyalty to a legacy of failed marriages may doom a person to failure in their own relationships. To do better might demonstrate a lack of loyalty.

Legacy refers to expectations within a family that may be spoken or unspoken, conscious or unconscious. These expectations are derived from being born to particular people and the belief that we owe family some measure of loyalty. Failure to meet legacy expectations can lead to loss of trustworthiness in the relationship and violate fairness to previous generations, even when the legacy is negative in nature. If one has a legacy obligation to a family, they may "pay it off" in kind to the next generation. For example, an abused child learns to abuse. He or she may pay the debt by continuing abuse into the next generation. A person may be dealt a legacy of failure and evidence loyalty to family by continuing to fail. Therapy involves conscious efforts to give up nonproductive legacies without blaming or cutting off from the prior generation. Instead, the person consciously develops constructive ways of balancing ledgers and paying debts instead of nonconstructive or damaging methods of paying that debt.

Entitlement is what people have due to them by virtue of the fact that they are born or give birth, plus any merit that they earn. Children are entitled to trustworthy parenting. If they don't receive it, they will provide for it themselves through **parentification,** thereby participating in an untrustworthy relationship. As children grow, they also are entitled to make efforts to pay back their obligations. Parents who do not allow children to do this contribute to unbalanced ledgers of entitlements and obligations. Parents are entitled to consideration by their children, depending upon the child's age and ability to repay the debt.

People earn **merit** by being trustworthy and considering the interests of others. Merit is specific to particular relationships and cannot be repaid in others. This is difficult, for example, between parents and children when children can never fully repay their parents for giving them life as well as the love and care (or lack thereof) they received when they were growing up. Merit is earned by crediting others with their contributions to relationships even when they are, at the same time, behaving in difficult ways. This can be seen when parents are able to love their children at the same time that they are angry with them. In this way, children "owe" their parents for their ethical fairness in the relationship. Children earn merit by exonerating their parents for failures and credit their parents by understanding them in a multigenerational perspective.

The family **ledger** is a balance sheet of entitlements and **obligations** and indebtedness. The ledger may appear unbalanced at any one point in time due to life cycle stages, particular circumstances, and the nature of human interaction. However, over time, it is expected that people will maintain their trustworthiness by paying back their debts through actions and exoneration. Relationships in which people are not allowed to pay their debts are not trustworthy and do not contribute to healthy growth and development. That is, parents do their children no favors by refusing to accept a child's efforts to acknowledge and repay debts. Over time, imbalances in ledgers may lead to **stagnation,** or lack of development toward autonomy and trustworthiness in the relationship. A person may never give up the search for ways to restore balance in the parental relationship.

As you can see, the idea of a ledger, borrowed from economics, speaks to an economy of what is owed and what is due in relationships. Some of these debts or obligations and entitlements exist from the simple fact of being born. Even when children are adopted and never know their biological parents, there is still a loyalty obligation to the biological parents. When attempts to forestall the oscillating balance of entitlement and obligation are successful, relationships stagnate and people may develop symptomatic ways of fulfilling the legacy. For example, an adopted daughter may give birth as a teenager. She may decide to keep the baby as a way of making up for what was missing in her own parent-child relationship or she may decide to give the baby up for adoption as a way of continuing the legacy her birth mother paid her, a way of demonstrating loyalty.

Nagy believed that problems in living are embedded in the numerous and complex relationships of multiple generations. To the extent that relationships are trustworthy, that is, balanced in terms of credits and debits, they serve as resources as people develop other relationships, even troubled ones. A reserve of trust can carry a person through an imbalanced period but a multigenerational deficit of trust, of negative loyalties and unfulfilled entitlements, can prevent someone from being trustworthy in other relationships. This reserve or lack thereof then affects future generations.

The **revolving slate** is the process by which entitlement is "paid back" through destructive actions, either to self or to others. Sometimes a child has not been treated fairly and has not had basic needs met by his or her parents, usually because the parents also were treated unfairly and had no merit or trust to give their child. In these circumstances, the child may enact his or her legacy by getting into trouble, treating others badly, using drugs, or doing poorly in school. This revolving slate of **destructive entitlement** will continue until something happens to balance the ledger and restore the family relationships to fairness and health. As you can see, this may mean examining ledgers over many generations.

Nagy believed that revolving slates of destructive entitlement are the chief factor in marital and family dysfunction. An imbalance in the ledger over time leads to discouragement and stagnation in relationships, a depletion of trust resources, and a lack of consideration for the interests of others. This lack of consideration leads to revolving slates of destructive entitlement. Therapy helps by drawing attention not to the particular issue or dysfunctional behavior but to the lack of fairness in important relationships. Attempts to make up for this lack of fairness, driven by invisible loyalties and the particular nature of one's legacy, appear in marital and family relationships as problems or acting out. Conflict or lack of intimacy in a marriage is more a reflection of a need to demonstrate loyalty to parents than lack of communication skills or poor problem-solving methods, according to Nagy. **Exploitation** (taking advantage of someone's dependency position in a relationship) and **scapegoating** (placing a negative legacy on a child instead of accepting it) are two ways that the revolving slate and stagnation can develop into symptoms or complaints.

Healthy Functioning

Imbalances in relationship ledgers are inevitable. Life is not always fair and people do not always treat one another fairly. However, in the well-functioning family, there is a balance over time, an oscillation of give and take that keeps the entitlements and obligations in balance. Children become more accountable for their debts as they mature and are allowed to make payments, although they may never be able to completely repay their parents. People are able to consider the interests of others in their actions and decisions. Trustworthy relationships are strong and encourage autonomy in children, which increases everyone's entitlement to take responsibility for their decisions and actions. Yes, people are *entitled* to accountability. This accountability and acknowledgment increases the trustworthiness of relationships, adding to the well of trust upon which people must draw from time to time.

The well-functioning family has no hidden ledgers or undue amounts of unpaid debts. Life cycle transitions offer opportunities for further growth as changes are negotiated among family members. There is mutual reciprocity of care, consideration, and interdependence. No one is unduly exploited or scapegoated, and no one is held in unhealthy dependencies as recipients of unhealthy attempts to pay back old debts. Resources of trust help people as they develop and navigate the stresses and strains of life. Symptoms are not necessary because relationships are trustworthy and everyone is overtly aware of and able to consider everyone else.

Symptom Development

The chief reason for **disjunction** is a breakdown in trustworthiness. This break leads to stagnation and a lack of flexibility in relationships over time. Nagy used the word *disjunction* rather than *dysfunction*. He believed that systems malfunction not because they are pathological or dysfunctional but because the ethical considerations that are necessary for healthy functioning are broken. This may seem to be word quibbling, but it is important to understand how Nagy saw the existential character and being of a family over time. The balance necessary for healthy functioning is not something that can easily be assessed, pinpointed for its brokenness, and "fixed." Rather, the very nature of the family interaction is amiss. People need to understand the ethical nature of relatedness and address it as a fundamental property of making relationships something that hold people in justice and fairness, increasing both autonomy and a sense of connectedness to the family goodness.

When relationships are not balanced, people become disengaged from caring for others and being accountable to them (as well as to self). This leads to destructive entitlement—vengeful or spiteful behaviors by the entitled one. This stunts personal growth and further destroys trustworthiness in relationships.

Sometimes, parents exploit their children's vulnerability and needs, parentifying them or engaging them in split loyalties. Parentifying is a process whereby children are inappropriately brought into the marriage or expected to take on responsibilities beyond their abilities. **Split loyalties** are those occasions when a child can be loyal to one parent only by being disloyal to the other. This is similar to triangling, discussed previously in the section on Bowen therapy, and is destructive, binding children in processes for which they cannot balance their ledgers. Paying back one parent (loyalty) is accomplished at the expense of trustworthiness in the other relationship (disloyalty). Asking a spouse not to give consideration to a parent results in a **loyalty conflict** and breaks trustworthiness in the marital relationship, leading to marital dissatisfaction and conflict.

When loyalties to past generations are unspoken, they may interfere with a person's loyalty to a partner or to children. These invisible loyalties are often very insidious and difficult to examine. They are very powerful, however, and sometimes seemingly paradoxical. For example, if a parent or grandparent did poorly in school, there may be an unspoken, invisible loyalty that keeps a child from doing better than his or her elder or succeeding in some other way. This is not "fear of success" but "fear of violating an invisible loyalty." These destructive legacies can lead to all sorts of problems and symptoms from indifference to depression or even homicide.

Pathology can also occur without apparent symptoms. For example, if one's legacy is to be the "good child," one may be bound and unable to develop autonomy by deciding what is "goodness" for oneself. Continuing to live the family lie can continue into future generations and account for the seeming "no reason" suicide, divorce, affair, breakdown, violence, or homicide.

Therapy and Change

The change that needs to occur, according to Nagy's contextual theory, is not merely behavioral or interactional. Behaviors and relationships can change and it can appear that the family has been restored to balance and fairness. However, this change may be very temporary and very much on the surface only. According to Nagy, the change that needs to occur is in the consideration of obligations in relationships, in the balance of entitlements and debts, and in the ways that people enact their loyalties and legacies.

The goal of therapy is to enable people to make efforts at **rejunction.** Rejunction is a healing of the breach or disengagement in important relationships. It is a reconnecting so that ledgers may be balanced and autonomy and trustworthiness established. Rejunction is the refusal to allow stagnation to prevent connection and fulfillment.

Rejunction is accomplished in therapy by first opening up a perspective of fairness in terms of considering others' views as well as one's own. Learning about and understanding (although not necessarily agreeing with) other people's perspectives and one's own behaviors, thoughts, and feelings can be placed in the larger relational context that includes multiple generations. Grievances are examined in their original contexts of loyalties, legacies, entitlements, and revolving slates and not just in terms of their present-day consequences. For example, an adolescent's behavior is understood in a context of how the youth is acting out a legacy that is bigger than even the parent-child relationship. People are held accountable; this is not a therapy that lets people off the hook for their behavior. Rather, the behavior is understood in a context bigger than the problem so that people can develop new, less destructive ways of balancing ledgers.

The therapist works as a guide to the process by assisting people in examining all interests and developing action plans that will be rejunctive or healing in relationships, rather than continuing legacies of problems and unhappiness.

Rejunction begins with an understanding of the dynamics in multiple generations of relationships, but must include actions or efforts to heal the breach. The therapist begins by demonstrating **multidirected partiality.** The therapist does not side with any one person, but takes in and even demands each person's position and views of the unfairness in the family, their own as well as others'. This is not *impartiality;* the therapist is very invested in holding all perspectives as important and valid for everyone to understand, not just the identified patient's (IP's), not just the parents' or the referral source's. By sequentially listening to family members with curiosity and genuine interest, the therapist demonstrates that everyone's interests and opinions are important and necessary to the process.

In marital therapy, the therapist demonstrates the principles of fairness to **posterity** (future generations) by pointing out how parenting is a part of marriage. When couples have no children, they are still accountable to their parents or to others who may have investments of trust in them. Thus, children's positions are important in marital therapy. For example, when spouses complain to and about each other, the therapist may ask the children how this affects them, whether they feel tugged and pulled, what their obligations are in the family in order for the parents to understand the effects of their legacies and behaviors on their children.

The therapist considers the interests of everyone involved, not just those present in therapy. This includes those who are absent, dead, and not yet born. To the extent that the therapist can hold this context as important, family members develop new understandings of their own and others' actions and the need to find other ways to balance ledgers and pay back debts.

Assessment includes an examination of relationships for their trustworthiness and resources of trust. All four dimensions of relationships are explored, although the relational ethics of balanced reciprocity transcend the others of facts, individual psychology, and transactional patterns. Each client is held accountable for assessing his or her own position and situation and for explaining it to others. In this way each person holds all others accountable for considering his or her interests. The therapist is flexible and sequential in understanding and being curious about each person's views of entitlements and obligations. Each person feels attended to and important.

After assessing each person's ability to engage in trustworthy interactions, the therapist helps each person understand where and how imbalances may be occurring. Discussion then centers around how rejunctive efforts are going to be made, how old debts and obligations are going to paid. Therapy is very much action oriented, but the therapist does not assign tasks. Rather, the therapist helps the clients decide what actions to take by being curious about reserves of trust and about possible consequences of certain actions. The therapist prods, encourages, confronts, and supports people in their efforts to rebalance relationships so that symptoms are not necessary, always considering the interests of everyone involved.

It is not necessary for rejunctive efforts to be successful in the sense that family members open their arms and harmony is restored. Payment may come from rejunctive efforts in themselves. That is, attempting to reconnect is rejunctive in and of itself. The therapist, by holding the therapeutic relationship trustworthy, helps the client develop ways of attempting rejunction and supports the client in both successes and failures.

The therapist **sides** with each and every client, holding each accountable for exposing injustices as well as making efforts to repay debts. Through this process, the therapist demonstrates and models fairness in relationships, allowing clients to, first, explain their own perspectives and positions; second, to understand how theirs and others' actions fit into the multigenerational patterns; and, third, develop plans for reconnecting with parents and others and exonerating them for past hurts. People must always be held accountable for their behavior regardless of its multigenerational context of loyalties and legacies. However, by understanding this context, people can allow themselves to accept these and other actions as attempts to balance ledgers, not because a parent wanted to hurt a child, but because all were bound up in revolving slates.

The therapist helps clients place seemingly negative behavior in a relational context partly through **loyalty framing.** Although Nagy did not claim to use positive connotation, reframing, or relabeling, loyalty framing certainly resembles these therapeutic techniques. For example, an acting-out teen's behavior may be explored by the therapist as a loyal attempt to fulfill a father's legacy, thereby drawing attention to the destructive nature of family relationships, forcing the family members to find other ways to deal with one another and past generations. This frees the teen from the hot seat and places him or her in a different role among all relationships, not just as the focus of the current family concern or anger.

Exoneration and rejunctive efforts are not always met with pleasant results. Sometimes people are so aware of possible negative reactions that they choose to not try. However, through engaging in a trustworthy relationship, the therapist can help them free themselves from negative legacies so that they and future generations do not repeat the same hurtful actions. Therapy may end without joyful reunions; it ends, however, when people are able to reestablish their own positions as trustworthy in relationships, building reserves of trust that can be used to repair and enhance current and future relationships. They are then able to make a commitment toward rejunctive action and behaving ethically in all relationships. This may take a few sessions or a few years.

JAMES FRAMO

James Framo started seeing couples and families in the late 1950s. Through his interactions with Nagy (Boszormenyi-Nagy and Framo, 1965) and others, Framo developed a therapy that integrated ideas from **object relations theory** and techniques of conjoint marital and family therapy. The chief idea from object relations theory that intrigued Framo was that of **projective identification.** During infancy, we are dependent upon caretakers to meet all of our needs. The primary caretaker has both good and bad characteristics. For example, the caretaker feeds the child when he or she is hungry (good), but may not always do so as soon as the infant would like (bad). Because there is no way for the infant to change the bad parts of the caretaker, these parts are incorporated into the psyche as **introjects** or representatives of the external object (caretaker). These introjects become part of the personality as unconscious objects, or "splits." People tend to view the world as though it were made up of the same kinds of objects with which one was familiar as a child, although this usually is an unconscious process. Mates select each other by "discovering" lost aspects of themselves in their partners, aspects that are familiar but not primary parts of the self. People project the introjected bad parts of themselves onto their spouses and children and then battle them. This is an attempt to resolve old issues in current relationships rather than in the parental generation, where they belong.

Therapy consists of first helping people understand these concepts, freeing them to interact with their partners in more constructive ways. They are not totally free, however, until they have understood their parents in the fullness of their persons, not just the introjected and badly remembered aspects. To accomplish this, Framo first prepared individuals and couples through conjoint marital and group marital therapy. He then invited whole families into therapy, usually in a marathon weekend of two two-hour sessions. In the family-of-origin session, Framo helped people to talk about things the way each of them remembered them, enlarging the perspective of clients so that it included parents and siblings as whole people, not just introjects. By understanding their parents differently and the role that past interactions play in current relationships, clients are further freed to interact with their spouses and children as real people, not battled, split-off projections of themselves. After the family-of-origin sessions, the couple could be free to explore their interactional dynamics in a larger context, reducing blame and opening opportunities for more intimate connections.

Framo believed that children's problems were reflections of their parents' unresolved marital and family-of-origin issues. He believed that the best way to help children was to help their families. Therefore, he did not typically see children in therapy. Framo also believed that cotherapy was useful to the extent that the cotherapists could assist each other in not becoming entangled in their own unresolved object relations issues. Similar to Bowen and Nagy, Framo believed that good therapists examined their own family-of-origin dynamics.

CASE STUDY

The following case study incorporates aspects of Bowen's, Nagy's, and Framo's theories and therapies. The student is reminded that there often are differences between *theory,* or explanations of phenomena, and *therapy,* or the ways that therapists behave. In many instances, the therapeutic technique may be more in the mind and intent of the therapist, the way the therapist thinks, than in any one particular action or technique. Therapists often use techniques and interventions from many models, keeping in mind the goals that they develop from their own ways of thinking. This is as true for these transgenerational therapies as for others. Similarly, explanations of what goes on in therapy or why it works may also be in the mind of the reader, the therapist, or clients.

Steve (thirty-eight) and Lauren (thirty-seven) came to therapy because of marital conflict and Lauren's depression. Lauren also was concerned with Steve's regular use of alcohol and occasional use of marijuana. They had two children: Molly (twelve) and Gregory (nine). Steve was an accountant who sometimes was rather tired of his job. He worked long hours, particularly during tax season, and often wondered what life would be like if he had gotten his MBA, as his father had wanted him to do. Instead, he had been anxious to get out from under his student loans and to "have fun."

Lauren majored in art in college and dreamed of having her own art gallery, displaying her paintings as well as those of others. She still liked to paint, but had gotten a teaching certificate so that she could have a steady income while Steve was building his practice. After Gregory was born, she substitute taught in order to have more time at home. Steve was quite busy and not available to help with housework, but Lauren described him as an attentive, patient, and involved father. She appreciated their lifestyle, but often wished she had more time to paint and dreamed about a gallery.

The therapist first assessed the couple for potential violence. During individual sessions, Steve and Lauren both said that there had never been any threats or actual violence, except once when they had been married about a year. They reported that that incident, which involved slamming a door so hard that it broke, scared both of them so badly that they each vowed to never let an argument get out of hand again. They had kept that vow. The therapist checked with the couple about this issue periodically during therapy. The therapist also assessed for alcohol or other drug use to determine that chemicals were not a part of the system in such a way as to interfere with therapy. Had there been alcohol or drug abuse or addiction, or if there was violence in the relationship, the therapist would have recommended other therapies before using transgenerational therapy. To do otherwise would be contraindicated because (1) the chemical itself or physiological addiction would interfere with progress and/or (2) one or both partners would not be safe in an atmosphere of threatened or actual violence that has the potential for escalating when couples deal with difficult issues.

The therapist did a detailed genogram with Steve and Lauren (see Figure 9.2). Steve was an oldest son with two younger brothers and a younger sister. Lauren was the second child of three, with an older brother and a younger sister. Both sets of parents were still alive. Steve's father ran a mechanic shop and his mother had been a music teacher. She was now retired except for giving occasional piano lessons. Steve's father was the youngest of four siblings with three older sisters, the oldest of whom had died ten years earlier of cancer. Their father, Steve's grandfather, had been a farmer and was now dead, as was their mother, a farmwife. They had deeded the farm to the families of their daughters but not their son, Steve's father, because they believed he would not do well managing it. Steve's mother was an only child, her mother having had three miscarriages before she was born. She helped her husband in the mechanic shop with the books as well as teaching music and managing the house. Steve described his father as "bitter" and his mother as "withdrawn; not there." Steve was not sure what his maternal grandparents did for a living because they died before he was born, when his mother was in her late teens.

Lauren's father was a banker whom she described as "stern." He had a younger sister and both of his parents were dead. Lauren's mother had told her that her paternal grandfather had been abusive and her grandmother had not been well. Lauren's mother was a homemaker who enjoyed keeping house, decorating, making crafts and doing "fun stuff" with her children. Lauren said that her mother tried to buffer her father's discipline. Lauren's mother had an older brother who died in the military. Her mother had been very close to this uncle and said that her father "never got over" his death. Lauren's maternal grandfather had been a merchant, running a retail store, and now was in a nursing home with Parkinson's disease. Her grandmother died twelve years ago of heart failure.

Molly, the twelve-year old, was in sixth grade and doing well. She was popular and well liked by her peers. The biggest complaint that Steve and Lauren had about her was that she was "pouty" and didn't clean her room. She enjoyed going to Lauren's mother's house and doing crafts with her. Steve had given up trying to get her to enjoy piano lessons. Gregory, nine, presented more of a challenge for

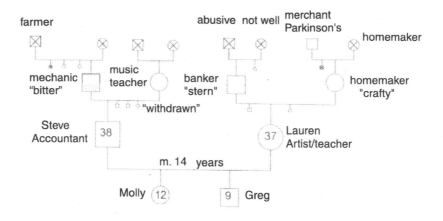

FIGURE 9.2. Steve and Lauren's Family Genogram

Steve and Lauren. He had difficulty reading and often became so frustrated that he had tantrums. Steve tried to discipline him, but Lauren did not approve of his methods and would sometimes yell at Steve when he was trying to work with Greg. Greg had been tested for learning disabilities and ADHD, but the psychologists said that he was only a "little immature." Steve thought this called for more discipline and stricter rules; Lauren thought it required reasoning and spending more time with Greg on his reading skills.

Molly and Greg were involved while the genogram was being drawn and the therapist asked them about their knowledge and opinions. It appeared to the therapist that both children were developing normally, although she realized that some might describe Gregory as immature. Neither parent seemed concerned about the children's behavior in therapy and the therapist suggested that they not come anymore. She believed that the children's difficulties would disappear and the parents would become more able to handle the problems as a team, or the behavior would become worse as therapy continued. The latter would be an indication of increased stress in the system and would signal slowing down or working more directly to detriangle the child. The therapist occasionally asked about the children's behavior during therapy.

The therapist helped Lauren and Steve understand the concepts of both Bowen and contextual theories. Steve identified his involvement in a triangle with his mother and father and one involving his father and his grandfather. He believed that his father had been acting out destructive entitlement by pushing Steve toward a business career. His father sometimes complained to him about his mother's lack of attention to the family business, even though she was busy with her own job as well as the house and children. Steve realized that he was caught in a split loyalty whenever he felt he should defend his mother. He recognized that the stress must have been triangled more onto one of his younger brothers who used alcohol excessively and had a hard time keeping a job. In therapy, he explored ways that he could detriangle from his father and grandfather by learning more about his grandfather. He learned that his grandfather had been very worried that Steve's father would hurt himself on the farm after running a tractor down an embankment. Rather than showing concern, however, Steve's grandfather had acted as though Steve's father was not competent.

Lauren became very interested in her mother's life and thought about detriangling herself from her parents' marriage by talking more with her father about how he might handle Gregory. She realized that she had married someone who would be more stern with her children so that she would not have to be. She learned that her father had been abused by his father and that his mother had not protected him. Lauren's father said that he had known he was too hard on his daughter and that he had married someone who would help temper his discipline. Lauren had thought he would tell her to be more strict with Greg, but was surprised when he suggested that she find ways to use her skills as an artist to help Greg be more creative about his difficulty in school. He also suggested that she encourage Greg, along with Steve, to play a musical instrument.

Lauren also learned that her mother had always felt lonely. Lauren's grandmother had been very busy and both of her parents had been focused on her brother. Although her brother had been good to her, he had been several years older and involved in his own activities. Lauren's mother devised ways of getting her father's attention by making signs for his store as well as crafty things for the house. She had married Lauren's father because he also seemed lonely and she was drawn to him as a helper.

In other therapies, the therapist might have encouraged Steve and Lauren to develop new communication skills and to talk directly to each other. In this case, however, the transgenerational therapist asked Steve and Lauren to tell their stories to her, each listening carefully while the other talked. Occasionally, the therapist asked each to comment on what the other had just said. When things seemed to get heated, the therapist would turn to the genogram as a way of reducing emotionality and to help the couple manage their anxiety by getting more ideas about how their actions fit into their original families. In this way, each learned about the typical patterns of conflict (abuse), symptoms, and triangling that their families had used to reduce marital tension. They also learned that turning to slightly different topics could help them stay connected when things became stressful between them.

The therapist coached each person in finding ways of both understanding and changing their roles in their families. They explored the legacies of work and family and the loyalties, including invisible ones tied to the legacies. They noticed patterns of abuse and made conscious efforts to change their own behaviors away from conflict in ways that acknowledged the good intentions of their parents and grandparents. Each made efforts to rejoin their families. When Lauren's mother became upset, Lauren asked her questions about other relatives. This helped Lauren to learn new information as well as keeping the emotionality low enough for Lauren and her mother to connect in new ways. Previously, Lauren had had a tendency to distance when her mother became upset. She enjoyed this new way of staying connected.

Steve, on the other hand, had more difficulty reworking family issues with his parents. When Steve's father criticized his mother, Steve switched tactics. Instead of defending his mother, Steve suggested that his father talk to his mother about his complaints. This resulted in Steve's father giving him the silent treatment. Apparently, he also gave Steve's mother the silent treatment because Steve's mother called him to ask what he had done to upset his father so much.

She also told Steve that she was upset that he did not do more to help his younger brother, who was out of work again. Steve's initial tendency was to fall back into old patterns and distance from his parents. He remarked that his efforts were not appreciated, so he probably would not try again. The therapist encouraged him to not give up, however, and suggested that he find another way of reconnecting with his family, one that considered his parents' positions and that might not be met with such resistance.

Steve began talking to his sister about their different experiences in the family. He had always dismissed her perspective because she was so much younger than he, so "what does she know anyhow? My parents always shielded her from real life." Steve discovered that his sister had known a lot about the family difficulties—their father's background and their parents' quarreling—for some time. She talked to Steve about their mother's family and how she had always tried to hide her loneliness, pretending that everything was okay. This helped Steve to see his mother in a new light, and he tried once more to pull himself out of his parents' marriage without cutting off. He called his mother and told her that he appreciated all that she had done for him and his siblings and asked if she would be interested in suggesting some new music for Gregory. This action exonerated Steve's mother by connecting her with the third generation in a valuable way, paying back a debt Steve owed her and changing the way he acted out a legacy with his son. By doing this, he increased both his own and his son's potential for differentiating and developing a trustworthy relationship.

Steve's father reacted to this change in dynamics by withdrawing from Steve and beginning to complain to Steve's second brother about him. Steve was disappointed about this, but was able to express his disappointment to Lauren rather than defending himself to his brother. He decided to maintain his position and hope that his father would come around in time. He knew, however, that he had repaid part of his debt with his effort and by not demanding things of his son that Gregory could not do.

This was not a miracle therapy. The initial stages of calming the system were accomplished fairly quickly, within a few months. Therapy continued about once a month as Steve and Lauren used the therapist as well as each other to develop new plans for reconnecting and differentiating in their families of origin. They reported less fighting between the two of them, although Steve continued to be the more strict of the two with the children. He reported feeling relieved about less stress and dread in his original family. He agreed to try again in a few months to reconnect with his father, this time with something less emotional.

Lauren began having coffee more often with her father and going with Molly to her mother's house for crafts. Molly seemed to resent this, so instead of either withdrawing *or* insisting, Lauren compromised by joining them occasionally. She also enlisted her parents' help in developing a show for her paintings. Lauren and Steve realized that they encouraged Gregory's dependency behavior but also did not want him to develop as lonely as did Steve or Steve's father. They discussed this dilemma a lot and decided that they would not give in to messages to make Greg "a man" by pushing him away (Silverstein, 1994). These discussions were not always easy, given Steve's legacy of pushing for independence, but they worked out a plan whereby Steve took over more of the homework help from Lauren. He and Greg began reading "boy" books together in Greg's room. Greg began whining less and turning more to his father for help in normal tones of voice. Molly began arguing with her mother about wearing makeup and still refused to clean her room.

GLOSSARY

anxiety: In Bowen theory, the natural state that arises when two people are in human relationship with each other. As people attempt to balance AUTONOMY and INTIMACY in relationships, natural differences and attempts to resolve those differences arise, leading to mild to moderate to severe anxiety. Difficulties arise in the ways that people attempt to manage anxiety, not from anxiety per se.

autonomy: In Bowen theory, a dimension of differentiation of self that allows a person to have a self separate from others.

balanced relationships: In contextual theory, balanced relationships are trustworthy, fair, and each person, over time, both receives and gives as situations require.

basic self: In Bowen theory, the maximal level of differentiation of self that one achieves. The basic self remains fairly constant over time, with minor fluctuations. *Contrast with* PSEUDOSELF.

conflict: In Bowen theory, one process that a system uses to manage ANXIETY. Conflict can range from moderate, reasoned discussions of differences, to yelling and arguing, to homicide. Conflict, as a concept, is not dysfunctional or symptomatic; it is part of the condition of being in human relationships.

dependent: A need to have others take care of oneself; may indicate normal, healthy functioning (when very young or ill, for example) or chronic underfunctioning.

destructive entitlement: In contextual theory, entitlements that are "paid back" in destructive ways to self and others. Attempts to get what one is due in negative and destructive ways; often related to INVISIBLE LOYALTIES and LEGACIES.

differentiation of self: In Bowen theory, the ability to maintain a separate self while remaining emotionally connected to one's family of origin. Differentiation of self includes two dimensions: INTIMACY and AUTONOMY.

differentiation of thinking from emotion: In Bowen theory, the ability to separate thinking and feeling, but stay connected to emotions or feelings. Lack of balance in this area of differentiation leads to reactivity (too much influence of emotions) or excessive rationality (too little influence of emotions).

disjunction: In contextual theory, moving away from trustworthy relatedness. Unbalanced ledger of debts and entitlements in a family.

distancing: In Bowen theory, one process by which a system manages anxiety. Distancing can be mild or severe, rare or frequent, short lived or long-lasting. It can include methods such as taking a time out or a more severe form of EMOTIONAL CUTOFF.

emotional cutoff: In Bowen theory, an excessive form of distancing that attempts to resolve emotional attachments by removing oneself from the emotional system. However, the person involved in the cutoff is not differentiated, which requires an ability to remain intimate in an emotional system. Rather, such a person is still REACTIVE and tends to make decisions that are overly influenced by emotions and anxiety.

enmeshment: In structural family therapy, Minuchin's term for loss of autonomy due to a blurring or lack of psychological and family boundaries.

entitlement: In contextual theory, this term refers to merit that accumulates as a result of behaving in an ethical manner with due consideration toward others. It is different from an arrogant attitude. Rather, it is what one is actually due either from acts of credit or from being part of a fair and trustworthy relationship.

ethical dimensions (of relationships): ethical dimensions in relationships include facts, individual psychology, systems transactional patterns, and merited trust. In contextual theory, the belief that relationships which are balanced in terms of facts, individual psychological factors, transactional patterns, and merited trust are healthy and lead to satisfied family members.

existential: In philosophy, the idea that humans experience life and a sense of existing as humans. In contextual theory, this also refers to the experience of existing in relationship with others and in relation to others.

exoneration: In contextual theory, a process of seeing the positive intent and intergenerational legacies and loyalties behind the behavior of members of previous generations. When exoneration occurs, negative holds from the past are loosened, releasing the client from INVISIBLE LOYALTIES and relational debts of others.

exploitation: Taking advantage of someone's dependency position in a relationship.

fact: In contextual theory, one of the four dimensions of ethical relatedness. Facts are things handed to one by destiny that cannot be changed: gender, particular parents, adoption, genetic predispositions and anomalies, etc.

fairness: In contextual theory, the notion that over time, people are given their due and are given chances to reciprocate in relationships. This leads to TRUSTWORTHINESS OF RELATIONSHIPS and a sense that the relationship is healthy and will serve the needs of its members.

family map: *See* GENOGRAM.

family projection process: In Bowen theory, the process by which unresolved lack of differentiation of parents is passed on to the children. Typically, one child is spared the triangling process and becomes more differentiated than the parents; and one child, who is triangled, becomes less differentiated and more likely to develop symptoms.

fusion: In Bowen theory, the tendency of one person to be so emotionally attached to another that his or her own sense of self and boundaries becomes dependent on the other. It is marked by a blurring of the intellectual and emotional systems within an individual and is the opposite of DIFFERENTIATION OF SELF.

fusion anxiety: In Bowen theory, the physiological anxiety that one feels when in danger of losing a sense of self within a relationship. Often leads to symptoms.

genogram: Developed by Bowen and now used in many therapies. A schematic drawing of a family, similar to a family tree, with information about the family, including the nature of emotional relationships and dynamics.

"I" statements: A technique in systems therapy in which the therapist encourages family members to speak for themselves in the form of "I think . . .," "I believe . . .," or "I feel . . ." rather than mind reading and speaking for another person (e.g., "She thinks . . ." or "He feels . . .").

indebtedness: In contextual theory, the fact of "owing" another either because the other has earned consideration in the relationship or because the other, a parent, is simply due consideration by virtue of having given birth to the person.

individual psychology: In contextual theory, one of the four dimensions of ethical relatedness. Individual psychology refers to the way that one processes information within oneself. This may include such things as intelligence, personality, and predispositions.

interdependent: The ability to care for others and be taken care of by others as needs require.

intergenerational: Having to do with patterns of behavior or family dynamics between generations. Often used interchangeably with TRANSGENERATIONAL.

intimacy: In Bowen theory, the dimension of differentiation of self that includes the ability to be emotionally connected to others.

introjects: In object relations theory, taking on aspects of other people which then become unconscious parts of the self-image.

invisible loyalty: In contextual theory, Boszormenyi-Nagy's term for unconscious commitments that children take on to help their families to the detriment of their own well-being.

ledger: A "balance sheet" of entitlements, obligations, and indebtedness for each individual in the family.

legacy: In contextual theory, expectations that originate not from the earnings of the parents but simply by being born of those parents. Legacies sometimes come in the form of INVISIBLE LOYALTIES, in that they are not in conscious awareness but are significant factors in relational dynamics and the ways that people live in the world.

loyalty: In contextual theory, the notion that internalized expectations, injunctions, and obligations in one's family of origin have powerful interpersonal influences. What to an outsider may seem an irrational or pathological behavior may, in fact, conform to a basic family loyalty. For example, a scapegoated, irresponsible child may be unconsciously acting out this loyalty message: "I will be the bad one to help you look good, because you have done so much for me."

loyalty conflict: In contextual theory, LOYALTIES can be helpful or nothelpful, healthy or dysfunctional. A loyalty conflict arises when loyalty to one's spouse is in conflict with loyalty to one's family of origin.

loyalty framing: In contextual theory, a therapeutic technique of describing a behavior in a new way that places it in the positive light, as being a way that the client attempts to live out a LEGACY or LOYALTY.

merit: In contextual theory, contributions to the balance of a relationship by considering and supporting the interests of the other.

multidirected partiality: The clinical stance whereby therapists are accountable to everyone whose well-being is potentially affected by their interventions. Everyone in therapy should feel that the therapist understands and "sides" with them. Therapists also take into account others who are affected by the therapy, especially children and future generations.

multigenerational transmission process: In Bowen theory, similar to family transmission process. Over time, as one branch of a family tree produces more and more differentiated individuals, other branches produce less and less differentiated individuals. This accounts for different branches of families that appear very different in maturity or differentiation. According to Bowen, it takes many generations (four to ten) to produce someone with symptoms of schizophrenia.

mutuality: In contextual theory, a sense that people in relationships can count on one another to be trustworthy in reciprocal fashion. That is, there is a sense of balance in relational credits and debits, with each receiving his or her due.

nuclear family emotional process: In Bowen theory, the dynamics that nuclear families use to manage stress. These processes include a physical or emotional SYMPTOM in one partner, CONFLICT, DISTANCING, or TRI-ANGLING. None of these, used in moderation, is by itself problematic. Using one to the exclusion of others or using one or more excessively can lead to individual or system dysfunction.

nuclear family projection process: In Bowen theory, this is the process by which parents transmit their immaturity and lack of differentiation to their children.

object relations theory: A theory based on notions of internalized images of self and others that occurred in early parent-child interactions. These affect a person's way of perceiving and relating to other people.

obligations: Acts and attitudes based on loyalty and on merit earned by another person in a relationship. Obligations are owed to the other in a balanced relationship.

parentification: A process in which a child is pulled into a caretaking role for one or both parents as well as siblings. A child assumes excessive responsibility in a pseudoadult role by emotionally and/or physically caring for parents or siblings.

posterity: Future generations; descendants.

projective identification: In object relations theory, a defense whereby unwanted aspects of the self are attributed to another person, which elicits these behaviors from the other person.

pseudoself: In Bowen theory, the self that fluctuates according to levels of stress in intimate and emotional situations. Pseudoself can look like basic or solid self: "This is who I am and what I believe." However, the pseudoself is more likely to be less differentiated in highly emotional or stressful situations.

psychoanalytic techniques: Techniques developed and used by early-twentieth-century psychoanalysts. The chief technique was for the analyst to allow the patient to free-associate so that unconscious material could be brought to consciousness and interpreted by the analyst.

reactive: In Bowen theory, excessive influence from emotions that leads to knee-jerk or reactive behaviors that have not been thought out. Opposite of RESPONSIVE.

rejunction: In contextual theory, the process of balancing an unbalanced ledger in a system of relationships. This often involves EXONERATING one or more parents or grandparents and giving up DESTRUCTIVE ENTITLEMENTS so that other relationships may also move toward balance.

relational ethics: In contextual theory, life is a chain of interlocking consequences in relationships between the generations. One's behavior is rooted in the past and, at the same time, will affect future generations. Because of this, individuals are ethically responsible for the consequences of their behaviors.

responsive: In Bowen theory, the ability to think clearly and choose behaviors or actions based on information and self-differentiation rather than purely on emotions. A responsive, angry person may *choose* to hit something or say something that others might find objectionable. The difference is that the responsive person has chosen these behaviors after carefully considering the consequences. Opposite of REACTIVE.

revolving slate: In contextual theory, the process by which entitlement is "paid back" through destructive actions, either to self or to others.

rigid triangle: In Bowen theory, a human-system triangle that is inflexible and endures over time. At times of great stress, the primary dyad favors the third party as a way of spreading anxiety. Over time, when a system uses triangling or a particular triangle excessively, the triangle becomes rigid and can lead to symptoms in one person.

scapegoating: In contextual theory, placing a negative legacy on a child instead of accepting responsibility for one's own legacy or debts.

sibling birth order: A concept borrowed by Bowen from Walter Toman suggesting that children in different birth order positions tend to take on typical characteristics of that position.

sides: Side taking. A clinical technique in contextual therapy in which the therapist deliberately takes one position over another. This is a temporary stance of MULTIDIRECTED PARTIALITY so that each person feels understood and supported.

societal emotional process: The application of Bowen's concept of multi-generational transmission process to society as a whole. The concept describes how a prolonged increase in social anxiety results in a gradual lowering of the functional level of differentiation in society and an increase in symptoms, particularly conflict and social ills.

split loyalties: In contextual theory, a situation in which the parents set up conflicting claims so that the child can offer loyalty to one parent only at the cost of his or her loyalty to the other.

stagnation: In contextual theory, ethically invalid attempts at solving life's problems that prevent the development of autonomy and trustworthy relationships.

symptom: In Bowen theory, a state or behavior that signals an unbalanced and dysfunctional system. Symptoms can be physical (headaches), emotional (depression), or social (stealing). They can include excessive conflict or fighting, excessive or chronic distancing, or triangling of a child or other third party. Symptoms can be mild or acute, short-lived or long-lived. Under stress, any person or system can become symptomatic. Systems that are more differentiated tend to suffer less severe and shorter-lived symptoms.

transactional patterns: In contextual theory, one of the four dimensions of ethical relatedness. This term refers to the patterns and dynamics that develop over time for individuals in relationships.

transgenerational: Between generations of families; often having to do with transmission of patterns, values, myths, etc., from one generation to another. Often interchangeable with INTERGENERATIONAL. In Bowen theory and others, often meaning more than two generations of patterns.

triangle: In Bowen theory, a three-person system; the smallest stable unit of human interaction. A two-person system is an unstable system that forms a triangle under stress. More than three people in a system form themselves into a series of interlocking triangles. *See* RIGID TRIANGLE.

triangling: In Bowen theory, the process of introducing a third person into a dyadic relationship to provide stability in the system.

trustworthiness of relationships: In contextual theory, the balance of debits and credits in a relationship that contributes to members' sense that the relationship is fair and will lead to fair dealings. The balance oscillates; however, over time, all parties receive their due.

typical family development: Developmental patterns that most families go through as members differentiate and form new attachments.

undifferentiated ego mass: In Bowen theory, a situation in which the family members are not able to distinguish their own feelings and thoughts from those of other family members. Often leads to dysfunctional behavior or symptoms.

BIBLIOGRAPHY

Boszormenyi-Nagy, I. (1987). *Foundations of contextual therapy: Collected papers of Ivan Boszormenyi-Nagy.* New York: Brunner/Mazel.

Boszormenyi-Nagy, I. and Framo, J. (Eds.) (1965). *Intensive family therapy.* New York: Harper and Row Medical Dept.

Boszormenyi-Nagy, I. and Krasner, B. (1986). *Between give and take: A clinical guide to contextual therapy.* New York: Brunner/Mazel.

Boszormenyi-Nagy, I. and Spark, G. (1973). *Invisible loyalties.* New York: Harper and Row.

Boszormenyi-Nagy, I. and Ulrich, D. N. (1981). Contextual family therapy. In A. Gurman and D. P. Kniskern (Eds.), *Handbook of family therapy* (pp. 159-186). New York: Brunner/Mazel.

Bowen, M. (1978). *Family therapy in clinical practice.* New York: Jason Aronson.

Bray, J., Williamson, D., and Malone, P. (1984). Personal authority in the family system. *Journal of Marital and Family Therapy, 10,* 167-178.

Fairbairn, W. (1954). *An object relations theory of the personality.* New York: Basic.

Framo, J. (1972). On the differentiation of self. *Family interaction: A dialogue between family researchers and family therapists.* New York: Springer Publishing Company.

Framo, J. L. (1982). *Explorations in marital and family therapy: Selected papers of James L. Framo, Ph.D.* New York: Springer Publishing Company.

Framo, J. L. (1992). *Family-of-origin therapy: An intergenerational approach.* New York: Brunner/Mazel.

Hovestadt, A., Anderson, W., Piercy, F., Cochran, S., and Fine, M. (1985). A family of origin scale. *Journal of Marital and Family Therapy, 11,* 287-298.

Kerr, M. (1981). Family systems theory and therapy. In A. S. Gurman and D. P. Kniskern (Eds.), *Handbook of family therapy* (pp. 226-264). New York: Brunner/Mazel.

Kerr, M. E. and Bowen, M. (1988). *Family evaluation: An approach based on Bowen theory.* New York: W. W. Norton and Company.

McGoldrick, M., Gerson, R., and Shellenberger, S. (1999). *Genograms in family assessment.* New York: W.W. Norton and Company.

Minuchin, S. (1974). *Families and family therapy.* Cambridge, MA: Harvard University Press.

Nelson, T. S. (1989). Differentiation in clinical and nonclinical women. *Journal of Feminist Family Therapy, 1*(2), 49-62.

Silverstein, O. (1994). *The courage to raise good men.* New York: Viking.

Slipp, S. (1984). *Object relations: A dynamic bridge between individual and family treatment.* Northvale, NJ: Jason Aronson.

Toman, W. (1961). *Family constellation.* New York: Springer Publishing Company.

van Heusden, A. and van den Eerenbeemt, E. (1987). *Balance in motion: Ivan Boszormenyi-Nagy and his vision of individual and family therapy.* New York: Brunner/Mazel.

Williamson, D. (1981). Personal authority via termination of the intergenerational hierarchical boundary: A "new" stage in the family life cycle. *Journal of Marital and Family Therapy, 7,* 441-452.

PART II:
SPECIAL ISSUES AND TOPICS
IN MARRIAGE AND FAMILY THERAPY

Chapter 10

Couple Therapy

Gary H. Bischof
Karen B. Helmeke

Typically couples come in and one partner wants one thing to happen;
the other partner wants something else. So satisfying both of them becomes very, very tricky. . . . Couple therapy is a very complicated form
of therapy. . . . It's always been the thing that has most fascinated me
and kept me captivated. . . . And even though I do workshops and am
presented as an expert on couple therapy, I still find it very difficult
to do.

Neil S. Jacobson, PhD (1949-1999)
Leading researcher and expert on couple therapy

In this chapter, we focus on therapy with one of the most intense and important family relationships, the intimate couple. In earlier times, this area
was known as "marriage counseling" or "marital therapy." The focus was on
improving relationships between married spouses. As family forms have
become increasingly diversified, many have found the term "marital therapy" limiting. It does not include, for example, cohabiting couples or same-
sex couples who may be in committed long-term relationships. We consider
a couple to be two partners who are in a serious, intimate, committed relationship, including gay, lesbian, or bisexual couples, cohabiting couples,
and married couples. Thus couple therapy addresses these serious, committed relationships.

Several areas related to couple therapy will be addressed in this chapter.
After a brief historical perspective, we consider recent trends in couple therapy. Next we describe some of the key clinical issues in doing therapy with
couples. Then we examine four well-established approaches to couple therapy and the increasing popularity of the use of preventive approaches for
couples. Common problems seen by couple therapists will be considered.
We also look at couple therapy with four especially challenging clinical

problems: domestic violence, affairs, substance abuse, and serious individual problems. We conclude by examining sex therapy and couple therapy with same-sex couples.

HISTORICAL BACKGROUND

The profession of marriage counseling began about 1930, nearly twenty years before the formal beginnings of the family therapy movement. Around that time, three professional centers for marriage counseling were established. Paul Popenoe opened a center in Los Angeles, and Abraham and Hannah Stone opened a similar clinic in New York. A third center was opened by Emily Mudd in Philadelphia in 1932 (Broderick and Schrader, 1981). Popenoe claims to be the first to introduce the term *marriage counseling,* and in 1930 he began seeing couples for three dollars per hour (no small sum during the Great Depression). He promoted public recognition of the marriage counseling profession through a monthly feature in *Ladies Home Journal* called "Can This Marriage Be Saved?" which began in 1945 and continues today. He also provided case material for an early television series, *Divorce Court,* which aired in the 1940s and 1950s.

Members of this new profession of marriage counseling began meeting in 1942 and formed the American Association of Marriage Counselors (AAMC) in 1945. This group developed outside the mainstream of the mental health establishment of psychiatry. Early marriage counselors included clergy, physicians, social workers, and family guidance professionals (Broderick and Schrader, 1981). The AAMC, along with the National Council on Family Relations, published standards for marriage counseling in 1949, and identified marriage counseling as a specialized field of family counseling. This diverse group continued to assist marriages using a variety of approaches without a unifying theory. In 1970, AAMC changed its name to the American Association of Marriage and Family Counselors to reflect the interest of its members in systems theory and the growing family therapy movement (Broderick and Schrader, 1981). This group became the current American Association for Marriage and Family Therapy (AAMFT) in 1978, as was discussed in the section on the history of the field of marriage and family therapy in Chapter 1.

In recent years, two leaders in couple therapy have suggested that couple therapy has indeed come of age, and they identify several significant developments and key trends for therapy with couples (Johnson and Lebow, 2000). The acceptance and utilization of couple therapy increased substantially in the last decade of the twentieth century. Johnson and Lebow report an increasing demand for this type of therapy, and a growing number of practitioners are trained to do couple therapy, including those specializing in couple therapy from the fields of psychology, social work, and counselor education. An understanding has also clearly emerged that couple therapy requires distinct training and a specific set of skills.

Johnson and Lebow (2000) identify nine key trends for couple therapy during the 1990s:

1. Couple therapy (CT) becoming firmly established as a legitimate treatment
2. Growing scientific understanding of committed relationships
3. Evidence of the effectiveness of CT for relationship problems and individual disorders
4. Greater understanding of the influence of gender on relationships
5. New respect for the diversity of family forms
6. Influence of postmodernism (see Chapter 6 for details on postmodernism)
7. Movement toward integration across models of treatment
8. Increased attention to the role of emotion in CT
9. Greater recognition of couple violence

(1) Couple therapy is becoming firmly established as the accepted treatment of choice for couple problems. Although this may seem obvious, some in the mental health profession have been slow to change from an approach focused upon individuals, and couples therapists still find it difficult at times to secure payment from insurance companies for treatment focused upon strengthening the couple's relationship. (2) There has been a growing understanding of the science of relationships. Some key developments in the scientific understanding of committed relationships from the research of John Gottman (1994; Gottman and Silver, 1999) are highlighted in Box 10.1. (3) There now exists strong evidence supporting the effectiveness of couple therapy for both relationship problems and individual mental health disorders.

Several of the trends in couple therapy identified by Johnson and Lebow (2000) reflect changes in the wider spheres of marriage and family therapy and society, and are addressed in other chapters in this text. These include (4) a greater understanding of the influence of gender; (5) new respect for the diversity of family forms; and (6) the influence of postmodernism and social constructivism as reflected in more collaborative, meaning- and language-oriented approaches to therapy. (7) Approaches to couple therapy have also become more integrated, and draw from multiple models of treatment.

BOX 10.1. Research on Couple Relationships

Dr. John Gottman, a psychologist at the University of Washington in Seattle, has spent over twenty-five years studying the intricacies of committed relationships. He can predict with 94 percent accuracy which marriages will succeed and which will fail (1994). Gottman's sophisticated labs include a mock apartment so couples can be observed and videotaped, and participants are hooked up to equipment that measures physical changes such as heart rate or sweat during a discussion with one's partner. He has identified three types of successful, long-term marriages (1994). **Validating couples** are good friends, listen well to each other, validate their partner's experience, and compromise easily. **Volatile couples** argue and bicker over lots of issues, try to persuade the other rather than understand or validate, show high levels of engagement, show anger, laughter, and affection easily, are passionate and good at making up. **Conflict-minimizing couples** seldom argue, preferring to see the overall relationship as more important than some issue over which they might differ. They lead calm, pleasant lives, often exhibit lower levels of companionship and sharing, and value separateness and personal space or interests. Interestingly, Gottman has found that regardless of the style of marriage, successful relationships across all three types were characterized by a *5:1 ratio of positive to negative* feelings and actions toward their partner. Some disagreement in working out differences is healthy, and anger itself in a relationship is not predictive of divorce, as long as the 5:1 ratio is maintained.

Gottman identified four especially corrosive behaviors that lead to the downfall of a marriage, termed the **Four Horsemen of the Apocalypse.** These are (1) **criticism**—attacking, blaming partner's personality or character, rather than a specific behavior; (2) **contempt**—insults or put-downs of partner, such as name-calling, hostile humor, sarcasm, or body language such as rolling of the eyes or facial grimaces; (3) **defensiveness**—warding off a perceived attack, manifested by denying responsibility, making excuses, playing one-upsmanship, or pointing out partner's faults when even legitimate concerns are raised; and (4) **stonewalling**—one partner, usually the man, removes himself, withdraws, becoming as a "stone wall," unresponsive and unmoved by the partner's complaints. Occasional withdrawal is not uncommon, but habitual use of stonewalling signals serious trouble for the relationship. Noting gender differences, Gottman found that men tended to become more physiologically aroused or "flooded" (pulse rate and blood pressure rise) when confronted with marital tension, perhaps explaining their tendency to withdraw to protect themselves and prevent blowing up. Gottman suggests that a key is for partners to be aware when they are getting overwhelmed (e.g., heart rate increases, muscles tense), and take a break and calm down before attempting further conversation. Listening and speaking nondefensively, validating the partner's point of view (without necessarily agreeing with that view), sharing power in the relationship, nurturing fondness and admiration for your partner, and making healthy habits of these ways of relating are also crucial for sustaining relationships in the long term. Gottman's work is presented in two useful and readable books, complete with self-tests and exercises designed to evaluate and improve your relationship: *Why Marriages Succeed or Fail* (1994), and *Seven Principles for Making Marriage Work* (1999 with co-author Nan Silver).

Two final trends more specific to couple therapy were identified. (8) One is the increased attention to the role of emotion, as evidenced by increased inquiry about the emotional experience of clients, and in the evoking of emotion in sessions of couple therapy. Emotionally Focused Therapy (Greenberg and Johnson, 1988) has been one of the most researched models of couple therapy and is described later. (9) Finally, the decade of the 1990s saw greater attention to the serious problems of violence in committed relationships. The underreporting of couple violence, even in couple therapy, is a major finding that has emerged over the past few decades of the twentieth century (Johnson and Lebow, 2000).

GENERAL CLINICAL ISSUES IN COUPLE THERAPY

Couple therapy is unique and presents particular challenges. In this section we examine some of the clinical issues faced by couple therapists. Among the various relationships in a family, the couple bond is the most fragile. Unlike other family relationships, such as those between parents and children or between siblings, which end only with death, the couple relationship is not a permanent one. Indeed, approximately 50 percent of first marriages and 60 percent of second marriages end in divorce (Gottman, 1994). One partner can decide independently if he or she wishes to terminate the marital or couple relationship, a factor not shared with any other family relationship. This threat of the termination of the relationship can significantly color therapy with a couple.

When couples do seek therapy, they are often experiencing significant conflict. Each often blames the other for their problems. He may focus on the fact that she does not show affection or respond to his initiations for sexual intimacy. She may attribute their problems to his failure to listen and to the fact that he does not communicate his feelings with her. Each holds that if only the other would change, things would be better. Positions on the issues in the relationship become very rigid and polarized. Each may attempt to win the therapist over to his or her point of view, or look for the therapist to play "judge" to settle disputes. It is crucial for the couple therapist to *remain neutral and not take sides.* The view of each partner is validated by the therapist. The *relationship* is the client. The contribution that *each* makes to their difficulties and can make to solve their problems are stressed. At times, the therapist may challenge one partner or the other, and at any one point in the therapy it may appear that the therapist is taking one person's side, yet this will shift at a later point, ideally yielding a balance overall in the process of therapy.

Couple therapy calls for an **active, directive approach,** especially early in treatment. The therapist redirects the couple's negative interactions and blocks hurtful patterns. Providing a clear sense of how therapy will begin and establishing mutually agreed upon goals will help to instill hope and engender confidence that the therapist can handle the couple's problems effectively. The therapist creates an atmosphere in which the couple can explore new behaviors and practice new ways of communicating. Active attention to what attracted the partners to each other and better times in the relationship also often helps to remind the couple of what they appreciate about each other and to place their current struggles in perspective.

Dealing with **secrets** is another key clinical issue when working with couples. The secret may be about an affair, or steps one partner has taken to end the relationship, unbeknownst to the other. Some couple therapists see couples together only in order to avoid being brought in on one partner's secret. Many couple therapists, though, include individual time with each partner, during which a secret may be revealed. Therapists differ as to how to handle secrets. Some prefer to have all the important information and may be willing to maintain a secret to this end. Others believe that sharing a secret with one partner compromises the therapy and prohibits the therapist from maintaining neutrality. Still others inform the couple early in treatment about their stand on secrets, perhaps stating that they see secrets as destructive to therapy and to the relationship, and that secrets will need to be shared if they become known during therapy. The couple, then, can decide what they wish to reveal. Each of these positions has some unique advantages and disadvantages. Couple therapists must think through their stand on the issue of secrets, as they are inevitable in work with couples.

The role of *sessions with individual partners in couple therapy* is another important clinical consideration. Many approaches begin with an initial interview with the couple together. This may be followed by an individual session with each partner to assess in more detail individual concerns and commitment to the relationship. Other couple therapists see couples only conjointly. Some clinical issues suggest the need for individual sessions. If partners are especially volatile, and cannot be seen together without intense arguing, individual sessions may be appropriate to de-escalate the conflict and work with each separately on what each can change to improve the relationship. When domestic violence is suspected or known, the therapist should meet separately with each partner to complete a more accurate assessment. Victims of violence often will limit what they reveal in front of the abusive partner, and revealing violence in front of the abusive partner could place the victim at risk for retaliation and further violence after the session. Individual sessions may also be utilized when there is a question about commitment to the relationship or when things are simply not adding up and the therapist senses that something else is going on that one or both partners are reluctant to reveal in conjoint sessions.

In some cases, *one partner may refuse to come* to therapy. Ideally, starting with the initial phone call, especially if the presenting problem is related to the relationship, the therapist emphasizes the importance of both partners attending therapy together. Therapy may proceed, though, even if only one partner attends. In this case, the therapist seeks to understand the reasons for the reluctance of the absent partner to attend and may offer to contact him or her. Parties are informed of the risk of one partner outgrowing the other if both do not attend (see Box 10.2). A family systems approach posits that it is possible to change relationships through work with one member of the couple, but this is not the preferred route in couple therapy.

Another relatively common situation occurs when therapy *begins as individual therapy* and, as therapy progresses, the need for couple therapy becomes evident. Two options are available, depending upon the nature of the relationship between the spouse attending therapy and the therapist, and the comfort of the other spouse in coming to see a therapist already well known to the first spouse. One option would be for the couple to be referred to a new therapist for couple therapy. Alternatively, the therapist could shift from individual to couple therapy if all parties are agreeable. In this case, it is useful for the therapist to meet individually with the partner who has not been attending, to join with him or her and obtain this partner's perspective on the relationship.

One final issue faced by clinicians involves the need for **cultural sensitivity.** All therapists will encounter couples whose cultural, ethnic, or racial

---

BOX 10.2. A Client's View of the Advantages of Couple Therapy

As part of a research study on clients' perceptions of pivotal moments in couple therapy (Helmeke and Sprenkle, 2000), one of the couples discussed the importance of attending therapy sessions as a couple:

BETH: I think I could work on me as much as I wanted, but if he wasn't here, we wouldn't be nearly where we are now.

JOE: No, Beth would have found the self-confidence and the happiness, and would have left me, and that would have been the end of it. I'd have been the one left behind. If she would have gone on by herself, she probably would have found answers for herself, but I wouldn't have been a part of it, if I had sat out of the process.

background is different from their own. Typically, in their training and supervision, therapists examine biases and assumptions that stem from their own cultural background and experiences. For instance, Sandy is a Caucasian therapist who grew up in a small community and had little contact with any minorities. A Latino couple from Puerto Rico with a strong Pentecostal religious background comes to see her. In addition to becoming aware of assumptions she is making regarding communication styles, gender roles, racial stereotypes, etc., Sandy might also need to do some research on themes affecting clinical work with Puerto Ricans and Pentecostals. She might even ask the couple to help educate her about cultural differences that will be important for her to be aware of in her work with them. Similarly, couple therapists may work with interracial couples; again, it is important for therapists to have some awareness and sensitivity toward issues that may confront these couples because of their different backgrounds. These issues—gender, culture, and spirituality—are covered in greater detail in Chapter 13.

WELL-ESTABLISHED APPROACHES TO COUPLE THERAPY

All the various models of family therapy described in other chapters in this text have been applied to work with couples. A Bowenian family-of-origin couple therapist would emphasize relationships with one's family of origin and differentiation as keys to resolving relationship problems. A solution-focused therapist would focus on what was different during better times in the relationship, how the couple had resolved problems in the past, and what kind of future the couple desires, emphasizing their individual and collective strengths and resources. A strategic therapist attends to problematic sequences of interaction; a feminist couple therapist is interested in the role of gender socialization and how power is distributed in the relationship. Increasingly, therapists draw from various approaches, depending upon the unique problems and dynamics of each couple.

In this section we take a look at four approaches to couple therapy that have been designed for use particularly with couples. The four are behavioral couple therapy and its more recent evolution to integrative behavioral couple therapy, emotionally focused therapy, Pinsof's integrative problem-centered couple therapy, and the imago approach to couple therapy. The first two were selected based upon strong research support for these approaches, and the fact that the developers of these approaches have adapted their approaches based upon sound research and feedback from clients. Pinsof's approach is an excellent representation of the move toward integrative couple therapy that draws upon various individual and family therapy models. Finally, the imago approach has been quite popular and is widely practiced across the United States. The following case example is presented to help in understanding how therapists, using each of these four approaches, would conceptualize therapy for this couple.

Amy and Ron have been married for eight years. They have two children, a daughter, five, and a son, three. Ron works full time in sales for a software company, and Amy also works full time managing accounts in an advertising agency. Amy called to arrange couple therapy, and reported that they have been arguing increasingly, and a recent especially volatile argument culminated in Ron moving out for a couple days. At the first session Amy complained of Ron not sharing fairly in household duties and child care, and that Ron does not listen to her concerns, often comes home late without warning, and leaves when she attempts to address problems in the marriage. Ron stated that Amy does not appreciate the demands placed upon him at work, fails to notice the things he does around the house, and constantly criticizes him, and that Amy is seldom responsive to his initiations of physical intimacy. Amy's parents have remained married. Her father had problems with alcohol when she was growing up, but is sober now. Ron's parents divorced when he was ten years old, and he was shuffled between his parents' homes through most of his teen years. Both express a desire to improve the marriage, and though divorce is mentioned at times in their arguments, neither has taken any steps to pursue a divorce.

Behavioral Couple Therapy

Behavioral couple therapy (BCT) has been one of the most widely utilized and researched types of couple therapy. Behavioral couple therapists generally assume that each partner's interactions are maintained and changed by environmental events following each partner's behavior (Jacobson and Margolin, 1979). Of particular interest are negative or "coercive" cycles in which partners attempt to control the behavior of the other with negative behaviors. In our case example, Amy's repeated complaints and Ron's tuning her out and leaving are examples of these types of negative interactions. The therapist does a thorough assessment of the couple's interaction, with an eye toward how each partner influences the other's marital satisfaction (Jacobson and Holtzworth-Monroe, 1986). Questionnaires, spouse observation checklists, and therapist observation of the couple's in-session behavior are often used in this approach.

Intervention in BCT involves two primary components. These are behavior exchange and communication/problem solving (Jacobson and Holtzworth-Monroe, 1986). **Behavior exchange strategies** are direct efforts to identify and change the frequency with which behaviors are reinforced and punished. Behavior exchange is often used early in the treatment process; its goal is to increase positive interactions and decrease negative, coercive cycles. Directives such as "caring days" (Stuart, 1980) or "love days" (Jacobson and Margolin, 1979) involve having the couple develop lists of behaviors that their partner would find pleasant and affirming, and selected behaviors are done on certain days in an effort to enhance positive aspects in the relationship. Thus, the therapist helps the couple identify behaviors that may be mutually positively reinforcing, and to encourage them to do more of these behaviors. Each is encouraged to ask directly for what he or she wants, perhaps providing a range of options that would be acceptable, and should not assume the other can read his or her mind. Partners are also trained to recognize and acknowledge the positive behaviors their partner has done for them (Jacobson and Holtzworth-Monroe, 1986). Increasing positive interactions and decreasing negative ones helps establish goodwill and hope, and sets the stage for the other primary type of intervention in BCT.

The other primary intervention in BCT is **communication** and **problem-solving skills training** (Jacobson and Holtzworth-Monroe, 1986; Jacobson and Margolin, 1979). Through systematic training, the therapist assists the partners to resolve current problems and equips them with skills they can apply to problems in the future. These skills include

1. defining problems in a nonblaming way and focusing on one problem at a time,
2. discussing one's own views rather than assuming a partner's view,
3. empathic listening and summarizing what has been heard,
4. generating solutions,
5. deciding upon a solution, and
6. implementing the solution.

Ron and Amy had worked to increase positive interaction between them; Amy was acknowledging the ways Ron helps out at home, and Ron became more attentive, listening to Amy's concerns. The therapist helped them address problems, such as Ron not calling when he was going to be late, and how they might manage work/home/parenting demands in a way that felt better to both.

BCT has been modified in recent years to promote **emotional acceptance** in addition to the traditional change strategies, resulting in **integrative behavioral couple therapy** (IBCT) (Christensen, Jacobson, and Babcock, 1995; Jacobson and Christensen, 1996). This addition was made to enhance the treatment and respond to studies which showed that although two-thirds showed improvement in the short term, about half the couples treated with traditional BCT were not achieving lasting benefit (Jacobson et al., 1984; Jacobson, Schmaling, and Holtzworth-Monroe, 1987). With IBCT, rather than focusing on change partners experience the problematic behavior or a facet of their partner in a new way. Though framed as "acceptance" this newer development in fact is a change in perception or meaning related to the once problematic behavior (Christensen, Jacobson, and Babcock, 1995). Behavior once viewed as intolerable may instead be seen as simply part of the imperfect package of qualities that makes up their mate. Attention is also paid to "softer" emotions, such as fear, hurt, or disappointment, which express vulnerability and are more likely to promote closeness between the partners. This attention to more vulnerable emotions will take center stage in the next approach.

Emotionally Focused Couple Therapy

Emotionally Focused Therapy (EFT) for couples integrates aspects of family systems and experiential therapies (Greenberg and Johnson, 1988; Johnson, 1996; Johnson and Greenberg, 1995). It proposes that due to problems with attachment (Bowlby, 1969) couples will hide their **primary emotions,** such as fear or insecurity, and instead exhibit secondary reactive emotions, such as defensiveness or anger. Partners assume rigid interactional positions that lead to repetitive negative cycles. Patterns such as pursue-distance (one partner continually pursues the other, while the other distances; as the pursuer presses harder for contact, the partner becomes even more distant) or blame-withdraw serve as a defense against expressing vulnerable emotions. Ongoing negative interactions reinforce that it is unsafe to be vulnerable, thus further burying primary emotions (Greenberg and Johnson, 1988). Ron and Amy are in a blame-withdraw cycle, with Ron withdrawing and not being attentive, Amy criticizing and blaming, and Ron withdrawing further and leaving at times, leaving Amy feeling even more frustrated and blaming and criticizing Ron further.

The goal of therapy is to access primary emotions, enhance the emotional bond, and alter negative interactional sequences (Greenberg and Johnson, 1988). The experience of primary affect serves as a means for couples to reframe their relationship and to see negative interactions as stemming from deeper unexpressed emotions. For example, Ron begins to see Amy's criticism as an expression of her overwhelming fear that he is abandoning her, perhaps reminiscent of her feelings that her alcoholic father was not available to her. Amy understands Ron's withdrawal as fear of being emotionally hurt and feeling as if he has never quite measured up, a common feeling from his childhood. As they experience each other differently, their interactions will change and they will develop a more stable bond.

EFT therapists create a safe environment for the exploration of these vulnerable feelings and at times work intensely with one partner as the other observes. The therapist attends to nonverbals and emotional tone that indicate deeper emotions and heightens the experience of these emotions. In our case, the therapist notices and gently points out Ron's slightly down-turned lip and moist eyes as he discussed what it is like for him to know he has disappointed Amy, thus deepening his expression of sadness in the session. The therapist then turns to Amy to check in with her about how it has been for her to see her husband's pain and to experience him in a novel way. Later, the therapist would focus more intently on Amy's primary emotions.

The following steps are typically followed in EFT, generally over twelve to twenty sessions (Greenberg and Johnson, 1988, p. 66):

1. Delineate the issues presented by the couple and assess how these issues express core conflicts in the areas of separateness/connectedness and dependence/independence.
2. Identify the negative interaction cycle.
3. Access unacknowledged feelings underlying interactional positions.
4. Redefine the problem(s) in terms of the underlying feelings.
5. Promote identification with disowned needs and aspects of self.
6. Promote acceptance by each partner of the other partner's experience.
7. Facilitate the expression of needs and wants to restructure the interaction.
8. Establish the emergence of new solutions.
9. Consolidate new positions.

Integrative Problem-Centered Couple Therapy

As the field of marriage and family therapy has evolved, less attachment to one particular model or approach is needed, and experienced clinicians draw from various sources to assist clients with a variety of problems. Indeed, integrative approaches were mentioned as one of the recent developments in the area of couple therapy. William Pinsof's **integrative problem-centered therapy** is a fine example of a sophisticated integrative approach that has been specifically applied to couples (Pinsof, 1995, 1999a,b). Pinsof draws upon his many years of clinical work and research in couple and family therapy. He focuses on transforming conflict and building love in his integrative work with couples.

Pinsof proposes an active, directive approach, particularly regarding stopping destructive patterns. The therapist identifies **displaced conflict,** which is fighting about *content* issues, other than core issues. An example is that Ron and Amy might fight about what movie to see on a night out. Couples are then coached to have **engaged conflict,** respectfully addressing core *process* issues in the relationship. For Amy and Ron, a core issue could be a fear of intimacy, which is not expressed but gets played out in the arguing about where to go for dinner, and may result in their deciding not to go out at all, thus preventing an opportunity for intimate conversation. Therapists explore opportunities in which love was possible, and what happened that kept it from occurring. Pinsof advocates integrating sex therapy, and from his clinical experience finds that many couples can make changes up to a point, but reach an impasse that often is related to issues of sexual intimacy (1999a).

Pinsof has introduced what he calls the **problem maintenance structure,** which involves the various issues at many different levels that keep the problem going. These levels include current patterns in a relationship, biological factors, unresolved issues from one's past, the client's core view of self, and more (1995, 1999b). For Pinsof, therapy then consists of a choosing among six different levels and opening "doors" of therapeutic approaches at a particular level that will assist the couple or individual to make desired changes. These doors are opened in order of cost-effectiveness, simplicity, and directness, and they provide information that helps identify the "logjam" that is constraining change. For example, with Ron and Amy, he would attempt direct behavioral and communication skills interventions first. If this direct approach proves unsuccessful, he considers the role of biology, and interventions might include biofeedback or medication. If biological influences are ruled out, or change has still not occurred, experiential or meaning-oriented therapies such as cognitive therapy, narrative therapy, or EFT might be employed. The next realm to consider is transgenerational family-of-origin involvement. If Ron or Amy needed this intervention, the therapist might explore family-of-origin influences through the use of genograms or involve their parents for a few sessions. If problems are still not resolved, the therapist turns his or her attention to more intrapsychic, individually oriented domains and draws from psychoanalysis and self-psychology in the final two areas. These latter two areas involve individual, longer-term therapy, and the therapist-client relationship becomes a primary vehicle for change. Pinsof suggests that more in-depth treatment is needed for some couples and individuals, and that integrative approaches prove superior for long-term outcomes for couple therapy (1999b).

Imago Relationship Therapy

In **imago relationship therapy** (IRT) the therapist would almost never meet individually with a partner, and each partner is seen as the vehicle of healing for the other (Hendrix and Hunt, 1999). IRT is a theory and therapy of committed relationships with a focus on marriage. Selection of a partner is believed to be the result of an unconscious match between a mental image of one's parents or caretakers created in childhood (called the *imago,* Greek for "image") and certain character traits of the attractive partner (Hendrix, 1988). It is no coincidence that partners get together, and each unconsciously chooses the other in an effort to heal childhood wounds. As romantic love inevitably wanes, and since the selected partner shares some of the same limitations as one's parents, each reexperiences frustrations from one's childhood. Creating a healing dialogue between the partners helps to create a "conscious marriage/committed relationship" in which they intentionally meet each other's unmet childhood needs (Hendrix and Hunt, 1999). Consistent use of the **couples dialogue** evolves into a spiritual practice, transforming the conscious marriage into a spiritual path.

This three-step couples dialogue is the cornerstone of IRT (Hendrix, 1988; Hendrix and Hunt, 1999). The therapist uses education and presents the steps of the dialogue to the couple. They are coached to follow the steps rigidly, especially initially. The three steps are **mirroring, validation,** and **empathy**. Partners take turns being the sender (speaker) and receiver (listener) during the dialogue. The sender uses "I" messages and speaks about his or her own experience, not blaming or attacking the other. Information on one issue at a time is communicated in small bits, particularly when the couple is first learning these skills. For example, Amy might say, "When you come home late without calling, I worry about what might have happened to you, and the kids get antsy about when you are coming home." The receiver then uses mirroring, essentially active listening, to reflect back the content of the sender's message. Thus, Ron would mirror back, "What I heard you say was that when I come home late without calling, you worry about . . . is that about right? Is there more?" In this way, the receiver invites further information from the sender and conveys to the sender that he or she has been heard and understood. This does not mean the receiver has to agree with what the sender has said, but it does give the sender a chance to know what he or she has said has "registered" with the receiver, something that rarely happens in a typical heated discussion, in which both partners are speaking over each other.

Validation, the second step, acknowledges that the sender's reality makes sense, given their perspective. Validating statements begin with an affirming phrase: "It makes sense that you would feel . . ." Using validation, Ron may say, "I can see how you would feel worried and upset when I don't call." This is often an important step for couples in conflict who talk past each other and are made to feel that their reactions are unreasonable or unjustified. Mirroring and validation help the sender feel heard and understood.

Empathy, the third and final step, involves the receiver not only recognizing how the partner could feel the way he or she does, but goes a step beyond that, asking the receiver to experience the sending partner's feelings. This step adds an emotional element and creates connection between the partners. As the receiver, Ron might say (and communicate nonverbally with his tone of voice and compassion), "Yes, I get it. I feel what you are feeling. I hear you." Although being able to remain a separate self, the receiver is still able to empathize with the sender. Through empathic attunement couples make a deep emotional connection, which is healing in itself (Hendrix and Hunt, 1999).

IRT uses the three steps of the couples dialogue with some variations for specific purposes. To "reimage" the partner, one might use the **parent-child dialogue,** where one partner assumes the role of the other's parent, and the sender assumes the role of herself or himself as a child and speaks to the partner-as-parent, addressing key issues. In the physically nurturing **holding exercise,** the sender reclines across the lap of the receiver and talks to the partner about his or her childhood wounds. Other variations of the couples dialogue include **behavior change requests,** or asking for what one needs from the partner, and the **container,** an intense seven-step procedure for expressing anger and turning this energy into a passionate connection. IRT therapists also encourage couples to "revision" their relationships, envisioning and creating the qualities and behaviors of their dream relationship (Hendrix, 1988; Hendrix and Hunt, 1999).

IRT has become quite popular. The Institute for IRT has certified over 1,400 therapists worldwide (Hendrix and Hunt, 1999). Couples in large numbers purchase books and videos on the approach. A professional journal dedicated to the approach, *The Journal of Imago Relationship Therapy,* has also been established. Luquet (1996) created a six-session adaptation of IRT in workbook form for use with time-limited managed care treatment. Research studies on IRT have been admittedly limited, but feedback and testimonials from couples attending IRT workshops have been encouraging (Hendrix and Hunt, 1999). IRT represents an increasingly common phenomenon in the area of couple therapy, as it has been used as either a form of therapy for distressed couples or as a method to enhance relationships or prevent problems in nonproblematic couples.

PREVENTIVE APPROACHES AND ENRICHMENT PROGRAMS

Since the late 1970s, there has been a proliferation of new prevention and couple enrichment programs (Berger and Hannah, 1999; Floyd et al., 1995). **Preventive approaches** and **enrichment programs** are generally geared toward relatively functional couples who have not yet experienced significant relationship problems. These approaches emphasize skill building (e.g., communication skills, problem solving) and the well-being of the couple. They are often structured, programmatic, time limited, affirmative, and usually economical and primarily group oriented. Couple therapy, on the other hand, usually targets distressed couples who have already experienced problems that have interfered with relationship satisfaction or relationship stability, or both. The line between these approaches has gradually blurred, and it is now common to see therapeutic models for couples that incorporate preventive ingredients, and preventive models modified for couple therapy.

Societal trends have also affected the growth of preventive approaches. Couples seem to be more open to focusing directly on improving their relationships, and attending workshops and retreats intended to strengthen marriages. Concerned about high divorce rates and attempting to promote "family values," legislators in several states have initiated efforts to make it more difficult to divorce and also require more preparation before marriage. Some states have proposed various forms of a special commitment, sometimes termed "covenant marriage," which may require premarital counseling or involve showing evidence of fault in order to end such a marriage in divorce. States have also considered incentives such as tax credits, lower marriage license fees, and shorter waiting periods for couples who complete premarital counseling.

There has also been an increasing use of **premarital inventories** to identify areas of relational strength and to identify potential problem areas that may predict later marital satisfaction versus dissatisfaction or divorce (Johnson and Lebow, 2000). It is common for couples being married through an organized religious institution to complete such inventories during their preparations for marriage. Typically, each partner completes the survey independently, sometimes predicting how the other might respond to the questions. The results reveal areas of agreement or disagreement for the couple and can be helpful in generating conversation about issues the couple had not fully considered. A widely used inventory is the PREPARE, developed by David Olson and colleagues (Olson, 1996). It includes 165 items designed to consider content areas such as Marriage Expectations, Communication, Sexual Relationship, Children and Parenting, and Financial Management, personality scales such as Assertiveness and Avoidance, and scales focusing on family-of-origin issues. Versions exist for married couples (ENRICH), remarrying couples with children, and older couples (Olson and Olson, 1999).

In addition to premarital inventories, there are several established preventive approaches in the field, such as the Prevention and Relationship Enhancement Program (PREP). In PREP, couples meet for a twelve-hour workshop, and focus on issues such as communication, conflict resolution and negotiation skills, and restructuring expectations and enhancing fun in the relationship (Markman, Stanley, and Blumberg, 1994; Stanley, Blumberg, and Markman, 1999). In PREP, partners use a piece of carpet or floor tile to symbolize when they are in the speaker position and have the "floor," while the other listens. Another widely researched and long-standing approach is the COUPLE COMMUNICATION program, based upon communication-systems theories, which has served more than half a million couples around the world (Miller et al., 1991; Miller and Sherrard, 1999). Using thirty-inch floor mats that display key concepts, couples focus on communication skills, behavior contracts, and increasing self-awareness. PAIRS (Practical Application of Intimate Relationship Skills) provides another well established, yet more intensive approach. It was developed as a four- to five-month, 120-hour comprehensive psychoeducational course for individuals or couples designed to enhance self-knowledge and to develop the ability to sustain a pleasurable intimate relationship (Gordon and Durana, 1999). PAIRS focuses more on individual growth and family-of-origin issues than do most preventive or enhancement approaches, although its originators have recently developed briefer adaptations that emphasize couple communication and conflict resolution skills. Expansions of PAIRS to high school and adolescent populations are in the pilot stage.

COMMON PROBLEMS IN COUPLE THERAPY

What are the most common types of problems that lead a couple to seek out a marriage and family therapist? Whisman, Dixon, and Johnson (1997) surveyed 122 couple therapists on the problems and therapeutic issues encountered in couple therapy, as well as the five problems they had the most difficulty treating and the five problems they believed were the most damaging to relationship functioning. The most commonly seen problems in couple therapy are presented in Table 10.1.

Problems that couple therapists saw in the 1997 study as the most difficult to treat and the most damaging to relationships are presented in Table 10.2. Note that the same ten problems were identified as both the most difficult to treat and most damaging to the couple's relationship. This 1997 study repeated a similar one published in 1981 by Geiss and O'Leary and the findings across the two studies are very similar. Of note: sexual problems, role conflict, and demonstration of affection all dropped out of the top ten most damaging problems from 1981 to 1997, to be replaced by physical abuse, incest, and addictive behavior other than alcohol.

Many of the problems listed in Table 10.2 as the most difficult to treat and most damaging to relationships are dealt with in most forms of couple therapy. These problems include lack of loving feelings, power struggles, com-

TABLE 10.1. Top Ten Problems in Couple Therapy

Problem	Rank in 1997 Study
Communication	1
Power struggles	2
Unrealistic expectations of marriage or spouse	3
Sex	4
Decision making, problem solving	5
Demonstration of affection	6
Money management, finances	7
Lack of loving feelings	8
Children	9
Serious individual problems	10

Source: Whisman, Dixon, and Johnson, 1997.

munication problems, and unrealistic expectations. Several problems on the list, such as domestic violence, affairs, substance abuse, and serious individual problems, require specialized approaches or attention to specific issues within the overall couple therapy.

DOMESTIC VIOLENCE

Domestic violence is a pervasive social problem that has devastating effects on all family members. As noted, increased attention to this problem has been identified as one of the recent significant trends in couple therapy. Physical violence occurs annually in 16 percent of marital relationships, a total of 8.7 million couples each year (Straus, 1999). Partner abuse often begins early in a relationship and, without intervention, tends to continue (O'Leary et al., 1989). For some couples, repeated aggression leads to marital distress and contributes to the likelihood of divorce. For others, aggression leads to battering, severe physical injury, homicide, or suicide (O'Leary, 1999). Communities across the United States face these extreme consequences of domestic violence on an all-too-frequent basis. Children in

TABLE 10.2. Problems in Couple Therapy Most Difficult to Treat and Most Damaging, 1997 Study

Problem	Most Difficult to Treat	Most Damaging Impact
Lack of loving feelings	1	4
Alcoholism	2	3
Extramarital affairs	3	2
Power struggles	4	7
Serious individual problems	5	9
Physical abuse	6	1
Communication	7	6
Unrealistic expectations of marriage or spouse	8	8
Addictive behavior other than alcohol	9	10
Incest	10	5

Source: Whisman, Dixon, and Johnson, 1997.

homes where violence occurs are also adversely affected; they are more likely to assault their siblings and parents, commit violent crimes outside the family, and assault their own partners and children than children who have not witnessed violence between their parents.

Although women sometimes use violence in their relationships, too, it is with a different frequency and degree than when men use violence, and thus experts emphasize that most violence is against women. For instance, it is estimated that 95 percent of the victims of domestic violence are women (Hyde, 1996). More than half (52 percent) of all women murdered in the United States are murdered by their partners (Hyde, 1996). Wives are more likely to suffer severe physical injuries and serious psychological and emotional consequences. A woman is more apt to use violence as a means of self-defense, and a man is apt to use aggression as a means of controlling his partner (Stets, 1988). Society's encouragement of women to value "relationship at any cost," and weak institutional responses to domestic violence, serve to entrap women in violent relationships (Hotaling, Straus, and Lincoln, 1990). Further, women in abusive relationships often lack the financial resources or job skills to live independently and may suffer from bruised self-esteem or fear for their own or their children's safety if they were to leave.

Although it is a pervasive problem, domestic violence is often not acknowledged by couples in therapy. This is likely related both to partners' reluctance to reveal physical abuse and to therapists' lack of skill in conducting a thorough assessment of this problem. In one study, only 6 percent of wives seeking counseling indicated on their intake form that marital violence was a significant problem (O'Leary, Vivian, and Malone, 1992), but when asked to complete a standardized assessment instrument, 53 percent indicated that their husbands had physically assaulted them. When asked directly in an interview, 44 percent indicated they had been assaulted.

Couple treatment for domestic violence has been controversial. Some experts strongly advocate for separate group or individual treatment for batterers and victims, and indeed some twenty states prohibit couple therapy in their standards for batterer interventions (Stith, 2000). Frequently, treatment is mandated after an assault has come to the attention of the legal system. Often perpetrators of violence are ordered to a psychoeducational group that covers topics such as anger management, problem solving, communication skills, gender roles, the need for control, and other issues related to partner violence. Two primary reasons are given for opposition to couple therapy. One is that including the victim of the violence in treatment sessions suggests that she is in part responsible for the violence, and the structure of treatment should reinforce that the batterer is responsible for his behavior. The other objection raised about couple therapy for domestic violence is that sessions with both partners might increase the risk of further abuse, as the perpetrator might retaliate later for issues that were raised in the sessions. These are legitimate concerns that need to be taken into account and addressed if couple therapy is utilized.

Proponents of couple therapy with couples for whom violence has been a problem argue that it has been demonstrated to be safe and appropriate in certain situations and should be included among potential treatment strategies for several reasons. Assuming a family systems perspective does not relieve the batterer of responsibility for violent behavior. Couple sessions can reveal dynamics that are never fully seen in group or individual therapy and may impact relational factors associated with violence (Bograd and Mederos, 1999). At least 50 percent of battered wives remain with their abusive partners or return to them after leaving a women's shelter (Stith, 2000). Domestic violence-focused couple therapy can offer a safe environment in which to resolve problems and improve conflict resolution skills together while the therapist keeps the anxiety and emotional intensity under control.

Criteria have been suggested to exclude couple therapy for domestic violence. These include current problems with alcohol or other drugs; the use of violence outside the home within the past two years; severe violence in the relationship within past two years; extreme obsession with one's partner or bizarre forms of violence; the use of weapons or refusal to remove guns from the home (Bograd and Mederos, 1999; Stith, 2000). Both partners need to be committed to the couple therapy as well. Some couple therapy approaches requires the male to complete a group domestic batterer program first.

Traditional couple therapy approaches are generally considered inappropriate for treating domestic violence. Special safeguards should be built into the treatment process to ensure ongoing safety (Stith and Rosen, 1990). In one of these safeguards, the partners commit to a **no-violence contract** that is reiterated throughout treatment and may specify what the consequences of further violence would be (e.g., batterer moving out). Another useful intervention is for the victim of violence to develop a **safety plan,** in which she thinks through the details of what she would do, where she would go, what important documents she might need, etc., in the case of the threat or occurrence of additional violence. Couples also work on anger management skills, and learn the use of **time out.** Partners agree on a prearranged cue to signal a time out, which can be called by either partner. During the time out, generally suggested to be about an hour, the partners leave the scene of conflict, take time to cool off, perhaps taking a walk, and think about what transpired, one's own feelings, and one's part in the argument. Angry partners should not drink or drive during the time out. After cooling down, the couple attempts to resolve the issue calmly, if both are agreeable to do so, or to arrange a later time to discuss their concerns.

Other aspects of couple therapy for domestic violence may include general interventions to improve couple communication and conflict resolution skills. Exploration of each partner's family of origin is also often helpful, particularly with attention to violence and substance abuse, and traditional gender role expectations. Some approaches also emphasize the role of cultural beliefs and practices that may perpetuate domestic violence (Almeida and Durkin, 1999). During these later phases of work with the couple, goals of increased personal and relationship flexibility, and less rigid gender and cultural role expectations are pursued. Therapists continue to monitor risks for further violence and to assist couples in decreasing overall stress in their relationship and lives in general. Couple therapy for domestic violence in one ongoing research study involves the use of a cotherapy team, with each cotherapist meeting with one of the partners individually for a brief period at the beginning and end of each session (Stith, 2000). The purpose of these pre- and postsession meetings is to assess for repeat violence and to process intense feelings that occur during the session. Over the three years the project has been operating, no incidence of violence has occurred after a couple therapy session or in relation to any in-session discussion.

EXTRAMARITAL AFFAIRS

Disclosure of an affair is one of the most common reasons couples seek therapy. Emotions are intense, ambivalence about continuing the marriage is common, and recurrent crises are the norm (Glass, 2000). Members of AAMFT reported that 46 percent of all clients sought help because of extramarital involvement (Humphrey, 1987). Several studies indicate that approximately 25 percent of women and 50 percent of men had experienced extramarital sex (Glass and Wright, 1977, 1985; Kinsey, Pomeroy, and Martin, 1953; Laumann et al., 1991). An additional 20 percent acknowledge extramarital **emotional affairs** and sexual intimacies without sexual intercourse (Glass, 2000). Although men consistently engage in affairs more often than women, current trends show that women are becoming involved in extramarital affairs at increasingly higher rates.

Experts on affairs conclude that not all affairs are alike. Emily Brown (1999), who has written and presented extensively on this topic, suggests five types of affairs. She believes that affairs signal problems in a relationship and are not really about sex. The **conflict avoidance affair** occurs for couples that are terrified to be anything but pleasant and nice, and fail to develop ways to resolve differences in the relationship, and so the marriage erodes. In the **intimacy avoidance affair,** the partners keep high barriers between them out of fear of closeness. The mirror opposite of the conflict avoiders, these couples often use frequent and intense conflict or affairs as a way to avoid intimacy, and often each spouse becomes involved in an affair. The **sexual addiction affair** is more common for men, and sex is used compulsively to numb inner pain and emptiness, much as alcoholics use alcohol. In a **split self affair** the partners have often sacrificed their own needs to take care of others, and the deprivation has caught up with one of them. The affair is usually serious, long term, and passionate, and this type is typically more common for men, although this may be changing. The partner involved in the affair focuses on deciding between the affair partner and the marriage and avoids looking at the internal split. Finally, in an **exit affair** one spouse has already decided to leave the marriage, and the affair provides the justification. The other partner usually blames the affair rather than looking at how their marriage got to that point.

Therapists should consider the type of affair and what purpose the affair might be serving in the relationship before embarking upon treatment of the couple. Several factors should be considered when assessing extramarital involvement. These include the degree of emotional and sexual involvement, duration of the involvement, extent of the deception used to conceal the affair, and the nature of the disclosure. **Combined-type involvement,** consisting of deep emotional attachment and sexual intercourse, is more prevalent for women, and has the most serious implications for the marriage (Glass and Wright, 1985). Subotnik and Harris (1999) propose a continuum of emotional involvement in which casual sex in serial affairs and one-night stands contrast with romantic love affairs and long-term affairs with a high degree of emotional investment.

The couple therapist attempts to establish the affair in the context of the overall marriage, while also trying to calm the crisis that may result from the disclosure or discovery of an affair. The symptoms of many betrayed spouses are very similar to the posttraumatic stress reactions of victims of abuse (Glass and Wright, 1997). These reactions may include obsessive thinking, flashbacks, hypervigilance, depression, anxiety, and suicidal or homicidal thoughts. Early stages of treatment may need to involve establishing safety and permitting emotional venting in individual sessions. A brief marital history, particularly of the two-year period preceding the onset of the affair, helps to establish whether marital distress is long-standing or of recent origin. Other issues such as communication patterns, conflict-resolution styles, regulation of power, intimacy, and symptoms of depression and anxiety should be assessed as well. Affairs may be perceived differently among various cultural groups, and therapists should be sensitive to the meaning of affairs in a particular culture (Penn, Hernandez, and Bermudez, 1997). Affairs by men or women may be viewed very differently within a culture as well.

An important consideration to address early in treatment is the nature of the continuing contact between the betraying spouse and the extramarital lover. If the affair is over and both spouses are satisfied that this is the case, and they are willing to work on the marriage, then couple therapy is preferred. On the other hand, if the betraying spouse is ambivalent or is continuing contact with the lover, couple therapy is not indicated; instead, individual sessions would be more appropriate, with a focus upon decision making and clarifying commitment to the marriage.

A dilemma occurs for the therapist when the affair is revealed in an individual session with the therapist and that spouse does not want the revelation to be made known to the other spouse. Some therapists refuse to see the couple for marital therapy, believing that keeping a secret will compromise therapy for the couple. Others are willing to provide both individual and couple sessions to deal with ambivalent feelings while attempting to improve the marriage at the same time. Disclosure may also serve no real purpose if the affair was long ago and an isolated incident, or if the involved spouse has ended the affair and is engaged in improving the relationship.

A well-regarded integrative approach that flows from research in this area is an **interpersonal trauma model** described by Glass and Wright (1997) and Lusterman (1995). It combines individual and relational issues in a three-stage model for treatment. The first stage establishes safety, manages affect, and validates the posttraumatic symptoms previously mentioned. Understanding the vulnerabilities for the extramarital involvement and telling the story of the affair constitutes the middle stage. The final stage of healing and recovery involves integrating the meaning of the affair into the present and moving on into the future. Some manner of atonement and forgiveness and putting the affair into perspective occur in this final stage.

Another central issue in couple treatment of affairs is telling the story of the affair. This has been viewed as a crucial aspect of recovery and rebuilding trust (Glass, 2000). Often, the betraying spouse prefers to disclose as little as possible, and the betrayed spouse may range in his or her preference from not wanting to know much to wanting to know it all. Glass sees the disclosure process as developing from an initial truth-seeking inquisition, to a neutral information-seeking phase, to a final process of empathic listening and mutual exploration. Simple facts such as who, what, when, and where can be answered during the early stage to relieve the pressure for information. Explicit details about sexual intimacy and questions about motivations should be delayed until some healing has occurred, or perhaps not shared at all. Some betrayed spouses will let go of the need to know sexual details, but others feel they cannot heal until every question has been answered. The guiding principle should be whether additional information would enhance healing. Comparisons between the betrayed spouse and the extramarital lover should be redirected by the therapist to what the betraying spouse liked best about himself or herself during the affair that can be expanded or integrated into the marriage.

Outcomes are less hopeful when the infidelity occurs early in a marriage, when the wife is the unfaithful partner, or when the extramarital involvement is a combined-type involvement, which includes both sexual and emotional intimacy.

SUBSTANCE ABUSE

Addictions to alcohol and other drugs constitute another significant problem that can have a large impact upon treatment. It is estimated that at least 13 to 16 percent of the population has been alcohol dependent at some point, and a third of Americans report family problems due to alcohol abuse (Stanton, 1999). Similar to domestic violence, abuse of or dependence upon substances is often underreported by couples seeking counseling, and clients often minimize or deny that problems exist in this area.

Various approaches to couple and family therapy address the social situation and relationships of the abuser. The therapist may use partners to engage the substance abuser in treatment, to support him or her in the process of change, and to address psychological factors such as depression. The couple therapist also attempts to modify typical behaviors regarding the abuser's habit in order to break the addictive cycle. The therapist helps the couple understand the role substances play in the relationship, and the role relational dynamics and power issues may play in the problematic use of substances. Relapse prevention can also be enhanced through involvement of one's partner (Piercy, 1996).

Family therapy approaches for alcohol and other drug abuse appear to be supported by a growing body of research. Reviews of research conclude that couple and family therapy are both successful and cost-effective in the treatment of alcoholism (Edwards and Steinglass, 1995; O'Farrell, 1993). Behavioral couple therapy (BCT), described previously, has been shown to be especially effective in maintaining abstinence and improving marital satisfaction compared to traditional individual treatment. Using a series of behavioral assignments, BCT increases positive feelings, shared activities, and constructive communication because these relationship factors are conducive to sobriety (O'Farrell, 1993, 1999). Among the assignments included are developing an individualized sobriety contract; "catching" your partner doing something nice; caring days; planning and doing shared rewarding activities; and teaching effective communication skills. Relapse prevention is also addressed, and the couple completes a continuing recovery plan that is reviewed at quarterly follow-up visits for an additional two years.

In a review of couple and family therapy for alcoholism, Edwards and Steinglass (1995) found that three factors influenced the effectiveness of treatment: gender, investment in the relationship, and perceived support of the spouse for abstinence. They showed that couple therapy for alcoholics tended to be more effective when the abuser was male, when the partners were committed to the relationship, and when the nonabusing partner showed strong support for abstinence.

A group of family therapy researcher-clinicians developed an integrative family systems approach for use with *female* alcoholics and drug abusers (Wetchler and DelVecchio, 1995; Wetchler et al., 1993). Their twelve-session systemic couple therapy incorporates aspects of structural, strategic, and transgenerational family therapies and was designed to be used in conjunction with an individual substance abuse treatment program. This approach addresses present-centered issues such as interactional sequences involving the substance use (e.g., having the couple describe what happens prior to or after use of substances) and the structural makeup of the relationship, such as power differentials and gender issues (e.g., examining how the couple makes decisions, exploring how substance use is related to power in the relationship). Family-of-origin information is gathered through the use of genograms. The therapist focuses on relationships and contact with members of one's family, substance abuse in the family, and ways in which substance abuse was a part of family rituals. These family issues have been found to be tied to substance abuse (Stanton, 1999; Steinglass et al., 1987). Couples are assisted in negotiating and resolving conflicts more effectively, altering dysfunctional sequences, neutralizing negative family-of-origin influences, and changing current relationships with one's family members. The final stage of therapy focuses on highlighting positive gains, consolidating changes that have been made, and planning for potential future problems.

SERIOUS INDIVIDUAL PROBLEMS

What role does couple therapy play in the treatment of disorders that are generally considered individual in nature? This is an emerging area of interest and considerable research is being generated using couple therapy as part of an overall plan of treatment for individual problems. Couple therapy has been utilized to treat mental health problems such as depression (Coyne, 1986; Kung, 2000), anxiety (Craske and Zoellner, 1995), bipolar disorder (Peven and Shulman, 1998), eating disorders (Root, 1995), and personality disorders (Slipp, 1995). In some cases, couple therapy may be the only form of treatment, but typically it is utilized along with individual therapy, group therapy, or medication. Recently, the impact of physical illness on couples' relationships has begun to be defined, and the role of couple therapy for conditions such as chronic illness, cancer, and infertility is receiving increased attention (Cooper-Hilbert, 1998; Diamond et al., 1999; Rolland, 1994).

It makes sense to a family systems-oriented therapist to include one's partner in the treatment of serious disorders. Relationship distress may contribute to the onset or worsening of individual problems. Likewise, individual difficulties are likely to affect one's significant relationships. Partners in long-term relationships often settle into roles that may be challenged if the other begins to make significant changes. For example, if one partner has tended to be the anxious and worrisome one and the other is the calming and reassuring one, there will likely be repercussions in the relationship if the anxious partner becomes less anxious and worried. The other partner may find that his or her familiar calming role is no longer needed, and relationship stability may be threatened. The reassuring partner may even inadvertently sabotage the positive change efforts of their partner to reestablish familiar roles and patterns (see *homeostasis* in Chapter 2). In another example, a couple seen by one of the authors included a wife who had experienced occasional recurrent episodes of severe depression. Upon her return from an especially inspiring service trip abroad, she was on an emotional high, and in light of her bright mood, her husband noticed he was feeling somewhat depressed and was prescribed an antidepressant medication for a brief period of time. Several months later, the wife experienced another episode of severe depression, perhaps rebalancing the couple to more familiar roles in their relationship.

Let us briefly examine further some of the issues related to *couple therapy with depression,* one of the most common mental health problems. A distressed couple relationship is a strong predictor of the risk of developing depression, particularly for women (Weissman, 1987). Changes in the social environment and the level of social support have been demonstrated to have a clear association with depression (Paykel and Cooper, 1992). In a study of depressed women, marital arguments were the most frequently reported life events prior to the onset of depression (Paykel et al., 1969). Ongoing marital problems are associated with poor prognosis for depression and higher rates of relapse (Hooley and Teasdale, 1989; Kung, 2000). Depression, likewise, impacts the relationship. Depressed women exhibit low rates of positive emotional expression and high rates of emotional distance with their partner, and depressed men tend to show more irritability and anger toward their spouses (Halford et al., 1999; Kung, 2000). Thus, marital distress and depression can become quite intertwined.

Several couple therapy models have been developed especially for treating couples with at least one depressed partner; yet fewer than ten systematic clinical trials have been reported (Kung, 2000; Prince and Jacobson, 1995). Overall, couple therapy for depression has been shown to be highly effective in reducing both relationship distress and depression where wives were depressed and the couples were maritally distressed. Couple therapy seems to be the treatment of choice when marital problems exist before the onset of depression, the marital problems are severe, and at least one spouse attributes the depression to marital problems. Couple therapy is also indicated when both partners are depressed, though little research has been done with this type of couple. The association of marital problems and men's depression also warrants additional research (Halford et al., 1999).

SEX THERAPY

A discussion about couple therapy would be lacking without some attention to a specialized form of therapy for couples—sex therapy. The field of sex therapy followed a different course than the field of marriage and family therapy, with the two converging only in the 1980s. Of all the human biological processes, sexual response was pretty much the last to be scientifically studied and observed (Charlton, 1997). Pioneers William Masters and Virginia Johnson (1970) conducted their work on the human sexual response cycle in the late 1960s and 1970s. From their laboratory observations of individuals and couples, they focused on the physiological changes that accompany sexual experience. They identified a four-stage model of the **human sexual response cycle** that includes excitement, plateau, orgasm, and resolution. Another pioneer in sex therapy, Helen Singer Kaplan (1979), extended their model by including **desire** as another important factor in human sexuality. Different types of sexual disorders are related to problems in one or more phases of the sexual response cycle.

Early methods in sex therapy included education, and reducing anxiety about sexual performance through the use of behavioral assignments. These assignments gradually increased the emotional and physical intimacy for the couple, so that successful, functional sexual intercourse could be achieved. A typical assignment, still employed by many sex therapists today, is the **sensate focus exercise** (Masters and Johnson, 1970). In this exercise, couples experiencing sexual problems, such as the inability to achieve or maintain an erection or the inability to achieve orgasm, engage in progressively more intimate exchanges. The couple starts with nondemand pleasuring, which includes exploring each other's bodies, with the breasts and genitals off limits, while paying attention to what they find pleasurable. They gradually increase sexual intimacy, moving to inclusion of the breasts and genitals, vaginal insertion of the penis without thrusting, and finally to sexual intercourse completed to orgasm. The intention of the exercise is to decrease anxiety and introduce a sense of exploration and focus on self- and partner pleasure without initial expectations of intercourse.

Beginning in the 1980s, family systems-oriented sex therapists emphasized the relational and systemic aspects of sexuality, expanding the previous emphasis on the physiological components of sexual response. David Schnarch (1991, 1998) stands out as a family systems sex therapist. His "sexual crucible" approach provides an excellent example of a systemic framework for human sexuality and sex therapy that moves beyond earlier behavioral and biological models. This model focuses on intimacy, passion, and meaning, issues that had been neglected in traditional sex therapy.

Schnarch's provocative ideas have been very popular, and he includes concepts such as "eyes-open orgasm" (partners keeping eyes open and making eye contact during orgasm) and "wall-socket sex" (uninhibited, electrifying sex) in his 1998 book *Passionate Marriage,* intended for a lay audience. Unlike many couple therapists who address sexual problems indirectly, believing that improving intimacy and communication often improves sexual interaction, Schnarch sees the couple's sexuality as a window into the dynamics of their relationship and directly addresses sexual matters early in treatment. His theoretical model is based on an integration of object relations and Bowenian theories (see Chapter 12). The therapeutic process is designed to resolve past personal or relational issues by increasing the *individual's* level of differentiation, thus paradoxically leading to increased potency and intimacy in the *relationship.*

COUPLE THERAPY WITH SAME-SEX COUPLES

Although couples share much in common regardless of sexual orientation, there are significant differences that therapists need to understand to work effectively with gay and lesbian couples (Brown, 1995; Carl, 1990). For instance, therapists need to be familiar with how antihomosexual bias and **homophobia,** the "fear and hatred of same-sex intimacy, love, and sexuality," affects their gay or lesbian clients (Brown, 1995, p. 274). These couples are also often oppressed by **heterosexism,** defined as "the privileging by the culture and its institutions of heterosexual forms of relating, while simultaneously devaluing non-heterosexual forms of relating" (Brown, 1995, p. 274). Examples of heterosexism include hate crimes directed at gays and lesbians, and the inability of same-sex couples to legally marry or for partners to have access to health care or inheritance rights that are assumed for heterosexual couples. Many same-sex couples also tend to internalize anti-gay bias and may view their relationships as less viable or stable than heterosexual relationships (Schiemann and Smith, 1996).

Gay and lesbian couples also face unique issues related to gender role socialization and where they are in the *coming-out process,* the process of acknowledging to oneself and revealing to others one's sexual orientation. Unlike heterosexual relationships, which are influenced by different gender-role socialization, same-sex couples share a common history of socialization to their gender and may share the same benefits and deficits of that development. Thus, a lesbian couple, with both partners socialized as females, may have difficulty accomplishing more stereotypical "male" qualities such as expression of anger, initiation of sexual activity, and tolerance of distance and difference (Brown, 1995). The partners may also be at different places in their coming out to co-workers or family members. This may result in tensions and issues related to public recognition as a couple. For example, if a gay man has not shared his sexual orientation with his family, he might describe his partner as a roommate, possibly leading the partner to question his commitment to the relationship.

Lesbian couples may also struggle with high expectations for nurturing and support, and face problems with boundaries, often manifested by intolerance for distance or difference within the couple. By virtue of having two women in a relationship, the likelihood of having at least one partner with a history of childhood physical or sexual abuse is much greater than for heterosexual couples (Brown, 1995). Gay male couples must confront the realities of AIDS and the HIV epidemic, which disproportionately affects the gay white male community within the United States. This may include dealing with the illness of one's partner or the death of close friends. Socialized as males and dealing with significant loss, gay male couples may struggle with the emotional work of relationship maintenance (Brown, 1995). Balancing commitment and sexual behavior outside the relationship (a relatively common and accepted occurrence for many gay male couples) must often be negotiated, and this can be complicated, especially with the risk of HIV infection.

CONCLUSION

This chapter has covered some of the main issues and trends in couple therapy. We have considered some of the challenges in doing therapy with intimate partners and examined well-established ways to help couples with their problems. Common problems for couples presenting for therapy have been identified. Some especially damaging problems were discussed in detail. Prevention programs are on the rise. Approaches to assist couples in conflict are becoming increasingly sophisticated and are supported by sound research. Couple therapy has indeed come of age. As partners continue to have expectations of their committed relationships that are unparalleled in previous generations, this specialized area of marriage and family therapy will likely continue to thrive.

GLOSSARY

active, directive approach: Therapist plays an active role, structuring the session, setting an agenda, directing the clients, suggesting homework assignments, etc.

behavior change requests: A structured variation of the couples dialogue in imago relationship therapy wherein one partner asks specifically for what one needs from the other partner, typically offering some acceptable alternatives rather than demanding a certain behavior.

behavior exchange strategies: Direct efforts to identify and change the frequency with which behaviors are reinforced and punished, often used early in the treatment process with a goal to increase positive interactions and decrease negative, coercive cycles.

behavioral couple therapy: Focused and structured form of couple therapy based upon social learning theory that attempts to improve effective communication skills and enhance positive interactions between the partners.

combined-type involvement: Consisting of deep emotional attachment and sexual intercourse, this form of extramarital affair is more prevalent for women and has the most serious implications for the marriage.

communication skills training: Direct efforts to teach and assist clients to develop effective communication skills, with emphasis upon things such as active listening and using "I" messages.

conflict avoidance affair: Type of extramarital affair that occurs for couples who are terrified to be anything but pleasant and nice, and fail to develop ways to resolve differences in the relationship; thus, the marriage erodes.

conflict-minimizing couples: These couples seldom argue and lead calm, pleasant lives, often exhibit lower levels of companionship and sharing, and value separateness and personal space or interests. A type of successful long-term couple identified by Gottman.

container: An intense seven-step procedure of imago relationship therapy for expressing anger and turning this energy into a passionate connection.

contempt: Insults or put-downs of one's partner, such as name-calling, hostile humor, sarcasm, or body language such as rolling of the eyes or facial grimaces.

couples dialogue: A structured communication exercise used in imago relationship therapy that involves partners taking turns assuming the roles of sender and receiver and includes three parts: MIRRORING, VALIDATION, and EMPATHY.

criticism: Attacking or blaming one's partner's personality or character, rather than a specific behavior.

cultural sensitivity: Being attuned to issues of diversity and cultural values and practices different from one's own or different from the dominant culture.

defensiveness: Warding off a perceived attack, manifested by denying responsibility, making excuses, playing one-upsmanship, or pointing out partner's faults when even legitimate concerns are raised.

desire: Aspect of human sexuality identified by pioneer sex therapist Helen Singer Kaplan that extended earlier models of human sexuality that had focused primarily upon the physical aspects of sex.

displaced conflict: Fighting about *content* issues, other than core issues.

emotional acceptance: Recent addition to traditional behavioral couple therapy, focuses on each partner accepting some of the human limitations of the partner and attends to "softer" emotions, such as fear, hurt, or disappointment, which express vulnerability and are more likely to promote closeness between the partners.

emotional affairs: Extramarital contact with another party that involves emotional intimacy and personal sharing but does not include physical intimacy or sexual contact.

Emotionally Focused Therapy (EFT): Approach to couple therapy that emphasizes emotions and attachment between the partners, the goal of which is to access primary emotions, enhance the emotional bond, and alter negative interaction patterns.

empathy: Generally, it is the ability to experience something from another's perspective. Specifically in imago relationship therapy, it is the third and final step of the couples dialogue, and involves the receiver experiencing and understanding the sending partner's feelings, helping to create an emotional connection between the partners.

engaged conflict: Respectful working out of disagreements about core *process* issues in the relationship.

enrichment programs: Structured group programs (e.g., Marriage Encounter) for relatively functional couples who have not experienced serious relationship difficulties, with the goal of strengthening the relationship.

exit affair: In this type of extramarital affair one spouse has already decided to leave the marriage, and the affair provides the justification. The other partner usually blames the affair rather than looking at how their marriage got to that point.

Four Horsemen of the Apocalypse: Four especially corrosive behaviors identified by researcher John Gottman that lead to the downfall of a marriage. *See* CRITICISM, CONTEMPT, DEFENSIVENESS, and STONEWALLING.

heterosexism: The privileging by the culture and its institutions of heterosexual forms of relating, and simultaneously devaluing nonheterosexual forms of relating.

holding exercise: A physically nurturing communication exercise used in imago relationship therapy in which the sender reclines across the lap of the receiver and talks to the partner about his or her childhood wounds.

homophobia: The fear and hatred of same-sex intimacy, love, and sexuality.

human sexual response cycle: Four-stage model of human sexual response developed by pioneering sexual researchers Masters and Johnson that includes: excitement, plateau, orgasm, and resolution.

imago relationship therapy: Form of couple therapy developed by Harville Hendrix and colleagues which stresses that partners choose a mate based upon an image of an ideal mate (*imago* is Greek for "image") that results from childhood experiences with primary caregivers. This approach utilizes structured communication exercises that empower partners to become a source of healing for each other.

integrative behavioral couple therapy: An approach to couple therapy, developed by Neil Jacobson and Andrew Christensen, that expands traditional behavioral couple therapy and its focus on change-oriented interventions by also including interventions designed to promote acceptance of one's partner and to elicit softer emotions regarding one's partner and the relationship.

integrative problem-centered therapy: Integrative approach to therapy that considers issues at several different levels, including current interactional patterns, family-of-origin influences, biochemical contributions, and psychoanalytic issues.

interpersonal trauma model: A three-stage model for understanding and treating couples in which an extramarital affair has occurred that views the affair as an individual and interpersonal trauma. Stages include establishing safety and managing emotions, exploring the vulnerabilities for the affair, and healing and recovery.

intimacy avoidance affair: Type of extramarital affair wherein the couple keeps high barriers between them out of fear of closeness and often uses frequent and intense conflict or affairs as a way to avoid intimacy.

mirroring: A form of active listening used in imago relationship therapy that involves the receiver reflecting back the content of the sender's message. For example, a mirroring statement might begin: "What I heard you say was . . . is that about right?"

no-violence contract: Intervention strategy used with couples in which domestic violence has been a problem. Partners agree verbally and/or in writing to remain nonviolent and commit themselves to healthier alternatives when upset, and may specify what the consequences of further violence would be (e.g., batterer moving out).

parent-child dialogue: Communication exercise from imago relationship therapy in which one partner assumes the role of the other's parent, and the sender assumes the role of herself or himself as a child and speaks to the partner-as-parent, addressing key issues.

premarital inventories: Typically completed by engaged couples, these questionnaires cover a range of issues pertinent to couples (e.g., finances, sexuality, children). They are usually completed separately by each partner and provide an overview of potential strengths and problem areas for the couple.

preventive approaches: Approaches that are applied to couples to help prevent the onset or worsening of problems. Typically involve education and skill building in areas such as communication skills and problem solving.

primary emotions: Emotions that are deeper and more core to one's experience, such as fear or insecurity, but instead are sometimes manifested as secondary reactive emotions, such as defensiveness or anger.

problem maintenance structure: In Pinsof's integrative problem-centered approach to therapy, the various issues at many different levels that maintain the problem.

problem-solving skills training: A component of behavioral couple therapy and other approaches that involves training and development of skills to help partners deal with conflict, including skills such as defining the problem, acknowledging each partner's role in the problem, brainstorming potential solutions, and establishing a plan for implementation of a mutually agreeable solution.

safety plan: Plan developed for victims of violence in which she thinks through the details of what she would do, where she would go, what important documents she might need, etc., in the case of the threat or occurrence of additional violence.

secrets: Information not known to all parties in the therapeutic process, e.g., one partner might reveal an affair to the therapist and not inform the other partner.

sensate focus exercise: Common intervention in sex therapy that encourages curious exploration of what one's partner and oneself finds pleasurable. Partners engage in a series of progressively intimate nondemanding explorations of each other's bodies, initially avoiding genital contact, and gradually moving toward intercourse.

sexual addiction affair: More common for men, in this type of extramarital affair sex is used compulsively to numb inner pain and emptiness, much the same way alcoholics use alcohol.

split self affair: Type of extramarital affair in which the partners have sacrificed their own needs to take care of others, and the deprivation has caught up with one of them. The affair is usually serious, long term, and passionate, and this type is typically more common for men, although this may be changing.

stonewalling: An especially corrosive behavior for couples; one partner, usually the man, removes himself, withdraws, becoming a "stone wall," unresponsive and unmoved by the partner's complaints.

time out: Strategy used for violent or especially volatile couples that involves partners agreeing that if either party becomes too angry, one partner leaves the scene for a designated amount of time providing the opportunity to cool off and reflect on one's behavior. Once calm, the couple then attempts to communicate effectively and resolve issues.

validating couples: Type of successful couple, partners are good friends, listen well to each other, validate their partner's experience, and compromise easily.

validation: The second step of imago's couples dialogue, in which the receiver acknowledges that the sender's reality makes sense, given his or her own perspective. Validating statements may begin, "It makes sense that you would feel . . ."

volatile couples: Another type of successful long-term couple, they argue and bicker over many issues, try to persuade the other rather than understand or validate, show high levels of engagement, show anger, laughter, and affection easily, and are passionate and good at making up.

REFERENCES

Almeida, R. V. and Durkin, T. (1999). The cultural context model: Therapy for couples with domestic violence. *Journal of Marital and Family Therapy, 25*, 313-324.

Berger, R. and Hannah, M. T. (Eds.) (1999). *Preventive approaches in couples therapy.* New York: Brunner/Mazel.

Bograd, M. and Mederos, F. (1999). Battering and couples therapy: Universal screening and selection of treatment modality. *Journal of Marital and Family Therapy, 25*, 291-312.

Bowlby, J. (1969). *Attachment and loss.* Volume 1: *Attachment.* New York: Basic Books.

Broderick, C. B. and Schrader, S. S. (1981). The history of professional marriage and family therapy. In A. S. Gurman and D. P. Kniskern (Eds.), *Handbook of family therapy* (pp. 5-35). New York: Brunner/Mazel.

Brown, E. M. (1999). *Affairs: A guide to working through the repercussions of infidelity.* San Francisco: Jossey-Bass.

Brown, L. S. (1995). Therapy with same-sex couples: An introduction. In N. S. Jacobson and A. S. Gurman (Eds.), *Clinical handbook of couple therapy* (pp. 274-291). New York: Guilford.

Carl, D. (1990). *Counseling same-sex couples.* New York: Norton.

Charlton, R. S. (Ed.) (1997). *Treating sexual disorders.* San Francisco: Jossey-Bass.

Christensen, A., Jacobson, N. S., and Babcock, J. C. (1995). Integrative behavioral couple therapy. In N. S. Jacobson and A. S. Gurman (Eds.), *Clinical handbook of couple therapy* (pp. 31-64). New York: Guilford.

Cooper-Hilbert, B. (1998). *Infertility and involuntary childlessness.* New York: Norton.

Coyne, J. C. (1986). Strategic marital therapy for depression. In N. S. Jacobson and A. S. Gurman (Eds.), *Clinical handbook of marital therapy* (pp. 495-511). New York: Guilford.

Craske, M. G. and Zoellner, L. A. (1995). Anxiety disorders: The role of marital therapy. In N. S. Jacobson and A. S. Gurman (Eds.), *Clinical handbook of couple therapy* (pp. 394-410). New York: Guilford.

Diamond, R., Kezur, D., Meyers, M., Scharf, C., and Weinshel, M. (1999). *Couple therapy for infertility.* New York: Guilford.

Edwards, M. E. and Steinglass, P. (1995). Family therapy treatment outcomes for alcoholism. *Journal of Marital and Family Therapy, 21*, 475-510.

Floyd, F. J., Markman, H. J., Kelly, S., Blumberg, S. L., and Stanley, S. M. (1995). Preventive intervention and relationship enhancement. In N. S. Jacobson and A. S. Gurman (Eds.), *Clinical handbook of couple therapy* (pp. 212-226). New York: Guilford.

Geiss, S. K. and O'Leary, K. D. (1981). Therapist ratings of frequency and severity of marital problems: Implications for research. *Journal of Marital and Family Therapy, 7*, 515-520.

Glass, S. P. (2000). *AAMFT Clinical update: Infidelity.* Washington, DC: AAMFT.

Glass, S. P. and Wright, T. L. (1977). The relationship of extramarital sex, length of marriage, and sex differences on marital satisfaction and romanticism: Athanasiou's data reanalyzed. *Journal of Marriage and Family, 39,* 691-703.

Glass, S. P. and Wright, T. L. (1985). Sex differences in type of extramarital involvement and marital dissatisfaction. *Sex roles, 12,* 1101-1119.

Glass, S. P. and Wright, T. L. (1997). Reconstructing marriages after the trauma of infidelity. In W. K. Halford and H. J. Markman (Eds.), *Clinical handbook of marriage and couples interventions* (pp. 471-507). New York: John Wiley and Sons.

Gordon, L. H. and Durana, C. (1999). The PAIRS program. In R. Berger, and M. T. Hannah (Eds.), *Preventive approaches in couples therapy* (pp. 217-236). New York: Brunner/Mazel.

Gottman, J. (1994). *Why marriages succeed or fail.* New York: Simon and Schuster.

Gottman, J. and Silver, N. (1999). *Seven principles for making marriage work.* New York: Crown.

Greenberg, L. and Johnson, S. (1988). *Emotionally focused therapy for couples.* New York: Guilford.

Halford, W. K., Bouma, R., Kelly, A., and Young, R. McD. (1999). Individual psychopathology and marital distress. *Behavior Modification, 23,* 179-216.

Helmeke, K. B. and Sprenkle, D. H. (2000). Clients' perceptions of pivotal moments in couple therapy: A qualitative study of change. *Journal of Marital and Family Therapy, 26,* 469-483.

Hendrix, H. (1988). *Getting the love you want: A guide for couples.* New York: Henry Holt.

Hendrix, H. and Hunt, H. (1999). Imago relationship therapy: Creating a conscious marriage or relationship. In R. Berger and M. T. Hannah (Eds.), *Preventive approaches in couples therapy* (pp. 169-195). New York: Brunner/Mazel.

Hooley, J. M. and Teasdale, J. D. (1989). Predictors of relapse in unipolar depressives: Expressed emotion, marital distress and perceived criticism. *Journal of Abnormal Psychology, 98,* 229-235.

Hotaling, G. T., Straus, M. A., and Loncoln, A. J. (1990). Intrafamily violence and crime and violence outside the family. In M. S. Straus and R. J. Gelles (Eds.), *Physical violence in American families* (pp. 431-470). New Brunswick, NJ: Transaction Publishers.

Humphrey, F. G. (1987). Treating extramarital sexual relationships in sex and couples therapy. In G. R. Weeks and L. Hof (Eds.), *Integrating sex and marital therapy: A clinical guide* (pp. 149-170). New York: Brunner/Mazel.

Hyde, J. S. (1996). *Half the human experience: The psychology of women,* Fifth edition. Lexington, MA: D. C. Heath.

Jacobson, N. S. and Christensen, A. (1996). *Integrative couple therapy.* New York: Norton.

Jacobson, N. S., Follette, W. C., Revenstorf, D., Baucom, D. H., Halhweg, K., and Margolin, G. (1984). Variability in outcome and clinical significance of behavioral marital therapy: A reanalysis of outcome data. *Journal of Consulting and Clinical Psychology, 52,* 497-564.

Jacobson, N. S. and Holtzworth-Monroe, A. (1986). Marital therapy: A social learning/cognitive perspective. In N. S. Jacobson and A. S. Gurman (Eds.), *Clinical handbook of marital therapy* (pp. 29-70). New York: Guilford.

Jacobson, N. S. and Margolin, G. (1979). *Marital therapy: Strategies based on social learning and behavior exchange principles.* New York: Brunner/Mazel.

Jacobson, N. S., Schmaling, K. B., and Holtzworth-Monroe, A. (1987). Component analysis of behavioral marital therapy: Two-year follow-up and prediction of relapse. *Journal of Marital Therapy, 13,* 187-195.

Johnson, S. M. (1996). *The practice of emotionally focused marital therapy: Creating connection.* New York: Brunner/Mazel.

Johnson, S. M. and Greenberg, L. (1995). The emotionally focused approach to problems in adult attachment. In N. S. Jacobson and A. S. Gurman (Eds.), *Clinical handbook of couple therapy* (pp. 121-141). New York: Guilford.

Johnson, S. and Lebow, J. (2000). The "coming of age" of couple therapy: A decade review. *Journal of Marital and Family Therapy, 26,* 23-38.

Kaplan, H. S. (1979). *Disorders of sexual desire.* New York: Brunner/Mazel.

Kinsey, A. C., Pomeroy, W. B., and Martin, C. E. (1953). *Sexual behavior in the human female.* Philadelphia: W. B. Saunders.

Kung, W. W. (2000). The intertwined relationship between depression and marital distress: Elements of marital therapy conducive to effective treatment outcome. *Journal of Marital and Family Therapy, 26,* 51-63.

Laumann, E., Gagnon, J., Michael, R., and Michaels, S. (1991). *The social organization of sexuality: Sexuality practices in the United States.* Chicago: University of Chicago Press.

Luquet, W. (1996). *Short-term couples therapy: The Imago model in action.* New York: Brunner/Mazel.

Lusterman, D. (1995). Treating marital infidelity. In R. Mikessell, D. Lusterman, and S. H. McDaniel (Eds.), *Integrating family therapy: Handbook of family psychology and systems theory* (pp. 259-270). Washington, DC: American Psychological Association.

Markman, H. J., Stanley, S. M., and Blumberg, S. L. (1994). *Fighting for your marriage: Positive steps for a loving and lasting relationship.* San Francisco: Jossey-Bass.

Masters, W. H. and Johnson, V.E. (1970). *Human sexual inadequacy.* Boston: Little, Brown.

Miller, S. L., Nunnally, E. W., Wachman, D. B., and Miller, P. A. (1991). *Talking and listening together.* Denver-Littleton, CO: Interpersonal Communications Programs.

Miller, S. L. and Sherrard, P. (1999). Couple communication: A system for equipping partners to talk, listen, and resolve conflicts effectively. In R. Berger and M. T. Hannah (Eds.), *Preventive approaches in couples therapy* (pp. 125-148). New York: Brunner/Mazel.

O'Farrell, T. J. (Ed.) (1993). *Treating alcohol problems: Marital and family interventions.* New York: Guilford.

O'Farrell, T. J. (1999). BCT offers good outcomes. *Family Therapy News, 29* (7), 1, 18-19.

O'Leary, K. D. (1999). Developmental and affective issues in assessing and treating partner aggression. *Clinical Psychology: Science and Practice, 6* (4), 400-414.

O'Leary, K. D., Barling, J., Arias, I., Rosenbaum, A., Malone, J., and Tyree, A. (1989). Prevalence and stability of aggression between spouses: A longitudinal analysis. *Journal of Consulting and Clinical Psychology, 57(2),* 263-268.

O'Leary, K. D., Vivian, D., and Malone, J. (1992). Assessment of physical aggression against women in marriage: The need for a multimodal assessment. *Behavioral Assessment, 14,* 5-14.

Olson, D. H. (1996). *PREPARE/ENRICH Counselors Manual: Version 2000.* Minneapolis, MN: Life Innovations.

Olson, D. H. and Olson, A. K. (1999). PREPARE/ENRICH program: Version 2000. In R. Berger and M. T. Hannah (Eds.), *Preventive approaches in couples therapy* (pp. 196-216). New York: Brunner/Mazel.

Paykel, E. S. and Cooper, Z. (1992). Life events and social stress. In E. S. Paykel (Ed.), *Handbook of affective disorders,* Second edition (pp. 149-270). New York: Guilford.

Paykel, E. S., Myers, J. K., Dienelt, M. N., Klerman, G. L., Lindenthal, J. J., and Pepper, M. P. (1969). Life events and depression. *Archives of General Psychiatry, 21,* 753-760.

Penn, C. D., Hernandez, S. L., and Bermudez, M. (1997). Using a cross-cultural perspective to understand infidelity in couples therapy. *The American Journal of Family Therapy, 25,* 169-185.

Peven, D. E. and Shulman, B. H. (1998). Bipolar disorder and the marriage relationship. In J. Carlson and L. Sperry (Eds.), *The disordered couple* (pp. 13-28). New York: Brunner/Mazel.

Piercy, F. (1996). Family therapy of drug and alcohol abuse. In F. Piercy, D. Sprenkle, J. Wetchler, and Associates (Eds.), *Family therapy sourcebook,* Second edition (pp. 319-324). New York: Guilford.

Pinsof, W. (1995). *Integrative problem-centered therapy: A synthesis of family, individual, and biological strategies.* New York: Basic Books.

Pinsof, W. (1999a). Building love and transforming conflict in couples therapy. Presentation at the annual meeting of the American Association for Marriage and Family Therapy, Chicago, IL, October 9.

Pinsof, W. (1999b). Choosing the right door. *Family Therapy Networker, 23* (1), 48-55, 66.

Prince, S. E. and Jacobson, N. S. (1995). A review and evaluation of marital and family therapies for affective disorders. *Journal of Marital and Family Therapy, 21,* 377-401.

Rolland, J. S. (1994). *Families, illness, and disability: An integrative treatment model.* New York: Basic Books.

Root, M. P. (1995). Conceptualization and treatment of eating disorders in couples. In N. S. Jacobson and A. S. Gurman (Eds.), *Clinical handbook of couple therapy* (pp. 437-457). New York: Guilford.

Schiemann, J. and Smith, W. L. (1996). The homosexual couple. In H. Kessler (Ed.), *Treating couples* (pp. 97-136). San Francisco: Jossey-Bass.

Schnarch, D. M. (1991). *Constructing the sexual crucible: An integration of sexual and marital therapy.* New York: Norton.

Schnarch, D. M. (1998). *Passionate marriage.* New York: Owl Books/Henry Holt.

Slipp, S. (1995). Object relations marital therapy of personality disorder. In N. S. Jacobson and A. S. Gurman (Eds.), *Clinical handbook of couple therapy* (pp. 458-470). New York: Guilford.

Stanley, S. M., Blumberg, S. L., and Markman, H. J. (1999). Helping couples fight for their marriages: The PREP approach. In R. Berger and M. T. Hannah (Eds.), *Preventive approaches in couples therapy* (pp. 279-303). New York: Brunner/Mazel.

Stanton, D. (1999). *AAMFT Clinical update: Alcohol use disorders.* Washington, DC: AAMFT.

Steinglass, P., Bennett, L. A., Wolin, S. and Reiss, D. (1987). *The alcoholic family.* New York: Basic Books.

Stets, J. E. (1988). *Domestic violence and control.* New York: Springer-Verlag.

Stith, S. M. (2000). *AAMFT Clinical update: Domestic violence.* Washington, DC: AAMFT.

Stith, S. M. and Rosen, K. H. (1990). Family therapy for spouse abuse. In S. M. Stith, M. B. Williams, and K. Rosen (Eds.), *Violence hits home: Comprehensive treatment approaches to domestic violence* (pp. 83-99). New York: Springer.

Straus, M. A. (1999). The controversy over domestic violence by women: A methodological, theoretical, and sociology of science analysis. In X. B. Arriaga and S. Oskamp (Eds.), *Violence in intimate relationships* (pp. 17-44). Thousand Oaks, CA: Sage.

Stuart, R. B. (1980). *Helping couples change: A social learning approach to marital therapy.* New York: Guilford.

Subotnik, R. and Harris, G. (1999). *Surviving infidelity: Making decisions, recovering from the pain.* Holbrook, MA: Bob Adams Press.

Weissman, M. M. (1987). Advances in psychiatric epidemiology: Rates and risks for major depression. *American Journal of Public Health, 77,* 445-451.

Wetchler, J. L. and DelVecchio, D. L. (1995). Systemic couples therapy for a female heroin addict. *Journal of Family Psychotherapy, 6*(4), 1-13.

Wetchler, J. L., McCollum, E., Nelson, T., Trepper, T., and Lewis, R. (1993). Systematic couples therapy for alcohol-abusing women. In T. J. O'Farrell (Ed.), *Treating alcohol problems: Marital and family interventions* (pp. 220-236). New York: Guilford.

Whisman, M. A., Dixon, A. E., and Johnson, B. (1997). Therapists' perspectives of couple problems and treatment issues in couple therapy. *Journal of Family Psychology, 11,* 361-366.

Chapter 11

Communication Training, Marriage Enrichment, and Premarital Counseling

Lee Williams

An ounce of prevention is worth a pound of cure.

Benjamin Franklin

Beginning in the 1960s, the divorce rate in the United States dramatically climbed to unprecedented levels. Although the divorce rate stopped rising in 1980, current estimates are that nearly one in two couples getting married today will divorce or separate. The high divorce rate has focused more attention on the need for programs designed to help couples develop happy and lasting marriages.

Unfortunately, messages from society often reinforce the notion that couples simply fall in and out of love, or that "love conquers all." Often overlooked, however, is the importance of couples learning skills to help them sustain their relationships over time. Indeed, it can be far more difficult to get a driver's license than a marriage license in some states, even though sustaining a successful marriage would appear to be a much more difficult endeavor, given the recent divorce statistics.

Given these messages from society about marriage, perhaps it is not surprising that few follow Benjamin Franklin's advice. Most couples, for example, do not seek out marriage preparation. Silliman and Schumm (1999) cite studies that indicate only 10 to 35 percent of couples receive any type of marriage preparation. Many couple therapists have also noted that many couples do not seek help for their marriages until they are highly distressed, if they seek help at all. When couples do seek help, typically at least one partner is seriously considering divorce.

This chapter describes **preventative approaches** that are intended to help couples develop healthy and lasting marriages. Preventative approaches dif-

fer from traditional **couple therapy** in their focus on enhancing couple relationships before significant problems arise. In contrast, couple therapy is
aimed at helping couples that are already experiencing significant problems
or relationship distress. In reality, couples frequently seek out the programs
described in this chapter because they are already experiencing problems in
their relationships. Fortunately, most of these programs are suitable for both
distressed and nondistressed couples. Indeed, many of the programs have
elements such as **communication training** that could be easily incorporated into traditional couple therapy.

The chapter focuses on six preventative approaches that have been used
in **premarital counseling** and **marriage enrichment.** Premarital counseling is distinguished from marriage enrichment in that premarital counseling
seeks to prepare engaged couples for marriage, and marriage enrichment
helps couples who are already married to strengthen or enhance their relationships. Most of the six programs described here are suitable for either engaged couples preparing for marriage or couples who are already married:

1. Relationship Enhancement (RE)
2. COUPLE COMMUNICATION
3. Prevention and Relationship Enhancement Program (PREP)
4. Practical Application of Intimate Relationship Skills (PAIRS)
5. PREPARE/ENRICH
6. ACME-style marriage enrichment

The six programs were selected because they are among the best known in
the marriage and family therapy field. *Preventive Approaches in Couples Therapy,* edited by Berger and Hannah (1999), is an excellent resource for those
seeking information on other preventative programs for couples. As the title
of this chapter suggests, communication training is an essential feature in
most of the programs described here. In addition to describing these programs, case examples of premarital counseling, as traditionally offered in
church settings, will also be presented.

THEORETICAL CONCEPTS

No one theoretical approach encompasses or embodies the premarital
counseling or marriage enrichment programs described in this chapter.
Most of the programs are eclectic in nature; that is, they draw upon a few
theories rather than just one. Relationship Enhancement, for example, is
based upon psychodynamic, behavioral, humanistic, and interpersonal theories. PAIRS also draws from a wide range of theories, including experien-

tial, object relations, communication, behavioral, and family systems (e.g., Satir, Bowen, Boszormenyi-Nagy). Due to the strong emphasis on teaching communication and conflict resolution skills, many of the programs have been influenced by **cognitive-behavioral, communication,** and **social learning theories.** In addition to theory, empirical research has heavily informed the development of some programs, such as PREP and PREPARE/ENRICH.

Despite the eclectic nature of these programs, they do share some common features. All of the programs share a preventive philosophy. They work from the assumption that it is better to prevent problems rather than fix them once they develop. All of the preventive approaches described in this chapter emphasize the importance of couples learning effective communication and conflict resolution skills. Upon mastery, these skills can be applied to a variety of issues the couple may need to address in their relationship. More comprehensive programs such as PREP and PAIRS share other commonalities, for example, emphasizing the importance of nurturing the couple's bond or intimacy, exploring expectations in the relationship, and exploring how family-of-origin experiences can influence the partners and their relationship.

MAJOR PROPONENTS OF MARRIAGE ENRICHMENT AND PREMARITAL COUNSELING

The programs discussed in this chapter are often identified with key individuals who were instrumental in program development. Bernard Guerney Jr., for example, is widely recognized as the primary developer of Relationship Enhancement. The idea for Relationship Enhancement came out of Guerney's effort to enlist parents as helpers by training them to behave in a therapeutic manner when interacting with their children (Cavedo and Guerney, 1999). Sherod Miller is the name most closely associated with Couples Communication, which was born out of research by Miller and his colleagues Elam Nunnally and Daniel Wackman that explored couples' transition from engagement to early marriage (Miller and Sherrard, 1999).

PREP's beginnings are also rooted in research. Howard Markman conducted a longitudinal study that showed communication to be a key predictor of whether couples would later become distressed (Stanley, Blumberg, and Markman, 1999). Based on this research, Markman developed an intensive, preventive program for couples, which evolved into PREP with the contribution of other individuals such as Scott Stanley and Susan Blumberg. Lori Gordon is the founder of PAIRS, another intensive workshop for couples. PAIRS was initially developed as a graduate school course that Gordon taught to marriage and family therapy students (Gordon and Durana, 1999).

David Mace would probably be considered the most prominent early proponent of marriage enrichment. He, along with his wife Vera, were co-founders of Association of Couples for Marriage Enrichment (ACME), an international organization that supports and trains couples to lead marriage enrichment groups.

Churches should also be recognized as one of the strongest proponents of premarital counseling. Individuals who are married within the Catholic Church, for example, are often required to go through some form of marriage preparation or premarital counseling. Many Protestant churches also require premarital counseling or marriage preparation for couples marrying. In fact, clergy perform the majority of premarital counseling (Stahmann and Hiebert, 1997).

Recently, another strong proponent of marriage education has been Diane Sollee, who is the founding director of the Coalition for Marriage, Family and Couples Education (CMFCE). CMFCE sponsors a national conference on marriage education for both professionals and the general public, and runs a Web site <www.smartmarriages.com> that provides numerous articles and resources for individuals seeking information on marriage education.

PATHOLOGY AND BEHAVIOR DISORDERS

A picture is emerging through marital research as to why some couples become distressed and eventually divorce and others do not. Stanley, Blumberg, and Markman (1999), developers of PREP, have described one common pathway through which relationships become distressed. As a couple spends time together, their attachment or bond to each other grows. A commitment to the relationship develops between the two to protect themselves from the feared loss of their loved one. For many couples, this commitment eventually leads to marriage. Satisfaction tends to be high for couples at this stage because they have not encountered many significant issues. Therefore, they have had little chance to test their abilities to handle conflict.

As time passes, couples must deal with an increasing number of life problems. Couples who do not have good skills for managing conflict often fall into patterns that damage the relationship. These negative patterns can include escalation, invalidation, withdrawal/avoidance, and negative interpretations (Markman, Stanley, and Blumberg, 1994). Through **escalation,** partners respond to one another with increasingly negative comments, creating a negative spiral of anger and frustration. **Invalidation** occurs when the partner denigrates the thoughts, feelings, or character of the other. **With-**

drawal/avoidance is a reluctance or unwillingness to talk about important issues. Men are more likely than women to be withdrawers or avoiders. **Negative interpretations** occur when an individual consistently believes the motives of his or her partner are more negative than they are in reality.

Over time, mismanaged conflict erodes the quality of the relationship. Eventually, "the presence of the partner becomes increasingly associated with pain and frustration, not pleasure and support" (Stanley, Blumberg, and Markman, 1999, p. 282). Negative interpretations about the partner become commonplace and further erode the commitment and bond in the relationship. At this point, individuals are faced with a decision either to stay in or leave the relationship. With fewer constraints to divorce in American society today, couples are now more likely to consider divorce rather than remain in a stable but unhappy marriage.

John Gottman is also noted for his research on examining why couples become distressed. Much of what he and his colleagues have learned about marriages has come from studying couples in **marriage labs,** and then following them longitudinally over time. In marriage labs, couples are closely videotaped as they discuss an area of disagreement. These videotapes are later analyzed by observing each person's words, gestures, and facial expressions to determine the emotions being felt and expressed. Individuals are also hooked up to a variety of instruments that measure their physiological reaction to the discussion. Electrodes are placed on each individual's chest to measure his or her heart rate. Other devices placed on the fingers measure the pulse rate or the amount of sweat produced in response to stress.

Through this research, it has been possible to predict with over 90 percent accuracy which couples will later divorce (Gottman and Gottman, 1999). One of the key findings from this research is that couples who stay married maintain a ratio of positive to negative feelings and behaviors of five to one (Gottman, 1994). In contrast, couples who divorce show only 8:1 positive to negative ratio. The presence of **criticism, contempt, defensiveness,** and **stonewalling** in couple interactions has also been found to be predictive of couples who will divorce. Gottman (1994) labels these the **Four Horsemen of the Apocalypse.** The first horseman, criticism, involves attacking an individual's personality or character rather than complaining about a specific behavior. The second horseman, contempt, reflects a disgust or lack of respect for the other partner. Contempt goes beyond criticism and is often expressed as a negative comment said with the intent to insult or psychologically hurt the other partner. Criticism and contempt often lead to the third horseman, defensiveness. Defensiveness can be manifested in a number of ways such as denying responsibility, making an excuse, or complaining about one's partner, to name just a few. Defensiveness is destructive because it tends to escalate rather than resolve conflict. The same is true for stonewalling, the fourth horseman. Stonewalling occurs when an individual, often a man, withdraws or stops participating in a discussion or argument, as if turning into a stone wall. Men are more likely than women to stonewall because men are more likely to become **flooded** during marital conflict, a state of physical arousal accompanied by negative thoughts and feelings. The inability to effectively handle conflict can lead to chronic flooding, which can eventually lead the individual to adopt a negative view of the partner and the marriage (Gottman, 1994). With repeated flooding, an individual can develop a negative response to his or her partner through **conditioning,** even when the partner makes a neutral or benevolent comment or exhibits a harmless behavior.

Chronic flooding can set in motion a **distance and isolation cascade** (Gottman, 1994; Gottman and Gottman, 1999). The individual begins to view the problems in the marriage as severe and believes there is no point in trying to work out the issues with the partner. The couple begins to do less and less together, thereby developing parallel lives. This, in turn, leads to each individual feeling lonely in the marriage. Based on this research, an intervention approach called the Marriage Survival Kit is currently being tested (Gottman and Gottman, 1999).

The research on how marriages become distressed clearly points to the need for couples to learn how to effectively manage conflict. Most of the programs in this chapter focus on teaching couples specific skills or strategies for communicating and handling conflict to avoid the destructive patterns that can erode and destroy the relationship. Programs such as PREP and PAIRS also examine the dysfunctional attitudes and beliefs that can impact the relationship, and encourage couples to nurture the positive aspects of their relationship.

TECHNIQUES

The goals and aims of the six programs are outlined, the formats of the programs are provided, and examples of interventions or techniques used in the programs to accomplish the goals are dicussed in this section.

Relationship Enhancement (RE)

Relationship Enhancement (RE) is a skills-based program that can be used with either married or engaged couples. Couples are taught a set of nine skills through RE to help them develop and maintain a healthy relationship (Cavedo and Guerney, 1999). Four of the skills focus on helping couples learn how to effectively communicate. The **expressive skill,** for example, helps individuals to better understand their own needs, desires, and feelings, and to express them in a way that will minimize the listener's defensiveness. The **empathic skill** helps individuals compassionately understand the emotional and psychological needs of the speaker, and how to effectively respond to the speaker's message. In RE, the emphasis is not on having the listener simply repeat or paraphrase what the expresser has said, but on getting the listener to try to comprehend the expresser's experience by asking himself or herself how similar circumstances would make the listener think and feel. An effective empathic response can help build compassion, trust, openness, and respect in the relationship. The **discussion and negotiation skill** is intended to help couples maintain a positive atmosphere when discussing difficult issues, and to uncover the deep feelings and root issues behind the difficult issues. Couples are also taught a **facilitative** (coaching) **skill** to help them exit negative communication cycles or spirals, and resume using the RE skills.

Couples are also taught a **problem/conflict resolution skill,** which facilitates their discovery of creative solutions to their problems that are mutually satisfying to both parties. The problem/conflict resolution skill enables couples to develop agreements on behavioral changes that are mutually satisfying to both parties. Two additional skills, **changing-self skill** and **helping-others-change skill,** are taught to help individuals bring about the desired changes. Changing-self skill helps individuals to alter their own behaviors for the purposes of self-improvement or to honor agreements to change they have made with their partners. The helping-others-change skill helps individuals change the attitudes, behaviors, or feelings of others.

Finally, individuals are taught the **transfer and generalization skill** and the **maintenance skill.** The transfer and generalization skill aids the individual in using the skills in their everyday life with others besides their partner; the maintenance skill helps individuals maintain their high level of skills over time. Continued use of these skills over time, in both the couple's and in all other relationships, can reduce stress and improve self-esteem, interpersonal effectiveness, and personal satisfaction.

Couples learn specific guidelines to help them effectively perform each of the skills. When individuals are taught the expresser skill, for example, they are instructed to state their views in a subjective manner (Guerney, 1977). Instead of saying, "The house is disorganized," which implies an objective reality, the individual is encouraged to say, "By my standards, the house is disorganized," which acknowledges the subjectivity of the individual's perceptions or judgments. Other guidelines instruct the expresser to broaden the statement to include his or her feelings, and to be as specific as possible to avoid overgeneralizations. The expresser might state, for example, "For the last few days when I come home from work, I find toys scattered around the living room and papers and toys scattered around the kitchen. By my standards, that means the house is disorganized, and I'm upset and annoyed about it." Individuals are also instructed to include a positive underlying feeling or expectation if they state an implied criticism (e.g., "I believe that you share my desire to have a house that is organized") and, if appropriate, the behavior they would like to see the other person display.

RE can be used for either distressed couples or nondistressed couples, and can be flexibly adapted to a variety of formats. It can be used in therapy with individuals, couples, or families, but is also suitable for a group format. RE can be provided in one long (one to two days) marathon session, or divided into multiple sessions over a period time. Regardless of the format, RE participants are first given the rationale for the skills, and then learn the skills through readings and demonstrations. Next, participants are given the opportunity to practice the skills through role-playing and discussing issues in the relationship. In role-playing, individuals might first listen to an audiotape of a speaker, and then stop the tape and try to give an empathic response. The individual can then compare his or her response to the one given on the tape by a skilled person. Couples practice the skills with less intense issues in the beginning, and work on more difficult issues as their skill level builds. An essential ingredient to RE is the use of coaches who provide participants feedback on how well the couples are using the skills.

COUPLE COMMUNICATION

The **COUPLE COMMUNICATION** program is designed to promote healthier and more satisfying relationships by teaching couples how to more effectively communicate and resolve conflicts (Miller and Sherrard, 1999). COUPLE COMMUNICATION has been used with both distressed and nondistressed couples, and can be used either as a component of therapy or as a program designed for premarital couples or couples seeking enrichment.

COUPLE COMMUNICATION helps individuals better understand themselves and their partners, and educates them on effective and ineffective means of communication. Couples are taught eleven specific communication skills for talking and listening, and are given guidelines for resolving issues. A key part of the COUPLE COMMUNICATION program is practicing the skills and getting feedback from coaches who observe the couples as they apply the skills.

When offered in a group format, COUPLE COMMUNICATION is typically divided into four two-hour sessions (Miller and Sherrard, 1999). The first session focuses on caring for self, and emphasizes themes of self-esteem and how each individual is unique. Couples are taught, for example, that individual differences are potential resources for the couple, and not just potential sources of conflict. Couples are taught how to use the **Awareness Wheel,** a tool used to help individuals increase self-awareness, understand issues or situations better, and use this information to communicate more effectively with others. The Awareness Wheel encourages individuals to explore and articulate different aspects of an issue, including their experiences, feelings, thoughts, wants for self or others, and current or future actions.

The focus of the second session is on caring for your partner. The participants are told that expanding their awareness of their partner is necessary for a healthy relationship. Expanding this awareness is developed by learning five listening skills and practicing the **Listening Cycle.** Individuals are taught, for example, how to allow the speaker to direct the conversation, rather than having the listener try to lead the conversation. The importance of seeking understanding first, before trying to reach an agreement, is also emphasized. Individuals are also taught how to communicate concern and validate the partner's experience through listening.

In the third section, couples learn about effective and ineffective strategies for resolving conflict. Couples are taught a process for resolving conflicts called **mapping an issue,** which includes the following eight steps (Miller and Sherrard, 1999, p. 142):

Step 1: Identify and define the issue.
Step 2: Contract to work through the issue.
Step 3: Understand the issue completely.
Step 4: Identify wants.
Step 5: Generate options.
Step 6: Choose actions.
Step 7: Test the action plan.
Step 8: Evaluate the outcome.

In the fourth session, the focus is on teaching couples about different negative and positive styles of communication. Couples are then encouraged to identify which styles they typically use. Finally, couples are given the opportunity to practice the positive communication styles while discussing an issue.

A unique aspect of the COUPLE COMMUNICATION program is the use of **skill mats,** which are thirty-inch square floor maps printed with either the Awareness Wheel or Listening Cycle frameworks. The skill mat with the Awareness Wheel is divided into different sections to help individuals explore or process their experiences. Individuals first step onto the skill mat and state the issue they want to talk about, and then step on other parts of the Awareness Wheel to explore and articulate different aspects of the issue, such as their experiences, feelings, thoughts, wants for self or others, and actions. The skill mats are intended to accelerate learning by using both the right brain (learning through words, concepts) and the left brain (learning through associated experience).

Prevention and Relationship Enhancement Program (PREP)

Prevention and Relationship Enhancement Program (PREP) is a twelve-hour program that is typically delivered to couples in a group format, although elements of PREP can easily be incorporated into couple therapy. PREP has a strong research or empirical base, and emphasizes a skills-oriented approach to addressing factors that can lead to marital breakdown. PREP is suitable for either engaged couples preparing for marriage or couples who are already married.

PREP has four primary goals (Stanley, Blumberg, and Markman, 1999). The first goal is to teach couples better communication and conflict resolution skills for managing conflict. The second goal is to help couples explore their expectations in the relationship. Couples can be at risk if one or both partners have expectations that are unreasonable or unexpressed. Unmet expectations often lead to disappointment and frustration in the relationship. The third goal of PREP is to have couples explore their attitudes and choices regarding commitment. The fourth goal enhances the couple's relationship bond through fun, friendship, and sensuality.

A variety of techniques or strategies is used throughout the program to achieve the four goals (Markman, Stanley, and Blumberg, 1994). To improve a couple's ability to handle conflict in a more positive manner, PREP teaches couples the **speaker-listener technique.** Using this technique, one individual is the speaker, and the other individual assumes the listener role. The speaker follows certain guidelines, such as speaking only about his or her own experiences, not the partner's, and keeping statements brief so the listener can paraphrase what is being said. The listener must paraphrase what the speaker says and avoid interjecting rebuttals while in the listener role. Couples are also taught how to take **time-outs** when their discussions escalate to the point that they are damaging or unproductive. They are also taught other **ground rules** to help them avoid negative or harmful strategies for handling conflict.

To help couples explore their expectations within the relationship, partners are given a set of questions to answer individually, and are then encouraged to share their responses with their partners. PREP asks couples to explore their expectations in a number of different areas, such as sexuality, children, spending time together, communication, and decision making. Another exercise encourages couples to identify and share with each other their core belief system. Individuals explore a number of aspects of their core belief system, including religious and spiritual values, core relationship values, and moral views.

To foster commitment, couples are educated regarding how thinking too much about alternatives to the relationship can ultimately lead to disappointment and even the breakup of a relationship. Couples are encouraged to focus their thoughts and energy on improving the current relationship rather than alternatives. They are also encouraged to take a long-term view of marriage, rather than a short-term view, which tends to be more reactive to current events in the relationship. PREP also invites individuals to explore whether their choices reflect their life priorities. The partners may discover, for example, that they need to devote more time to nurturing their relationship.

PREP helps couples enhance their relationship through fun, friendship, and sensuality using a number of techniques. Couples are asked to brainstorm fun activities they can do together, for example, and are then encouraged to set aside time for these activities. To nurture the friendship aspect of the relationship, they are asked to find time to spend with each other in order to share and talk together. Discussing issues or problem solving should be avoided during these times in order to protect the relationship from conflict. Couples are taught how to separate sexuality from sensuality, and are encouraged to do exercises that promote physical affection (e.g., hugging, massage) outside of sexual intercourse.

The PAIRS Program

The **Practical Application of Intimate Relationship Skills (PAIRS)** program is a comprehensive **psychoeducational** course designed to enhance participants' knowledge of self and their ability to sustain a pleasurable intimate relationship (Gordon and Durana, 1999). The program not only emphasizes learning skills but also an in-depth exploration of the self. PAIRS is offered in a group format and consists of 120 hours of training typically spread over four to five months. Participants range from well-functioning couples to highly distressed couples.

PAIRS is divided into five sections (Gordon and Durana, 1999). In the first section, participants learn communication skills such as empathic listening and speaking for oneself. Participants, for example, are taught how to use the PAIRS **Dialogue Guide** to express a range of thoughts, feelings, and assumptions by completing sentences that begin with word phrases such as "I notice," "I assume," "I am hurt by," and "I appreciate." This section also addresses negative communication styles and teaches skills for effectively resolving conflict. Participants also learn to identify **caring behaviors** and uncover hidden expectations or beliefs about love and relationships.

The second section focuses on exploration of the self. Participants uncover the early messages they learned about love and relationships, and explore how family-of-origin rules, myths, or loyalties may affect their current relationships. The creation of a **genogram,** a multigenerational family map, is used to facilitate this exploration. The impact that different roles or personality styles can have on intimacy is also addressed in this section.

The third section focuses on bonding. PAIRS emphasizes that accepting one's need for bonding is crucial to sustaining an intimate relationship. Participants learn, for example, attachment behaviors to build empathy for one's partner, to differentiate the need for bonding from the need for sex, and to free repressed emotions from the childhood and recent past. Couples are asked to identify, for example, caring behaviors they would like to see in their partners, as well as identify "turn-ons/turn-offs."

Enhancing the couple's physical intimacy is the focus of the fourth section. Couples explore the pleasures of physical bonding and touch, as well as their sensuality and sexuality. Early sexual decisions, sexual myths, and jealousy are other topics addressed in this section.

The fifth and final section is devoted to clarifying expectations and goals. Using the skills and insights developed throughout the program, couples negotiate a contract or set of expectations for their relationship.

PREPARE/ENRICH Program: Version 2000

A popular and commonly used premarital inventory among family therapists is **PREPARE/ENRICH.** PREPARE is used for couples preparing for marriage, and has a special version (PREPARE-MC) for couples with children. ENRICH was designed for married couples seeking enrichment, or for couples who have cohabited for more than two years. A fourth inventory, MATE, has been designed specifically for older couples who are fifty or over. The inventories are intended to facilitate couples talking about their relationships and to help them identify strengths and areas of growth within their relationship.

The PREPARE/ENRICH inventories contain 165 items, which measure the couple's relationship in twenty different areas (Olson and Olson, 1999). The inventories contain twelve content areas, including: Idealistic Distortion (which assesses the extent to which an individual is idealistic or realistic), Marriage Expectations (PREPARE and PREPARE-MC), or Marital Satisfaction (ENRICH), Personality Assessment, Communication, Conflict Resolution, Financial Management, Leisure Activities, Sexual Relationship, Children and Parenting, Family and Friends, Role Relationship, and Spiritual Beliefs. For each of these areas, couples receive feedback on whether it is a potential strength or potential growth area. Areas in which the partners are in close agreement with each other are identified as strengths, and areas in which the couple disagrees are identified as growth areas.

The inventories also contain four personality scales that measure Assertiveness, Self-Confidence, Avoidance, and Partner Dominance. Assertiveness measures a person's ability to express his or her feelings and desires to the partner; Self-Confidence measures how good the individual feels about himself or herself. Assertiveness and self-confidence mutually reinforce each other in a positive cycle (Olson and Olson, 1999). Avoidance measures an individual's reluctance to deal directly with issues. Partner Dominance measures how much the individual perceives that the partner tries to control him or her. Avoidance and partner dominance also mutually reinforce each other, but in a negative or undesirable cycle.

The inventories contain four scales that examine the level of **cohesion** and **flexibility** in the individual's family of origin and the level of cohesion and flexibility in the current couple relationship. The results from both partners are plotted on the Couple and Family Map to help the couple explore the relationship between the family of origin and the couple's relationship. A couple might explore, for example, how different levels of closeness or cohesion in their families of origin may influence their perceptions or expectations about closeness in their own relationship.

In addition to the inventory results, couples receive the twenty-five-page *Building a Strong Marriage Workbook,* which contains six exercises to develop skills and strengthen the couple's relationship. In the first exercise, each partner shares what he or she believes are the three strengths and three areas for growth in the relationship. Each partner's perceptions are discussed and compared with the feedback from the inventory. In the second exercise, each partner takes a turn sharing a three-item "wish list" with his or her partner, which is intended to help develop assertiveness and active listening skills. Couples discuss a growth area in their relationship using a ten-step model for resolving couple conflict in the third exercise. Steps in this model include, for example, clearly defining the problem, examining how each partner contributes to the problem, brainstorming possible solutions, and choosing and implementing one of the solutions. In the fourth exercise, couples go over the Couple and Family Map to discuss how their families of origin influence their relationship. In the fifth exercise, couples complete a budget worksheet and a list of short- and long-term financial goals. In the final exercise, partners share with each other their list of personal, couple, and family goals.

ACME-Style Marriage Enrichment

The Association for Couples in Marriage Enrichment (ACME) is a nonprofit organization whose mission is "to promote enrichment opportunities and resources that strengthen couple relationships and enhance personal growth, mutual fulfillment and family wellness" (ACME, 1993, p. 9). ACME trains couples to lead marriage enrichment groups in support of its mission.

ACME-style marriage enrichment typically has been done in one of four formats: (1) weekend retreats with a small number of couples; (2) one-and-a-half-day workshops, or miniretreats, for either a large or small groups of couples; (3) weekly meetings for a small group of couples that run four to six weeks; or (4) groups for a small number couples that meet regularly for a year or more (Dyer and Dyer, 1999). ACME leader couples determine the amount of structure and which exercises are used during an ACME event.

Leader couples, regardless of the format used, are trained to follow a five-stage process (Dyer and Dyer, 1999). In the first stage, security and community building, group leaders attempt to reduce the anxiety or ambivalence that couples may have about participating, and to develop a sense of connection among the couples in the group. Couples are encouraged to identify, for example, their fears and hopes about participating in marriage enrichment, and get acquainted with one another through ice-breaking erercises. In the second stage, development of awareness, couples are encouraged to evaluate their relationship, identifying both areas of strength and areas requiring change to make the relationship more fulfilling. Each partner, for example, might be asked to identify what he or she likes about the marriage, what could be better in the marriage, and what he or she is willing to do to make it better.

Development of knowledge and skills is the focus of the third stage. Communication, handling anger and conflict, and ways to build intimacy are among the skills emphasized in this stage. In the fourth stage, planning for growth, couples are encouraged to commit to intentional relationship growth and develop a specific plan for changing their marital interactions.

Couples develop three specific goals for their relationship and map out specific steps or actions they can take to meet their goals. In the fifth and final stage, celebration and closure, the goals are to reinforce commitment to the relationship and give appreciation to one's partner and others for the enrichment experience. Commitment may be reinforced by having couples share their growth plans with one another, or by having couples renew their marriage vows.

Throughout the five stages, a strong emphasis is given to couple dialogue. Couples typically discuss their relationship in private during the event to practice the skills or apply the ideas to their relationship. Another technique, **open couple dialogue,** is also used, in which couples talk about their relationship in front of other couples. Open couple dialogue is most often used by leader couples to model an exercise or skill for others in the group.

CASE EXAMPLES OF PREMARITAL COUNSELING IN CHURCH SETTINGS

The six programs discussed throughout this chapter represent the programs most commonly known to family therapists for communication training, marriage enrichment, and premarital counseling. The majority of premarital counseling today, however, continues to be offered through churches. Many churches require couples to participate in some form of marriage preparation or premarital counseling before getting married within that church. Through brief case examples, this section describes a variety of approaches that couples may encounter as they receive premarital counseling in church settings.

Case Example 1

Janna and Bill are both twenty-seven, and are preparing for their first marriage. Both are Lutheran, and they plan to have their wedding at the church that Janna currently attends. Pastor Dan agrees to meet with the couple for three sessions. He begins by asking the couple questions about their expectations regarding the marriage. Over time, Pastor Dan has developed a list of eight questions that he asks all couples. He begins by asking Janna and Bill to identify twelve reasons each why they want to marry the other person. After listening to their answers, Pastor Dan tells them that most couples will feel good about their marriage a year later if ten out of the twelve items still hold true, but adds that individuals are generally unhappy if the marriage is fulfilling six or fewer of the items. Next, he asks them to state their personal and collective goals for the next five, ten, and fifteen years. He informs them that their goals should be specific, measurable, compatible, and time bound. Janna and Bill both state they want to buy a home within the next five years. Pastor Dan encourages them to be more specific by asking them what size house they want. What size of down payment will they need? How much will they need to save each year to realize their goal? In the second session, the couple and Pastor Dan go over other questions, such as the couple's definition of love and marriage. Pastor Dan emphasizes that marriage equals commitment, and explores their reaction to this comment. In the third and final session, the couple and Pastor Dan go over the couple's wedding plans.

Case Example 2

Thomas and Virginia, thirty-three and twenty-nine years old respectively, are also preparing for their first marriage. Thomas is a practicing Catholic; Virginia identifies herself as Methodist, but does not regularly attend church. Thomas notified his priest of the couple's intention to get married at least six months in advance of the wedding as required by his church. Father Jerry met initially with the couple and explained that all couples preparing for marriage must take a premarital inventory called **FOCCUS** (Stahmann and Hiebert, 1997). Father Jerry explained to the couple that FOCCUS would give the couple feedback on their relationship in a variety of areas such as communication, problem solving, personality match, sexuality, and extended family. He added that the results from the inventory would be used as a springboard for the couple to discuss both strengths and areas of growth in their relationship. Thomas and Virginia were instructed to answer the questions without consulting each other, and to complete the questions on interfaith marriages since they were from different denominational backgrounds. Father Jerry spent two sessions going over the results of the inventory and asking the couple to discuss their responses with each other. The couple scored strongly in communication, problem solving, friends and interests, lifestyle expectations, and sexuality. The inventory showed the couple to have uncertainty or lack of agreement in four key areas: finances, family of origin, religion and values, and interfaith marriage. The couple spent considerable time, facilitated by Father Jerry, discussing their thoughts, feelings, and expectations in these areas.

Father Jerry also had the couple participate in an **Engaged Encounter** weekend, which is similar to Marriage Encounter (Elin, 1999), but is designed specifically for couples who are preparing for marriage. Father Jerry explained to Thomas and Virginia that the Engaged Encounter weekend was led by a team of married couples who would give several presentations based on their personal experiences. After each presentation, Thomas and Virginia would be given the opportunity to privately reflect on the presentation and discuss with each other the meaning the topic had for their relationship. After completing the Engaged Encounter weekend, the couple met with Father Jerry a final time to discuss the wedding ceremony.

Case Example 3

Heather and Brandon, twenty-one-year-old students, both Catholic, notified their priest that they were planning to marry in nine months. The couple was assigned to Linda and Craig, both who were in their late thirties and had been married for ten years. Linda and Craig were among six couples in the church who provided marriage preparation to couples such as Heather and Brandon through a mentoring program. Linda and Craig invited Heather and Brandon to their home for an initial meeting. After getting to know one another through conversation, Linda and Craig introduced Heather and Brandon to a workbook that both couples would complete together. Linda and Craig explained that the workbook would help Heather and Brandon explore important areas in their relationship through reflection and discussion. Linda and Craig indicated that they would also complete the exercises and share their answers with Heather and Brandon so they could benefit from their experiences. Heather and Brandon were encouraged to ask the couple any questions as they went through the process. Once a week during the next month, Linda and Craig invited the couple to their home where the two couples shared their responses to the reflective questions in the workbook.

Case Example 4

Dennis and Diane are a couple in their early forties, both previously married. The couple sought out premarital counseling from their church because they desired to be better prepared for marriage and avoid the mistakes from their earlier marriages. When the couple notified the church of their plans to marry, they were referred to a counselor with whom the church had contracted to do premarital counseling. The counselor, Dr. Ramirez, contracted with the couple to do a **Dynamic Relationship History** (Stahmann and Hiebert, 1997), a detailed history of the couple's relationship intended to uncover relational dynamics, issues, and patterns. Dr. Ramirez asked Dennis and Diane each to describe how they first met, their initial impressions of each other, and how their first dating experiences were. Questions of this nature helped to uncover what attracted Dennis and Diane to each other. Dr. Ramirez also explored how the partners decided to date seriously and how they became engaged, revealing how the couple developed a bond and commitment to each other. The couple's first fights and decisions were also explored, giving insight into the couple's conflict resolution skills and the distribution of power or influence within the relationship. Since both Dennis and Diane were previously married, a brief history of those marriages was explored. They also agreed to briefly explore their families of origin to see what potential influence they had on their relationships. One session each was devoted to constructing a three-generation family map or genogram of Dennis's and Diane's family of origin. Dr. Ramirez explored a variety of areas during the construction of the genogram, asking questions about individual family members, sibling interactions, parent-child interactions, and husband-wife interactions (Stahmann and Hiebert, 1997).

At the end of the relationship history and family-of-origin exploration, Dr. Ramirez gave the couple a summary of what he learned about their relationship. He shared with the couple how they seemed to have many strengths, such as their similar interests and shared religious and moral values. He also complimented them on their realistic expectations regarding finances and their sexual relationship. Dr. Ramirez noted, however, that Dennis and Diane seemed to have difficulty with issues of conflict and described how they seem to follow a distance-pursuing pattern. When Diane would raise an issue in the relationship, Dennis would often be a reluctant participant in the conversation. This would upset Diane, leading her to complain that Dennis did not seem to care about her or her concerns. Dennis would offer little in reply, trying to avoid escalating the fight. This would only make Diane more upset. After pointing out the pattern to Dennis and Diane, Dr. Ramirez helped the couple see how each person experienced the other's behavior and why each responded as they did. Dr. Ramirez talked about, for example, how men sometimes withdraw in order to avoid conflict, never recognizing how their action actually escalates the conflict. He also suggested that the couple's family-of-origin experiences could be contributing to the pattern. He noted, for example, how Dennis withdrawing could trigger Diane's fear of being abandoned, a fear she developed as a child growing up in a home with emotionally unavailable parents. Likewise, he observed that Dennis grew up in home with an alcoholic father who was abusive when drunk. Dennis learned to stay away from his father when he showed any signs of being upset, which likely contributed to him being fearful of conflict. The couple found the summary session very informative and agreed to continue seeing the counselor for an additional three sessions to address better ways of handling conflict in the relationship.

These case examples or vignettes illustrate the diversity of premarital counseling that is currently being practiced today. As in the first two vignettes, a common format for premarital counseling is to have the couple meet privately with a clergy member from the church in which the wedding will be held. The number and nature of these meetings can vary widely depending upon the clergy member. On one end of the spectrum, clergy may have only one session with the couple and focus primarily on wedding plans, with little attention given to preparing the couple for marriage. On the other end of the spectrum, clergy may devote several sessions to marriage preparation, exploring a variety of areas in the relationship. The most common areas addressed in premarital counseling include communication, conflict resolution, egalitarian roles, sexuality, commitment, finances, and personality issues (Silliman and Schumm, 1999).

The vignettes illustrate a variety of approaches that can be used in premarital counseling, such as using premarital inventories, conducting a relationship history, or exploration of the family of origin. In some cases, couples may participate in daylong or weekend programs, such as Engaged Encounter, with other engaged couples. These programs often include presentations or lectures in combination with opportunities for couples to discuss their relationship privately or with other couples. Premarital counseling in church settings may also include training in communication and conflict resolution skills through instruction or participation in a skills-based program such as PREP. **Christian PREP,** for example, incorporates scriptural guidelines into PREP (Stanley and Trathen, 1994).

Premarital counseling within a church setting is not the exclusive domain of clergy, as evidenced by the last three vignettes. Married couples may lead weekend retreats such as Engaged Encounter, or act as mentor or sponsor couples. In some churches, married couples, rather than clergy, administer and discuss the premarital inventory results with couples preparing for marriage. Some churches also turn to counseling professionals to perform the premarital counseling. These counselors may be part of the church staff, or they may be professionals within the community who are contracted to provide the services on an as-needed basis.

RELEVANT RESEARCH

Three areas of research related to premarital counseling and marriage enrichment are discussed in this section. The first part discusses the research that examines the general effectiveness of marriage enrichment and premarital counseling programs. The second part briefly highlights the available research on each of the six programs highlighted in this chapter. The third and final part examines research on designing effective premarital counseling programs.

Effectiveness of Marriage Enrichment and Premarital Counseling

One of the key studies that evaluated the effectiveness of preventative programs was a meta-analysis study by Giblin, Sprenkle, and Sheehan (1985). **Meta-analysis** is a powerful research tool that enables researchers to combine and compare results across different experimental studies. This in turn permits researchers to draw conclusions between and across studies using statistical analyses rather than judgments as used in traditional literature reviews. To conduct a meta-analysis, the results from the different studies must be standardized to a common unit of measure. This is accomplished by converting the original statistics (e.g., r, t, or F statistics) in the studies into a common statistic called the **effect size.** The effect size reflects how powerful the treatment effects were in comparison to the control (no treatment) or alternative treatment groups in the experiment.

Giblin, Sprenkle, and Sheehan found an average effect size of .44 for all types of premarital, marital, and family enrichment programs combined. An effect size of .44 means that the average person participating in a treatment program was better off than 67 percent of those who received no treatment. Further analyses revealed an effect size of .53 for premarital programs, an effect size of .42 for marital enrichment programs, and an effect size of .54 for family enrichment programs. Hahlweg and Markman (1988) also did a meta-analysis of behavioral premarital intervention programs and found an effect size of .55 for these programs relative to no treatment controls. Effect sizes of these magnitudes are considered in the medium range (Wampler and Serovich, 1996). Giblin, Sprenkle, and Sheehan (1985) noted that the effect size for the preventive approaches is smaller than the effect size of .85 for psychotherapy in general (see Smith, Glass, and Miller, 1980).

A survey by the Center for Marriage and Family at Creighton University found that married couples who had marriage preparation within the Catholic Church generally found the experience to be valuable (Williams et al., 1999), but the perceived value declined the longer the individual had been married. Among those who had been married twelve months or less, 87.5 percent agreed marriage preparation had been a valuable experience. By the seventh and eighth year of marriage, approximately half of the respondents (50.0 percent among those married seven years and 52.7 percent among those married eight years), agreed marriage preparation had been a valuable experience. This decline over time could be due to three possible factors. It is possible that individuals may simply forget the value of marriage preparation with the passage of time. Or, like some immunizations, it is possible that the benefits may wear off with time. Couples may need periodic booster sessions of marriage education throughout the marriage (Stanley and Markman, 1997). Finally, it is possible that marriage preparation, as currently practiced, is most helpful to couples during their initial adjustment to marriage. It may be less helpful for developmental tasks that couples may face in the future, such as raising children. Ideally, programs would also be available to prepare married couples for these later marital transitions, such as programs for first-time parents (Stanley and Markman, 1997).

Empirical Support for Specific Programs

Relationship Enhancement (RE)

RE has been one of the more extensively studied preventive programs. Cavedo and Guerney (1999) state that RE has been compared to several couple programs and "was found to be generally superior to the alternative treatment on either outcome or process measures" (p. 99). They cite, for example, several studies that show RE to be superior compared to a problem-solving program and relationship discussion program for premarital couples. They also note that in the meta-analysis by Giblin, Sprenkle, and Sheehan (1985), RE demonstrated the largest effect size (.96) among marriage enrichment programs.

COUPLE COMMUNICATION

COUPLE COMMUNICATION, similar to RE, has been extensively studied, with Miller and Sherrard (1999) reporting that over forty independent outcome studies have been conducted on the program. These studies support that COUPLE COMMUNICATION leads to the following changes: (1) improved communication behavior within couples; (2) improved perception by the couple of their ability to communicate; (3) improved perception of relationship quality; (4) increased self-disclosure; and (5) improved self-esteem. A meta-analysis comparing COUPLE COMMUNICATION to no treatment control found an effect size of .52 using relationship satisfaction as the outcome measure (Wampler and Serovich, 1996).

PREP

In their summary of the empirical evaluation and research on PREP, Stanley, Blumberg, and Markman (1999) state "that there are three streams of research that support the approach embodied in PREP" (p. 297). The first stream of research, discussed earlier in the chapter, centers on factors that put couples at risk for distress and divorce. PREP targets those factors that are amenable to change by teaching couples skills that improve their interactions and by educating them about the role that expectations, beliefs, and attitudes can play in relationships.

The second stream of research that the authors point to is the outcome studies conducted on PREP. In the United States, PREP therapy has been compared to matched control couples who received no treatment and followed longitudinally over time (Markman et al., 1988, 1993; Stanley et al., 1995). Couples who received PREP were better than control couples on a number of communication measures. They also reported fewer instances of physical violence and were less likely to divorce. At the five-year follow-up, for example, the incidence of divorce and separation was 8 percent for PREP couples, and 19 percent for the control group. After twelve years, 19 percent of PREP couples were divorced or separated compared to 28 percent of the control couples, although the difference was no longer statistically significant. Another outcome study in Germany compared a version of PREP to a mixed control group of couples, in which half received no treatment and half received treatment from alternative premarital programs (Stanley, Blumberg, and Markman, 1999). At the three-year follow-up, PREP couples were more satisfied than controls and had a lower incidence of divorce (1.6 percent versus 12.5 percent). After five years, PREP couples continued to report a lower incidence of divorce (4 percent versus 24 percent) compared to control couples. A third study in the Netherlands (Van Widenfelt et al., 1996) did not show the same promising results as those reported in U.S. and German studies. Stanley, Blumberg, and Markman

(1999) argue that methodological problems make interpretation of these results difficult; they are currently conducting a large-scale outcome study that will address some of these concerns.

One of the most impressive aspects of the PREP research is the length of time that couples are followed. Following couples longitudinally over a significant period of time is important for two reasons (Stanley, Blumberg, and Markman, 1999). First, differences between treatment and no-treatment groups are difficult to break out initially because most engaged couples are highly satisfied with their relationships, which researchers call a *ceiling effect*. Second, one of the outcomes of most interest is whether a couple stays married or divorces. Couples need to be followed over a sufficient length of time to see whether the interventions impact the long-term stability of the relationship.

Survey research is the third stream of research supporting PREP. In the study by the Center for Marriage and Family (Williams et al., 1999), which found that communication, commitment, and conflict resolution were rated as the most helpful areas of marriage preparation. PREP emphasizes the importance of each of these topics in the program.

PAIRS

In their summary of the research, Gordon and Durana (1999) discuss several studies that suggest PAIRS can lead to improvements in several areas, such as marital satisfaction, cohesion, and emotional well-being. A key limitation of the research, however, is that PAIRS participants have not been compared to control groups, giving less confidence in the results. They cite only one unpublished study by Turner that compared PAIR participants to control participants, which found that the PAIRS intervention had a positive impact on interaction style, social support, and marital discord. More empirical research using controlled, randomized experiments is clearly needed to confirm the initial, promising results for PAIRS.

PREPARE/ENRICH

According to Olson and Olson (1999), the PREPARE/ENRICH inventory has strong reliability and validity. They report that the **internal reliability** coefficients range from .74 to .89 for PREPARE; .73 to .84 for PREPARE-MC; and .74 to .89 for ENRICH. They also report the instrument has strong **test-retest reliability.** Studies have assessed the **predictive validity** of PREPARE (Fowers and Olson, 1986; Larsen and Olson, 1989), demonstrating that PREPARE has some ability to predict marital success after two to three years. Another study (Fowers and Olson, 1989) showed that ENRICH scores could successfully distinguish between happily and unhappily married individuals, giving evidence to its **discriminant validity.** The validity of PREPARE and ENRICH was established on earlier versions of the inventories; no published studies have assessed the predictive or discriminant validity of the inventories since their revision in 1996.

ACME-Style Marriage Enrichment

Dyer and Dyer (1999) report that limited research has been done on ACME-style marriage enrichment. They cite the lack of a prescribed program and the independence of leader couples as factors making it difficult to conduct a systematic evaluation of ACME-style marriage enrichment. Dyer and Dyer point to three studies in which participants in ACME-style marriage enrichment events did better than no-treatment controls on measures such as positive relationship change. One key limitation of these studies is that random assignment of participants to treatment and no-treatment groups was not used. Though initial results are promising, further research is needed to develop empirical confidence in this approach.

Research on Designing Premarital Counseling Programs

A study by the Center for Marriage and Family on marriage preparation among Catholics examined several aspects of marriage preparation design (Williams et al., 1999). Although the study was conducted among Catholics who received preparation primarily in a church setting, the results do provide important clues on designing marriage preparation programs. The study found, for example, that marriage preparation was most helpful to couples if it enabled them to spend time together and learn more about each other. Learning more about marriage, deepening one's relationship with God, and learning more about oneself were also important elements or benefits of marriage preparation. Consistent with previous research (Silliman, Schumm, and Jurich, 1992), the study found that marriage preparation was most helpful if presented by a team of providers. The findings suggest that both clergy and married couples should be included in marriage preparation if conducted through a church setting. The study also found that private meetings with clergy, weekend programs, and meetings with married couples were the three formats rated most helpful, which is consistent with another study that explored what engaged couples wanted from marriage preparation (Williams, 1992). The use of premarital inventories was found to be a helpful component of marriage preparation, probably because it helps couples learn more about their relationship and provides a springboard for couples to discuss their relationship. In their review of premarital inventories, Larson and his colleagues (1995) found PREPARE, FOCCUS, and PREP-M to be the most psychometrically sound of the inventories they reviewed. PREP-M has since been replaced by a newer version of the inventory called **RELATE.**

In terms of length of preparation, the study clearly showed that one session was not very helpful. Rather, eight to nine sessions appeared to provide optimum results, with more sessions not necessarily being more helpful. These results are consistent with research by Wright (1981), who found that only 15 percent of respondents who had attended only one session reported that marriage preparation definitely helped their marriage. In comparison, 75 percent of individuals who had attended seven or more sessions reported that marriage preparation had definitely helped their marriage. The topics rated most helpful in marriage preparation in the Center for Marriage and Family study were collectively labeled the "Five C's": communication, commitment, conflict resolution, children, and church. The fifth C, church, was a composite of religion and values with marriage covenant. The importance of communication and conflict resolution in this study is consistent with the emphasis that programs described in this chapter focus on teaching couples skills in these areas.

CONCLUSION

This chapter reviewed six well-known programs within the family therapy field that are used in premarital counseling and marital enrichment. This chapter also presented a variety of approaches and techniques used in premarital counseling within a church setting since premarital counseling is offered predominantly in this setting. Teaching couples skills for effectively communicating and managing conflict is an essential feature in each of the six programs presented in this chapter. The emphasis on these skills is supported by marital research, which shows the couple's ability to communicate and handle conflict is predictive of later marital success. Although the aim or goals of these programs are preventive in nature, distressed couples often seek out and participate in these programs as well. Elements of these programs can also be incorporated into couple therapy. To varying degrees, there is empirical support for the efficacy of these programs, although some programs clearly require additional research.

ADDITIONAL RESOURCES

The following resource list is provided for those would like more information on the programs highlighted in this chapter. The Coalition for Marriage, Family and Couples Education also sponsors a Web site <www.smartmarriages.com> that provides a listing of programs and resources for marriage education.

ACME-Style Enrichment—Contact Association for Couples in Marriage Enrichment (ACME), P.O. Box 10596, Winston-Salem, NC 27108; phone 1-800-634-8325; or <http://home.swbell.net/tgall/acme.htm>.

COUPLE COMMUNICATION—Contact Interpersonal Communication Programs, 7201 S. Broadway, Suite 11, Littleton, CO 80122; phone 1-800-328-5099.

FOCCUS—Contact Family Life Office, 3214 N. 60th Street, Omaha, NE 68104; phone 1-888-874-2684; or <http://www.foccusinc.com>.

PAIRS—Contact 1-888-742-7748; or <http://www. pairs.com>.

PREP—Contact PREP, Inc., P.O. Box 102530, Denver, CO 80250; phone 1-303-759-9934; or <http://www.PREPINC. com>.

PREPARE/ENRICH—Contact Life Innovations, P.O. Box 190, Minneapolis, MN 55440; phone 1-800-331-1661; or <http://www.life innovation.com>.

RELATE—Contact the Marriage Study Consortium, P.O. Box 25391, Provo, UT 84602 5391; phone 1-801-378-4359; or <http://relate. byu.edu>.

Relationship Enhancement (RE)—Contact the National Institute of Relationship Enhancement at 1-800-432-6454; or <http://www. nire.org>.

GLOSSARY

ACME-style marriage enrichment: Marriage enrichment programs led by couples trained through the Association for Couples in Marriage Enrichment (ACME). Through a five-stage process, couples develop greater awareness of their relationship, learn new skills and knowledge, and develop a plan for relationship growth.

Awareness Wheel: A tool used in COUPLE COMMUNICATION to help individuals explore and articulate different aspects of an issue, such as their feelings, thoughts, desires, and actions.

caring behaviors: Actions that demonstrate love and concern for an individual.

changing-self skill: A skill taught in Relationship Enhancement that helps individuals alter their own behavior.

Christian PREP: A version of PREP (Prevention and Relationship Enhancement Program) that integrates and reflects a commitment to traditional Christian principles.

cognitive-behavioral theory: A psychological theory that seeks to change feelings and behavior through challenging faulty thinking or beliefs.

cohesion: The amount of emotional closeness or distance within a couple or family.

communication theory: The study of relationships in terms of the exchange of verbal and nonverbal messages.

communication training: Any approach that emphasizes learning skills to effectively communicate and resolve conflict with other individuals.

conditioning: A process in which two stimuli are paired together and eventually become associated with one another.

contempt: Demonstrating disgust or lack of respect for an individual.

COUPLE COMMUNICATION: A preventative program designed to enhance couple relationships through teaching couples how to more effectively communicate and resolve conflicts.

couple therapy: Therapy that is intended to help couples who are already distressed or experiencing significant problems.

criticism: An attack against an individual's personality or character rather than complaining about a specific behavior.

defensiveness: A response to a complaint or criticism that implies the individual did nothing wrong. Defensiveness can manifest itself in many forms, such as making excuses or blaming another for the problem.

Dialogue Guide: A sentence completion exercise used in PAIRS to help individuals uncover and express their thoughts, feelings, and assumptions.

discriminant validity: Evidence as to whether an instrument is measuring what it is supposed to be measuring based on its ability to differentiate between two groups.

discussion and negotiation skill: A communication skill taught in Relationship Enhancement that helps individuals to uncover root issues and maintain a positive atmosphere when discussing difficult topics.

distance and isolation cascade: A process in which individuals begin to view their problems as severe, with the additional belief that there is no point in trying to work out problems with their partner. This can result in couples doing less and less together, creating feelings of loneliness in the relationship.

Dynamic Relationship History: An assessment technique in which a couple's relational dynamics, issues, and patterns are uncovered through collecting a detailed relationship history.

effect size: A statistic that measures the strength of the treatment effects in comparison to the control (no treatment) or alternative treatment conditions. Effect size can be used to standardize results across studies, allowing researchers to compare different studies through a technique called meta-analysis.

empathic skill: A communication skill taught in Relationship Enhancement that helps individuals understand the needs of a speaker.

Engaged Encounter: A weekend experience for engaged couples that emphasizes reflection and communication between couples.

escalation: A negative sequence of interaction in which partners respond to each other with increasingly negative comments or actions.

expressive skill: A communication skill taught in Relationship Enhancement that helps individuals communicate about themselves in a way that minimizes listener defensiveness.

facilitative skill: A communication skill taught in Relationship Enhancement that helps individuals exit negative communication cycles and resume using the RE skills.

flexibility: The degree of adaptability within a couple or family. At the extremes, couples can be either too rigid or chaotic.

flooded: A state of physical arousal accompanied by negative thoughts and feelings that can occur during conflict.

FOCCUS: A widely used premarital inventory that encourages couples to explore and discuss their relationships in a variety of topic areas.

Four Horsemen of the Apocalypse: Four characteristics in couple interactions that have been found through research to be predictive of divorce in couples. They are criticism, contempt, defensiveness, and stonewalling.

genogram: A multigenerational family map or family tree that is used to explore important events and psychological processes in the family of origin.

ground rules: Strategies in PREP that couples can use to protect a relationship from poorly handled conflict.

helping-others-change skill: A skill taught in Relationship Enhancement that helps individuals change the attitudes, behaviors, or feelings of others.

internal reliability: An indication of how consistent items are in what they measure. Higher scores (closer to 1.0) indicate greater consistency.

invalidation: Putting down the thoughts, feelings, or character of another person.

Listening Cycle: A conceptual map and tool used in COUPLE COMMUNICATION to help individuals develop better listening skills.

maintenance skill: A skill taught in Relationship Enhancement that helps individuals sustain using the other RE skills over time.

mapping an issue: An eight-step problem-solving approach to resolving conflict that is used in the COUPLE COMMUNICATION program.

marriage enrichment: Preventative programs designed to enhance and enrich relationships for married couples.

marriage labs: Laboratories designed to resemble living quarters to allow researchers to observe couple interactions in a setting that approximates real life.

meta-analysis: A statistical approach that allows one to compile and compare the results across several experimental studies. Results across studies can be compared by transforming the results into a common statistic called effect size.

negative interpretations: When an individual consistently believes the motives of his or her partner are more negative than they are in reality.

open couple dialogue: A technique in ACME-Style Marriage Enrichment in which a couple dialogues in front of other couples as a way of demonstrating and modeling effective communication skills.

Practical Application of Intimate Relationship Skills (PAIRS): A comprehensive course designed to enhance participants' knowledge of self and how to sustain a satisfying intimate relationship.

predictive validity: Evidence as to whether an instrument is measuring what it is supposed to be measuring based on its ability to predict some phenomenon.

premarital counseling: Programs designed to enhance engaged couples' relationships and prepare them for marriage.

PREPARE/ENRICH: PREPARE is a widely used premarital inventory that encourages unmarried couples to explore and discuss their relationship in a variety of topic areas before marriage. ENRICH is similar to PREPARE, but is intended for couples who are already married.

preventative approaches: Programs that generally attempt to teach couples skills and enhance relationships before the onset of major problems.

Prevention and Relationship Enhancement Program (PREP): A preventive program designed to teach couples effective communication and conflict resolution skills as well as enhance commitment and bonding within the relationship.

problem/conflict resolution skill: A skill taught in Relationship Enhancement that helps couples discover creative solutions to their problems.

psychoeducational: An approach that emphasizes educating clients about psychological processes.

RELATE: A widely used premarital inventory that encourages couples to explore and discuss their relationship in a variety of topic areas.

Relationship Enhancement (RE): A skills based program that primarily focuses on teaching couples effective communication and conflict resolution skills.

skill mats: Thirty-inch square floor mats with either the Awareness Wheel or Listening Cycle printed on them. Skill mats are a technique used in COUPLE COMMUNICATIONS.

social learning theory: A psychological theory that stresses learning by observation and imitation.

speaker-listener technique: A technique in which one person is designated as the speaker and the other person the listener. The speaker must follow certain guidelines, such as speaking only about his or her own experience, while the listener paraphrases only what the speaker is saying without interjecting his or her own thoughts or feelings.

stonewalling: When an individual withdraws or stops participating in a discussion or argument.

test-retest reliability: An indication of how consistently an instrument performs over time.

time-outs: A technique in which either partner requests that the couple temporarily suspend discussing an issue when the conflict reaches a point where it is destructive or unproductive.

transfer and generalization skill: A skill taught in Relationship Enhancement that helps individuals utilize the other RE skills in everyday life with people other than their partners.

withdrawal/avoidance: A reluctance to talk about important issues.

REFERENCES

Association for Couples in Marriage Enrichment (ACME) (1993). *Strategic plan.* Winston-Salem, NC: Author.

Berger, R. and Hannah, M. T. (Eds.) (1999). *Preventive approaches in couples therapy.* Philadelphia: Brunner/Mazel.

Cavedo, C. and Guerney, B. J. (1999). Relationship enhancement enrichment and problem-prevention programs: Therapy-derived, powerful, versatile. In R. Berger and M. T. Hannah (Eds.), *Preventive approaches in couples therapy* (pp. 73-105). Philadelphia: Brunner/Mazel.

Dyer, P. M. and Dyer, G. H. (1999). Marriage Enrichment, A.C.M.E. style. In R. Berger and M. T. Hannah (Eds.), *Preventive approaches in couples therapy* (pp. 28-54). Philadelphia: Brunner/Mazel.

Elin, R. J. (1999). Marriage Encounter: A positive preventive enrichment program. In R. Berger and M. T. Hannah (Eds.), *Preventive approaches in couples therapy* (pp. 55-72). Philadelphia: Brunner/Mazel.

Fowers, B. J. and Olson, D. H. (1986). Predicting marital success with PREPARE: A predictive validity study. *Journal of Marital and Family Therapy, 12,* 403-413.

Fowers, B. J. and Olson, D. H. (1989). ENRICH marital inventory: A discriminant validity and cross-validation assessment. *Journal of Marital and Family Therapy, 15,* 65-79.

Giblin, P., Sprenkle, D. H., and Sheehan, R. (1985). Enrichment outcome research: A meta-analysis of premarital, marital and family interventions. *Journal of Marital and Family Therapy, 11,* 257-271.

Gordon, L. H. and Durana, C. (1999). The PAIRS Program. In R. Berger and M. T. Hannah (Eds.), *Preventive approaches in couples therapy* (pp. 217-236). Philadelphia: Brunner/Mazel.

Gottman, J. M. (1994). *Why marriages succeed or fail.* New York: Simon and Schuster.

Gottman, J. M. and Gottman, J. S. (1999). The Marriage Survival Kit: A research-based marital therapy. In R. Berger and M. T. Hannah (Eds.), *Preventive approaches in couples therapy* (pp. 304-330). Philadelphia: Brunner/Mazel.

Guerney, B. G. (1977). *Relationship Enhancement*. San Francisco: Jossey-Bass.

Hahlweg, K. and Markman, H. J. (1988). Effectiveness of behavioral marital therapy: Empirical status of behavioral techniques in preventing and alleviating marital distress. *Journal of Consulting and Clinical Psychology, 56,* 440-447.

Larsen, A. S. and Olson, D. H. (1989). Predicting marital satisfaction using PREPARE: A replication study. *Journal of Marital and Family Therapy, 15,* 311-322.

Larson, J. H., Holman, T. B., Klein, D. M., Busby, D. M., Stahmann, R. F., and Peterson, D. (1995). A review of comprehensive questionnaires used in premarital education and counseling. *Family Relations, 44,* 245-252.

Markman, H. J., Floyd, F. J., Stanley, S. M., and Storaasli, R. D. (1988). Prevention of marital distress: A longitudinal investigation. *Journal of Consulting and Clinical Psychology, 56,* 210-217.

Markman, H. J., Renick, M. J., Floyd, F. J., Stanley, S. M., and Clements, M. (1993). Preventing marital distress through communication and conflict management training: A 4- and 5-year follow-up. *Journal of Consulting and Clinical Psychology, 61,* 1-8.

Markman, H., Stanley, S., and Blumberg, S. (1994). *Fighting for your marriage: Positive steps for preventing divorce and preserving a lasting love.* San Francisco: Jossey-Bass.

Miller, S. and Sherrard, P. (1999). COUPLE COMMUNICATION: A system for equipping partners to talk, listen, and resolve conflicts effectively. In R. Berger and M. T. Hannah (Eds.), *Preventive approaches in couples therapy* (pp. 125-148). Philadelphia: Brunner/Mazel.

Olson, D. H. and Olson, A. K. (1999). PREPARE/ENRICH Program: Version 2000. In R. Berger and M. T. Hannah (Eds.), *Preventive approaches in couples therapy* (pp. 196-216). Philadelphia: Brunner/Mazel.

Silliman, B. and Schumm, W. R. (1999). Improving practice in marriage preparation. *Journal of Sex and Marital Therapy, 25,* 23-43.

Silliman, B., Schumm, W. R., and Jurich, A. P. (1992). Young adults' preference for premarital preparation designs: An exploratory study. *Contemporary Family Therapy, 14,* 89-100.

Smith, M., Glass, G., and Miller, T. (1980). *Benefits of psychotherapy.* Baltimore: John Hopkins Press.

Stahmann, R. F. and Hiebert, W. J. (1997). *Premarital and remarital counseling: The professional's handbook.* San Francisco: Jossey-Bass.

Stanley, S. M., Blumberg, S. L., and Markman, H. J. (1999). Helping couples fight for their marriages: The PREP approach. In R. Berger and M. T. Hannah (Eds.), *Preventive approaches in couples therapy* (pp. 279-303). Philadelphia: Brunner/Mazel.

Stanley, S. M. and Markman, H. J. (1997). Acting on what we know: The hope of prevention. Paper presented at the Family Impact Seminar, Washington, DC, June.

Stanley, S. M., Markman, H. J., St. Peters, M., and Leber, B. D. (1995). Strengthening marriages and preventing divorce. *Family Relations, 44,* 392-401.

Stanley, S. M. and Trathen, D. W. (1994). Christian PREP: An empirically based model for marital and premarital intervention. *Journal of Psychology and Christianity, 13,* 158-165.

Van Widenfelt, B., Hosman, C., Shaap, C., and van der Staak, C. (1996). The prevention of relationship distress for couples at risk: A controlled evaluation with nine-month and two-year follow-ups. *Family Relations, 45,* 156-165.

Wampler, K. S. and Serovich, J. M. (1996). Meta-analysis in family therapy research. In D. H. Sprenkle and S. M. Moon (Eds.), *Research methods in family therapy* (pp. 286-303). New York: Guilford Press.

Williams, L. M. (1992). Premarital counseling: A needs assessment among engaged individuals. *Contemporary Family Therapy, 14,* 505-518.

Williams, L. M., Riley, L. A., Risch, G. S., and Van Dyke, D. T. (1999). An empirical approach to designing marriage preparation programs. *American Journal of Family Therapy, 27,* 271-283.

Wright, H. N. (1981). *Premarital counseling,* Second edition. Chicago: Moody Press.

Chapter 12

Sexual Dysfunctions and Sex Therapy

Joan D. Atwood

The demand for treatment for sexual problems has increased in the past three decades. This is in large part due to increased public knowledge that effective treatments are available and the growing recognition that these problems are comparable to other behavioral difficulties and therefore often respond to behavioral treatment (Hawton, 1983). There is also increased awareness within the fields of marriage and family therapy, social work, and clinical psychology that sex therapy should be a primary part of training in these areas. Thus, professionals in these disciplines are now more likely to ask couples about the sexual aspects of their relationship. As De Silva (1992) points out, training in sex therapy need not be an elective specialization; rather, it should be an essential component of the training of every practitioner.

SEXUAL PROBLEMS

Sexual dysfunctions or problems are impairments or disturbances in sexual desire, arousal, or orgasm. They are usually considered to be a group of problems within "normal" sexuality, different from **sexual deviations** or **paraphilias** (although overlap can occur, for example, a male presenting with erectile dysfunction with his wife may, upon close inquiry, show a history of paraphiliac sexual activity) and the two are treated as separate clinical categories. It is also important to keep in mind that sexual dysfunctions cannot be considered mutually exclusive from the nondysfunctions. Functional and dysfunctional presentations are considered to be on the same continuum. In other words, there are degrees of dysfunction and, in one person or in a couple, areas of satisfactory sexual activity alongside areas of difficulty. Also consider the social aspect: what is considered dysfunctional may vary from person to person, from couple to couple, and from society to society. In addition, many couples would consider their sexuality a normal and therefore would not become a part of a clinical population; yet a certain proportion of them would report their sexual behavior as less than satisfactory. Frank, Anderson, and Rubinstein (1978) reported that 80 percent of their happily married couples reported that their sexual relations were happy and satisfactory, even though 40 percent of the men reported erectile or ejaculatory problems and over 60 percent of the women reported problems of arousal or orgasm.

Several factors appear to be associated with sexual dysfunctions, including sexual ignorance, attitude, anxiety level, fears of performance, and the quality of the couple's relationship. Sexual ignorance, or lack of proper information about the various aspects of sex, is sometimes a major contributory factor in these disorders (Bancroft, 1989; Zilbergeld, 1978). Another important factor is the person's attitude toward sex and sexual activity (Spence, 1991; Zilbergeld, 1978, 1992). Anxiety is associated with sexual dysfunction in that some difficulties can be caused by anxiety and others can be maintained by it (Bancroft, 1989; Lief, 1977; Masters and Johnson, 1970). For example, a young male may fear getting caught by his parents when he is having sex and this may keep him from achieving erection. In another situation, he may become anxious about getting an erection in the first place.

Fears of performance are a significant factor in sexual difficulties. Fears of performance may affect males or females, although it is most obvious in males. These fears of performance may lead to an avoidance of sex, loss of self-esteem, loss of spontaneity in the relationship, or it may negatively affect the relationship in general. In this case, one or both partners assume a spectator role, often judging personal sexual performance. This creates less of an involvement in the sexual activity and eventually a loss of arousal and/or erection. In addition, this could lead to a loss of intimacy in the relationship as couples often report that it feels as if a third person is in the room rating their sexual performance.

Generally speaking, a **self-fulfilling prophecy** occurs when this "spectator" rates his or her own sexual performance, which creates less of an involvement in natural spontaneous sexuality, which often leads to a decreased state of arousal, causing the spectator to believe his or her sexual performance is less than adequate, causing more performance fears, etc. This is also known as **spectatoring** (Masters and Johnson, 1970). This refers to the tendency of a person to watch and possibly judge himself or herself during sexual activity. This may lead to inhibited sexual action and enjoyment or true failure of the sexual experience.

The association between the quality of the couple's relationship and their sexual problems is evident (Crowe and Ridley, 1990; Woody, 1992). Sexual difficulties can emerge in a poor marital relationship. Jealousy fears and worries about infidelity or constant conflicts in areas other than sex may contribute to, or be reflected by, a sexual problem. Sex sometimes may become a battleground for marital conflicts, such as those associated with dominance, jealousy, and punitiveness (Harbin and Gamble, 1977). Equally, a sexual problem can cause wider relationship difficulties and when couples present with marital problems it is not unusual for a specific sexual problem to be present as well.

Some sexual problems are caused by or associated with physical factors. The relevance of such factors as alcoholism, diabetes, aging, neurological damage, prescription drug and street drug use, and so on, to sexual activity is well established (Bancroft, 1989; Kolodny, Masters, and Johnson, 1979). The presenting sexual problem may be a manifestation of the underlying physical problem.

Sexual problems can produce as much anguish and sorrow in those who suffer from them as any psychological disorder. Many people cannot help but feel that their masculinity or femininity is affected if a sexual problem is present. Failing to achieve sexual gratification in a relationship often affects the couple's experience of the whole relationship as well.

Many useful classifications of sexual dysfunctions exist (see American Psychiatric Association, 1987; Bancroft, 1989; De Silva, 1994; Hawton, 1985; Kaplan, 1974; Masters and Johnson, 1970). See Table 12.1 for a simple list of possible sexual dysfunctions that occur for each gender.

Dysfunctions may be considered **primary sexual problems** (total, present in all circumstances) or **secondary sexual problems** (situational, present in some circumstances only) depending upon whether the individual has ever been asymptomatic. A man with primary impotence has never had the ability to maintain a successful erection or ejaculation. The anorgasmic female has never had an orgasm. Secondary problems occur where the individual was sexually functional and then, because of situational factors, develops the dysfunction, such as when premature ejaculation happens in sexual intercourse but not during masturbation.

The two major areas of male dysfunction include disorders of potency and ejaculation.

Impotence or Erectile Dysfunction

Impotence or **erectile dysfunction** is defined as the inability to achieve or maintain an erection. Primary impotence tends to be rare and, according to **Masters and Johnson** (1970), occurs in 1 percent of males under age thirty-five. Secondary erectile dysfunction is said to occur if erection is insufficient to engage in sexual intercourse. This occurs approximately 25

TABLE 12.1. Sexual Dysfunctions

Males	Females
Low sexual interest	Low sexual interest
Erectile dysfunction	Lack of response
Premature ejaculation	Anorgasmia
Retarded ejaculation	Vaginismus
Dyspareunia	Dyspareunia
Sexual aversion	Sexual aversion

percent of the time. The basic premise of the therapy for this disorder is that anxiety disrupts erectile response. Thus, the object of therapy is to diminish the anxiety sufficiently.

Although current psychological treatment for erectile dysfunction has changed very little since its inception (Zilbergeld, 1992), medical treatment options have increased dramatically. The use of sensate focus is supplemented with cognitive techniques used to promote relaxation, positive self-statements, sexual fantasy, and the restoration of self-confidence. For men with lifelong erectile problems, individual psychodynamic treatment has been suggested along with sex therapy (Althof, 1989). Beck and Barlow (1984) have found that men with erectile dysfunction pay more attention to how much of an erection they have and less attention to their feelings of arousal.

The treatment of erectile dysfunction has become increasingly medical in the past ten to fifteen years. Drugs, devices, and surgery dominate the field. Recently there has been a report of successful treatment using an adrenergic antagonist drug (Assalian, 1988). Sildenafil citrate (Viagra), a Type-V phosphodiesterase inhibitor, also has been demonstrated to be an effective medication for the treatment of erectile dysfunction via arteriolar smooth muscle relaxation in the **corpus cavernosum,** which increases blood flow to promote penile **tumescence** (Goldstein et al, 1998; Moreland, Goldstein, and Traish, 1998; Wise, 1999). Although this drug may be successful as a medical treatment for erectile dysfunction, it is important to explore with the couple the psychological changes that have occurred in the marital relationship as a result. For example, unrealistic expectations, inadequate information regarding sexuality, and marital difficulties could be problems associated with poor outcomes. In some cases, marriages may dissolve following successful sexual results due to medical or psychotherapeutic intervention. It is possible that the marriages were stable with the sexual dysfunction and once the dysfunction was removed, instability ensued. Research is greatly needed in this area.

Although most urologists believe that the vast majority of erectile problems have an organic basis (LoPiccolo, 1992), there are several problems with this view. For example, it is often quoted that 50 to 90 percent of erectile problems have an organic basis, but this definition is usually made without examination of age. If one looks at men under the age of fifty with erectile dysfunction, the percentage drops drastically (Seagraves and Seagraves, 1992). The other problem is inattention to normal changes in erectile response that occur with age (Schiavi et al., 1990). Healthy men over age fifty who report good sexual function have tumescence test results (tests that measure how much blood is in the penis or how erect the penis is) that look just as abnormal as men reporting erectile dysfunction (Schiavi et al., 1990). This means that there is erectile variety in the male sexual response.

It is important to note that even when urologists see a man with a purely psychological basis to his sexual problem, they often prescribe nonsurgical treatment such as **intracavernous injection therapy** or **vacuum erection devices.** They contend their patients will not go to a mental health professional, or perhaps there are no sex therapists in their community, or that sex therapy is too expensive and insurance does not cover it. Some evidence suggests that a combination of sex therapy with injection therapy might be helpful in alleviating a man's anxiety, which would help him later achieve firmer erections without the medication (Bahren et al., 1989; Kaplan, 1990; Turner et al., 1989). It is important to keep in mind, however, that these studies tend to downplay an important side effect of injection therapy, which is the incidence of **fibrosis** (scarring of the soft tissue of the penis) (Lakin et al., 1990). Severe cases of fibrosis, which occurs in about a third of men using injection therapy, can cause pain and curvature of the penis during erection. Support for men with erectile dysfunction can be obtained from Impotence Anonymous, a national organization located at 119 South Rush Street, Maryville, Tennessee 37801. This organization offers therapy for men and their partners.

Premature Ejaculation

Masters, Johnson, and Kolodny (1985) believe that **premature ejaculation** affects 15 to 20 percent of all men. It is difficult to define premature ejaculation. A common definition is: given a normal, healthy, functioning partner, premature ejaculation is the inability to delay ejaculation long enough to bring the partner to orgasm.

The treatment of premature ejaculation is based on the assumption that it is possible to exert conscious control over ejaculation, and the man can learn to prolong erection when sexually aroused. The main components of this treatment program involve couple communication and increasing the ability of the male to perceive impending orgasm.

The **squeeze technique** is a common approach used to treat this disorder. The couple is encouraged to engage in foreplay until the male achieves erection. He is asked to let his partner know when he is approaching the feeling of inevitability of orgasm. The partner then can use the squeeze technique or stop activity until the sensation subsides. The squeeze technique involves squeezing the penis just below the glans, with the thumb on one side and forefinger on the opposite side, gently but with sufficient force to diminish the impending sensation of orgasm. The exercise can be repeated several times. Next, intercourse in the female superior position is suggested so that the squeeze technique may be more easily applied and/or intercourse can be interrupted. In addition, several self-help techniques have been proposed. For example, the use of a condom seems to help lower the sensitivity of the penis because the glans is not stimulated directly. Some men drink an alcoholic beverage to decrease the rapidity of their response; others masturbate before intercourse knowing that the second orgasm will take longer. Kaplan suggests using the **stop-start technique** (in which intercourse proceeds until the feeling of impending orgasm and then stops until the male determines that the feeling has subsided) first developed by Semans (1956).

Retarded Ejaculation or Ejaculatory Incompetence

Ejaculatory incompetence is the inability of an erect penis to ejaculate. Masters and Johnson (1970) say that it occurs in less than 5 percent of men, usually those who are younger and sexually inexperienced. If a man has never ejaculated within the vagina, he is said to have primary ejaculatory incompetence. If he has been able to ejaculate in the vagina previously but currently cannot, then he has secondary ejaculatory incompetence. These men may be able to ejaculate via masturbation or oral sex.

An unintended side effect that could occur with this disorder is that the male is able to maintain sexual intercourse for long periods of time without ejaculating. This may be considered a positive effect by the particular male and his partner. On the other hand, in some cases the male may begin to question his partner's sexual abilities, or the female may feel that her partner is not physically attracted to her. **Sensate focus exercises** are used to treat retarded ejaculation. Sensate focus is basically sensual touching. The partners touch each other first in nonerogenous zone areas focusing on the pleasurable sensations. This enables the man to focus on his sexual and sensual feelings. In a stepwise fashion, the man learns to ejaculate via masturbation alone, then by masturbating with his partner present, and then having his partner masturbate him to the point of **ejaculatory inevitability,** eventually inserting the penis in the vagina to actually ejaculate.

Low Sexual Interest

Lief (1977) and Kaplan (1979) are responsible for the labeling of low sexual desire as a sexual dysfunction. This was based on their observations that the lack of motivation to have sex was a crucial factor in unsuccessful sex therapy cases. In the case of males, no erection occurs and no urges to engage in sexual behavior are felt. In the case of females, she experiences a lack of sexual arousal. Physically, she does not lubricate vaginally and no change in the vaginal size occurs to accommodate the penis. The causes of **low sexual interest** may include organic as well as **psychogenic factors.** Approximately 10 to 20 percent of men with low sexual interest have pituitary tumors that cause too much of the hormone **prolactin** to be produced. This hormone reduces the amount of testosterone and can lead to low sexual interest or erectile dysfunction (Schwartz, Bauman, and Masters, 1983). Sexual unresponsiveness can also be caused by psychogenic factors such as shame, poor self-esteem, a bad relationship, guilt, or embarrassment about sexual activity or one's body, or a history of sexual abuse. Before any treatment can begin, the etiological factors must be identified.

The goal here is to create a nondemanding, relaxed, and sensuous environment in which mutually gratifying sexual activity can take place. For the woman, the sensate focus exercise is critical in assisting her to relax and in some cases to help her learn about her own sexuality. The female superior position is often helpful because it increases female sensitivity. However, a review of the current treatment programs for sexual desire disorders reveals that current approaches are more eclectic than the original behavioral techniques (see Leiblum and Rosen, 1988).

Anorgasmia or Orgasmic Dysfunction

Not all women experience orgasm. This is known as **anorgasmia** or **orgasmic dysfunction.** Orgasmic dysfunction occurs in a woman who is sexually responsive but does not reach orgasm when aroused. Many women report that they enjoy sexual intercourse even though they do not orgasm. Primary orgasmic dysfunction occurs in women who have never had an orgasm by any means. If a woman has experienced an orgasm at one time in her life, the current problem is said to be secondary orgasmic dysfunction. Situational orgasmic dysfunction occurs situationally. For example, a woman may have an orgasm during masturbation but not during sexual intercourse, or with one partner and not another.

Kaplan (1974) reports that approximately 8 percent of women are anorgasmic by any means for unknown reasons. Approximately 10 percent of women are coitally anorgasmic (Kinsey, Pomeroy, and Martin, 1953; Levin and Levin, 1975). Only 30 to 40 percent of women report that they regularly experience orgasm through sexual intercourse without having the clitoris manually stimulated at the same time (Hite, 1976; Ellison, 1980). Only about 5 percent of the cases of orgasmic dysfunction are the result of organic factors (Masters, Johnson, and Kolodny, 1985). The organic causes involved include diabetes, alcoholism, hormone deficiencies, or pelvic infections. The other 95 percent are the result of psychogenic causes, such as guilt or shame associated with sexual activity. These states of mind tend to interfere with a woman's ability to relax and let go.

In general, the basic task is to facilitate the female to let go of an over-controlled response. This involves maximizing clitoral stimulation and at the same time diminishing those forces that inhibit orgasm. The major objective is for the woman to have an orgasm. Masturbation is encouraged. Vibrators may be used. She is encouraged to fantasize, to try thrusting movements. She is encouraged to use **Kegeling exercises** (starting and stopping the flow of urine in order to strengthen the vaginal muscles) to strengthen the muscle used in orgasm. Next, once the woman has achieved an orgasm, she may work with her partner to achieve orgasm through intercourse. First, he should manually stimulate her. Next, the bridge technique can be used, in which he continues to stimulate her clitoris during intercourse. Female superior position is used since this maximizes female stimulation and allows her freedom of movement. These techniques were all set forth in the 1970s. The only alternatives have been the incorporation of systemic and psychodynamic marital therapy into the sex therapy sessions. The outcome studies report that more success occurs with women who have never had an orgasm than with women who enter therapy because they want to increase their ability to have orgasms with their partners (DeAmicis et al., 1985; Hawton et al., 1986).

Vaginismus

Vaginismus is defined as the involuntary spastic contraction of the outer one-third of the vagina. Vaginismus may cause severe pain (**dyspareunia**) and as a result the female may avoid sexual activity. Masters, Johnson, and Kolodny (1985) estimate that 2 to 3 percent of all postadolescent women experience vaginismus. Generally, they do not have a problem with sexual arousal. The causes of vaginismus are usually psychogenic and generally related to shame, fear, and embarrassment. Dyspareunia can sometimes lead to vaginismus. Masters and Johnson (1970) found that vaginismus is associated with erectile dysfunction in a woman's partner, strong religious teachings against sexuality, homosexual feelings, a history of sexual assault, and negative or hostile feelings for one's partner.

The successful treatment of vaginismus most often utilizes behavioral techniques focused on modifying a conditioned response. Often **vaginal dilators** of progressive size are used, combined with Kegel exercises to teach control of circumvaginal muscles, cognitive restructuring to alleviate guilt about sexuality or to resolve past sexual trauma, and attention to systemic marital issues or intrapsychic problems. The dilators are generally used in the doctor's office with or without the partner's presence. The woman must learn to allow for the presence of the dilator without the conditioned fear response. The goal is to decrease the woman's fear and anxiety sufficiently so that penetration can occur. Encouragement and support by the partner is crucial (Lazarus, 1989; Leiblum, Pervin, and Cambell, 1989).

Dyspareunia

Dyspareunia is painful intercourse, and it may occur in men as well as women. In men, dyspareunia may be caused by infection in the penis, foreskin, testes, urethra, or the prostate, as well as allergic reactions to spermicidal creams or foams. Some men complain of sensitivity to the string of the IUD if their partner has an intrauterine device. They experience dyspareunia as pain in the penis, the testes, or the glans area. In women, pelvic inflammatory disease, endometriosis, tumors, rigid **hymen,** yeast infections, creams, or many other factors, may cause dyspareunia. Although many women experience pain at some point during sexual intercourse, dyspareunia is chronic. The pain could manifest as a burning sensation or a cramping. It could occur externally in the vaginal area or internally in the pelvic area. Masters and Johnson estimate that approximately 1 to 2 percent of women experience dyspareunia on a regular basis.

Sexual Aversion

Some people have an irrational fear—a **phobia**—of sexual activity, which leads them to avoid it. Not much has been written about sexual aversion. There are little data concerning the prevalence of the disorder or success of any type of treatment program. Individuals with this disorder respond to sexual activity in a phobic way, including avoidance. When they are approached for sexual behavior, they may experience nausea, stress reaction, increased heart rate, muscle tension, and/or diarrhea. Sexual aversion is usually caused by severe negative attitudes toward sexuality expressed by the individual's parents during childhood (LoPiccolo, 1985). Also related is the consistent pressuring by a partner or gender confusion in men (Masters, Johnson, and Kolodny, 1985). Many clients with sexual aversion disorder have a history of childhood molestation or adult sexual trauma.

Most clinicians would agree that treatment of sexual aversion should include some sort of **systematic desensitization** to the aversive sexual behavior, along with an introduction and focus on the ability to experience sexual pleasure. Treatment techniques also include suggestions for avoiding **flashbacks** in sexual situations and the necessity of recovering memories in psychotherapy (Maltz and Holman, 1987). Kaplan's (1987) model of sexual phobias broadened the concept of aversion to sex. She suggested pharmacological treatment as an important adjunct to sex therapy. Her view, however, still needs to be empirically tested.

DIAGNOSIS AND ASSESSMENT

Couple therapists dealing with sexual issues are involved in four areas of assessment that are not adequately described in the literature. They are the identification of organic causes; the identification of psychological issues; the examination of interpersonal factors; and the assessment of **systemic** issues.

Organic Factors

Organic factors can affect sexual functioning. They may be the direct cause, the primary cause, or a contributing factor. Even in sexually dysfunctional clients who are seemingly organically intact, usually some biophysiological processes can be implicated in the sexual dysfunction (for a more detailed description of these factors, see Kolodny, Masters, and Johnson, 1979). For this reason, the marriage and family therapist should have a basic knowledge of the potential organic factors that can cause sexual symptoms.

Some Physical Causes of Sexual Dysfunctions

- Biochemical/physiological disorders may serve to decrease sexual interest or energy. This category includes **cardiopulmonary, hepatic, renal, endocrine,** and **degenerative diseases** as well as **malignancies.**
- Diseases such as mumps, tuberculosis, or tumors may serve to affect **libido** or arousal. In addition, tumors, infections, or invasive surgeries can negatively impact libido.
- Anatomic or mechanical interference includes **endometriosis, prostatitis, urethritis, pelvic inflammatory disease (PID),** and conditions such as **priapism, phimosis, clitoral adhesions** can make intercourse painful.
- Postsurgery with neurological or vascular damage can affect sexual drive. Included in this group are problems in abdominal aortic surgery, complications from a hysterectomy, or problems related to a prostatectomy.
- Neurological disorders include damage to the higher nerve centers as in **spina bifida, temporal or frontal lobe damage, multiple sclerosis,** or surgery or trauma to the sacral or lumbar cord. In this case, the effect is generally to increase or decrease sexual drive. When there is spinal damage, sexual drive may not be affected but erectile response, ejaculation, or orgasm in females might be.
- **Vascular disorders** may cause erectile problems in males by interfering with vascular flow to the penis.
- Endocrine disorders can depress sexual drive by decreasing androgen levels.
- Genetic or congenital disorders such as **Klinefelter's syndrome** may result in impotence in males. Undescended testes in males may affect sexual response.
- Drugs and medication may have a direct or indirect effect on sexual functioning. Although many drugs are said to be **aphrodisiacs,** this is more myth than fact. Currently, no drug can be considered a specific aphrodisiac.

Assessment and diagnosis should include some of these relevant questions:

- Is there a physical disease or disability (e.g., renal failure, circulatory problems, diabetes)?
- Does the partner of the person who is presenting the sexual dysfunction have a disease? The person may be responding to the partner's

postcardiac vulnerability, cancer, **prostatectomy,** or **mastectomy.** If illness or injury permanently affects sexual function of the partner, body image and sexual role behavior may be ignored.

- Is the client taking any drugs that could affect sexual function (e.g., hypertensive medicine, alcohol, methadone, and even over-the-counter medications)? The author once had a client who had seen a psychologist for painful intercourse for two years. As it turned out, the client was addicted to Dristan, an over-the-counter medication that dries up mucous membranes. The problem was that it dries up *all* mucous membranes, including the vagina! This client could have gone for psychotherapy for twenty years and, unless the therapist asked the right questions, the true problem would have remained uncovered and the sexual problem would have prevailed.
- Has the person had any surgery such as **prostate gland** removal or **vulvectomy?**
- Is there an escalation in the aging process that is impairing sexual functioning?

Identification of Psychological Issues

Briefly, psychological issues refer to the complex and unique elements in each individual that can shape sexual attitudes and behavior (e.g., adequate or inadequate sex information and education). The psychological sequences that mediate most dysfunctions are an unwillingness to make love, an inability to relax, and an inability to concentrate on sensation. A major assessment issue here is to identify the inhibitions that serve to block sexual desire. The most common inhibitions are anxiety, guilt, and reaction to sexual trauma. Once they are identified they need to be conveyed to the couple in a nonblaming, nonjudgmental manner.

Generally speaking, the following psychological issues are involved in sexual dysfunction:

- Early sexual attitudes and experiences may affect sexual functioning. These would include early rape, incest, or other sexual trauma; attitudes that sex is bad or dirty; or early homosexual experiences that served to confuse sexual preference.
- Lack of information about sexuality may result in ignorance of technique, fear of pregnancy, or unrealistic expectations concerning sexuality and/or orgasm.
- Situational factors such as unemployment, family stresses, and marital problems.

- Communication problems between the partners can be expressed in the sexual arena.
- Intrapsychic issues such as **performance anxiety** or depression can produce sexual symptoms. With depression, it is important to understand whether the individual is depressed because of the sexual dysfunction, the depression caused the sexual dysfunction, or both problems are influencing each other. Low self-esteem or poor body image can also play a role in sexual dysfunction.

These diagnosis and assessment issues focus primarily on the biological or organic bases of sexual dysfunctions. However, most sexual dysfunctions are psychologically based. Other factors are relevant to gathering information concerning psychological factors.

Sex History Interview

1. History of sexual behavior, including a psychosexual/developmental overview/exploration of the client's childhood personal history and religious upbringing
2. Current sexual behavior
3. Attitudinal and cognitive factors
4. How do clients think about their sexual dysfunction? Do they have negative attitudes about sex in general? (For a more detailed sex information instrument, see Masters and Johnson, 1970.)

Examination of Interpersonal Issues

Interpersonal issues can affect sexual functioning through ineffective sexual communication styles (e.g., not openly discussing sexual needs.) In other words, the couple may have dysfunctional communicational patterns with respect to sexual issues. Some relevant assessment areas follow:

1. *Conflict resolution*—the ease with which differences of opinion are resolved
2. *Affection*—the degree to which feelings of emotional closeness are expressed by the couple
3. *Sexuality*—the degree to which sexual needs are communicated and fulfilled by the marriage
4. *Identity*—the couple's level of self-confidence and self-esteem

5. *Compatibility*—the degree to which the couple is able to work and play together comfortably, along with commitment to their marriage and similar attitudes, belief systems, and preferred activities
6. *Intellectual and affectual expressiveness*—the degree to which thoughts, beliefs, attitudes, and feelings are shared within the marriage, as well as self-disclosure
7. *Autonomy*—the success with which the couple gains independence from their families of origin and their offspring as individuals and as a couple
8. *Relational structure*—the degree to which the couple has explicit rules and roles that provide structure and definition
9. *Sexual boundary rigidity*—the degree of enmeshment or disengagement of the couple. Disengagement in a relationship could lead to stimulus and touch deprivation, sexual isolation, and/or body image anxiety
10. *Disruptions of established power hierarchies*—a possible disruption within the couple or family subsystem occurring at about the time when the sexual dysfunction began, for example, a challenge to the husband's decision-making authority that resulted in inhibited sexual desire or erectile dysfunction
11. *Life cycle crisis*—the capacity of the family structure to transform in response to predictable major life crises

Systemic Issues

Zimmer (1987) believes that clinicians should carefully evaluate the couple's general relationship at the beginning of therapy. Some sexual dysfunction is usually exhibited by couples in marital distress. These dysfunctions, however, could play various important roles in the maintenance of the marital system. For example, they may divert the couple from other family interactions. They may help the couple to maintain emotional distance. They may provide the couple with outlets for power positions or hostility, etc. They may sustain role-specific behavior. In these cases, treating the sexual dysfunction in a sex therapeutic modality alone is likely to meet with failure as the sexual dysfunction must be sustained in order to maintain the stability of the marriage.

This type of conceptualization enables the therapist to accomplish the following:

- Assess and understand the place of influences within the marriage in the etiology and maintenance of the sexual dysfunction

- Assess the relative strength of relationship-enhancing forces that could potentially facilitate and support the process of sex therapy
- Assess the relative strength of relationship-diminishing forces that would potentially inhibit and perhaps even undermine the process of sex therapy

Therefore, a comprehensive and multidimensional approach to the treatment of sexual dysfunctions must include a thorough evaluation of the marital relationship. Focusing on marital problems helps to facilitate more rapid changes in both marital and sexual functioning.

APPROACHES TO SEX THERAPY

Presently, three widely accepted theoretical orientations are used to treat sexual problems. They are the psychoanalytic; the cognitive-behavioral, including the newer sex therapies; and the systemic. It is important to note that there also needs to be a consideration of "normal" sexuality or at least the physiological aspects of the normal human sexual response. Before the publication of *Human Sexual Response* by Masters and Johnson in 1966, no data or information existed on what was considered "normal" physiological functioning.

The Psychoanalytic Perspective

Prior to 1970, the treatment of sexual problems was based on anecdotal observations and was considered the domain of psychiatry. The typical therapies for sexual problems that have evolved from this tradition are dyadic. Their aim is not to focus on the sexual symptom but rather to achieve a more complete understanding of the person's mental life. The first implication of the psychoanalytic view of sexual dysfunction is that the dysfunction itself is not the problem. It is a symptom of a deeper pathology. The second implication is that sexual problems are symptomatic of an underlying personality conflict that requires intense psychiatric therapeutic intervention and resolution. For example, a psychoanalytic interpretation of premature ejaculation would be that the man with this problem has intense, unconscious feelings of hatred toward women. Such a man supposedly has orgasms rapidly because it satisfies his sadistic impulses and ensures that his partner will receive little or no pleasure from the act. Vaginismus (previous section, Vaginismus, this chapter) is seen as one way a woman may deal with her **penis envy**—which is thought to occur in all girls during the **phallic stage of**

development. The problem is an expression of their unconscious desire to castrate their partner.

The therapeutic goal is not just to relieve the symptom, but to resolve its infrastructure—the underlying conflict. Insight, understanding, mastery, and psychological growth are highly valued therapeutic goals. The means of symptom removal used by the other therapeutic approaches are considered "transference cures" or "suggestion," likely to be followed by symptom substitution. This psychodynamic or psychoanalytically based treatment approach requires a lengthy treatment often with questionable outcomes. After the evaluation phase, a married patient with a sexual problem is usually seen alone as interpersonal problems within the marital relationship tend to be viewed as the acting out of the patient's internal conflicts.

A Cognitive-Behavioral Model: Masters and Johnson

The major treatment approach presented in this chapter is that of Masters and Johnson (1966, 1970) which is focused on because it forms the basis for all sexual therapy programs available today. With the Masters and Johnson (1966) publication of *Human Sexual Response* and their 1970 publication of *Human Sexual Inadequacy,* a new approach emerged, one that appeared to be an effective treatment approach of much shorter therapeutic duration. This new approach, known as the Masters and Johnson's approach, challenged psychoanalytic attitudes and suggested a radically different therapeutic approach. The first book was based on a study that examined the physiological changes that took place during sexual activity. The second book was based on data that explored a new treatment model for sexual disorders.

The Human Sexual Response Cycle

In this section, the Masters and Johnson (1966) **human sexual response cycle** is presented. One of their major contributions is that for the first time there was a description of the physiological responses that occurred during the human sexual response cycle. To have a better understanding of the sexual dysfunctions, it is important to first grasp the nature of sexual functioning.

There are four phases of the human sexual response cycle. Individuals generally progress sequentially through the four phases. There are detailed descriptions of the changes that occur during these phases. For a complete description of these changes, the reader is referred to Masters and Johnson's *Human Sexual Response* (1966). There are two generalized responses to sexual stimulation: **vasocongestion** and **myotonia.** Vasocongestion refers to increased blood flow to the penile and vaginal area, and myotonia refers to increased muscle tension. These responses occur in both males and females. Following are descriptions of each of the four phases of the human sexual response cycle.

1. *The Excitement Phase* is characterized by increased penile and vaginal vasocongestion.
2. *The Plateau Phase* occurs when maximal enlargement and congestion of pelvic organs has been reached. In the female, the orgasmic platform occurs as the uterus elevates. In the male, secretions from the **Cowper's gland** occur. This liquid secretion contains semen and may cause impregnation even though it is released prior to ejaculation. Immediately prior to ejaculation in the male, a period of ejaculatory inevitability occurs, at which point the male is no longer able to voluntarily inhibit ejaculation.
3. *Orgasm* consists of involuntary contractions occurring at 0.8-second intervals in both the penis and vagina. The frequency of contractions is related to the subjective report of intensity of orgasm (see Atwood and Gagnon, 1987). Respondents reported more subjectively intense orgasms the more contractions they had.
4. *The Resolution Phase* consists of a return to a resting state. For the male there is a refractory period during which the excitement phase cannot recur. This refractory phase increases with age. For the female, no such phase is evident, suggesting a physiological basis for multiple orgasms.

In addition, both genders experience **tachycardia** whereby heart rate increases from about 70 beats per minute to about 180 beats per minute. Both males and females experience a **sex flush** during sexual stimulation and orgasm. This refers to a blushing of the face, neck, chest, and arms. Keep in mind that although there is much overlap, there is also variation in the human sexual response among individuals and between the genders. Females tend to be more varied on their response than males. Some proceed to orgasm similar to the male response; others proceed to the plateau phase and move into the resolution phase without orgasm, and some are multiorgasmic. Females tend to spend more time in the excitement phase and their resolution phase is not as long as the male's. Vaginal and penile **plethysmograph** are devices used in the laboratory to measure vasocongestion (Geer and Quartararo, 1976). Basically, a plethysmograph is a photo light sensor. It indirectly measures blood volume density. If there is an increased amount of blood in the penile or vaginal area, less light is reflected. If there is a decreased amount of blood, more light is reflected.

In *Human Sexual Inadequacy,* Masters and Johnson (1970) presented a comprehensive treatment approach which is still the main basis for most sex therapy programs today. In this view, sexual dysfunctions are learned disorders rather than symptoms of underlying personality disorders. The dysfunctional man or the woman with an orgasmic disorder is viewed as a person who was exposed to an environment that taught him or her to be anxious in a particular situation. In addition, the psychoanalytic view would see the person's sexual problems, interpersonal relationships, and attitudes toward his or her parents as understandable in terms of one single underlying conflict, while the cognitive-behavioral view would suggest that each aspect of the patient's functioning might be caused by separate variables. The rapid acceptance of this new form of therapy by both the lay and the professional public testified to the inadequacy of psychoanalytic tradition in dealing with the widespread presence of sexual problems.

The general program most widely used in sex therapy is the conjoint therapy of Masters and Johnson (1970) modified in its detail by Bancroft, 1989; Gillan, 1987; Hawton, 1985; Spence, 1991; and Wincze and Carey, 1991. The knowledge gained from their original research formed the basis of their treatment model and, since that time, their work has been reviewed, evaluated, and followed-up. For the most part, the model has been upheld with the changes representing refinements of the original approach rather than departures from basic concepts. In any form of sexual therapy, the goal is to assist people to enjoy sexuality with natural abandonment, to free themselves from self-control. Sexual problems are often multifaceted and therefore, to deal with them effectively, one needs several methods.

Annon (1976) suggested that some sexual dysfunctions respond relatively well to short brief therapy and others require a more long-term approach. Based on this belief, he developed the **PLISSIT model,** which is an acronym for Permission, Limited Information, Specific Suggestions, and Intensive Therapy. This therapeutic approach advances from the simple to the more in depth.

During the **permission stage** the therapist assists individuals in accepting their sexual feelings, fantasies, and desires. The therapist, depending on the situation, encourages the clients not to have sexual intercourse if they do not want to. The therapist suggests that the couple not compare themselves to any other couple, nor to compare their sexual behavior with any statistics they might have read. During the **limited information stage,** the therapist provides information about sexuality in general, giving clients more realistic information for their knowledge base. In the third phase, **specific suggestions,** the therapist may suggest limited tasks to the couple, such as self-stimulation, sensate focus, or the squeeze technique. A more **intensive ther-**

apy may be necessary if the sexual dysfunction is still not resolved after the individuals have progressed through the previous steps. This therapy is more long term and aims at identifying deep-seated reasons that might interfere with sexual functioning.

The Masters and Johnson treatment procedure consists of three phases. The first phase, which lasts three days, involves *history taking*—both medical and psychological. The goal is to learn as much as possible about the clients' lives and personalities. The second phase consists of a *roundtable discussion* with the husband, wife, and cotherapists present. The therapists offer their hypotheses about possible causes of the dysfunction and correct any misconceptions the clients may have. Here too, the therapists promote communication between the partners. The third phase consists of *training the couple* in sensate-focus exercises and other techniques specific to their disorder. Sensate focus involves the couple providing each other with sensual pleasure that is not explicitly sexual. They basically explore each other's bodies with their hands. Some couples become sexually aroused for the first time in years. They are told not to have intercourse because so often it has become their preoccupation and indicator of failure. This approach may be termed conjoint behavioral therapy. The program is behavioral in that there is no attempt to interpret the presenting symptoms in terms of psychodynamic constructs, and that behavioral tasks are a major part of the package. The degree to which an approach geared toward unraveling conflicts and relationship problems is incorporated into this varies from therapist to therapist and case to case (Woody, 1992). Anxiety reduction is key to this therapy. Prohibitions against intercourse help to achieve this because performance fears and fears of pain are immediately removed. Some basic assumptions of this approach follow.

The problem is believed to be a joint problem. In a relationship, behaviors, attitudes, values, judgments, and anxieties often impact both individuals. It is never only the problem of one person if that person is in a relationship. This does not necessarily imply causality or fault but rather that when in a relationship, what one person does impacts the other. In terms of a sexual problem, it is possible that the problem could have preceded the relationship; but it could also have an impact on the relationship and an effect on the other partner. In these cases conjoint therapy is often helpful. Both partners, regardless of the specific etiology of the disorder, share the responsibility for treatment. Thus, a husband cannot blame his wife for his premature ejaculation and vice versa. One partner is not seen as the "at fault" one or the "sick" one. The couple is encouraged to view the disorder as a common problem and to view the solution as needing a team effort. With conjoint therapy, the emphasis is always on the relationship; it is the relationship that is in therapy. This reduces the risk that the partner with the sexual difficulty will be labeled as the one with the problem while the other partner sees himself or herself as the partner with the disorder's therapist, or as having no problem. This type of attitude can create therapeutic difficulties.

Sex is seen as a natural function. Sexual behavior is enormously affected by social learning, family definitions and values, individual personality dynamics, and biology, but it is also considered a natural function. Sex as a natural function means that the reflexes of sexual behavior are present from birth. Erections happen; vaginal lubrication happens. These reflexes are not taught; they occur automatically. However, this does not mean that they cannot be disrupted. Many obstacles to healthy sexual expression can be learned through increased stress, health-related problems, or psychological factors. The therapist provides an atmosphere of acceptance of sexuality as a natural function and gives permission for sexual enjoyment. The partners are encouraged to view sexuality as a means of giving each other pleasure, of relaxing with each other, and not as a performance that is supposed to occur at specific times and in specific ways.

The couple is educated in sexual knowledge. Information about clients' anatomy and physiology is gathered by conducting a thorough medical history, physical examination, and laboratory evaluation of both partners. Couples are given information about anatomy, physiology, different coital positions, etc. Here it is important to work hand in hand with medical personnel in order to flush out accurate information regarding any organically based etiology of the sexual dysfunction.

Some of the anxiety is reduced. This is usually achieved by restricting any attempt at intercourse. The couple is told not to engage in intercourse at this time. This removes the immediate pressure to perform and thus tends to reduce anxiety. Relaxation skill training may be used. The emphasis is on enjoyment and pleasure and not necessarily on orgasm or intercourse.

The couple is taught to develop sexual communication skills. Generally, sexual difficulties are concomitant with communication difficulties. It is helpful to include both partners when assisting the couple with more constructive communication techniques. Effective communication skills can be taught and often lead to a more pleasurable and satisfying sexual relationship. In addition, when both partners are included in the therapy, both partners' feelings and expectations can be addressed. For example, a male with erectile dysfunction may believe that he does not experience firm erections during intercourse. His partner may feel otherwise and is therefore an additional source of information. Sometimes a partner may raise a question that the other has been reluctant to ask. In other situations, a partner, during the sexual history taking, may provide information that the other knew nothing about. Verbal and physical communication, and acceptance of the partner's desires, values, and differences are emphasized. In addition, couples are taught to describe their own motivations rather than attributing motivations to the other. For example, "I feel unattractive" rather than "You do not find me attractive."

The Basic Concepts

A biopsychosocial approach. The Masters and Johnson model employs a **biopsychosocial approach,** which is a basic recognition of the importance of the underlying physiological and anatomical bases of human sexual behavior. This knowledge is integrated into their treatment program and is considered a crucial component primarily because it will discover those clients whose sexual dysfunction has an organic etiology, which would render psychotherapy unwarranted. In addition, it takes into account the health status and physical functioning of the clients, as well as providing a basis for answering clients' questions related to sexual anatomy and physiology.

Dual-sex therapy teams. Masters and Johnson believe that a **dual-sex therapy team** of a male and a female therapist is important because only a female can understand female sexuality and only a male can understand male sexuality. In this way, each partner's sexual expression, attitudes, problems, and feelings can be understood in the broader social context. A woman who is trying to explain to her husband that she likes to be romanced outside of the bedroom can be helped immeasurably by a female therapist. The therapists do not take sides, so to speak, or advocate for one partner over the other. Rather, they share the responsibility for assisting the partners with their relationship. The function of the dual-sex therapy team is to educate, model, and provide both overt and covert permission for the couple to be sexual.

A rapid treatment approach. The Masters and Johnson treatment program consists of an intensive daily treatment format that occurs over two weeks. This type of therapy format assists couples in staying focused and gives them an intense, effective, educational, and therapeutic experience without outside distractions. The critique of such a format is that the couple is "on vacation," so to speak. They have been removed from the day-to-day stresses of life.

History Taking and Initial Assessments

History taking occurs the first day with each therapist interviewing the same-sex partner. This session typically lasts from one to two hours. In this session, a detailed social history is taken as well as a detailed sexual history.

Some of the questions considered are: What are the specific sexual dysfunctions? What are the etiologies of these dysfunctions? Does the couple have nonsexual problems? Do they have any other sexual problems? Are there any underlying psychopathologies in either partner? Are there any physical problems? How motivated are they? Are there any secrets? Are there any major discrepancies in the histories taken? What objectives do the partners have for therapy? Are these objectives realistic? Is this treatment modality appropriate for this couple? After a lunch break the opposite-sex therapist interviews each partner. Additional information is taken. Next a thorough medical examination is given.

Beginning Treatment

The basic therapy program of Masters and Johnson involves two weeks away from home and work devoted completely to therapy. Although this approach has good success rates, it is not practical and too expensive for most couples. However, some aspects of it are common of most sex therapy programs:

- Usually there is a period of coital abstinence to reduce performance anxiety and facilitate communication.
- There is a focus on giving and receiving pleasure rather than on orgasm per se.
- Sensate focus exercises involving tactile stimulation are used. These exercises are the cornerstone of any sex therapy program. They begin with an emphasis on nonverbal and then on verbal communication.
- The couple is encouraged to find a mutually agreed-upon time and place to focus on sexual interaction without distractions. They are encouraged to spend time together engaging in communication and nongenital touching.
- They are asked to verbalize to their partner how the touching feels and what aspects they like. They are asked to fondle and touch each other for the specific purposes of giving and receiving pleasure. Again, the emphasis is neither on sexual intercourse nor on orgasm.
- **Handriding techniques** are used to assist the partners in showing each other what feels pleasurable. Each partner takes turns placing his or her hand on the hand of his or her partner and gently moving the partner's hand over the body, showing what is pleasurable.

As therapy progresses the therapist encourages additional exercises. Genital stimulation is suggested, and the partners are encouraged to discuss how they feel. The exercises progress in a nondemand manner, and the clients progress eventually to sexual intercourse. Couples are asked to explore alternative positions and discuss which ones are preferable. Rest periods are suggested, as sexual tension mounts, in order to prolong sexual pleasure.

There is a sequencing of sexual activities and techniques that facilitate success. Specific techniques are suggested that will meet the specific needs of the couple, for example, the squeeze technique for delaying premature ejaculation.

In sum, at the time that Masters and Johnson first published their results, there were very little data on human sexuality practices utilizing good methodology with generalizable samples. Even less exploration into effective treatment approaches had occurred. Masters and Johnson's (1966, 1970) data represented the first study examining sexual functioning and dysfunctioning. Their work suggested a number of interesting possibilities for dealing with dysfunctions. Both partners were included in the treatment, and the concerns of each partner were considered without placing blame for the dysfunction. The symptoms belonged to the marital pair, not to the **symptom bearer.** They believed that the psychological mechanisms of dysfunction were largely related to current rather than past influences, e.g., performance anxiety, spectatoring, anger at the dysfunctional spouse. A new emphasis was placed on social forces rather than on past intrapsychic causes, e.g., cultural expectations that prevent the normal development of female or male sexual expression, or religious orthodoxy. Masters and Johnson believed that male and female **cotherapy teams** were uniquely suited to foster communication and mutual understanding between the spouses. They felt the therapy team was also more effective in identifying and dealing with the high frequency of serious interpersonal problems. Correction of misinformation and imparting of knowledge were facilitated by cotherapists.

Their model did not go without criticism—primarily from Zilbergeld and Evans (1980) and their publication of "The Inadequacy of Masters and Johnson." Zilbergeld and Evans challenged Masters and Johnson's outcome statistics and their research methodology as well. They felt that Masters and Johnson worked primarily with highly motivated and educated middle-class couples, many of whom were health professionals in their community. Thus, they felt they were dealing with a highly select population with an unusually high prognosis. Second, they felt that the Masters and Johnson model did not really measure success rates; instead, they measured failure rates, and these were vaguely defined. They felt a more operationalized definition of the human sexual response and sexual problems were needed. However, although modified, the Masters and Johnson treatment model still forms the basis of most sex therapy programs today.

Masters and Johnson reported very low failure rates (see Masters and Johnson, 1966). The unfortunate effect of the Masters and Johnson study was that their outstanding results were not replicated in other studies. Their sample was preselected so that the couples' motivation for change was probably higher than that of the general population. Their results were so outstanding that controlled evaluative studies were largely ignored. There was some attention paid to comparing sex therapy to other forms of therapies, but the designs were often inferior; couples with different dysfunctions were lumped together with little attention paid to prognostic factors. The question as to whether sex therapy was more effective than no therapy at all was not addressed until 1983. At this time, Heiman and LoPiccolo (1988) demonstrated that the sexual and general adjustment of couples with a variety of sexual dysfunctions was much improved after sex therapy in comparison to changes that occurred to them while on a waiting list. Two additional studies compared sex therapy with treatment by self-help instructions and limited therapist contact (Mathews, Whitehead, and Kellett, 1983; Dow, 1981) and demonstrated that sex therapy was more effective. The Mathews, Whitehead, and Kellett study also compared systematic desensitization plus counseling and found that sex therapy was more effective.

The original Masters and Johnson Program included daily treatment sessions conducted with cotherapists. Studies have shown that this could be modified. On the basis of several treatment studies, it appears that weekly or biweekly treatment sessions were actually preferable to daily sessions (Clement and Schmidt, 1983; Heiman and LoPiccolo, 1988; Mathews, Whitehead, and Kellett, 1983). Four studies have shown no differences in outcome between treatment conducted by cotherapists or therapists working alone (Crowe, Gillian, and Golombok, 1981; Clement and Schmidt, 1983; Mathews, Whitehead, and Kellett, 1983; LoPiccolo et al., 1985). In two of these studies (Clement and Schmidt, 1983; LoPiccolo et al., 1985), there was no evidence of an intervening therapeutic effect between the gender of the therapist and that of the presenting partner. Currently in most clinical settings, individual therapists provide sex therapy in weekly treatment sessions.

The New Sex Therapy

The New Sex Therapy, written by Helen Singer Kaplan (1974), represented a blending of two approaches. Her approach involved a synthesis of the theory and procedures of psychodynamic theory with the more behavioral perspectives. It was an attempt to modify the antecedents to a couple's sexual difficulty, with recognition that it could have deeper roots. In this theory, Masters and Johnson's (1970) learning theory principles were brought into the process of identifying the mechanisms by which transactions are maintained and reinforced in order to provide appropriate behavioral modifications. The symptoms are considered the disorder rather than the underlying cause. This view is systemic in that for the most part the relationship, not the individuals, is seen as the problem. This approach involves the couple, so if one of the partners cannot tolerate the anxiety or change, then this treatment based on behavioral principles will not work. The goal here is more limited than traditional psychodynamic therapies in that the focus here is on alleviating symptom distress rather than personality overhaul.

Originally Helen Singer Kaplan (1974) proposed a **biphasic model** of human sexuality. The first phase involved vasocongestion of the genitals and the second phase consisted of the reflective muscular contractions of orgasm. Later Kaplan's (1979) biphasic model evolved into a **triphasic model** consisting of a **desire phase,** an **excitement phase,** and a **resolution phase.** She also believed that sexual dysfunctions could fall into one of these categories and that these categories are separate and distinct—that is, one phase can function well even if the individual is having problems with another. Adding the desire phase to the human sexual response cycle was an important contribution because, in many cases, sexual desire is not always present. This phase basically expanded Masters and Johnson's model and has been incorporated into their basic paradigm. Zilbergeld and Ellison (1980) believed that both Masters and Johnson's and Kaplan's models ignored the cognitive and subjective aspects of the sexual response, which they thought should be considered. Zilbergeld and Ellison's five components of the sexual response cycle are: Interest or desire, defined as how frequently a person wants to engage in sexual activity; arousal, defined as how excited one gets during sexual activity; physiological readiness (erection or vaginal lubrication); orgasm; and satisfaction (one's evaluation of how one feels). Thus they were interested in the cognitive elements of sexual experiences.

Systems Theory

A major problem in the field is that sex therapy for the most part has not been grounded or related to **systems theory,** meaning that sex continues to be treated as a special area both theoretically and clinically within the couple therapy field. In other words, little effort has been made to elaborate the conceptual connections between the family theories and theories of sexual behavior. Systems theorists generally see sexuality only as a symptom or a metaphor for the relationship in order that the couple might avoid dealing with the more essential couple issues. Similarly, there are a variety of ways in which systems theorists, depending on the context of the relationship, may view sexual issues. This viewpoint stresses that sexual dysfunctions do not exist in a vacuum but that they are often related to problems in the couple's emotional relationship, such as poor communication, hostility and competitiveness, or sex role problems. Even in those cases in which the sexual dysfunction is not related to relationship problems, the couple's emotional relationship is often damaged by the sexual problem and feelings of guilt, inadequacy, and frustration that usually accompany sexual dysfunction.

In this view, sexual problems hold a cyclical position in the couple's interaction. One's demands may be the result of his or her own sexual frustration and feelings of rejection. The partner's anxiety may be a combination of sexual conflict, self-doubt about sexuality, and fear of failure to please the partner. Thus, the important features of therapy include interrupting whatever cycle has been developed, separating the sexual problem from the relationship as a whole, exploring the roots of the sexual problem, and then integrating it with feelings of love. Therapy from this viewpoint tends to focus on the couple's interactions and the system dynamics that are maintaining the problematic sexual patterns.

In essence, the major approaches to sex therapy can be separated into two camps. On one hand, using the Masters and Johnson and the newer sex therapies' models, sexual dysfunction is treated seriously and the sexual issue presented is the problem to be worked on. On the other hand, using the psychoanalytic and the more systemically based therapies, sexual dysfunction is seen as a manifestation of some underlying conflict or as a metaphor or a symptom of a problem relationship. These two major divisions represent the division between the fields of sex therapy and couple therapy. However, it is one purpose of this chapter to suggest that it does not make sense to train people to practice marriage and family therapy without giving them adequate training in human sexuality. Neither is it fruitful to train people to practice sex therapy without giving them the context in which to apply it. Atwood and Weinstein (1989) suggest that it is time for the two fields to be brought together. Sager (1976) also believed that marriage and family therapists need to be versed in sex therapy and ready to shift focus when necessary, rather than refer clients to a "sex therapist." Lief (1977) also believes it is impossible to undertake sex therapy without exploring the quality of the couple's relationship.

Recently, **postmodern** approaches to therapy with couples have begun. For a description of one such postmodern approach, see Atwood (1993).

RESEARCH OUTCOMES

There has been considerable variation in outcome among different types of sexual problems and some other important prognostic factors. This information has been enhanced by evidence from long-term follow-up studies of couples who have received sex therapy (DeAmicis et al., 1985; Hawton et al., 1986). In terms of male problems, sex therapy appears to produce satisfactory results in both the short and long term for erectile dysfunctions, but less sustained results for premature ejaculation. Men with low sexual desire appear to have a very poor prognosis. With regard to female problems, the result of sex therapy for vaginismus are excellent and sustained, whereas the results of treatment of desire disorders are often disappointing, especially in the long term.

There now needs to be a considerable rethinking about the problem of low sexual desire both in order to develop more understanding of its nature and causes, and to establish alternative treatment approaches. A text directed solely at this problem (Lieblum and Rosen, 1988) represents an excellent first step. Zimmer's (1987) demonstration that sex therapy combined with marital therapy was more effective than sex therapy plus placebo treatment of distressed couples with female sexual dysfunctions might serve as a basis for more broad-based approaches to this problem.

Other factors shown to be of prognostic significance in sex therapy include the quality of the couple's general relationship, pretreatment motivation, especially of the male partner, the degree of attraction between partners, and early progress in terms of carrying out homework assignments (Whitehead and Mathews, 1977; Hawton and Catalin, 1990; Whitehead and Mathews, 1986).

Of relevance to the psychological treatment of sexual dysfunctions is the explosion that has occurred in physical treatments, especially the use of intracavernosal injections and vacuum devices for men with erectile dysfunctions. Although these undoubtedly represent important advances in treatment, especially for men with organic disorders, it is worrying that some clinicians are readily using them to treat apparent psychogenic cases. In the future more collaboration should occur between those specialists experienced in psychologically based treatment approaches and those, such as urologists, who largely provide only physical treatment.

The most pressing need in the field is for the development of an understanding of low sexual desire. It appears that there is no physiological factor present in healthy premenopausal women that could be responsible for the disorder, leading to the idea that social affective and cognitive factors may be present in this disorder. Bringing in marital therapy might result in an approach likely to help couples experiencing this and other difficulties. In addition, the fields of couple therapy and sexual therapy need to see more of an overlap with respective courses present to a larger degree in the training programs.

MULTICULTURAL INFLUENCES

It is also important to keep in mind that these approaches assume that sex is a primary way of exchanging pleasure, that it is a natural activity, that both partners are equally involved, that people should be educated about sexuality, and that communication is a necessary factor in sexual relationships. However, culture also has a great influence on sexual attitudes, **sexual scripts,** and behavior. In egalitarian relationships, the major goals are sexual pleasure and psychological disclosure and intimacy. However, for example, in Hispanic cultures men are permitted to engage in sexually pleasurable activities, but the norm for women is purity. In these cultures, women view sex as an obligation to satisfy the husband's needs. For the men, sexuality is an expression of their masculinity.

All of us have ideas about sexuality that are infused with our own value system based on the sociocultural milieu. Therapists carry with them their own sexual scripts and, because the therapy itself is grounded in the cultural environment, it is crucial for the therapist to keep in mind that clients have their own ideas about the meaning of their sexuality, what role gender plays, and what a good sexual relationship is for them. They also have ideas about what constitutes the sexual dysfunctions, what causes them, what the role of a good therapist is, and what the goals of the therapy should be. The therapist needs to be respectful of what the clients bring to therapy in terms of their own definitions and meanings.

WHEN TO REFER

Under any circumstances it is important for marriage and family therapists to have a basic understanding of sexual dysfunction etiology. The following may be used as a guide for when to refer for the therapist who does not have specific training in sexual therapy. Refer when the following conditions are present:

1. Clinical depression underlying the sexual complaint
2. Significant past psychiatric history

3. Problems complicated by homosexual conflict or gender confusion, overt or latent
4. Patients who present with marked personality or characterological disorders
5. Primary sexual dysfunction
6. Lack of commitment to the relationship or to the partner
7. Significant secrets, such as ongoing infidelity
8. Major reality concerns such as major family or work problems that would detract from the therapy
9. Major relationship difficulties with the partner
10. Lack of commitment to the therapy by one or both partners

SUMMARY

The major sexual dysfunctions, impairments in one of the phases of the human sexual response cycle, were presented and explored. They included erectile dysfunction, premature ejaculation, retarded ejaculation, orgasmic dysfunction, vaginismus, dyspareunia, and inhibited sexual desire. Diagnosis and assessment issues were discussed. Organic factors contributing to sexual dysfunction were discussed, along with psychological influences. Several sex therapy approaches are available, and these were presented and explored. Some of the programs deal specifically with the sexual problem while others focus on the relationship and psychological issues. Masters and Johnson's program is basically a cognitive-behavioral approach with the main treatment being temporary coital abstinence and the sensate focus technique. Their model forms the basis for most sexual therapy programs today. Kaplan's approach combines features of traditional insight therapy with Masters and Johnson's approach. One of her most important contributions is in the area of inhibited sexual desire. Systems theory was presented, along with an examination of the way sexual issues may be a metaphor for couple or relationship issues. Multicultural influences on sexual behavior were presented, along with a discussion of when sex therapy was contraindicated.

GLOSSARY

anorgasmia: A condition marked by the absence of or inability to experience orgasm.

aphrodisiacs: Agents that arouse or increase sexual response or desire.

biopsychosocial approach: Viewing the necessary relationship between a person's health and his or her mental and social conditions (mind and body connection).

biphasic model: The concept of the biphasic nature of the sexual response provides a theoretical framework which will further the understanding of sexual physiology and anatomy. The sexual response is not a single entity. Rather, it consists of two distinct independent components: a genital vaso-congestive reaction and the muscular contractions which constitute orgasm in both genders.

cardiopulmonary: Relating to the heart and lungs.

clitoral adhesions: The clitoral hood adheres to the glans, making orgasm difficult or impossible.

corpus cavernosum: The paired, cylindrical, spongelike bodies of the penis or clitoris that transverse the length of the shaft, one on either side.

cotherapy teams: The simultaneous involvement of two therapists in working with an individual, couple, or family.

Cowper's gland: Two pea-sized glands at the base of the penis, under the prostate, that secrete a clear fluid into the urethra during sexual intercourse.

degenerative diseases: A retrogressive pathological change in cells and tissues that may cause their functions to be impaired or destroyed.

desire phase: The first of three general divisions of the sexual response cycle in which the desire for sexual activity increases, leading to the physiological changes of sexual arousal in the excitement phase.

dual-sex therapy teams: The use of male and female cotherapists in the treatment of sexual inadequacy and dysfunction.

dyspareunia: A term for a sexual dysfunction characterized by difficult or painful intercourse or by an inability to enjoy sexual intercourse; recurrent or persistent genital pain in a male or female before, during, or after sexual intercourse.

ejaculatory incompetence (or retarded ejaculation): The inability of a male to reach an orgasm and ejaculate during vaginal intercourse and/or during masturbation.

ejaculatory inevitability: The feeling, occurring in the emission phase of ejaculation, when a male becomes aware his arousal has passed the point where he can control ejaculation and where it is now a reflexive process.

endocrine: Pertaining to internal secreting; hormonal; producing secretions that are distributed in the body by way of the bloodstream.

endometriosis: A painful condition caused by the growth of endometrial tissue outside the uterus, such as over the ovaries and fallopian tubes.

erectile dysfunction: The inability of a male to have or maintain an erection sufficient to vaginal intercourse or sufficient masturbation.

excitement phase: The first phase in the sexual response cycle. This phase can last for just a few minutes or extend for several hours. Characteristics of this phase include an increasing level of muscle tension, a quickened heart rate, flushed skin (or for some people blotches of redness may occur on the chest and back), hardened or erect nipples, and the onset of vasocongestion. Vasocongestion results in swelling of the woman's clitoris and labia minora and erection of the man's penis.

fibrosis: The formation of excessive fibrous tissue.

flashback: A recurring, intensely vivid mental image of a past traumatic experience.

handriding technique: A nonverbal technique used to improve sexual interactions.

hepatic: Relating to the liver.

human sexual response cycle: The four stages that humans go through from the beginning of arousal to the time after orgasm. These phases are excitement, plateau, orgasm, and resolution.

hymen: A thin membrane partially covering the entrance to the human vagina.

impotence: The inability of the male to have or maintain an erection sufficient for complete penile-vaginal intercourse. This condition is now called erectile dysfunction.

intensive therapy: Therapy that occurs with a skilled professional sex therapist, aimed at resolving the sexual concerns a client brings to therapy. Therapy sessions continue until complaints are resolved.

intracavernous injection therapy: A method used to treat erectile dysfunction administered through injection.

Kegeling exercises: A regimen of isometric exercises in which a woman executes a series of voluntary contractions of the muscles in her pelvic diaphragm in an effort to increase the muscle contractibility of the vaginal muscles.

Klinefelter's syndrome: The most common numerical sex chromosome anomaly in males, involves at least one extra X chromosome.

libido: The sexual drive, urge, or desire for pleasure or satisfaction; also a term used to denote sexual motivation.

limited information stage: The therapeutic effects of permission giving are usually reinforced and enhanced by providing limited information related to the patient's specific problem.

low sexual interest: The lack of desire to have sexual intercourse.

malignancy: Tendency to a fatal issue; a cancer.

mastectomy: Surgical removal of the glandular tissue of the breasts, often as a treatment for cancer.

Masters and Johnson: William Masters and Virginia Johnson, pioneers of observational sexual research who developed new methods of sex therapy.

multiple sclerosis: A disease of the central nervous system, the nerves that constitute the brain and spinal cord.

myotonia: The buildup of muscle tone or tension, especially during sexual arousal.

orgasmic dysfunction: The inability of a male or female to reach orgasm following normal sexual stimulation, either alone or with a partner.

paraphilias: Sexual actions that are pleasurable and gratifying, yet whose object (with whom or what one has intercourse) and/or aim (a goal other than seeking sexual intercourse) deviate from the norm.

pelvic inflammatory disease (PID): An inflammatory condition of the female pelvic organs, especially one due to bacterial or other sexually transmitted infection.

penis envy: In psychoanalytic theory, an alleged unconscious sense of sexual inadequacy and inferiority in a female because she lacks a penis and as a result envies the male.

performance anxiety: The fear that one will not be able to perform adequately in a sexual relationship—by failing to achieve an erection or have an orgasm, by not being able to be aroused and lubricated, or by not being able to satisfy one's partner.

permission stage: On the simplest level of sexual therapy, the dysfunctional person is given permission to be sexual and to discuss any sexual issue of concern.

phallic stage of development: In psychoanalytic theory, the third of five stages in psychosexual development; the period when a boy becomes aware of the pleasure-giving possibilities of his penis and girls become aware of its symbolic equivalent.

phimosis: The narrowing of an opening; tightness of the prepuce or foreskin of the penis, which prevents its retraction over the glans.

phobia: An anxiety disorder characterized by an obsessive, irrational, intense, and morbid dread or fear of something. An irrational or persistent fear.

plethysmograph: An instrument for measuring and recording changes in the sizes and/or volumes of organs by measuring changes in their blood volume.

PLISSIT model: A model for the use of different levels of sex therapy, PLISSIT stands for four levels of therapy, starting with permission giving and often limited information, moving to specific suggestions, and finally in problems that are not resolved by the efforts of the first three levels, culminating in intensive therapy.

postmodern: A philosophical outlook that rejects the notion that there exists an objectively known universe discoverable by impartial science, and instead argues that there are multiple views of reality.

premature ejaculation: A sexual dysfunction in which an individual is unable to sustain the preorgasmic period of arousal so that ejaculation occurs too soon relative to the individual's own expectation or that of the partner.

priapism: A rare, pathological condition involving prolonged and painful erection of the penis, usually without sexual desire.

primary sexual problem: Any sexual dysfunction that has always been experienced by an individual.

prolactin: The hormone that stimulates milk production, produced and secreted by the posterior pituitary gland.

prostate gland: A golfball-sized muscular and glandular structure in the urogenital system of males.

prostatectomy: A partial excision of the prostate to enlarge the prostatic urethra when it is closed.

prostatitis: An acute or chronic infection or inflammation of the prostate, treatable with antibiotics, bed rest, and fluids.

psychogenic factors: Originating in the mind.

renal: Relating to the kidney.

resolution phase: This phase occurs after orgasm in the sexual response cycle. The heart rate, blood pressure, breathing, and muscle contraction return to normal levels. Swelled and erect body parts return to normal and skin flushing disappears. Women may return from the resolution phase to the orgasm phase with minimal stimulation. Mean experience for the refractory period is from a few minutes to several days; there is great variance in the length of the refractory period among men.

secondary sexual problem: Any sexual dysfunction that follows a period of satisfactory sexual functioning.

self-fulfilling prophecy: Predictions about a future event that in turn increase the probability of the occurrence of that event.

sensate focus exercises: Noncoital, nondemand, graduated pleasuring exercises for use in behavioral therapy of various sexual dysfunctions.

sex flush: A temporary reddish rash or color change in the skin that sometimes develops in both men and women as a result of vasocongestion during the plateau stage of sexual arousal.

sexual deviations: Any sexual behavior regarded as abnormal by society.

sexual dysfunction: The inability to react emotionally and/or physically to sexual stimulation in a way expected of the average healthy person according to one's own standards.

sexual scripts: A cultural script whose goal is to enhance, reduce, or permit sexual arousal under acceptable conditions; an individual's unique set of attitudes, expectations, and values regarding sexual behavior, emotions, and relationships.

specific suggestions: If the sexual dysfunction is not resolved with application of permission giving and limited information, the sex therapist may make specific suggestions such as the use of sensate focus, stop-start, and squeeze behavioral exercises.

spectatoring: A psychological response whereby a person acts as an observer, monitor, or judge of his or her own sexual performance and/or that of his or her partner. It is a common outcome and cause for sexual dysfunction.

spina bifida: An abnormal development of the neural tube characterized by defective closure of the bony encasement of the spinal cord.

squeeze technique: Used to subside orgasmic sensation by squeezing the penis just below the glans with the thumb on one side and the forefingers on the opposite side until sensation diminishes.

stop-start technique: A therapeutic behavioral exercise to teach male control of orgasm and premature ejaculation.

symptom bearer: An individual in a structured group who manifests symptoms of a disorder.

systematic desensitization: A behavioral therapy in which deep relaxation is used to reduce anxiety associated with certain situations; a therapeutic technique in which a person is gradually exposed to increasing amounts of anxiety-producing stimuli.

systemic: Relating to systems or a system.

systems theory: Refers to the view of interacting units or elements making up an organized whole.

tachycardia: A rapid pulse.

temporal or frontal lobe damage: The lower lateral portion of the cerebral hemisphere. Damage in the temporal lobe can be caused by lack of oxygen. .

triphasic model: Classifies a sexual dysfunction as a disturbance of sexual desire, sexual excitement, or the orgasmic response. It recognizes that orgasm, excitement, and desire phase impairment are separate diseases, and each responds to different and specific therapeutic interventions.

tumescence: A swelling; the erection and enlargement of the sexual organs, particularly the clitoris and the penis, resulting from the vasocongestion accompanying sexual stimulation.

urethritis: An infection of the urethra.

vacuum erection devices: A method used to treat erectile dysfunction whereby the penis is placed into a cylinder and a vacuum is created, which causes blood to flow into the penis, thereby creating an erection.

vaginal dilators: A treatment used in a medical setting to help resolve vaginismus by helping a woman gain voluntary control over the pelvic muscles and gently widen the vagina.

vaginismus: Involuntary spasms of the muscles surrounding the lower third of the vagina when penetration of the penis is attempted.

vascular disorders: Disorder of the blood vessel system.

vasocongestion: A normal increase in the amount of blood concentrated in certain body tissues, especially in the genitals and female breasts, during sexual arousal.

vulvectomy: Surgical removal of part or all of the vulvar tissue.

REFERENCES

Althof, S. E. (1989). Psychogenic impotence: Treatment of men and couples. In S. R. Leiblum and R. C. Rosen (Eds.), *Principles and practice of sex therapy: Update for the 1990s* (pp. 237-265). New York: Guilford Press.

American Psychiatric Association (1987). *Diagnostic and Statistical Manual of Mental Disorders* (DSM-IIIR). Washington, DC: American Psychiatric Association.

Annon, J. S. (1976). *The behavioral treatment of sexual problems: Brief therapy.* New York: Harper and Row.

Assalian, P. (1988). Clomipramine in the treatment of premature ejaculation. *Journal of Sex Research, 24,* 213-215.

Atwood, J. D. (1993). Social constructionist couples therapy. *The Family Journal: Counseling and Therapy for Couples and Families, 1*(2), 116-129.

Atwood, J. D. and Gagnon, J. (1987). Masturbatory behavior in college youth. *Journal of Sex Education and Therapy, 13*(2), 35-42.

Atwood, J. D. and Weinstein, E. (1989). The couple relationship as the focus of sex therapy. *The Australian and New Zealand Journal of Family Therapy, 10*(3), 161-168.

Bahren, W., Scherb, W., Gall, H., Beckert, R., and Holzki, G. (1989). Effects of intracavernosal pharmacotherapy on self-esteem, performance anxiety and partnership in patients with chronic erectile dysfunction. *European Journal of Urology, 16,* 175-180.

Bancroft, J. (1989). *Human sexuality and its problems.* New York: Churchill Livingstone.

Beck, J. G. and Barlow, D. H. (1984). Current conceptualization of sexual dysfunction: A review and an alternative perspective. *Clinical Psychology Review, 4,* 363-378.

Clement, U. and Schmidt, G. (1983). The outcome of couple therapy for sexual dysfunctions using three different formats. *Journal of Sex and Marital Therapy, 9*(1).

Crowe, M., Gillian, P., and Golombok, S. (1981). Form and content in the conjoint treatment of sexual dysfunction: A controlled study. *Behavior Research and Therapy, 19,* 47-54.

Crowe, M. and Ridley, J. (1990). *Therapy with couples. A behavioral systems approach to marital and sexual problems.* Oxford: Blackwell.

DeAmicis, L., Goldenberg, D. C., LoPiccolo, J., Friedman, J., and Davies, L. (1985). Clinical follow-up of couples treated for sexual dysfunction. *Archives of Sexual Behavior, 14,* 467-489.

De Silva, P. (1992). Sexual and marital therapy in clinical psychology training. *Bulletin of the British Association of Sexual and Marital Therapists, 8,* 16-18.

De Silva, P. (1994). Psychological treatment of sexual problems. *International Review of Psychiatry, 6,* 163-173.

Dow, S. (1981). Retarded ejaculation as a function of nonaversive conditioning and discrimination: A hypothesis. *Journal of Sex and Marital Therapy, 7*(1), 49-53.

Ellison, C. (1980). A critique of the clitoral model of female sexuality. Paper presented at the Annual Meeting of the American Psychological Association, Montreal, Canada, September.

Frank, E., Anderson, C., and Rubinstein, D. (1978). The frequency of sexual dysfunction in couples. *New England Journal of Medicine, 299,* 111-115.

Geer, J. H. and Quartararo, J. D. (1976). Vaginal blood volume responses during masturbation. *Archives of Sexual Behavior, 5*(5), 403-413.

Gillan, P. (1987). *Sex therapy manual.* Oxford: Blackwell.

Goldstein, I., Lue, T. F., Padma-Nathan, H., Rosen, R. C., Steers, W. D., and Wicker, P. A. (1998). Oral sildenafil in the treatment of erectile dysfunction. *New England Journal of Medicine, 338,* 1397-1404.

Harbin, H. T. and Gamble, B. (1977). Sexual conflicts related to dominance and submission. *Medical Aspects of Human Sexuality, 11,* 84-89.

Hawton, K. (1983). Behavioral approaches to the management of sexual deviations. *British Journal of Psychiatry, 143,* 248-255.

Hawton, K. (1985). *Sex therapy: A practical guide.* Oxford: Oxford Medical Publications.

Hawton, K. and Catalin, J. (1990). Sex therapy for vaginismus: Characteristics of couples treatment and outcome. *Sexual and Marital Therapy, 5,* 39-48.

Hawton, K., Catalin, J., Martin, P., and Fagg, J. (1986). Long-term outcome of sex therapy. *Behavior Research and Therapy, 24,* 665-675.

Heiman, J. R. and LoPiccolo, J. (1988). *Becoming orgasmic.* Englewood Cliff, NJ: Prentice-Hall.

Hite, S. (1976). *The Hite report.* New York: Macmillan.

Kaplan, H. S. (1974). *The new sex therapy.* New York: Brunner/Mazel.

Kaplan, H. S. (1979). *The disorders of sexual desire.* New York: Brunner/Mazel.

Kaplan, H. S. (1987). *Sexual aversion, phobias, and panic disorder.* New York: Brunner/Mazel.

Kaplan, H. S. (1990). The combined use of sex therapy and intrapenile injections in the treatment of impotence. *Journal of Sex and Marital Therapy, 16,* 195-207.

Kinsey, A. C., Pomeroy, W. B., and Martin, C. E. (1953). *Sexual behavior in the human female.* Philadelphia: Saunders.

Kolodny, R., Masters, W., and Johnson, V. (1979). *A textbook of sexual medicine.* Boston: Little, Brown and Co..

Lakin, M. M., Montague, D. K., Medendorp, S. V., Tesar, L., and Shovar, L. R. (1990). Intracavernous injection therapy: Analysis of results and complications. *Journal of Urology, 143,* 1138-1141.

Lazarus, A. A. (1989). Dyspareunia: A multimodal psychotherapeutic perspective. In S. R. Leiblum and R. C. Rosen (Eds.), *Principles and practice of sex therapy: Update for the 1990s* (pp. 89-112). New York: Guilford Press.

Leiblum, S. R., Pervin, L. A., and Cambell, E. H. (1989). The treatment of vaginismus: Success and failure. In S. R. Leiblum and Rosen (Eds.), *Principles and practice of sex therapy: Update for the 1990s* (pp. 89-112). New York: Guilford Press.

Leiblum, S. R. and Rosen, R. C. (1988). Changing perspective on sexual desire. In S. R. Leiblum and R. C. Rosen (Eds.), *Sexual desire disorder* (pp. 1-20). New York: Guilford Press.

Levin, R. and Levin, A. (1975). Sexual pleasure: the surprising preferences of 100,000 women. *Redbook,* September, pp. 51-58.

Lief, H. I. (1977). Inhibited sexual desire. *Medical Aspects of Human Sexuality, 7,* 94-95.

LoPiccolo, J. (1985). Diagnosis and treatment of male sexual dysfunction. *Journal of Sex and Marital Therapy, 11*(4), 215-231.

LoPiccolo, J. (1992). Postmodern sex therapy for erectile failure. In R. C. Rosen and S. R. Leiblum (Eds.), *Erectile disorders: Assessment and treatment* (pp. 171-179). New York: Guilford Press.

LoPiccolo, J., Hieman, J. R., Hogan, D. R., and Roberts, C. W. (1985). Effectiveness of single therapists versus co-therapy teams in sex therapy. *Journal of Consultation and Clinical Psychology, 53*(3), 287-294.

Maltz, W. and Holman, B. (1987). *Incest and sexuality: A guide to understanding and healing.* Lexington, MA: Lexington Books.

Masters, W. H. and Johnson, V. E. (1966). *Human sexual response.* Boston: Little, Brown and Co.

Masters, W. H. and Johnson, V. E. (1970). *Human sexual inadequacy.* Boston: Little, Brown and Co.

Masters, W., Johnson, V., and Kolodny, R. (1985). *Human sexuality,* Second edition. Boston: Little, Brown and Co.

Mathews, S. A., Whitehead, A., and Kellett, J. (1983). Psychological and hormonal factors in the treatment of female sexual dysfunction. *Psychological Medicine, 13,* 83-92.

Moreland, R. B., Goldstein, I., and Traish, A. (1998). Sildenafil: A novel inhibitor of phosphodiesterase type 5 in human corpus cavernosum smooth muscle cells. *Life Science, 62,* 309-318.

Sager, C. J. (1976). *Marriage contracts and couple therapy.* New York: Brunner/Mazel.

Schiavi, R. C., Schreiner-Engel, P., Mandeli, J., Schanzer, H., and Cohen, E. (1990). Healthy aging and male sexual function. *American Journal of Psychiatry, 147,* 766-771.

Schwartz, M. F., Bauman, J. E., and Masters, W. H. (1983). Hyperprolactinemia and sexual dysfunction in men. *Biological Psychiatry, 17,* 861-876.

Seagraves, R. T. and Seagraves, K. B. (1992). Aging and drug effect on male sexuality. In R. C. Rosen and S. R. Leiblum (Eds.), *Erectile disorders: Assessment and treatment* (pp. 96-140). New York: Guilford Press.

Semans, J. H. (1956). Premature ejaculation: A new approach. *Southern Medical Journal, 49,* 353-358.

Spence, S. H. (1991). *Psychosexual therapy: A cognitive-behavioral approach.* London: Chapman and Hall.

Turner, L. A., Althof, S. E., Levine, S. B., Risen, C. B., Bodner, D. R., Kursh, E. D., and Resnick, M. I. (1989). Self-injection of papaverine and phentolamine in the treatment of psychogenic impotence. *Journal of Sex and Marital Therapy, 15,* 63-176.

Whitehead, A. and Mathews, A. (1977). Attitude change during behavioral treatment of sexual inadequacy. *British Journal of Social and Clinical Psychology, 16,* 275-281.

Whitehead, A. and Mathews, A. (1986). Factors related to successful outcome in the treatment of sexually unresponsive women. *Psychological Medicine, 16,* 373-375.

Wincze, J. P. and Carey, M. P. (1991). *Sexual dysfunction: A guide for assessment and treatment.* New York: Guilford Press.

Wise, T. N. (1999). Psychological side effects of sildenafil therapy for erectile dysfunction. *Journal of Sex and Marital Therapy, 25,* 145-150.

Woody, J. D. (1992). *Treating sexual distress: Integrative systems therapy.* Newbury Park: Sage Publications.

Zilbergeld, B. (1978). *Male sexuality: A guide to sexual fulfillment.* Boston: Little, Brown and Co.

Zilbergeld, B. (1992). *The new male sexuality.* New York: Bantam Books.

Zilbergeld, B. and Ellison, C. R. (1980). Desire discrepancies and arousal problems in sex therapy. In S. Leiblum, L. Pervin (Eds.), *Principles and practice of sex therapy.* New York: Guilford Press.

Zilbergeld, B. and Evans, M. (1980). The inadequacy of Masters and Johnson. *Psychology Today,* August, pp. 29-43.

Zimmer, D. (1987). Does marital therapy enhance the effectiveness of treatment for sexual dysfunction? *Journal for Sex and Marital Therapy, 12*(3), 193-207.

Chapter 13

Contextual Issues
in Marital and Family Therapy:
Gender, Culture, and Spirituality

Kevin P. Lyness
Shelley A. Haddock
Toni Schindler Zimmerman

Rather than gender being a peripheral issue, gender is the basic category on which the world is organized.

Rachel T. Hare-Mustin
In *Women and Families*

Diversity is a valuable resource for the growth and enrichment of all societies.

Douglas C. Breunlin, Richard C. Schwartz,
and Betty MacKune-Karrer
Metaframeworks

At its best, the very process (of family therapy) becomes a spiritual well-spring for healing and resilience.

Froma Walsh
Spiritual Resources in Family Therapy

There has been increasing attention to contextual issues in the practice of couple and family therapy in recent years. Issues of gender and power were the first to come to the fore, closely followed by issues of culture, ethnicity, and race (Leslie, 1995). More recently, issues of spirituality and religion have gained prominence (Walsh, 1999a). Much of the discussion about gender and culture has been driven by the feminist critique of the field (Leslie, 1995). Central to this discussion has been attention to power differences between the sexes and cultures in our society, and more recently in spirituality as well.

One of the primary initial criticisms of family therapy was the failure of family therapy to see relationships *in context* (Taggart, 1985). As family therapy has evolved through the years, therapists have come to recognize the powerful influence that context has on individuals and their relationships. Individuals and families live in a society in which contexts such as gender, culture, and spirituality are important and life shaping, and to ignore the influence of these issues is to do a disservice to families. For example, a large body of literature shows that more egalitarian couples are more satisfied in their relationships (Gottman and Silver, 1999; Larson, Hammond, and Harper, 1998; Rabin, 1996; Schwartz, 1994; Steil, 1997) and that there are benefits for both men and women (Kessler and McRae, 1982; Steil, 1997) in egalitarian relationships. Not only are there positive consequences for egalitarian relationships, but there are many negative consequences for both women and men when they adhere to traditional gender expectations and develop intimate relationships based on power differentials (e.g., Canary and Stafford, 1992; Erickson, 1993; Gottman, 1991; Rabin, 1996; Steil, 1997; Suitor, 1991; Walker, 1989).

Marital and family therapy theories themselves typically do not address contextual issues (although the contextual therapy of Ivan Boszormenyi-Nagy [Boszormenyi-Nagy and Krasner, 1986] addresses the context of relationships, it does not specifically address gender, culture, or spirituality). Instead, many scholars argue that contextual issues—such as gender, culture, and spirituality—should be overarching principles that are infused throughout all models of marital and family therapy. One direction the field has taken is to look at contextual issues as **metaframeworks** (Breunlin, Schwartz, and MacKune-Karrer, 1992). Another way to think about a metaframework is through the metaphor of an umbrella. Each of these domains (e.g., gender, culture, and spirituality) can be seen as an umbrella that "covers" all of the other theories of MFT. It is important to think about gender, culture, and spirituality regardless of whether you are working from a structural perspective or a narrative perspective (see Figure 13.1).

Spirituality has been explored by some (Breunlin, Schwartz, and MacKune-Karrer, 1992) as part of a multicultural perspective, but Berenson (1990) recommends that family therapists should use spirituality as a "meta-objective" (p. 70) or umbrella as well. Our view is that marital and family therapists should "cover" their theories with these umbrellas of gender, culture, and spirituality to protect from biases. Not only should MFTs use these umbrellas, but they should keep them fully open, bringing these is-

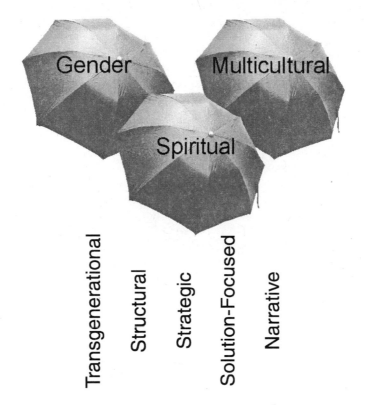

FIGURE 13.1. The Umbrellas of Gender, Multiculturalism, and Spirituality

sues into therapy directly. If you extend the metaphor of the umbrella a bit further, by having your umbrella open only a little or not at all you cannot cover much. In terms of contextual issues, having your umbrella closed means you are not attending to these issues and may be encouraging stereotypes by supporting the status quo. If you have your umbrella open fully, you will be attending to and bringing issues of gender, culture, and spirituality to the forefront of therapy. All therapists' behaviors lie somewhere along a continuum of having either a closed or open umbrella, and the hope is that all therapists will move toward having their umbrellas open wide.

Through this chapter the reader will become familiar with the history of our field's struggles with opening these umbrellas, with techniques and interventions for addressing these issues, and with research that relates to each area. First discussed is the role of gender in family therapy, followed by culture, and then spirituality.

GENDER

What Is Gender?

Gender "refers to the psychological, social, and cultural features and characteristics that have become strongly associated with the biological categories of male and female" (Gilbert and Scher, 1999, p. 3). Gender is not just biological sex but includes many features associated with that sex which are imposed by sociocultural context. Gender, therefore, includes all of the societal expectations of who we should be, based upon American sex. There is perhaps no place in American society where gender expectations are more prevalent than in the family.

Our society is filled with gender messages about who we should be and who we should not be. For example, men are typically assigned the *public sphere* of work, and women are assigned the *private sphere* of homemaking, child care, and maintaining family relationships. Each gender is also expected to have qualities that will help them in these spheres (e.g., men should be stoic and women should be nurturing and emotional). These gender messages often serve to keep people stuck in a "gender box" and increase power differentials between men and women at the same that they keep women and men apart. (See Box 13.1 for an exercise in gender stereotypes.)

Many of these gender messages also tell us who we should be within our marriages, our relationships, and our families. For example, men are seen as less emotional, even though they may have the same internal experiences as females (Gottman and DeClaire, 1997), and women are often socialized that to be good mothers they should not work, yet a mother's working may have positive rather than negative impacts on children, and it is often the marital relationship and not the mothers' working that impacts child development (Benokraitis, 1999). In the past, marriage and family therapy theories were also guided by these messages about what is right and appropriate within the family and in family therapy. In marriage and family therapy, it is important to question these societal ideals about the family and about what is "normal." Feminists have led the way for this discussion in marriage and family therapy. (See Gilbert and Scher, 1999, and Rabin, 1996, for more detailed discussions of gender role socialization in relation to counseling and therapy.)

Gender expectations even influence the perception of therapists by society. Bischoff and Reiter (1999) explored how mental health clinicians are portrayed in movies and found that women clinicians are typically sexualized and male clinicians are portrayed as incompetent. Gender plays such a

BOX 13.1. In the Box/Out of the Box Exercise

Females

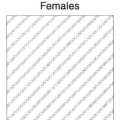

Males

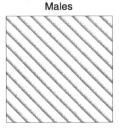

In small groups, brainstorm traits, characteristics, attitudes, and/or behaviors that society encourages for each gender. These are "in the box" behaviors and traits. For example, "in the box" traits for females might include nurturing, emotional, passive, wants children, while "in the box" traits for males might include aggressive, rational, enjoy sports, and nonemotional. Come up with as many traits and attitudes for each gender as you can that society expects. Often these are stereotypes that govern behavior.

The next step is to discuss what consequences women and men experience for stepping "out of the box." Consequences might include what others would say about you if you step out (women who are "out of the box" are often referred to as a "bitch," while men who step out of the box might be called a "wimp" or "fag") or personal consequences as you step out (such as feeling strange because you are going against norms). Consequences can be both positive and negative. Explore the following questions: What are the benefits of stepping "out of the box"? What are the benefits of staying "in the box" for each gender?

Next, consider the benefits and consequences of "in the box" versus "out of the box" behavior for couples and families. For example, "in the box" behaviors often encourage women to have less say about major aspects in their lives (e.g., finances, careers) and encourage men to feel overly responsible for breadwinning and underinvolved in fathering and child care.

Finally, consider how couples in therapy need to find a "common gender box" where they can interact with less constraint and conflict. Examples of "common box" behaviors include interdependence, assertiveness, and a sharing of major life responsibilities such as housework, child care, and breadwinning.

Source: Adapted from Creighton and Kivel (1992).

powerful role in our society that it permeates our culture and creates expectations and stereotypes for everyone and restricts our behavior. Two videos are recommended for therapists and students in helping to understand how socialization affects both women and men. These are *Myths That Maim*

(Lucas, 1992), which explores the social construction of gender identity and gender violence, and *Tough Guise: Violence, Media, and the Crisis in Masculinity* (Katz and Earp, 1999). The constraining aspects of gender expectations must be addressed in American society, and one avenue toward this end is marital and family therapy.

The Feminist Critique of Marital and Family Therapy

The feminist critique of family therapy began in the 1970s (Hare-Mustin, 1978; Humphrey, 1975), and Hare-Mustin's article in particular was seen as an impetus for heated dialogue within the family therapy field. This article not only challenged the theories of family therapy, but it served to challenge the very definition of the family. In fact, much of the early feminist critique focused on the traditional definition of the family. The family was traditionally defined in family therapy as it was in the larger society; that is, men should be in the public sphere and women's domain was the private. In this type of family, the power of the male is guaranteed by societal expectations that he will be older, more educated, of higher social status, and more economically viable than his wife (Hare-Mustin, 1978). Family therapy, by not challenging this definition, ended up devaluing women and "women's work" and supporting power imbalances. Because traditional family therapy focused on building families who conformed to the traditional family model, family therapy itself was seen as supporting male power and not allowing women to have power, or by pathologizing the women who did.

In particular, family therapy has been criticized by feminists for its adherence to theories of **circular causality.** Taggart (1985) in particular raised the question of whether this concept has inhibited the development of gender equity in family therapy. Circular causality and systems theory, in their traditional forms, fail to account for imbalances of power within relationships—it is assumed that each part of the system carries the same weight in contributing to problems and to change. Within many relationships, both parties do not have the same options for behavior due to differences in **power,** particularly within the family, where traditional roles give males the bulk of the power. Economics provides one simple example of power in families: the partner who has the most resources typically has the most power. Since men typically earn more than women for the same work, and are more likely to work full time, they have more economic resources and hence often have a great deal of decision-making power (Benokraitis, 1999). Men also have more choices about ending relationships because they have the economic means to survive and many women do not (Benokraitis, 1999). A more severe example is in cases of domestic violence, in which men have more physical power than women do (Benokraitis, 1999; Bograd, 1999). For example, women are six times more likely than men to be assaulted by an intimate relation, and are more likely to sustain serious physical injury as a result of domestic violence than are men (Gelles, 1988).

Power has been a key issue in the feminist critique, particularly in challenging how the field views therapy. As Bograd (1986) points out, some leading theorists in the field stated that power was merely a metaphor and not a reality (Keeney, 1983). This denies the very real impact of power in many relationships. Much of the early critique dealt with domestic violence and the role of power in those relationships as a way to argue against the field's position that power was a nonissue (Hansen, 1993).

Related to this discussion of power in relationships is the idea of **therapeutic neutrality** (Bograd, 1986). Early family therapists attempted to remain neutral so as not to impose their ideals of family functioning on others. One criticism of neutrality is that it in effect supports the status quo. If you do not take a stand against power imbalances and gender inequity, you are silently supporting it. As such, feminist-informed family therapy is inherently political—it seeks to bring about changes to reduce or eliminate such inequities. More recently, Doherty (1995) has argued against therapeutic neutrality in family therapy as well.

An additional critique of traditional family therapy is that it is based upon prototypically male ideals and standards of health (Bograd, 1986). One specific example is Murray Bowen's Differentiation of Self scale, which defines well-adjusted individuals as rationally objective and able to free themselves from relational contexts—qualities that have been associated with men (see Bograd, 1986; Hare-Mustin, 1978).

Since the feminist critique of family therapy began, much has changed in family therapy. Many introductory graduate texts for family therapy have sections discussing either the feminist critique and/or gender sensitivity in practice (e.g., Avis, 1986; Becvar and Becvar, 1996; Brock and Barnard, 1992; Gladding, 1998; Goldenberg and Goldenberg, 2000; Hanna and Brown, 1995; Thomas, 1992). Interested readers are encouraged to read the following articles on the feminist critique: Bograd (1986), Goldner (1985), Hare-Mustin (1978), and Taggart (1985), as well as the book *Women in Families: A Framework for Family Therapy*, edited by McGoldrick, Anderson, and Walsh (1989). Unfortunately, although much has changed, much has stayed the same. Sexism in our society, our relationships, and even in therapy is still pervasive. An example is the recent finding by Werner-Wilson et al. (1997) that therapists interrupt female clients at a much higher rate than they interrupt male clients during family therapy sessions.

A Note About Feminism

Although you do not have to be a feminist to pay attention to issues of gender in marriage and family therapy, the literature on gender in family therapy is derived from feminist thought and has evolved from feminist critique (in fact, as you begin to think about, practice, and pay attention to these issues, you may find yourself feeling more and more feminist as time goes on).

Feminism is defined as "a recognition of women's subordination and inferior social position, an analysis of the forces that maintain it, a commitment to changing it, and a vision of future equality between men and women" (Avis, 1986, p. 221). One does not have to be female to agree with or practice feminist principles; within family therapy, some of the leading feminist writers have been men (e.g., Morris Taggart and Robert-Jay Green).

The phrase *feminist-informed family therapy* may scare some people off, but there is no question that not paying attention to issues of gender in therapy will result in less effective therapy (Gottman and Silver, 1999; Schwartz, 1994). It is important to point out that men benefit from such a model as well as women (see Bograd, 1991, for a discussion of feminist approaches to men in family therapy). Power imbalances within relationships have been linked to lack of intimacy and engagement for both partners (Horst and Doherty, 1995; Rabin, 1996; Steil, 1997). Gender-aware therapy benefits all parties in developing balanced and collaborative relationships (Gottman and Silver, 1999; Rabin, 1996).

Gender and the Practice of Marital and Family Therapy

A gender-aware approach to therapy should include the following:

- Recognition of *oppression* based on gender, race, and class (Gilbert and Scher, 1999)
- Reducing *power* differentials between clients and therapists (Gilbert and Scher, 1999; Haddock, Zimmerman, and MacPhee, 2000; Whipple, 1996)
- Ongoing *self-examination* of values on the part of the therapist (Gilbert and Scher, 1999)
- Emphasis on *change* both in therapy and in society (Gilbert and Scher, 1999)
- Valuing the *female perspective* (Gilbert and Scher, 1999; Whipple, 1996)

- Focusing on *women's empowerment* (Gilbert and Scher, 1999; Haddock, Zimmerman, and MacPhee, 2000; Whipple, 1996)
- *Balance* (Breunlin, Schwartz, and MacKune-Karrer, 1992, p. 248), which is attained through collaboration, both within the family and between the family and therapist

Collaboration has been identified as a key not only to feminist or gender-aware therapy, but also to feminist supervision (Wheeler et al., 1989), and to intimacy in couples (Horst and Doherty, 1995).

Therefore, gender-aware or gender-informed therapy seeks to value all clients' experiences while seeking to reduce power differentials, both within couples and within the therapeutic system, in part through balance. In exploring specific ways to work with clients from a gender-aware perspective, there are two major areas of focus: assessment and intervention.

Assessment

Many authors have noted the importance of assessing gender dynamics in the initial stages of marital and family therapy (Breunlin, Schwartz, and MacKune-Karrer, 1992; Haddock, Zimmerman, and MacPhee, 2000; Rabin, 1996; Patterson et al., 1999). There are several specific areas to focus on in assessment.

Rabin (1996) makes several specific suggestions regarding assessment. In general, Rabin suggests that clinicians assess the following areas:

1. In what ways do the presenting problems reflect gender power issues?
2. How does each partner define equality and to what extent are the partners in agreement about these definitions?
3. To what extent does each partner perceive the other as a real friend?
4. To what extent does the relationship empower both partners?
5. To what extent is the communication work of the relationship equally shared?
6. To what extent has the couple developed a shared ideology fostering their relationship?

Patterson et al. (1999) note that oftentimes partners in a relationship may be coming from different gender backgrounds, which often causes conflict. For example, a man who grows up in a family where "women's work" is as valued as "men's work" may clash in a marriage to a woman from a family with traditional gender values and expectations. Not everyone comes from families that value traditional roles.

Breunlin, Schwartz, and MacKune-Karrer (1992) take this a bit further and suggest that couples and families often fit into one of five transitional positions in the evolution of gender balance, falling along a continuum from traditional to balanced. They describe each of these positions, along with ways for therapists to assess the positions, and possible interventions (see Table 13.1).

Finally, therapists should assess couple interactions for gender and power themes, including family dynamics such as who opens the conversation, who chooses the topic, who interrupts whom, who talks more, who pays for the session, and who decides if there will be a next session (Rabin, 1996). Each of these areas can reveal power dynamics in a relationship, although initial hypotheses should always be tentative if they are based on little information.

TABLE 13.1. Transitional Gender Positions Continuum

Position	Goals	Interventions
Traditional	Promote gender awareness	Question narrow gender expectations
		Question explanations that justify patriarchy
Gender-aware	Amplify experiences of gender imbalance	Support increasing awareness
		Question when family adheres to narrow gender definitions
Polarized	Decrease polarization and encourage balanced roles	Validate individuals' experiences
		Question extreme descriptions
		Encourage balancing extreme positions
In transition	Amplify changes toward egalitarian roles	Support and validate beliefs
		Discuss consequences of change in all family members
		Clarify new roles
Balanced	Support egalitarian roles and expand changes into other social areas	Discuss trade-offs and consequences of beliefs
		Examine potential social traps
		Discuss impact of lack of social support

Source: Adapted from Breunlin, Schwartz, and MacKune-Karrer (1992), pp. 265-266.

Intervention

In marriage and family therapy, gender can be used as a lens for examining and enacting interventions. It is important to thoroughly assess where the couple falls on the gender-balance continuum in order to develop appropriate interventions. Breunlin, Schwartz, and MacKune-Karrer (1992), make specific intervention suggestions for clients at each of their five transitional stages (traditional through balanced). See Table 13.1 for some interventions suggested for these transitional stages. They note that "the treatment of gender imbalance consists of validating experiences and of expanding descriptions as well as explanations of female/male interactions" (p. 259). Whipple (1996) notes that in bringing up gender as a topic, the therapist questions the source of gender messages while helping clients explore the effects of gender messages and stereotypes in their relationships. It is important to be explicit (i.e., having one's umbrella wide open) in pointing out these connections in clients' lives (Breunlin, Schwartz, and MacKune-Karrer, 1992; Haddock, Zimmerman, and MacPhee, 2000; Whipple, 1996).

Empowering and valuing women is a consistent theme in gender-aware therapy (Breunlin, Schwartz, and MacKune-Karrer, 1992; Haddock, Zimmerman, and MacPhee, 2000; Parker, 1997a,b; Whipple, 1996). One way of empowering clients is to help them explore all of the options available to them, including nonstereotypical ones (Whipple, 1996), as well as by examining, and discarding if necessary, traditional gender expectations. Much of empowerment for clients is about helping them develop new identities as stronger people. Haddock, Zimmerman, and MacPhee (2000) recommend that therapists encourage female clients to be more attentive to self-care, to be assertive and independent, to pursue personal time and space, and to develop their own support systems. Therapists should help male clients to be more attentive to relationship maintenance, to be more emotionally expressive and available, to be more vulnerable in relationships, and to develop support systems that include men (Haddock, Zimmerman, and MacPhee, 2000).

Gender-aware therapy seeks to balance imbalances by affirming women (Whipple, 1996). There are several useful techniques in valuing and affirming women: take women seriously rather than discounting them; encourage women by supporting their decisions and noting their strengths; and validate women's anger and encourage them to express it constructively.

On the other hand, it is also important to be gender aware when working with men (Bograd, 1991; Deinhart and Avis, 1994; Font, Dolan-Del Vecchio, and Almeida, 1998; Green, 1998). Green (1998) and Font, Dolan-Del Vecchio, and Almeida (1998), discuss traditional and expanded norms of masculinity (see Table 13.2 for norms for both men and women) with the suggestion that men in particular need to challenge the traditional norms that keep them in traditional roles. As men learn to expand their roles within the family and within society, space is created for women to be able to change their own roles. One way of helping men to expand their roles is to empower them to develop an identity around these expanded roles. As an example, therapists could empower men to balance work and family by valuing their partner's work as much as their own (Schwartz, 1994) and by in-

TABLE 13.2. Traditional and Nontraditional Norms

Traditional Norms	Expanded Norms
Males	
Suppression of emotional vulnerability	Expanded emotionality
Avoiding feminine behavior	Embracing femininity
Primacy of the work role	Balancing work and family
Independence	Embracing relatedness over individualism
Aggression	Valuing collaboration in conflict resolution
Toughness and stoicism	Maintaining flexibility
Striving for dominance	Valuing shared power of relatedness
Provider/protector of the family	
Treating sexual partners as objects	Relational attitude toward sexuality
Females	
Passivity	Expanded assertiveness and proactive behavior
Submissive in relationship with partner	Valuing shared power of relatedness
Dependence	Valuing relatedness and independence
High emotionality	
Self-sacrificing	Caring for both self and others
Primacy of partner and mother role	Balancing family and work
Repression of anger	Comfort with assertive expression

Source: Adapted from Green (1998) and Font, Dolan-Del Vecchio, and Almeida (1998).

creasing their role in parenting. An important aspect of gender-aware therapy is empowerment for both women and men.

Deinhart and Avis (1994) found in a study of marriage and family therapists that the interventions most endorsed for working with men were in the areas of developing the therapists' skills in thinking about and noticing gender, promoting mutual responsibility (e.g., valuing work), and challenging stereotypical behaviors and attitudes (e.g., encouraging males to be active caregivers). Although Deinhart and Avis did not find therapists endorsing interventions geared toward increasing affective expression for men in therapy, other authors have stressed the importance of encouraging men to develop more intimate relationships and become more emotionally expressive (Ganley, 1991; Haddock, Zimmerman, and MacPhee, 2000).

In intervening to reduce gender imbalance, Breunlin, Schwartz, and MacKune-Karrer (1992) use universal statements about gender (e.g., "It is painful when family members experience limitations," p. 259), directives about behavior (e.g., "Would the two of you think about how you prepare your daughters for adulthood in the 1990s?" p. 260), and questions about gender in the family (e.g., "What do each of you think about the way responsibilities and decisions are shared in your house?" p. 260). Breunlin, Schwartz, and MacKune-Karrer (1992) and Roberts (1991) both recommend using circular questions (Selvini Palazzoli et al., 1978; Tomm, 1987) as gender interventions. Circular questions are useful in allowing people to take another person's perspective in looking at themselves. See Box 13.2 for some suggestions in using circular questions with gender (as well as with culture and spirituality).

Unfortunately, family therapists may not see many truly egalitarian couples in therapy. Schwartz (1994) suggests that many couples are "near-peers" (p. 2) (e.g., he is helpful to her around the house, but there is not an equal division of labor). Therefore, moving couples toward a truly peer relationship may be needed for couples to experience the full benefits of equality (Schwartz, 1994).

Power is one of the most important issues to deal with in considering gender in therapy. In fact, power may be the key concept. In reducing power differentials, Haddock, Zimmerman, and MacPhee (2000) discuss several dimensions of power within the family to which the therapist must attend. These include decision making; communication, and conflict resolution; work, life goals, and activities; housework; finances; sex; relationship maintenance; abuse and violence; and parental responsibility and parental style. It is also important to pay attention to and address issues of separation and divorce as they relate to power when these issues arise (Haddock, Zimmerman, and MacPhee, 2000). Many other writers have talked about the importance of utilizing gender-aware therapy specifically in the treatment of domestic

BOX 13.2. Circular Questions
About Gender, Culture, and Spirituality

In groups of two or three, practice asking one another some of the following questions to expand your ability to think about gender, culture, and spirituality. Think about how these questions could be used in therapy.

In terms of relationships generally:
- Who in your family of origin taught you the most about being a girl or boy/man or woman?
- What did your parents model for you about gender relationships in their interactions?

In terms of differences in behavior:
- Who would you consider to be the most stereotypically feminine in your family of origin? Masculine?
- Who gave you the most messages about what it was to be "a man" or "a woman"? About what it is to be white or black or Latino? About what it is to be of your religion?

Ranking by various members of the family regarding specific behaviors:
- Who in your family of origin most approves of you as a man/woman? As a member of your religion? As a member of your race or culture? Who least approves of those characteristics?

Explanation questions:
- What is your explanation of why society seems to ascribe different behaviors to different genders? Races? Religions?

Differences related to hypothetical circumstances:
- If your mother (father) had worked outside of the home (or had not), how do you think family relationships might have been different?
- If you had been born a different gender, how do you think your life would have been different as a child? What if you had been born a different race?
- If you were a different gender, how do you think your style as a therapist would be different? What if you were a different race or religion?

Normative comparison questions:
- Do you think your family was more or less flexible about gender roles than other families? Would others in your family agree with you or disagree?

(continued)

(continued)
- Did you learn similar things about your race as other children in your neighborhood, or did you learn different things within your family? How about regarding gender? Religion?

Conservative needs questions:
- Assume there are important reasons for your family to continue its patterns around gender, race, and religious roles. What would those reasons be?

Process interruption questions:
- What part of you is most comfortable talking about these topics? Least comfortable?
- If we were to stop this discussion, what would your reaction be?

Source: Adapted from Roberts (1991).

violence. For example, see Almeida and Durkin (1999), Bograd (1999), Goldner (1999), and Jory and Anderson (1999) in a recent special section of the *Journal of Marital and Family Therapy* on the treatment of domestic violence.

Parker (1997a,b) has explored power issues in couple therapy and makes some recommendations for how therapists can attend to power dynamics. Parker (1997b) recommends four strategies for broaching power issues. These are (1) structuring the session for consciousness raising; (2) boldly naming power issues; (3) indirectly raising the power issues; and (4) meeting with partners separately to raise the issues.

An additional power variable to consider in looking at gender in therapy involves power differentials between the therapist and the clients. Therapy inherently involves power differentials—clients come to therapists for help with a problem that they cannot solve themselves, and they often expect therapists to be experts. However, it is important to maintain a collaborative stance when working with clients to ensure that the imbalance of power remains manageable and is made explicit (Haddock, Zimmerman, and MacPhee, 2000).

Gender plays a role in how clients perceive therapy, including the goals and tasks of therapy (Gregory and Leslie, 1996; Werner-Wilson, 1997) and how therapists perceive clients, including whose goals are attended to, and who is interrupted (Stabb, Cox, and Harber, 1997; Werner-Wilson et al., 1997; Werner-Wilson, Zimmerman, and Price, 1999). Therapists need to keep in their awareness the potential for power imbalance and the different ways that men and women may react to therapy and therapists.

Though there has been very little research on the topic of gender in marital and family therapy practice, studies that have been done are informative. Women and men react differently in how they develop a therapeutic alliance in therapy (Werner-Wilson, 1997). This suggests that therapists must pay attention to gender as a variable as they develop alliances with their clients. Clients' gender also impacts how therapists interact with them in other ways. Werner-Wilson et al. (1997) found that MFT doctoral students interrupted women clients three times more often than male clients, even while controlling for amount of talking and gender of therapist. Werner-Wilson, Zimmerman, and Price (1999) found that gender influenced therapeutic goals as well, with women's goals being attended to more in marital therapy while men's goals were attended to more in family therapy.

Gender is a critical part of marital and family therapy; gender is inescapable because people are gendered and our society is gendered. To ignore gender in therapy is to do an injustice to women and to men. These interventions focus on making gender and power dynamics an explicit part of therapy. If therapists do not address gender in their work, they are, in effect, supporting the status quo of gender inequality, which is bad for women, bad for men, and bad for relationships (Kessler and McRae, 1982; Steil, 1997).

Case Example

Sheila (twenty-nine) and Don (thirty-three) are a Caucasian, middle-class couple. They have a nine-month old daughter, Jesse. Sheila works full time as a physical therapist and Don works full time as a real estate agent.

The couple has come to therapy because of marital difficulties that have been causing them to argue a lot and to feel a loss of emotional closeness with each other. Sheila reports that she is frustrated because "right at the time that Don should be cutting back at work to spend more time with his daughter," he has begun working late almost every night. She is exhausted and angry because she is doing the bulk of the child care and housework. She also mentions that the "straw that broke the camel's back" was Don telling his parents that they could spend the holidays with them without even consulting Sheila. Don reports he feels that Sheila does not even notice him—"She is so wrapped up with the baby." He says that when he does get time with Sheila, she is angry and emotionally unavailable. He also feels that Sheila does not understand that he cannot cut back at work—"We need the money I earn now more than ever."

Using the gender umbrella, the therapist recognizes the gender and power dynamics that are underlying the couple's marital difficulties. Her assessment of the couple's difficulties includes the influence of the social context that defines men as primary breadwinners and women as primary caretakers, and places the couple as traditional along the continuum of gender positions. The therapist brings up the topic of gender and explores with the couple the possible influences of gender socialization on the presenting problem. For instance, she may use circular questions (see Box 13.2) to explore whether Don's increased focus on work is related to pressures that he be the primary breadwinner for his family.

The therapist makes efforts to validate the internal struggles of both Don and Sheila.

Following a collaborative exploration of the influence of gender socialization on the behaviors of each partner, the therapist normalizes that many couples encounter similar difficulties upon the birth of their first child. She then overtly states that these gender messages can be harmful to individuals and their relationships, inviting the couple to consider some of these negative effects (e.g., loss of intimacy and friendship in marriage, a compromised emotional connection between fathers and children, exhaustion and anger for women). She also encourages the couple to consider the benefits of resisting these messages, and invites both partners to articulate what they would like their marriage to "look like." Both indicate that they want to enjoy their friendship again and to share all aspects of their life as partners.

Based on this information, the therapist assists the couple in collaboratively setting the following goals: (1) to involve Don more in the parenting of his daughter, (2) to divide household labor equitably between Don and Sheila, (3) to allow Sheila time for self-care, (4) to develop skills for negotiating decisions together, and (5) to share financial responsibility for the family and to equally value their careers.

CULTURE

In some ways, the field of marital and family therapy has embraced addressing ethnicity, culture, and race, more fully than it has embraced gender. For example, the *Handbook of Family Therapy,* Volume II (Gurman and Kniskern, 1991) devoted a chapter to ethnicity and family therapy (McGoldrick et al., 1991), but did not address gender in any significant way. However, the feminist critique helped to spur our field on to explore issues of culture, race, and ethnicity (Leslie, 1995).

Our field has also had some debate over how to address issues of culture, ethnicity, and/or **race.** McGoldrick et al. (1991) refer to **ethnicity** as "a concept of a group's 'peoplehood' based on a combination of race, religion, and cultural history, whether or not members realize their commonalities with one another" (p. 547). Interestingly, McGoldrick and Giordano (1996) define ethnicity as "a common ancestry through which individuals have evolved shared values and customs" (p. 1), which is a somewhat more narrow definition. Ethnicity has, at times, been even more narrowly defined as simply a group that is regarded as a group due to its common ancestry (Preli and Bernard, 1993). Further distinctions have been made between ethnicity and **ethnic minority groups,** with the term ethnic minority being perhaps more relevant because we all have an ethnic background, but only some of us fit into ethnic minority groups and are targeted for discrimination and prejudice.

At a more general level, others have talked about and defined the word **culture**. Falicov (1995) provides perhaps the best multidimensional definition of culture, culminating from years of her published work:

> shared world views, meanings and adaptive behaviors derived from simultaneous membership and participation in a multiplicity of contexts, such as rural, urban or suburban setting; language, age, gender, cohort, family configuration, race, ethnicity, religion, nationality, socioeconomic status, employment, education, occupation, sexual orientation, political ideology; migration and stage of acculturation. (p. 375)

This definition is much broader than an ethnic-focused one in that it allows for the examination of a multitude of variables. This broad definition of culture has led to the adoption of a **multicultural** perspective by many (Breunlin, Schwartz, and MacKune-Karrer, 1992; Preli and Bernard, 1993).

So why is a multicultural framework important in therapy? The United States is one of the most ethnically and culturally diverse nations in the history of the world (McGoldrick et al., 1991). A multicultural perspective validates the variety of ways that culture influences our humanity (Breunlin, Schwartz, and MacKune-Karrer, 1992). Just as in dealing with gender, to ignore multicultural influences is to legitimize only one reality—that of the dominant culture. However, by taking a multicultural view one can see that, given the multitude of variables subsumed into the view, there is no truly dominant culture. Yet our history books, our research studies, our popular media, and our societal messages tend to compare all of us to a "dominant culture."

Each of us fits into different "levels" of culture—different ages, educational levels, social class, race, ethnicity, sexual orientation, religion, etc. Falicov (1995) notes that each person is raised in a number of cultural subgroups, and each of us draws selectively from these groups' relative influences. Family therapy has been accused of holding monolithic views of the family based upon ideals of the majority culture (Breunlin, Schwartz, and MacKune-Karrer, 1992; Preli and Bernard, 1993), but, as McGoldrick (1998) notes, "all families, not just 'minorities' are seen as embedded in and bounded by class, culture, gender, and race. Moreover, how a society defines gender, race, culture, and class relationships is viewed as critical to understanding how *all* family processes are structured" (p. 17, italics in original). To not pay attention to culture is to deny the embeddedness of families in culture.

It is also important that therapists, and majority-group therapists in particular, understand the role of prejudice and discrimination in our culture.

The first ethical issue listed in the American Association for Marriage and Family Therapy's (AAMFT) *Code of Ethics* is that "Marriage and family therapists do not discriminate against or refuse professional service to anyone on the basis of race, gender, religion, national origin, or sexual orientation" (AAMFT *Code of Ethics,* Line 1.1). At another level, *Code of Ethics* specifies that marriage and family therapists (MFTs) cannot practice outside of their competence. Therapists need to understand issues of culture in particular so that they do not practice in areas outside their realm of knowledge (Thomas, 1992).

A powerful resource for therapists and students can be found in two videos that discuss prejudice and discrimination in the United States. These are *The Color of Fear* (Mun Wah, 1994), which discusses prejudice in relation to men, and *The Way Home* (Butler, 1998), which provides a similar discussion about women. Prejudice and discrimination are a fact of life for minority groups by definition. To be truly effective in working with clients who are members of minority groups, therapists should be aware of the levels of. prejudice and discrimination in our society and the impact that they have on our clients. However, a multicultural approach needs to include more than just sensitivity training in order to be relevant (Preli and Bernard, 1993); a truly relevant approach helps majority-culture therapists understand their own experience from an ethnic and cultural perspective.

Culture and the Practice of Marital and Family Therapy

There are many things to consider when working with families from a multicultural perspective. One is that families are unique within cultural groups (Gladding, 1998; Hanna and Brown, 1995). Family therapists should distinguish among a family's patterns that are universal and common to a wide variety of families, patterns that are culture specific, and patterns that are idiosyncratic to that particular family (Goldenberg and Goldenberg, 2000). One way for therapists to increase their understanding of families from a multicultural perspective is to learn as much as possible about a variety of cultural groups. One particularly useful resource in exploring the impact of ethnicity on families is the book *Ethnicity and Family Therapy* (Second Edition) by McGoldrick, Giordano, and Pearce (1996). This book has chapters on nine general ethnic groups and forty different specific ethnic family types (e.g., Jamaican families, Korean families, Hungarian families, Russian families, Soviet Jewish families, etc.). This is perhaps the most comprehensive exploration of ethnic families available to family therapists. However, its authors caution that therapists should not feel that they have to know everything about every ethnic group; of primary importance is an awareness of difference and similarity (McGoldrick and Giordano, 1996).

Because family therapists cannot know everything about every family type (though therapists should always strive to learn more about diversity), there are some general guidelines that are perhaps even more important to consider. Falicov (1995) believes that existing theories, practices, and beliefs should be viewed through a "cultural lens." She asserts there are key parameters that therapists should keep in mind as they assess families and plan interventions. These four parameters of assessment and intervention are *ecological context, migration and acculturation, family organization,* and *family life cycle.* Ecological context might include such areas as a family's community, work, living conditions, school environment, and so on. Migration is another factor to view with this cultural lens. It includes if and when a family migrated and whether that migration was forced or voluntary. Family organization refers to how a family is arranged according to its "cultural code." This code influences family hierarchy, family values, communication styles, and emotional expressivity. When family life cycle is viewed through a cultural lens, therapists do not look at developmental norms but rather at what is normal to a particular culture. Established norms and developmental processes may not fit for some cultures, but therapists should be wary about assuming health or pathology based on norms that may be asynchronous with the culture at hand. These areas are of particular importance in both assessment and intervention with families.

Assessment

Having a multicultural perspective while assessing families is very important (Breunlin, Schwartz, and MacKune-Karrer, 1992; Falicov, 1995; Patterson et al., 1999). It is particularly important to keep this perspective in mind when the client's culture is different from that of the therapist so that the therapist does not misinterpret as pathological behavior which may be culturally based (Breunlin, Schwartz, and MacKune-Karrer, 1992; Hanna and Brown, 1995; Patterson et al., 1999). For example, in seeing an Asian-American family, young children may be indulged more than is typical in U.S. culture (Berg and Jaya, 1993). A non-Asian therapist seeing this might interpret pathology where there is none if she or he does not have at least a basic understanding of Asian-American families.

Therapists should assess the degree of fit between the therapist and client regarding immigration and acculturation status, economics, education, ethnicity, religion, gender, age, race, majority/minority status, and regional background (Breunlin, Schwartz, and MacKune-Karrer, 1992). Each of these areas may impact values and behavior and, if not assessed, therapists may assume more similarity (or difference) than actually exists. Breunlin, Schwartz, and MacKune-Karrer list a variety of questions therapists can explore in assessing this degree of fit. However, it is equally important to know that there are both advantages and disadvantages to being in the same cultural group as your client (McGoldrick and Giordano, 1996). One of the potential disadvantages of belonging to the same group is that you may believe that you understand them fully even though families and individuals differ.

Hanna and Brown (1995) offer a number of questions for assessing racial and cultural factors in therapy:

- How does your racial/cultural/religious heritage make your family different from other families you know?
- Compared to other families in your cultural group, how is your family different?
- What are the values that your family identifies as being important parts of your heritage?
- At this particular time in your family's development, are there issues related to your cultural heritage that are being questioned by anyone?
- What is the hardest part about being a minority in U.S. culture?
- When you think of living in America versus the country of your heritage; what are the main differences?
- What lessons did you learn about your people? About other peoples?
- What did you learn about disloyalty?
- What were people in your family really down on? [i.e., what did they dislike?]
- What might an outsider not understand about your racial/cultural/religious background? (p. 101)

Many of these questions should be modified based upon the majority/minority status of the client and the degree of match between therapist and client.

Additional assessment factors include exploring the importance of culture with clients and families (McGoldrick and Giordano, 1996) and considering cultural background when evaluating other assessment materials (e.g., assessment instruments such as the Dyadic Adjustment Scale), since behaviors may have different meanings within different cultures (Patterson et al., 1999). Once again, power comes into play as well, as different cultural groups experience different levels of power in society. Being aware of and assessing power dynamics within the family and of the family within society is of vital importance (Patterson et al., 1999).

One of the more ignored aspects of culture in family therapy has been social class and poverty. However, often more differences exist within a cultural group based upon class than across cultural groups of the same class. Every cultural group has social class divisions (Goldenberg and Goldenberg, 2000) and therapists should assess and attend to these factors as well. In particular, social class often determines access to power within society (Goldenberg and Goldenberg, 2000). Aponte's *Bread and Spirit: Therapy with the New Poor* (1994) provides an excellent resource for the family therapist in understanding work with the poor.

One final way to conceptualize assessment from a multicultural perspective is to assess both opportunities and constraints (Breunlin, Schwartz, and MacKune-Karrer, 1992). Many families are constrained by their culture, and many families feel particularly constrained when coming to therapy. The therapist can open room for unexplored opportunity as well as explore the sense of constraint within the family. Opening room for opportunity can also be one target of intervention.

Hines and Boyd-Franklin (1996) illustrate one way prejudice and discrimination affect African-American couples:

> Usually, African American women initiate the therapy process. Therapists may get frustrated with women who express intense dissatisfaction yet resist change in dysfunctional relationships. Their discontent frequently is coupled with an awareness of the torment that generations of racism have caused for both African American men and women, and empathy for their husbands' frustration and sense of powerlessness. (p. 70)

Intervention

Although our field has much to say on the use of a multicultural perspective in assessment, little has been done with specific interventions. Most of the literature seems to focus on training therapists to think multiculturally (e.g., Falicov, 1995). However, some specific suggestions for intervention have been made.

Perhaps the most basic intervention is that of making culture the central metaphor for therapy (Laird, 1998). Culture as a metaphor for therapy implies understanding people within their own context. This helps clients and families by empowering them to change within their context and to change their context, while recognizing that context can provide both opportunity and constraint. McGill (1992) spells out the core metaphors and themes of different cultural stories. For example, one core metaphor for Native Americans is harmony with nature. Metaphor in general can be an excellent way of introducing topics from within a client's perspective (see Lyness and Thomas, 1995, for an illustration of using metaphor within a narrative framework).

Marital and family therapists need also to validate and strengthen cultural identity. When families are placed under stress—as client families typically are—their sense of identity can become diffuse. Therapists can foster a sense of identity by strengthening the sense of cultural heritage helping the family to find resources in that identity (McGoldrick and Giordano, 1996).

Therapists also need to be aware of and support client support systems from a cultural perspective. Many families are unconnected from traditional support systems, and therapists need to be aware of ways to connect individuals and families with support in the community (e.g., community organizations and supports such as El Centro or Lambda centers) (McGoldrick and Giordano, 1996). Therapists can also serve as "culture brokers" (McGoldrick and Giordano, 1996, p. 23) and help the family identify and resolve value conflicts. Conflicts often exist both intrapersonally and within the family about aspects of cultural background, including pride in some aspects and shame about others. Family therapists can help families explore and resolve these conflicts (McGoldrick and Giordano, 1996).

Perhaps one of the most important interventions from a multicultural perspective is to move beyond polarizing discussions (McGoldrick and Giordano, 1996). When families are polarized, they are constrained from other options. Black-versus-white or male-versus-female polarizations keep people stuck. Therapists need to notice and address such polarizations. One way of reducing polarization is for the therapist to validate both sides, rather than take sides. For example, in families with generations at different levels of acculturation, the different generations may become polarized. The therapist should try to validate the older and younger generations together to reduce polarized discussion (see the following case example).

Many of the interventions suggested for a gender-aware therapy, particularly including attention to power dynamics, are equally useful in multicultural therapy. The most important intervention in working from a multicultural perspective is to maintain a collaborative stance with your clients. By maintaining collaboration, therapists can avoid pitfalls of power and can empower families to change.

Case Example

Lupe (forty-two), is seeking therapy because she is concerned about her daughter, Rose (fourteen). Lupe is divorced from Rose's father, Manuel, but he is in the community and has visitation rights with Rose. Lupe does not feel that Manuel is a resource for helping Rose at this time. Lupe was born in Mexico but immigrated to the United States when she was an adolescent.

The therapist begins by asking Lupe about her concerns regarding her daughter. She reports that Rose has been getting into trouble—breaking curfew, getting poor grades, skipping school, and dating boys that are "no good." Lupe also expresses disappointment that Rose is gone from home too much and does not eat meals or attend church with her. Lupe is concerned that Rose will not be able to find a suitable husband if she does not start "acting like a lady."

The therapist then asks Rose to respond to her mother's concerns. Rose claims that her mother "just doesn't want me to have friends," and is "trying to keep me her little girl." Rose argues that she is not doing anything that her friends are not doing, and that her mother just does not understand how difficult it has been for her to make friends and fit in at her school. Rose says that she does not spend more time with her mom because "it is boring to hang out with Mom" and "church is stupid."

While listening to Lupe and Rose share their perspectives, the therapist recognizes that the mother and daughter are experiencing common difficulties with emancipation. However, using a cultural umbrella, the therapist seeks to understand these difficulties within a cultural context. For instance, does the daughter feel that she must deny her cultural beliefs and practices to "fit in" at a school that is predominantly Caucasian? Is Rose's "pulling away" from her mother influenced in part by racist messages that her mother's (her culture's) ways are inferior? How are different levels of acculturation influencing the emancipation process?

The therapist collaboratively explores these questions with Lupe and Rose. Using culture as the central metaphor of therapy, the therapist helps Lupe and Rose understand their difficulties within a cultural context. This exploration allows mother and daughter to see their difficulties from a new perspective, and provides a means for reconnection and commonality. The therapist helps reconnect Rose with her cultural background by encouraging her involvement in a youth group at her church where she can interact with people her own age and still connect with her cultural background. The therapist also explores the racism that Rose encounters at school and facilitates a conversation between mother and daughter about ways to cope with it.

In addition, the therapist inquires about the process by which daughters emancipate within the Mexican culture. As a result of these efforts, Lupe and Rose decide that, when Rose turns fifteen years old, they will hold a *quinceañera*—a Mexican tradition that marks a girl's passage from childhood into adulthood and renews baptism vows in the Catholic Church. One significant part of this tradition is that the girl's first dance is with her father; this will provide a way for Rose to reconnect with her father, and for Lupe and Manuel to work together. Recognizing that it is time to begin planning a *quinceañera* allows Lupe to realize that her daughter is becoming a woman. Her daughter's enthusiasm for the ceremony alleviates some of her fears about her daughter "losing her way" in the dominant culture.

SPIRITUALITY

In the past, **religion** and **spirituality** were often considered only under the umbrella of culture (see Breunlin, Schwartz, and MacKune-Karrer, 1992, for an example). However, interest has been growing recently regarding spirituality and religion in clinical practice (Harris, 1998; Prest, Russel, and Souza, 1999; Stander et al., 1994; Walsh, 1999c), and some have noted that it is not enough to discuss religion or spirituality from a cultural perspective (Stander et al., 1994). As one example of growing interest in spirituality in family therapy, the *Family Therapy Networker*'s cover headline for the January/February 2000 issue is "Christian Counseling: A Journey Beyond the self" and the lead article is "Inside Christian Counseling" (Wylie, 2000).

In some form or another, spirituality and religion have been a part of our field for many years (Humphrey, 1983). One branch of our history as a profession (MFT), the marriage counselors, often consisted of pastors or ministers. Marriage often has a religious basis; weddings are often religious ceremonies. Yet in general, as marriage and family therapists, we have attempted to maintain a *secular* outlook, keeping religion and therapy strictly apart. As Wylie (2000) notes, however, a large number of counselors consider themselves Christian and believe that part of their counseling job requires counseling in religion and religious beliefs. The American Association of Christian Counselors had approximately 18,000 members in 2000. By contrast, the American Association for Marriage and Family Therapists states that they represent the interests of 23,000 therapists (see <www. AAMFT.org>). Clearly, a great deal of clinical interest in religion and spirituality exists and seems to be growing.

Religion has been defined as "an organized belief system that includes shared, and usually institutionalized, moral values, beliefs about God or a Higher Power, and involvement in a faith community" (Walsh, 1999b, p. 5). Spirituality is an overarching construct which "refers more generally to transcendent beliefs and practices" (Walsh, 1999b, p. 6). Spirituality can be experienced either within or without organized religion; it is more often seen as a general construct that does not necessarily have to do with a specific Higher Power. In fact, some define it as a sense of connection to others, the world, and the universe (Walsh, 1999b). Spirituality has also been defined as "the multifaceted relationship or connection between human and metaphysical systems" (Prest and Keller, 1993, p. 138).

Spirituality has four elements, according to one model (Haug, 1998b). These dimensions include (1) the cognitive, wherein spirituality prompts us to reflect upon our lives, relationships, and the meaning we give to experiences; (2) the affective, wherein spiritual beliefs help people to experience a sense of safety and security, confidence and hope, and belonging and connection; (3) the behavioral, wherein spiritual experiences and beliefs lead to lifestyle choices; and (4) the developmental, wherein beliefs are transmitted through religious affiliations, values, and beliefs in the family of origin and continue to evolve over the life span.

In summarizing literature on spirituality and religion in the family, Walsh (1999b) notes that nearly 90 percent of adults say religion is important in their lives and 96 percent of Americans believe in God or a universal spirit. Among teenagers, 93 percent believe in God. Americans adhere to a number of different religions, but are primarily Christian (85 percent), with 57 percent considering themselves Protestant. Major Protestant denominations include Baptist (19 percent of all adults), Methodist (9 percent), Lutheran (6 percent), Presbyterian (4 percent), Episcopalian (4 percent), and Pentecostal (1 percent). Twenty-six percent of all Americans are Catholic, an additional 2 percent are Mormon, and 1 percent are Eastern Orthodox (Walsh, 1999b). The non-Christian population in the United States has grown from 3.6 percent in 1900, to 9.9 percent in 1970, to 14.6 percent in 1995 (Gallup, 1996); it is expected to grow to 14.8 percent in the mid-2000's (*Encyclopedia Britannica,* 1998). Two percent of Americans identify as Jewish, and Islam, Hinduism, and Buddhism each are currently at 1 percent.

As these statistics show, religion and belief in a Higher Power are important to the vast majority of Americans. For many, religion and spirituality are a great source of strength. Research on healthy families (Beavers and Hampson, 1990; Curran, 1983; Stinnett and DeFrain, 1985; see Thomas, 1992 for an additional review) shows consistently that spiritual beliefs and practices are key ingredients in healthy family functioning, helping people to cope with the negative experiences life inevitably provides and giving meaning and ritual to daily life. Spiritual and religious beliefs are also seen as ways to strengthen family resilience (Walsh, 1999b,c; Wolin et al., 1999).

Unfortunately, although religion and spirituality are a great source of strength for many, for others religion is another symbol of patriarchy, sexism, and heterosexism (Walsh, 1999b). In addition, some religious cults have created serious problems for families and their members (Walsh, 1999b). Many fundamentalist religions continue to promote traditional gender expectations in which women are considered second-class citizens and homosexuality is condemned. Fundamentalist religions have also been blamed for high levels of domestic violence because of their high levels of patriarchy (Benokraitis, 1999). The message to women in some religions in cases of domestic violence is that they must not be a good-enough wife. As an example, Barnett and LaViolette (1993) quote a woman who saw a Christian counselor:

> The counselor told me in front of my husband to be a better wife and mother, to pray harder, to be more submissive. He told my husband that he shouldn't hit me. When we got home, my husband only remembered the part about how I should be more submissive. (p. 32)

One resource for therapists and students in understanding the role of religion in domestic violence can be found in the video *Broken Vows—Religious Perspectives on Domestic Violence,* Parts I and II (Center for the Prevention of Sexual and Domestic Violence, 1994).

Of course, most religions do not condone domestic violence. For the majority of people, religion is a source of strength and positivity. However, the underlying patriarchy of many religions supports gender power imbalances. Some organizations that are meant to bring men closer to their families (e.g., the Christian Promise Keepers groups) have had a patriarchal stance that keeps men as the heads of household. Patriarchy, sexism, and heterosexism have driven many away from organized religion (Walsh, 1999b).

Spirituality and the Clinical Practice of Marital and Family Therapy

Marital and family therapy's exploration of spirituality is a relatively recent phenomenon (Harris, 1998; Prest and Keller, 1993; Walsh, 1999b). Kelly (1992) reviewed family therapy journals and found that, among over 3,600 articles, only 1.3 percent included religion as a major component, and only 0.7 percent in a major and positive way. In the past, MFT has been interested in establishing a scientific authenticity that has interfered with the embracing of spirituality—a decidedly unscientific pursuit. In addition, the field has steered away from spirituality because of rigid conceptions of spirituality and religion as requiring evangelism.

In part, this has been due to therapists attempting to be attentive to power issues—telling clients how to live their spiritual lives was seen as a potential abuse of power (Prest and Keller, 1993). In fact, it is important to consider the ethical considerations in discussing spirituality, as with any therapeutic endeavor (Haug, 1998a; Prest and Keller, 1993). As an example, therapists who identify themselves as working from a spiritual perspective may have clients that seek them out as a result. One of the ethical challenges is avoiding being perceived as colluding with the "spiritually one-up spouse" (Rotz, Russell, and Wright, 1993, p. 369).

As in working from a multicultural perspective, in working with spirituality it is helpful to have an understanding of the varieties of spiritual experience (Stewart and Gale, 1994; Ross, 1994). Also, as with approaches to gender and culture, it is important to assess spirituality and religion in families (Breunlin, Schwartz, and MacKune-Karrer, 1992; Gottman, 1999; Stewart and Gale, 1994; Ross, 1994).

Assessment

Assessment of spirituality and religion within the family are vital to incorporating spirituality in clinical practice. There are several frameworks for assessment of spirituality and religion in families. Raider (1992) suggests four general areas in which to assess spirituality: family structure, family processes, boundaries, and family system equilibrium. Table 13.3 spells out some specific assessment questions for each of these four areas. Additional discussion regarding assessment of spirituality can be found in Breunlin, Schwartz, and MacKune-Karrer (1992), Haug (1998b), and Walsh (1999a).

As always, it is also important to assess the degree of fit or lack of fit between therapist and client regarding belief systems (Anderson and Worthen, 1997; Breunlin, Schwartz, and MacKune-Karrer, 1992; Haug, 1998b; Rotz, Russell, and Wright, 1993). If there is difference between the belief systems of the therapist and client, these differences should be processed and recognized. For example, if a therapist is Catholic and has clients who are Muslim, these differences should be acknowledged and made explicit in the therapy. When beliefs are similar, such beliefs may be a source of therapeutic strength (Anderson and Worthen, 1997). Even if beliefs differ, however, spirituality can be integrated into intervention.

Intervention. Therapists must explore spiritual issues in four areas: (a) the client's belief systems; (b) the therapist's own belief systems; (c) the relationship between clients, therapists, and religious communities; and (d) the field of family therapy itself, that is, in the theories and models of family therapy (Stander et al., 1994). Each of these areas has implications for practice and intervention.

Regarding the field of MFT, many theories have spiritual dimensions to them (Harris, 1998). In particular, contextual theory (Boszormenyi-Nagy and Krasner, 1986) deals with the ethical nature of relating in what could be construed as a spiritual way (although it is not necessarily presented that way). Therapists should explore their own theories as they think about utilizing spirituality in their practice.

Religiously or spiritually sensitive therapists should have respect for the "ethic of religious autonomy" (Stander et al., 1994, p. 31). Spiritually sensitive therapists should also pay attention to clients' personal struggles to grow religiously yet approach potentially religious issues (e.g., divorce, abortion, sexual orientation, etc.) without allowing his or her own struggles to interfere with the clients' therapy (Stander et al., 1994).

At the most basic level, similar to working with gender and multiculturalism, a collaborative stance of the therapist in working with clients regarding spirituality and religion is again important (Joanides, 1996). Because power

TABLE 13.3. Some Examples of Spirituality Assessment Questions

Dimension of Family Functioning	Questions
Family structure	To what extent does the family's religion specify rules and norms concerning marriage, divorce, contraception, fidelity, etc.?
	To what extent does the family's religion specify sex roles?
	To what extent does the family's religion value family life?
Family processes	What is the religious orthodoxy of each member of the family? Are the members of the family similar to one another?
	To what extent does the family's religion emphasize emotional closeness, nurturance, and intimacy among family members?
	To what extent does the family's religion influence the family's capacity to tolerate diversity and different points of view?
Boundaries	To what extent does the family's religion influence family rules, norms, and expectations that determine family members' behavior?
	To what extent does the family's religion influence family morals, values, and ethical positions?
	To what extent does the family's religion influence the family's boundaries within the neighborhood and community?
Family system equilibrium	To what extent does the family's religion emphasize tradition, order, and stability?
	To what extent does the family's religion shape the family's identity?
	To what extent does the family's religion prescribe family rituals characterized by repetition, stylization, and order?

Source: Adapted from Raider (1992).

dynamics can again come into play, reducing power differentials between client and therapist is important, and similar techniques may be used (see Haddock, Zimmerman, and MacPhee, 2000, for suggestions regarding reducing power differentials in therapy). Joanides (1996) notes that adopting a collaborative approach reduces the tendency to mislabel religious issues as pathological, prevents the therapist from misinterpreting subtle religious issues as irrelevant to therapy, and helps keep therapists from inadvertently imposing their worldview on client families while allowing a broader and deeper discussion of the family's religious and spiritual experiences.

One model of spirituality versus religion in therapy comes from Alcoholics Anonymous (AA) (Berenson, 1990; Walsh, 1999b). Twelve-step programs such as AA are built upon essentially Christian ideals (confession, service to others), but these are stripped of their religious trappings and boiled down to their essential spirituality. One basic principle of twelve-step programs is trying to live according to spiritual principles. This "soft" approach to spirituality has been healing for many people, and family therapists might find ways to incorporate twelve-step principles into their practice as a way of increasing attention to spirituality.

Several general themes can be used by therapists in working with spirituality. To promote the strengths and healing that religion can provide, therapists can help clients search for and explore their religious roots (Walsh, 1999a). Different religious practices can also be fostered or explored with families, including prayer, meditation, and rituals (Imber-Black and Roberts, 1992; Roberts, 1999; Walsh, 1999a). Evan Imber-Black and Janine Roberts explore nonreligious ways to build rituals in family life in *Rituals for Our Times: Celebrating, Healing, and Changing Our Lives and Our Relationships* (1992).

One of the more positive aspects of utilizing spirituality is in the encouragement of faith-based activism (Walsh, 1999a). Walsh points out that studies of resilient people often find that they gain strength from collaborative efforts to right wrongs or bring about change. Other spiritual writers have also espoused the benefits of service (e.g., Doherty, 1995, in *Soul Searching: Why Psychotherapy Must Promote Moral Responsibility*). One such resource for therapists and clients is Thomas Moore's (1992) *Care of the Soul: A Guide for Cultivating Depth and Sacredness in Everyday Life*.

Rotz, Russell, and Wright (1993) offer some specific suggestions for working with religious families, particularly when there is a spiritually "one-up" spouse. One basic intervention with religious families is to ask the partners their expectations of therapy. This makes explicit the agendas of family members and can bring to the forefront any religious goals the family may have. It is also important to make the issue of spiritual differences explicit within the couple dynamics. This goes back to previous suggestions about addressing power differentials within families—spirituality can be a source of power in religious families; that is, the more spiritual or religious members can use this as a power dynamic over those in the family who are less so when spirituality or religion is highly valued. Therapists are encouraged to disavow conversion efforts; that is, therapists should not get involved in family conflict over converting a family member. At a more basic level, it is also important to balance the therapeutic agenda (as in most family therapy). With some families who have destructive religious agendas, the therapist may, in fact, have to limit or disallow "God talk" (Rotz, Russell, and Wright, 1993, p. 373).

Prest and Keller (1993) make suggestions for working with families within both traditional and nontraditional belief systems, particularly when spirituality and religion have become part of the presenting problem. When working with families with traditional belief systems, the therapist may identify solutions that have become part of the problem, as sometimes spiritual solutions become problematic. Therapists are encouraged to elicit fundamental beliefs or values that provide foundations for clients' spiritual beliefs and that seem to be contributing to the presenting problem. Dialogues regarding incongruent spiritual maps can also be very helpful for family members who are struggling with a lack of fit between one's situation and beliefs (or spiritual map). If the therapist is comfortable with this type of intervention, use of quotations from religious texts can be used. This can often be a powerful way of reinforcing a therapeutic message. However, there should be a degree of fit between the intervention and the therapist's belief systems, as well as the client's beliefs. Finally, therapists are encouraged to use themselves in the process, by sharing their own spiritual process. However, therapists must develop a degree of comfort when using the self in therapy (Prest and Keller, 1993). One warning, however, is that therapists must reassess some basic therapeutic practices based upon client's religious beliefs. For example, the use of masturbation in the treatment of sexual dysfunction might cause some clients difficulty (Stander et al., 1994).

There is a basic difference in approach to therapy from a spiritual perspective—the concept of healing versus treatment (Walsh, 1999a). Healing implies "a gathering of resources within the person, the family, and the community, and is fostered through the therapeutic relationship" (Walsh, 1999a, p. 33), whereas treatment is "externally administered by experts" (p. 33). One consistent aspect of healing is that it does not necessarily involve the removal of symptoms (Moore, 1992; Wright, 1999). In caring for the soul, versus treating the person, there are times when suffering is helpful. However, clients do not always want to hear that. I (KL) once was treating a client who was getting over a divorce. He asked at one point how he could stop hurting, and I told him, "Sometimes you just have to hurt for awhile." I never saw that client again. Clients want answers and relief, but by taking a spiritual perspective we can help them value their suffering and benefit from it.

Further resources are available for learning about the use of spirituality in therapy. Walsh's (1999c) *Spiritual Resources in Family Therapy* goes into great depth on many topics related to spirituality.

Research

To date, there appear to be only two studies of spirituality and religion in the training and practice of family therapy (Prest, Russel, amd Sauza, 1999; Carlson et al., 2002). This study found that MFT graduate students value the role of spirituality and religion in their own lives and in the lives of their clients, see themselves as both spiritual and religious, view spirituality as connected to other aspects of life, and devote energy to developing their spiritual lives. However, these students felt constrained from discussing spirituality in their professional lives, even though they reported that spirituality often influenced their choice of career. Those with clinical experience consider spiritual issues in their practice, for the most part, and believe that spirituality enhances their work. One finding of note was that students were more likely to emphasize spirituality over religion, most likely in an attempt to avoid proselytizing.

Although the majority of students in this study valued and used spirituality, fewer than half had any training regarding the use of spirituality in clinical work. Clearly the field is making some progress regarding spirituality, but more advances need to be made.

Case Example

Michelle and Pete have recently decided to get married. Both have two children from previous marriages. The couple has sought therapy for help in blending their families and are primarily concerned about how to manage their difference in faith—Michelle and her children are Catholic, and Pete and his children are Jewish. They state that their concerns came to a head when they were planning the wedding ceremony.

The therapist congratulates the couple on their proactive stance in dealing with potential difficulties in their relationship, and normalizes that virtually all stepfamilies encounter difficulties in blending their families. The therapist states that differences in faith can present additional challenges, but that many couples have found ways to effectively manage these challenges.

After a thorough assessment of the couple's situation and beliefs, the therapist makes several recommendations. First, the therapist discusses with the couple the possibility of accepting and honoring multiple realities (i.e., more than one faith) and encourages each partner to learn about the other's religion. The therapist encourages the couple to explore any negative views they may hold about the other's faith. For instance, given that anti-Semitic views are not uncommon in the United States, the therapist invites Michelle to consider the influence these views have on her openness to celebrate and practice more than one faith.

The therapist also encourages the couple to explore various options for managing these differences. For instance, the therapist helps the couple consider (1) celebrating all the rituals of both of their faiths, and exposing their children to both faiths; (2) developing their own rituals; and (3) one of them adopting the religion of the other. In exploring these options, the therapist recommends that the couple interview other couples that married despite differences in faith to gain additional perspectives.

SUMMARY AND CONCLUSIONS

As the field of marital family therapy has matured, therapists' abilities to address issues of gender, culture, and spirituality have improved. Each of these contextual issues plays a role in the everyday life of every member of our society, in both positive and negative ways. There are clear benefits to addressing power and equality in marriage, to addressing power and equality in society, and to addressing issues of power in the larger sense (i.e., a higher power).

It is vital that therapists continue to address these issues in their practice. As MFT continues to develop, we are recognizing that ignoring these factors is even unethical. Our hope is that your umbrellas are a bit more open now, and that as you continue learning about marital and family therapy, you always keep in mind how gender, culture, and spirituality impact families and MFT theories.

GLOSSARY

circular causality: This term refers to a nonlinear, reciprocal sequence of events whereby one event modifies another event, which in turn modifies another event, which eventually modifies the *original* event. In linear causality there is a single cause-and-effect relationship; in circular causality, events, behaviors, and interactions are seen as mutually influencing one another (through feedback loops). In families, each member is influenced by every other member of the family system in a never-ending cycle. Families affect individuals; individuals affect their families in a recursive manner. Because of this, family therapists will focus on present interactions rather than past, and the process of those interactions rather than their content.

culture: Having a shared worldview and behaviors that come about by belonging to and participating in a specific contexts, such as age, gender, family configuration, race, ethnicity, religion, socioeconomic status, geographic location, employment, education, sexual orientation, and/or political ideology.

ethnic minority groups: Groups of people with distinct ethnic backgrounds who experience prejudice, stereotyping, and discrimination.

ethnicity: A way to describe people who have a common ancestry and shared values, customs, and rituals, frequently based on a combination of race, religion, and cultural background.

feminism: The realization of women's subordination and inferior position in society, understanding how this position is maintained in society, and a commitment to moving from this position to one of equality.

gender: The characteristics that are associated with the biological categories of male and female. These characteristics include social, cultural, emotional, and psychological aspects.

metaframework: An overarching conceptual framework or principle that helps explain underlying phenomena or patterns.

multicultural: An approach to therapy that recognizes culture as an overarching metaframework and that utilizes a multidimensional definition of culture.

power: The ability to impose one's will on others. Those who have power are seen to have influence and authority. Power is involved in hierarchy, and typically derives from both tangible (e.g., money) and intangible (e.g., love, interest) resources. Power is also often ascribed to specific roles by society, often by gender.

race: Often serves as a basis for differential treatment. This treatment is a social construction, meaning it is not merely based on biology or inherited physical characteristics but in fact is the basis for hierarchy in our society.

religion: An organized and agreed-upon belief system that involves beliefs about God or a Higher Power. Religion typically involves institutionalized beliefs, a shared community, and shared rituals.

spirituality: An overarching and more general construct referring to beliefs in a Higher Power. These beliefs generally include transcendent practices and beliefs.

therapeutic neutrality: In systems theory, the therapist focuses on the processes of relationships. Therefore, a neutral therapist would not see anyone as causing the problems, and would be unable to align with any one family member on issues due to a belief in circular causality.

REFERENCES

Almeida, R. V. and Durkin, T. (1999). The cultural context model: Therapy for couples with domestic violence. *Journal of Marital and Family Therapy, 25,* 313-324.

Anderson, D. A. and Worthen, D. (1997). Exploring a fourth dimension: Spirituality as a resource for the couple therapist. *Journal of Marital and Family Therapy, 23,* 3-11.

Aponte, H. J. (1994). *Bread and spirit: Therapy with the new poor.* New York: Norton.

Avis, J. M. (1986). Feminist issues in family therapy. In F. P. Piercy, D. H. Sprenkle, and Associates, *Family therapy sourcebook* (pp. 213-242). New York: Guilford.

Barnett, O. W. and LaViolette, A. D. (1993). *It could happen to anyone: Why battered women stay.* Thousand Oaks, CA: Sage.

Beavers, W. R. and Hampson, R. B. (1990). *Successful families: Assessment and intervention.* New York: Norton.

Becvar, D. S. and Becvar, R. J. (1996). *Family therapy: A systemic integration* (Third edition). Boston: Allyn and Bacon.

Benokraitis, N. V. (1999). *Marriage and families: Changes, choices and constraints* (Third edition). Upper Saddle River, NJ: Prentice-Hall.

Berenson, D. (1990). A systemic view of spirituality: God and twelve-step programs as resources in family therapy. *Journal of Strategic and Systemic Therapies, 9,* 59-70.

Berg, I. K. and Jaya, A. (1993). Different and same: Family therapy with Asian-American families. *Journal of Marital and Family Therapy, 19,* 31-38.

Bischoff, R. J. and Reiter, A. D. (1999). The role of gender in the presentation of mental health clinicians in the movies: Implications for clinical practice. *Psychotherapy, 36,* 180-189.

Bograd, M. (1986). A feminist examination of family therapy: What is women's place? *Women and Therapy, 5,* 95-106.

Bograd, M. (Ed.) (1991). *Feminist approaches for men in family therapy.* Binghamton, NY: The Haworth Press.

Bograd, M. (1999). Strengthening domestic violence theories: Intersections of race, class, sexual orientation, and gender. *Journal of Marital and Family Therapy, 25,* 275-290.

Boszormenyi-Nagy, I. and Krasner, B. (1986). *Between give and take: A clinical guide to contextual therapy.* New York: Brunner/Mazel.

Breunlin, D. C., Schwartz, R. C., and MacKune-Karrer, B. (1992). *Metaframeworks: Transcending the models of family therapy.* San Francisco: Jossey-Bass.

Brock, G. W. and Barnard, C. P. (1992). *Procedures in marriage and family therapy* (Second edition). Boston: Allyn and Bacon.

Butler, S. (Producer/Director) (1998). *The way home.* VHS. Oakland, CA: World Trust.

Canary, D. J. and Stafford, L. (1992). Relational maintenance strategies and equity in marriage. *Communication Monographs, 59,* 243-267.

Carlson, T., Kirkpatrick, D., Hecker, L., and Killmer, M. (2002). A study of marriage and family therapists' beliefs about the appropriateness of addressing religious and spiritual issues in therapy. *American Journal of Family Therapy, 30*(2), 157-171.

Center for the Prevention of Sexual and Domestic Violence (Producer) (1994). *Broken vows—Religious perspectives on domestic violence,* Parts I and II. VHS. Seattle, WA.

Creighton, A. and Kivel, P. (1992). *Helping teens stop violence: A practical guide for educators, counselors, and parents.* Alameda, CA: Hunter House.

Curran, D. (1983). *Traits of a healthy family.* San Francisco: Harper and Row.

Deinhart, A. and Avis, J. M. (1994). Working with men in family therapy: An exploratory study. *Journal of Marital and Family Therapy, 20,* 397-417.

Doherty, W. J. (1995). *Soul searching: Why psychotherapy must promote moral responsibility.* New York: Basic Books.

Encyclopedia Britannica (1998). *Encyclopedia Britannica yearbook 1998.* Chicago, IL: Encyclopedia Britannica.

Erickson, R. J. (1993). Reconceptualizing family work: The effect of emotion work on perceptions of marital quality. *Journal of Marriage and the Family, 55,* 888-900.

Falicov, C. J. (1995). Training to think culturally: A multidimensional comparative framework. *Family Process, 34,* 373-388.

Font, R., Dolan-Del Vecchio, K., and Almeida, R. V. (1998). Finding the words: Instruments for a therapy of liberation. *Journal of Feminist Family Therapy, 10*(1), 84-97.

Gallup, G., Jr. (1996). *Religion in America: 1996 report.* Princeton, NJ: Princeton Religion Research Center.

Ganley, A. (1991). Feminist therapy with male clients. In M. Bograd (Ed.) *Feminist approaches for men in family therapy* (pp. 1-24). Binghamton, NY: The Haworth Press.

Gelles, R. J. (1988). Violence and pregnancy: Are pregnant women at greater risk of abuse? *Journal of Marriage and the Family, 50,* 841-847.

Gilbert, L. A. and Scher, M. (1999). *Gender and sex in counseling and psychotherapy.* Boston: Allyn and Bacon.

Gladding, S. T. (1998). *Family Therapy: History, theory, and practice* (Second edition). Upper Saddle River, NJ: Merrill.

Goldenberg, I. and Goldenberg, H. (2000). *Family therapy: An overview* (Fifth edition). Pacific Grove, CA: Brooks/Cole.

Goldner, V. (1985). Feminism and family therapy. *Family Process, 24,* 31-47.

Goldner, V. (1999). Morality and multiplicity: Perspectives on the treatment of violence in intimate life. *Journal of Marital and Family Therapy, 25,* 325-336.

Gottman, J. M. (1991). Predicting the longitudinal courses of marriage. *Journal of Marriage and Family Therapy, 17,* 3-7.

Gottman, J. M. (1999). *The marriage clinic: A scientifically based marital therapy.* New York: Norton.

Gottman, J. M. and DeClaire, J. (1997). *Raising an emotionally intelligent child: The heart of parenting*. New York: Fireside.

Gottman, J. M. and Silver, N. (1999). *The seven principles for making marriage work*. Now York: Crown.

Green, R. (1998). Traditional norms of masculinity. *Journal of Feminist Family Therapy, 10*(1), 81-83.

Gregory, M. A. and Leslie, L. A. (1996). Different lenses: Variations in clients' perception of family therapy by race and gender. *Journal of Marital and Family Therapy, 22,* 239-251.

Gurman, A. S. and Kniskern, D. P. (Eds.) (1991). *Handbook of family therapy* (Volume II). New York: Brunner/Mazel.

Haddock, S. A., Zimmerman, T. S., and MacPhee, D. (2000). The power equity guide: Attending to gender in family therapy. *Journal of Marital and Family Therapy, 26,* 153-170.

Hanna, S. M. and Brown, J. H. (1995). *The practice of family therapy: Key elements across models*. Pacific Grove, CA: Brooks/Cole.

Hansen, M. (1993). Feminism and family therapy: A review of feminist critiques of approaches to family violence. In M. Hansen and M. Harway (Eds.), *Battering and family therapy: A feminist perspective* (pp. 69-81). Newbury Park, CA: Sage.

Hare-Mustin, R. T. (1978). A feminist approach to family therapy. *Family Process, 17,* 181-193.

Harris, S. M. (1998). Finding a forest among trees: Spirituality hiding in family therapy theories. *Journal of Family Studies, 4,* 77-86.

Haug, I. E. (1998a). Including a spiritual dimension in family therapy: Ethical considerations. *Contemporary Family Therapy, 20,* 181-194.

Haug, I. E. (1998b). Spirituality as a dimension of family therapists' clinical training. *Contemporary Family Therapy, 20,* 471-483.

Hines, P. M. and Boyd-Franklin, N. (1996). African American families. In M. McGoldrick, J. Giordano, and J. K. Pearce (Eds.), *Ethnicity and family therapy* (Second edition) (pp. 66-84). New York: Guilford.

Horst, E. A. and Doherty, W. J. (1995). Gender, power, and intimacy. *Journal of Feminist Family Therapy, 6*(4), 63-85.

Humphrey, F. G. (1975). Changing roles for women: Implications for marriage counselors. *Journal of Marriage and Family Counseling, 4,* 33-40.

Humphrey, F. G. (1983). *Marital therapy*. Englewood Cliffs, NJ: Prentice-Hall.

Imber-Black, E. and Roberts, J. (1992). *Rituals for our times: Celebrating, healing, and changing our lives and our relationships*. San Francisco: Harper and Row.

Joanides, C. J. (1996). Collaborative family therapy with religious family systems. *Journal of Family Psychotherapy, 7*(4), 19- 35.

Jory, B. and Anderson, D. (1999). Intimate justice II: Fostering mutuality, reciprocity, and accommodation in therapy for psychological abuse. *Journal of Marital and Family Therapy, 25,* 349-364.

Katz, J. and Earp, J. (Writers) (1999). *Tough guise: Violence, media, and the crisis in masculinity*. VHS. Northampton, MA: Media Education Foundation.

Keeney, B. (1983). *Aesthetics of change*. New York: Guilford.

Kelly, E. W. (1992). Religion in family therapy journals: A review and analysis. In L. A. Burton (Ed.), *Religion and the family: When God helps* (pp. 185-208). Binghamton, NY: The Haworth Pastoral Press.

Kessler, R. and McRae, J. (1982). The effect of wives' employment on the mental health of married men and women. *American Sociological Review, 47,* 216-227.

Laird, J. (1998). Theorizing culture: Narrative ideas and practice principles. In M. McGoldrick (Ed.), *Re-visioning family therapy: Race, culture, and gender in clinical practice* (pp. 20-36). New York: Guilford.

Larson, J. H., Hammond, C. H., and Harper, J. M. (1998). Perceived equity and intimacy in marriage. *Journal of Marital and Family Therapy, 24,* 487-506.

Leslie, L. A. (1995). The evolving treatment of gender, ethnicity, and sexual orientation in marital and family therapy. *Family Relations, 44,* 359-367.

Lucas, R. (Director) (1992). *Myths that maim.* VHS. Encinitas, CA: Encinitas Center for Family and Personal Development.

Lyness, K. P. and Thomas, V. (1995). Fitting a square peg in a square hole: Using metaphor in narrative therapy. *Contemporary Family Therapy, 17,* 127-142.

McGill, D. W. (1992). The cultural story in multicultural family therapy. *Families in Society, 73,* 339-349.

McGoldrick, M. (1998). Introduction: Re-visioning family therapy through a cultural lens. In M. McGoldrick (Ed.), *Re-visioning family therapy: Race, culture, and gender in clinical practice* (pp. 3-19). New York: Guilford.

McGoldrick, M., Anderson, C. M., and Walsh, F. (Eds.) (1989). *Women in families: A framework for family therapy.* New York: Norton.

McGoldrick, M. and Giordano, J. (1996). Overview: Ethnicity and family therapy. In M. McGoldrick, J. Giordano, and J. K. Pearce (Eds.), *Ethnicity and family therapy* (Second edition) (pp. 1-29). New York: Guilford.

McGoldrick, M., Giordano, K., and Pearce, J. K. (Eds.) (1996). *Ethnicity and family therapy* (Second edition). New York: Guilford.

McGoldrick, M., Preto, N. G., Hines, P. M., and Lee, E. (1991). Ethnicity and family therapy. In A. S. Gurman and D. P. Kniskern (Eds.), *Handbook of family therapy* (Volume 2) (pp. 546-582). New York: Brunner/Mazel.

Moore, T. (1992). *Care of the soul: A guide for cultivating depth and sacredness in everyday life.* New York: HarperCollins.

Mun Wah, L. (Producer/Director) (1994). *The color of fear.* VHS. Oakland, CA: Stirfry Seminars.

Parker, L. (1997a). Keeping power issues on the table in couples work. *Journal of Feminist Family Therapy, 9*(3), 1-24.

Parker, L. (1997b) Unraveling power issues in couples therapy. *Journal of Feminist Family Therapy, 9*(2), 3-20.

Patterson, J., Williams, L., Grauf-Grounds, C., and Chamow, L. (1999). *Essential skills in family therapy: From the first interview to termination.* New York: Guilford.

Preli, R. and Bernard, J. M. (1993). Making multiculturalism relevant for majority culture graduate students. *Journal of Marital and Family Therapy, 19,* 5-16.

Prest, L. A. and Keller, J. F. (1993). Spirituality and family therapy: Spiritual beliefs, myths, and metaphors. *Journal of Marital and Family Therapy, 19,* 137-148.

Prest, L. A., Russel, R., and Souza, H. D. (1999). Spirituality and religion in training, practice, and personal development. *Journal of Family Therapy, 21,* 60-77.

Rabin, C. (1996). *Equal partners, good friends: Empowering couples through therapy.* New York: Routledge.

Raider, M. C. (1992). Assessing the role of religion in family functioning. In L. A. Burton (Ed.), *Religion and the family: When God helps* (pp. 165-184). Binghamton, NY: The Haworth Pastoral Press.

Roberts, J. (1991). Sugar and spice, toads and mice: Gender issues in family therapy training. *Journal of Marital and Family Therapy, 17,* 121-132.

Roberts, J. (1999). Heart and soul: Spirituality, religion, and rituals in family therapy training. In F. Walsh (Ed.), *Spiritual resources in family therapy* (pp. 256-271). New York: Guilford.

Ross, J. L. (1994). Working with patients within their religious contexts: Religion, spirituality, and the secular therapist. *Journal of Systemic Therapies, 13*(3), 7-15.

Rotz, E., Russell, C. S., and Wright, D., W. (1993). The therapist who is perceived as "spiritually correct": Strategies for avoiding collusion with the "spiritually one-up" spouse. *Journal of Marital and Family Therapy, 19,* 369-375.

Schwartz, P. (1994). *Love between equals: How peer marriage really works.* New York: Free Press.

Selvini Palazzoli, M., Cecchin, G., Prata, G., and Boscolo, L. (1978). *Paradox and counterparadox.* Northvale, NJ: Jason Aronson.

Stabb, S. D., Cox, D. L., and Harber, J. L. (1997). Gender-related therapist attributions in couples therapy: A preliminary multiple case study investigation. *Journal of Marital and Family Therapy, 23,* 335-346.

Stander, V., Piercy, F. P., Mackinnon, D., and Helmeke, K. (1994). Spirituality, religion and family therapy: Competing or complementary worlds? *American Journal of Family Therapy, 22,* 27-41.

Steil, J. M. (1997). *Marital equality: Its relationship to well-being of husbands and wives.* Thousand Oaks, CA: Sage.

Stewart, S. P. and Gale, J. E. (1994). On hallowed ground: Marital therapy with couples on the religious right. *Journal of Systemic Therapies, 13*(3), 16-25.

Stinnett, N. and DeFrain, J. (1985). *Secrets of strong families.* Boston: Little, Brown.

Suitor, J. J. (1991). Marital quality and satisfaction with the division of household labor across the family life cycle. *Journal of Marriage and the Family, 53,* 221-230.

Taggart, M. (1985). The feminist critique in epistemological perspective: Questions of context in family therapy. *Journal of Marital and Family Therapy, 11,* 113-126.

Thomas, M. B. (1992). *An introduction to marital and family therapy: Counseling toward healthier family systems across the lifespan.* New York: Merrill.

Tomm, K. (1987). Interventive interviewing. Part II: Reflexive questions as a means to enable self-healing. *Family Process, 26,* 3-14.

Walker, A. J. (1989). Gender in families: Women and men in marriage, work, and parenthood. *Journal of Marriage and the Family, 51,* 845-871.

Walsh, F. (1999a). Opening family therapy to spirituality. In F. Walsh (Ed.), *Spiritual resources in family therapy* (pp. 28-58). New York: Guilford.

Walsh, F. (1999b). Religion and spirituality: Wellsprings for healing and resilience. In F. Walsh (Ed.), *Spiritual resources in family therapy* (pp. 3-27). New York: Guilford.

Walsh, F. (Ed.). (1999c). *Spiritual resources in family therapy.* New York: Guilford.

Werner-Wilson, R. J. (1997). Is therapeutic alliance influenced by gender in marriage and family therapy? *Journal of Feminist Family Therapy, 9*(1), 3-16.

Werner-Wilson, R. J., Price, S. J., Zimmerman, T. S., and Murphy, M. J. (1997). Client gender as a process variable in marriage and family therapy: Are women clients interrupted more than men clients? *Journal of Family Psychology, 11,* 373-377.

Werner-Wilson, R. J., Zimmerman, T. S., and Price, S. J. (1999). Are goals and topics influenced by gender and modality in the initial marriage and family therapy session? *Journal of Marital and Family Therapy, 25,* 253-262.

Wheeler, D., Avis, J. M., Miller, L., and Chaney, S. (1989). Rethinking family therapy training and supervision: A feminist model. In M. McGoldrick, C. M. Anderson, and F. Walsh (Eds.), *Women in families: A framework for family therapy* (pp. 135-151). New York: Norton.

Whipple, V. (1996). Developing an identity as a feminist family therapist: Implications for training. *Journal of Marital and Family Therapy, 22,* 381-396.

Wolin, S. J., Muller, W., Taylor, F., and Wolin, S. (1999). Three spiritual perspectives on resilience: Buddhism, Christianity, and Judaism. In F. Walsh (Ed.), *Spiritual resources in family therapy* (pp. 121- 135). New York: Guilford.

Wright, L. (1999). Spirituality, suffering, and beliefs: The soul of healing with families. In F. Walsh (Ed.), *Spiritual resources in family therapy* (pp. 61- 75). New York: Guilford.

Wylie, M. S. (2000). Inside Christian counseling: Soul therapy. *Family Therapy Networker, 24*(1), 26-37.

Chapter 14

Special Topics in Family Therapy

Connie J. Salts
Thomas A. Smith Jr.

Family therapy approaches were first conceived and implemented in response to specific types of mental health issues that challenged the practitioners of the time. The first "special problems" addressed by the pioneering family therapists were those of the seriously mentally ill (Nichols and Schwartz, 2001). This chapter follows in this longest of family therapy traditions: the application of family therapy perspectives to particular mental health and relational problems. Four specific problem areas are addressed: substance abuse, divorce, family violence, and schizophrenia. Each problem area is reviewed in relation to the contribution that marriage and family therapy approaches have made to the understanding and treatment of problems that arise in individuals (children and adults), couples, and families where these four issues surface.

SUBSTANCE ABUSE

It is widely accepted that addiction generally develops within a family context, frequently reflects and promotes other family difficulties, and is usually maintained and exacerbated by family interactive processes. (Stanton and Heath, 1995, p. 530)

Substance abuse is a substantial problem in the United States. Nearly 20 percent of the population will suffer a substance abuse problem at some time in their lives (Helzer and Pryzbeck, 1988). In 1990, 13 million Americans were diagnosed with alcoholism and more than 14 million used illegal drugs (Institute of Medicine, 1990).

Definitions

In the *Diagnostic and Statistical Manual of Mental Disorders,* Fourth Edition, Text Revision (American Psychiatric Association, 2000, pp. 181-183), substance dependence is defined as:

> A maladaptive pattern of substance use, leading to clinically significant impairment or distress, as manifested by three (or more) of the following, occurring at any time in the same 12-month period:
>
> (1) tolerance, as defined by either of the following:
>   (a) a need for markedly increased amounts of the substance to achieve intoxication or desired effect
>   (b) markedly diminished effect with continued use of the same amount of the substance
> (2) withdrawal, as manifested by either of the following:
>   (a) the characteristic withdrawal syndrome for the substance (refer to Criteria A and B of the criteria sets for Withdrawal from the specific substances)
>   (b) the same (or a closely related) substance is taken to relieve or avoid withdrawal symptoms
> (3) the substance is often taken in larger amounts or over a longer period than was intended
> (4) there is a persistent desire or unsuccessful efforts to cut down or control substance use
> (5) a great deal of time is spent in activities necessary to obtain the substance (e.g., visiting multiple doctors or driving long distances), use the substance (e.g., chain-smoking), or recover from its effects
> (6) important social, occupational, or recreational activities are given up or reduced because of substance use
> (7) the substance use is continued despite knowledge of having a persistent or recurrent physical or psychological problem that is likely to have been caused or exacerbated by the substance (e.g., current cocaine use despite recognition of cocaine-induced depression, or continued drinking despite recognition that an ulcer was made worse by alcohol consumption)

Substance abuse is defined as:

A. A maladaptive pattern of substance use leading to clinically significant impairment or distress, as manifested by one (or more) of the following, occurring within a 12-month period:

(1) recurrent substance use resulting in a failure to fulfill major role obligations at work, school, or home (e.g., repeated absences or poor work performance related to substance use; substance-related absences, suspensions, or expulsions from school; neglect of children or household)

(2) recurrent substance use in situations in which it is physically hazardous (e.g., driving an automobile or operating a machine when impaired by substance use)

(3) recurrent substance-related legal problems (e.g., arrests for substance-related disorderly conduct)

(4) continued substance use despite having persistent or recurrent social or interpersonal problems caused or exacerbated by the effects of the substance (e.g., arguments with spouse about consequences of intoxication, physical fights).

B. The symptoms have never met the criteria for Substance Dependence for this class of substance. (Reprinted with permission from the Diagnostic and Statistical Manual of Mental Disorders, Fourth Edition, Text Revision. Copyright 2000 American Psychiatric Association.)

Substance Abuse and Family Therapy

"Family therapy approaches have been established as viable interventions for drug and alcohol abuse" (Liddle and Dakof, 1995, p. 512). In spite of this, family therapy is still inconsistently offered as part of treatment in most drug abuse treatment settings (Liddle and Dakof, 1995). Compelling research literature suggests that there is a **family predisposition** toward alcoholism and that families play a significant role in the course of alcoholism. Similar to drug treatment, alcoholism treatment has not embraced family intervention as integral to successful treatment, in spite of the evidence that suggests it should be (Edwards and Steinglass, 1995). It is important to note that most clinicians and researchers operating from a family perspective do not believe that the family *causes* the abuse or that family members are responsible for the abuser's use. Often families may feel blamed by a poorly skilled therapist's efforts to highlight family involvement. Family members' involvement often should be presented as critical to their loved one's recovery (Walitzer, 1998).

Marriage and Family Therapy for Alcoholism

Edwards and Steinglass (1995) undertook a major review of the efficacy of marriage and family therapy for alcoholism and reported evidence for using marriage and family therapy in all phases of treatment (treatment initiation, primary treatment, and aftercare). They did not find specific support for one type of family therapy over any other. The strongest association of family therapy to positive outcomes was in relation to bolstering the alcoholic's initiation into therapy. The most well-known family approach in relation to initiating treatment is known as **intervention.** This approach was made famous when it was disclosed that former President Gerald Ford and his family motivated his wife Betty into treatment using intervention. An intervention involves the family and other loved ones receiving eight to ten hours of training focused on how to effectively confront the alcoholic with his or her drinking. This model is based on the assumption that one of the key issues to be dealt with, if an alcoholic is going to stop drinking, is the drinker's denial that he or she is not in control. The power of the family and loved ones together facing the alcoholic with the consequences of drinking, in stark confrontation, often supplies the force to break through the drinker's denial. Only after taking responsibility for their drinking do alcoholics have a true chance for recovery. This approach was successful in a published outcome study (Liepman, Silvia, and Nirenberg, 1989).

Steinglass et al. (1987) detail the application of a systemically based family therapy approach with alcoholics. They distinguish between **alcoholic families** and "families with an alcoholic member." The former is a family in which alcohol is the structuring principle for their lives together. The family's activities, daily routines, important interactions, and rituals are all organized around the drinker's pattern of abuse. The authors suggest that these families are good candidates for family therapy. Their model has four stages: the first stage is diagnosing alcoholism and defining it as a family problem. The second stage involves removing alcohol from the family. The first two stages often occur in close proximity and fairly quickly. The third stage, which involves dealing with the emotional issues that invariably surface when the alcoholic is sober, often takes longer to complete. The fourth stage involves **family reorganization,** establishing new patterns of interaction without the alcohol to define their lives. There is limited empirical support for this model (Walitzer, 1998). Edwards and Steinglass (1995) concluded, in their review of four clinical studies of family systems treatments, that the initial effects of the treatments were clearly superior in relation to either individual therapy or no treatment. They also reported that the effects decayed significantly over time. Further examination of these studies reveals that none of them included any prevention relapse interventions after the primary therapy was completed.

Stanton and Heath (1995) make note of an important issue in relation to family treatment and alcoholism when they discuss **codependence.** This term is used very broadly in the substance abuse field. It is defined by Schaef (1986) as a disease that parallels the alcoholic's disease process. Manifestations of codependence in a partner or someone close to the alcoholic include caretaking, selflessness, control issues, perfectionism, and fear. Stanton and Heath suggest that the codependent concept be used with caution, because it can be pejoratively used as a label for women. This caution is most clearly elaborated by Bepko and Kresten (1988) who suggest that instead of using codependence, the terms **overresponsible and underresponsible** be applied to the nonabusing partner and abuser, respectively. They argue that these terms more accurately reflect the behaviors associated with the common relational pattern that is referred to by others when discussing the pattern of interaction between an abuser and his or her "codependent" partner.

Walitzer (1998) presented **behavioral marital therapy** (BMT) as a viable treatment for alcoholism in adults who are in a couple relationship. Theoretically, improved marital functioning should encourage the couple to undertake behaviors that assist the primary goal of abstinence. BMT is often offered after completion of an in- or outpatient substance abuse treatment program, although it may be offered in conjunction with an outpatient program. The primary components of BMT, which Walitzer suggests are important to alcoholism improvement, are increasing the goodwill and commitment to the relationship by the partners, and increased effectiveness of their negotiation and communication skills. BMT is an empirically supported treatment for marital difficulties and has empirical support as an **adjunctive therapy** in the treatment of alcoholism (McCrady, 1990). BMT has not been similarly researched in relation to other substance abuse problems. Edwards and Steinglass (1995) also reported that marital and/or family involvement in **aftercare** (formal contact designed to maintain treatment gains, in this case sobriety, over time) is empirically supported as helping to prevent **relapse,** at least for two years posttreatment.

When the various outcome studies are evaluated in more detail, several other significant family-related variables emerge as important. For example, it seems clear that marriage and family approaches are more effective for families with male (versus female) alcoholics (Edwards and Steinglass,

1995). Low commitment to the couple relationship by the nondrinking partner is associated with poor outcomes. Finally, increased family support for **abstinence** is associated with more positive outcomes. These two latter findings suggest that it may be important to determine the partner's and/or family's commitment to recovery before deciding to include them in the treatment.

In summary, Edwards and Steinglass (1995) state that as part of a treatment regimen for alcoholism, family involvement is effective, but it has yet to be empirically proven to be sufficient to bring about recovery as the only treatment. Stanton and Heath (1995) echoed the same opinion, stating, "Only by collaborating with extended families, self-help programs, specialists in the field of chemical dependency, and physicians monitoring pharmacotherapy can substance abuse be controlled" (p. 531). It is quite likely that the sentiment presented at the beginning of this section—that family involvement is commonly not part of a typical treatment plan—may have come about because family therapists have not been effectively collaborative with other, more established professionals in the substance abuse field.

Marriage and Family Therapy for Drug Abuse

Liddle and Dakof (1995) completed an extensive review of the research applying various family treatments to drug abuse. As previously stated, although they found ample evidence warranting the use of family therapy and family-based treatments with drug abuse cases, it is not an integral part of most published treatments, nor are family applications well or often researched.

In relation to adolescent drug abuse treatment, family treatments have been developed, applied, and evaluated. Szapocznik and colleagues (1983, 1986, 1988) undertook a program of outcome research to explore the effectiveness of several different applications of family therapy with drug abusing adolescents and their families. Their studies used **structural family therapy** as well as a one-person version of family-focused therapy, both of which demonstrated significant treatment gains in abstinence (measured as days without drug use) by the time of treatment termination. They also demonstrated family therapy's effectiveness in engaging adolescent abusers and their families in treatment.

Several other clinical trials were conducted that focused on various family therapies in application to adolescent drug abusers (Henggeler et al., 1991; Joanning et al., 1992; Lewis et al., 1990). Liddle and Dakof (1995) report that all of the trials found family-based models were effective in **engaging** and **retaining** abusers in treatment. All of the evaluations reported that the family-based treatments reduced drug use significantly in their participants. These studies also reported decreases in drug-related problem behaviors. In summary, Liddle and Dakof (1995) report that not only can family therapy retain families in treatment and contribute to decreases in adolescent substance abuse, but that **integrative family models**—models that were designed to specifically address adolescent substance abuse—seemed more effective than several more traditional drug abuse treatments, such as peer-group therapy and individual therapy, and more generic family-based treatments, such as multifamily groups and parent training.

The research is not as clear in relation to adult drug abusers. The seminal work of Duncan Stanton and Tom Todd (1979; Stanton, Todd, and Associates, 1982; Stanton et al., 1984), working with young adult heroin addicts to compare a structural-strategic family therapy approach, traditional individual treatment, and a no-treatment group, produced findings that strongly supported the effectiveness of family therapy. The results of this study have not been found in replication attempts. In fact, Liddle and Dakof (1995) conclude their review of family therapy with adult abusers by saying that family therapy alone cannot be supported by current standards but can be considered appropriate to offer as part of a treatment regimen. They echo the observations mentioned in relation to alcoholism treatment: collaboration between family therapists and drug abuse professionals will be important to further family therapy's cause in the treatment of drug abuse.

DIVORCE

> To change our thinking about divorced families—to remove from them the label of deviance or pathology . . . we must unambiguously acknowledge and support them as normal, prevalent family types that have resulted from major societal trends and changes. (Ahrons and Rodgers, 1987, pp. 201-202)

Divorce is one solution to an unsatisfactory marriage. Currently 45 percent of all first marriages in the United States end in divorce (Lamb, Sternberg, and Thompson, 1997). Couples most likely to divorce are those who are twenty years of age or younger when they marry. Individuals with lower incomes and education tend to divorce more than those with higher education and incomes. One exception to this general rule is that women with five or more years of college with good incomes have higher rates of divorce than do poorer and less educated women. Demographers predict that 40 to 60 percent of all current marriages will eventually end in divorce, due in part to women's and men's changing roles and women's increasing financial independence (Bumpass, 1990).

Although divorce is a common event in today's families, it is an unscheduled transition that alters the traditional family life cycle and interrupts developmental tasks (Carter and McGoldrick, 1999). It is a multidimensional process involving many decisions, changes, and adjustments. How the divorce is handled emotionally is the key to whether the process becomes a transitional crisis or has a permanent crippling effect on the adults and children of the nuclear family as well as the extended family. Although an individual's experience and adjustment needs vary considerably from case to case, most divorcing families must address common issues and each spouse must face challenges. In addition to the emotional divorce, the couple will be faced with the implications of the legal divorce, economic divorce, coparental divorce, community divorce, and psychic divorce (Bohannan, 1970; Kaslow, 1991).

Because divorce is not a single event, it usually takes a minimum of one and a half to three years after the initial **separation** to successfully adjust to the changes, stabilize one's feelings, and move through the divorce process. When families cannot adequately resolve the issues of the emotional divorce, they can remain stuck for years struggling with various family and individual developmental issues. Models of divorce therapy have divided the process into sequential stages (Kaslow, 1991; Salts, 1985; Sprenkle, 1989) and transitions (Ahrons and Rodgers, 1987; Ahrons, 1999) that, when presented as a normative process rather than one of pathology or dysfunction, can be used by clinicians to help client families cope more effectively during this painful and complex process. These stages consist of the predivorce decision-making stage, the divorce restructuring stage, and the postdivorce recovery stage.

Predivorce Decision-Making Stage

During the **predivorce stage** at least one partner has become disenchanted with the marriage or his or her marital partner, thus beginning the **emotional divorce**. Unfulfilled emotional needs, financial and job-related problems, third-party involvement, different values and goals, communication difficulties, bad personal habits, parenting differences, substance abuse, and violence are examples of the multitude of reasons the nagging feelings of dissatisfaction begin (Textor, 1989). As these feelings grow, the spouse may exhibit flares of anger toward his or her partner, or privately simmer in unhappiness and depression. In many cases, the marital relationship is unsatisfactory and/or unstable for a long time; in others, the marriage deteriorates suddenly and fast. In some families open conflict occurs between the spouses; in others, a distancing and withdrawal of **emotional investment** in the marriage and/or family life takes place. As the individual struggles with the loss of love for the partner, it is not unusual for that individual to have an **affair** and/or consult a therapist. Whether the spousal relationship is highly conflictual or cold and distant, children living in the home frequently develop emotional or behavioral problems (Ahrons, 1999).

Few couples actually enter therapy at this stage with the presenting problem as a mutual desire to work toward an amicable divorce. Often one partner will seek individual therapy for the purpose of dealing with an unhappy marriage. In such cases, most therapists warn the client that excluding one spouse from therapy may be an intervention in favor of divorce. A marriage and family therapist will see many couples in which one or both partners have contemplated divorce and are attending therapy for the purpose of "giving it one last try" before moving to end the marriage. In other cases, the disengaged partner may seek a therapist who can become the caretaker of the soon-to-be-left spouse.

Although a divorce often ends up being a mutual decision, one person usually takes the first step to begin the process. The decision to separate is a difficult and complex one, often fraught with trepidation, confusion, inadequacy, rejection, and anger. For some, it may take two or more years to make the final decision, especially for those who have been in the marriage for a long time. Whether the person is the "leaver" or the "left," the vehemence of the couple's conflict, the interaction style of the couple at the time the decision to divorce is made, the process used to make the final decision, and the individuals' personal explanation for the failure of the marriage will impact the emotional aspects of divorce for each individual.

During the predivorce stage, most parents are not likely to seek a therapist to find help for a child in coping with the effects of **marital discord** and/or a dissolving marriage unless the child has displayed severe behavior problems. Many adults are too caught up in their own emotional divorce to recognize the negative impact their actions have on the children. Parents may deny this possibility by rationalizing that the children are either too young to understand what is going on or that older children are too involved with their own friends and activities to be bothered. Although the first major task of the therapist during the predivorce stage is to help the couple assess and work toward a resolution of the marital conflict, the second major task is to assist the parents to begin addressing their children's needs during the process (Nichols, 1985).

Conjoint marital therapy is the most likely treatment in this stage of divorce, and couples who are able to identify and resolve their conflicts do not move to the next stage. In some cases, marital therapy provides the opportunity for a couple to come to a mutual realization that ending the marriage may be the best decision. For many couples who may or may not have sought therapy, the conflict becomes too intense and a decision to separate is made by at least one partner. It is estimated that in the United States and most European countries between two-thirds and three-quarters of all divorces are initiated by women. The recent increase in women's economic independence is one of the biggest factors leading to this current statistic (Ahrons, 1999).

Once the decision to separate is made, announcing the end of the marriage in not an easy task. Rarely are the two spouses at the same point in the emotional divorce process. Therefore, while the process is legally **no-fault divorce** in all states, blame often plays a big role. Grief over the severe losses of one's present lifestyle and future plans and dreams can be very powerful. Anger, unresolved grief, and depression are major deterrents to making a healthy adjustment to divorce. Family therapy during this time may help to de-escalate the anger. It can help both children and adults to handle their fears about the major changes that divorce will bring, and it can provide an opportunity to plan how the separation will occur.

Divorce Restructuring Stage

The predivorce stage ends when the decision to divorce is made and the separation begins. Separation day is a major life transition and has the potential for severe stress and crisis. If there has been time for some preparation and planning before the actual physical separation occurs, the adults and especially the children will have the opportunity for a more orderly experience and will have time to process some of the emotional trauma. Abrupt departures frequently result in severe crises for those left behind. It is shocking; the feelings of abandonment often leave adults and children feeling totally helpless (Ahrons, 1999).

In the short term, some negative emotions can have beneficial value. Anger may help provide the energy one needs to get through the crisis of separation. Appropriate grief and sadness are healthy ways to mourn the many losses experienced in divorce. Unfortunately, far too many couples enter this stage with high negative emotional intensity and with both parties taking an adversarial stance in the fight over property and/or children. In other situations, one partner may still be in denial of the end of the marriage due to continued attachment to his or her spouse. Although constructive caring or friendship between former intimates can facilitate the adjustment process, one person attempting to win back a partner who does not wish to be in the relationship can constrain the individual's long-term adjustment and interfere with cooperative coparenting.

Healthy separations have two common factors: **good management** and **firm relationship rules** about how the spouses will interact and will not interact. Good management requires knowing about and preparing for the transitions of divorce, defusing tension at high stress points, and giving everyone enough time to begin adjustment. For relationship rules or boundaries to remain firm, spouses need to recognize how their roles have changed, which means coping with **role losses** and establishing new roles (Ahrons, 1999).

When couples begin the actual physical separation, the legal, economic, and coparental issues of divorce come to the forefront, contributing to a high degree of stress among family members. When both spouses have accepted the end of the marriage, **divorce mediation** is an avenue the partners may choose to aid them with their decisions about custody, visitation, and distribution of property and financial assets. Mediation is a process that involves consideration of the best interest of all involved and is based on cooperative problem solving. Although therapists trained in divorce mediation can assist couples in making decisions regarding these issues, financial and tax professionals may need to be consulted regarding the financial implications of custody and the distribution of assets. Divorce mediation is estimated to be beneficial for about 80 percent of divorcing couples, but it will not be successful if the couple maintains high emotional intensity or if one partner has not accepted the end of the marriage (James, 1997).

The **legal divorce** involves the parties, jointly or separately, taking action to legally end their marriage. If couples can effectively use divorce mediation, the legal divorce becomes a formality. When couples use the court system to continue their marital battle, a long "cold war" may result in which children, extended family, and friends are forced to take sides. When couples use the adversarial system to make decisions regarding their lives, it then becomes difficult to separate the emotional divorce from the legal, economic, and coparental aspects.

The **economic divorce** interfaces with the legal divorce when decisions are made on how to divide the accumulated property and financial assets, as well as settle issues of alimony and child support. Couples who have accumulated property and other financial resources frequently battle over what is considered an equitable division of these assets. Other couples, however, must contend with assigning responsibility for the couple's debts. The economic divorce also entails individual decisions about where one can now afford to live and the lifestyle that can be financially sustained. Some individuals will also be faced with the task of learning how to handle their own finances.

When the divorcing couple has children still living at home, the complexity of the legal and economic divorce increases. Even when there is no dispute regarding which parent the children will live with, issues of financial and parental responsibility will greatly affect the adjustment of the parents and the children. As part of the **coparental divorce,** parents should focus on how to deal with the children's perceptions and responses, interpreting what is happening to them, and helping them express their fears, feelings, and hopes. Involving children in family therapy and/or mediation can help provide for this. Frequently, however, parents are so invested in the decisions of who will be financially responsible for the children's current and future expenses, as well as which parent gets to have them for the holidays, that the children's emotional needs are overlooked.

Healthy adjustment for children of divorce requires that their basic economic and psychological needs be met. It is important for children to be able to maintain the familial relationships in their lives that were significant and meaningful prior to the divorce, including not only parents but extended family, such as grandparents. Children will benefit when the relationship between their parents is supportive and cooperative. When divorcing couples can reorganize their family into a **binuclear family,** the opportunity for these elements of child adjustment can be met. In most binuclear families, children divide their living time between the households. Although the division of time spent in each household varies greatly from one binuclear family to another, the important factor is that the family remains a family—it just has a very different structure than before the divorce (Ahrons, 1999).

Five types of relationships between former spouses and coparental units have been observed through research: perfect pals, cooperative colleagues, angry associates, fiery foes, and dissolved duos (Ahrons and Rodgers, 1987). **Perfect pals** are a small group of divorced spouses who remain close friends, have good problem-solving skills and few conflicts, share child-rearing responsibilities, and generally have joint custody. **Cooperative colleagues,** although not friends, are able to remain child focused and can separate their marital issues from their parental roles. Both parents remain important and involved in their children's lives. When conflicts arise that the parents cannot resolve, they choose a mediator or therapist to help rather than enter the court system. Studies have found that about half of the divorced parents fit into this group. **Angry associates** continue to interact and have involvement in their children's lives, but these former spouses cannot separate their parental and marital issues. Their power struggles contribute to often-lengthy custody disputes and long legal battles over financial matters. **Fiery foes** are hostile and angry all the time. They are unable to coparent; their emotional battles frequently involve extended family and friends, and their legal battles continue for many years after the divorce. Children usually suffer from devastating loyalty conflicts and often lose significant relationships with extended kin when parents are angry associates and fiery foes. **Dissolved duos** are ex-spouses who have no further contact with each other, and one parent assumes full responsibility for the children. The dissolved duos, according to Ahrons (1999), are the only families of divorce who fit the "single-parent" category and, therefore, are not considered a binuclear family.

When the families move to separate households, there is an undertaking of new activities and the establishment of new daily routines to which individuals must adjust. Separation also marks the time when friends and extended family are often first informed of the impending divorce, thus moving the process beyond the couple and into the community. Included in the **community divorce** is the social support of formal and informal contacts with individuals and groups that provide emotional and material resources. Social support and participation are related to low stress and better adjustment for the divorcing individual. Unfortunately for some, this may be a time when one's support network is reduced as family and friends take sides (Kaslow, 1991).

Due to the multidimensional aspects of the **divorce restructuring stage,** individuals may present to therapy in a state of high stress and crisis. It is important for clinicians to help clients become aware of the many transitions in the divorce process and to help clients cope more effectively during this difficult time. In addition to helping the clients deal with their emotional pain, clinicians can teach problem-solving approaches, conflict reduction techniques, and stress management skills to help individuals and families to manage the emotional divorce in order for them to be able to make decisions about the legal, economic, coparental, and community divorce.

The physical separation is generally the most stressful time for children of all ages. "The needs of children in divorce situations can be stated very simply: They need whatever will provide them with continuing assistance to develop as normally as possible" (Nichols, 1989, p. 73). Children need a clear explanation of what is happening and what it means them. They need parents to adequately handle the adult developmental tasks so that the children are free to continue their own development in relation to the divorce and their normal life cycle tasks. Children need adequate parenting so that age-appropriate dependency-independency needs are maintained, and they need attention and support to minimize the expected abandonment anxiety issues (Nichols, 1989). Research supports the importance of a healthy parent-child relationship as being the key to child adjustment to marital disruption (Simons et al., 1999).

Postdivorce Recovery Stage

As decisions are made and changes continue, the divorce restructuring stage moves toward the **postdivorce recovery period** and what has been termed by some as the **psychic divorce** (Bohannon, 1970; Kaslow, 1991). This can be a stage of devastation or of exciting new challenges. Some of the personal challenges at this time include coping with loneliness, regaining self-confidence, and rebuilding social relationships. If the former spouses can reduce their negativism, **emotional closure** regarding the divorce can be gained. For adults, a divorce adjustment group (Salts, 1989) or individual therapy may be beneficial in helping individuals adjust to the status and roles of singlehood and their continuing responsibilities as parents.

The measure of how successfully one traverses the tasks and stages of divorce has been termed **divorce adjustment.** It involves the development of an identity for oneself that is not tied to the status of being married or to the ex-spouse, an ability to function adequately in the role responsibilities of daily life, being relatively free of symptoms of psychological disturbance, and having a positive sense of self-esteem. As indicated previously, successful divorce adjustment takes time, and the more complex the process, the longer individuals and families need to move forward in meeting the development tasks of their particular life stage.

For 35 percent of divorced American women, the end of the divorce process occurs when they settle into their lives as single individuals and, those with children, participating in a binuclear or single parent family structure. For 65 percent of divorced American women and 75 percent of American men, an additional transitional crisis occurs when either or both spouses **remarry.** Unfortunately, the redivorce rate is about 14 percent higher than the first-marriage rate, with about half of remarriages terminating in less than five years.

FAMILY VIOLENCE

The application of marriage and family therapy theory and practice to the issue of **relationship/family violence** has been at times interesting, promising, and frustrating. For the purpose of this chapter, when we talk about relationship/family violence, we are specifically limiting our focus to partner/spousal violence and intrafamilial violence perpetrated upon children.

We recognize that other important types of relational/family violence such as dating/premarital and elder violence also occur at staggering rates.

Partner/Spouse Violence

The incidence of partner/spouse violence occurring in the United States is epidemic. Straus and Gelles (1990) estimate that over 2 million wives are severely beaten by their husbands each year. From another data set, Gelles and Straus (1988) reported that 16 percent of couples—one in six—experienced an incident of physical assault in 1985. Using that formula in application to the 1985 population in the United States meant that approximately 8.7 million couples were involved in **spousal abuse** that year.

Part of the challenge in trying to understand and subsequently intervene in relationally violent or abusive situations begins at the simplest level: determining what is meant by violence and abuse. The terms **abuse** and **violence** are often used interchangeably or exclusively by various groups of professionals (Walker, 1999). For example, in the professional literature couple violence is referred to as "spouse abuse," "wife abuse," "battering," "domestic violence," and "wife beating," among other terms. Definitions can have unintended effects; for example, in many law enforcement circles "domestic violence" can include street fights between strangers. Using the "official" statistics in that law enforcement district would not be an accurate account of violent action between partners—what is regularly labeled "domestic violence" by mental health professionals. Another important definitional consideration concerns the question, Is **psychological** or **verbal abuse** considered violence? There are no uniformly agreed-upon terms or definitions for the types of relational violence in this chapter. Therefore, all reports of statistics, research findings, and treatment program evaluations must be clearly considered in light of how violence was operationalized/ conceptualized in that specific situation. The definition used highlights the purpose of the abusive behaviors, while broadly defining them. **Partner/ spouse abuse** is a pattern of abusive behaviors including physical, sexual, and/or psychological maltreatment used by one person in an intimate relationship against another to gain power unfairly or to maintain that person's misuse of power, control, and/or authority (Walker, 1999). A single act of even moderate violence that is not accompanied by psychologically abusive or coercive behavior would not fit this definition of abuse.

The next discourse important to understanding the history and future of marriage and family therapy in relation to partner/spouse abuse are the issues of **gender, patriarchy,** and **feminism.** It is impossible to discuss partner/spouse abuse without considering gender. Researchers have reported that women are violent toward men in roughly equal numbers to the number of men violent toward women (Steinmetz, 1977a,b; Straus and Gelles, 1986). Feminists counter that gross numbers from national surveys do not reflect the true situation. They cite research that reports men are more likely to be more violent, less likely to be intimidated by their partner's violence, and less likely to be injured (Cantos, Neidig, and O'Leary, 1994; Cascardi and Vivian, 1995), and that women are more likely to use violence in self-defense, escape, and retaliation (Hamberger et al., 1997; Stets and Straus, 1990). Flynn (1990) recounted the political uproar that began when Steinmetz (1977a) described what she called "The Battered Husband Syndrome." Flynn describes the feminist response that denounced the data, the researcher, and her conclusions as drawing attention away from what feminists consider to be the more important issue of the patriarchy, maintaining that serious male-to-female violence occurs. In fact, Anderson (1997) states that the heart of the debate between feminists and family violence professionals revolves around the relative importance of patriarchy as the cause of domestic violence. Patriarchy, in application to family relationships, refers to a structure in which males are the dominant gender. It is generally agreed that the dominant family structure in the United States is patriarchal. A feminist explanation for partner/spouse abuse states that men perpetrate violence against women to maintain power and control of the heterosexual relationships they are in. This theory is the support for what Flynn (1990) calls "selective inattention" to the issue of female-to-male violence.

Marriage and Family Therapy and Partner/Spouse Abuse

A similar struggle ensued among therapists, especially marriage and family therapists. The following quote seems to succinctly sum up the current state of marriage and family therapy in relation to partner/spouse abuse:

> There is little consensus among marriage and family therapists about how to conceptualize and treat domestic violence cases, as demonstrated by the polarized controversy about whether couples or conjoint therapy for battered women and their partners is or is not dangerous, unethical, or ineffective. (Bograd and Mederos, 1999, p. 291)

Since the 1980s it has been clear to many that marriage and family therapists have not been in the forefront of the mental health response addressing partner/spouse abuse (Avis, 1992). In 1995, the *Journal of Marital and Family Therapy,* one of the preeminent family therapy journals, published a special issue to examine the effectiveness of marriage and family therapy in relation to many major mental health concerns. Conspicuous in its absence was any article addressing intrafamilial violence. In fact, the application of **systemically based marriage and family therapy treatments** to partner/spouse abuse cases has been the focus of some of family therapy's most strident criticism, especially by feminist clinicians and advocates (Bograd, 1992). The emphasis in systemic theory on shared, **reciprocal causality/responsibility** for patterns of interaction has been at the heart of the criticism. Any implication that the victim, typically a woman, "caused" her own abuse is considered totally unacceptable. Implicating a woman as responsible for her abuse is revictimizing the woman. One of the immediate outcomes of this criticism was the idea that doing conjoint couple treatment, by the very fact that the couple was seen together, signified the clinician's belief that the victim played a part in her own abuse. Subsequently, few if any articles, presentations, or books focused on couple-oriented, systemically based theory and/or therapy were offered. In essence, marriage and family therapists became silent concerning partner/spousal abuse (Avis, 1992). This does not mean that clinicians stopped working with violent couples conjointly. There is no way to know how many therapists have seen and continue to see violent couples together. It means only that marriage and family therapists and other couple therapists stopped writing and talking about working this way.

Historical Developments

In the absence of a marriage and family therapy voice in relation to partner/spousal abuse treatment, the primary treatment modalities presented through the usual professional outlets of journals, books, and workshops predominately involved combinations of **concurrent individual therapy** and/or separate **group treatment** for the victim and abuser, respectively. In concert with this, the predominant perspective requiring the focus to be on male-to-female violence meant that *perpetrator* meant "he" and *victim* meant "she".

The key factor in the offender component of the predominant treatment approaches had as its primary goal the development in the offender the resolution that he is responsible for his actions, that no one else made him perpetrate. It was suggested that as a result of this realization, he can then begin to take responsibility for using more constructive means of interacting with his partner, ways that do not involve the use of violence to maintain his dominance. It is widely reported that the potential success of offender treatment is maximized through a specialized group therapy setting, in which groups of violent offending males are seen together. The dynamics of peer pressure and the leadership of more treatment-advanced offenders are believed to be optimal in "breaking through" the offender's resistance to feeling and accepting responsibility in comparison to individual counseling.

Victim treatment primarily involves her acceptance of the same premise important in offender treatment: the offender is responsible for his actions; she did nothing to deserve the violence. She is also counseled to develop plans for herself and her children, if she has them, to be safe. This important aspect of treatment often involves leaving home and taking up temporary residence at a **battered women's shelter.** Shelter programs began emerging during the 1970s and have evolved into a broad network of **safe houses** that offer a wide variety of social and therapeutic services for victims and their children (Chalk and King, 1998). One of the primary challenges for the shelter movement has and continues to be adequate funding. For many therapists, another goal of working with the victim is to educate her in relation to the gender issues that many believe are at the heart of the perpetuation of couple violence, namely the use of violence in an effort for males to maintain the inequitable status quo of the patriarchal society. The victim's treatment may occur in either individual therapy, victim group therapy, or a combination of both. Throughout most of the 1980s and 1990s conjoint therapy for violent couples was generally considered inappropriate, contraindicated, and/or unethical (Bograd, 1992).

Current Marriage and Family Therapy Trends

Only recently (Bograd and Mederos, 1999; Almeida and Durkin, 1999; Goldner, 1999) have conjoint models for treatment of partner/spousal abuse begun to resurface in the literature. The primary difference between the recent treatment literature and the earlier, conjoint offerings is the current emphasis on the **contextual issues** of gender, **power differential,** race, and ethnicity. This important shift coincides with various researchers/theoreticians' call for finding a perspective that does not continue the dichotomous thinking that has polarized family theorists and practitioners—a perspective that, when informed by the pertinent contextual issues, may well allow for an integration of systemic and feminist theory in relation to partner/spousal violence. (Anderson, 1997; Bograd, 1999). Postmodern **constructivist theoretical perspectives** seem to be providing the groundwork for resolving the ethical dilemmas of trying to focus on individual responsibility while maintaining a relational perspective (McConaghy and Cottone, 1998). An example of the positive outcome inclusion of contextual variables brings to the effort to more fully understand and effectively treat partner/spouse violence is sexual orientation. The previously discussed issue of **gender polarization** and political action often left any depiction of partner/spouse abuse to be **gender typed,** typically male to female. This depiction, in essence, completely denied the very real situation of gay and lesbian relationship violence (Bograd, 1999). This unfortunate fact stands in sharp contrast to the reported conservative estimation that one half million gay men are battered annually (Island and Letellier, 1991).

Several potential advantages have been mentioned in association to couple treatment for partner/spouse abuse: conjoint interviews may more readily and truly reveal actual patterns of couple interaction (Rosenbaum and Maiuro, 1990); working together may more readily reveal whether the relationship can be reformulated without violence (Johnston and Campbell, 1993); interactional patterns displayed during the conjoint sessions are available to use in treatment immediately, sometimes allowing for additional therapeutic effectiveness (Jory, Anderson, and Greer, 1997); and couple therapy meets the request that many couples make to work together on the violence in their relationship (Lipchik, 1991).

The recent emergence of **conjoint couple treatment,** described in the previous paragraph, although reflective of the most current thought is still offered with hesitation (Bograd and Mederos, 1999). Sprenkle (1994) offers probably the clearest caveat when he notes that clinical research has not been published that directs us as to what circumstances, when, or even if couple treatment should occur. Since Sprenkle's pronouncement, the only major empirical research that seems to inform the issue was the research carried out by the late Neil Jacobson, John Gottman, and their colleagues at the University of Washington. This research describes a subset of male batterers (approximately 20 percent in their sample) who can be categorized based upon physiologic markers of heart rate reactivity. These batterers heart rate calms as they become more violent. The researchers state that these batterers appear to be sociopathically violent toward their partners, a group that Jacobson and colleagues caution probably will not respond to any known treatments (Gottman et al., 1995; Jacobson et al., 1994).

It seems clear that the most important guide for the clinician in deciding if couple therapy is indicated or not must revolve first around the issue of physical and psychological safety for the victim. Bograd and Mederos (1999) sensibly argue that to reach the "minimize risk, maximize safety goal," a focused, even structured interview process is necessary. They further suggest that because violence is often not presented as a problem, a **universal screening** should occur. The standard procedure for initiating couple therapy should include an initial couple session followed by an individual session with each partner before any agreement to begin conjoint couple therapy is made. These authors believe that a detailed **lethality assessment** should occur. Finally, they suggest that all seven of the following conditions should be met before a clinician considers undertaking conjoint couple therapy:

1. Both partners/spouses freely agree to couple therapy.
2. The violence is limited to a few episodes or less of minor (e.g., slaps, shoves, grabbing, restraining) violence.
3. Psychological abuse has been used infrequently or only mildly.
4. No risk factors for lethality are present and the woman does not fear retaliation.
5. The perpetrator admits and takes responsibility for the abuse.
6. The victim does not feel that she is responsible for the abuse.
7. The perpetrator must demonstrate an ongoing commitment to effectively deal with his explosive feelings without blaming others or acting out.

If one or more of these criteria are not met, then the authors suggest that couples work should not occur and the more traditional separate individual and/or group modalities should be employed (Bograd and Mederos, 1999). Almeida and Durkin (1999) represent a common current perspective in their description of a treatment regimen that includes a combination of individual, specialized group, and couple therapy. The couple therapy is the final phase of treatment, only undertaken if the prior individual and/or group treatment has been successful. In sum, given the wide variety of situations in which partner/spouse abuse occurs, it is unlikely that a single treatment method will be maximally effective (Lipchik, Sirles, and Kubicki, 1997).

Partner/Spouse Abuse and Child Abuse

Three important research findings that contribute significantly to a fuller understanding of the broader ramifications of family violence follow: (1) there is a growing body of evidence that child and partner/spouse abuse co-occur at alarming rates, conservatively placed at 40 percent (Appel and Holden, 1998); (2) the impact on children of *witnessing* partner/spouse abuse in their homes may effect them just as adversely as being the victim of abuse directly (Anderson and Cramer-Benjamin, 1999); and (3) children who are exposed to violence as either witnesses or victims are more likely to grow up to be either victims and/or perpetrators or perpetrators, respectively (Anderson and Cramer-Benjamin, 1999). When you consider these three research trends it is possible to more clearly visualize the potential for perpetuation of the various forms of family violence.

An additional implication can be derived from these research findings, pertinent to partner/spouse abuse treatment and prevention, is the idea that inclusion of direct screening of a violent couple's children for the purpose of uncovering either or both direct and indirect abuse experiences is important (Anderson and Cramer-Benjamin, 1999). The disruption to children's development, the potential assault to their self-esteem, the loss of their sense of personal safety and control, as well as trust in intimate relationships can be profound and lasting. Some of the potential long-term effects of untreated child abuse include lower socioeconomic status, increased risk for sexual dysfunction, adult couple relationship problems, lower self-esteem, substance abuse, and higher probability for diagnosis of a wide variety of mental health disorders (Mullen and Fleming, 1998). These research outcomes underline the importance of identifying and halting abuse experiences of children and attempting to address them as soon as possible.

Child Abuse

Child abuse is a significant problem in the United States. The National Committee for Prevention of Child Abuse reports that approximately 1.4 million children are maltreated each year, with 160,000 children suffering serious or life-threatening injuries, and approximately 2,000 dying as a result of abuse or neglect (Wissow, 1995). According to the National Child Abuse and Neglect Data System (NCANDS), for the year 2000 almost two-thirds of child victims (63 percent) suffered neglect (including medical neglect); 19 percent were physically abused; 10 percent were sexually abused; and 8 percent were psychologically maltreated (NCANDS, 2002).

Child abuse and neglect are defined in many ways. The specifics are important especially in relation to the generalizability of research findings and comparison of incidence and prevalence statistics. For the purpose of this chapter, **child abuse** is defined as the intentional harm or threat of harm to a child by someone acting in the role of caretaker, for even a short period of time (Wissow, 1995), and it may be **physical, emotional,** or **sexual abuse. Neglect** is defined as the lack of provision of the basic needs of a child.

More family therapy literature exists addressing child sexual abuse, so the current section focuses on sexual abuse to illustrate how family therapy can be utilized to address child abuse. Most of the following should be similarly applicable to the other forms of child abuse. Child sexual abuse occurs more frequently to children from socially deprived and disorganized family backgrounds that have higher rates of couple conflict, separation, and violence. The presence of a stepparent, poor parent-child attachment, and physical separation of the child from the home are also more highly associated with abuse (Mullen and Fleming, 1998). Mullen and Fleming also report that there is significant co-occurrence of the different forms of child abuse (physical, emotional, sexual, and neglect).

Child Abuse Treatment

In their review of child sexual abuse treatment, Finkelhor and Berliner (1995) summarize the treatment outcome studies by saying that the child victims show improvements that are consistent with the belief that therapy helps children recover. They further report that the results of these studies are promising, but the definitive studies have yet to be done. They continue by reporting that **externalizing** (or acting out) and **sexualized symptoms** are most resistant to change and that some children show no improvement with therapy. Most studies of child sexual abuse therapy report length of treatment at six to twenty sessions.

Finkelhor and Berliner (1995) make a very important point when they say "One important consideration distinguishes sexual abuse treatment from much other child psychotherapy: sexual abuse is an experience, not a syndrome or a disorder" (p. 1415). Disorders may develop, but often children are sent to treatment because of an experience. This means that the treatment population is very diverse, much more so than with most disorders or syndromes. The lists of associated symptoms is also very diverse.

Only about 30 percent of sexually abused children disclose their abuse during childhood (Finkelhor, 1984). The fact that the majority of sexual abuse cases do not present for therapy as a child highlights another aspect of diversity in relation to child sexual abuse, namely the age diversity of victims in treatment. A significant portion of the victim population is treated as children, demanding that the clinician possess experience and skill in child therapy, and parent-child and family issues. Another significant portion of the victim population is treated in adolescence, a distinctly different challenge than working with a younger child population. Finally, the third significant portion of the victim population presents for treatment as adults, often referred to as **adult survivors of sexual abuse.** These clients demand another, different set of treatment skills, often focused on a combination of individual, family-of-origin, and couple issues. Based on the diversity of abuse victims, it is very unlikely that any one treatment approach will be effective for all or even most victims.

Another unique consequence of abuse as an experience is that many children are referred for treatment without having any symptoms. This is almost unheard of in relation to other potential child problems. Referral of **asymptomatic** children is a controversial issue, especially when examined in light of another commonly discussed outcome of child sexual abuse: the **sleeper effect**. Sleeper effects refer to serious symptoms that may not surface until years after the abuse (Briere, 1992). A common example of the sleeper effect is when sexual abuse occurs with a prepubescent child, and then symptoms develop when the child is older, such as during puberty with sexual acting out. The idea of sleeper effects is widely accepted among child abuse professionals, in spite of the fact that there is little, if any, empirical support for it (Finkelhor and Berliner, 1995). Finkelhor and Berliner point out that the belief in sleeper effects has had several profound consequences for child sexual abuse clinicians and researchers. The fear that sleeper effects will eventually appear leaves many clinicians suspicious of short-term treatment success and outcome evaluations. They are skeptical of asymptomatic children, often believing they are in denial or repressing their trauma. Another outcome of this, which many in the field believe is unfortunate, is that children are kept in treatment, sometimes lengthy, prescribed treatment regimens, regardless of whether their symptoms improve or if they even display symptoms. This is done in the name of undertaking **prophylactic measures** to help avoid sleeper effects.

Treatment dropouts are a significant problem in child abuse treatment, maybe because of the lengthy treatment recommended despite actual symptom patterns. Deblinger (1994, as cited in Finkelhor and Berliner, 1995) found that the most likely victims to drop out of treatment were males, low-symptom children, minority children, and parent treatment only cases (in which children are not involved in treatment). One approach with promise for dealing with treatment dropouts would be to offer a more or less standardized brief intervention to all victims that focused on assessment and dealing with the central messages of establishing (1) the lack of blame for the victim, (2) safety/prevention skills, and (3) a stable nonoffending adult relationship. Treatment would continue only for those cases where (1) these were not present or easily established, and/or (2) significant distress or symptoms were continuing, and/or (3) the family and child desired to continue (Finkelhor and Berliner, 1995).

Stevenson (1999) reports that **cognitive-behavioral treatments** are the most effective at reducing abused children's behavioral symptoms as well as modifying their parents' behaviors. He goes on to report that at present evidence is inconclusive regarding which forms of treatment are most effective at treating the actual sexual abuse. Both Briere (1992) and Finkelhor and Berliner (1995) report that **abuse-specific treatment** is generally accepted to be a critical component to successful therapy. The common elements of abuse specific treatment are (1) encouraging the expression of **abuse-induced feelings,** (2) dealing with any **self-blame issues,** (3) teaching **abuse**

prevention skills, and (4) diminishing any sense of isolation through reassurance or group therapy with other victims (Finkelhor and Berliner, 1995). The exact means by which these elements are operationalized vary greatly from clinician to clinician. For example, abuse-specific features can be undertaken in individual, relational (parent-child), group, or family therapy.

Family Therapy for Child Abuse

> Obviously, the effectiveness of treatment for children is likely to be strongly influenced by the family context, and addressing it should be a very important priority for intervention. (Finkelhor and Berliner, 1995, p. 1416)

One of the most important and consistent findings by child abuse researchers is that family—in particular, nonoffending parent support—is a consistent predictor of better recovery outcomes for child victims (Mullen and Flemming, 1998). Cohen and Mannarino (1997) reported that parental emotional support was the strongest predictor variable for a positive treatment outcome. In spite of the previous statements based on child abuse research, family therapy approaches have been little researched in relation to child abuse treatment. One of the few studies undertaken thus far reported that providing parents and children with treatment was associated with parents perceiving more symptom reduction in their children than in cases that received child therapy only. Conversely, in the same study, children who received treatment either alone or with parents perceived their own symptoms to improve more than those children who received no therapy while their parents were treated (Deblinger, 1994, as cited in Finkelhor and Berliner, 1995). Most of the other studies that have tested a family therapy treatment, at least when employing a **generic family treatment regimen,** have not resulted in significant treatment improvements for children (Finkelhor and Berliner, 1995). These outcomes are consistent with the suggestion offered in the previous section that abuse-specific elements offered through a variety of techniques are probably the most effective treatments. Therefore, the remainder of this section addressing family therapy and child abuse will focus on an integrative child-family, abuse-specific approach.

Filial Therapy

Louise Guerney and Bernard Guerney (1987) coined the term *filial therapy* to describe a type of child-centered play therapy administered by the child's parents. Filial comes from the Latin terms for "son" *(filius)* and "daughter" *(filia)*. Though currently conceptualized as a treatment with individual families, originally filial therapy was practiced as a family group therapy in which parents were trained as play therapists during ten two-hour sessions. Between the 1960s and 1990s very little literature addressed filial therapy. During the 1990s the idea of an integration of play therapy and family therapy had a resurgence (Gil, 1991, 1994; Johnson et al., 1999; VanFleet, 1994b).

To fully explicate the therapeutic effect of filial therapy, a brief background addressing the play therapy component is offered. Play therapy has a history dating to Sigmund Freud's work with the famous case of "Little Hans" in 1909. **Play therapy** can be conceptualized as child therapy using play as the medium through which the child will primarily express his or her feelings as well as seek mastery of conflicts. Axline (1947) offered a play therapy model that seems to include the core beliefs of most modern play therapy practitioners. At the heart of these methods is the relationship of the child and practitioner that develops over time. Axline's method involves nondirective, unconditional acceptance of the child and the child's actions in the play setting. Play therapy traditionally is considered to be an approach that encourages the child to deal with his or her intrapsychic conflicts through the accepting therapeutic relationship, which includes the opportunity for the child to symbolically work through the conflict using play. Play therapy requires that the therapist has a variety of materials available for the child's use. These materials may include dolls, dollhouses, toy soldiers, stuffed toys, toy animals, household types of toys such as furniture and kitchenware, puppets, and objects that may be smashed or hit. Art supplies are particularly useful, including crayons, paint, finger paints, sand art, and so on. Gil finds that in addition to these materials, telephones, sunglasses, feelings cards (i.e., illustrations of faces expressing feelings), therapeutic stories, mutual storytelling technique, puppet play, sand play, nursing bottles, dishes and utensils, and video therapy are particularly effective in working with abused children.

The idea of integrating play therapy and family therapy is supported by the previously noted research which emphasizes the critical role that family, particularly nonoffending parents, can have in positive outcomes for abused children. Directly involving the child's nonoffending parent(s) may greatly facilitate their support for the child.

The following are the core beliefs of a filial therapist, according to VanFleet (1994b):

1. Play is an essential element of child development and is therapeutically beneficial.

2. Nonoffending parent involvement is associated with more positive and longer lasting results.
3. Most child problems are environmentally induced (e.g., abuse), therefore education and skill development are usually associated with positive outcomes for children and their families.
4. Child-centered play therapy is associated with positive child outcomes.

As previously mentioned, originally filial therapy was conceptualized and practiced as a group therapy method. For a discussion of current thought on how to operationalize a group filial model, see Landreth (1991). An example of a comprehensive program for child abuse treatment that includes group filial therapy as a primary component is the Cedar House program (Kendig and Lowry, 1998). The following briefly outlines how VanFleet (1994a) proposes a filial application proceed:

1. Initial assessment of the child and family using interviews, family play observations, and measures of parent-child behaviors, attitudes, and skills.
2. As appropriate, recommendation of filial therapy to parents, including full discussion of its rationale, content, and process.
3. Therapist demonstrations of child-centered play sessions with the children as parents observe.
4. Training period for parents to learn play session skills, which includes skills-training exercises and mock play sessions with therapist feedback.
5. Office-based parent play sessions with their own children, followed by supervisory feedback from the filial therapist.
6. Ongoing home-based play sessions, followed by regular therapist-parent meetings to discuss play themes, parents' concerns, additional parenting skills, and generalization of skills.
7. As needed, and prior to discharge, follow-up office-based play sessions with **live supervision** by the therapist for maintenance.
8. At discharge, evaluation of filial therapy by parents and therapist; post-therapy assessment of parent-child behaviors, attitudes, and skills.

Although the filial therapy model seems to include various elements that have been found to be associated with better child outcomes following abuse (e.g., nonoffending parent involvement, abuse-specific treatment focus, utilizing cognitive-behavioral elements through a play environment), only limited empirical support has been published (Bavin-Hoffman, Jennings, and Landreth, 1996). Similar to other applications of family therapy models, carefully designed outcome research is needed to determine the true effectiveness of this innovative approach.

PSYCHOEDUCATIONAL FAMILY THERAPY
FOR SCHIZOPHRENIA

The training of practitioners in psychoeducational family models should not be separated from training in traditional family therapy methods, including techniques for joining and alliance building, maintaining neutrality, reframing and relabeling, and thinking in terms of recursive processes. (Goldstein and Miklowitz, 1995, p. 374)

According to the DSM-IV (American Psychiatric Association, 1994), **schizophrenia** is a mental disorder with characteristic symptoms that fall into two broad categories—those that reflect an excess or distortion of normal functions (positive symptoms) and those that reflect a diminution or loss of normal functions (negative symptoms). **Positive symptoms** include delusions, hallucinations, disorganized speech, and grossly disorganized or rigid behavioral response. **Negative symptoms** include restrictions in the range and intensity of emotional expression, in the fluency and productivity of thought and speech, and in the initiation of goal-directed behavior. When assessing for schizophrenia, the patient must display two or more of the five characteristic symptoms (negative symptoms are lumped together), with each being present for a significant portion of the time during a one-month period. This is referred to as the **active phase** or **psychotic episode.** In addition, the individual must have continuous signs of **social dysfunction** and/or **occupational dysfunction** that have persisted for at least a six-month period.

In the 1950s, research investigating the family's role in the development of schizophrenia led to the idea that it was caused by dysfunctional family interaction patterns rather than being an intrapsychic disorder. Although this research lead to the development of many of the models underlying family systems theory, it did not find the cause of or cure for schizophrenia. There is no determined single causative factor for schizophrenia. Biological, environmental, and psychosocial factors can all play a role (Maxmen and Ward, 1995). The advent and widespread use of **neuroleptic drugs** and the more recent **antipsychotic drugs,** as well as various social changes including the **deinstitutionalization** of patients from large mental hospitals, the shortening of the length of hospital stays during active phases of schizophrenia, and the reliance on community care for most of the recovery process, led to a three-phase model of treatment for schizophrenia. These included medication during the acute phase in the hospital, use of **pharmacological** and **psychosocial therapy** to provide stabilization during the **outpatient period,** and maintenance of a **stable state** through ongoing **multimodal treatments** (Goldstein and Miklowitz, 1995).

With less time spent in treatment facilities during the stabilization periods, patients with schizophrenia had a greater opportunity to be in contact with their families. Clinicians noted not only the impact of the family on the patient's clinical state, but also the burdens and effects a member with schizophrenia brought to the family. Studies of patients following their release from the hospital showed a direct relationship between the degree to which intense emotion was expressed in the family and the degree of relapse (Brown et al., 1962; Kavanagh, 1992). The theory of **expressed emotion (EE)** emerged, suggesting that schizophrenia is a thought disorder in which the individual is especially vulnerable to, and highly responsive to, stress involving the expression of intense, negative emotions. This opened the idea that positive family involvement in the treatment process could enhance the potential of a better outcome for the patient and ultimately for the family (Goldstein and Miklowitz, 1995).

A series of intervention studies was conducted (Falloon et al., 1987; Goldstein et al., 1978; Hogarty et al., 1986; Leff et al., 1989; Randolph et al., 1994; Tarrier, Barrowclough, and Porceddu, 1988) to compare groups of patients that had a **psychoeducational family component** added to their regular treatment program and those who did not have the family component. All comparison groups involved regular medication management alone or in combination with another form of psychosocial treatment, along with crisis intervention as needed. Success of the treatment modality was measured in part by the rate of relapse during follow-up time periods, from six months to two years. These studies confirmed that programs containing some form of family intervention, combined with routine care, are more effective than routine care alone (Goldstein and Miklowitz, 1995). Studies (Falloon et al., 1987; Hogarty et al., 1991) also show that over a two-year period family interventions are more effective in delaying relapses and improving social functioning than are the individual supportive or skill-oriented interventions. However, providing only a few sessions of family education, with or without the patient, does not bring about long-term changes.

Several different types of family interventions have been tested. These include

(a) individual family treatment which includes the patient as well as key relatives and usually consists of home- or clinic-based education, skill building, problem solving, and crisis-intervention sessions; (b) **relatives' groups** which exclude patients and are oriented around helping relatives to cope with the disorder; and (c) **multiple-family groups** which, like relatives' groups, are educational and coping-based but do include patients. (Goldstein and Miklowitz, 1995:372)

The success of any of the family treatments is dependent on the attendance by family members; therefore, the best program may be dependent on the family's comfort zone with selected programs. Box 14.1 provides a set of guidelines from psychoeducators for managing rehabilitation following a schizophrenic episode. Box 14.2 provides a listing of the common ingredients found in almost all effective psychoeducational family programs.

BOX 14.1.
Psychoeducational Guidelines
for Families and Friends
of Persons with Schizophrenia

- Understand recovery takes time. Go slowly and understand that things will get better in their own time.
- Keep things calm and cool. Understand disagreements are normal; tone them down as much as possible.
- Give the person his or her space.
- Set some limits and rules. Rules help to keep things orderly and calm.
- Communicate clearly and simply. Say what you need to say calmly, clearly, and in a positive manner.
- Follow doctor's orders. Take medications only as prescribed.
- Reestablish rituals and routines in your family life. Stay in touch with family and friends for social support.
- Don't take street drugs or alcohol; they make symptoms worse.
- If you notice changes, consult with your family clinician as soon as possible.
- Take things one step at a time. Change is gradual.
- Temporarily lower your expectations. Compare things month to month instead of year to year.

Source: Adapted from McFarlane, 1991, p. 375.

**BOX 14.2. Common Ingredients
in Effective Family Intervention Programs**

- The family is engaged *early* in the treatment process.
- The atmosphere is one of nonblaming.
- Families are educated about schizophrenia.
- The rationale for the treatment is provided.
- Coping recommendations are made.
- Communication training is provided.
- Information is provided on how to give positive and negative feedback within the family in a constructive manner.
- Problem-solving training is provided with the goals of:
  a. day-to-day management of the schizophrenia and its ramifications
  b. stress management
  c. providing specific problem-solving skills
- Crisis intervention can occur, with specific attention to signs of stress and possible recurrence of active schizophrenic episodes.

Source: Adapted from Goldstein and Miklowitz, 1995, p. 363.

GLOSSARY

abstinence: Continued success by a client in completely avoiding the targeted symptom. For example, in the case of alcoholics, the client attempts to completely avoid ingesting alcohol in any form.

abuse: Physical, sexual, and/or psychological maltreatment used by one person against another.

abuse prevention skills: Behaviors taught to an abuse victim that, if practiced, should decrease the possibility of further abuse.

abuse-induced feelings: Feeling that occur because an individual has suffered abuse.

abuse-specific treatment: Any treatment approach that is specifically designed to address abuse.

active phase: The period of time lasting at least one month when an individual with schizophrenia is displaying two or more of the characteristic symptoms; also called a psychotic episode.

adjunctive therapy: Any therapy that is suggested to be secondary but supportive of another therapeutic intervention that is considered to be primary.

adult survivors of sexual abuse: Individual adults who were victims of sexual abuse at some point during their childhood.

affair: When a marital partner either has a sexual relationship or makes an emotional investment with someone other than his or her spouse.

aftercare: Formal contact with clients, designed to maintain treatment gains after the primary therapy is completed.

alcoholic families: Families in which alcohol is the structuring principle for their lives together.

angry associates: One of five types of relationships between former spouses and coparental units in which the divorced spouses continue to interact and have involvement in their children's lives, but they cannot separate their parental and marital issues, resulting in continuing power struggles.

antipsychotic drugs: Generalized term for drugs used to improve the symptoms of schizophrenia.

asymptomatic: The lack of any symptoms when the expectation based on what has happened previously suggests that symptoms should be present.

battered women's shelter: Places designed to offer refuge to women who are victims or potential victims of abuse.

behavioral marital therapy (BMT): An approach to couple therapy that is based on the principles of behaviorism.

binuclear family: A coparental divorce arrangement in which the family remains a family, and children divide their living time between the two separate households.

child abuse: The intentional harm or threat of harm to a child by someone acting in the role of caretaker, for even a short period of time.

codependence: Manifestations of behavior in a partner or someone close to the alcoholic that usually includes caretaking, selflessness, control issues, perfectionism, and fear.

cognitive-behavioral treatments: Therapy approaches that are based upon the principle that changing how a client thinks (cognition) and acts (behavior) is often the key to improvement.

community divorce: The dimension of the divorce process involving the social support of formal and informal contacts with individuals and groups that provide emotional and material resources for the person experiencing divorce.

concurrent individual therapy: Individual therapy performed at the same general time that the client is also involved in another type of therapy.

conjoint couple treatment: Any therapy approach that recommends that couples be seen for treatment together.

constructivist theoretical perspectives: Theoretical perspectives based upon the principle that what is stated to be true depends on how the observer perceives it, not on qualities that actually make up the entity in question.

contextual issues: Issues that add a richer meaning to the understanding of a particular entity. For example, ethnicity may help explain the difference of experiences that two people similar in other ways manifest.

cooperative colleagues: One of five types of relationships between former spouses and coparental units in which the divorced spouses, although not friends, are able to remain child focused and can separate their marital issues from their parental roles.

coparental divorce: The dimension of the divorce process in which divorcing parents must address the continuing developmental needs of their children, including their perceptions and responses to the divorce.

deinstitutionalization: Changes in the treatment for schizophrenia that resulted in the removal of patients from long-term confinement in mental hospitals.

dissolved duos: One of five types of relationships between former spouses and coparental units in which the divorced spouses have no further contact with each other and one parent assumes full responsibility for the children.

divorce: The ending of a marriage by an act of law, and the multidimensional process through which the marital couple transition as a result of their changed marital relationship.

divorce adjustment: A measure of how successful one is in completing the tasks of and moving through the divorce process.

divorce mediation: A process in which a divorcing couple works with a mediator to make decisions regarding custody, visitation, and distribution of property and financial assets, based on the best interest of all involved and on cooperative problem solving.

divorce restructuring stage: The stage in the divorce process when the decision to divorce is made and the separation begins.

economic divorce: The dimension of the divorce process involving division of accumulated property and financial assets, issues of alimony and child support, and decisions by the individuals resulting from no longer having a shared financial base.

emotional abuse: Child abuse that includes actions which traumatize the child yet do not include physical harm, such as verbal berating or cursing.

emotional closure: When the various different emotions the individual has experienced as a result of the divorce process no longer play a significant role in his or her life.

emotional divorce: The dimension of the divorce process in which the individual is faced with various different emotions regarding his or her marriage and the life changes resulting from the divorce.

emotional investment: A commitment of one's emotions to a relationship with the expectation that one's partner will reciprocate.

engaging: In relation to therapy, the ability to successfully attract someone into initially attending therapy.

expressed emotion (EE): The degree of affect expressed within a family—especially noteworthy in families with schizophrenic members—in which emotionally intense and negative interactions are considered a factor in the schizophrenic's relapse.

externalizing symptoms: Symptoms that are directed or manifested toward others, such as misbehavior.

family predisposition: The probability that membership in a particular family increases the possibility of a particular characteristic, such as alcoholism, manifesting in any member.

family reorganization: In reference to alcoholic families, establishing new patterns of interaction without the alcohol to define the family members' lives.

feminism: Doctrine that advocates equal rights for men and women.

fiery foes: One of five types of relationships between former spouses and coparental units in which the divorced spouses are hostile and angry all the time and unable to coparent, their emotional battles frequently involve extended family and friends, and their legal battles continue for many years after the divorce.

filial therapy: A type of child-centered play therapy administered by the child's parents.

firm relationship rules: Having expectations that are not subject to change about what is and is not suitable behavior between ex-spouses.

gender: Sets of behaviors that are associated with the two biological sexes, i.e., masculine or feminine.

gender polarization: The idea that males and females will take positions that are in opposition to each other.

gender typed: The idea that a particular behavior is predominantly associated with either males or females.

generic family treatment regimen: Refers to any one of the generally accepted family therapy approaches not specifically designed to deal with a specific client population or symptom group.

good management: Learning about and preparing for the transitions resulting from divorce, using effective life skills to make decisions and to control one's life.

group treatment: Any therapeutic model that is practiced on more than two clients gathered together.

integrative family models: Therapy approaches that attempt to incorporate the best aspects of several distinct therapy approaches into a cohesive and comprehensive therapy model.

intervention: A therapeutic technique that involves the family and other loved ones receiving eight to ten hours of training focused on how to effectively confront the alcoholic with his or her drinking.

legal divorce: The dimension of the divorce process in which the parties jointly or separately take action to legally end their marriage

lethality assessment: An assessment that is intended to determine the potential for death associated with actions on the part of an individual.

live supervision: The oversight of a therapist's therapy session by a more experienced therapist through direct observation of the session as it occurs. Usually this will be accomplished by using one-way mirrors or a video camera.

marital discord: When a marital couple fails to get along well together, has conflict, or has lack of agreement.

multimodal treatments: The use of more than one type of treatment at the same time, i.e., the concurrent use of pharmacological and psychosocial therapy.

multiple-family groups: A form of treatment in which members of several families meet together as a group, along with the schizophrenic patients, for educational and coping-based information and support.

negative symptoms: Schizophrenic symptoms that reflect a diminution or loss of normal functions, such as restrictions in the range and intensity of emotional expression, in the fluency and productivity of thought and speech, and in the initiation of goal-directed behavior.

neglect: The lack of provision of the basic needs of a child.

neuroleptic drugs: Drugs used for schizophrenia that have been found beneficial in reducing hallucinations and delusions in the early and middle stages of the disorder. The term *neuroleptic* derives from the side effects, the most common involving the nerves and muscles controlling movement and coordination.

no-fault divorce: A legal divorce option in which neither party is required to show that a spouse is responsible or to blame; irreconcilable differences.

occupational dysfunction: Impaired functioning in task-related activities.

outpatient period: The time following the schizophrenic's release from the hospital when the patient continues treatment in order to maintain a stable state.

overresponsible and underresponsible: Bepko and Kresten (1988) suggest that instead of using codependence, the terms *overresponsible* and *underresponsible* be applied to the nonabusing partner and abuser, respectively. They argue that these terms more accurately reflect the behaviors associated with the common relational pattern between an abuser and someone close to him or her.

partner/spouse abuse: A pattern of abusive behaviors including physical, sexual, and/or psychological maltreatment used by one person in an intimate relationship against another to gain power unfairly or to maintain that person's misuse of power, control, and/or authority.

patriarchy: A social structure that places the male or father as the ultimate authority.

perfect pals: One of five types of relationships between former spouses and coparental units in which the divorced spouses remain close friends, have good problem-solving skills and few conflicts, share child-rearing responsibilities, and generally have joint custody.

perpetrator: The person who commits an act of violence or abuse.

pharmacological therapy: Treatment consisting of the use of prescribed medications.

physical abuse: Child abuse that includes acts of violence against the child's person.

play therapy: A type of therapy that can be conceptualized as child therapy using play as the medium through which the child will primarily express his or her feelings as well as seek mastery of conflicts.

positive symptoms: Schizophrenic symptoms that reflect an excess or distortion of normal functions such as delusions, hallucinations, disorganized speech, and grossly disorganized or rigid behavioral response.

postdivorce recovery period: The stage in the divorce process following the restructuring stage when individuals are continuing to make decisions and changes in their lives as a result of the divorce.

power differential: The concept that there is an unequal distribution of power between any two units of comparison.

predivorce stage: The time period that falls between the beginning of the deterioration of the marriage and the decision by the couple to divorce.

prophylactic measures: Actions taken with the goal of preventing something from occurring.

psychic divorce: The dimension of the divorce process in which the individual addresses issues such as coping with loneliness, regaining self-confidence, and rebuilding social relationships.

psychoeducational family component: A therapeutic effort offering educational programs directed at helping families better understand and learn skills for dealing with a seriously disturbed family member, such as a schizophrenic recently released from a psychiatric hospital.

psychological abuse: Maltreatment by one person against another that does not include any physical elements but is nonetheless damaging to the internal makeup of the victim.

psychosocial therapy: A treatment of both individual and relational mental health concerns using individual and family therapy.

psychotic episode: The period of time lasting at least one month when an individual with schizophrenia is displaying two or more of the characteristic symptoms; also called the active phase.

reciprocal causality/responsibility: The concept that events do not cause each other in a sequential fashion but in fact affect each other in a more circular or recursive manner.

relapse: The return of symptoms after treatment goals to lessen or eradicate those same symptoms appear to have been met; to regress after partial recovery from an illness.

relationship/family violence: Physical, sexual, and/or psychological maltreatment used by one person in an intimate relationship against another.

relatives' groups: A form of treatment in which family members of schizophrenic patients meet without the patient for the purpose of helping relatives cope with the disorder.

remarry: To enter into marriage with a new partner following the dissolution of a previous marriage.

retaining: In relation to therapy, the ability to successfully attract someone to continue to commit to therapy.

role losses: When an individual no longer functions in a certain role, e.g., as a spouse following a divorce.

safe houses: Places designed to offer protection to a victim or potential victim of abuse.

schizophrenia: A mental disorder with characteristic symptoms that reflect either an excess or distortion of normal functions (positive symptoms) or a diminution or loss of normal functions (negative symptoms) accompanied by social and/or occupational dysfunction.

self-blame issues: The idea that often abuse victims blame themselves for their abuse instead of blaming the perpetrator.

separation: A time during which the marital couple is not living together. When occurring as part of the divorce process, a legal separation agreement may be implemented.

sexual abuse: Child abuse that includes actions that are sexual with or toward the child, such as the performance of any sexual act with a child.

sexualized symptoms: Symptoms that are sexual in nature, such as attempting sex acts.

sleeper effect: The concept that a particular outcome may not occur immediately proceeding its cause but may in fact occur well after the precipitating event.

social dysfunction: Impaired functioning in interpersonal relations.

spousal abuse: A pattern of abusive behaviors including physical, sexual, and/or psychological maltreatment used by one person in a marital relationship against another to gain power unfairly or to maintain that person's misuse of power, control, and/or authority.

stable state: The time during which the schizophrenic patient is not displaying symptoms.

structural family therapy: A therapy approach designed to be utilized with entire families that focuses on the manner in which families are organized as key to their ability to function successfully.

substance abuse: A maladaptive pattern of substance use leading to clinically significant impairment or distress.

systemically based marriage and family therapy treatments: Therapy approaches that are primarily based upon the principles of general systems theory and are focused upon the treatment of relationships.

treatment dropouts: Clients who do not complete therapy before their goals are realized.

universal screening: The idea that all potential therapy cases should be assessed for the presence of a particular symptom pattern.

verbal abuse: Maltreatment by one person against another that does not include any physical elements but is verbal in nature.

violence: Physical, sexual, and/or psychological maltreatment used by one person against another.

REFERENCES

Ahrons, C.R. (1999). Divorce: An unscheduled family transition. In B. Carter and M. McGoldrick (Eds.), *The expanded family life cycle: Individual, family and social perspectives,* Third edition (pp. 381-398). Boston, MA: Allyn and Bacon.

Ahrons, C.R. and Rodgers, R.H. (1987). *Divorced families: A multidisciplinary developmental view.* New York: W.W. Norton and Company.

Almeida, R. and Durkin, T. (1999). The cultural context model: Therapy for couples with domestic violence. *Journal of Marital and Family Therapy, 25,* 313-324.

American Psychiatric Association (2000). *Diagnostic and statistical manual of mental disorders* (Fourth edition, Text revision). Washington, DC: American Psychiatric Association.

Anderson, K. (1997). Gender, status, and domestic violence: An integration of feminist and family violence approaches. *Journal of Marriage and the Family, 59,* 655-669.

Anderson, S. and Cramer-Benjamin, D. (1999). The impact of couple violence on parenting and children: An overview and clinical implications. *American Journal of Family Therapy, 27,* 1-19.

Appel, A. and Holden, G. (1998). The co-occurrence of spouse and physical child abuse: A review and appraisal. *Journal of Family Psychology, 12,* 578-599.

Avis, J. (1992). Where are all the family therapists? Abuse and violence within families and family therapy's response. *Journal of Marital and Family Therapy, 18,* 225-232.

Axline, V. (1947). *Play therapy.* Cambridge, MA: Riverside Press.

Bavin-Hoffman, R., Jennings, G., and Landreth, G. (1996). Filial therapy: Parental perceptions of the process. *International Journal of Play Therapy, 5,* 45-58.

Bepko, C. and Krestan, J. (1988). *The responsibility trap.* New York: The Free Press.

Bograd, M. (1992). Values in conflict: Challenges to family therapists' thinking. *Journal of Marital and Family Therapy, 18,* 245-256.

Bograd, M. (1999). Strengthening domestic violence theories: Intersections of race, gender, class, sexual orientation, and gender. *Journal of Marital and Family Therapy, 25,* 275-290.

Bograd, M. and Mederos, F. (1999). Battering and couples therapy: Universal screening and selection of treatment modality. *Journal of Marital and Family Therapy, 25,* 291-312.

Bohannan, P. (1970). The six stations of divorce. In P. Bohannan (Ed.), *Divorce and after* (pp. 33-62). Garden City, NY: Doubleday.

Briere, J. (1992). *Child Abuse Trauma: Theory and Treatment of the Lasting, Effects.* Newbury Park, CA: Sage Publications, Inc.

Brown, G.W., Monck, E.M., Carstairs, G.M., and Wing, J.K. (1962). Influence on family life in the course of schizophrenic illness. *British Journal of Psychiatry, 16,* 55-68.

Bumpass, L. (1990). What's happening to the family? Interactions between demographic and institutional change. *Demography, 17,* 483-498.

Cantos, A., Neidig, P., and O'Leary, K. (1994). Injuries of women and men in a treatment program for domestic violence. *Journal of Family Violence, 9,* 113-124.

Carter, B. and McGoldrick M. (1999). The divorce cycle: A major variation in the American family life cycle. In B. Carter and M. McGoldrick (Eds.), *The expanded family life cycle: Individual, family and social perspectives,* Third edition (pp. 362-372). Boston, MA: Allyn and Bacon.

Cascardi, M. and Vivian, D. (1995). Context for specific episodes of marital violence: Gender and severity of violence differences. *Journal of Family Violence, 10,* 265-293.

Chalk, R. and King, P. (Eds.) (1998). *Violence in families: Assessing prevention and treatment programs.* Washington, DC: National Academy Press.

Cohen, J. and Mannarino, A. (1997). Factors that mediate treatment outcome of sexually abused preschool children: Six and 12 month follow up. *Journal of the American Academy of Adolescent Psychiatry, 37,* 44-51.

Deblinger, E. (1994). Update on treatment outcome studies. Presented at the American Psychological Association convention, Los Angeles, CA.

Edwards, M. and Steinglass, P. (1995). Family therapy treatment outcomes for alcoholism. In W. Pinsof and L. Wynn (Eds.), *Family therapy effectiveness: Current research and theory* (pp. 475-510). Washington, DC: AAMFT.

Falloon, I.R., McGill, C.W., Boyd, J.L. and Pederson, J. (1987). Family management in the prevention of morbidity of schizophrenia: Social outcome of a two-year longitudinal study. *Psychological Medicine, 17,* 59-66.

Finkelhor, D. (1984). *Child sexual abuse: new theory and research,* New York: Free Press.

Finkelhor, D. and Berliner, L. (1995). Research on the treatment of sexually abused children: A review and recommendations. *Journal of the American Academy of Child and Adolescent Psychiatry, 34,* 1408-1423.

Flynn, C. (1990). Relationship violence by women: Issues and implications. *Family Relations, 39,* 194-198.

Gelles, R. and Straus, M. (1988). *Intimate violence: The causes and consequences of abuse in the American family.* New York: Simon and Schuster.

Gil, E. (1991). *The healing power of play: Working with abused children.* New York: Guilford.

Gil, E. (1994). *Playing in family therapy.* New York: Guilford.

Goldner, V. (1999). Morality and multiplicity: Perspectives on the treatment of violence in intimate life. *Journal of Marital and Family Therapy, 25,* 325-336.

Goldstein, M.J. and Miklowitz, D.J. (1995). The effectiveness of psychoeducational family therapy in the treatment of schizophrenic disorders. *Journal of Marital and Family Therapy, 21*(4), 361-376.

Goldstein, M.J., Rodnick, E.H., Evans, J.R., May, P.R.A., and Steinberg, M.R. (1978). Drug and family therapy in the aftercare of acute schizophrenics. *Archives of General Psychiatry, 42,* 887-986.

Gottman, J., Jacobson, N., Rushe, R., Shortt, J., Babcock, J., La Taillade, J., and Waltz, J. (1995). The relationship between heart rate reactivity, emotionally aggressive behavior, and general violence in batters. *Journal of Family Psychology, 9,* 227-248.

Guerney, L. and Guerney, B., Jr. (1987). Integrating child and family therapy. *Psychotherapy, 24,* 609-614.

Hamberger, L.K., Lohr, J., Bonge, D., and Tolin, D. (1997). An empirical classification of motivations for domestic violence. *Violence Against Women, 3,* 401-423.

Helzer, J.E. and Pryzbeck, T.R. (1988). The co-occurrence of alcoholism with other psychiatric disorders in the general population and its impact on treatment. *Journal of Studies on Alcohol, 49,* 219-224.

Henggeler, S.W., Borduin, C.M., Melton, G.B., Mann, B.J., Smith, L.A., Hall, J.A., Cone, L., and Fucci, B.R. (1991). Effects of multisystemic therapy on drug use and abuse in serious juvenile offenders: A progress report from two outcome studies. *Family Dynamics Addiction Quarterly, 1,* 40-51.

Hogarty, G.E., Anderson, C.M., Reiss D.J., Kornblith, S.J., Greenwald, D.P., Jaine, C.D., and Madonia, M.J. (1986). Family psychoeducation, social skills training, and maintenance chemotherapy in the aftercare of schizophrenia. I. One-year effects of a controlled study on relapse and expressed emotion. *Archives of General Psychiatry, 43,* 633-642.

Hogarty, G.E., Anderson, C.M., Reiss, D.J., Kornblith, S.J., Greenwald, D.P., Ulrich, R.F., and Carter, M. (1991). Family psychoeducation, social skills training, and maintenance chemotherapy in the aftercare of schizophrenia. II. Two-year effects of a controlled study on relapse and adjustment. *Archives of General Psychiatry, 48,* 340-347.

Institute of Medicine (1990). *Treating drug problems: A study of the evolution, effectiveness, and financing of public and private drug treatment systems* (Report by the Institute of Medicine Committee for the Substance Abuse Coverage Study, Division of Health Care Services). Washington, DC: National Academy Press.

Island, D. and Letellier, P. (1991). *Men who beat the men who love them: Battered gay men and domestic violence.* Binghamton, NY: Harrington Park Press.

Jacobson, N.S., Gottman, J.M., Waltz, J., Rushe, R., Babcock, J., and Holtzworth-Munroe, A. (1994). Affect, verbal content, and psychophysiology in the arguments of couples with a violent husband. *Journal of Consulting and Clinical Psychology, 62*(5), 982-988.

James, P. (1997). *The divorce mediation handbook: Everything you need to know.* San Francisco: Jossey-Bass Publishers.

Joanning, H., Thomas, F., Quinn, W., and Mullen, R. (1992). Treating adolescent drug abuse: A comparison of family systems therapy, group therapy, and family drug education. *Journal of Marital and Family Therapy, 18,* 345-356.

Johnson, L., Bruhn, R., Winek, J., Krepps, J., and Wiley, K. (1999). The use of child-centered play therapy and filial therapy with Head Start families: A brief report. *Journal of Marital and Family Therapy, 25,* 169-176.

Johnston, J. and Campbell, L. (1993). A clinical typology of interparental violence in dispute-custody divorces. *American Journal of Family Therapy, 19,* 351-362.

Jory, B., Anderson, D., and Greer, C. (1997). Intimate justice: Confronting issues of accountability, respect and freedom in treatment of abuse and violence. *Journal of Marital and Family Therapy, 23,* 399-419.

Kaslow, F. (1991). The sociocultural context of divorce. *Contemporary Family Therapy, 13*(6), 583-607.

Kavanagh, D.J. (1992). Recent developments in expressed emotion and schizophrenia. *British Journal of Psychiatry, 160,* 601-620.

Kendig, B. and Lowry, C. (1998). *Cedar House: A model child abuse treatment program.* Binghamton, NY: The Haworth Press.

Lamb, M., Sternberg, K., and Thompson, R. (1997). The effects of divorce and custody arrangements on children's behavior, development, and adjustment. *Family and Conciliation Courts Review, 35,* 393-404.

Landreth, G. L. (1991). *Play therapy: The art of the relationship.* Muncie, IN: Accelerated Development.

Leff, J., Berkowitz, R., Shavit, N., and Stachen, A. (1989). A trial of family therapy versus a relatives' groups for schizophrenia. *British Journal of Psychiatry, 154,* 58-66.

Lewis, R.A., Piercy, F.P., Sprenkle, D.H., and Trepper, T.S. (1990). Family-based interventions for helping drug-abusing adolescents. *Journal of Adolescent Research, 5,* 82-95.

Liddle, H. and Dakof, G. (1995). Efficacy of family therapy for drug abuse: Promising but not definitive. *Journal of Marital and Family Therapy, 21,* 511-543.

Liepman, M.R., Silvia, L.Y., and Nirenberg, T.D. (1989). The use of family behavior loop mapping for substance abuse. *Family Relations, 38,* 282-287.

Lipchik, E. (1991). Spouse abuse: Challenging the party line. *Family Therapy Networker, 5,* 59-63.

Lipchik, E., Sirles, E., and Kubicki, A. (1997). Multifaceted approaches in spouse abuse treatment. In R. Geffner, S. Sorenson, and P. Lundberg-Love (Eds.), *Violence and sexual abuse at home: Current issues in spousal battering and child maltreatment* (pp. 131-148). Binghamton, NY: The Haworth Press.

Maxmen, J.S. and Ward, N.G. (1995). Schizophrenia and related disorders. *Essential psychopathology and its treatment,* Second edition. New York: W.W. Norton and Company (pp. 173-205).

McConaghy, J. and Cottone, R. (1998). The systemic view of violence: An ethical perspective. *Family Process, 37,* 51-63.

McCrady, B. (1990). The marital relationship and marital treatment. In R. Collins, K. Leonard, and J. Searles (Eds.), *Alcohol and the family: Research and clinical perspectives* (pp. 338-355). New York: Guilford.

McFarlane, W.R. (1991). Family psychoeducational treatments. In A.S. Gurman and D.P. Kniskern (Eds.), *Handbook of family therapy,* Volume II. (pp. 363-395). New York: Brunner/Mazel.

Mullen, P. and Fleming, J. (1998). Long-term effects of child sexual abuse. *Issues in Child Abuse Prevention, 9,* 1-11.

National Child Abuse and Neglect Data System (NCANDS) (2002). Summary of key findings from calendar year 2000. Retrieved online October 22, 2002, from the National Clearinghouse on Child Abuse and Neglect Information via the U. S. Department of Health and Human Services: <http://www.calib.com/nccanch/pubs/factsheets/canstats.cfm>.

Nichols, M.P. and Schwartz, R.C. (2001). *Family therapy: Concepts and methods* (Fifth edition). Boston, MA: Allyn and Bacon.

Nichols, W.C. (1985). Family therapy with children of divorce. *Journal of Psychotherapy and the Family, 1*(3), 55-68.

Nichols, W.C. (1989). Problems and needs of children. In M.R. Textor (Ed.), *The divorce and divorce therapy handbook* (pp. 61-76). Northvale, NJ: Jason Aronson Inc.

Randolph, E.T., Eth, S., Glynn, S.M., and Paz, G.G. (1994). Behavioral family management in schizophrenia: Outcome of the clinic-based intervention. *British Journal of Psychiatry, 164,* 501-506.

Rosenbaum, A. and Maiuro, R. (1990). Perpetrators of spouse abuse. In R. Ammerman and M. Hersen (Eds.), *Treatment of family violence: A sourcebook* (pp. 385-405). New York: Plenum.

Salts, C.J. (1985). Divorce stage theory and therapy: Therapeutic implications throughout the divorcing process. *Journal of Psychotherapy and the Family, 1*(3), 13-23.

Salts, C.J. (1989). Group therapy for divorced Adults. In M.R. Textor (Ed.), *The divorce and divorce therapy handbook* (pp. 285-300). Northvale, NJ: Jason Aronson Inc.

Schaef, A. (1986). *Codependence misunderstood/mistreated.* New York: Harper and Row.

Simons, R.L., Lin, K., Gordan, L.C., Conger, R.D., and Lorenz, F.O. (1999). Explaining the higher incidence of adjustment problems among children of divorce compared with those in two-parent families. *Journal of Marriage and the Family, 61*(4), 1020-1033.

Sprenkle, D.H. (1989). The clinical practice of divorce therapy. In M.R. Textor (Ed.), *The divorce and divorce therapy handbook* (pp. 171-195). Northvale, NJ: Jason Aronson Inc.

Sprenkle, D. (1994). Wife abuse through the lens of systems theory. *Counseling Psychologist, 22,* 598-602.

Stanton, M. and Heath, A. (1995). Family treatment of alcohol and drug abuse. In R. Mikesell, D. Lusterman, and S. McDaniel (Eds.), *Integrating family therapy: Handbook of family psychology and systems theory* (pp. 529-544). Washington, DC: American Psychological Association.

Stanton, M.D., Steier, F., Cook, L., and Todd, T.C. (1984). Narcotic detoxification in a family and home context: Final report 1980-1983. March. Unpublished manuscript.

Stanton, M.D. and Todd, T.C. (1979). Structural family therapy with drug addicts. In E. Kaufman and P. Kaufman (Eds.), *The family therapy of drug and alcohol abuse* (pp. 55-70). New York: Gardner.

Stanton, M.D., Todd, T.C., and Associates (1982). *The family therapy of drug abuse and addiction.* New York: Guilford.

Steinglass, P., Bennett, L.A., Wolin, S.J., and Reiss, D. (1987). *The alcoholic family.* New York: Basic Books.

Steinmetz, S.K. (1977a). The battered husband syndrome. *Victimology: An International Journal, 2*(3-4), 499-509.

Steinmetz, S. (1977b). *The cycle of violence: Assertive, aggressive and abusive family interaction.* New York: Praeger.

Stets, J. and Straus, M. (1990). Gender differences in reporting marital violence and its medical and psychological consequences. In M. Straus and R. Gelles (Eds.), *Physical violence in American families: Risk factors and adaptations to violence in 8,145 families* (pp. 227-244). New Brunswick, NJ: Transaction Publishers.

Stevenson, J. (1999). The treatment of long-term sequelae of child abuse. *Journal of Child Psychiatry and Psychology, 40,* 89-111.

Straus, M.A. and Gelles, R.J. (1986). Societal change and family violence from 1975 to 1985 as revealed by two national surveys. *Journal of Marriage and the Family, 48,* 465-479.

Straus, M.A. and Gelles, R.J. (1990). How violent are American families? Estimates from the National Family Violence Resurvey and other studies. In M.A. Strauss and R.J. Gelles (Eds.), *Physical violence in American families* (pp. 95-112). New Brunswick, NJ: Transaction Publishers.

Szapocznik, J., Kurtines, W.M., Foote, F.H., Perez-Vidal, A., and Hervis, O. (1983). Conjoint versus one-person family therapy: Some evidence for the effectiveness of conducting family therapy through one person. *Journal of Consulting and Clinical Psychology, 51,* 881-899.

Szapocznik, J., Kurtines, W.M., Foote, F.H., Perez-Vidal, A., and Hervis, O. (1986). Conjoint versus one-person family therapy: Further evidence for the effectiveness of conducting family therapy through one person with drug-abusing adolescents. *Journal of Consulting and Clinical Psychology, 54,* 395-397.

Szapocznik, J., Perez-Vidal, A., Brickman, A.L., Foote, F.H., Stantisteban, D., Hervis, O., and Kurtines, W. (1988). Engaging adolescent drug-abusers and their families in treatment: A strategic structural systems approach. *Journal of Consulting and Clinical Psychology, 56,* 552-557.

Tarrier, N., Barrowclough, D., and Porceddu, K. (1988). The community management of schizophrenia: A controlled trial of a behavioral intervention with families to reduce relapse. *British Journal of Psychiatry, 153,* 532-542.

Textor, M.R. (1989). The divorce transition. In M.R. Textor (Ed.), *The divorce and divorce therapy handbook* (pp. 3-43). Northvale, NJ: Jason Aronson Inc.

VanFleet, R. (1994a). Filial therapy for adoptive children and parents. In K.J. O'Connor and C.E. Schaefer (Eds.), *Handbook of play therapy,* Volume Two: *Advances and innovations* (pp. 371-385). New York: Wiley.

VanFleet, R. (1994b). *Filial therapy: Strengthening parent-child relationships through play.* Sarasota, FL: Professional Resource Press.

Walitzer, K. (1998). Family therapy. In P. Ott, R. Tarter, and R. Ammerman (Eds.), *Sourcebook on substance abuse.* (pp. 337-349). Needam Heights, MA: Allyn and Bacon.

Walker, L. (1999). Psychology and domestic violence around the world. *American Psychologist, 54,* 21-29.

Wissow, L. (1995). Child abuse and neglect. *New England Journal of Medicine, 34*(5), 1425-1430.

Chapter 15

Ethical, Legal, and Professional Issues in Marriage and Family Therapy

Lorna L. Hecker

Mrs. Chapman has called for therapy because her sixteen-year-old son, Randy, has been failing school. You, the family therapist, ask to see the entire family at the initial intake session. Everyone attests to the problems of Randy, except Randy, who remains silent. You decide to see Randy alone, to get to know him. During your session with Randy, he opens up and tells you that he regularly drinks vodka as a way to "chill out." He reports carrying vodka to school in his backpack.

What do you do with this new information regarding Randy?

Your treatment of the Chapman family, as with all family therapy, now involves ethical and potentially legal issues. Many ethical and legal questions are posed by the dilemma described, including the following:

- *Who is the client?* Is it the Chapman family, the parents, or Randy?
- What are the rights of Randy to *confidentiality* or *privilege?* Are there any legal statutes governing treatment of a minor? What are the rights of the parents to know of Randy's drinking behavior?
- Is Randy's behavior dangerous? Would his behavior fall under a *duty to warn?*
- How does the therapist handle this situation clinically so that Randy and his family are most likely to get the help they need, while balancing the rights of the individuals involved?
- What might happen to the therapist's relationship with the parents if he or she does not tell Mr. and Mrs. Chapman about Randy's behavior? What might happen to the therapist's relationship with Randy if he or she does tell?

Each time a family therapist sees a client, potential ethical, legal, and professional issues can arise. Therapists must be educated on these issues, or they may inadvertently hurt individuals or families, they may make poor clinical judgments, or they may violate existing laws.

First, we define and discuss ethics and ethical decision making in family therapy. Entrenched in this decision making is the need for the therapist to be aware of legal issues, including state statutes (which will not be specifically discussed because they vary from state to state). The importance of therapists and therapists-in-training receiving therapy will also be discussed. Last, an overview of the field of marriage and family therapy will be provided, including information on how one becomes a family therapist.

ETHICS IN MARRIAGE AND FAMILY THERAPY

Ethics is "the study of what constitutes good and bad human conduct, including related actions and values" (Barry, 1982, p. 4). When clients enter therapy, they place their lives (sometimes literally) in the hands of the therapist. Without ethical standards, clients would have no reason to trust a therapist with their most private information. Thus, without ethical practices there would be no marriage and family therapy profession.

To guide ethical practice, all mental health professions have **professional codes of ethics** if the therapist is a member of a professional organization such as the American Association for Marriage and Family Therapy (AAMFT), the American Psychological Association (APA), The American Counseling Association (ACA), or the National Association of Social Workers (NASW). A code of ethics is a written statement established and distributed by a discipline or profession that expresses how a profession should and should not conduct itself. (See Appendix A to view the AAMFT code of ethics [2001].) Ethical codes perform the following functions (Schlossberger and Hecker, 1996):

1. *Ethical codes define the role of the profession.*
   - The codes express the dominant morality of the field.
   - They define values and goals of the profession.
   - They define the standards that both the professionals and users of the professionals' services can expect in any professional interaction.
2. *Ethical codes guide the conduct of professions and can provide specific guidance about conduct in the form of advice or mandates.*

Ethical codes serve as a basis for sanctions. Sanctions may vary from censure to fines, revocation of licensure or certification, denial of privileges, or incarceration.

If an AAMFT clinical member violates the AAMFT Code of Ethics, for example, a consumer may file a complaint with AAMFT. The AAMFT has a specific decision tree (1992a) and *Procedures for Handling Ethical Matters* (1992b) that are followed for every ethical complaint filed. In addition, a consumer may also file a complaint with the state's attorney general.

Ethical codes are important guides for clinicians practicing marriage and family therapy, but ethical practice constitutes much more than just following ethical codes. Each day a therapist practices, he or she is faced with ethical issues, many of which are not discussed in the Code of Ethics. In addition, a therapist must weigh out three factors when making ethical decisions: the *ethical* implications of the decision, any *legal* implications of the decision, and any *clinical* implications of the decision.

In this chapter we focus on what constitutes ethical practice by marriage and family therapists, and we also discuss how ethical decisions are made.

ETHICAL CLINICAL PRACTICE

What constitutes ethical clinical practice? Ethical practice by a therapist generally occurs when the therapist has good moral sense (knows, understands, and behaves in accordance to what is right), follows his or her professional code of ethics, is knowledgeable about existing laws impacting his or her clients, and has good clinical expertise.

As part of ethical practice, many states now require therapists to provide written professional disclosure statements. A **professional disclosure statement** should minimally tell the client about the education and qualifications of the therapist. Disclosure statements introduce clients to the therapist's qualifications, the nature of the therapeutic process, and other important issues involved in marriage and family therapy. The therapist in a marriage and family therapist's disclosure statement may address the following issues (Gill, 1982; Gross, 1977; Swanson, 1979; Witmer, 1978):

- What is the purpose of psychotherapy?
- What do you believe helps persons lead more satisfying lives?
- What should clients expect as a result of engaging in therapy efforts?
- How will clients and therapist know if progress is made?
- What is the therapist's primary responsibility during therapy?
- What types of presenting problems have you been most effective in assisting clients with in the past?
- Under what circumstances might clients be offered referral to another sort of assistance?

- How do you handle the confidential nature of the therapeutic relationship?
- What are limits to confidentiality? Are your clients entitled to legal privilege under your treatment? How is confidentiality to be handled when there is more than one client?
- What are your qualifications? What are the limitations to your practice?
- What are your office procedures for collection of fees, handling of emergencies, and so on?

See Appendix B for an example of a professional disclosure statement.

Although some therapists dispense this information in a disclosure statement, some integrate the information in their **informed consent.** An informed consent is a document that the client reads about the specifics of therapy treatment. After reading and understanding the document, the client consents to treatment by signing the informed consent document. Therapists should generally provide the following information to the client via informed consents (Beamish, Navin, and Davidson, 1994; Hare-Mustin, 1980; Huber, 1994; Margolin, 1982):

- Procedures and goals of therapy
- Any potential of harm or risks to the client(s)
- A reasonable summation of the benefits of therapy
- Qualifications and policies of the therapist
- Theoretical orientation of the therapist
- Assurance that family members may withdraw their consent to treatment at any time
- Reassurance of alternative referrals sources for treatment (generally at least three recommended sources is standard)

See Appendix C for an example of an informed consent document.

One of the largest concerns that clients have when educated about therapy is concern for their privacy. Clients expect that their exchanges with marriage and family therapists will be kept confidential. In our society, to some extent, we think people should be entitled to privacy: freedom from intrusions from the state or third parties (Smith-Bell and Winslade, 1994). In marriage and family therapy, professional therapists grant their clients **confidentiality.** Confidentiality is the ethical obligation of the therapists to keep communications between themselves and the client strictly private, not privy to any outside parties. However, although MFTs are expected to keep therapy confidential by their professional duty, a therapist may be charged with contempt of court if he or she refuses to testify about a client (Smith-Bell and Winslade, 1994). In addition, legal exceptions to confidentiality exist in all fifty states, which is discussed next. Consider the following case example of an issue surrounding client confidentiality.

Case Example and Analysis

Mrs. Johnson calls the Marriage and Family Therapy Center where Ms. Moore works to inquire about her son, Terry, who is a client at the center. Terry is Ms. Moore's client. He is a forty-three-year-old male who is struggling with issues of independence from his family of origin, with whom he still lives. Mrs. Johnson tells Ms. Moore that Terry has been progressively getting worse since attending therapy, and that he has been fighting continuously with both Mr. Johnson and herself. Ms. Moore defends her treatment of Terry and discusses the possibility of Mr. and Mrs. Johnson joining Terry for family therapy sessions.

Ethical implications: Ethically, Ms. Moore has violated the AAMFT Code of Ethics, section 2.2, which states that "Marriage and Family Therapists do not disclose client confidences except by written authorization or waiver, or where mandated or permitted by law." Ms. Moore violated Terry's right to confidentiality not only by telling to his mother about his treatment, but *by even acknowledging that Terry was in treatment at the Marriage and Family Therapy Center at all.* The simple fact that a client is in therapy must be kept confidential.

Legal implications: Ms. Moore has violated Terry's right to confidentiality. Depending upon counselor licensure by state, Ms. Moore may have also violated the law. The therapist may have also violated client-therapist privilege.

Clinical implications: The profession of marriage and family therapy rests on the trust that clients place in their therapists to keep confidential information they divulge. The therapist, Ms. Moore, violated that trust. This could impact Terry's feelings about the therapeutic relationship. Most clients would feel very betrayed by Ms. Moore's actions. In addition, if the client is struggling with issues of independence from his family of origin, Ms. Moore inadvertently created "more of the same" by discussing Terry's treatment to become more independent with his mother.

In many states, in addition to the ethical obligation to maintain client confidentiality, the therapist is expected to uphold a legal obligation of client privilege. **Privilege** is a legal right, *typically owned by the client,* that is governed by state statute. In some states, clients of marriage and family therapists own privilege; in others, they do not. Privilege is "an exception to the general rule that the public has a right to relevant evidence in a court proceeding" (Smith-Bell and Winslade, 1994, p. 184). If a client is entitled by state law to privilege, information revealed in therapy sessions is not privy to the courts.

There are notable legal exceptions to confidentiality or privilege. All states have some form of **child abuse reporting laws** that mandate therapists to report suspected child abuse or neglect. (In some states *all* citizens are required to report suspected child abuse or neglect, not just counselors or psychologists.) Thus, if an MFT suspects child abuse or neglect, he or she is legally mandated to violate client confidentiality and report the information to the proper authorities. In addition, since the now famous *Tarasoff v. Regents of University of California* case (1976), most states have ruled that therapists have a duty to warn if they believe a client has intent to hurt someone else.

The details of the Tarasoff case are thus: While in psychotherapy, Prosenjit Poddar threatened to kill Tatiana Tarasoff. Tarasoff was a fellow student in Poddar's square-dancing class. Although Tarasoff was not mentioned by name, the therapist knew her identity. Tarasoff was not informed of this threat against her life. Two months later, Poddar murdered Tatiana Tarasoff. The Tarasoff family filed suit, and the court ruled that "When a therapist determines or pursuant to the standards of the profession determine, that his patient presents a serious danger of violence to another, he incurs an obligation to use reasonable care to protect the intended victim against such danger" (*Tarasoff v. Regents of University of California,* 1976, p. 346). Either by law and/or ethical duty, therapists also have **duty to warn** when the following three criteria are met:

1. The therapist has established there is likelihood that the client will cause harm to himself or herself or to someone else.
2. A "special" (i.e., therapeutic) relationship exists between the therapist and client.
3. There is a foreseeable victim (Lamb et al., 1990). (Courts have at times ruled that a victim can also be a group or class of people as well.)

Last, confidentiality or privilege may be violated if a courtroom judge so orders, or if the therapist is a defendant in legal action arising from the therapy itself. In all cases, if the therapist attains a written waiver of confidentiality from the client, the therapist may discuss issues with those persons the client specifically designates in writing.

All therapists have the responsibility to be well trained and to follow what the courts deem an **appropriate standard of care.** An appropriate standard of care is how most therapists would treat a case under similar circumstances. Although this may vary widely, depending upon the training and theoretical orientation of the therapist, there are standards of practice that therapists must follow. Therapists who do not provide an appropriate standard of care leave themselves at risk for **malpractice.** Malpractice claims are legal actions taken against a therapist for actions that are believed to fall below the appropriate standard of care and cause injury to a client or clients. Therapists can be sued for malpractice if they do not provide sufficient care for clients if the following circumstances are met:

1. There was proximate cause, that is, what the therapist did appeared to cause injury to the client.
2. The care of the therapist fell below the appropriate standard of care.
3. An injury actually occurred. (Schultz, 1982)

According to Stromberg and Dellinger (1993, p. 3), common types of malpractice claims include the following:

- Misdiagnosis
- Practicing outside one's area of competence
- Failure to obtain informed consent for treatment
- Negligent or improper treatment
- Physical contact or sexual relations with patients
- Failure to prevent patients from harming themselves or others
- Improper release of hospitalized patients
- Failure to consult another practitioner or refer a patient
- Failure to supervise students or assistants
- Abandonment of patients

Upon analysis, most of these claims include areas that have to do with therapist competence and knowing one's field of expertise, as well as the limits of that expertise. We discuss later in this chapter the options for obtaining competent training. The other area that causes ethical complaints and legal malpractice claims has to do with **dual relationships.** Dual relationships occur when a professional does not keep appropriate boundaries and blends a personal or business relationship with the professional therapeutic relationship (Gottlieb, 1993; Kagle and Giebelhausen, 1994; Borys and Pope, 1989; Ramsdell and Ramsdell, 1993; Pope, 1991; Kitchener, 1998; Borys, 1992). Consider the following case example.

Case Example and Analysis

Rhonda is distraught over a breakup with her abusive boyfriend. Although she knows that she made the right decision, she misses her boyfriend and seeks the help of a marriage and family therapist to deal with her grief over the loss of her relationship, as well as to explore her history of getting into bad relationships. Rhonda feels very vulnerable and lonely as she begins therapy with Mr. Mason, a master's-level marriage and family therapist. Mr. Mason compliments Rhonda on her ability to leave her relationship and begins to explore her vulnerabilities which lead Rhonda into abusive relationship patterns. Mr. Mason is extremely complimentary to Rhonda, often commenting about her hairstyle or clothing. He even states he enjoys her perfume. Rhonda is struck by his sincerity and begins to trust Mr. Mason. Throughout the course of treatment, Mr. Mason continues to be complimentary to Rhonda, holds her hand during sessions as she cries about her past relationships with men, and always sits next to her on the couch. He massages her shoulders as she talks, and even asks her for a kiss on his birthday.

Ethical implications: Mr. Mason has clearly violated section 1.3 of the AAMFT code of ethics (2001). Although he has not (yet) engaged in sexual relations with the client, he has engaged in a dual relationship with Rhonda. He is fostering a close personal relationship with Rhonda that is inappropriate in the context of the professional relationship of therapy.

Legal implications: Legally, Mr. Mason has broken no laws as yet. He has acted unprofessionally and unethically, and if he moves the relationship into one clearly defined by law as a sexual relationship, he will, in some states, have committed a crime. Some state statutes make sexual intimacies between a client and therapist a felony.

Clinical implications: The clinical implications of Mr. Mason's actions are numerous. Rhonda came to therapy in a vulnerable position, and Mr. Mason exploited that vulnerability and the trust of the therapist/client relationship. Since Rhonda wanted to learn how to avoid abusive relationships, which invariably involve a misuse of power, Mr. Mason has re-created her problem in the context of the therapeutic relationship. Write Haas and Malouf (1995, p. 80), "The therapist's elevated power position, combined with the fact that the client expects the therapist to act in a fiduciary capacity, make it virtually impossible for a client to make an autonomous decision regarding sexual involvement."

Because a therapist always holds more power than a client in the relationship, the risk of a dual relationship becoming exploitive always exists. Although all therapy is indeed personal, it is the therapist's responsibility to maintain appropriate boundaries and protect the client's best interests.

In addition to following one's professional code of ethics, the therapist needs to know how to make ethical decisions for the many gray areas not covered in codes. Ethical decision making can be a frustrating process because often there is no "one right answer." One must choose from many possible answers to a problem and weigh out the costs and benefits to each possible decision carefully.

ETHICAL DECISION MAKING

Marriage and family therapists face ethical issues in practice on a daily basis. Often, ethical issues are entwined with legal issues. Generally, a model for making ethical decisions can be discussed in simple terms, but the process of weighing ethical, legal, and clinical considerations can be complex. Generally, the following steps are part of the ethical decision-making process:

Step 1: Awareness of Potential Ethical Issues

In addition to being knowledgeable of the ethical codes of one's professional organization, therapists should know the literature regarding additional potential ethical issues. For example, when seeing a family, one potential pitfall for the therapist occurs when a family member independently shares a secret with the therapist. This puts the therapist in a sticky position of either unwillingly aligning with one family member because the therapist is a "knower" of the secret and others are not, or being forced to ask the family member to share the secret. In any scenario such as this, the therapist's **maneuverability** (ability to intervene effectively) is compromised.

Over time, wise therapists learn potentially problematic clinical issues that may arise into ethical dilemmas and work to preempt ethical problems. For example, many therapists develop secret policies (Karpel, 1980) to avoid potential problems with conflicts of interest that occur when one family member shares a secret about himself or herself or another family member. **Secret policies** are written statements about how information shared privately with the therapist shall be handled by the therapist, signed by the involved parties.

Imagine if you will that a therapist unwittingly sees a spouse separately, only to be told by the client that he or she is having an extramarital affair. At this point, the therapist is immediately put in a situation of having a secret. What should the therapist do? If the therapist shares the secret, he or she violates the revealing client's trust. In addition, some ethical codes deem that information shared by an individual in couple, family, or group therapy should be held confidential (see AAMFT code of ethics [2001], section 2.2; ACA Code of Ethics [1995], section B.2.b.), and others leave it to therapist/family verbal agreement (see section 4.03, APA Code of Ethics, 1992). If the therapist does not take action, the therapist has put himself or herself in alignment with the revealing client at the expense of the unknowing spouse. These types of situations can be thwarted by the therapist coming to agreement with the couple about how information should be handled at the onset of therapy. Some therapists alleviate this problem by never seeing partners individually. However, with the high prevalence of domestic violence in couples, this may preclude a therapist from ever learning about abusive situations occurring within the family. Heightened awareness of potential ethical conflicts and practicing good ethics constitutes an appropriate standard of practice.

Case Analysis

Recall the Chapman family mentioned at the beginning of the chapter. A wise therapist would have been aware of the potential for a conflict of interest if he or she promises Randy confidentiality, yet finds himself or herself faced with an adolescent who may confess to being in danger. The therapist instead should have agreed on a secrets policy with the family. Most parents will agree to adolescent confidentiality with the exception that if the therapist learns the child is doing something that may jeopardize his or her health, the therapist should share that information with the parents. This would have given the therapist the ability to share Randy's behavior with Mr. and Mrs. Chapman. The downside of this agreement is that Randy may not have shared the information of his alcohol abuse if this type of agreement had been established.

Step 2: Define the Ethical Problem

What is the ethical issue or dilemma? What immediate facts have the most bearing on the decision you must make? Are there any economic, social, or political pressures to take into consideration? What do you think each of the clients or people involved would want you to do regarding this issue?

Case Analysis

The ethical dilemma for the therapist is that Randy is behaving in a way that could hurt or kill him. The therapist now knows the information, but if he tells the parents about Randy's drinking he risks alienating Randy from therapy or perhaps any future therapy or therapists. On the other hand, the therapist is fearful Randy may hurt himself. The therapist may also consider whether Randy is driving after he drinks. Surely the parents would want to know if their child is at risk, but will the therapist be clinically effective if he tells the parents at this point in therapy? What risks are there if the therapist does not tell the parents?

Step 3: Gather Information from All Relevant Sources

What sources may be of help in solving the problem? Sources to consult may be your professional code of ethics, other professionals, and state or federal laws.

Case Analysis

The AAMFT code of ethics addresses confidentiality between family members. Section 2.2 states: "In the context of couple, family or group treatment, the therapist may not reveal any individual's confidences to others in the client unit without the prior written consent of the individual." The code of ethics clearly errs on the side of protecting client confidentiality, yet in most states parents could legally get access to the information.

The therapist must struggle with what will happen if the parents are not alerted to Randy's behavior. Might he drink and drive? Might he drink to the point of poisoning himself? Yet again, the therapist has to consider whether Randy is telling the truth. Some teens might make up bravado stories to impress a therapist. On the other hand, if Randy is drinking, underage drinking is against the law. What do you suppose would happen if Randy does hurt himself through his drinking behaviors and the parents find out the therapist knew but did not inform them?

Step 4. Define the Ethical Principles or Values That Influence Your Thinking of the Problem

Ethical guidelines are guided by moral principles. Several authors have discussed the need for ethics to be guided by the following moral principles (Kitchener, 1984; Rosenbaum, 1982; Stadler, 1986; Forester-Miller and Davis, 1996):

> *Autonomy:* This is the belief that people should be allowed freedom of choice and action.
> *Nonmaleficence:* This is an important maxim for all therapists. This principle means that above all else, the therapist should do no harm.
> *Justice:* This principle states that humans should be treated fairly and that goodness and badness be distributed justly among them. This can be done by
> 1. distributing good and bad to people based on their merits,
> 2. equal distribution of good and bad, or
> 3. distributing good and bad according to their needs and abilities or both (Thiroux, 1980, p. 125).
> *Fidelity:* Refers to the value of honoring commitments and promoting trust.
> *Veracity:* Refers to the importance of truth-telling.
> *Beneficence:* Refers to promoting good.

Case Analysis

Let's explore the Chapman case using moral principles to guide us.

Autonomy: Should the therapist violate Randy's autonomy as an individual by telling the parents about his drinking behavior? Would the therapist be violating the autonomy of others (those who might be driving when an intoxicated Randy is driving) if he does not tell? Does the therapist violate the parents right to know about a child's dangerous behaviors so that the parents can keep the child safe?

Nonmaleficience: What do you think will do the least amount of harm in this situation? Telling the parents may cause the therapeutic relationship with Randy great harm. Not telling the parents may cause Randy or others harm, and/or injure the therapeutic relationship between the therapist and Randy.

Fidelity: If you promised Randy confidentiality, then you should honor that commitment. If you told the family you were there to help them, yet do not reveal the information, are you being deceptive to the parents?

Beneficence: What course of action could the therapist take that would do the most good for the most amount of people? Would this be accomplished by telling the parents or by keeping Randy's confidence?

Step 5. Formulate and Weigh All Possible Alternatives

The therapist must consider all courses of action and the possible ramifications of each decision.

Case Analysis

If the therapist tells Randy's parents, will he increase the chances of keeping Randy safe? Will the damage done with Randy be irreparable? Might the therapist consider asking Randy to tell his parents about his behavior? The therapist could work with Randy individually to curb his behavior in the hopes that the drinking problem resolves. The therapist could tell the parents and then work closely with the family to regain trust and communication so that Randy could talk about his problems and not engage in drinking behavior to mask them. The therapist could work with Randy and his parents to increase family structure so that the parents were more aware of Randy's behaviors and decrease the chances that Randy would be allowed in environments where alcohol would be available. A sensitive therapist can find many solutions to difficult problems.

Step 6: Choose the Best Ethical Alternative and Implement the Decision

After a therapist has gathered all the information and weighed possible outcomes of various courses of action, he or she chooses what is considered to be the best course and acts on his or her decision.

Case Analysis

The therapist decides to wait and assess the situation for a little longer before deciding what to do about Randy's drinking behavior. Indeed, he is not even sure at this point that Randy is telling the truth because he knows little about Randy. The therapist decides to work on the structure of the family by putting the parents in charge of the family again, so that Randy has fewer chances for illegal drinking. He also decides to work on improving family communication so that Randy has an outlet to discuss his feelings, and he works with Randy individually as well to identify sources of coping, such as positive peers and other social circles from which Randy could obtain support.

Step 7: Monitor Your Decision and the Outcome of Your Decision; Reevaluate If Necessary

Ethical decisions are evaluated and reevaluated repeatedly.

Case Analysis

If the therapist senses Randy's situation is declining, or finds that the situation is even worse than Randy originally described it, he may choose to reconsider telling the parents of the behavior. The therapist, meanwhile, may learn more about the legal implications of telling, consulting an attorney to obtain advice about the validity of breaking confidentiality, and to see if there are any state laws governing the situation.

In summary, making ethical decisions is a complex task. The therapist strives to do the right thing but ethical decision making, clinical expertise, and legal knowledge must guide him or her.

COMMON ETHICAL DILEMMAS FACED BY MARRIAGE AND FAMILY THERAPISTS

The list of ethical issues faced by marriage and family therapists is endless. Family therapists must have a good working knowledge of law, their code of ethics, and an ethical decision-making model in order to traverse the daily entanglements of performing marriage and family therapy. Pulling from the work of Margolin (1982), Zygmond and Borhem (1989), Beamish, Navin, and Davidson (1994), Green and Hansen (1989), and personal experience, some ethical dilemmas faced by marriage and family therapists are outlined next.

Balancing the Interests of More Than One Client

Therapists generally have a responsibility to promote the best interests of their clients. But if therapists have multiple clients, such as with marriage or family therapy, these interests may diverge. Consider the marital couple that comes to therapy. The wife has agreed to come to therapy because she wants a divorce but also wants the best possible outcome for her children, so she agrees to meet with the therapist to discuss the children. The husband, however, wishes the marriage to be saved, and does not want a divorce. Whose agenda does the therapist follow? If the therapist follows the wife's agenda, the husband will feel that the therapist is supporting divorce. If the therapist follows the husband's agenda, the wife may leave treatment, and the issues concerning the children's welfare will remain untended. Promoting the welfare of one or more family members may not support the welfare of others (Fenell and Weinhold, 1989; Jensen, Josephson, and Frey, 1989).

Maintaining Multiple Client Confidences

Therapists must maintain client confidences, but in the face of multiple clients this can get convoluted. For example, if a family member shares a secret with the therapist about another member during a call to reschedule a missed session, does the therapist honor that confidence? If the therapist does honor the confidence, he or she is now in the unique position of being a secret holder—an unwitting ally to the person who told the secret. This type of confidence keeping can severely limit the therapist's effectiveness.

Conflicting Values Between the Therapist and Client

What happens when a client has values opposing those of the therapist? For example, a client wants counseling regarding her decision to have an abortion, but the therapist is a staunch antiabortion advocate. Another example might be a child who is brought to counseling because her parent caught her masturbating. Although the therapist may see masturbation as a normal part of sexual development, the parents, based on religious convictions, consider it a sin.

Theoretical Purity versus Real-World Demands

The goal of systems theory is to see health and dysfunction as a function of the entire system, not just one individual. Many couples or families present one person in therapy as the **identified patient** (such as the Chapman example at the beginning of the chapter), the person bearing the symptomology of the family system. The therapist's job is to "spread the symptoms around" in the family and decrease the pathologizing of this individual family member.

If the therapist is to be paid by an insurance company, however, he or she usually must identify one family member and give this person a diagnosis in order to make the services reimbursable by insurance. The therapist may risk the family not receiving reimbursement and being denied services if the therapist does not assign a diagnosis to the identified patient or another family member. This clash between systems theory and the mental model can leave the therapist with continuing ethical issues (Denton, 1989).

Choice and Implementation of Therapeutic Theory

The theory or model from which ones chooses to practice marriage and family therapy also may pose ethical dilemmas. For example, some systems therapists refuse to treat family members unless all family members participate directly (O'Shea and Jessee, 1982). Thus, if one or more family members refuse to participate in treatment, the others are denied needed treatment. On the other hand, some systems therapists believe their work will not be effective if all family members do not participate in therapy (Haley, 1980). Refusing to treat motivated family members when others will not participate poses an ethical problem (Tiesmann, 1980).

Feminists (Avis, 1985; Bograd, 1984; Goldner, 1985a,b; Hare-Mustin, 1978, 1979, 1980; Jacobson, 1983) have criticized that the notion of *circularity* (see Chapter 2 for further discussion on this concept) as well as other systems concepts do not take into account the power dynamics in relationships and the very real inequities women face on a daily basis in relationships. Feminists charge that women do not hold equal power in relationships and, for example, in the case of domestic violence certainly do not hold "equal influence" on the present system.

Another example of how theory poses ethical dilemmas is evident in a popular newer postmodern movement called **social constructivism.** Social constructionist family therapies grew out of a philosophy which maintains that there is no objective reality—we simply create and perpetuate our realities through the stories that we tell and live by (Friedman, 1993). Social constructivism argues that facts do not exist, only our stories exist. When the stories of two people are vastly different for the same event, whose narrative do therapists listen to? For example, if the story of a child is that her stepfather sexually abused her, but the stepfather's story denies this, whose story or "narrative" does the therapist follow? Social constructivism does not answer these difficult questions posed daily in clinical work (see Chapter 6 for further information on social constructionist family therapies).

Often criticized on ethical grounds has been strategic therapy (Schwartz, 1989; Slipp, 1989). Strategic therapy typically employs therapeutic paradox, including prescribing the symptom and restraining change. For example, a strategic family therapist might prescribe a client to be depressed, in an attempt to ameliorate the depression. Strategic therapists might also indicate that they have concerns about clients becoming cheerful too quickly, and tell them that they feel clients should be depressed for a little while longer. Again, the goal is to paradoxically cure or lessen the depression. Although some would conclude that integrity and authenticity is needed when guiding clients (Wendorf and Wendorf, 1985), others would argue that family change is a more important goal. Some authors have provided guidelines for how to utilize this type of therapy while maintaining ethical integrity (Fisher, Anderson, and Jones, 1981; O'Shea and Jessee, 1982; Rohrbaugh et al., 1981).

In summary, marriage and family therapists face thorny ethical issues on a daily basis. Knowledge of the law, one's professional ethical codes, and ethical decision making is important to the profession of marriage and family therapy. The importance of good training cannot be overemphasized. Following is a discussion regarding the profession of marriage and family therapy and how a prospective student can gain information on the field and apply to graduate school.

WHAT IS MARRIAGE AND FAMILY THERAPY?

Marriage and family therapy has been recognized as a separate and distinct mental health discipline since 1978. At that time, the U.S. Department of Health, Education, and Welfare designated the AAMFT Commission on Accreditation for Marriage and Family Therapy Education as the sole accrediting agency for both graduate and postdegree educational and training programs in MFT. In addition, the National Institute of Mental Health lists marriage and family therapy as a core mental health profession.

The American Association for Marriage and Family Therapy (AAMFT), as mentioned in Chapter 1, is charged with ensuring that the public receives quality care in marriage and family therapy. AAMFT promotes understanding, research, and education within marriage and family therapy. Parishioners who become clinical members of AAMFT have completed masters' degrees, doctoral degrees, or postgraduate training in marriage and family therapy, as well as 1,000 hours of supervised clinical experience with individuals, couples, or families. Clinical members of AAMFT have met stringent requirements set by the organization which tell the public that the professional is qualified for independent practice. AAMFT has approximately 23,000 members in the United States, Canada, and abroad, and has helped to regulate marriage and family therapy in forty-two states and Quebec (AAMFT, n.d.).

An estimated 46,000 marriage and family therapists are in practice throughout the United States, meaning that the remaining family therapists do not identify with AAMFT, but likely identify with related fields of psychology, social work, counseling, and so on. Some see marriage and family therapy as a separate profession; others see it as part of other mental health disciplines. Although AAMFT as well as the International Family Therapy Association (IFTA) and the International Association of Marriage and Family Counselors (IAMFC) would see family therapy as a separate profession, other mental health disciplines (such as psychology or social work) may see family therapy as a professional specialty or an area of elective study within another mental health profession.

One can become a marriage and family therapist in one of two ways. One is to obtain a master's or doctoral degree specifically in marriage and family therapy. The other is to earn a graduate degree in another mental health field and do postgraduate clinical training that provides clinical education in MFT. By whatever method a therapist becomes trained in family therapy, he or she must meet the training requirements to practice marriage and family therapy (or a related profession) established by his or her particular state. Forty-two states regulate the practice of marriage and family therapy through **licensure** or **certification.** Licensure includes protection of the title of family therapist. Licensure regulates that those not licensed may not use the title "licensed marriage and family therapist." Licensure generally also regulates and defines the practice of those being licensed. Certification ensures that the profession being certified has met specified criteria. Registration protects the title but not the practice of a profession. Generally states require a minimum of a master's degree in a related field (MFT, psychology, social work, counseling), and supervised experience practicing MFT. A written exam is also required. See Appendix D for advice on pursuing graduate education.

THERAPISTS RECEIVING THERAPY

For persons entering a helping profession, it is often helpful if not mandatory that they receive counseling for themselves. Some programs actually expect students to receive therapy; others strongly recommend it. There are many benefits to counselor trainees receiving therapy:

- Increasing self-esteem
- Understanding therapy from the client perspective
- In vivo learning of therapist techniques
- Recognizing blind spots that may interfere with providing effective therapy for clients

- Increased self-awareness, which enhances ability to intervene as a therapist
- Becoming comfortable with the degree of interpersonal intensity required in therapy
- Gaining an understanding of one's own needs so that they do not interfere with providing therapy to others
- Understanding how and why one may react to certain clients based on personal beliefs and values or certain issues that may cause reactivity in the trainee

Finding a therapist is not always an easy task. The following strategies are recommended to find a therapist who fits your needs as a developing family therapist:

- Discuss with other students and faculty whom they would recommend for personal growth counseling.
- Check to see if your insurance covers psychotherapy; if it does, there may be requirements as to the type of therapist allowed. If you do not have insurance and cannot afford a private practice clinician, try community agencies with sliding fee scales. In addition, university campuses have counseling or psychological centers where therapy is provided free or at low cost to students.
- Upon contacting a therapist, ask the following questions:

  1. What are the therapist's training and qualifications? Ask specifically what type of degree he or she has. Ask whether he or she belongs to any professional organizations (APA, AAMFT, NASW, ACA). Ask whether he or she is certified or licensed in your state. You may also ask whether he or she has ever been accused of any ethics code violations.
  2. What theoretical orientation does the therapist utilize? The therapist should be able to articulate the models or schools of therapy they utilize.
  3. Ask about fees and payment policies.
  4. Discuss concerns about confidentiality. As a therapist in training, you will want to be careful to whom you divulge information.
  5. *Do not* use people with whom you may have future contact in the role of faculty or employer, if at all possible. You want to avoid any future dual relationships that may make you feel uncomfortable. It would be difficult to be evaluated by someone down the road who knows your personal history.

6. Ask if the therapists have seen other therapists prior in their practice. Some therapists become "the therapist's therapist" and are the best sources to seek out. These practitioners have experience with providing therapy to therapists, and they understand the unique concerns of seeking therapy within your own profession.

In summary, some graduate programs require therapists in training to receive therapy; others do not. If a therapist in training is reluctant to obtain therapy, his or her reasons for the reluctance should be examined.

PROFESSIONAL RESOURCES

Associations for Professional Therapists

The following associations oversee the practice of counseling and psychology related professions. Each one has codes of ethics that members agree to abide by, and which set standards for the profession.

American Association for Marriage and Family Therapy (AAMFT)
1133 15th Street, NW, Suite 300
Washington, DC 20005-2710
202-452-0109
Web site: http://www.aamft.org

American Counseling Association
5999 Stevenson Avenue
Alexandria, VA 22304-3300
703-823-9800 or 800-347-6647
Web site: http://www.counseling.org

American Psychological Association
1200 17th Street, NW
Washington, DC 20036
202-955-7600
Web site: http://www.apa.org

National Association of Social Workers
750 First Street, NE, Suite 700
Washington, DC 20002-4241
202-408-8600 or 800-638-8799
Web site: http://www.naswdc.org

Journals

The following is a list of journals that publish research, theory, or clinical practice information related to the field of marriage and family therapy.

The Journal of Marital and Family Therapy (the journal of AAMFT)
Journal of Counseling and Development
Family Process
Journal of Marriage and Family Counseling
Family Journal: Counseling and Therapy for Couples and Families
The American Journal of Family Therapy
Journal of Couple and Relationship Therapy
The Journal of Family Psychotherapy (the journal of the International Family Therapy Association)
The Journal of Family Psychology
Contemporary Family Therapy
Journal of Marriage and the Family
Journal of Orthopsychiatry
Family Therapy
Journal of Systemic Therapies
Journal of Sex and Marital Therapy
Child and Family Behavior Therapy
Family Relations
Family, Systems, and Health
Journal of Feminist Family Therapy
Journal of Couples Therapy
Journal of Divorce and Remarriage
Journal of Family Issues
American Psychologist
Social Work
The Australian and New Zealand Journal of Family Therapy
Journal of Gay and Lesbian Psychotherapy
Psychotherapy
The Family Journal: Counseling and Therapy for Couples and Families

APPENDIX A: AAMFT CODE OF ETHICS
(EFFECTIVE JULY 1, 2001)

Summary of Changes
Preamble

The Board of Directors of the American Association for Marriage and Family Therapy (AAMFT) hereby promulgates, pursuant to Article 2, Section 2.013 of the Association's Bylaws, the Revised AAMFT Code of Ethics, effective July 1, 2001.*

The AAMFT strives to honor the public trust in marriage and family therapists by setting standards for ethical practice as described in this Code. The ethical standards define professional expectations and are enforced by the AAMFT Ethics Committee. The absence of an explicit reference to a specific behavior or situation in the Code does not mean that the behavior is ethical or unethical. The standards are not exhaustive. Marriage and family therapists who are uncertain about the ethics of a particular course of action are encouraged to seek counsel from consultants, attorneys, supervisors, colleagues, or other appropriate authorities.

Both law and ethics govern the practice of marriage and family therapy. When making decisions regarding professional behavior, marriage and family therapists must consider the AAMFT Code of Ethics and applicable laws and regulations. If the AAMFT Code of Ethics prescribes a standard higher than that required by law, marriage and family therapists must meet the higher standard of the AAMFT Code of Ethics. Marriage and family therapists comply with the mandates of law, but make known their commitment to the AAMFT Code of Ethics and take steps to resolve the conflict in a responsible manner. The AAMFT supports legal mandates for reporting of alleged unethical conduct.

The AAMFT Code of Ethics is binding on Members of AAMFT in all membership categories, AAMFT-Approved Supervisors, and applicants for membership and the Approved Supervisor designation (hereafter, AAMFT

---

*This code is published by the American Association for Marriage and Family Therapy, 1133 15th Street, NW Suite 300, Washington, DC 20005-2710; (202) 452-0109; (202) 223-2329 FAX; <www.aamft.org>. Violations of this code should be brought in writing to the attention of AAMFT Ethics Committee, 1133 15th Street, NW, Suite 300, Washington, DC 20005-2710; telephone (202) 452-0109; e-mail: <ethics @aamft.org>. Copyright 2001. American Association for Marriage and Family Therapy. Reprinted with permission.

Member). AAMFT members have an obligation to be familiar with the AAMFT Code of Ethics and its application to their professional services. Lack of awareness or misunderstanding of an ethical standard is not a defense to a charge of unethical conduct.

The process for filing, investigating, and resolving complaints of unethical conduct is described in the current Procedures for Handling Ethical Matters of the AAMFT Ethics Committee. Persons accused are considered innocent by the Ethics Committee until proven guilty, except as otherwise provided, and are entitled to due process. If an AAMFT Member resigns in anticipation of, or during the course of, an ethics investigation, the Ethics Committee will complete its investigation. Any publication of action taken by the Association will include the fact that the Member attempted to resign during the investigation.

Contents

1. Responsibility to clients
2. Confidentiality
3. Professional competence and integrity
4. Responsibility to students and supervisees
5. Responsibility to research participants
6. Responsibility to the profession
7. Financial arrangements
8. Advertising

Principle I
Responsibility to Clients

Marriage and family therapists advance the welfare of families and individuals. They respect the rights of those persons seeking their assistance, and make reasonable efforts to ensure that their services are used appropriately.

1.1 Marriage and family therapists provide professional assistance to persons without discrimination on the basis of race, age, ethnicity, socioeconomic status, disability, gender, health status, religion, national origin, or sexual orientation.

1.2 Marriage and family therapists obtain appropriate informed consent to therapy or related procedures as early as feasible in the therapeutic relationship, and use language that is reasonably understandable to clients. The content of informed consent may vary depending upon the client and treatment plan; however, informed consent generally necessitates that the client: (a) has the capacity to consent; (b) has been adequately informed of significant information concerning treatment processes and procedures; (c) has been adequately informed of potential risks and benefits of treatments for which generally recognized standards do not yet exist; (d) has freely and without undue influence expressed consent; and (e) has provided consent that is appropriately documented. When persons, due to age or mental status, are legally incapable of giving informed consent, marriage and family therapists obtain informed permission from a legally authorized person, if such substitute consent is legally permissible.

1.3 Marriage and family therapists are aware of their influential positions with respect to clients, and they avoid exploiting the trust and dependency of such persons. Therapists, therefore, make every effort to avoid conditions and multiple relationships with clients that could impair professional judgment or increase the risk of exploitation. Such relationships include, but are not limited to, business or close personal relationships with a client or the client's immediate family. When the risk of impairment or exploitation exists due to conditions or multiple roles, therapists take appropriate precautions.

1.4 Sexual intimacy with clients is prohibited.

1.5 Sexual intimacy with former clients is likely to be harmful and is therefore prohibited for two years following the termination of therapy or last professional contact. In an effort to avoid exploiting the trust and dependency of clients, marriage and family therapists should not engage in sexual intimacy with former clients after the two years following termination or last professional contact. Should therapists engage in sexual intimacy with former clients following two years after termination or last professional contact, the burden shifts to the therapist to demonstrate that there has been no exploitation or injury to the former client or to the client's immediate family.

1.6 Marriage and family therapists comply with applicable laws regarding the reporting of alleged unethical conduct.

1.7 Marriage and family therapists do not use their professional relationships with clients to further their own interests.

1.8 Marriage and family therapists respect the rights of clients to make decisions and help them to understand the consequences of these decisions. Therapists clearly advise the clients that they have the responsibility to make decisions regarding relationships such as cohabitation, marriage, divorce, separation, reconciliation, custody, and visitation.

1.9 Marriage and family therapists continue therapeutic relationships only so long as it is reasonably clear that clients are benefiting from the relationship.

1.10 Marriage and family therapists assist persons in obtaining other therapeutic services if the therapist is unable or unwilling, for appropriate reasons, to provide professional help.

1.11 Marriage and family therapists do not abandon or neglect clients in treatment without making reasonable arrangements for the continuation of such treatment.

1.12 Marriage and family therapists obtain written informed consent from clients before videotaping, audio recording, or permitting third-party observation.

1.13 Marriage and family therapists, upon agreeing to provide services to a person or entity at the request of a third party, clarify, to the extent feasible and at the outset of the service, the nature of the relationship with each party and the limits of confidentiality.

Principle II
Confidentiality

Marriage and family therapists have unique confidentiality concerns because the client in a therapeutic relationship may be more than one person. Therapists respect and guard the confidences of each individual client.

2.1 Marriage and family therapists disclose to clients and other interested parties, as early as feasible in their professional contacts, the nature of confidentiality and possible limitations of the clients' right to confidentiality. Therapists review with clients the circumstances where confidential information may be requested and where disclosure of confidential information may be legally required. Circumstances may necessitate repeated disclosures.

2.2 Marriage and family therapists do not disclose client confidences except by written authorization or waiver, or where mandated or permitted by law. Verbal authorization will not be sufficient except in emergency situations, unless prohibited by law. When providing couple, family or group treatment, the therapist does not disclose information outside the treatment context without a written authorization from each individual competent to execute a waiver. In the context of couple, family or group treatment, the therapist may not reveal any individual's confidences to others in the client unit without the prior written permission of that individual.

2.3 Marriage and family therapists use client and/or clinical materials in teaching, writing, consulting, research, and public presentations only if a written waiver has been obtained in accordance with Subprinciple 2.2, or when appropriate steps have been taken to protect client identity and confidentiality.

2.4 Marriage and family therapists store, safeguard, and dispose of client records in ways that maintain confidentiality and in accord with applicable laws and professional standards.

2.5 Subsequent to the therapist moving from the area, closing the practice, or upon the death of the therapist, a marriage and family therapist arranges for the storage, transfer, or disposal of client records in ways that maintain confidentiality and safeguard the welfare of clients.

2.6 Marriage and family therapists, when consulting with colleagues or referral sources, do not share confidential information that could reasonably lead to the identification of a client, research participant, supervisee, or other person with whom they have a confidential relationship unless they have obtained the prior written consent of the client, research participant, supervisee, or other person with whom they have a confidential relationship. Information may be shared only to the extent necessary to achieve the purposes of the consultation.

Principle III
Professional Competence and Integrity

Marriage and family therapists maintain high standards of professional competence and integrity.

3.1 Marriage and family therapists pursue knowledge of new developments and maintain competence in marriage and family therapy through education, training, or supervised experience.

3.2 Marriage and family therapists maintain adequate knowledge of and adhere to applicable laws, ethics, and professional standards.

3.3 Marriage and family therapists seek appropriate professional assistance for their personal problems or conflicts that may impair work performance or clinical judgment.

3.4 Marriage and family therapists do not provide services that create a conflict of interest that may impair work performance or clinical judgment.

3.5 Marriage and family therapists, as presenters, teachers, supervisors, consultants and researchers, are dedicated to high standards of scholarship, present accurate information, and disclose potential conflicts of interest.

3.6 Marriage and family therapists maintain accurate and adequate clinical and financial records.

3.7 While developing new skills in specialty areas, marriage and family therapists take steps to ensure the competence of their work and to protect clients from possible harm. Marriage and family therapists practice in specialty areas new to them only after appropriate education, training, or supervised experience.

3.8 Marriage and family therapists do not engage in sexual or other forms of harassment of clients, students, trainees, supervisees, employees, colleagues, or research subjects.

3.9 Marriage and family therapists do not engage in the exploitation of clients, students, trainees, supervisees, employees, colleagues, or research subjects.

3.10 Marriage and family therapists do not give to or receive from clients (a) gifts of substantial value or (b) gifts that impair the integrity or efficacy of the therapeutic relationship.

3.11 Marriage and family therapists do not diagnose, treat, or advise on problems outside the recognized boundaries of their competencies.

3.12 Marriage and family therapists make efforts to prevent the distortion or misuse of their clinical and research findings.

3.13 Marriage and family therapists, because of their ability to influence and alter the lives of others, exercise special care when making public their professional recommendations and opinions through testimony or other public statements.

3.14 To avoid a conflict of interests, marriage and family therapists who treat minors or adults involved in custody or visitation actions may not also perform forensic evaluations for custody, residence, or visitation of the minor. The marriage and family therapist who treats the minor may provide the court or mental health professional performing the evaluation with information about the minor from the marriage and family therapist's perspective as a treating marriage and family therapist, so long as the marriage and family therapist does not violate confidentiality.

3.15 Marriage and family therapists are in violation of this Code and subject to termination of membership or other appropriate action if they: (a) are convicted of any felony; (b) are convicted of a misdemeanor related to their qualifications or functions; (c) engage in conduct which could lead to conviction of a felony, or a misdemeanor related to their qualifications or functions; (d) are expelled from or disciplined by other professional organizations; (e) have their licenses or certificates suspended or revoked or are otherwise disciplined by regulatory bodies; (f) continue to practice marriage and family therapy while no longer competent to do so because they are impaired by physical or mental causes or the abuse of alcohol or other substances; or (g) fail to cooperate with the Association at any point from the inception of an ethical complaint through the completion of all proceedings regarding that complaint.

Principle IV
Responsibility to Students and Supervisees

Marriage and family therapists do not exploit the trust and dependency of students and supervisees.

4.1 Marriage and family therapists are aware of their influential positions with respect to students and supervisees, and they avoid exploiting the trust and dependency of such persons. Therapists, therefore, make every effort to avoid conditions and multiple relationships that could impair professional objectivity or increase the risk of exploitation. When the risk of impairment or exploitation exists due to conditions or multiple roles, therapists take appropriate precautions.

4.2 Marriage and family therapists do not provide therapy to current students or supervisees.

4.3 Marriage and family therapists do not engage in sexual intimacy with students or supervisees during the evaluative or training relationship between the therapist and student or supervisee. Should a supervisor engage in sexual activity with a former supervisee, the burden of proof shifts to the supervisor to demonstrate that there has been no exploitation or injury to the supervisee.

4.4 Marriage and family therapists do not permit students or supervisees to perform or to hold themselves out as competent to perform professional services beyond their training, level of experience, and competence.

4.5 Marriage and family therapists take reasonable measures to ensure that services provided by supervisees are professional.

4.6 Marriage and family therapists avoid accepting as supervisees or students those individuals with whom a prior or existing relationship could compromise the therapist's objectivity. When such situations cannot be avoided, therapists take appropriate precautions to maintain objectivity. Examples of such relationships include, but are not limited to, those individuals with whom the therapist has a current or prior sexual, close personal, immediate familial, or therapeutic relationship.

4.7 Marriage and family therapists do not disclose supervisee confidences except by written authorization or waiver, or when mandated or permitted by law. In educational or training settings where there are multiple supervisors, disclosures are permitted only to other professional colleagues, administrators, or employers who share responsibility for training of the supervisee. Verbal authorization will not be sufficient except in emergency situations, unless prohibited by law.

Principle V
Responsibility to Research Participants

Investigators respect the dignity and protect the welfare of research participants, and are aware of applicable laws and regulations and professional standards governing the conduct of research.

5.1 Investigators are responsible for making careful examinations of ethical acceptability in planning studies. To the extent that services to research participants may be compromised by participation in research, investigators seek the ethical advice of qualified professionals not directly involved in the investigation and observe safeguards to protect the rights of research participants.

5.2 Investigators requesting participant involvement in research inform participants of the aspects of the research that might reasonably be expected to influence willingness to participate. Investigators are especially sensitive to the possibility of diminished consent when participants are also receiving clinical services, or have impairments which limit understanding and/or communication, or when participants are children.

5.3 Investigators respect each participant's freedom to decline participation in or to withdraw from a research study at any time. This obligation requires special thought and consideration when investigators or other members of the research team are in positions of authority or influence over participants. Marriage and family therapists, therefore, make every effort to avoid multiple relationships with research participants that could impair professional judgment or increase the risk of exploitation.

5.4 Information obtained about a research participant during the course of an investigation is confidential unless there is a waiver previously obtained in writing. When the possibility exists that others, including family members, may obtain access to such information, this possibility, together with the plan for protecting confidentiality, is explained as part of the procedure for obtaining informed consent.

Principle VI
Responsibility to the Profession

Marriage and family therapists respect the rights and responsibilities of professional colleagues and participate in activities that advance the goals of the profession.

6.1 Marriage and family therapists remain accountable to the standards of the profession when acting as members or employees of organizations. If the mandates of an organization with which a marriage and family therapist is affiliated, through employment, contract or otherwise, conflict with the AAMFT Code of Ethics, marriage and family therapists make known to the organization their commitment to the AAMFT Code of Ethics and attempt to resolve the conflict in a way that allows the fullest adherence to the Code of Ethics.

6.2 Marriage and family therapists assign publication credit to those who have contributed to a publication in proportion to their contributions and in accordance with customary professional publication practices.

6.3 Marriage and family therapists do not accept or require authorship credit for a publication based on research from a student's program, unless the therapist made a substantial contribution beyond being a faculty advisor or research committee member. Coauthorship on a student thesis, dissertation, or project should be determined in accordance with principles of fairness and justice.

6.4 Marriage and family therapists who are the authors of books or other materials that are published or distributed do not plagiarize or fail to cite persons to whom credit for original ideas or work is due.

6.5 Marriage and family therapists who are the authors of books or other materials published or distributed by an organization take reasonable precautions to ensure that the organization promotes and advertises the materials accurately and factually.

6.6 Marriage and family therapists participate in activities that contribute to a better community and society, including devoting a portion of their professional activity to services for which there is little or no financial return.

6.7 Marriage and family therapists are concerned with developing laws and regulations pertaining to marriage and family therapy that serve the public interest, and with altering such laws and regulations that are not in the public interest.

6.8 Marriage and family therapists encourage public participation in the design and delivery of professional services and in the regulation of practitioners.

Principle VII
Financial Arrangements

Marriage and family therapists make financial arrangements with clients, third-party payors, and supervisees that are reasonably understandable and conform to accepted professional practices.

7.1 Marriage and family therapists do not offer or accept kickbacks, rebates, bonuses, or other remuneration for referrals; fee-for-service arrangements are not prohibited.

7.2 Prior to entering into the therapeutic or supervisory relationship, marriage and family therapists clearly disclose and explain to clients and supervisees: (a) all financial arrangements and fees related to professional services, including charges for canceled or missed appointments; (b) the use of collection agencies or legal measures for nonpayment; and (c) the procedure for obtaining payment from the client, to the extent allowed by law, if payment is denied by the third-party payor. Once services have begun, therapists provide reasonable notice of any changes in fees or other charges.

7.3 Marriage and family therapists give reasonable notice to clients with unpaid balances of their intent to seek collection by agency or legal recourse. When such action is taken, therapists will not disclose clinical information.

7.4 Marriage and family therapists represent facts truthfully to clients, third-party payors, and supervisees regarding services rendered.

7.5 Marriage and family therapists ordinarily refrain from accepting goods and services from clients in return for services rendered. Bartering for professional services may be conducted only if: (a) the supervisee or client requests it, (b) the relationship is not exploitative, (c) the professional relationship is not distorted, and (d) a clear written contract is established.

7.6 Marriage and family therapists may not withhold records under their immediate control that are requested and needed for a client's treatment solely because payment has not been received for past services, except as otherwise provided by law.

Principle VIII
Advertising

Marriage and family therapists engage in appropriate informational activities, including those that enable the public, referral sources, or others to choose professional services on an informed basis.

8.1 Marriage and family therapists accurately represent their competencies, education, training, and experience relevant to their practice of marriage and family therapy.

8.2 Marriage and family therapists ensure that advertisements and publications in any media (such as directories, announcements, business cards, newspapers, radio, television, Internet, and facsimiles) convey information that is necessary for the public to make an appropriate selection of professional services. Information could include: (a) office information, such as name, address, telephone number, credit card acceptability, fees, languages spoken, and office hours; (b) qualifying clinical degree (see subprinciple 8.5); (c) other earned degrees (see subprinciple 8.5) and state or provincial licensures and/or certifications; (d) AAMFT clinical member status; and (e) description of practice.

8.3 Marriage and family therapists do not use names that could mislead the public concerning the identity, responsibility, source, and status of those practicing under that name, and do not hold themselves out as being partners or associates of a firm if they are not.

8.4 Marriage and family therapists do not use any professional identification (such as a business card, office sign, letterhead, Internet, or telephone or association directory listing) if it includes a statement or claim that is false, fraudulent, misleading, or deceptive.

8.5 In representing their educational qualifications, marriage and family therapists list and claim as evidence only those earned degrees: (a) from institutions accredited by regional accreditation sources recognized by the United States Department of Education, (b) from institutions recognized by states or provinces that license or certify marriage and family therapists, or (c) from equivalent foreign institutions.

8.6 Marriage and family therapists correct, wherever possible, false, misleading, or inaccurate information and representations made by others concerning the therapist's qualifications, services, or products.

8.7 Marriage and family therapists make certain that the qualifications of their employees or supervisees are represented in a manner that is not false, misleading, or deceptive.

8.8 Marriage and family therapists do not represent themselves as providing specialized services unless they have the appropriate education, training, or supervised experience.

APPENDIX B:
EXAMPLE DISCLOSURE STATEMENT

Ima Goodhelper, PhD
Licensed Marriage and Family Therapist
Center for Family Change
2415 Golden Street
Regionville, Indiana
555-555-2938

Disclosure Statement

Introduction to Services

Ima Goodhelper, PhD, offers private practice, consisting of individual, couple, or family therapy. Since therapy can be conducted in a number of different ways, this statement has been prepared to inform you about Dr. Goodhelper and her qualifications and practice.

Therapist Qualifications

Dr. Goodhelper has a PhD in marriage and family therapy from Purdue University, obtained in 1991. She also holds a master's degree in counselor education, and a bachelor's degree in psychology. She has been a psychotherapist for fifteen years. Dr. Goodhelper has been affiliated with the Center for Family Change for ten years. Areas of clinical expertise include couples counseling, family therapy, and specific presenting concerns of depression, anxiety, and adolescent behavioral problems. Dr. Goodhelper is

- a clinical member of the American Association for Marriage and Family Therapy,
- an approved supervisor of the American Association for Marriage and Family Therapy,
- and a licensed marriage and family therapist in the state of Indiana (License #555511110).

What to Expect Your First Session

Initially, Dr. Goodhelper will spend some time getting to know you and what concerns you bring to counseling. In addition, confidentiality and office procedures will be explained to you. Then, Dr. Goodhelper will spend some time discerning the goals that you have for therapy, and working with you to set realistic goals from which to evaluate your progress. Typically people come to therapy because there is something they would like changed about their lives. Dr. Goodhelper will want to understand exactly what your expectations are so that she can help you meet your goals.

Privacy and Confidentiality

As a client, you have the right to confidentiality. Information obtained during counseling sessions will be held strictly confidential and will not be disclosed to anyone outside of therapy without your written consent. There are a few legal exceptions to confidentiality, which will be explained to you during your first session (for example, it is legally required that suspected child abuse or neglect be reported to authorities).

Office Procedures and Fees

Fees are $95 per fifty-minute session. Payment is required at the end of each session. If you prefer to have your insurance company billed, you will be required to pay your copay at each session.

Emergency Phone Service

The Center for Family Change has emergency services available twenty-four hours per day. If an emergency arises that cannot wait until your next appointment, dial 555-HELP (3457) for a consultation with a therapist on call.

APPENDIX C:
EXAMPLE INFORMED CONSENT DOCUMENT

Ima Goodhelper, PhD,
Licensed Marriage and Family Therapist
Center for Family Change
2415 Golden Street
Regionville, Indiana
555-555-2938

Informed Consent for Treatment

Some Things You Should Know About Your Therapist and Therapy

Since therapy is conducted in a number of different ways, depending upon the therapist and his or her orientation, this description has been prepared to inform you about Dr. Goodhelper's qualifications, the therapeutic process, and general knowledge about what to expect from therapy. Please feel free to ask Dr. Goodhelper any questions you may have prior to signing this consent for treatment.

Therapist Qualifications

Dr. Goodhelper has a PhD in marriage and family therapy from Purdue University, obtained in 1991. She also holds a master's degree in counselor education, and a bachelor's degree in psychology. She has been a psychotherapist for fifteen years. Dr. Goodhelper has been affiliated with the Center for Family Change for ten years. Areas of clinical expertise include couples counseling, family therapy, and specific presenting concerns of depression, anxiety, and adolescent behavioral problems. Dr. Goodhelper is also a clinical member and approved supervisor of the American Association for Marriage and Family Therapy. She is a licensed marriage and family therapist in the state of Indiana (License #555511110).

What to Expect from Therapy

If you decide to enter therapy with Dr. Goodhelper, she will initially spend time with you exploring the problems that brought you to therapy. Next, you and Dr. Goodhelper will work together to set specific goals that you wish to work toward in therapy. Periodically your progress in therapy will be reviewed. The length of therapy will vary depending upon the type and amount of concerns you bring to therapy. At times, changes brought about by your efforts in therapy may cause you discomfort or anxiety; your feelings should be discussed with Dr. Goodhelper. These feelings often accompany behavioral change and are often a sign of progress. However, as part of your treatment, you may experience an array of feelings such as guilt, sadness, anxiety, anger, frustration, loneliness, and helplessness. In addition, although you may be coming to therapy to benefit a relationship you are currently in, one danger of therapy is that change in relationships is not always predictable. That is, although positive change is expected, this does not always occur for every relationship brought to therapy. Last, you should be aware that therapy does not work for every person. Considerable research confirms therapy can have significant benefits for those who seek treatment. Benefits to therapy can include progress toward meeting your therapeutic goals and/or alleviating the problem for which you are seeking help. Additional benefits may also include feeling understood, improved communication, improved clarity of issues and goals, decreased depression and/or anxiety, increased self-esteem, or improvement in relationships. You will have the opportunity in therapy to talk about all of the feelings, positive and negative, that may accompany your work in therapy.

At the beginning of therapy, counseling generally occurs on a weekly basis. As therapy progresses, meetings may occur on a less frequent basis until goals are met and termination is completed. Sessions are fifty minutes in length, unless other arrangements have been made with your therapist.

Dr. Goodhelper is a family therapist, and her theoretical orientations includes family systems theory, structural family therapy, strategic family therapy, solution-focused therapy, and emotionally focused therapy, among others. Her approach will depend upon your unique needs as client(s). Dr. Goodhelper is not a physician and cannot prescribe or provide any medication. If medical treatment is indicated, she will recommend a physician or psychiatrist to you, depending upon the nature of your concerns. If it appears your concerns are outside the treatment range of Dr. Goodhelper, you will be given options for referral to a more appropriate treatment choice.

Confidentiality/Privilege

As a client, one of your most important rights is that of confidentiality. Conversations with your therapist and written records are legally protected by state law, as well as professional ethical principles. Information obtained during therapy sessions will be held confidential and will not be disclosed to anyone outside of therapy without your written consent. There are few exceptions to confidentiality. Dr. Goodhelper will be required to break confidentiality if one or more of the following conditions exist:

1 If Dr. Goodhelper has reason to think that you (clients involved in therapy) may be harmful to yourself or others.
2. If Dr. Goodhelper suspects that child abuse or neglect has occurred or will occur.
3. If a court orders the release of information regarding your treatment.

If you are attending therapy *as part of a couple or family,* you may be seen individually in addition to the couple or family therapy that you are attending. If this occurs, your therapist needs to be advised as to how you would like information you divulge to her to be handled. There are several ways that information can be handled between family members. Please read carefully the following options for how you would like information between you and your spouse or family members handled.

☐ _____ (Initials) I give permission for any information I divulge to be shared with family members.

☐ _____ (Initials) I *do not* give permission for information I divulge to be shared with family members.

> I understand if I choose this option, I limit the type of help that I can receive from Dr. Goodhelper. In this instance, if information is divulged to Dr. Goodhelper that she thinks is important for you to share with your partner or other family members, she will ask you to divulge this information before therapy continues. If you refuse to divulge important information, the ramifications of such a decision will be discussed in detail. In some cases, a referral to another treating therapist may be made.

☐ _____ (Initials) I *do not* give permission for information I divulge to be shared with family members except under instances in which my life may be threatened or someone else's life may be in danger due to my _____.

To ensure quality control in therapy, Dr. Goodhelper reserves the right to consult with therapist-colleagues regarding your treatment. This is similar to a physician "getting a second opinion" and can be very helpful in therapeutic treatment. These professionals are required to maintain the same strictest confidentiality as Dr. Goodhelper.

Your Rights As a Client

As a client you have the right to:

1. ask questions at any point in time regarding therapeutic or office procedures;
2. offer feedback and your views on therapy;
3. be actively involved in formulating your goals and collaborating with your therapist to promote change;
4. terminate therapy at any time (you may ask Dr. Goodhelper for a list of possible referral sources);

5. confidentiality as designated in this consent document;
6. be apprised of fees and fee changes;
7. ask about alternative procedures available for meeting your goals;
8. review your case records or (with your written release) obtain written copies.

Office Procedures and Fees

If you are unable to attend an appointment, it is your responsibility to cancel your session at least twenty-four hours in advance of the session. Failure to do so will result in your being charged the full fee for the session. Certain exceptions will be made to this policy in the event of emergencies, provided that the therapist is informed prior to the time of the appointment.

Fees are $95 per fifty-minute session. Payment is expected at the end of each session. If you have health insurance, it is your responsibility to (a) make your copayment and (b) complete and sign the necessary insurance forms so that we might share information with your insurer. Ultimately it is the client, not the insurer, who is responsible for the payment of the fee.

Telephone calls lasting longer than five minutes will be billed in quarter-hour increments at your set fee. Therapeutic phone calls are not generally reimbursable by insurance. Consultations with outside sources (attorneys, courts, teachers, etc.) will be billed in quarter-hour increments at the regular fee. Expert witness fees are $120 per hour. Emergency services are billed at your normal fee rate.

Last, unpaid bills will be sent to collection should payment not be made in a reasonable period of time.

Emergency Services

During normal business hours, calls are taken by staff at the regular office phone number (555-555-2938). The Center for Family Change has emergency services available twenty-four hours per day. If an emergency arises that cannot wait until your next appointment, dial 555-HELP (3457) for a consultation with a therapist on call. The Center for Family Change is not an emergency service. If you have an immediate psychiatric emergency, go to a hospital emergency room and indicate to them it is a psychiatric emergency so that the appropriate personnel can be summoned to evaluate your situation.

Informed Consent

By signing below, I agree that I have read and understand the above information, and agree to the terms of therapy stated above. My signature indicates that I am giving my consent for Dr. Goodhelper to treat me (us) in therapy. My signature also indicates that Dr. Goodhelper has permission to treat any of my minor children whom I bring to therapy.

Signature _____ · Date _____
(Client)

Signature _____ Date _____
(Client)

Signature _____ Date _____
(Client)

Signature _____ Date _____
(Therapist)

APPENDIX D: FIRST STEPS IN PURSUING GRADUATE EDUCATION—ADVICE TO STUDENTS

For those considering an occupation as a helping professional, graduate school should be explored relatively early in one's undergraduate career. A college student should do several things to prepare for graduate school.

1. *Explore the various areas of mental health that interest you:* Counseling, psychology, marriage and family therapy, social work—compare and contrast the professions while considering your career goals. Take an introductory overview class in the field or fields that interest you.

2. *Gain experience in working with people.* You may be able to understand more thoroughly how to guide your career if you work with people and understand your likes and dislikes, strengths and weaknesses. Try to find jobs in which you are exposed to people, preferably jobs in mental health settings. If you cannot find a job, volunteer. Volunteer experience is invaluable and can be added to your developing professional résumé.

3. *Talk to professors and other professionals in the field you are considering entering.* Ask about their training, their job market, and their opinions on the various types of training available, and any general advice they might have for someone wanting to pursue an education in a mental health field.

4. *Take courses in both statistics and research methods.* As a mental health professional, you will be expected to keep apprised of research. In order to provide the appropriate standard of care, you need to be familiar with the latest research findings of the problem you are treating. For example, if you are treating a child for enuresis, there may be a new, proven technique that works well for children with bed-wetting problems. If you are unable to consume research, you will be an ineffective practitioner. For your immedi-

ate career future, almost all graduate schools in the helping professions require these courses. Faculty in graduate programs look for students who understand and value research.

5. *Gain experience in research.* Volunteer to be a research assistant to your professors. This experience provides three things. It provides valuable experience in the research process; it gives you a competitive edge for your application to graduate school; and it allows the professor to get to know you and your skills much more closely than he or she would be able to do in the classroom alone. This exposure to the professor can also give you a resource for someone who can write a letter to support your application to graduate school.

6. *Begin to put a professional résumé together.* Tailor your volunteering, work, and collegiate experiences toward your career goal.

7. *Call or write for application packets from the graduate programs that interest you.* Look over the materials and apply to several. Do not choose just one graduate school to apply to; entrance to graduate schools can be quite competitive.

8. *Study for and take the Graduate Record Exam (GRE) early.* Most graduate programs have application deadlines long before you would be starting classes, and you must have taken your GRE and sent your scores in to the graduate program to which you are applying before the application deadline. A common mistake is that students wait until it is too late to take the GRE and are disqualified from the application process. Your college counseling or career center should have applications for the GRE. Find out if the graduate programs you are applying to require a subject test (e.g., psychology subject test). You will need to have your GRE scores sent directly from the testing organization to your colleges of interest.

9. *Get good grades.* Your grade point average is an important consideration when getting into graduate school. If there was a period of time where your grade point average wavered due to a personal crisis, but then you pulled your grades back up, explain your situation briefly in your application packet.

10. *Get to know your present professors and others professionals in the mental health field.* You will need letters of recommendation to get into graduate school. Three letters of recommendation are typically required (some colleges have required forms that must be filled out by the recommending source). You want your professors to be able to write a detailed letter about you. Take the time to get to know them and let them know you. Do not send recommendation letters in your application packet from family, friends, or family friends; stick to letters from professionals. Letters from personal, rather than profesional sources are biased and will be discounted by those who read them. Give your professor who is writing your letter

plenty of lead time to write the letter so you meet your application deadline. Check to be sure he or she completed the letter prior to the deadline. If the graduate school you are applying to requires three letters of recommendation and they receive only two, your application will likely not be considered. Remember to thank your professor for the letter; it takes time to compose a good letter.

11. *If possible, visit the program prior to the application deadline.* This action shows an interest and investment in the program. Ask to meet with the program director, tell him or her you are interested in applying and would like to come and learn more about their program. Bring along a list of questions you have regarding the training.

12. *If finances are in question, ask the graduate program about scholarships and graduate assistantships.* Many graduate programs offer graduate assistantships in which you become a teaching assistant or research assistant. In exchange for your work, you receive a small monthly stipend and a tuition waiver. Some students choose to take out student loans during their graduate program.

GLOSSARY

appropriate standard of care: How most professionals would treat a case under similar circumstances.

certification: State legislation that prohibits the use of a particular professional title without a certificate.

child abuse reporting laws: All states have some form of child abuse reporting laws requiring professional therapists (and sometimes laypersons as well) to report child abuse or neglect.

confidentiality: The ethical obligation of therapists to keep communications between themselves and the client strictly private, not privy to any outside parties.

dual relationship: Having a professional relationship with a client and also a personal, business, or intimate type of relationship with him or her.

duty to warn: The responsibility of the therapist to inform an intended victim if a client is threatens to harm a person or group of persons.

ethics: The study of what constitutes good and bad human conduct, including related actions and values.

identified patient: The person bearing the symptoms of a dysfunctional family (or couple) system.

informed consent: Therapists inform clients in writing about their rights and what to expect during therapeutic treatment.

licensure: This term refers to a state statute that prohibits the practice of a profession without a license from the state.

malpractice: Practicing in a way that causes injury to a client as a result of the therapist's action.

maneuverability: Ability to intervene effectively.

privilege: Legal right to privacy owned by the client, typically regulated by state statute.

professional codes of ethics: Written codes of conduct set by professional organizations stating acceptable and unacceptable behaviors and standards for the discipline.

professional disclosure statement: A written statement introducing clients to the therapist's qualifications, the nature of the therapeutic process, and other important issues entailed in martial and family therapy.

secret policies: The therapist sets a written or verbal agreement with marital or family therapy clients on how information will be handled in therapy with respect to information shared individually with the therapist (separate from the other member of the couple or the other members of the family).

social constructivism: A philosophy that maintains that there is no objective reality.

REFERENCES

American Association for Marriage and Family Therapy (AAMFT) (1992a). *Decision tree: AAMFT ethics cases.* Washington, DC: Author.

American Association for Marriage and Family Therapy (AAMFT) (1992b). *Procedures for handling ethical matters.* Washington, DC: Author.

American Association for Marriage and Family Therapy (AAMFT) (2001). *AAMFT code of ethics.* Washington, DC: Author.

American Association for Marriage and Family Therapy (AAMFT) (n.d.). About the American Association for Marriage and Family Therapy. Retrieved October 2001, <http://www.aamft.org/about/aamft.htm>.

American Counseling Association (1995). *Code of ethics and standards of practice.* Alexandria, VA: Author.

American Psychological Association (1992). *Ethical principles of psychologists and code of conduct.* Washington, DC: Author.

Avis, J. M. (1985). The politics of functional family therapy: A feminist critique. *Journal of Marital and Family Therapy, 11,* 127-138.

Barry, V. C. (1982). *Moral aspects of health care.* Pacific Grove, CA: Brooks/Cole.

Beamish, P. M., Navin, S. L., and Davidson, P. (1994). Ethical dilemmas in marriage and family therapy: Implications for training. *American Mental Health Counselors Association Journal, 16*(1), 129-142.

Bograd, M. (1984). Family systems approaches to wife battering: A feminist critique. *American Journal of Orthopsychiatry, 54,* 558-568.

Borys, D. S. (1992). Non-sexual dual relationships. *Innovations in Clinical Practice,* (11), 443-454.

Borys, D. S. and Pope, K. S. (1989). Dual relationships between therapist and client. *Professional Psychology: Research and Practice, 20*(5), 283-293.

Denton, W. (1989). A family systems analysis of the DSM-III-R. *Journal of Marital and Family Therapy, 16*(2), 113-125.

Fenell, D. L. and Weinhold, B. K. (1989). *Counseling families: An introduction to marriage and family therapy.* Denver, CO: Love.

Fisher, L., Anderson, A., and Jones, J. E. (1981). Types of paradoxical interventions and indications/contraindications for use in clinical practice. *Family Process, 20,* 25-35.

Forester-Miller, H. and Davis, T. E. (1996). *A practitioner's guide to ethical decision making.* Alexandria, VA: American Counseling Association. Retrieved October 24, 2001, <http://www.counseling.org/resources/pracguide.htm>.

Friedman, S. (Ed.) (1993). *The new language of change: Constructive collaboration in psychotherapy.* New York: Guilford Press.

Gill, S. J. (1982). Professional disclosure and consumer protection in counseling. *Personnel and Guidance Journal, 60,* 443-446.

Goldner, V. (1985a). Feminism and family therapy. *Family Process, 24,* 31-47.

Goldner, V. (1985b). Warning: Family therapy may be dangerous to your health. *Family Therapy Networker, 9,* 19-23.

Gottlieb, M. C. (1993). Avoiding exploitive dual relationships: A decision-making model. *Psychotherapy, 30*(1), 41-48.

Green, S. L. and Hansen, J. C. (1989). Ethical dilemmas faced by family therapists. *Journal of Marital and Family Therapy, 15,* 149-158.

Gross, S. J. (1977). Professional disclosure: An alternative to licensure. *Personnel and Guidance Journal, 55,* 586-588.

Haas, L. J. and Malouf, J. L. (1995). *Keeping up the good work: A practitioner's guide to mental health ethics* (Second edition). Sarasota, FL: Professional Resource Exchange.

Haley, J. (1980). *Problem-solving therapy.* San Francisco: Jossey-Bass.

Hare-Mustin, R. T. (1978). A feminist approach to family therapy. *Family Process, 17,* 181-194.

Hare-Mustin, R. T. (1979). Family therapy and sex-role stereotypes. *The Counseling Psychologist, 8,* 31-32.

Hare-Mustin, R. T. (1980). Family therapy may be dangerous to your health. *Professional Psychology, 11,* 935-938.

Huber, C. H. (1994). *Ethical, legal, and professional issues in the practice of marriage and family therapy* (Second edition). New York: Macmillan Publishing Company.

Jacobson, N. S. (1983). Beyond empiricism: The politics of marital therapy. *American Journal of Family Therapy, 11,* 11-24.

Jensen, P. S., Josephson, A. M., and Frey, J. (1989). Informed consent as a framework for treatment: Ethical and therapeutic considerations. *American Journal of Psychotherapy, 43,* 378-386.

Kagle, J. D. and Giebelhausen, P. N. (1994). Dual relationships and professional boundaries. *Social Work, 39*(2), 213-220.

Karpel, M. A. (1980). Family secrets. I. Conceptual and ethical issues in the relational context. II. Ethical and practical considerations in therapeutic management. *Family Process, 19,* 295-306.

Kitchener, K. S. (1984). Intuition, critical evaluation and ethical principles: The foundation for ethical decisions in counseling psychology. *The Counseling Psychologist, 24*(1), 92-97.

Kitchener, K. S. (1998). Dual role relationships: What makes them so problematic? *Journal of Counseling and Development, 67*(4).

Lamb, D. H., Clark, C., Drumheller, P., Frizzell, K., and Surrey, L. (1990). Applying "Tarasoff " to AIDS-related psychotherapy issues. *Professional Psychology: Research and Practice, 20*(1), 37-43.

Margolin, G. (1982). Ethical and legal considerations in marriage and family therapy. *American Psychologist, 37,* 788-802.

O'Shea, M. and Jessee, E. (1982). Ethical, value, and professional conflicts in systems therapy. In L. L'Abate (Ed.), *Values, ethics, and legalities and the family therapist* (pp. 1-21). Rockville, MD: Aspen Systems Corporation.

Pope, K. S. (1991). Dual relationships in psychotherapy. *Ethics and Behavior, 1*(1), 21-34.

Ramsdell, P. S. and Ramsdell, E. R. (1993). Dual relationships: Client perceptions of the effect of client-counselor relationship on the therapeutic process. *Clinical Social Work Journal, 21*(2), 195-212.

Rohrbaugh, M., Tennen, H., Press. S., and White, L. (1981). Compliance, defiances, and therapeutic paradox: Guidelines for strategic use of paradoxical interventions. *American Journal of Orthopsychiatry, 41,* 454-467.

Rosenbaum, M. (1982) *Ethics and values in psychotherapy: A guidebook.* New York: Free Press.

Schlossberger, E. and Hecker, L. (1996). Purposes, content, and uses of professional codes: Enhancing the identity of family sciences. Unpublished manuscript, Purdue University Calumet, Hammond, IN.

Schultz, B. M. (1982). *Legal liability in psychotherapy.* San Francisco: Jossey-Bass.

Schwartz, R. (1989). Maybe there is a better way: Response to Duncan and Solvey. *Journal of Marital and Family Therapy, 15,* 11-12.

Slipp, S. (1989). A different viewpoint for integrating psychodynamic and systems approaches. *Journal of Marital and Family Therapy, 15,* 13-16.

Smith-Bell, M. and Winslade, W. J. (1994). Privacy, confidentiality, and privilege in psychotherapeutic relationships. *American Journal of Orthopsychiatry, 64*(2), 180-193.

Stadler, H. A. (1986). Making hard choices: Clarifying controversial ethical issues. *Counseling and Human Development, 19*(1), 1-10.

Stromberg, C. and Dellinger, A. (1993). A legal update on malpractice and other professional liability. *The Psychologist's Legal Update,* (3), 3-15.

Swanson, J. L. (1979). Counseling directory and consumer's guide: Implementing professional disclosure and consumer protection. *Personal and Guidance Journal, 58,* 190-193.

Tarasoff v. Regents of University of California, 17 Cal. 3 d425, 551 P 2d. 334, 131 Cal. Rptr. 14 (1976).

Thiroux, J. P. (1980). *Ethics: Theory and practice* (Second edition). Encino, CA: Glencoe Pub. Co.

Tiesmann, M. (1980). Convening strategies in family therapy. *Family Process, 19,* 393-400.

Wendorf, D. J. and Wendorf, R. J. (1985). A systemic view of family therapy ethics. *Family Process, 24,* 443-453.

Witmer, J. M. (1978). Professional disclosure in licensure. *Counselor Education and Supervision, 18,* 71-73.

Zygmond, M. J. and Borhem, H. (1989). Ethical decision making in family therapy. *Family Process, 28*(3), 269-280.

Chapter 16

Research in Marriage and Family Therapy

Richard J. Bischoff

In my undergraduate program in family studies, I had an instructor who during a class asked students to raise their hands if they disliked research, statistics, and math. Nearly every hand shot up amid chuckles of recognition. He then commented that this was just as he had expected, and that in his opinion this is one of the primary reasons students gravitate toward family science and other social sciences, including marriage and family therapy. He explained that students of family science in particular and the social sciences in general can succeed without analytical and research skills and without interest! (A point with which I absolutely disagree.) I do not remember the specific reasons he gave for this—I think he said something about family studies and therapy are driven more by informal theory than by formal theory and the results of research. As a faculty member in a family science/family therapy program now, I have observed that many, if not most, of my students do not have a particular interest in research and that most profess a lack of analytic skill. This is true not only at the undergraduate level. Research methods and statistics courses are often dreaded and, in many cases, put off until they cannot be avoided any longer. It is almost as if students are secretly hoping that the program requirements will change so that these courses will be eliminated as requirements before they have to take them. In fact, I would guess that most of you reading this chapter are doing so begrudgingly.

In teaching graduate-level research courses, I have been struck with the level of anxiety that my family therapy students bring to the first few class sessions. Student anxiety is almost palpable. I have actually structured my class to address this anxiety directly during the first few sessions, which seems to help—temporarily. The anxiety typically subsides as the semester progresses, only to skyrocket again when we begin discussing statistics six to eight weeks into the semester.

Now, I would not say that aversion to math, statistics, and research is the reason that people choose family science and family therapy as major areas of study, but I do believe it is a factor. If we are doing it correctly, all of us gravitate toward areas of study and professions that capitalize on our natural strengths and skills, that are of most interest to us, and that do not excessively emphasize our weaknesses. Frankly, not everyone has the inclination to become a researcher or statistician. Although I do not have statistics to back up my next claim, it may just so happen that many people who do not have inclinations to become researchers or statisticians have natural skills for helping others with problems. This may be due to their ability to see people in context and to appreciate each person's uniqueness. It may be due to the value they place on natural intuition to help both themselves and others. It may be due to a host of other variables. Whatever the reason, quantifying behavior and experiences or conducting **observations** in ways that follow rules of **disciplined inquiry** often flies in the face of intuition and appreciating uniqueness. Frankly, the characteristics of successful treatment have perpetually been difficult to **operationalize** and **quantify.** Even when researchers are able to operationalize and quantify them, understanding them through the aggregation of data and the comparison of **means** and **standard deviations** can easily result in loss of meaning.

Consequently, many clinicians (and students) complain that research provides little to inform their clinical work. Many clinicians say that the laboratory nature of research—with its tight **controls** on **extraneous variables**—often does not reflect the real world of working with clients. In fact, treatments that are conducted as part of a study often are so tightly controlled that they cannot and, in fact, should not be duplicated in the real world of clinical practice (Pinsof and Wynne, 2000). Client **inclusion criteria** are often so exclusive that they act to eliminate clients representing those typically seen by most clinicians.

To give a specific example, in an excellently designed (tightly controlled) study, Jose Szapocznik and his colleagues (Szapocznik et al., 1988) looked at the degree to which a structural-strategic-systems engagement (SSSE) strategy was an improvement over the engagement as usual (EAU) strategies when attempting to engage adolescent substance abusers and their families in treatment. The problem is an important one for study because adolescent substance abusers and their families are notorious for being difficult to engage in treatment.

The SSSE strategy the investigators developed is essentially one in which the therapist attempts to overcome the resistance to participating in treatment of each member of the family prior to the first session. Using SSSE, joining, assessment, and restructuring begin at the first contact, which is typically the point at which the first request for treatment is made. For the purposes of the study, these investigators operationalized engagement as existing on six levels. At the lowest level, at the point of first contact (the first telephone call) an inquiry about the problem situation and an expression of polite concern is made by the therapist and an appointment to meet with the family is set. At the lowest level, or EAU, at the point of first contact (e.g., the first telephone call) the therapist inquired about the problem situation and expressed polite concern and then set an appointment to meet with the family. This type of interaction represented engagement as usual because it represented what would typically occur when a potential client calls to set up an appointment. Four higher levels of engagement were attempted, that grouped together were considered SSSE. SSSE interactions were ones in which the therapist assertively attempted to address or restructure the resistance of family members in order to engage them in treatment. For example, although rarely used, at the highest level, the therapist would make a visit in the family home before the first session in the therapist's office to restructure the family resistance and thereby engage them in treatment.

Szapocznik and his colleagues found the SSSE condition to produce engagement rates at 93 percent while the EAU condition produced engagement rates at 42 percent. Also, of those engaged in treatment, those in the SSSE condition were much more likely to complete treatment than those in the EAU condition.

The findings are interesting, and appear to have immediate clinical application; however, the application of these findings to clinical work for many clinicians is impractical. In order to implement a SSSE strategy such as the one under investigation, a clinician would need to spend a significant amount of unreimbursable time in engaging client families. This is something that most clinicians and agencies are unwilling to do. So, although the tight controls that eliminated error were important to finding the differences between the two types of engagement strategies, these same controls make the application of the findings impractical for many clinicians.

THE ROLE OF RESEARCH IN THE PRACTICE OF MARRIAGE AND FAMILY THERAPY

Despite the fact that very few clinicians report an interest in research, there is probably no more important time than now for marriage and family therapists to be actively involved in the generation of both **quantitative** and **qualitative research.** Mental health care has unwittingly become caught up in the rapidly changing health care marketplace. Third-party payers, other professionals, governmental entities, and clients are increasingly demanding evidence to support claims of the effectiveness of couples and family therapy. Although it has always been the ethical responsibility of those within the field to legitimate treatments through rigorous research methods (see Cavell and Snyder, 1991; Gurman, 1983; Liddle, 1991; Pinsof and Wynne, 1995b; Sprenkle and Bischoff, 1995), we now have added motivation to conduct this research—our livelihoods depend on it.

It is the ethical responsibility of members of a profession to substantiate the effectiveness of the services being provided. This is especially important in the continually elusive mental health care field in which standards for diagnosis and standard of care practices are difficult to determine. It is difficult to justify as ethical the provision of services for something as important as a person's mental and relationship health without **substantive evidence** as to its effectiveness. Yet we continue to do so. In fact, the number of new, untested approaches to therapy continues to grow. In 1987, Rollo May estimated that there were over 300 distinct models of therapy. That is an incredible number of published approaches to psychotherapy, the majority of which have no **empirical** support to justify their use.

Research in marriage and family therapy is important to the field for a number of reasons (see Sprenkle and Bischoff, 1995). First, and probably most important, *research can improve the practice of couple and family therapy.* Research that targets the outcomes of couple and family therapy as it is used to treat specific problems in specific contexts will lead to better treatment planning and treatment decision making when it comes to finding the most effective treatment approach for specific situations and contexts. In 1967, Gordon Paul explained that psychotherapy research should be most concerned with attempting to determine which treatment works best for which clients under which treatment circumstances. Although as a field we are far from an answer to this question, clinical research has begun to address it in a way that is leading to improved treatment outcomes. Of course, outcome research, especially that which attempts to determine the **efficacy** of a treatment, is fraught with problems that limit **generalizability.** Yet much can be learned from this research that can inform decision making in treatment.

For example, in a well-designed outcome study of the use of family therapy in the treatment of eating disorders, the investigators (Dare et al., 1990) found that their modified structural family therapy approach was superior to individual therapy when the age of onset of the eating disorder (anorexia nervosa) was younger than eighteen years. However, they also found that individual therapy was superior to family therapy when the age of onset was older than eighteen years. These findings have important implications for treatment planning when working with eating-disordered clients and their families, regardless of the theoretical model being used to guide treatment.

Research that investigates the **process of therapy** (what happens during therapy that produces change and that leads to an outcome) can help clinicians understand how change takes place given certain conditions or problems and the role of the therapist in facilitating those changes. As we better understand the process by which therapeutic change takes place, therapy can become more efficient, thus improving both the delivery of therapeutic services and client outcomes. Also, as we learn more about the various factors that account for variation in treatment outcomes, we can attempt to use these factors in a way that improves treatment outcomes.

Second, *research can add legitimacy to the field of family therapy with other mental health clinicians.* Relatively speaking, marriage and family therapy is the new kid on the mental health care scene. Psychiatry, social work, and psychology have been around for fifty to seventy years longer than family therapy as a profession. Many professionals in other mental health fields consider couple and family therapy as subspecialties of their own professions, and definitely not one that warrants the status of legitimate profession. Cleave Shields and his colleagues (Shields et al., 1994) have identified marriage and family therapy as a marginalized mental health profession. Although there are advantages to being on the margins (e.g., flexibility to creatively develop treatments), there are also disadvantages—the primary one being the lack of legitimacy afforded by one's peers in other mental health disciplines. These authors have cautioned that until the clinical effectiveness of the approach is legitimated through scientific means, the field will continue to be marginalized in the professional community.

Third, *research can provide evidence to the larger mental health community that family therapy is a treatment of choice for many mental health problems.* The mental health care environment of the 1990s and early twenty-first century is different than it was previous to this time. Third-party payer and managed care companies are increasingly reluctant to pay for treatments that do not have "proven effectiveness," and the evidence these entities are looking for comes from research.

Fourth, *research can legitimate family therapy with the public at large.* Because of the newness of the field of marriage and family therapy, consumers of mental health care generally do not know about the role of marriage and family therapy in the treatment of mental health problems. In general, when average consumers of mental health care consider finding a therapist, they think of either a psychologist or psychiatrist. This is true even for those with relationship problems such as marital conflict or family problems. The term *psychologist* has become synonymous with the term *therapist* for many people, including many mental health professionals.

Although as a marriage and family therapist I have known this for some time, it became even more clear to me when examining the results of a study conducted by a colleague and me to determine how therapists are presented in the movies (Bischoff and Reiter, 1999). For this study we examined over a ten-year period of time sixty-six movies that presented therapists and therapy. Of the ninety-nine therapists presented in these movies, only four had a professional identification as a marriage therapist, couple's therapist, family therapist, marriage and family therapist, or marriage, family, and child counselor. Yet, there were many more instances of therapists providing marital or couples therapy or in working with families.

Marriage and family therapy research will increase the visibility of the field and profession with consumers of marriage and family therapy. Research into the utility of marriage and family therapy for treating relationship problems and mental health concerns, and the impact of relationship function on mental and physical health and well-being, will improve the legitimacy of the field and profession for the treatment of serious mental health problems.

THE EVOLUTION OF RESEARCH WITHIN THE FIELD OF MARRIAGE AND FAMILY THERAPY

That research is an enigma for marriage and family therapists is especially interesting given that the practice of couple and family therapy actually originated from the research efforts of its founders (e.g., Broderick and Schrader, 1981; Nichols and Schwartz, 1998; Sprenkle and Bischoff, 1995; Wynne, 1983). Murray Bowen, Lyman Wynn, Theodore Lidtz, the members of the Mental Research Institute (MRI) group, and other founders of family therapy developed their models of family therapy as a result of their attempts to understand problem families through research. Through their research on schizophrenia and other serious adult pathologies, these early researchers began to recognize the influence of family communication and other family interactions on the exacerbation of symptoms. As these researchers began to understand the influence of the family on individual functioning, they began to experiment with family intervention in an attempt to alleviate pathology. It worked! These early researchers found that as they mobilized the family differently, the symptoms of pathology lessened. So, through basic research efforts they developed models of intervention that could later be tested for effectiveness (through applied research).

Miklowitz and Hooley (1998) have identified this as the ideal process for conducting modern clinical research: The results of basic research lead to the development of interventions and/or treatment manuals that are then tested. However, the research efforts of today do not really resemble the research efforts of the founders of family therapy (Wynne, 1983). According to Lyman Wynne (1983), there was little distinction between the researcher and the clinician in the early days of family therapy. In fact, both the research interview and the clinical interview were designed to intervene into the family pathology, and both were designed to provide data for the development and refinement of clinical theory. Researchers/clinicians would meet with subjects or patients and their families, interviewing them, as others observed through one-way mirrors or listened to the audiotaped session after it had taken place. They would then get together to discuss "each session, formulating **hypotheses** and criticizing the hypotheses for many, many hours" (Wynne, 1983, p. 114; emphasis added). In fact, this sounds more like an intensive clinical training experience than it does the research of today. Current research, including qualitative research, is truly a disciplined inquiry: Observations are carefully planned and recorded and follow strict guidelines that ensure confidence in the results of these observations. It is truly different from the early research effort of the founders of family therapy, but this blending of research and clinical work in the early days of family therapy provided a foundation for the growth of the field.

Fortunately, the research of today has become much more sophisticated and rigorous. Elusive **constructs** have been operationalized in ways that allow them to actually be measured. Measures have been developed and tested to determine their **psychometric qualities.** We now have measures of very complex constructs that show **reliability** (showing consistent results across time and situation) and **validity** (we are actually measuring what we think we are measuring). Studies are now designed to eliminate **competing explanations** to the results. **Programmatic research** has been conducted that allows for the results from sequential studies to build upon one another. This increased sophistication has allowed researchers to place greater confidence in their results. We know more now about what makes therapy work and the effectiveness of therapy than we would have ever known with the research methods of the past. In fact, many of the claims forwarded by these early researchers have been discounted or at least tempered as a result of later research efforts.

RESEARCH-PRACTICE GAP

Unfortunately, however, the increased sophistication of research methods today have distanced research efforts from clinical work to the point that many clinicians now avoid research findings, saying that they have little bearing on their clinical work (Cohen, Sargent, and Sechrest, 1986). In fact, one study of clinician attitudes toward research found that less than 14 percent said they use research findings to inform their clinical work[1] (Morrow-Bradley and Elliott, 1986). Clinicians often say that research is too reductionistic to be helpful clinically, and that the presentation of **clinical case studies** (Cohen, Sargent, and Sechrest, 1986; Jacobson, 1985a; Kaye, 1990) and their own experience as clinicians is more helpful than is research (Atkinson, Heath, and Chenail, 1991; Morrow-Bradley and Elliott, 1986). This is supported by Mahrer's (1988) observation that the charisma of the proponents of the approach to therapy, its fit with the personality of the therapist, and the therapist's intuition and life experience are more important in determining which approach to treatment will be used than research is. Given that this unscientific approach to treatment selection is normative, it is surprising that therapy is as successful as it is—or is it? It may be that the specific approach to treatment is not nearly as important as other factors in determining treatment success.

In fact, attempts to compare models of therapy have been fraught with difficulty and many prominent researchers have encouraged the field to move away from such efforts (e.g., Jacobson, 1985b). Studies comparing one model of therapy against another typically do little more than polarize individuals within the field. Like it or not, therapists are not going to adopt a new approach to therapy just because research says their favored one is not the best. No study of this type is ever so rigorously designed that reasonable competing explanations do not exist. You can be assured that therapists adopting the therapy that "lost" or that does not have research support will be quick to point out the deficiencies in that research. This type of research has done nothing to improve the services provided to clients.

Take for example the study by Douglas Snyder and Robert Wills (1989) comparing insight-oriented marital therapy with behavioral marital therapy. Snyder and Wills found fairly convincingly that insight-oriented marital therapy produced better outcomes than did behavioral marital therapy. Neil Jacobson (1991b) published a paper critiquing the Snyder and Wills study and defending behavioral marital therapy. His contention was that Snyder and Wills misrepresented behavioral marital therapy by eliminating essential aspects of this approach from their treatment manual. In addition, he contended that Snyder and Wills, as insight-oriented therapists, could not adequately train the insight-oriented therapists used in the study to fully or correctly implement behavioral therapies. This article was followed by a lively debate on behavioral marital therapy and on the value of comparing approaches to marital therapy by researchers throughout the field (Baucom and Epstein, 1991; Gurman, 1991;

Jacobson, 1991a; Johnson and Greenberg, 1991; Markman, 1991; Snyder and Wills, 1991).

This debate was beneficial in several ways. First, it identified as futile the efforts of researchers to compare models of therapy with the intention of proving one therapy superior to another. These attempts are counterproductive to improving treatment outcomes. Therapists are not going to abandon their beloved approaches to treatment just because research suggests that another approach produces better results than the one they are accustomed to using. This debate also reinforced the idea that psychotherapy research cannot be free of confounding variables. Although Snyder and Wills designed a fairly well controlled study, it did not sufficiently control for error to protect the integrity of both approaches to treatment. In order to do this, behavioral therapists should research behavioral therapies and insight-oriented therapists should research insight-oriented therapies. Intraschool studies of therapeutic approaches are the best-known way of assuring that the therapies are being represented fairly.

Comparative research studies are especially counterproductive now that **cooperative research** efforts to enhance the general delivery of services are most needed. This may be most appropriate anyway, given the burgeoning evidence which suggests that there are more similarities across therapies with successful outcomes than there are differences.

Attempts to Address the Research-Practice Gap

This problem is of such a serious concern for those within the field that numerous articles have been written in an attempt to address the practice gap between research and clinical work (e.g., Eisler and Dare, 1992; Griffith and Griffith, 1990; Kaye, 1990; Liddle, 1991; Olson, 1976; Pinsof and Wynne, 2000; Safran, Greenberg, and Rice, 1988; Schwartz and Breunlin, 1983). Meetings, conferences, and special caucuses as well have been sponsored by the National Institute of Mental Health, the American Association for Marriage and Family Therapy, the American Psychological Association, and other professional organizations in an attempt to overcome this gap. However, the practice gap between research and clinical work still exists.

This is not to say that research is not occurring. In fact, it is, and researchers are generating research results at a very rapid pace. The number of excellently designed studies is growing exponentially, spurred on by advances in **research design** and **analytic methodology** that have expanded the types of questions that can be asked through research. The expected result of these advances is that research will become increasingly more applicable to clinical practice.

In general, researchers/clinicians acknowledge this gap. The cynical part of me believes that this acknowledgment comes from their frustration in seeing that their great research efforts are not being used in clinical practice. So, as is true for most problems, those most interested in seeing the problem resolved are the first to offer solutions to its resolution (and yet by virtue of being the ones most interested, they are precisely those with the least relational power to effect the change). It is not surprising that suggestions from these researchers-clinicians have included socializing clinicians in graduate training programs to research, redesigning graduate curricula to emphasize research, modeling the use of research to inform clinical work, and standing on the proverbial soapbox to call for clinicians to use research more.

Complicating this problem within the profession of marriage and family therapy is the fact that most of the most prominent researchers within the field are professionals identifying themselves primarily with psychiatry, psychology, and social work to a greater extent than to marriage and family therapy (Hawley, Bailey, and Pennick, 2000). In fact, the most prominent researchers in the field are psychologists who publish in psychology journals as much as or more than in family therapy journals. It is also important to note that although the research literature on couple and family therapy is becoming quite large, most of this research is separated into couple therapy research and family therapy research (Alexander, Holtzworth-Munroe, and Jameson, 1994). Research studying the effectiveness of marriage and family therapy (as an integrated treatment approach) is rare. This is probably because most researchers consider couple therapy to be significantly different from family therapy and a subspecialization to one of the other mental health disciplines.

This has several implications (only two of which will be mentioned). First, couple and family therapy research is not research on the profession of marriage and family therapy, it is research on the practice of couple and family therapy. Second, marriage and family therapists who want to be up to date on the research must keep up with the research published in psychology and social work journals as well as in family therapy journals if they hope to not become marginalized (Liddle, 1991; Shields et al., 1994). This is a daunting task, and one that is filled with a large number of barriers to its accomplishment. I believe this maintains the gap between research and practice—not because of clinician disinterest in research, but because of the inaccessibility of this information to those whose primary affiliation is marriage and family therapy.[2]

Two advances hold the most promise for bridging the practice-research gap. First, there has been a call to move away from the tightly controlled studies of the efficacy of psychotherapy to the study of the effectiveness of psychotherapy (Pinsof and Wynne, 2000). Second, there has been a trend toward the more frequent use of qualitative methodologies in studies of marriage and family therapy (Moon, Dillon, and Sprenkle, 1990).

Movement Toward Effectiveness Studies

Efficacy studies are those that have tight controls on extraneous variables that might influence the results. These studies typically have a carefully designed **treatment manual** and a **no-treatment control group.** These studies are designed to determine whether a particular type of psychotherapy is more effective than no treatment or another type of treatment. Efficacy studies are as close to a laboratory setting as can be achieved in the study of mental health treatment.

The problem with efficacy studies is that by virtue of their exceedingly tight designs the results are often of little relevance to the real-life practice of psychotherapy. This is not to say that efficacy studies are not important; they are. It is through efficacy studies that we know that treatment is better than no treatment for most mental health and relationship problems.

Effectiveness studies are those that evaluate the real world of clinical practice. Rather than the tight controls that limit the participation in the study to just certain clients meeting certain criteria, and the restrictions on how the model of therapy can be implemented, these studies investigate the real world of clinical practice, as messy as it is. The result of the more widespread use of these type of studies is that the results will be more applicable to the practitioner.

The Increased Use of Qualitative Methodology

In 1990, Sidney Moon and her colleagues published an article in the *Journal of Marital and Family Therapy (JMFT)* advocating the increased use of qualitative methods in family therapy research. Each of the mental health disciplines had seen a growing interest in the use of qualitative research prior to 1990, but this article appeared to punctuate and legitimize the trend in the field of marriage and family therapy. The article, although over twelve years old, is still important reading for serious marriage and family therapy students interested in qualitative research.

Through this paper, Moon, Dillon, and Sprenkle (1990) argued that the increased use of qualitative methods could in fact facilitate the use of research findings in clinical work. They explained that qualitative methods are similar to clinical interviewing and discovery as it occurs in the context of therapy. In both clinical interviewing and most qualitative research, the richness of individual experience is preserved in context and is valued over gross generalizations and group averages. This, they reasoned, would appeal to clinicians and facilitate the use of research findings to inform clinical work.

Although it is unclear whether the increased use of qualitative research has resulted in a lessening of the research-practice gap, I can speak from my own experience—as the director of a marriage and family therapy training program—that most master's-level students appear to be more attracted to qualitative methods in completing their thesis requirements than they are to quantitative methods. This is a consistent phenomena, even when given the option of conducting less time-consuming quantitative investigations within the same area of interest. My students generally explain that they want to produce a thesis that has practical applicability, and they find it difficult to see how quantitative investigations result in the same practical applicability as do qualitative investigations.

WHAT IS RESEARCH?

After discussing the contemporary context of marriage and family therapy research, and before progressing any further in this discussion, it is important to clarify what is considered research in the field of marriage and family therapy. Despite all the talk about statistics, experiments, surveys, sampling, and scientific methods, research is really no more than disciplined inquiry, or in other words, the use of systematic, **replicable procedures** for obtaining and evaluating information. Although I admit that "research" (and even more so the synonymous term "science") can be intimidating, when it is realized that research really is no more than using **systematic procedures** in trying to understand the world, it becomes less scary. To a certain extent, most everyone reading this book is a researcher, because nearly everyone, at one time or another, has used systematic procedures for obtaining information. More important, nearly everyone can become researchers, whether the results of the findings are published or not.

In order to understand research, however, you must realize that it is not the only way of knowing about the world. In his introductory research text, Earl Babbie (1995) explained that a number of commonly used ways of knowing about the world cannot be classified as research. He calls these ways of knowing **natural human inquiry (NHI)** and notes that each of them are prone to producing errors in knowing, primarily because the pursuit of knowledge through each of them is not disciplined. The purpose of research is to arrive at knowledge by overcoming the errors associated with undisciplined inquiry.

Because NHI is such a popular way of learning about the world—and of learning how to do therapy—I will review some of the most popular forms of NHI (see Babbie [1995] for an expanded discussion). My personal favorite form of natural human inquiry—and, I think, a favorite of many of my colleagues—is **personal experience.** Through personal experience one learns about the world firsthand, through trial and error. There is no mistaking the power of this kind of knowledge! Everyone has had experience with this type of learning and, if you are like me, some of these experiences are very good, and some so bad that I hope to never repeat them. The problem with this type of learning is that I often *do* repeat experiences, or I come to a mistaken conclusion about what I learned. So I end up learning the same thing over and over again, with slight variations in experience each time. Another problem with this type of learning is that I never know how transferable it is to other people in other situations. Knowledge obtained in this way is mine and mine only, no matter how much in error my conclusions are. Learning through personal experience is a popular method of knowing used by mental health clinicians. Much of what clinicians know about how to conduct therapy comes from their experience of conducting therapy (Cohen, Sargent, and Sechrest, 1986; Morrow-Bradley and Elliott, 1986). Therapists even gravitate toward therapies or approaches to therapy that fit with their personal experience in relationships and with the world—more so than through research findings (Mahrer, 1988).

Tradition is another popular way of knowing about the world, both in and out of the world of therapy. Tradition is often knowledge that is assumed to be known by everyone because it has been passed down throughout the generations. The problem is that it is not known by everyone, even by those who should be in the know. It is through tradition that I conduct therapy as I was taught in my graduate program, whether that approach to treatment is based on evidence of helpfulness or not. It is through tradition (and convenience) that I conduct therapy in fifty-minute increments. However, the problem with tradition is that it often prevents us from exploring new possibilities and from seeing the obvious.

To obtain knowledge through **authority** is possibly a variation on obtaining knowledge through tradition, but can be distinguished in two important ways. First, knowledge obtained through authority is obtained through people we believe have special knowledge (whether this is true or not) because of their positions of power. Because we see them as authorities, the information they give us carries more weight and we tend to believe it more. Second, knowledge obtained from authorities is typically overt and available to us in the conscious mind. However, information gained through tradition is typically passed to us through covert means and is often not readily available in the conscious mind (many have had the experience of someone questioning why they do something the way they are currently doing it and have become stupefied and can respond only with a "because that's how its always been done"). This isn't necessarily a bad way of knowing (researchers are often seen as authority figures!), but errors in knowing occur when authority figures speak outside their area of expertise or provide information as fact that has little factual support. Politicians, doctors, lawyers, teachers, clergy, parents, and even therapists are examples of authority figures that have great power to influence people in Western societies.

Research, or science, attempts to overcome the deficits of obtaining knowledge through natural human inquiry by subjecting the search for knowledge to principles of disciplined inquiry. Procedures are followed in asking questions and in obtaining data in such a way that error and bias are eliminated. This is really not too much different from what happens in good clinical interviewing (Atkinson, Heath, and Chenail, 1991). The clinician obtains information through a variety of well-designed questions, tasks, or instruments—from a variety of sources that have been planned in advance to elicit certain information.

TYPES OF MARRIAGE AND FAMILY THERAPY RESEARCH

Research in marriage and family therapy is not homogeneous. It takes many different forms, has a variety of purposes, and uses a large number of strategies. To understand marriage and family therapy research, you must understand the different varieties.

Basic and Applied Research

Basic research is done when a researcher wants to understand something better, whereas **applied research** is done when a researcher wants to find solutions to problems (Ellis, 1994). Basic research is undertaken when a researcher is interested in learning more about a particular condition. For example, a researcher who is interested in understanding marital affairs might attempt to identify the degree to which various factors are associated with the occurrence of affairs. The researcher may attempt to determine if factors such as gender, years married, number of children, type of employment, religiosity, permissiveness, and marital satisfaction are associated with the occurrence of affairs. To use a clinical example, a researcher may be interested in the degree to which a particular population, such as Mexican Americans, has access to mental health care. Although both of these research areas may have clinical applicability, they are not applied research.

Applied research on the other hand would attempt to determine the best way of intervening to help couples whose relationships are distressed by an affair, or would attempt to determine how access to mental health care can be improved. As can be imagined, applied research typically follows basic research. As researchers gain a greater understanding for the phenomenon under study, they then are able to develop interventions designed to address the problems being studied (Miklowitz and Hooley, 1998). However, basic and applied research efforts are not necessarily mutually exclusive endeavors. In fact, a single study may have both basic and applied aspects.

Although it has been generally presumed that the sine qua non of applied research has traditionally been the **clinical trial** (developing an intervention or treatment program, implementing it under strict controls, and then evaluating its success), there is significant criticism about this approach to research. In fact, prominent researchers within the field have even criticized this type of research as not clinically applicable (Pinsof and Wynne, 2000). Pinsof and Wynne explain that we should be concerned about two types of applied research. The first, efficacy research, follows strict experimental design principles. The basic question being asked through efficacy research is whether the treatment in question is better than no treatment at all. In general, the answer is a resounding "yes" for nearly every type of therapy studied and for every type of problem studied. Although this information is important, it falls short of being clinically helpful and it really confirms only what is already presumed by nearly every mental health clinician, regardless of discipline or treatment approach. The primary problem with efficacy research is that to ensure that alternative explanations for findings are ruled out, the therapy being evaluated becomes sterile and does not look like the therapy as it would be applied in the real world.

This is where the second type of applied research, effectiveness research, can step in. Through effectiveness research, researchers evaluate the effectiveness of therapy as it is actually conducted in the messy, real world of clinical practice. The drawback to this type of research is that confounding variables abound. It can be unclear whether it was actually the treatment that made the difference or some other variable, such as the exceptional skill of the therapist implementing the treatment or the good advice the client got from his or her hairdresser. The advantage to effectiveness research is that it is actually a test of therapy as it is conducted in the nonlaboratory world of clinical practice and so has immediate relevancy to clinical work.

Qualitative and Quantitative Research

Since the mid-to late 1980s, research in family therapy has undergone a transformation that has resulted in greater acceptability of qualitative research methods (Sprenkle and Moon, 1996). That this transformation occurred within the MFT research community is interesting because it was primarily qualitative research methodologies used by the first family therapists to create their approaches to treatment. However, as one of these founders points out, the research efforts of the past do not resemble the research efforts of today (Wynne, 1983). These early researchers used loosely defined qualitative research strategies with very little concern for controlling **investigator bias.** These early research attempts resulted in study findings that were generally impressionistic. Probably in reaction to the mildly disciplined research of the founders of family therapy and the resulting claims of universal success of their approaches to treatment, researchers attempted to adopt more "scientific" principles in the evaluation of therapies and the study of clinically related material. Research became more experimental, and consequently, almost exclusively quantitative in nature. During this period of time a large number of outcome studies were conducted. Most of these were ones that compared one couple or family treatment to another, or that compared a couple or family treatment to an individual psychotherapy or no treatment. As this transformation in research emphasis became complete, clinicians began to lament that research was no longer applicable to their clinical work. They began to turn away from the exclusive reliance on quantitative methods and to reexplore the value of qualitative methodologies. Although this transformation began before the early 1990s, the publication of the paper by Sidney Moon and her colleagues in *JMFT* (Moon, Dillon, and Sprenkle, 1990) appeared to usher in the acceptability of qualitative research to the study of marriage and family therapy by stimulating a very public debate of the role of both qualitative and quantitative methods (Atkinson, Heath, and Chenail, 1991; Cavell and Snyder, 1991; Moon, Dillon, and Sprenkle, 1991). Until this time, it was difficult if not impossible to find an article based on qualitative research in the leading MFT journals. Yet this paper and the resulting debate appeared to open the minds of journal editors to accept these papers and to stimulate researchers to adopt more rigorous qualitative methodologies in conducting these studies. Today, it seems that the debate has subsided and both quantitative and qualitative methods are accepted as legitimate (Sprenkle and Moon, 1996). To understand the difference between these two methods (and the reason for the debate), you must understand that qualitative and quantitative research are led by different types of research questions, methods, and purposes, resulting in different knowledge.

Quantitative investigations are deductive in nature (the theory or hypothesis drives the collection of data and how the data are interpreted) (Sprenkle and Bischoff, 1995); in essence, "quantitative research aims for rigorous scientific empiricism by counting, comparing, measuring, and subjecting data to statistical analysis" (p. 543). In conducting a quantitative investigation, the researcher articulates questions and hypotheses prior to designing the study and collecting the data, and then designs the study to specifically answer the question being asked. Strict controls are built into the study to limit the effect of the investigator and to limit the degree to which alternative explanations for the results are possible. To control for bias and alternative explanations, variables are well defined beforehand and are reduced to their simplest forms so as to eliminate complexity. Because generalizability of results to a broader population is often the goal, **sampling theory** is often used to guide the identification and recruitment of subjects from whom data will be collected.

Qualitative investigations are inductive (the theory or explanation emerges from the data itself). Using qualitative methods, researchers try not to limit or place restrictive controls on the data or data collection with the hope that this openness will lead to previously undiscovered knowledge. Qualitative investigations tend to be exploratory in nature and recognize the influence of the investigator on the data being collected. Investigator bias is addressed through the identification and articulation of the sources of bias and through the use of multiple data collection methods and data sources (a quality control measure called **triangulation**) and **time in the field** (the amount of time the investigator spends with the **participants** [subjects] or with the data). Data are analyzed using narrative analytic strategies that facilitate theory development and that preserve the richness of the data in the results.

To make a gross generalization (meaning that there are exceptions), quantitative investigations focus on the verification of knowledge, whereas qualitative investigations focus on the discovery of knowledge. Quantitative investigations focus on the elimination of alternative explanations, whereas qualitative investigations attempt to facilitate the discovery of alternative explanations, if they exist. Quantitative investigations focus on reducing data to something that can be counted and numerically compared, whereas qualitative investigations focus on the narrative nature of the data and the context from which the data come. Quantitative investigations are designed so that results will be generalizable to the larger population, whereas qualitative investigations are designed so that the uniqueness of this set of subjects is emphasized.

Outcome and Process Research

Clinical research can be described in terms of outcome and process. **Outcome research** is designed to determine the results of a course of therapy generally or of an intervention or set of interventions specifically. For example, a researcher may attempt to determine the long-term or short-term outcomes as a result of a particular treatment. Those engaged in outcome research are often interested in the degree to which change has taken place, change is sustained over time, the intervention impacts other aspects of functioning, and the treatment of interest produced better results than another treatment (or no treatment).

Process research is designed to determine what happens during therapy. For example, determining changes in client resistance throughout the course of therapy would be an example of process research. Those engaged in process research are often interested in moment-by-moment changes in client experience of treatment, the interaction between the therapist and client or among family members, or the processes involved in change.

Although the earliest family therapy research was concerned using the process dimensions of therapy, including how families interacted with one another and the way in which intervention into the family took place, researchers quickly began concentrating more on the outcomes of treatment as family therapy developed. The most prominent research of the 1970s and early 1980s tended to be outcome-oriented research. However, beginning in the 1980s—probably due to the increased sophistication of research and the realization that significant differences among therapies were hard to find—researchers began to return to the study of the process of therapy. At this time, publications of studies on moment-by-moment in-session changes, clients' experience of therapy, and the nature of intervention began to appear. This resurgence in interest in the process of therapy within the context of the proliferation of outcome studies led to what was called by Alan Gurman and his colleagues "the new process perspective" (Gurman, Kniskern, and Pinsof, 1986). Through this perspective, researchers will often not conduct an exclusively process or outcome study, but will integrate both process and outcome indices within the same study. To do this, researchers focus on **incremental outcomes** within the context of therapy that lead up to the overall outcome of treatment. In this way, researchers are able to understand the incremental processes of change that occur within the course of treatment as well as the incremental outcomes associated with specific interventions. Two examples of this new process perspective will help you understand the value of integrating process and outcome research.

Gerald Patterson and his colleagues at the Oregon Social Learning Center (Chamberlain et al., 1984; Patterson and Chamberlain, 1988; Patterson and Forgatch, 1985) examined the relationship between therapist interventions and client resistance. These investigators developed a measure for evaluating client resistance on a incident-by-incident basis at the beginning, middle, and end phases of treatment. They also developed a measure of moment-by-moment therapist techniques that could be grouped into categories of support, confront, and teach. They measured both therapist use of technique at the various stages of therapy and the associated client expression of resistance. They found client resistance to be at its lowest at the beginning and ending phases of treatment and highest in the middle phase. The middle phase of treatment was also the time when therapists were more likely to engage in teach and confront interventions. Poorer outcomes (e.g., dropping out of treatment) were associated with a higher proportion of teach and confront techniques in the beginning phases of treatment (and consequently with more resistance at the beginning phase as well). This research has immediate treatment implications.

Leslie Greenberg and Susan Johnson refined their approach to couple therapy, emotionally focused couple therapy, through the implementation of an integrated process and outcome research approach (Greenberg et al., 1993; Greenberg, James, and Conry, 1988; Johnson and Greenberg, 1988). These researchers studied specific events and occurrences in therapy where, according to theory, they expected change to occur. They found that emotionally focused couple therapy promotes more **affiliative behaviors** in couples during the latter stages of treatment, that experiencing underlying emotions is positively associated with conflict resolution, and that one partner's **intimate self-disclosure** is positively associated with affiliative responsiveness in the other. They also found that clients identified the **critical incidents** of successful therapy to be expressing underlying emotions, understanding one's own experience of the relationship, taking responsibility for one's own experience, and having experience and emotion validated by one's partner. The result of this research is a refined approach to couple therapy that emphasizes empirically validated treatment processes for successful outcomes.

WHAT DOES THE RESEARCH LITERATURE SAY?

Marriage and family therapy research has moved away from the comparative studies of the past that pit one therapy against another. The state of the art of family therapy outcome research concerns the outcomes of couple or family therapy in the treatment of specific problem areas (Gurman, Kniskern, and Pinsof, 1986; Piercy and Sprenkle, 1990; Sprenkle and Bischoff, 1995). However, most of the studies conducted to determine the effectiveness of couple and family therapy have used a very small number of the hundreds of therapies that exist. The reason for this is quite practical. To study the effectiveness of a therapy on a specific problem area, the outcomes of the therapy must be able to be operationalized. In other words, to conduct an outcome study, it must be possible to measure change in some way. Pragmatically, this means that therapies that are primarily focused on behavioral change are more amenable to empirical study. Probably more important, therapists who espouse such therapies are more likely to ask questions about the effectiveness of their therapies that are more likely to be able to be operationalized.

Therefore, in the field of marriage and family therapy, behavioral, structural, and strategic therapies or therapies that have ties to these models of treatment are more likely to be those used in studies of the effectiveness of marriage and family therapy. Therapies that are focused on producing growth or change, which is difficult to operationalize, have only rarely been subjected to empirical investigation. For example, therapies that are narrative, experiential, or transgenerational in nature have rarely been used when evaluating family therapy outcomes. I suspect there are two primary reasons that these therapies are underrepresented in the research literature: first, their desired outcomes are difficult to operationalize and consequently measure. For example, how do you measure the authoring of a new story or detriangulation? Second, advocates of these therapies (especially narrative therapy) often criticize traditional research methods (Gurman, Kniskern, and Pinsof, 1986) as reductionistic, arbitrary, and not useful to the real world of clinical practice (e.g., Griffith and Griffith, 1990; Kaye, 1990; Tomm, 1983). Studies that are conducted investigating these more **aesthetic therapies** (Keeney and Sprenkle, 1983) tend not to be published in refereed journals. When they are published, they are often found in more obscure journals with a limited readership.

It would be a mistake to assume that this means aesthetic therapies are less effective than **pragmatic therapies** just because they do not lend themselves to study using traditional research methodology, especially in light of the common factors research that is currently being conducted. It may be that the key determining factor to the success of couple and family therapy is the marshaling of couple or family resources through the involvement in therapy of multiple members of the family (Russell Crane, personal communication, 2000). This would certainly be consistent with the commonly used definition of family therapy found in the research literature: family therapy is therapy which is conducted with more than one family member involved in the session greater than 50 percent of the time (Shadish et al., 1985).

In October 1995, William Pinsof and Lyman Wynne (1995a) guest-edited a special issue of *JMFT* subtitled "The Effectiveness of Marital and Family Therapy" in which leading researchers in the field summarized the research findings within the mental health field as they pertained to the practice of marriage and family therapy. Although published in 1995, the research reviews found in this special issue are consistent with what is currently known about the effectiveness of the practice of couple and family therapy in the treatment of a wide variety of presenting problems. I recommend this issue of *JMFT* to any student seriously interested in learning more about what we know about the effectiveness of MFT. Other excellent recent reviews have also been published (see Alexander et al., 1994; Baucom et al., 1998; Bergin and Garfield, 1994; Friedlander, 1998; Pinsof, Wynne, and Hambright, 1996). In 2000, the editors of the special issue of *JMFT* reiterated the general conclusions of this endeavor by reasserting that as a result of research in this area, the following can be stated fairly conclusively:

1. Couple therapy (CT) or family therapy (FT) is better than treatment that does not involve family members for treating adult schizophrenia (FT), depression in women in distressed marriages (CT), marital distress (CT), adult alcoholism and drug abuse (FT), adolescent conduct disorders (FT), adolescent drug abuse (FT), anorexia in young adolescent females (FT), childhood autism (FT), aggression and noncompliance in attentioin deficit-hyperactivity disorder (FT), dementia (FT), and cardiovascular risk factors (FT).
2. CT or FT is better than no treatment for all of the above clients and disorders as well as for adult obesity (CT), adult hypertension (CT), adolescent obesity (FT), anorexia in younger adolescents (FT), childhood conduct disorders (FT), childhood obesity (FT), and almost all childhood chronic illnesses (FT).
3. There are no studies that show that CFT has negative or destructive effects. [Note: CFT refers to couple and family therapy.]
4. There are insufficient data to support the superiority of any particular form of CFT over any other (meta-analytic findings).
5. CFT appears to be more cost effective than standard hospital treatment for adult schizophrenia and unipolar depression as well as residential treatment for adolescent conduct disorders.
6. CFT is not sufficient unto itself to treat a number of severe and chronic mental disorders such as schizophrenia, major unipolar and bipolar affective disorders, addictions, autism, and severe conduct disorders. However, CFT significantly enhances the treatment packages for these disorders. (Pinsof and Wynne, 2000, p. 2)

My intention is not to provide an exhaustive review of the extant research literature. However, it will be instructive to review a few of some of the most important areas of research in the field.

The General Effectiveness of Couple Therapy

Couple therapy has consistently been found effective for reducing marital conflict and increasing marital satisfaction (Alexander et al., 1994;

Baucom et al., 1998; Bray and Jouriles, 1995; Johnson and Lebow, 2000; Pinsof, Wynne, and Hambright, 1996). This is true regardless of the therapeutic approach being studied (Dunn and Schwebel, 1995). However, the degree of effectiveness is debatable. Couple therapy has been found to produce superior outcomes to no treatment and wait list/placebo controls in efficacy studies. Some evidence even suggests that couple interventions reduce the likelihood of divorce within two years after the completion of treatment (Jacobson, Schmaling, and Holtzworth-Munroe, 1987). However, other studies have found that although the short-term benefits of couple therapy are evident, it is difficult to maintain these benefits over longer periods of time.

The primary outcome measures used for studying the success of couple therapy are the continued presence of relationship conflict and the occurrence of dissolution or divorce. It is reasonable to assume that a desirable outcome of couple therapy would be greater relationship satisfaction and stability, but this may not be a reasonable expectation for all couple therapy. Jacobson and Addis (1993) explain that couples who have better outcomes are those whose partners at the beginning of treatment are less distressed and more emotionally engaged with each other. These couples also tend to be younger, with less relationship history, and with less individual psychopathology. This may mean that couples whose relationships are healthier and who have had fewer attempts to solve relationship difficulties are more likely to benefit from couple therapy. It also may mean that for some couples seeking couple therapy, their problems may be insurmountable. For these couples, relationship dissolution may in fact be a *successful* outcome of a course of treatment. It is interesting to note that no investigators have asked couples who dissolved their relationships after therapy whether they felt helped by therapy (Bray and Jouriles, 1995).

A large number of studies have been conducted to determine both the process and outcome of couple therapy; however, nearly all of these studies have examined just three models of therapy: behavioral marital therapy (or cognitive-behavioral marital therapy), emotionally focused couple therapy, and insight-oriented marital therapy. So, although it can be said that couple therapy is generally effective, it must be said with reservation because of the limited number of clinical models that have been subjected to inquiry. However, the three models that have been subjected to the most rigorous investigation each represent very different underlying assumptions about the nature of change and the role of the therapist in producing change. For example, the behavioral marital therapy model emphasizes the role of overt behavioral and interactional change with the therapist intervening actively into the interactional sequence. However, emotionally focused couple therapy and insight-oriented couple therapy, while also addressing the overt interactional experience between intimate adults, have as underlying assumptions the role of internal emotional experience and internal subconscious experience respectively. So, emotional experience and subconscious experience become the targets of therapeutic intervention. Although the investigated models are few, in their fundamental differentness they do account for a broad range of ways in which problem development and change can be conceptualized, making it easy to justify a statement of therapeutic effectiveness.

Couple and Family Therapy in the Treatment of Specific Problem Areas

Schizophrenia

It is fitting that the discussion of the effectiveness of family interventions on specific problem areas begin with schizophrenia. Many of the prominent early family therapy models were derived from the study of individuals showing schizophrenic symptoms and their families (Broderick and Schrader, 1981; Goldstein and Miklowitz, 1995). These early models have provided the foundation for many of the family therapy approaches currently being practiced. This area of study also exemplifies the differences in family therapy research since the 1950s, demonstrating change in focus toward multimodal treatments, the acknowledgement of the role biology plays in the development of psychopathology, and the limitations of family intervention. It is also fitting because some of the best-designed studies in the field have addressed the impact of family intervention on the management of schizophrenia.

That family therapy has its roots in the study of one of the most severe forms of psychopathology is interesting and perplexing for many students. However, when you consider that family dynamics are more obvious under conditions of chronic distress than under conditions of the waxing and waning of normal life stress, the birth of family therapy from the study of families in which one member has schizophrenic symptoms makes sense. If interventions designed to change the family dynamic in this extreme situation were found to be effective (and they were found to be effective using the impressionist methodology of the 1950s), then it makes sense that they would also apply to less extreme situations.

As early family therapy researchers began studying individuals with schizophrenia, their attentions were quickly directed toward the families of their subjects and patients. It was the obviousness of the family dynamics associated with severe psychopathology that attracted the early researchers to this area of study and that resulted in their early experimentation with interventions designed to create changes in the family dynamic with the hope of alleviating schizophrenic functioning. However, unlike the research on schizophrenia today, the research of the late 1950s and early 1960s considered family pathology to be the root cause of schizophrenia. The assumption was that an individual essentially developed schizophrenia in reaction to, as a defense against, or as a result of severe family pathology. The belief was that under the most severely pathological of family interactions, psychotic symptomotology in one member would be a logical result. This also led to the belief that symptoms point to underlying systemic pathology. Therefore, symptoms carry a function within the family either to point toward underlying systemic pathology (e.g., strategic-based approaches) or to scapegoat one member so the rest of the family can be free to be more functional (e.g., transgenerational approaches).

As family interventions gained in popularity and began to be used more generally, family research in the area of schizophrenia essentially stopped. In fact, nearly twenty years passed before renewed research and treatment interest in this area emerged. In the 1970s clinicians began again to see the influence of the family on schizophrenic symptoms and to take notice of the family dynamics associated with schizophrenic symptomology. As clinicians more frequently used aftercare treatment programs that would place patients in greater proximity to their families sooner after stabilization, they began to notice the resurgence of symptomatic behavior once the patients were placed in prolonged contact with their families (Goldstein and Miklowitz, 1995). However, this time around, a new set of assumptions about the **etiology** of schizophrenia and improved research methodologies informed both the studies and the treatments.

Underlying both the current research and family treatments being studied is the use of a **stress-vulnerability model** to explain etiology. In other words, unlike the assumption informing the early research efforts, this model states that environmental stress alone is probably not sufficient to result in the development of schizophrenia. Biological predispositions to schizophrenia are also assumed to exist. It is these biological factors that create a vulnerability to schizophrenia. Given sustained environmental stress coupled with this biological vulnerability, the condition may develop (Anderson, Reiss, and Hogarty, 1986).

In my opinion, two very important developments have come out of the modern family research on schizophrenia. These developments have since been successfully applied to other psychopathological conditions. First is the development of the construct of **expressed emotion** and second is the emphasis on **psychoeducational family treatments** within the context of a multimodal treatment package.

Expressed emotion (EE) refers to the degree to which a person is subjected to behaviors such as criticism or harsh tones of voice from family members, spouse, or partner (Anderson, Reiss, and Hogarty, 1986). When criticism of the person characterizes his or her most intimate interactions, that individual is said to be subjected to high EE. Low EE is present when these close family relationships are free of criticism and other belittling and degrading behaviors. High EE families tend to be very emotionally reactive to the patient and his or her expression of symptoms. EE has been the primary measure of environmental stress in family studies of schizophrenia and both observational (e.g., Falloon et al., 1985) and self-report (Shields et al., 1994) measures have been developed to assess the level of EE. Thus, it is believed that schizophrenia occurs as the result of an interaction between biological vulnerability and environmental stress.

Research has found that individuals with schizophrenia subjected to high EE after discharge from hospitalization are more likely to relapse than those for whom treatment was able to produce decreases in EE (Leff et al., 1982; Falloon et al., 1985). The Leff et al. (1982) study was specifically designed to determine the curative characteristics of the treatment they provided. They found that it was the aspects of the treatment designed to produce decreases in EE that accounted for the greatest variation in treatment outcome. In other words, individuals who have schizophrenia who also have family members that are critical, demanding, and judgmental in words and actions are more likely to relapse and to have more severe symptomotology than those who do not have critical family members. It is difficult to say whether high EE creates schizophrenia, or the stress of living with someone who has schizophrenia creates critical responses by family members, but it is instructive to note that treatment focused on reducing EE is associated with fewer relapses and greater compliance with medication regimens.

The second major advancement produced by this line of research concerns the development of psychoeducational family treatment models that are provided in the context of a multimodal treatment program. First, psychotic symptomotology is controlled through the use of neuroleptic medication. Environmental stress is primarily addressed through a behaviorally based psychoeducational treatment package that includes the family in treatment. Research has found that neither the therapeutic nor the educational components alone (with medication) are as effective as the integrated psychoeducational family treatment, and that medication alone has the highest relapse rates of any treatment (Hogarty et al., 1986).

The psychoeducational family treatments studied are founded in behavioral therapy treatment principles. These treatments emphasize

1. the early engagement of the family,
2. family education about schizophrenia including its etiology, course, and symptoms,
3. recommendations for coping with the disorder,
4. communication skills training,
5. problem-solving training, and
6. crisis intervention. (Goldstein and Miklowitz, 1995)

The family is taught that schizophrenia is a disorder that resides in the individual and is biologically determined and that it can be exacerbated or calmed by the family's influence.

Goldstein and Miklowitz (1995) have summarized the findings regarding family treatment of schizophrenia. They conclude that convincing evidence suggests that medication management coupled with behaviorally based psychoeducational family therapy are more effective than medical management alone and than medical management with individual therapy.

Affective Disorders

Most of the research on the effectiveness of psychotherapies in the treatment of depression and other mood disorders has been conducted using individually based therapies (Prince and Jacobson, 1995). In general, these studies have found that individual therapies (typically cognitive or interpersonal therapy) are successful in treating depression. Some studies have even found that psychotherapy-only treatments are as effective as medication-only treatments (Krupnick et al., 1996). Treatments combining both medication management and individual psychotherapy tend to produce the most successful outcomes, with close to 60 percent of patients recovering from unipolar depression in clinical trials (Elkin et al., 1989).

However, do not forget the 40 percent of patients who do not show improvement. Although there is a statistically significant difference in **recidivism** (the recurrence of symptoms) between depressives who are treated and those who are not, the recurrence rate of symptoms (Maxmen and Ward, 1995) in the treated population is about 50 percent! Therefore, although psychotherapy may be important in reducing the severity of acute symptomotology, it is far from being overwhelmingly successful in producing longitudinal absence of symptoms.

Depression and other mood disorders are especially resistant to intervention. This is made evident not only by the high rate of recidivism in the treated population but also by the surprisingly high rate of patients not completing treatment (Prince and Jacobson, 1995). Some prominent couple and family researchers (e.g., Prince and Jacobson, 1995) have speculated that one of the reasons for this resistance might be the recursive influence of depression and couple and family relationships. Because of this contextual influence, couple and family therapy has been seen as a preferred treatment for depression by many within the field.

Research on depression has shown that a strong association exists between depression and couple and family dysfunction (Prince and Jacobson, 1995). Studies have shown that the presence of intrafamily conflict is common for people who are depressed and that individuals from families in which conflict is common are at higher risk for developing depression. Research has also shown that the presence of couple and family conflict is predictive of relapse in treated populations and that depressive episodes are more likely to occur after episodes of couple conflict or intimate relationship disruption or interpersonal loss.

Of course, not all people with depression are in conflictual relationships, so one cannot say that couple or family conflict causes depression—but it certainly appears to make it worse. Additional support for the importance of the relationship between depression and couple and family relating is found in research addressing the protective and curative features of these relationships on the development and recurrence of depressive symptomotology (e.g., Jacobson et al., 1993). Studies have shown that depression is less common among people who are married than those who are single. Although the quality of the marital relationship has been found to be more of a protective factor than just the fact of being married, the protective function of the couple relationship has not been found to be compensated for in its absence through relationships with family and friends. When someone who is prone to develop depression or who is depressed has a supportive spouse and family, he or she is less likely to have severe symptoms and is less likely to relapse.

As mentioned before, it would be impossible—based on the existing research—to conclude that couple and family relationship dysfunction causes depression. Frankly, it is difficult to live with (and provide therapy for) someone who is chronically depressed. Their hopelessness and unhappiness is frustrating, discouraging, and just plain not very fun for partners and family members. Depression wreaks havoc not only on the individual, but also on those with whom they are in intimate relationships (e.g., Beach and O'Leary, 1993; Billings and Moos, 1983).

The research previously cited, which found that interactions between spouses in which one is depressed are more conflictual and less caring than in relationships where depression is not present, could also be explained in terms of the influence of depression on these relationships. Parenting and relationships with children have also been found to be impacted by depression. Some researchers have found that depressed women are likely to experience greater hostility and resentment toward their children than women who are not depressed. The children of depressed women are more likely to experience emotional and behavioral problems. The effects of depression on the family do not stop when the depressive episode is over or when it has been successfully treated. Coryell and colleagues (1993) found in their five-year posttreatment follow-up of successfully treated patients that relationship conflict and other relationship impairment continued in 40 to 50 percent of the patients studied.

Because of the reciprocal influence of environmental stress and depression, researchers and clinicians have hypothesized that couple and family therapy would produce superior outcomes to individual therapy in the treatment of depression. However, disappointingly, this has not been found to be the case. Probably the most secure statement that can be made based on the research done to this point is that couple therapy is no less or no more effective than individual therapy in the treatment of depression when evaluating success based on the amelioration of symptoms and relapse rates. Both treatments are more effective than no treatment.

Couple therapies (behavioral marital therapies [BMT]) have been those subjected to the most careful empirical investigation. Family therapies have been investigated only rarely and, although promising, we do not have sufficient information to comment on their effectiveness.

Results produced by the research programs of Beach and O'Leary (1993; O'Leary and Beach, 1990; O'Leary, Risso, and Beach, 1990) and Jacobson (Jacobson et al., 1991, 1993) serve as examples of the type of research being done in this area. In both of these research programs behavioral marital therapy was compared with individual cognitive therapy and a wait list control condition. Both sets of researchers used women with depression as subjects. Women in both studies were randomly assigned to treatment conditions and were evaluated for severity of depression and relationship satisfaction using the **Dyadic Adjustment Scale (DAS)** (Spanier, 1976) both before and after receiving the assigned treatment. Neither group of researchers found significant differences between those clients receiving BMT and those receiving individual cognitive therapy. However, both found that those receiving BMT were likely to score higher on their measure of couple satisfaction. Long-term follow-up with these couples also indicated that they were able to maintain these improvements in relationship satisfaction. Jacobson's studies examined treatment outcomes more carefully and found that in the BMT condition increased DAS scores were evident only when at least one spouse indicated relationship distress. If the relationship was not determined to be in distress, then BMT and individual cognitive therapy were equally effective at reducing depressive symptoms and in producing improvements in relationship satisfaction. Interestingly, neither Beach and O'Leary nor Jacobson were able to find significant differences in relapse rates at one-year follow-up after treatment was completed, further indicating no significant differences between individual and couple therapy in the treatment of depression.

Why devote so much attention to the discussion of the treatment of depression when no significant differences between treatment are found? There are two reasons: First, depression is one of the most prominent and frequently occurring forms of psychopathology (especially among women) (Maxmen and Ward, 1995). Therapists working with couples and families will need to be competent in working with depression.

Second, this area of research is a perfect example of the difficulty in making inferences to inform treatment from the results of basic research. In this case, research evidence linking couple and family relationship distress with depression leads logically to the hypothesis that addressing relationship distress in the context of therapy will result in improved treatment outcomes for depression. Yet this very reasonable hypothesis has not been supported through clinical trials; no significant differences among therapies have been found. This is not to say that couple and family therapy is not preferable in the treatment of depression over individual psychotherapy—especially when treating women in distressed relationships. In fact, we can extrapolate from the research literature that increased support from the nondistressed partner—regardless of the pretreatment level of relationship distress—assists in recovery and the prevention of relapse (Prince and Jacobson, 1995). At least a few conjoint sessions should be conducted during the course of treatment, even in cases of nondistressed relationship and individual treatment.

Eating Disorders

Similar to schizophrenia, eating disorders is an area of special historical interest in the field of family therapy. When they think about structural family therapy, most serious students will recall Salvador Minuchin's studies on the role of environmental stress (or family dysfunctional interactions) regarding the exacerbation of psychosomatic symptoms, first in individuals with diabetes and second in individuals with anorexia nervosa (Minuchin, 1978; Minuchin et al., 1975; Minuchin, Rosman, and Baker, 1978). As with the early studies of schizophrenia, the family dynamics associated with eating disorders were so striking and obvious that they became a source of interest for Minuchin. He found that through family intervention, exacerbation of symptoms was decreased.

A more recent, well-designed, and highly acclaimed research program (Dare et al., 1990; Russell et al., 1987; Szmukler et al., 1985) has been carried out that has evaluated the effectiveness of family therapy in the treatment of eating disorders. These researchers developed a treatment program based on structural and strategic family therapies and compared this family-based treatment to an individual supportive treatment that appears to be similar to a treatment-as-usual condition. Through random assignment of patients to the various conditions and the comparison of differential effectiveness based on age of the patient at the time of onset of the eating disorder, the researchers found some interesting results. First, the findings suggest that family therapy is generally more effective than individual therapy when the age of onset of the eating disorder is younger than eighteen years old. However, evidence suggests that individual supportive psychotherapy is more effective when the age of onset is eighteen years old and older.

In addition to providing evidence for the effectiveness of family therapy in the treatment of eating disorders, the primary significance of this line of research is underscoring the importance of contextual issues, such as the age of the patient, when designing treatment plans. Although it would be inappropriate to conclude that family therapy should not be used in cases of later onset anorexia, it did call into question the universal application of family therapy to all eating-disordered cases. Clinicians should carefully consider the needs of the individual client before rushing to a judgment regarding which treatment modality is best.

Substance Abuse

Research in the area of substance abuse has essentially followed three lines of inquiry. The first two concern the family treatment of drug abuse in adolescents and adults; the third is the family's treatment of alcoholism. Probably not so surprisingly, the study of the family treatment of adolescent drug abuse has far outpaced the study of the other two lines of research (Liddle and Dakof, 1995; Sprenkle and Bischoff, 1995; Stanton and Shadish, 1997). I say "not surprising" because the well-established and well-organized treatment provider milieu has a long tradition of providing substance abuse treatment using individual and group treatment formats. This tradition is especially prominent in the treatment of adult substance abuse disorders. Therefore, it is probably more acceptable within the treatment provider community to accept the prospect of the effectiveness of family therapy in the treatment of adolescent substance abuse than in the area of adult substance abuse. However, as Liddle and Dakof (1995) point out, the U.S. federal government has a long history of encouraging studies of the effectiveness of family therapy in the treatment of substance abuse disorders across the life span. Yet family therapy studies of adult substance abuse disorders have not been forthcoming, and those that were started have ended prematurely. This is an example of how the current mental health treatment environment influences which studies are conducted and even the implementation of research findings to practice. There are several fine studies of the effectiveness of family therapy in the treatment of substance abuse problems in both adolescents and adults, and yet clinicians are still reluctant to change their practice to reflect these research findings.

Although there are several excellently designed research programs that have investigated the effectiveness of family therapy in the treatment of adolescent drug abuse (e.g., Azrin et al., 1994; Joanning et al., 1992; Lewis et al., 1990; Stanton, Todd, and Associates, 1982), the research of Jose Szapocznik and his colleagues in Miami Florida was the first to verify the effectiveness of family therapy in this area (Liddle and Dakof, 1995).

Szapocznik and his colleagues conducted a series of studies, published throughout the 1980s and 1990s, in which they evaluated the effectiveness of an integrated structural-strategic family therapy treatment model. They found that the application of their family therapy treatment model was profoundly effective—reducing drug abstinence rates from 7 to 80 percent (Szapocznik et al., 1983, 1986, 1989, 1990). These changes were maintained by adolescents for up to one year after the completion of treatment. Not only did adolescents stop using substances as a result of therapy, the researchers also were able to document improved family functioning and overall target adolescent behavior. Interestingly, these treatment benefits were found regardless of whether the therapist was working with the whole family or with just the adolescent from the structural-strategic family therapy model. This is significant because this is one of the first (and only) attempts to demonstrate that family therapy works regardless of the number of participants in the therapy room.

The Szapocznik et al. (1988) research has also validated the effectiveness of engagement strategies. It is a well-known fact that dropout rates in the treatment of substance abusers in general and adolescent substance abusers in particular is incredibly high (Liddle and Dakof, 1995). Szapocznik tested the effectiveness of an intensive family therapy-based model of engagement. He found that the intensive family therapy engagement strategy that included phone calls to and visits with family members in their homes prior to the first session of therapy significantly improved the therapist's ability to engage adolescents and their families in therapy. Those that were engaged using the intensive engagement strategy were also more likely to complete treatment than those engaged using a less intensive engagement as usual procedure. Szapocznik and colleagues found that use of the intensive engagement procudure was successful in 93 percent of the cases, compared with 42 percent in the engagement as usual group.

M. Duncan Stanton and Thomas Todd (Stanton, Todd, and Associates, 1982) began a research program in the late 1970s that serves as the best example of research on the efficacy of family therapy in the treatment of adult substance abuse disorder. Stanton and Todd randomly assigned male heroine addicts who were all in their early to midtwenties and veterans to a paid family therapy condition, an unpaid family therapy condition, an anthropological/educational movie condition, and a standard nonfamily therapy treatment condition. Family therapy treatment was conducted using an integrated structural-strategic family therapy treatment approach. These researchers found that family therapy produced significantly better outcomes than did the educational treatment and the nonfamily therapy treatment. In fact, the differences between family therapy and nonfamily therapy treatments were quite striking, with more than double the rate of improvement in the family therapy conditions. Unfortunately, the Stanton and Todd research program was not continued by the investigators, and subsequent nonprogrammatic studies by other investigators have not found the dramatic results of effectiveness that Stanton and Todd achieved. However, these other studies have at least found family interventions to be as effective as individually based or group-based interventions.

Behavior Disorders in Children

Most therapists, regardless of their approach to treatment, would not think twice about using a family-based treatment for child behavior problems. This may be a reason why there are literally hundreds of studies on the treatment of child behavior problems (Kazdin, 1994). In the field of marriage and family therapy, the systemic family therapies (e.g., structural, strategic) could be considered logical choices to guide treatment plans addressing childhood behavior problems. However, studies of the efficacy and effectiveness of these models of therapy are surprisingly absent. Despite this absence of traditional family therapies, there appears to be consensus among writers within the field that family-based treatments are the treatments of choice when it comes to treating childhood behavior problems (Estrada and Pinsof, 1995; Kazdin, 1987, 1991, 1994; Hazelrigg, Cooper, and Borduin, 1987; Henggeler, Borduin, and Mann, 1992; Tolan, Cromwell, and Brasswell, 1986).

The most well-researched approach to treatment in this area is a behaviorally based set of approaches to treatment called parent management training (Estrada and Pinsof, 1995). Parent management training is conducted by working primarily with parents. Parents are instructed in how to observe their child's behavior and how to design interventions based on behavioral principles to change the behavior of their child. All the primary interventions take place at home and are implemented by the parents themselves. Work with the therapist is typically time limited and sessions are highly structured and consistent across therapists.

This approach to treating conduct problems in children has been found to be very successful, with treatment outcomes being maintained years after work with the therapist has stopped. It has also been found that the gains resulting from parent management training are generalized to other behaviors in the child and the siblings. Improvements in marital quality and other areas of family functioning that have not been the focus of treatment have also been documented. Research in this area is so far advanced that investigators have even attempted to determine those client and therapist variables that mediate successful outcome (no other area of family therapy research is this far advanced). Researchers have found that socially and economically disadvantaged families and families who are isolated fair worse in treatment than those who do not possess these risk factors. Treatments based on the parent management training principles have been developed specifically to address these risk factors. These modified treatments have also been found to be effective.

Delinquency in Adolescents

Delinquency refers specifically to adolescents who are in legal trouble. Although many delinquent adolescents are still treated individually and in isolation of their families, research has generally shown family therapy to be a treatment with better and more sustainable outcomes than individual therapy, probation and work programs (Tolan, Cromwell, and Brasswell, 1986). These findings have led reviewers of the literature to generally conclude that family therapy is the treatment of choice based upon outcome research in the treatment of adolescent delinquency (Chamberlain and Rosicky, 1995; Gurman and Kniskern, 1978; Henggeler, Borduin, and Mann, 1992; Kazdin, 1994; Tolan, Cromwell, and Brasswell, 1986).

One of the most original and noteworthy programs of research in the area of adolescent delinquency was begun by James Alexander and his colleagues in the early 1970s. Alexander developed what he calls functional family therapy (FFT) which is an integrated behavioral, structural, and strategic approach to treatment. The goal of FFT is to develop and implement a treatment plan to address the family and individual needs for proximity and distance. The idea behind this therapy is that all behavior is an attempt to meet needs for proximity or distance. Successful treatment must respect the family members' attempts to meet these needs. Functional family therapists do not attempt to challenge the validity of the needs; rather, they offer alternative meanings to behaviors used to meet these needs or suggest alternative behaviors that can be used to accomplish the same goals of proximity or distance (Alexander and Parsons, 1982).

Alexander began his program of research by studying adolescents referred by the courts to therapy because of "soft delinquency" behavior (e.g., minor theft, truancy, running away) (Alexander and Parsons, 1982; Parsons and Alexander, 1973). He randomly assigned adolescents to an FFT condition, a family group therapy condition, a psychodynamic family therapy condition, and a no-treatment condition. The FFT condition was found to produce results superior to each of the other conditions, and these results were sustained up to two and a half years later. They also found that siblings of adolescents treated with FFT also had lower rates of delinquent behavior at the two-and-a-half-year follow-up than did siblings of those adolescents receiving the alternative treatments (Klein, Alexander, and Parsons, 1977). This research has been successfully replicated throughout the United States by many different research teams (Alexander, Holtzworth-Munroe, and Jameson, 1994).

FFT has grown in popularity, especially among psychologists, to become one of the most well researched approaches to therapy in existence today. It is unfortunate that the approach is not as well recognized in the profession of marriage and family therapy, especially given the strong research support for the approach that is based on systemic principles. This may be due to the fact that James Alexander himself is a psychologist and so he has done most of his publishing in psychology journals.

Process Research and Common Factors

Couple and family therapy is successful. What accounts for success? What are those factors or characteristics of the therapy, the therapist, the client, or context in which treatment is conducted that lead to success? Although there are some exceptions, researchers generally rely on process research to answer these questions.

In general, process research is not as well developed as is outcome research. This is especially true in the study of couple and family therapies (Alexander, Holtzworth-Munroe, and Jameson, 1994). In fact, most of what is known about the process of change has come from the study of psychotherapy in general (typically individually focused treatments) and not from the study of couple and family therapy.

One of the most notable exceptions to this has been the study of emotionally focused couple therapy (Johnson and Greenberg, 1988; Greenberg and Johnson, 1988). In fact, Johnson and Greenberg claim that the refinement of their model of therapy is the direct result of process research. For example, they conducted a study of the most successful emotionally focused couples therapy sessions. Sessions were chosen based on both therapist and client ratings of success. Transcripts were made of the identified sessions and were intensively analyzed using a previously established coding system. The results of this research demonstrated that the most productive sessions were ones in which the members of the couple showed higher levels of experiencing (explorations of new feelings and experiences) and greater frequencies of self-disclosure, sharing with the spouse, and understanding responses directed toward the spouse.

Of course, findings such as these have direct implications for treatment. In this case, the investigators used these findings to refine their treatment approach to emphasize the importance of designing interventions that specifically target these indicators of success. However the degree to which therapy- or model-related factors contribute, in and of themselves, to therapy outcomes is unclear. I mention this because a growing body of research suggests that client variables and, to a lesser extent, therapist variables account for the greatest amount of variation in treatment outcome, regardless of treatment approach used. These factors have come to be known as **common factors,** meaning that they are present in and affect all therapeutic approaches.

The Most Important Determinant of Treatment Success

Research has found that what the client brings to bear contributes the most to determining treatment success (Garfield, 1994). Client perception of the presenting problem and motivation to change, chronicity of the problem and pretreatment relationship conflict (Bray and Jouriles, 1995), socioeconomic status and ethnicity (Sue, Zane, and Young, 1994), and years married and number of children (Allgood and Crane, 1991) are all examples of variables clients bring to bear that exert great impact on treatment outcomes. However, it is interesting that the variable exerting the greatest impact on outcomes is the client's perception of the client-therapist relationship.

Janice Krupnick and her colleagues (Krupnick et al., 1996) published the results of a large multisite study comparing the effectiveness of interpersonal psychotherapy, cognitive-behavioral therapy, medication management, and a medication placebo treatment in the treatment of depression. Surprisingly, they found little difference among treatment approaches on outcomes. However, when they investigated client and therapist contributions to the therapist-client relationship (therapeutic alliance) and outcomes, they found that the therapist contributions (and type of therapy) were not significant. In other words, it did not matter to treatment outcomes how the therapist rated the therapeutic alliance (strong or weak) or how the therapist's contribution was evaluated by the researchers. What mattered and what accounted for the greatest variation in client outcome was the client's perception of the therapeutic alliance. If the client believed that the therapist or psychiatrist was being helpful—that he or she had a good working relationship with the mental health provider—then a positive outcome was more likely than if the client did not believe he or she had a good working relationship with the mental health provider.

Now, lest you throw up your hands and say, "Well, why do I need to go to school for years to learn how to do therapy if all that really matters is the client's perception of our relationship?" you must first realize that therapeutic skill accounts for a portion of the variation in treatment outcomes as well (Beutler, Machado, and Neufeldt, 1994; Crits-Christoph et al., 1991; Green and Herget, 1991). This portion, although smaller than that accounted for by the degree to which clients feel they have a helpful relationship with the therapist, is significant. Studies have been conducted in which technique-based therapies (typically behavioral or structural and strategic) have been compared against supportive therapies (those that emphasize the relationship between therapist and client but are devoid of identifiable, programmatic techniques). These studies have repeatedly found that technique-based therapies produce better treatment outcomes than do supportive therapies. However, the supportive therapies still produce change! It's just that a strong therapeutic alliance coupled with the skillful administration of technique produces more success.

SOME FINAL THOUGHTS ABOUT MFTs AND RESEARCH

Although there is room for many more talented researchers within the field of marriage and family therapy, I am not naive enough to think that the majority of those reading this textbook have ambitions to become researchers. However, I do believe that it is imperative for all marriage and family therapists to have a working knowledge of research principles and to be actively involved in research. At a minimum, I think every responsible clinician should be involved in research in the following two ways.

Clinicians As Consumers of Research

Everyone is a consumer of research. Practically every product produced is the result of research—from soap to cars to how to treat depression. Everything in life is informed, at least in part, by research. We live in a world in which the results of disciplined inquiry are generally given high priority. Yet despite the importance of research in our lives, most people do not understand it. Most are not informed consumers of research.

Therapists are no exception. If the degree to which therapists say they use research to inform their clinical work is any indication of their consumerism of research (and I think it is), therapists are not informed consumers of the excellent burgeoning research that exists. Yet there is probably no more important time in the history of the profession for therapists to be consumers of research. The practice of mental health is at a crossroads. Gone are the days in which unsubstantiated claims could be made, as well as claims based on undisciplined inquiry, anecdotal account, and intuition accepted without· question by employers, third-party payers, and clients. Clients and third-party payers are increasing their demands for substantiated treatment plans and interventions with proven results. To compete in the mental health marketplace, therapists in the twenty-first century need to become informed and active consumers of research. In order to do this, one needs to understand research principles, needs to be able to read research reports and evaluate the quality of the research that was conducted, and needs to know how to integrate research into practice.

The field of marriage and family therapy can learn from the field of medicine, which is increasingly turning to what is referred to as evidenced-based practice (Guyatt, 1993). This is essentially the practice of medicine driven by research evidence. Although evidence-based medical practice is supported by a more developed and advanced research literature than exists in the mental health field, mental health practice would behooved to be informed by the research literature. Clinicians working in this way would understand how to read and interpret research articles and how to apply research findings to their clinical work.

Clinicians As Researchers

As I mentioned before, I'm not suggesting that every clinician be a researcher in the traditional sense of the word. However, all clinicians can and should use research principles and methods in conducting therapy and in evaluating the services they provide. From the discipline of education comes the term **action research,** a practitioner-led research activity that is as appropriate for mental health providers as it is for educators.

Action research is essentially the application of research principles to real-life situations by practitioners. The goal of action research is not the generalization of findings to a larger population as is the goal of traditional research endeavors. Rather, the goal of action research is the application of research findings to specific situations. For example, a particular clinician may want to evaluate the services he or she is providing to a specific population or in working with a particular client problem. This clinician would then develop a question that would allow him or her to evaluate what he or she is doing with clients and implement a "study" of that question using those clients. The results of this clinician's investigation would then result in changes to his or her own practice.

GLOSSARY

action research: A term referring to the application of research principles to real-life situations by practitioners, not for the purposes of the general dissemination of findings but for the purpose of informing and evaluating one's own clinical work.

aesthetic therapies: A term used by Bradford Keeney and Douglas Sprenkle (1983) to refer to treatments that are focused more on emotion, sensation, or intrapsychic processes that are difficult to operationalize than on more easily operationalized behaviors or outward, observable characteristics of a person or relationship. These therapies often focus on producing growth or change in perception of the person or relationship rather than behavioral change.

affiliative behaviors: A description used by emotionally focused therapists to refer to a set of behaviors that promotes or encourages togetherness in couple interactions.

analytic methodology: The methods, techniques, and strategies used for guiding the analysis and analyzing data.

applied research: Refers to studies designed to find solutions to problems (e.g., the best therapy for helping couples struggling with the chronic illness of one of the partners).

authority: This form of normal human inquiry refers to knowledge obtained through people who are believed to have special knowledge because of their status or position.

basic research: Refers to studies designed to better understand something (e.g., a condition, situation, interaction, phenomenon, construct) and to generate knowledge about that something.

clinical case studies: Narrative descriptions of the course of treatment with one or more client systems. They are typically designed to describe how treatment should be conducted, to identify important treatment considerations, or to discuss a client population or problem area. Rather than promoting knowledge through research they promote knowledge through experience.

clinical trial: Refers to research evaluating the efficacy of a particular intervention or treatment program. For a clinical trial, an intervention is operationalized with the use of a treatment manual, implemented under strict controls and the experimental method, and evaluated for its success.

common factors: Those factors that account for variations in treatment outcomes regardless of the treatment being provided. For example, therapist warmth and empathy are important regardless of the treatment approach used. Client motivation and the degree to which the client believes therapy will be helpful and a strong therapeutic alliance exists are also important common factors. Common factors have often been found to account for more of the variation in treatment outcome than factors unique to the treatment approach.

comparative research studies: Studies comparing one model of therapy against another. The result of this kind of study usually polarizes individuals within the field and results in few improvements to the services provided to clients.

competing explanations: Plausible alternative explanations of the results of a study that occur due to insufficient controls.

constructs: Theoretical creations based on observations which cannot be observed directly or indirectly.

controls: Research designs and procedures used by the investigator to lessen the effects of any variable other than the independent variable on the dependent variable. In general, the assumption is that the more tightly controlled the study, the more confidence can be placed in the results.

cooperative research: Research efforts that bring together researchers working from differing theoretical clinical perspectives or differing mental health professions to solve clinical problems or generate knowledge through joint research.

critical incidents: Those events or points in time in treatment when change takes place or to which change is attributed. This term was used in the study of change events in emotionally focused couple therapy.

disciplined inquiry: The use of systematic, replicable procedures for obtaining and evaluating information. Observations (data collection) are carefully planned and recorded and follow strict guidelines that ensure confidence in the results of these observations.

Dyadic Adjustment Scale (DAS): A paper-and-pencil measure developed by Graham Spanier designed to measure an adult's satisfaction with his or her relationship with an intimate partner or spouse.

effectiveness: Positive outcomes attributable to a course of therapy that suggest the value of that therapy. The research design used to study the value of the therapy reflects the real world of clinical practice.

efficacy: Positive outcomes attributable to a course of therapy which suggest the value of that therapy. The research design used to study the value of the therapy is experimental with tight controls that limit the influence of extraneous variables on treatment outcome. Treatment manuals are followed which standardize the treatment across providers and clients.

empirical: Based on or verifiable through disciplined inquiry and observation. Although this definition also includes qualitative investigations, many argue that empirical studies are quantitative in nature or more specifically experimental in nature.

etiology: The cause or causes of a condition.

expressed emotion (EE): A construct referring to the degree to which a person is subjected to behaviors such as criticism or harsh tone of voice from family members, spouse, or partner.

extraneous variable: A variable that makes possible an alternative explanation of the results.

generalizability: The extent to which the results obtained from a sample reflect the characteristics of the population from which the sample was drawn.

hypothesis: A tentative, testable assertion about something. This assertion typically involves the prediction of outcomes or the occurrence of certain behaviors, events, or phenomena—in other words, a prediction of the effect of the independent variable on the dependent variable. Although this is nothing more than a scientific (educated) guess, it is a guess that is informed by previous research and scientific knowledge and that is stated in a way that makes it testable or subject to scientific study.

inclusion criteria: Predetermined rules or guidelines designed to accomplish the goals of the research that define the characteristics of those who will be invited to participate in the study. The researcher determines the criteria to be used for inclusion, so criteria will vary from study to study depending on the goals of the research. Although the term suggests inclusion in the study, these rules and guidelines also exclude potential subjects from participation.

incremental outcomes: Short-term outcomes that contribute to the final outcome of the treatment. These outcomes may be the result of specific interventions, individual sessions, or series of sessions.

intimate self-disclosure: A term used by emotionally focused therapists to refer to self-disclosure driven by the most basic of human emotions, the disclosure of which would normally result in feelings of vulnerability.

investigator bias: Refers to the influence the investigator has on observations and results. A researcher's training, culture, gender, past experience, political agenda, and hypotheses may be among those investigator characteristics or attributes that bias a study and consequently influence what is seen and how it is interpreted. Although it is impossible to eliminate all investigator bias, there are methods of disciplined inquiry designed to reduce the impact of this bias on the outcomes of a study.

mean: The true statistical average derived by adding a group of scores and dividing this sum by the number of scores in the group.

natural human inquiry (NHI): Refers to the common, undisciplined way of learning about the world. These ways of learning about the world are typically not systematic or reproducible. Knowledge obtained in these ways is subject to the effects of bias. Common methods of natural human inquiry are personal experience, tradition, and authority.

no-treatment control group: A treatment condition used in experimental research in which no treatment is administered. This treatment condition is used to control for the effects of natural maturation and other sources of internal validity on the outcomes of the experiment.

observation: (1) An act of carefully watching something for a scientific purpose. The act of watching is directed by rules or guidelines that either restrict or expand what might be otherwise seen or noted; (2) a term used to refer to what is noted, seen, or concluded as a result of an instance of careful watching for scientific purposes.

operationalize: Defining the variable in such a way that it becomes observable. This entails an explicit description of those behaviors or processes that point to the variable in question. These behaviors or processes are then presented in such a way that reliable observations can be made regardless of who is doing the observing, when the observations are being made, and the context in which the observations are made.

outcome research: Research designed to determine the results of a course of therapy or of an intervention or set of interventions.

participants: A qualitative research term referring to the subjects of a study. The term *participants* is preferred over the term *subjects* because *subject* does not reflect the participatory and collaborative nature of qualitative research.

personal experience: A form of natural human inquiry that refers to learning about the world firsthand, through trial and error.

pragmatic therapies: Treatments whose processes, interventions, and outcomes can be easily operationalized and measured.

process of therapy: That which happens during the course of treatment that produces change and leads to an outcome.

process research: Research designed to determine what happens throughout the course of a treatment.

programmatic research: A research agenda followed by the same researcher or team of researchers that allows the results of one study to inform the development of the next study. The research agenda is thematic and directional with researchers designing sequential studies that build upon one another with the goal of better understanding the phenomenon under study over time.

psychoeducational family treatments: A treatment of major mental illness that includes pharmacological treatments, psychotherapy, and educational components. At a minimum, family members are involved in the educational component of treatment that typically includes information about the mental health condition being treated (including the typical course of the illness and what can be expected of the person with the condition) and the application of behavioral principles to modify the environment and interactions family members have with one another. Typically, professionals representing various areas of expertise are involved in the treatment provision.

psychometric qualities: The degree to which a measure of a construct or observable behavior is reliable and valid. Statistics are used to determine the reliability and validity of a measure or instrument. Generally, instruments that have reliability and validity coefficients of over .80 are considered psychometrically solid.

qualitative research: Disciplined inquiry focused on collecting narrative accounts, text, or observations that are analyzed without the benefit of predetermined categories or assumptions. In qualitative research the investigator becomes the primary data analytic tool, and the generation of research questions, data collection, and data analysis are often recursive processes. Although data can be quantified and statistics can be used as analysis strategies, more narrative analytic strategies designed to preserve the richness of the data are typically preferred. Qualitative research is typically inductive in nature.

quantify: Assigning numerical value to variables or characteristics of variables to aid in scientific observation or to facilitate the analysis of data obtained from scientific observations.

quantitative research: Disciplined inquiry focused on collecting data that can be summarized numerically (with numbers). The hallmark of quantitative research is the scientific experiment designed to determine the causal relationship of the independent and dependent variables. However, quantitative research also relies on survey and other methodologies that result in correlation findings (in which it is inappropriate to conclude causality). Inferential statistics are used to analyze quantitative research. Although there are exceptions, quantitative research is typically deductive in nature.

recidivism: The recurrence of symptoms after they have previously abated.

reliability: The degree to which the results of a measure of something are consistent across time, situation, and observer.

replicable procedures: Procedures that can be repeated or reproduced in other contexts or even within the same research study.

research design: The overall plan guiding all aspects of disciplined inquiry including subject recruitment and sampling, treatment administration, data collection and analysis, and results dissemination. Often the term is used to refer exclusively to the structure of the administration of treatment and control groups (e.g., pretest/posttest design) or to the genre of the study (e.g., survey design, qualitative design, experimental design).

sampling theory: A theory that suggests an entire population does not need to be observed to know the characteristics of that population. By randomly or systematically selecting a sufficiently large subgroup of that population (when every member of the population has an equal chance of being selected) the population characteristics can be known.

standard deviation: A standard unit of measurement that describes variation from the mean when scores cluster about the mean according to a normal (bell-shaped) curve. According to this measure of variability, 68 percent of the scores fall within one standard deviation (SD) of the mean, 95 percent fall within two SD, and 99 percent fall within three SD.

stress-vulnerability model: A model to explain the etiology of serious mental health conditions that says although some individuals have a predisposition (whether determined by genetics or sociobiology) to a class of mental health conditions, pathology will not develop in the absence of environmental stress. In other words, it is not sufficient to have a predisposition to the condition for the development of pathology. Other environmental factors producing stress on the system must also be present. Likewise, environmental stress alone is not sufficient to produce the condition in the absence of a genetic or sociobiological predisposition to the condition.

substantive evidence: Verifiable proof as to the reality of an observation, conclusion, or claim.

systematic procedures: Procedures that follow a method or plan.

time in the field: One of the most important determinants of the quality of a qualitative research study. This refers to the amount of time an investigator spends with subjects and is often accomplished by observing and interviewing the subjects in their natural environment.

tradition: A way of knowing about the world that is not guided by disciplined inquiry (*see* NATURAL HUMAN INQUIRY). Knowledge obtained in this way is assumed to be known by everyone because it has been passed down throughout the generations.

treatment manual: A detailed description of the treatment to be provided. These are typically step-by-step descriptions and are designed to eliminate or reduce the amount of variability in treatment administration across clients and treatment providers.

triangulation: A qualitative research strategy designed to improve the confidence one can have in the results of the study. Using triangulation, the investigators collect data from multiple sources (each of whom brings a unique perspective) using multiple methods.

validity: The degree to which a measure of something is actually measuring what it is purported to measure.

NOTES

1. Cohen, Sargent, and Sechrest (1986) found that a full 27 percent of the respondents in their study claimed that they could identify no trace of the influence of research on their clinical practice.

2. The research-practice gap is not exclusively a marriage and family therapy problem, however. Numerous articles identifying and addressing this problem are found in psychology journals. Studies consistently find that clinicians who use research to inform their clinical work are in the minority, with less than 15 to 20 percent of psychologists reporting that research is useful in their clinical practice.

REFERENCES

Alexander, J. F., Holtzworth-Munroe, A., and Jameson, P. (1994). The process and outcome of marital and family therapy: Research review and evaluation. In A. E. Bergin and S. L. Garfield (Eds.), *Handbook of psychotherapy and behavior change* (Fourth edition) (pp. 595-630). New York: John Wiley and Sons.

Alexander, J. F. and Parsons, B. V. (1982). *Functional family therapy.* Monterey, CA: Brooks/Cole Publishing.

Allgood, S. M. and Crane, D. R. (1991). Predicting marital therapy dropouts. *Journal of Marital and Family Therapy, 17,* 73-79.

Anderson, C. M., Reiss, D. J., and Hogarty, G. E. (1986). *Schizophrenia and the family.* New York: Guilford.

Atkinson, B., Heath, A., and Chenail, R. (1991). Qualitative research and the legitimization of knowledge. *Journal of Marital and Family Therapy, 17,* 175-180.

Azrin, N. H., Donohue, B., Besalel, V. A., Kogan, E. S., and Acierno. R. (1994). Youth drug abuse treatment: A controlled outcome study. *Journal of Child and Adolescent Substance Abuse, 3,* 1-16.

Babbie, E. (1995). *The practice of social research* (Seventh edition). Belmont, CA: Wadsworth Publishing Company.

Baucom, D. H. and Epstein, N. (1991). Will the real cognitive-behavioral marital therapy please stand up? *Journal of Family Psychology, 4,* 394-401.

Baucom, D. H., Shoham, V., Mueser, K. T., Daiuto, A. D., and Stickle, T. R. (1998). Empirically supported couple and family interventions for marital distress and adult mental health problems. *Journal of Consulting and Clinical Psychology, 66,* 53-88.

Beach, S. R. H. and O'Leary, K. D. (1993). Dysphoria and marital discord: Are dysphoric individuals at risk for marital maladjustment? *Journal of Marital and Family Therapy, 19,* 355-368.

Bergin, A. E. and Garfield, S. L. (Eds.) (1994). *Handbook of psychotherapy and behavior change* (Fourth edition). New York: John Wiley and Sons.

Beutler, L. E., Machado, P. P. P., and Neufeldt, S. A. (1994). Therapist variables. In A. E. Bergin and S. L. Garfield (Eds.), *Handbook of psychotherapy and behavior change* (Fourth edition) (pp. 229-269). New York: John Wiley and Sons.

Billings, A. G. and Moos, R. H. (1983). Comparisons of children of depressed and nondepressed parents: A social-environmental perspective. *Journal of Abnormal Psychology, 11,* 463-486.

Bischoff, R. J. and Reiter, A. D. (1999). The role of gender in the presenyation of mental health clinicians in the movies: Implications for clinical practice. *Psychotherapy, 36,* 180-189.

Bray, J. H. and Jouriles, E. N. (1995). Treatment of marital conflict and prevention of divorce. *Journal of Marital and Family Therapy, 21,* 461-473.

Broderick, C. B. and Schrader, S. S. (1981). The history of professional marriage and family therapy. In A. S. Gurman and D. P. Kniskern (Eds.), *Handbook of family therapy* (pp. 5-35). New York: Brunner/Mazel.

Cavell, T. A. and Snyder, D. K. (1991). Iconoclasm versus innovation: Building a science of family therapy—comments on Moon, Dillon, and Sprenkle. *Journal of Marital and Family Therapy, 17,* 181-185.

Chamberlain, P., Patterson, G. R., Reid, J. B., Kavanagh, K., and Forgatch, M. S. (1984). Observation of client resistance. *Behavior Therapy, 15,* 144-155.

Chamberlain, P. and Rosicky, J. G. (1995). The effectiveness of family therapy in the treatment of adolescents with conduct disorders and delinquency. *Journal of Marital and Family Therapy, 21,* 441-459.

Cohen, L. H., Sargent, M. M., and Sechrest, L. B. (1986). Use of psychotherapy research by professional psychologists. *American Psychologist, 41,* 198-206.

Coryell, W., Scheftner, W., Keller, M., Endicott, J., Maser, J., and Klerman, G. L. (1993). The enduring psychosocial consequences of mania and depression. *American Journal of Psychiatry, 150,* 720-727.

Crits-Christoph, P., Baranackie, K., Kurcias, J. S., Beck, A. T., Carroll, K., Perry, K., Luborsky, L., McLellan, A. T., Woody, G. E., Thompson, L., Gallagher, D., and Zitrin, C. (1991). Meta-analysis of therapist effects in psychotherapy outcome studies. *Psychotherapy Research, 1*(2), 81-91.

Dare, C., Eisler, I., Russell, G. F. M., and Szmukler, G. I. (1990). The clinical and theoretical impact of a controlled trial of family therapy in anorexia nervosa. *Journal of Marital and Family Therapy, 16,* 39-57.

Dunn, R. L. and Schwebel, A. I. (1995). Meta-analytic review of marital therapy outcome research. *Journal of Family Psychology, 9,* 58-68.

Eisler, I. and Dare, C. (1992). You can't teach an old dog new tricks: Teaching research to family therapy trainees. *Journal of Family Psychology, 5,* 418-431.

Elkin, I., Shea, T., Watkins, J. T., Imber, S. C., Satsky, S. M., Collins, J. F., Glass, D. R., Pilkonis, P. A., Leber, W. R., Fiester, S. J., Docherty, J., and Parloff, M. B. (1989). NIMH treatment of depression collaborative research program. *Archives of General Psychiatry, 46,* 971-982.

Ellis, L. (1994). *Research methods in the social sciences.* Madison, WI: WCB Brown and Benchmark Publishers.

Estrada, A. U. and Pinsof, W. M. (1995). The effectiveness of family therapies for selected behavioral disorders of childhood. *Journal of Marital and Family Therapy, 21,* 403-440.

Falloon, R. H., Boyd, J. L., McGill, C. W., Williamson, M., Razani, J., Moss, H. B., Gilderman, A. M., and Simpson, G. M. (1985). Family management in the prevention of morbidity of schizophrenia: Clinical outcome of a two-year longitudinal study. *Archives of General Psychiatry, 42,* 887-896.

Friedlander, M. L. (1998). Family therapy research: Science into practice, practice into science. In M. P. Nichols and R. C. Schwartz (Eds.), *Family therapy: Concepts and methods* (Fourth edition) (pp. 503-533). Boston: Allyn and Bacon.

Garfield, S. L. (1994). Research on client variables in psychotherapy. In A. E. Bergin and S. L. Garfield (Eds.), *Handbook of psychotherapy and behavior change* (Fourth edition) (pp. 190-228). New York: John Wiley and Sons.

Goldstein, M. J. and Miklowitz, D. J. (1995). The effectiveness of psychoeducational family therapy in the treatment of schizophrenic disorders. *Journal of Marital and Family Therapy, 21,* 361-376.

Green, R. J. and Herget, M. (1991). Outcomes of systemic/strategic team consultation. III. The importance of therapist warmth and active structuring. *Family Process, 30,* 321-336.

Greenberg, L. S., Ford, C. L., Alden, L. S., and Johnson, S. M. (1993). In-session change in emotionally focused therapy. *Journal of Consulting and Clinical Psychology, 61,* 78-84.

Greenberg, L. S., James, P. S., and Conry, R. F. (1988). Perceived change processes in emotionally focused couples therapy. *Journal of Family Psychology, 2,* 5-23.

Greenberg, L. S. and Johnson, S. M. (1988). *Emotionally focused therapy for couples.* New York: Guilford.

Griffith, M. and Griffith, J. (1990). Can family therapy research have a human face? *Dulwich Centre Newsletter, 2,* pp. 11-20.

Gurman, A. S. (1983). Family therapy research and the "new epistemology." *Journal of Marital and Family Therapy, 9,* 227-234.

Gurman, A. S. (1991). Back to the future, ahead to the past: Is marital therapy going in circles? *Journal of Family Psychology, 4,* 402-406.

Gurman, A. S. and Kniskern, D. P. (1978). Family therapy outcome research: Knowns and unknowns. In S. L. Garfield and A. E. Bergin (Eds.), *Handbook of family therapy* (Second edition) (pp. 817-901) New York: John Wiley and Sons.

Gurman, A. S., Kniskern, D. P., and Pinsof, W. M. (1986). Research on the process and outcome of marital and family therapy. In S. L. Garfield and A. E. Bergin (Eds.), *Handbook of psychotherapy and behavior change* (Third edition) (pp. 742-775). New York: John Wiley and Sons.

Guyatt, G. H. (1993). Editorial: Users' guides to the medical literature. *Journal of the American Medical Association, 270,* 2096-2097.

Hawley, D. R., Bailey, C. E., and Pennick, K. A. (2000). A content analysis of research in family therapy journals. *Journal of Marital and Family Therapy, 26,* 9-16.

Hazelrigg, M. D., Cooper, H. M., and Borduin, C. M. (1987). Evaluating the effectiveness of family therapies: An integrative review and analysis. *Psychological Bulletin, 101,* 428-442.

Henggeler, S. W., Borduin, C. M., and Mann, B. J. (1992). Advances in family therapy: Empirical foundations. In T. H. Ollendick and R. J. Prinz (Eds.), *Advances in clinical child psychology* (Volume 15) (pp. 207-241). New York: Plenum.

Hogarty, G. E., Anderson, C. M., Reiss, D. J., Kornblith, S. J., Greenwald, D. P., Javna, C. D., Madonia, M. J., and the EPICS Schizophrenia Research Group (1986). Family psychoeducation, social skills training, and maintenance chemotherapy in the aftercare treatment of schizophrenia. I. One year effects of a controlled study on relapse and expressed emotion. *Archives of General Psychiatry, 43,* 633-642.

Jacobson, N. S. (1985a). Family therapy outcome research: Potential pitfalls and prospects. *Journal of Marital and Family Therapy, 11,* 149-158.

Jacobson, N. S. (1985b). Toward a nonsectarian blueprint for the empirical study of family therapies. *Journal of Marital and Family Therapy, 11,* 163-165.

Jacobson, N. S. (1991a). To be or not to be behavioral when working with couples: What does it mean? *Journal of Family Psychology, 4,* 436-445.

Jacobson, N. S. (1991b). Toward enhancing the efficacy of marital therapy and marital therapy research. *Journal of Family Psychology, 4,* 436-445.

Jacobson, N. S. and Addis, M. E. (1993). Research on couples and couple therapy: What do we know? Where are we going? *Journal of Consulting and Clinical Psychology, 61,* 85-93.

Jacobson, N. S., Dobson, K., Frizzetti, A. E., Shmaling, K. B., and Suluski, S. (1991). Marital therapy as a treatment for depression. *Journal of Consulting and Clinical Psychology, 59,* 547-557.

Jacobson, N. S., Fruzzetti, A. E., Dobson, K., Whisman, M., and Hops, H. (1993). Couple therapy as a treatment for depression. II. The effects of relationship quality and therapy on depressive relapse. *Journal of Consulting and Clinical Psychology, 61,* 516-519.

Jacobson, N. S., Schmaling, K. B., and Holtzworth-Munroe, A. (1987). Component analysis of behavioral marital therapy: Two-year follow-up and prediction of relapse. *Journal of Marital and Family Therapy, 13,* 187-195.

Joanning, H., Quinn, W., Thomas, F., and Mullen, R. (1992). Treating adolescent drug abuse: A comparison of family systems therapy, group therapy, and family drug education. *Journal of Marital and Family Therapy, 18,* 345-356.

Johnson, S. M. and Greenberg, L. S. (1988). Relating process to outcome in marital therapy. *Journal of Marital and Family Therapy, 14,* 175-183.

Johnson, S. M. and Greenberg, L. S. (1991). There are more things in heaven and earth than are dreamed of in BMT: A response to Jacobson. *Journal of Family Psychology, 4,* 407-415.

Johnson, S. M. and Lebow, J. (2000). The "coming of age" of couple therapy: A decade review. *Journal of Marital and Family Therapy, 26,* 23-38.

Kaye, J. (1990). Toward meaningful research in psychotherapy. *Dulwich Centre Newsletter, 2,* 27-38.

Kazdin, A. E. (1987). Treatment of antisocial behavior in children: Current status and future directions. *Psychological Bulletin, 102,* 187-203.

Kazdin, A. E. (1991). Effectiveness of psychotherapy with children and adolescents. *Journal of Consulting and Clinical Psychology, 59,* 785-798.

Kazdin, A. E. (1994). Psychotherapy for children and adolescents. In A. E. Bergin and S. L. Garfield (Eds.), *Handbook of psychotherapy and behavior change* (Fourth edition) (pp. 543-594). New York: John Wiley and Sons.

Keeney, B. P. and Sprenkle, D. H. (1983). Ecosystemic epistemology: Critical implications for the aesthetics and pragmatics of family therapy. *Family Process, 21,* 1-19.

Klein, N. C., Alexander, J. F., and Parsons, B. V. (1977). Impact of family systems intervention on recidivism and sibling delinquency: Preliminary findings. *Journal of Consulting and Clinical Psychology, 45,* 469-474.

Krupnick, J. L., Sotsky, S. M., Simmens, S., Moyer, J., Elkin, I., Watkins, J., and Pilkonis, P. A. (1996). The role of the therapeutic alliance in psychotherapy and pharmacotherapy outcome: Findings in the National Institute of Mental Health treatment of depression collaborative research program. *Journal of Consulting and Clinical Psychology, 64,* 532-539.

Leff, J. P., Kuipers, L., Berkowitz, R., Eberlein-Vries, R., and Sturgeon, D. (1982). A controlled trial of social intervention in the families of schizophrenic patients. *British Journal of Psychiatry, 141,* 121-134.

Leff, J. P., Kuipers, L., Berkowitz, R., and Sturgeon, D. (1985). A controlled trial of social intervention in the families of schizophrenic patients: Two-year follow-up. *British Journal of Psychiatry, 146,* 594-600.

Lewis, A., Piercy, F. P., Sprenkle, D. H., and Trepper, T. S. (1990). Family-based interventions for helping drug-abusing adolescents. *Journal of Adolescent Research, 13,* 35-44.

Liddle, H. A. (1991). Empirical values and the culture of family therapy. *Journal of Marital and Family Therapy, 17,* 327-348.

Liddle, H. A. and Dakof, G. A. (1995). Efficacy of family therapy for drug abuse: Promising but not definitive. *Journal of Marital and Family Therapy, 21,* 511-543.

Mahrer, A. R. (1988). Discovery-oriented psychotherapy research: Rationale, aims and methods. *American Psychologist, 43,* 694-702.

Markman, H. J. (1991). Backwards into the future of couples therapy and couples therapy research: A comment on Jacobson. *Journal of Family Psychology, 4,* 416-425.

Maxmen, J. S. and Ward, N. G. (1995). *Essential psychopathology and its treatment* (Second edition). New York: W.W. Norton.

May, R. R. (1987). Therapy in our day. In Zeig, J. K. (Ed.), *The evolution of psychotherapy* (pp. 212-219). New York: Brunner/Mazel.

Miklowitz, D. J. and Hooley, J. M. (1998). Developing family psychoeducational treatments for patients with bipolar and other severe psychiatric disorders: A pathway from basic research to clinical trials. *Journal of Marital and Family Therapy, 24,* 419-435.

Minuchin, S. (1978). *Families and family therapy.* Cambridge, MA: Harvard University Press.

Minuchin, S., Baker, L., Rosman, B., Liebman, R., Milman, L., and Todd, T. (1975). A conceptual model of psychosomatic illness in children. *Archives of General Psychiatry, 32,* 1031-1038.

Minuchin, S., Rosman, B., and Baker, L. (1978). *Psychosomatic families.* Cambridge, MA: Harvard University Press.

Moon, S. M., Dillon, D. R., and Sprenkle, D. H. (1990). Family therapy and qualitative research. *Journal of Marital and Family Therapy, 16,* 357-373.

Moon, S. M., Dillon, D. R., and Sprenkle, D. H. (1991). On balance and synergy: Family therapy and qualitative research revisited. *Journal of Marital and Family Therapy, 17,* 173-178.

Morrow-Bradley, C. and Elliott, R. (1986). Utilization of psychotherapy research by practicing psychotherapists. *American Psychologist, 41,* 188-197.

Nichols, M. P. and Schwartz, R. C. (1998). *Family therapy: Concepts and methods* (Fourth edition). Boston: Allyn and Bacon.

O'Leary, K. D. and Beach, S. R. H. (1990). Marital therapy: A viable treatment for depression and marital discord. *American Journal of Psychiatry, 147,* 183-186.

O'Leary, K. D., Risso, L. P., and Beach, S. R. H. (1990). Attributions about marital discord/depression link and therapy outcome. *Behavior Therapy, 21,* 413-422.

Olson, D. H. (1976). Bridging research, theory, and application: The triple threat in science. In D. H. Olson (Ed.), *Treating relationships* (pp. 565-579). Lake Mills, IA: Graphic Publishing.

Parsons, B. V. and Alexander, J. F. (1973). Short-term family intervention: A therapy outcome study. *Journal of Consulting and Clinical Psychology, 41,* 195-201.

Patterson, G. R. and Chamberlain, P. (1988). Treatment process: A problem at three levels. In L. C. Wynne (Ed.), *The state of the art in family therapy research: Controversies and recommendations* (pp. 189-223). New York: Family Process Press.

Patterson, G. R. and Forgatch, M. S. (1985). Therapist behavior as a determinant for client noncompliance: A paradox for the behavior modifier. *Journal of Consulting and Clinical Psychology, 53,* 846-851.

Paul, G. L. (1967). Strategy of outcome research in psychotherapy. *Journal of Consulting Psychology, 31,* 109-118.

Piercy, F. P. and Sprenkle, D. H. (1990). Marriage and family therapy: A decade review. *Journal of Marriage and the Family, 52,* 1116-1126.

Pinsof, W. M. and Wynne, L. C. (1995a). The effectiveness and efficacy of marital and family therapy: Introduction to the special issue. *Journal of Marital and Family Therapy, 21,* 341-343.

Pinsof, W. M. and Wynne, L. C. (1995b). The efficacy of marital and family therapy: An empirical overview, conclusions, and recommendations. *Journal of Marital and Family Therapy, 21,* 585-613.

Pinsof, W. M. and Wynne, L. C. (2000). Toward progress research: Closing the gap between family therapy practice and research. *Journal of Marital and Family Therapy, 26,* 1-8.

Pinsof, W. M., Wynne, L. C., and Hambright, A. B. (1996). The outcomes of couple and family therapy: Findings, conclusions, and recommendations. *Psychotherapy, 33,* 321-331.

Prince, S. E. and Jacobson, N. S. (1995). A review and evaluation of marital and family therapies for affective disorders. *Journal of Marital and Family Therapy, 21,* 377-401.

Russell, G. F. M., Szmukler, G. I., Dare, C., and Eisler, I. (1987). An evaluation of family therapy in anorexia nervosa and bulimia nervosa. *Archives of General Psychiatry, 44,* 1047-1056.

Safran, J. D., Greenberg, L. S., and Rice, L. M. (1988). Integrating psychotherapy research and practice: Modeling the change process. *Psychotherapy, 25,* 1-17.

Schwartz, R. C. and Breunlin, D. (1983). Research: Why clinicians should bother with it. *Family Therapy Networker,* July-August, pp. 23-27, 57-59.

Shadish, W., Ragsdale, K., Glaser, R. R., and Montgomery, L. M. (1985). The efficacy and effectiveness of marital and family therapy: A perspective from meta-analysis. *Journal of Marital and Family Therapy, 21,* 345-360.

Shields, C. G., Wynne, L. C., McDaniel, S. H., and Gawinski, B. (1994). The marginalization of family therapy: A historical and continuing problem. *Journal of Marital and Family Therapy, 20,* 117-138.

Snyder, D. K. and Wills, R. M. (1989). Behavioral versus insight-oriented marital therapy: Effects on individual and interspousal functioning. *Journal of Consulting and Clinical Psychology, 57,* 39-46.

Snyder, D. K. and Wills, R. M. (1991). Facilitating change in marital therapy and research. *Journal of Family Psychology, 4,* 426-435.

Spanier, G. B. (1976). Measuring dyadic adjustment: New scales for assessing the quality of marriage and similar dyads. *Journal of Marriage and the Family, 38,* 15-28.

Sprenkle, D. H. and Bischoff, R. J. (1995). Research in family therapy: Trends, issues and recommendations. In M. P. Nichols and R. C. Schwartz (Eds.), *Family therapy: Concepts and methods* (Third edition) (pp. 542-580). Boston: Allyn and Bacon.

Sprenkle, D. H. and Moon, S. M. (1996). Toward pluralism in family therapy research. In D. H. Sprenkle and S. M. Moon (Eds.), *Research methods in family therapy* (pp. 3-19). New York: Guilford.

Stanton, M. D. and Shadish, W. R. (1997). Outcome, attrition, and family-couples treatment for drug abuse: A meta-analysis and review of the controlled, comparative studies. *Psychological Bulletin, 122,* 170-191.

Stanton, M. D., Todd, T. C., and Associates (1982). *Family therapy of drug abuse and addiction.* New York: Guilford.

Sue, S., Zane, N., and Young, K. (1994). Research on psychotherapy with culturally diverse populations. In A. E. Bergin and S. L. Garfield (Eds.), *Handbook of psychotherapy and behavior change* (Fourth edition) (pp. 783-817). New York: John Wiley and Sons.

Szapocznik, J., Kurtines, W. M., Foote, F. H., Perez-Vidal, A., and Hervis, O. (1986). Conjoint versus one-person family therapy: Further evidence for the effectiveness of conducting family therapy through one person with drug abusing adolescents. *Journal of Consulting and Clinical Psychology, 54,* 385-387.

Szapocznik, J., Kurtines, W. M., Foote, F. H., Perez-Vidal, A., and Hervis, O. (1983). Conjoint versus one-person family therapy: Some evidence for the effectiveness of conducting family therapy through one person. *Journal of Consulting and Clinical Psychology, 51,* 889-899.

Szapocznik, J., Kurtines, W., Santisteban, D. A., and Rio, A. T. (1990). Interplay of advances between theory, research, and application in treatment interventions aimed at behavior problem children and adolescents. *Journal of Consulting and Clinical Psychology, 58,* 696-703.

Szapocznik, J., Perez-Vidal, A., Brickman, A. L., Foote, F. H., Santisteban, D., Hervis, O., and Kurtines, W. (1988). Engaging adolescent drug abusers and their families in treatment: A strategic structural systems approach. *Journal of Consulting and Clinical Psychology, 56,* 552-557.

Szapocznik, J., Rio, A., Murray, E., Cohen, R., Scopetta, M., Rivas-Vazquez, A., Hervis, O., Posada, V., and Kurtines, W. (1989). Structural family versus psychodynamic child therapy for problematic Hispanic boys. *Journal of Consulting and Clinical Psychology, 57,* 571-578.

Szmukler, G. I., Eisler, I., Russell, G. F. M., and Dare, C. (1985). Anorexia nervosa, parental "expressed emotion" and dropping out of treatment. *British Journal of Psychiatry, 147,* 265-271.

Tolan, P. H., Cromwell, R. E., and Brasswell, M. (1986). Family therapy with delinquents: A critical review of the literature. *Family Process, 25,* 619-649.

Tomm, K. (1983). The old hat doesn't fit. *Family Therapy Networker,* July-August, pp. 39-41.

Wynne, L. C. (1983). Family research and family therapy: A reunion? *Journal of Marital and Family Therapy, 9,* 113-117.

Index